REFERENCE

DISCARDED

**Great Lives from History**

# African Americans

## Great Lives from History

# African Americans

## Volume 5
Sojourner Truth – Whitney Young
Appendixes
Indexes

*Editor*
**Carl L. Bankston III**
*Tulane University*

Salem Press
Pasadena, California    Hackensack, New Jersey

*Editor in Chief:* Dawn P. Dawson

*Editorial Director:* Christina J. Moose    *Photo Editor:* Cynthia Breslin Beres
*Development Editor:* R. Kent Rasmussen    *Research Supervisor:* Jeffry Jensen
*Manuscript Editors:* Stacy Cole and Constance Pollock    *Production Editor:* Andrea E. Miller
*Acquisitions Manager:* Mark Rehn    *Graphics and Design:* James Hutson
*Administrative Assistant:* Paul Tifford, Jr.    *Layout:* Mary Overell and William Zimmerman

*Cover photos* (pictured left to right, from top left): Frederick Douglass (Archive Photos/Getty Images); Barack Obama (Official presidential portrait/Pete Souza, White House photographer); Diana Ross (AP/Wide World Photos); Malcolm X (Time & Life Images/Getty Images); Willie Mays (AP/Wide World Photos); Spike Lee (AP/Wide World Photos); Booker T. Washington (The Granger Collection, New York); Bessie Smith (The Granger Collection, New York); Colin Powell (Archive Photos/Getty Images)

∞ The paper used in these volumes conforms to the American National Standard for Permanence of Paper for Printed Library Materials, Z39.48-1992 (R1997).

**Library of Congress Cataloging-in-Publication Data**

Great lives from history. African Americans / editor, Carl L. Bankston III.
    <5>v. ;
 Includes bibliographical references and index.
   ISBN 978-1-58765-747-4 (set : alk. paper) — ISBN 978-1-58765-748-1 (vol. 1 : alk. paper) —
ISBN 978-1-58765-749-8 (vol. 2 : alk. paper) — ISBN 978-1-58765-750-4 (vol. 3 : alk. paper) —
ISBN 978-1-58765-751-1 (vol. 4 : alk. paper) — ISBN 978-1-58765-752-8 (vol. 5 : alk. paper)
   1. African Americans—Biography—Encyclopedias.   2. African Americans—History—Encyclopedias.
I. Bankston, Carl L. (Carl Leon), 1952 -   II. Title: African Americans.
 E185.96.G736 2011
 920.009296′073—dc23
 [B]

2011018008

# Contents

Key to Pronunciation . . . . . . . . . . . . . . . . . xcix
Complete List of Contents . . . . . . . . . . . . . . ci

Sojourner Truth . . . . . . . . . . . . . . . . . 1441
Harriet Tubman . . . . . . . . . . . . . . . . 1444
C. DeLores Tucker . . . . . . . . . . . . . . 1447
Big Joe Turner . . . . . . . . . . . . . . . . . 1448
Henry McNeal Turner . . . . . . . . . . . 1450
Ike Turner . . . . . . . . . . . . . . . . . . . . 1451
Nat Turner . . . . . . . . . . . . . . . . . . . . 1453
Tina Turner . . . . . . . . . . . . . . . . . . . 1455
McCoy Tyner . . . . . . . . . . . . . . . . . 1458
Cicely Tyson . . . . . . . . . . . . . . . . . . 1460
Mike Tyson . . . . . . . . . . . . . . . . . . . 1462
Neil deGrasse Tyson . . . . . . . . . . . . 1464
Wyomia Tyus . . . . . . . . . . . . . . . . . 1466

Leslie Uggams . . . . . . . . . . . . . . . . . 1468
Blair Underwood . . . . . . . . . . . . . . . 1470
Gene Upshaw . . . . . . . . . . . . . . . . . 1472
Usher . . . . . . . . . . . . . . . . . . . . . . . 1474

Courtney B. Vance . . . . . . . . . . . . . 1476
James Van Der Zee . . . . . . . . . . . . . 1477
Mario Van Peebles . . . . . . . . . . . . . 1480
Melvin Van Peebles . . . . . . . . . . . . . 1482
Sarah Vaughan . . . . . . . . . . . . . . . . 1483
Ben Vereen . . . . . . . . . . . . . . . . . . . 1485
Denmark Vesey . . . . . . . . . . . . . . . 1487
C. T. Vivian . . . . . . . . . . . . . . . . . . 1488

Jersey Joe Walcott . . . . . . . . . . . . . 1491
Alice Walker . . . . . . . . . . . . . . . . . . 1493
David Walker . . . . . . . . . . . . . . . . . 1495
George Walker . . . . . . . . . . . . . . . . 1497
Jimmie Walker . . . . . . . . . . . . . . . . 1498
Madam C. J. Walker . . . . . . . . . . . . 1500
Margaret Walker . . . . . . . . . . . . . . . 1503
Fats Waller . . . . . . . . . . . . . . . . . . . 1504
Eric Walrond . . . . . . . . . . . . . . . . . 1507
Alexander Walters . . . . . . . . . . . . . . 1508
Dionne Warwick . . . . . . . . . . . . . . . 1510
Booker T. Washington . . . . . . . . . . . 1513
Denzel Washington . . . . . . . . . . . . . 1515
Harold Washington . . . . . . . . . . . . . 1518

Kenny Washington . . . . . . . . . . . . . 1521
Maxine Waters . . . . . . . . . . . . . . . . 1523
Muddy Waters . . . . . . . . . . . . . . . . 1525
Faye Wattleton . . . . . . . . . . . . . . . . 1526
J. C. Watts . . . . . . . . . . . . . . . . . . . 1528
Robert C. Weaver . . . . . . . . . . . . . . 1530
Chick Webb . . . . . . . . . . . . . . . . . . 1531
Ida B. Wells-Barnett . . . . . . . . . . . . 1533
Cornel West . . . . . . . . . . . . . . . . . . 1535
David West . . . . . . . . . . . . . . . . . . . 1537
Dorothy West . . . . . . . . . . . . . . . . . 1538
Kanye West . . . . . . . . . . . . . . . . . . 1540
Togo West . . . . . . . . . . . . . . . . . . . 1541
Clifton Reginald Wharton, Jr. . . . . . . . 1543
Phillis Wheatley . . . . . . . . . . . . . . . 1545
Tyrone Wheatley . . . . . . . . . . . . . . . 1547
Forest Whitaker . . . . . . . . . . . . . . . 1548
Bill White . . . . . . . . . . . . . . . . . . . . 1550
Walter White . . . . . . . . . . . . . . . . . 1552
John Edgar Wideman . . . . . . . . . . . . 1555
L. Douglas Wilder . . . . . . . . . . . . . . 1557
Lenny Wilkens . . . . . . . . . . . . . . . . 1558
Roy Wilkins . . . . . . . . . . . . . . . . . . 1560
Bert Williams . . . . . . . . . . . . . . . . . 1563
Billy Dee Williams . . . . . . . . . . . . . 1565
Cootie Williams . . . . . . . . . . . . . . . 1566
Daniel Hale Williams . . . . . . . . . . . 1567
Gus Williams . . . . . . . . . . . . . . . . . 1569
Hosea Williams . . . . . . . . . . . . . . . 1571
Juan Williams . . . . . . . . . . . . . . . . . 1573
Mary Lou Williams . . . . . . . . . . . . . 1574
Montel Williams . . . . . . . . . . . . . . . 1576
Robert Franklin Williams . . . . . . . . . 1578
Serena Williams . . . . . . . . . . . . . . . 1579
Vanessa Williams . . . . . . . . . . . . . . 1581
Venus Williams . . . . . . . . . . . . . . . 1583
Willie L. Williams . . . . . . . . . . . . . . 1584
Maury Wills . . . . . . . . . . . . . . . . . . 1586
August Wilson . . . . . . . . . . . . . . . . 1587
Flip Wilson . . . . . . . . . . . . . . . . . . . 1590
Jackie Wilson . . . . . . . . . . . . . . . . . 1592
William Julius Wilson . . . . . . . . . . . 1593
Paul Winfield . . . . . . . . . . . . . . . . . 1595
Oprah Winfrey . . . . . . . . . . . . . . . . 1597
James Winkfield . . . . . . . . . . . . . . . 1600

Ernest Withers . . . . . . . . . . . . . . . . . . 1601
George C. Wolfe . . . . . . . . . . . . . . 1603
Stevie Wonder . . . . . . . . . . . . . . . . 1605
Alfre Woodard . . . . . . . . . . . . . . . . 1607
Lynette Woodard . . . . . . . . . . . . . . 1609
Granville T. Woods . . . . . . . . . . . . . . 1610
Tiger Woods . . . . . . . . . . . . . . . . . 1612
Carter G. Woodson . . . . . . . . . . . . . 1615
Rod Woodson . . . . . . . . . . . . . . . . . 1617
Jane Cooke Wright . . . . . . . . . . . . . 1619
Jeffrey Wright . . . . . . . . . . . . . . . . . 1620
Jeremiah Wright . . . . . . . . . . . . . . . 1622
Louis T. Wright . . . . . . . . . . . . . . . . 1624
Richard Wright . . . . . . . . . . . . . . . . 1625

Frank Yerby . . . . . . . . . . . . . . . . . . . 1628
Al Young . . . . . . . . . . . . . . . . . . . . 1631

Andrew Young . . . . . . . . . . . . . . . . 1632
Coleman Young . . . . . . . . . . . . . . . . 1635
Whitney Young . . . . . . . . . . . . . . . . 1637

**Appendixes**
Chronological List of Entries . . . . . . . . . . 1641
Mediagraphy . . . . . . . . . . . . . . . . . . 1651
Literary Bibliography . . . . . . . . . . . . . . 1658
Organizations and Societies . . . . . . . . . . 1665
Research Centers and Libraries . . . . . . . . . 1669
Bibliography . . . . . . . . . . . . . . . . . . 1673
Web Site Directory . . . . . . . . . . . . . . 1682

**Indexes**
Category Index . . . . . . . . . . . . . . . . . 1689
Personages Index . . . . . . . . . . . . . . . . 1705
Subject Index . . . . . . . . . . . . . . . . . 1731

# KEY TO PRONUNCIATION

Many of the names of personages covered in *Great Lives from History: African Americans* may be unfamiliar to students and general readers. For difficult-to-pronounce names, guidelines to pronunciation have been provided upon first mention of the name in each essay. These guidelines do not purport to achieve the subtleties of all languages but will offer readers a rough equivalent of how English speakers may approximate the proper pronunciation.

*Vowel Sounds*

| Symbol | Spelled (Pronounced) |
|---|---|
| a | answer (AN-suhr), laugh (laf), sample (SAM-puhl), that (that) |
| ah | father (FAH-thur), hospital (HAHS-pih-tuhl) |
| aw | awful (AW-fuhl), caught (kawt) |
| ay | blaze (blayz), fade (fayd), waiter (WAYT-ur), weigh (way) |
| eh | bed (behd), head (hehd), said (sehd) |
| ee | believe (bee-LEEV), cedar (SEE-dur), leader (LEED-ur), liter (LEE-tur) |
| ew | boot (bewt), lose (lewz) |
| i | buy (bi), height (hit), lie (li), surprise (sur-PRIZ) |
| ih | bitter (BIH-tur), pill (pihl) |
| o | cotton (KO-tuhn), hot (hot) |
| oh | below (bee-LOH), coat (koht), note (noht), wholesome (HOHL-suhm) |
| oo | good (good), look (look) |
| ow | couch (kowch), how (how) |
| oy | boy (boy), coin (koyn) |
| uh | about (uh-BOWT), butter (BUH-tuhr), enough (ee-NUHF), other (UH-thur) |

*Consonant Sounds*

| Symbol | Spelled (Pronounced) |
|---|---|
| ch | beach (beech), chimp (chihmp) |
| g | beg (behg), disguise (dihs-GIZ), get (geht) |
| j | digit (DIH-juht), edge (ehj), jet (jeht) |
| k | cat (kat), kitten (KIH-tuhn), hex (hehks) |
| s | cellar (SEHL-ur), save (sayv), scent (sehnt) |
| sh | champagne (sham-PAYN), issue (IH-shew), shop (shop) |
| ur | birth (burth), disturb (dihs-TURB), earth (urth), letter (LEH-tur) |
| y | useful (YEWS-fuhl), young (yuhng) |
| z | business (BIHZ-nehs), zest (zehst) |
| zh | vision (VIH-zhuhn) |

# COMPLETE LIST OF CONTENTS

## VOLUME 1

Contents. . . . . . . . . . . . . . . . . . . . . . . . v
Publisher's Note . . . . . . . . . . . . . . . . . . . vii
Contributors . . . . . . . . . . . . . . . . . . . . . xi
Key to Pronunciation. . . . . . . . . . . . . . . xvii
Complete List of Contents . . . . . . . . . . . xix

Aaliyah . . . . . . . . . . . . . . . . . . . . . . . . . 1
Hank Aaron. . . . . . . . . . . . . . . . . . . . . . 3
Robert S. Abbott . . . . . . . . . . . . . . . . . . 5
Kareem Abdul-Jabbar . . . . . . . . . . . . . . 8
Ralph David Abernathy . . . . . . . . . . . . . 11
Faye Adams . . . . . . . . . . . . . . . . . . . . . 14
Cannonball Adderley . . . . . . . . . . . . . . 15
Alvin Ailey . . . . . . . . . . . . . . . . . . . . . 18
George Edward Alcorn . . . . . . . . . . . . . 20
Ira Frederick Aldridge. . . . . . . . . . . . . . 22
Elizabeth Alexander. . . . . . . . . . . . . . . 24
Muhammad Ali . . . . . . . . . . . . . . . . . . 26
Noble Drew Ali . . . . . . . . . . . . . . . . . . 29
Damon Allen . . . . . . . . . . . . . . . . . . . . 31
Debbie Allen . . . . . . . . . . . . . . . . . . . . 33
Marcus Allen . . . . . . . . . . . . . . . . . . . . 34
Richard Allen . . . . . . . . . . . . . . . . . . . 36
Allen Allensworth . . . . . . . . . . . . . . . . 38
Charles Alston. . . . . . . . . . . . . . . . . . . 40
Gene Ammons. . . . . . . . . . . . . . . . . . . 41
Wally Amos . . . . . . . . . . . . . . . . . . . . . 43
Eddie "Rochester" Anderson . . . . . . . . . 45
Marian Anderson . . . . . . . . . . . . . . . . . 47
Maya Angelou. . . . . . . . . . . . . . . . . . . 50
Henry Armstrong . . . . . . . . . . . . . . . . . 53
Lillian Hardin Armstrong . . . . . . . . . . . 55
Louis Armstrong . . . . . . . . . . . . . . . . . 57
Molefi Kete Asante . . . . . . . . . . . . . . . 60
Arthur Ashe . . . . . . . . . . . . . . . . . . . . . 63
Evelyn Ashford . . . . . . . . . . . . . . . . . . 65
Crispus Attucks . . . . . . . . . . . . . . . . . . 66

Babyface. . . . . . . . . . . . . . . . . . . . . . . 69
Pearl Bailey . . . . . . . . . . . . . . . . . . . . 71
Dusty Baker . . . . . . . . . . . . . . . . . . . . 73
Ella Baker . . . . . . . . . . . . . . . . . . . . . . 75
Houston A. Baker, Jr. . . . . . . . . . . . . . . 77

Josephine Baker . . . . . . . . . . . . . . . . . 78
James Baldwin. . . . . . . . . . . . . . . . . . . 81
James Presley Ball. . . . . . . . . . . . . . . . 84
Toni Cade Bambara . . . . . . . . . . . . . . . 86
Ernie Banks . . . . . . . . . . . . . . . . . . . . 88
Tyra Banks. . . . . . . . . . . . . . . . . . . . . 90
Benjamin Banneker . . . . . . . . . . . . . . . 92
Edward Mitchell Bannister . . . . . . . . . . 94
Amiri Baraka . . . . . . . . . . . . . . . . . . . 96
Charles Barkley . . . . . . . . . . . . . . . . . . 99
Steven Barnes . . . . . . . . . . . . . . . . . . 101
Gerald William Barrax . . . . . . . . . . . . 102
Marion Barry. . . . . . . . . . . . . . . . . . . 104
Richmond Barthé. . . . . . . . . . . . . . . . 107
Count Basie . . . . . . . . . . . . . . . . . . . 109
Jean-Michel Basquiat . . . . . . . . . . . . . 111
Charlotta Spears Bass . . . . . . . . . . . . . 113
Angela Bassett . . . . . . . . . . . . . . . . . . 115
Daisy Bates. . . . . . . . . . . . . . . . . . . . 116
Alvin Batiste . . . . . . . . . . . . . . . . . . . 118
Kathleen Battle. . . . . . . . . . . . . . . . . . 119
Elgin Baylor . . . . . . . . . . . . . . . . . . . 121
Bob Beamon . . . . . . . . . . . . . . . . . . . 123
Andrew Jackson Beard. . . . . . . . . . . . . 125
Romare Bearden . . . . . . . . . . . . . . . . 126
Louise Beavers . . . . . . . . . . . . . . . . . 129
Tyson Beckford . . . . . . . . . . . . . . . . . 130
Jim Beckwourth . . . . . . . . . . . . . . . . . 132
Julius Wesley Becton, Jr.. . . . . . . . . . . 134
Harry Belafonte . . . . . . . . . . . . . . . . . 136
Cool Papa Bell . . . . . . . . . . . . . . . . . . 138
James Madison Bell . . . . . . . . . . . . . . 140
Chuck Berry . . . . . . . . . . . . . . . . . . . 141
Halle Berry. . . . . . . . . . . . . . . . . . . . 144
Blind Tom Bethune . . . . . . . . . . . . . . 145
Mary McLeod Bethune . . . . . . . . . . . . 148
James Bevel . . . . . . . . . . . . . . . . . . . 150
Chauncey Billups . . . . . . . . . . . . . . . . 152
David Harold Blackwell . . . . . . . . . . . 153
Edward Blackwell . . . . . . . . . . . . . . . 156
Henry Blair. . . . . . . . . . . . . . . . . . . . 158
Eubie Blake . . . . . . . . . . . . . . . . . . . 159
Art Blakey . . . . . . . . . . . . . . . . . . . . 162

Bobby Blue Bland . . . . . . . . . . . . . . . . 163
James Bland . . . . . . . . . . . . . . . . . . 165
Jimmy Blanton . . . . . . . . . . . . . . . . . 167
Mary J. Blige . . . . . . . . . . . . . . . . . . 168
Vida Blue . . . . . . . . . . . . . . . . . . . . 170
Guion Bluford . . . . . . . . . . . . . . . . . 171
Charles F. Bolden, Jr. . . . . . . . . . . . . . 173
Jane Matilda Bolin . . . . . . . . . . . . . . . 175
Horace Mann Bond . . . . . . . . . . . . . . 177
Julian Bond . . . . . . . . . . . . . . . . . . . 179
Barry Bonds . . . . . . . . . . . . . . . . . . 182
Margaret Allison Bonds . . . . . . . . . . . . 185
Marita Bonner . . . . . . . . . . . . . . . . . 186
Arna Bontemps . . . . . . . . . . . . . . . . . 188
Ralph Boston . . . . . . . . . . . . . . . . . . 190
Sister Thea Bowman . . . . . . . . . . . . . . 192
Otis Boykin . . . . . . . . . . . . . . . . . . . 193
Perry Bradford . . . . . . . . . . . . . . . . . 195
David Bradley . . . . . . . . . . . . . . . . . 196
Ed Bradley . . . . . . . . . . . . . . . . . . . 198
Tom Bradley . . . . . . . . . . . . . . . . . . 200
William Stanley Braithwaite . . . . . . . . . 202
Carol E. Moseley Braun . . . . . . . . . . . . 204
Anthony Braxton . . . . . . . . . . . . . . . . 206
Toni Braxton . . . . . . . . . . . . . . . . . . 208
Cyril V. Briggs . . . . . . . . . . . . . . . . . 210
Andrew Felton Brimmer . . . . . . . . . . . . 212
Lou Brock . . . . . . . . . . . . . . . . . . . . 213
Edward W. Brooke . . . . . . . . . . . . . . . 215
Gwendolyn Brooks . . . . . . . . . . . . . . . 217
Big Bill Broonzy . . . . . . . . . . . . . . . . 220
Charles Brown . . . . . . . . . . . . . . . . . 222
Charlotte Hawkins Brown . . . . . . . . . . . 223
Claude Brown . . . . . . . . . . . . . . . . . . 225
Clifford Brown . . . . . . . . . . . . . . . . . 227
Dorothy Lavinia Brown . . . . . . . . . . . . 229
Elaine Brown . . . . . . . . . . . . . . . . . . 230
H. Rap Brown . . . . . . . . . . . . . . . . . . 232
James Brown . . . . . . . . . . . . . . . . . . 234
Jim Brown . . . . . . . . . . . . . . . . . . . . 237
Ray Brown . . . . . . . . . . . . . . . . . . . . 239
Ron Brown . . . . . . . . . . . . . . . . . . . 241
Sterling A. Brown . . . . . . . . . . . . . . . 243
Tim Brown . . . . . . . . . . . . . . . . . . . 245
Tony Brown . . . . . . . . . . . . . . . . . . . 246
Willie Brown . . . . . . . . . . . . . . . . . . 249
Blanche Kelso Bruce . . . . . . . . . . . . . . 251
John E. Bruce . . . . . . . . . . . . . . . . . . 254
Antonio Bryant . . . . . . . . . . . . . . . . . 255

Kobe Bryant . . . . . . . . . . . . . . . . . . 256
Eugene Jacques Bullard . . . . . . . . . . . . 259
Ed Bullins . . . . . . . . . . . . . . . . . . . . 260
Ralph Bunche . . . . . . . . . . . . . . . . . . 262
Solomon Burke . . . . . . . . . . . . . . . . . 265
Yvonne Brathwaite Burke . . . . . . . . . . . 267
Harry T. Burleigh . . . . . . . . . . . . . . . . 268
Roland Burris . . . . . . . . . . . . . . . . . . 271
Nannie Helen Burroughs . . . . . . . . . . . . 273
LeVar Burton . . . . . . . . . . . . . . . . . . 275
George Washington Bush . . . . . . . . . . . . 277
Octavia E. Butler . . . . . . . . . . . . . . . . 279

Lee Calhoun . . . . . . . . . . . . . . . . . . . 282
Cab Calloway . . . . . . . . . . . . . . . . . . 283
Godfrey Cambridge . . . . . . . . . . . . . . . 286
Roy Campanella . . . . . . . . . . . . . . . . . 288
Bebe Moore Campbell . . . . . . . . . . . . . 290
E. Simms Campbell . . . . . . . . . . . . . . . 292
Earl Campbell . . . . . . . . . . . . . . . . . . 294
Irene Cara . . . . . . . . . . . . . . . . . . . . 296
Francis Lewis Cardozo . . . . . . . . . . . . . 298
Rod Carew . . . . . . . . . . . . . . . . . . . . 300
Mariah Carey . . . . . . . . . . . . . . . . . . 301
John Carlos . . . . . . . . . . . . . . . . . . . 303
Stokely Carmichael . . . . . . . . . . . . . . . 305
Harry Carney . . . . . . . . . . . . . . . . . . 308
William H. Carney . . . . . . . . . . . . . . . 309
Leroy Carr . . . . . . . . . . . . . . . . . . . . 311
Diahann Carroll . . . . . . . . . . . . . . . . . 312
Benny Carter . . . . . . . . . . . . . . . . . . 314
Nell Carter . . . . . . . . . . . . . . . . . . . . 316
Stephen L. Carter . . . . . . . . . . . . . . . . 318
George Washington Carver . . . . . . . . . . . 319
Lorene Cary . . . . . . . . . . . . . . . . . . . 322
Bernie Casey . . . . . . . . . . . . . . . . . . 324
Cedric the Entertainer . . . . . . . . . . . . . 325
Wilt Chamberlain . . . . . . . . . . . . . . . . 327
James Chaney . . . . . . . . . . . . . . . . . . 330
Dave Chappelle . . . . . . . . . . . . . . . . . 333
Ezzard Charles . . . . . . . . . . . . . . . . . 334
Ray Charles . . . . . . . . . . . . . . . . . . . 336
Suzette Charles . . . . . . . . . . . . . . . . . 338
Barbara Chase-Riboud . . . . . . . . . . . . . 339
Benjamin Chavis . . . . . . . . . . . . . . . . 341
Don Cheadle . . . . . . . . . . . . . . . . . . . 343
Henry Plummer Cheatham . . . . . . . . . . . 344
Chubby Checker . . . . . . . . . . . . . . . . . 347
James E. Cheek . . . . . . . . . . . . . . . . . 349

# VOLUME 2

Contents. . . . . . . . . . . . . . . . . . . xxxv
Key to Pronunciation . . . . . . . . . . . xxxvii
Complete List of Contents . . . . . . . . . . xxxix

Kenneth Chenault . . . . . . . . . . . . . 351
Charles Waddell Chesnutt . . . . . . . . . . 353
Cyrus Chestnut. . . . . . . . . . . . . . . 355
Alice Childress. . . . . . . . . . . . . . . 356
Shirley Chisholm. . . . . . . . . . . . . . 359
Joseph Cinque . . . . . . . . . . . . . . . 361
Kenneth Clark . . . . . . . . . . . . . . . 363
Septima Poinsette Clark . . . . . . . . . . 365
John Henrik Clarke. . . . . . . . . . . . . 367
Albert Buford Cleage, Jr. . . . . . . . . . . 369
Eldridge Cleaver . . . . . . . . . . . . . . 371
Roberto Clemente . . . . . . . . . . . . . 374
Michelle Cliff . . . . . . . . . . . . . . . 377
Lucille Clifton . . . . . . . . . . . . . . . 378
George Clinton. . . . . . . . . . . . . . . 380
James E. Clyburn. . . . . . . . . . . . . . 382
Alice Coachman . . . . . . . . . . . . . . 384
Johnnie Cochran . . . . . . . . . . . . . . 386
Daniel Coker . . . . . . . . . . . . . . . . 388
Nat King Cole . . . . . . . . . . . . . . . 390
Natalie Cole . . . . . . . . . . . . . . . . 393
Bessie Coleman . . . . . . . . . . . . . . 394
Ornette Coleman . . . . . . . . . . . . . . 396
Wanda Coleman . . . . . . . . . . . . . . 399
Honi Coles and Cholly Atkins . . . . . . . . 400
Marva Collins . . . . . . . . . . . . . . . 403
Patricia Hill Collins . . . . . . . . . . . . 405
Alice Coltrane . . . . . . . . . . . . . . . 407
John Coltrane. . . . . . . . . . . . . . . . 409
James H. Cone . . . . . . . . . . . . . . . 411
John Conyers, Jr. . . . . . . . . . . . . . . 413
Sam Cooke. . . . . . . . . . . . . . . . . 415
J. California Cooper . . . . . . . . . . . . 417
Sam Cornish . . . . . . . . . . . . . . . . 418
Jayne Cortez . . . . . . . . . . . . . . . . 420
Bill Cosby . . . . . . . . . . . . . . . . . 422
William and Ellen Craft . . . . . . . . . . 425
Kimberlé Williams Crenshaw . . . . . . . . 426
Scatman Crothers . . . . . . . . . . . . . 428
Andraé Crouch . . . . . . . . . . . . . . . 430
Stanley Crouch . . . . . . . . . . . . . . . 432
Big Boy Crudup . . . . . . . . . . . . . . 433

Alexander Crummell . . . . . . . . . . . . 435
Paul Cuffe . . . . . . . . . . . . . . . . . 437
Countée Cullen. . . . . . . . . . . . . . . 439
Dorothy Dandridge. . . . . . . . . . . . . 442
Julie Dash . . . . . . . . . . . . . . . . . 445
Willie Davenport . . . . . . . . . . . . . . 446
Angela Davis. . . . . . . . . . . . . . . . 448
Benjamin J. Davis . . . . . . . . . . . . . 451
Benjamin O. Davis, Sr. . . . . . . . . . . . 452
Benjamin O. Davis, Jr. . . . . . . . . . . . 455
Ernie Davis. . . . . . . . . . . . . . . . . 457
Henrietta Vinton Davis. . . . . . . . . . . 459
Miles Davis. . . . . . . . . . . . . . . . . 461
Ossie Davis. . . . . . . . . . . . . . . . . 464
Sammy Davis, Jr. . . . . . . . . . . . . . . 466
Shani Davis . . . . . . . . . . . . . . . . 469
Viola Davis. . . . . . . . . . . . . . . . . 471
Dominique Dawes . . . . . . . . . . . . . 472
Darryl Dawkins . . . . . . . . . . . . . . 474
Roy DeCarava . . . . . . . . . . . . . . . 476
Ruby Dee. . . . . . . . . . . . . . . . . . 478
Anita DeFrantz . . . . . . . . . . . . . . . 479
Martin Robison Delany . . . . . . . . . . . 481
Samuel R. Delany . . . . . . . . . . . . . 484
Ron Dellums . . . . . . . . . . . . . . . . 485
Oscar DePriest . . . . . . . . . . . . . . . 488
R. Nathaniel Dett. . . . . . . . . . . . . . 489
Gail Devers. . . . . . . . . . . . . . . . . 491
Eric Dickerson . . . . . . . . . . . . . . . 493
Bo Diddley. . . . . . . . . . . . . . . . . 494
David Dinkins . . . . . . . . . . . . . . . 497
Ivan Dixon . . . . . . . . . . . . . . . . . 499
Willie Dixon . . . . . . . . . . . . . . . . 500
Larry Doby. . . . . . . . . . . . . . . . . 502
Dr. Dre . . . . . . . . . . . . . . . . . . . 504
Owen Dodson . . . . . . . . . . . . . . . 506
Fats Domino . . . . . . . . . . . . . . . . 508
Thomas A. Dorsey . . . . . . . . . . . . . 510
Aaron Douglas . . . . . . . . . . . . . . . 512
Frederick Douglass. . . . . . . . . . . . . 513
Rita Dove. . . . . . . . . . . . . . . . . . 516
Charles R. Drew . . . . . . . . . . . . . . 518
W. E. B. Du Bois . . . . . . . . . . . . . . 520
Henry Dumas. . . . . . . . . . . . . . . . 523
Paul Laurence Dunbar . . . . . . . . . . . 524

Alice Dunbar-Nelson . . . . . . . . . . . . . . . 527
Tim Duncan . . . . . . . . . . . . . . . . . 528
Katherine Dunham . . . . . . . . . . . . . . . 530
Oscar James Dunn . . . . . . . . . . . . . . . 532
Charles S. Dutton . . . . . . . . . . . . . . 533
Mervyn Dymally . . . . . . . . . . . . . . . 535

Billy Eckstine . . . . . . . . . . . . . . . . 538
Marian Wright Edelman . . . . . . . . . . . . 540
Lee Elder . . . . . . . . . . . . . . . . . . 542
Joycelyn Elders . . . . . . . . . . . . . . . 543
Duke Ellington . . . . . . . . . . . . . . . . 545
Ralph Ellison . . . . . . . . . . . . . . . . 548
James A. Emanuel . . . . . . . . . . . . . . . 551
Omar Epps . . . . . . . . . . . . . . . . . . 552
Julius Erving . . . . . . . . . . . . . . . . 554
Mike Espy . . . . . . . . . . . . . . . . . . 556
James Reese Europe . . . . . . . . . . . . . . 559
James Carmichael Evans . . . . . . . . . . . . 560
Lee Evans . . . . . . . . . . . . . . . . . . 562
Mari Evans . . . . . . . . . . . . . . . . . . 563
Charles Evers . . . . . . . . . . . . . . . . 565
Medgar Evers . . . . . . . . . . . . . . . . . 566
Myrlie Evers-Williams . . . . . . . . . . . . . 568
Patrick Ewing . . . . . . . . . . . . . . . . 571

James L. Farmer, Jr. . . . . . . . . . . . . . 573
Louis Farrakhan . . . . . . . . . . . . . . . 575
Father Divine . . . . . . . . . . . . . . . . 577
Marshall Faulk . . . . . . . . . . . . . . . . 580
Jessie Redmon Fauset . . . . . . . . . . . . . 582
Samuel Ferguson . . . . . . . . . . . . . . . 584
Stepin Fetchit . . . . . . . . . . . . . . . . 586
50 Cent . . . . . . . . . . . . . . . . . . . 588
Laurence Fishburne . . . . . . . . . . . . . . 590
Ella Fitzgerald . . . . . . . . . . . . . . . 592
Henry Ossian Flipper . . . . . . . . . . . . . 595
Curt Flood . . . . . . . . . . . . . . . . . . 596
William Thomas Fontaine . . . . . . . . . . . . 598
George Foreman . . . . . . . . . . . . . . . . 600
James Forman . . . . . . . . . . . . . . . . . 602
Leon Forrest . . . . . . . . . . . . . . . . . 604
James Forten . . . . . . . . . . . . . . . . . 606
Amos Fortune . . . . . . . . . . . . . . . . . 608
John R. Fox . . . . . . . . . . . . . . . . . 609
Jamie Foxx . . . . . . . . . . . . . . . . . . 611
Redd Foxx . . . . . . . . . . . . . . . . . . 613
Aretha Franklin . . . . . . . . . . . . . . . 614
John Hope Franklin . . . . . . . . . . . . . . 617

Joe Frazier . . . . . . . . . . . . . . . . . 620
Walt Frazier . . . . . . . . . . . . . . . . . 621
Morgan Freeman . . . . . . . . . . . . . . . . 623
Charles Fuller . . . . . . . . . . . . . . . . 625
Mary Hatwood Futrell . . . . . . . . . . . . . 626

Ernest J. Gaines . . . . . . . . . . . . . . . 629
Henry Highland Garnet . . . . . . . . . . . . . 631
Kevin Garnett . . . . . . . . . . . . . . . . 633
Marcus Garvey . . . . . . . . . . . . . . . . 635
Arthur George Gaston . . . . . . . . . . . . . 637
Henry Louis Gates, Jr. . . . . . . . . . . . . 640
Marvin Gaye . . . . . . . . . . . . . . . . . 643
Addison Gayle, Jr. . . . . . . . . . . . . . . 645
Helene Doris Gayle . . . . . . . . . . . . . . 646
Althea Gibson . . . . . . . . . . . . . . . . 648
Bob Gibson . . . . . . . . . . . . . . . . . . 650
Josh Gibson . . . . . . . . . . . . . . . . . 652
Dizzy Gillespie . . . . . . . . . . . . . . . 654
Nikki Giovanni . . . . . . . . . . . . . . . . 657
Danny Glover . . . . . . . . . . . . . . . . . 658
Savion Glover . . . . . . . . . . . . . . . . 660
Whoopi Goldberg . . . . . . . . . . . . . . . 662
Cuba Gooding, Jr. . . . . . . . . . . . . . . 663
Dexter Gordon . . . . . . . . . . . . . . . . 665
Ed Gordon . . . . . . . . . . . . . . . . . . 667
Lewis Gordon . . . . . . . . . . . . . . . . . 668
Annette Gordon-Reed . . . . . . . . . . . . . 670
Berry Gordy, Jr. . . . . . . . . . . . . . . . 672
Louis Gossett, Jr. . . . . . . . . . . . . . . 674
Meredith C. Gourdine . . . . . . . . . . . . . 676
Evelyn Boyd Granville . . . . . . . . . . . . . 678
Earl G. Graves, Sr. . . . . . . . . . . . . . 679
Macy Gray . . . . . . . . . . . . . . . . . . 681
William H. Gray III . . . . . . . . . . . . . 682
Al Green . . . . . . . . . . . . . . . . . . . 684
Joe Greene . . . . . . . . . . . . . . . . . . 686
Dick Gregory . . . . . . . . . . . . . . . . . 688
Frederick Drew Gregory . . . . . . . . . . . . 690
Wilton D. Gregory . . . . . . . . . . . . . . 692
Pam Grier . . . . . . . . . . . . . . . . . . 694
Ken Griffey, Jr. . . . . . . . . . . . . . . . 695
Johnny Griffin . . . . . . . . . . . . . . . . 697
Florence Griffith-Joyner . . . . . . . . . . . 699
Angelina Weld Grimké . . . . . . . . . . . . . 701
Charlotte L. Forten Grimké . . . . . . . . . . 703
Robert Guillaume . . . . . . . . . . . . . . . 706
Bryant Gumbel . . . . . . . . . . . . . . . . 707
Tony Gwynn . . . . . . . . . . . . . . . . . . 708

# VOLUME 3

Contents . . . . . . . . . . . . . . . . . . lv
Key to Pronunciation . . . . . . . . . . . . . . lix
Complete List of Contents . . . . . . . . . . . lxi

Alex Haley . . . . . . . . . . . . . . . . . . 711
Arsenio Hall . . . . . . . . . . . . . . . . . 714
Prince Hall . . . . . . . . . . . . . . . . . 716
Fannie Lou Hamer . . . . . . . . . . . . . . 717
Virginia Hamilton . . . . . . . . . . . . . . 720
M. C. Hammer . . . . . . . . . . . . . . . . 721
Lionel Hampton . . . . . . . . . . . . . . . 723
Herbie Hancock . . . . . . . . . . . . . . . 725
W. C. Handy . . . . . . . . . . . . . . . . . 727
Lorraine Hansberry . . . . . . . . . . . . . . 728
Austin Hansen . . . . . . . . . . . . . . . . 731
Frances Ellen Watkins Harper . . . . . . . . . 732
Michael S. Harper . . . . . . . . . . . . . . 734
Franco Harris . . . . . . . . . . . . . . . . 735
Patricia Roberts Harris . . . . . . . . . . . . 737
Donny Hathaway . . . . . . . . . . . . . . . 739
Connie Hawkins . . . . . . . . . . . . . . . 740
Bob Hayes . . . . . . . . . . . . . . . . . . 742
Elvin Hayes . . . . . . . . . . . . . . . . . 745
Isaac Hayes . . . . . . . . . . . . . . . . . 746
Roland Hayes . . . . . . . . . . . . . . . . 748
Patrick F. Healy . . . . . . . . . . . . . . . 750
Dorothy Height . . . . . . . . . . . . . . . 752
Sally Hemings . . . . . . . . . . . . . . . . 754
Rickey Henderson . . . . . . . . . . . . . . 756
Jimi Hendrix . . . . . . . . . . . . . . . . . 758
Matthew Alexander Henson . . . . . . . . . . 761
Alexis M. Herman . . . . . . . . . . . . . . 763
Anita Hill . . . . . . . . . . . . . . . . . . 764
Lauryn Hill . . . . . . . . . . . . . . . . . 767
Asa Grant Hilliard III . . . . . . . . . . . . 768
Chester Himes . . . . . . . . . . . . . . . . 770
Earl Hines . . . . . . . . . . . . . . . . . . 772
Gregory Hines . . . . . . . . . . . . . . . . 774
Milt Hinton . . . . . . . . . . . . . . . . . 776
Mellody Hobson . . . . . . . . . . . . . . . 778
Eric Holder . . . . . . . . . . . . . . . . . 779
Billie Holiday . . . . . . . . . . . . . . . . 781
Evander Holyfield . . . . . . . . . . . . . . 784
John Lee Hooker . . . . . . . . . . . . . . . 786
Bell Hooks . . . . . . . . . . . . . . . . . . 788
Benjamin Hooks . . . . . . . . . . . . . . . 789

John Hope . . . . . . . . . . . . . . . . . . 791
Lena Horne . . . . . . . . . . . . . . . . . 794
Charles Hamilton Houston . . . . . . . . . . 797
Whitney Houston . . . . . . . . . . . . . . . 798
Dwight Howard . . . . . . . . . . . . . . . 800
Jennifer Hudson . . . . . . . . . . . . . . . 802
Langston Hughes . . . . . . . . . . . . . . . 803
Charlayne Hunter-Gault . . . . . . . . . . . 807
Zora Neale Hurston . . . . . . . . . . . . . 808

Ice Cube . . . . . . . . . . . . . . . . . . . 812
Gwen Ifill . . . . . . . . . . . . . . . . . . 814
India.Arie . . . . . . . . . . . . . . . . . . 815
Roy Innis . . . . . . . . . . . . . . . . . . 817
Allen Iverson . . . . . . . . . . . . . . . . 819

Bo Jackson . . . . . . . . . . . . . . . . . . 822
Janet Jackson . . . . . . . . . . . . . . . . 825
Jesse Jackson . . . . . . . . . . . . . . . . 826
Jesse Jackson, Jr. . . . . . . . . . . . . . . . 829
Mahalia Jackson . . . . . . . . . . . . . . . 831
Maynard Jackson . . . . . . . . . . . . . . . 833
Michael Jackson . . . . . . . . . . . . . . . 835
Reggie Jackson . . . . . . . . . . . . . . . . 838
Samuel L. Jackson . . . . . . . . . . . . . . 840
Shirley Ann Jackson . . . . . . . . . . . . . 842
Sheila Jackson Lee . . . . . . . . . . . . . . 844
T. D. Jakes . . . . . . . . . . . . . . . . . . 846
Etta James . . . . . . . . . . . . . . . . . . 847
LeBron James . . . . . . . . . . . . . . . . 849
Jay-Z . . . . . . . . . . . . . . . . . . . . 852
Benjamin T. Jealous . . . . . . . . . . . . . 853
Wyclef Jean . . . . . . . . . . . . . . . . . 855
Leonard Jeffries . . . . . . . . . . . . . . . 856
Mae C. Jemison . . . . . . . . . . . . . . . 858
Derek Jeter . . . . . . . . . . . . . . . . . 860
Charles S. Johnson . . . . . . . . . . . . . . 862
Dwayne Johnson . . . . . . . . . . . . . . . 864
Jack Johnson . . . . . . . . . . . . . . . . . 865
James Weldon Johnson . . . . . . . . . . . . 868
John H. Johnson . . . . . . . . . . . . . . . 872
Joshua Johnson . . . . . . . . . . . . . . . 874
Katherine G. Johnson . . . . . . . . . . . . 876
Magic Johnson . . . . . . . . . . . . . . . . 877
Michael Johnson . . . . . . . . . . . . . . . 880
Rafer Johnson . . . . . . . . . . . . . . . . 882

Robert L. Johnson . . . . . . . . . . . . . . 884
Sargent Johnson . . . . . . . . . . . . . . . 886
William H. Johnson . . . . . . . . . . . . . 888
Absalom Jones . . . . . . . . . . . . . . . . 889
Bill T. Jones . . . . . . . . . . . . . . . . . 891
Gayl Jones . . . . . . . . . . . . . . . . . . 893
James Earl Jones . . . . . . . . . . . . . . . 895
Marion Jones . . . . . . . . . . . . . . . . . 897
Quincy Jones . . . . . . . . . . . . . . . . . 899
Sissieretta Jones . . . . . . . . . . . . . . . 902
Scott Joplin . . . . . . . . . . . . . . . . . . 903
Barbara Jordan . . . . . . . . . . . . . . . . 905
June Jordan . . . . . . . . . . . . . . . . . . 907
Michael Jordan . . . . . . . . . . . . . . . . 909
Vernon Jordan . . . . . . . . . . . . . . . . 912
Jackie Joyner-Kersee . . . . . . . . . . . . . 914
Master Juba . . . . . . . . . . . . . . . . . . 916
Hubert Fauntleroy Julian . . . . . . . . . . . 917
Percy Lavon Julian . . . . . . . . . . . . . . 919
Ernest Everett Just . . . . . . . . . . . . . . 921

Maulana Karenga . . . . . . . . . . . . . . . 923
Ulysses Kay . . . . . . . . . . . . . . . . . . 925
William Melvin Kelley . . . . . . . . . . . . 926
Adrienne Kennedy . . . . . . . . . . . . . . 928
Alan Keyes . . . . . . . . . . . . . . . . . . 930
Alicia Keys . . . . . . . . . . . . . . . . . . 932
Jamaica Kincaid . . . . . . . . . . . . . . . 934
B. B. King . . . . . . . . . . . . . . . . . . 936
Coretta Scott King . . . . . . . . . . . . . . 939
Martin Luther King, Jr. . . . . . . . . . . . . 941
Eartha Kitt . . . . . . . . . . . . . . . . . . 944
Gladys Knight . . . . . . . . . . . . . . . . 946
Beyoncé Knowles . . . . . . . . . . . . . . . 948
Yusef Komunyakaa . . . . . . . . . . . . . . 949

L. L. Cool J. . . . . . . . . . . . . . . . . . 952
Patti LaBelle . . . . . . . . . . . . . . . . . 953
Willie Lanier . . . . . . . . . . . . . . . . . 955
Nella Larsen . . . . . . . . . . . . . . . . . 957
Lewis Howard Latimer . . . . . . . . . . . . 959
Jacob Lawrence . . . . . . . . . . . . . . . . 961
Robert H. Lawrence, Jr. . . . . . . . . . . . . 963
James Lawson . . . . . . . . . . . . . . . . . 964
John Lawson . . . . . . . . . . . . . . . . . 966
Canada Lee . . . . . . . . . . . . . . . . . . 967
Spike Lee . . . . . . . . . . . . . . . . . . . 969
Hughie Lee-Smith . . . . . . . . . . . . . . 971
Meadowlark Lemon . . . . . . . . . . . . . . 972
Sugar Ray Leonard . . . . . . . . . . . . . . 974

Lisa Leslie . . . . . . . . . . . . . . . . . . 976
Carl Lewis . . . . . . . . . . . . . . . . . . 978
Edmonia Lewis . . . . . . . . . . . . . . . . 980
John Robert Lewis . . . . . . . . . . . . . . 982
Ray Lewis . . . . . . . . . . . . . . . . . . 984
C. Eric Lincoln . . . . . . . . . . . . . . . . 985
Sonny Liston . . . . . . . . . . . . . . . . . 987
Cleavon Little . . . . . . . . . . . . . . . . 989
Little Richard . . . . . . . . . . . . . . . . . 990
Little Walter . . . . . . . . . . . . . . . . . 992
Earl Lloyd . . . . . . . . . . . . . . . . . . 994
Alain Locke . . . . . . . . . . . . . . . . . . 995
Audre Lorde . . . . . . . . . . . . . . . . . 997
Joe Louis . . . . . . . . . . . . . . . . . . . 999
Joseph Lowery . . . . . . . . . . . . . . . . 1001

Moms Mabley . . . . . . . . . . . . . . . . . 1003
Bernie Mac . . . . . . . . . . . . . . . . . . 1005
Hattie McDaniel . . . . . . . . . . . . . . . 1006
Audra McDonald . . . . . . . . . . . . . . . 1008
Claude McKay . . . . . . . . . . . . . . . . 1010
Jackie McLean . . . . . . . . . . . . . . . . 1012
Terry McMillan . . . . . . . . . . . . . . . . 1014
Donovan McNabb . . . . . . . . . . . . . . . 1016
Ronald E. McNair . . . . . . . . . . . . . . 1017
Clyde McPhatter . . . . . . . . . . . . . . . 1019
John McWhorter . . . . . . . . . . . . . . . 1020
Haki R. Madhubuti . . . . . . . . . . . . . . 1022
Malcolm X . . . . . . . . . . . . . . . . . . 1024
Karl Malone . . . . . . . . . . . . . . . . . 1027
Vance Hunter Marchbanks . . . . . . . . . . 1029
Ellis Marsalis, Jr. . . . . . . . . . . . . . . . 1030
Wynton Marsalis . . . . . . . . . . . . . . . 1032
Kerry James Marshall . . . . . . . . . . . . . 1034
Paule Marshall . . . . . . . . . . . . . . . . 1035
Thurgood Marshall . . . . . . . . . . . . . . 1037
Kenyon Martin . . . . . . . . . . . . . . . . 1039
Jan Ernst Matzeliger . . . . . . . . . . . . . 1041
Benjamin E. Mays . . . . . . . . . . . . . . 1043
Willie Mays . . . . . . . . . . . . . . . . . . 1045
John Willis Menard . . . . . . . . . . . . . . 1048
James Meredith . . . . . . . . . . . . . . . . 1049
Louise Meriwether . . . . . . . . . . . . . . 1052
Kweisi Mfume . . . . . . . . . . . . . . . . 1053
Oscar Micheaux . . . . . . . . . . . . . . . . 1055
Cheryl Miller . . . . . . . . . . . . . . . . . 1057
Dorie Miller . . . . . . . . . . . . . . . . . 1058
Florence Mills . . . . . . . . . . . . . . . . 1060
Charles Mingus . . . . . . . . . . . . . . . . 1061
Arthur Mitchell . . . . . . . . . . . . . . . . 1064

Brian Stokes Mitchell . . . . . . . . . . . . . 1065
Clarence M. Mitchell, Jr. . . . . . . . . . . . 1067
Thelonious Monk . . . . . . . . . . . . . . . 1068

Little Brother Montgomery . . . . . . . . . . 1071
Archie Moore . . . . . . . . . . . . . . . . . 1073
Garrett Augustus Morgan . . . . . . . . . . . 1075

# Volume 4

Contents . . . . . . . . . . . . . . . . . . . lxxvii
Key to Pronunciation . . . . . . . . . . . . . lxxxi
Complete List of Contents . . . . . . . . . . lxxxiii

Dutch Morial . . . . . . . . . . . . . . . . . 1077
Garrett Morris . . . . . . . . . . . . . . . . 1078
Toni Morrison . . . . . . . . . . . . . . . . . 1080
Jelly Roll Morton . . . . . . . . . . . . . . . 1082
Edwin Moses . . . . . . . . . . . . . . . . . 1084
Walter Mosley . . . . . . . . . . . . . . . . 1086
Elijah Muhammad . . . . . . . . . . . . . . . 1088
Eddie Murphy . . . . . . . . . . . . . . . . . 1090
Isaac Burns Murphy . . . . . . . . . . . . . . 1093
Albert Murray . . . . . . . . . . . . . . . . . 1094
Pauli Murray . . . . . . . . . . . . . . . . . 1095
Walter Dean Myers . . . . . . . . . . . . . . 1097

Ray Nagin . . . . . . . . . . . . . . . . . . . 1100
Diane Nash . . . . . . . . . . . . . . . . . . 1102
Fats Navarro . . . . . . . . . . . . . . . . . 1103
Gloria Naylor . . . . . . . . . . . . . . . . . 1105
Aaron Neville . . . . . . . . . . . . . . . . . 1106
Huey P. Newton . . . . . . . . . . . . . . . . 1108
Fayard and Harold Nicholas . . . . . . . . . . 1110
Herbie Nichols . . . . . . . . . . . . . . . . 1112
Nichelle Nichols . . . . . . . . . . . . . . . 1114
E. D. Nixon . . . . . . . . . . . . . . . . . . 1116
Jessye Norman . . . . . . . . . . . . . . . . 1117
Eleanor Holmes Norton . . . . . . . . . . . . 1119

Barack Obama . . . . . . . . . . . . . . . . . 1121
Michelle Obama . . . . . . . . . . . . . . . . 1124
Odetta . . . . . . . . . . . . . . . . . . . . . 1126
Hakeem Olajuwon . . . . . . . . . . . . . . . 1128
Hazel R. O'Leary . . . . . . . . . . . . . . . 1130
King Oliver . . . . . . . . . . . . . . . . . . 1132
Shaquille O'Neal . . . . . . . . . . . . . . . 1133
Buck O'Neil . . . . . . . . . . . . . . . . . . 1136
Clarence Otis, Jr. . . . . . . . . . . . . . . . 1137
Chris Owens . . . . . . . . . . . . . . . . . . 1139
Jesse Owens . . . . . . . . . . . . . . . . . . 1140
Terrell Owens . . . . . . . . . . . . . . . . . 1143

Clarence E. Page . . . . . . . . . . . . . . . 1145
Rod Paige . . . . . . . . . . . . . . . . . . . 1146
Satchel Paige . . . . . . . . . . . . . . . . . 1148
Charlie Parker . . . . . . . . . . . . . . . . . 1151
Pat Parker . . . . . . . . . . . . . . . . . . . 1153
Gordon Parks, Sr. . . . . . . . . . . . . . . . 1155
Rosa Parks . . . . . . . . . . . . . . . . . . . 1157
David A. Paterson . . . . . . . . . . . . . . . 1159
Deval Patrick . . . . . . . . . . . . . . . . . 1161
Floyd Patterson . . . . . . . . . . . . . . . . 1163
Frederick D. Patterson . . . . . . . . . . . . 1165
Chris Paul . . . . . . . . . . . . . . . . . . . 1166
Walter Payton . . . . . . . . . . . . . . . . . 1168
Calvin Peete . . . . . . . . . . . . . . . . . . 1170
Rodney Peete . . . . . . . . . . . . . . . . . 1172
Tyler Perry . . . . . . . . . . . . . . . . . . 1173
Brock Peters . . . . . . . . . . . . . . . . . . 1175
Ann Petry . . . . . . . . . . . . . . . . . . . 1177
Bill Pickett . . . . . . . . . . . . . . . . . . 1179
Paul Pierce . . . . . . . . . . . . . . . . . . 1181
Samuel R. Pierce, Jr. . . . . . . . . . . . . . 1183
P. B. S. Pinchback . . . . . . . . . . . . . . . 1184
Scottie Pippen . . . . . . . . . . . . . . . . . 1186
Leonard Pitts . . . . . . . . . . . . . . . . . 1187
Jean Baptiste Pointe du Sable . . . . . . . . . 1188
Sidney Poitier . . . . . . . . . . . . . . . . . 1190
Fritz Pollard . . . . . . . . . . . . . . . . . . 1193
Alvin Francis Poussaint . . . . . . . . . . . . 1194
Adam Clayton Powell, Jr. . . . . . . . . . . . 1196
Colin Powell . . . . . . . . . . . . . . . . . . 1199
Leontyne Price . . . . . . . . . . . . . . . . 1202
Lloyd Price . . . . . . . . . . . . . . . . . . 1204
Charley Pride . . . . . . . . . . . . . . . . . 1206
Pearl Primus . . . . . . . . . . . . . . . . . 1208
Prince . . . . . . . . . . . . . . . . . . . . . 1210
Professor Longhair . . . . . . . . . . . . . . 1212
Richard Pryor . . . . . . . . . . . . . . . . . 1214
Puff Daddy . . . . . . . . . . . . . . . . . . . 1217

Benjamin Quarles . . . . . . . . . . . . . . . 1219
Queen Latifah . . . . . . . . . . . . . . . . . 1221

Albert Raby . . . . . . . . . . . . . . . . . . . 1224
Ma Rainey . . . . . . . . . . . . . . . . . . . 1226
A. Philip Randolph . . . . . . . . . . . . . 1228
Charles Rangel . . . . . . . . . . . . . . . . 1231
Phylicia Rashad . . . . . . . . . . . . . . . . 1233
Otis Redding . . . . . . . . . . . . . . . . . 1235
Ed Reed . . . . . . . . . . . . . . . . . . . . . 1236
Ishmael Reed . . . . . . . . . . . . . . . . . 1238
Tim Reid . . . . . . . . . . . . . . . . . . . . 1240
Hiram Rhoades Revels . . . . . . . . . . 1241
Sylvia M. Rhone . . . . . . . . . . . . . . . 1243
Condoleezza Rice . . . . . . . . . . . . . . 1245
Jerry Rice . . . . . . . . . . . . . . . . . . . . 1247
Linda Johnson Rice . . . . . . . . . . . . . 1249
Lloyd Richards . . . . . . . . . . . . . . . . 1251
Lionel Richie . . . . . . . . . . . . . . . . . 1252
Rihanna . . . . . . . . . . . . . . . . . . . . . 1255
Norbert Rillieux . . . . . . . . . . . . . . . 1256
Faith Ringgold . . . . . . . . . . . . . . . . 1258
Max Roach . . . . . . . . . . . . . . . . . . . 1260
Oscar Robertson . . . . . . . . . . . . . . . 1261
Paul Robeson . . . . . . . . . . . . . . . . . 1263
Bill Robinson . . . . . . . . . . . . . . . . . 1266
David Robinson . . . . . . . . . . . . . . . 1269
Frank Robinson . . . . . . . . . . . . . . . . 1270
Jackie Robinson . . . . . . . . . . . . . . . 1272
Jo Ann Gibson Robinson . . . . . . . . . 1275
Max Robinson . . . . . . . . . . . . . . . . . 1277
Randall Robinson . . . . . . . . . . . . . . 1278
Smokey Robinson . . . . . . . . . . . . . . 1280
Spottswood W. Robinson III . . . . . . . 1282
Sugar Ray Robinson . . . . . . . . . . . . 1284
Chris Rock . . . . . . . . . . . . . . . . . . . 1286
Al Roker . . . . . . . . . . . . . . . . . . . . 1287
Sonny Rollins . . . . . . . . . . . . . . . . . 1289
Diana Ross . . . . . . . . . . . . . . . . . . . 1291
Darius Rucker . . . . . . . . . . . . . . . . . 1294
Wilma Rudolph . . . . . . . . . . . . . . . . 1295
Bill Russell . . . . . . . . . . . . . . . . . . . 1298
George Russell . . . . . . . . . . . . . . . . 1300
John Brown Russwurm . . . . . . . . . . 1302
Bayard Rustin . . . . . . . . . . . . . . . . . 1303

Betye Saar . . . . . . . . . . . . . . . . . . . 1306
Sonia Sanchez . . . . . . . . . . . . . . . . 1307
Barry Sanders . . . . . . . . . . . . . . . . . 1309
Deion Sanders . . . . . . . . . . . . . . . . 1311
Pharoah Sanders . . . . . . . . . . . . . . . 1314
David Satcher . . . . . . . . . . . . . . . . . 1315
Augusta Savage . . . . . . . . . . . . . . . 1317

Arturo Alfonso Schomburg . . . . . . . . . . 1319
George S. Schuyler . . . . . . . . . . . . . 1321
Dred Scott . . . . . . . . . . . . . . . . . . . . 1324
Briana Scurry . . . . . . . . . . . . . . . . . 1326
Bobby Seale . . . . . . . . . . . . . . . . . . 1328
Betty Shabazz . . . . . . . . . . . . . . . . . 1330
Ilyasah Shabazz . . . . . . . . . . . . . . . 1332
Tupac Shakur . . . . . . . . . . . . . . . . . 1333
Ntozake Shange . . . . . . . . . . . . . . . 1335
Al Sharpton . . . . . . . . . . . . . . . . . . 1337
Bernard Shaw . . . . . . . . . . . . . . . . . 1340
Art Shell . . . . . . . . . . . . . . . . . . . . 1341
Archie Shepp . . . . . . . . . . . . . . . . . 1344
Wayne Shorter . . . . . . . . . . . . . . . . 1345
Fred Shuttlesworth . . . . . . . . . . . . . 1347
Horace Silver . . . . . . . . . . . . . . . . . 1349
Joseph Simmons . . . . . . . . . . . . . . . 1350
Kimora Lee Simmons . . . . . . . . . . . 1352
Russell Simmons . . . . . . . . . . . . . . . 1354
Ruth Simmons . . . . . . . . . . . . . . . . 1356
Willie Simms . . . . . . . . . . . . . . . . . 1357
Nina Simone . . . . . . . . . . . . . . . . . 1359
O. J. Simpson . . . . . . . . . . . . . . . . . 1361
Mike Singletary . . . . . . . . . . . . . . . 1364
Benjamin Singleton . . . . . . . . . . . . . 1366
John Singleton . . . . . . . . . . . . . . . . 1367
John Brooks Slaughter . . . . . . . . . . . 1369
Robert Smalls . . . . . . . . . . . . . . . . . 1371
Tavis Smiley . . . . . . . . . . . . . . . . . . 1373
Anna Deavere Smith . . . . . . . . . . . . 1374
Barbara Smith . . . . . . . . . . . . . . . . . 1376
Bessie Smith . . . . . . . . . . . . . . . . . . 1377
Emmitt Smith . . . . . . . . . . . . . . . . . 1379
Huey "Piano" Smith . . . . . . . . . . . . 1381
Tommie Smith . . . . . . . . . . . . . . . . 1382
Will Smith . . . . . . . . . . . . . . . . . . . 1385
Wesley Snipes . . . . . . . . . . . . . . . . . 1386
Snoop Dogg . . . . . . . . . . . . . . . . . . 1388
Thomas Sowell . . . . . . . . . . . . . . . . 1390
Claude M. Steele . . . . . . . . . . . . . . . 1392
Michael Steele . . . . . . . . . . . . . . . . 1393
Shelby Steele . . . . . . . . . . . . . . . . . 1395
Maria Stewart . . . . . . . . . . . . . . . . . 1397
William Grant Still . . . . . . . . . . . . . . 1398
Sonny Stitt . . . . . . . . . . . . . . . . . . . 1401
Woody Strode . . . . . . . . . . . . . . . . . 1402
Leon H. Sullivan . . . . . . . . . . . . . . . 1404
Donna Summer . . . . . . . . . . . . . . . . 1405
Sun Ra . . . . . . . . . . . . . . . . . . . . . 1407

Taj Mahal . . . . . . . . . . . . . . . . 1410
Henry Ossawa Tanner. . . . . . . . . . . 1412
Lawrence Taylor . . . . . . . . . . . . . 1413
Mildred D. Taylor. . . . . . . . . . . . . 1415
Mary Church Terrell . . . . . . . . . . . 1416
Clarence Thomas . . . . . . . . . . . . . 1418
Debi Thomas . . . . . . . . . . . . . . . 1421
Frank Thomas. . . . . . . . . . . . . . . 1423
Isiah Thomas . . . . . . . . . . . . . . . 1424

Vivien Thomas . . . . . . . . . . . . . . 1427
Larry D. Thompson . . . . . . . . . . . . 1428
Henry Threadgill . . . . . . . . . . . . . 1430
Emmett Till . . . . . . . . . . . . . . . . 1432
Melvin B. Tolson . . . . . . . . . . . . . 1434
Jean Toomer . . . . . . . . . . . . . . . 1435
Robert Townsend . . . . . . . . . . . . . 1438
William Monroe Trotter . . . . . . . . . . 1439

# VOLUME 5

Contents. . . . . . . . . . . . . . . . . xcvii
Key to Pronunciation . . . . . . . . . . . xcix
Complete List of Contents . . . . . . . . . ci

Sojourner Truth . . . . . . . . . . . . . . 1441
Harriet Tubman . . . . . . . . . . . . . . 1444
C. DeLores Tucker . . . . . . . . . . . . 1447
Big Joe Turner . . . . . . . . . . . . . . 1448
Henry McNeal Turner . . . . . . . . . . . 1450
Ike Turner. . . . . . . . . . . . . . . . . 1451
Nat Turner . . . . . . . . . . . . . . . . 1453
Tina Turner . . . . . . . . . . . . . . . . 1455
McCoy Tyner . . . . . . . . . . . . . . . 1458
Cicely Tyson . . . . . . . . . . . . . . . 1460
Mike Tyson . . . . . . . . . . . . . . . . 1462
Neil deGrasse Tyson . . . . . . . . . . . . 1464
Wyomia Tyus . . . . . . . . . . . . . . . 1466

Leslie Uggams . . . . . . . . . . . . . . 1468
Blair Underwood . . . . . . . . . . . . . 1470
Gene Upshaw. . . . . . . . . . . . . . . 1472
Usher . . . . . . . . . . . . . . . . . . 1474

Courtney B. Vance . . . . . . . . . . . . 1476
James Van Der Zee . . . . . . . . . . . . 1477
Mario Van Peebles . . . . . . . . . . . . 1480
Melvin Van Peebles. . . . . . . . . . . . 1482
Sarah Vaughan . . . . . . . . . . . . . . 1483
Ben Vereen . . . . . . . . . . . . . . . . 1485
Denmark Vesey . . . . . . . . . . . . . . 1487
C. T. Vivian . . . . . . . . . . . . . . . . 1488

Jersey Joe Walcott . . . . . . . . . . . . 1491
Alice Walker . . . . . . . . . . . . . . . 1493
David Walker . . . . . . . . . . . . . . . 1495

George Walker . . . . . . . . . . . . . . 1497
Jimmie Walker . . . . . . . . . . . . . . 1498
Madam C. J. Walker . . . . . . . . . . . . 1500
Margaret Walker . . . . . . . . . . . . . 1503
Fats Waller . . . . . . . . . . . . . . . . 1504
Eric Walrond . . . . . . . . . . . . . . . 1507
Alexander Walters . . . . . . . . . . . . 1508
Dionne Warwick . . . . . . . . . . . . . 1510
Booker T. Washington . . . . . . . . . . . 1513
Denzel Washington . . . . . . . . . . . . 1515
Harold Washington . . . . . . . . . . . . 1518
Kenny Washington . . . . . . . . . . . . 1521
Maxine Waters . . . . . . . . . . . . . . 1523
Muddy Waters . . . . . . . . . . . . . . 1525
Faye Wattleton . . . . . . . . . . . . . . 1526
J. C. Watts. . . . . . . . . . . . . . . . . 1528
Robert C. Weaver . . . . . . . . . . . . . 1530
Chick Webb. . . . . . . . . . . . . . . . 1531
Ida B. Wells-Barnett . . . . . . . . . . . 1533
Cornel West. . . . . . . . . . . . . . . . 1535
David West . . . . . . . . . . . . . . . . 1537
Dorothy West . . . . . . . . . . . . . . . 1538
Kanye West . . . . . . . . . . . . . . . . 1540
Togo West. . . . . . . . . . . . . . . . . 1541
Clifton Reginald Wharton, Jr. . . . . . . . 1543
Phillis Wheatley . . . . . . . . . . . . . 1545
Tyrone Wheatley . . . . . . . . . . . . . 1547
Forest Whitaker . . . . . . . . . . . . . . 1548
Bill White. . . . . . . . . . . . . . . . . 1550
Walter White . . . . . . . . . . . . . . . 1552
John Edgar Wideman . . . . . . . . . . . 1555
L. Douglas Wilder . . . . . . . . . . . . 1557
Lenny Wilkens . . . . . . . . . . . . . . 1558
Roy Wilkins. . . . . . . . . . . . . . . . 1560
Bert Williams . . . . . . . . . . . . . . . 1563

Billy Dee Williams . . . . . . . . . . . . . . . 1565
Cootie Williams. . . . . . . . . . . . . . . . 1566
Daniel Hale Williams . . . . . . . . . . . . . 1567
Gus Williams . . . . . . . . . . . . . . . . . 1569
Hosea Williams . . . . . . . . . . . . . . . . 1571
Juan Williams . . . . . . . . . . . . . . . . . 1573
Mary Lou Williams . . . . . . . . . . . . . . 1574
Montel Williams . . . . . . . . . . . . . . . 1576
Robert Franklin Williams . . . . . . . . . . . 1578
Serena Williams. . . . . . . . . . . . . . . . 1579
Vanessa Williams . . . . . . . . . . . . . . . 1581
Venus Williams . . . . . . . . . . . . . . . . 1583
Willie L. Williams . . . . . . . . . . . . . . 1584
Maury Wills. . . . . . . . . . . . . . . . . . 1586
August Wilson . . . . . . . . . . . . . . . . 1587
Flip Wilson . . . . . . . . . . . . . . . . . . 1590
Jackie Wilson . . . . . . . . . . . . . . . . . 1592
William Julius Wilson . . . . . . . . . . . . 1593
Paul Winfield . . . . . . . . . . . . . . . . . 1595
Oprah Winfrey . . . . . . . . . . . . . . . . 1597
James Winkfield . . . . . . . . . . . . . . . 1600
Ernest Withers . . . . . . . . . . . . . . . . 1601
George C. Wolfe . . . . . . . . . . . . . . . 1603
Stevie Wonder . . . . . . . . . . . . . . . . 1605
Alfre Woodard . . . . . . . . . . . . . . . . 1607
Lynette Woodard . . . . . . . . . . . . . . . 1609
Granville T. Woods . . . . . . . . . . . . . 1610
Tiger Woods . . . . . . . . . . . . . . . . . 1612

Carter G. Woodson . . . . . . . . . . . . . . 1615
Rod Woodson . . . . . . . . . . . . . . . . . 1617
Jane Cooke Wright . . . . . . . . . . . . . . 1619
Jeffrey Wright. . . . . . . . . . . . . . . . . 1620
Jeremiah Wright . . . . . . . . . . . . . . . 1622
Louis T. Wright . . . . . . . . . . . . . . . . 1624
Richard Wright . . . . . . . . . . . . . . . . 1625

Frank Yerby . . . . . . . . . . . . . . . . . . 1628
Al Young . . . . . . . . . . . . . . . . . . . 1631
Andrew Young . . . . . . . . . . . . . . . . 1632
Coleman Young. . . . . . . . . . . . . . . . 1635
Whitney Young . . . . . . . . . . . . . . . . 1637

## Appendixes

Chronological List of Entries . . . . . . . . . . 1641
Mediagraphy . . . . . . . . . . . . . . . . . 1651
Literary Bibliography. . . . . . . . . . . . . . 1658
Organizations and Societies . . . . . . . . . . 1665
Research Centers and Libraries. . . . . . . . . 1669
Bibliography . . . . . . . . . . . . . . . . . 1673
Web Site Directory . . . . . . . . . . . . . . 1682

## Indexes

Category Index . . . . . . . . . . . . . . . . 1689
Personages Index . . . . . . . . . . . . . . . 1705
Subject Index . . . . . . . . . . . . . . . . . 1731

# SOJOURNER TRUTH
## Activist

*Truth, born a slave, walked to freedom to become an example of courage and survival. Although she was an illiterate woman, she was able to reach white and black audiences through her speeches and her biography. She challenged white supremacy, claiming her rights through legal action and civil disobedience, and proposed ideas to alleviate the suffering of her people.*

**BORN:** c. 1797; Hurley, Ulster County, New York
**DIED:** November 26, 1883; Battle Creek, Michigan
**ALSO KNOWN AS:** Isabella Baumfree (birth name); Isabella Van Wagenen
**AREAS OF ACHIEVEMENT:** Abolitionism; Social issues; Women's rights

### EARLY LIFE

Sojourner Truth (soh-JUHRN-uhr) was born a slave around 1797 in Hurley, Ulster County, New York, near the Hudson River. She was the second youngest of ten or twelve children of James and Elizabeth, but as a child she knew only one sibling. Her birth name was Isabella Baumfree.

Truth and her family were the property of Colonel Johannes Hardenbergh, who owned nearly two million acres between the Hudson and Delaware rivers in Ulster County. Hardenbergh died when Truth was an infant, and she and her family became the property of his son, Charles.

In 1807, after the death of Charles Hardenbergh, Truth was sold to John Neely, a merchant from Twaalfskill, New York (near present-day Kingston). She was about nine years old. After one or two years, the Neelys sold her to Martinus Shryver, a fisherman and tavern keeper. Shryver, in turn, sold Truth in 1810 to John J. Dumont of New Paltz Landing, where she remained until 1826.

With the Dumont family, Truth did farm work and household chores. In 1814, she married another slave named Thomas, whom Dumont seems to have selected for her, and they lived together for about ten years. They had five children, four of whom—Diana, Peter, Elizabeth, and Sophia—lived past infancy. The fifth may have died in infancy or early childhood.

In 1817, the New York state legislature passed a law decreeing that all New York slaves born before July 4, 1799, would be freed on July 4, 1827. Dumont promised Truth and Thomas that he would free them on July 4,

1826, a year earlier than the law required. However, Truth subsequently injured her hand and lost her ability to work quickly; Dumont, arguing that she owed him additional work because of her inefficiency, broke his promise. In the fall of 1826, Truth walked off the Dumonts' property carrying her infant daughter, Sophia. She went to the home of Levi Rowe, a Quaker whom she expected to help her. However, she found him on his deathbed. Rowe sent her to the home of Isaac and Maria Van Wagenen in Wagondale, New York (present-day Bloomington).

The Van Wagenens took in Truth and gave her work as a free person. However, when Dumont learned that she was at the Van Wagenen house, he went to claim her as his property. To prevent Truth's reenslavement, the Van Wagenens paid him twenty-five dollars for Truth and Sophia. Truth remained with them for about a year and adopted their last name, becoming Isabella Van Wagenen. While working for the family, Truth learned that her five-year-old son, Peter, had been sold illegally and taken to Alabama. Determined to rescue her son, she confronted the Dumonts, who did not recognize her claim. With support from Quaker friends, she hired a lawyer who, in 1828, succeeded in having Peter returned to his mother.

*Sojourner Truth.* (Courtesy, University of Texas at Austin)

---

## TRUTH AND THE ABOLITIONIST MOVEMENT

Throughout her life, Sojourner Truth was illiterate, and most accounts of her life and accomplishments as an abolitionist and activist have been relayed by third parties who evaluated her based on their own agendas and priorities. Thus, Truth's fame has been attributed to the publication of Harriet Beecher Stowe's 1863 article "Sojourner Truth, the Libyan Sibyl" and Frances Gage's "Reminiscence," which described Truth's "Ain't I a Woman?" speech at the Ohio Woman's Rights Convention of 1851. However, Truth had started her abolitionist activism well before these articles introduced her to wider audiences. Truth had given speeches telling her story and sold copies of her memoir as a way of supporting herself. She had toured with the British radical George Thompson and met Frederick Douglass. During her journeys she was able to build her network of abolitionist, feminist, and spiritualist supporters; indeed, she bridged many of these disparate movements, connecting the plights of women and slaves and championing all people's equality under God. Her impressive figure—almost six feet tall and gaunt—her natural eloquence, and her courage to speak to white audiences gave her the power to move white abolitionists, women's suffragists, and other important figures to appropriate her as a symbol of struggle against injustice.

---

Truth and Peter moved to New York City in late 1828, leaving Sophia with the Van Wagenens. She joined the Zion African Church and worked as a housekeeper for various families. In 1835, Truth was accused of poisoning her employer but was able to prove that she did not commit the crime. During her fourteen years in New York City, Truth came into contact with employers and other African Americans who were very religious. Several went on to become prominent abolitionists. In this context, Truth had a spiritual experience in which she felt called to become a traveling evangelist. To pursue this calling, she adopted the name "Sojourner Truth." "Sojourner" reflected that she would travel the land, and "Truth" her determination to speak the truth. Thus, in 1843, she set out from New York on her mission.

### LIFE'S WORK

Truth began preaching in Connecticut and Northampton, Massachusetts; there, she found many supporters associated with the Northampton Association, which had been founded by abolitionists, idealists, and workers to pursue equal rights for all. Truth remained with the association until 1846, working as a laundress. During her stay with the Northampton Association, she met prominent abolitionists such as William Lloyd Garrison, editor of The *Boston Liberator* and president of the American Anti-Slavery Society, and Frederick Douglass. In 1846, Truth began dictating her autobiography to Olive Gilbert;

in 1850, it was published as *Narrative of Sojourner Truth* and marked her emergence as an abolitionist and women's suffrage advocate.

In 1851, Garrison invited Truth to accompany him and his friend George Thompson, a radical member of the British parliament, on a trip into western New York. Truth made the trip with Thompson, making speeches and selling her book. In Ohio, Truth assisted the Ohio Woman's Rights Convention and delivered a famous speech on equal rights for African American women, which was later published as "Ain't I a Woman?" In 1853, Truth journeyed to Andover, Massachusetts, and asked Harriet Beecher Stowe, the author of *Uncle Tom's Cabin* (1852), to help promote her autobiography. Stowe wrote a short article about the book. Ten years later, based on this brief encounter, Stowe wrote "Sojourner Truth, the Libyan Sibyl" for *Atlantic Monthly*.

In 1857, Truth joined the community of Harmonia, a racially mixed settlement of progressive abolitionists and spiritualists, located six miles west of Battle Creek, Michigan. She was joined there by her daughters, Diana, Elizabeth, and Sophia, who had been legally freed. Her grandsons, James Caldwell and Samuel Banks, became her traveling companions. In 1860, Truth moved to the town of Battle Creek.

With the outbreak of the Civil War in 1861, Truth became deeply involved in politics. She openly challenged slavery and championed the Union cause. In 1862, Truth accompanied Josephine Griffing, a radical feminist, to Indiana, violating a state law prohibiting the entry of black people. She was chased by a mob and arrested. In 1863, when President Abraham Lincoln signed the Emancipation Proclamation and gave orders to recruit African American troops to fight for the Union, Truth went door to door to collect Thanksgiving food for the soldiers of the First Michigan Colored Regiment, stationed at Camp Ward in Detroit. In 1864, Truth collected more food and clothing from the people of Battle Creek for the Camp Ward troops. Around this time, she addressed the troops and sang a song that she had composed in honor of the regiment.

The Civil War and social struggles of the 1860's

moved Truth to make her first trip to Washington, D.C., in 1864, accompanied by her grandson, Banks. She carried a new edition of her autobiography and her portrait printed on postcards. Under her picture was printed the message "The Shadow Supports the Substance." In Washington, Truth and her white companion Lucy Colman met Lincoln; he signed her autograph book, "For Auntie Sojourner Truth, October 29, 1864." In later years, Truth would also visit presidents Andrew Johnson and Ulysses S. Grant.

Truth stayed in Washington from 1864 to 1867. During her stay, she saw and experienced the racial discrimination that pervaded everyday life. Although streetcars had been desegregated by federal law in 1865, conductors did not want to stop for black passengers. Truth insisted on riding in the streetcars, even when she was humiliated and assaulted, forcing conductors to respect the law.

In Washington, D.C., Truth worked for the National Freedmen's Relief Association and the Freedmen's Bureau, aiding black refugees from the southern states. The poor conditions in which freed African Americans lived—characterized by cramped housing, crime, and joblessness—led her to argue that her people needed work, not government money. Truth proposed that the government provide land for free African Americans. Massachusetts senator Charles Sumner advised her to collect signatures to pressure Congress to authorize land grants. From 1870 to 1871, Truth and Banks toured New England and the mid-Atlantic region collecting signatures. Her tour was cut short when Banks fell ill, and they returned to Battle Creek, where he died in 1875. Subsequently, the exodus of many freed African Americans to Kansas in 1879 upstaged Truth's plan, but she supported it enthusiastically.

In Battle Creek, at the urging of her friend Frances Titus, Truth updated her *Narrative of Sojourner Truth*, adding her speeches and scrapbook. During the fall of 1883, Truth fell gravely ill. She died before dawn on November 26.

## SIGNIFICANCE

Truth was born a slave and became a nationally known advocate for the abolition of slavery and equal rights for women. Truth viewed her advocacy as a religious calling to put her faith into practice. Her escape from slavery and her adherence to her principles in the face of personal hardship and tragedy made her a powerful symbol of the abolitionist and women's rights causes.

*—F. Sonia Arellano-Lopez*

## FURTHER READING

Bordewich, Fergus M. *Bound for Canaan: The Underground Railroad and the War for the Soul of America*. New York: HarperCollins, 2005. Offers historical background on the activities of the abolitionists who befriended and assisted Truth.

Claflin, Edward Beecher. *Sojourner Truth and the Struggle for Freedom*. New York: Barron's Educational Series, 1987. Provides a brief and straightforward account of Truth's life.

Gilbert, Olive. *Narrative of Sojourner Truth, a Bondswoman of Olden Time*. 1878. Reprint. New York: Oxford University Press, 1994. This reprint is the version updated with support from Frances Titus, which includes Stowe's article on Truth, excerpts of letters, speeches, and scrapbook material.

Mabee, Carleton. "Sojourner Truth and President Lincoln." *The New England Quarterly* 61, no. 4 (December, 1988): 519-529. A compelling article demystifying the diverse versions of the meeting between Truth and Lincoln.

Painter, Nell Irvin. *Sojourner Truth: A Life, a Symbol*. New York: W. W. Norton, 1996. Scholarly biography of Truth that includes information on the social, economic, and political conditions under which she lived.

SEE ALSO: William Craft and Ellen Craft; Martin Robison Delany; Frederick Douglass; James Forten; Henry Highland Garnet; Frances Ellen Watkins Harper; Maria Stewart; Harriet Tubman; David Walker.

# HARRIET TUBMAN
## Abolitionist

*Tubman escaped slavery and then dedicated her life to helping others do the same. Her commitment to freedom fueled an intense passion for the abolitionist movement and led her to serve as a Union Army nurse and spy during the Civil War. She also forged ties with the women's suffrage movement and spoke eloquently in support of women's and African Americans' rights.*

**BORN:** c. 1820; Bucktown, Dorchester County, Maryland
**DIED:** March, 10, 1913; Auburn, New York
**ALSO KNOWN AS:** Harriet Ross Tubman; Araminta Ross (birth name); Minty; Moses
**AREAS OF ACHIEVEMENT:** Abolitionism; Social issues; Women's rights

### EARLY LIFE

Harriet Ross Tubman was born Araminta Ross around 1820 to Harriet and Benjamin Ross in Bucktown, Dorchester County, Maryland. She decided to take her mother's name when she was older. Tubman and her eight siblings were born on the plantation of Edward Brodess. She began work as a domestic servant at the age of about six years and also was rented out to other households for the same purpose. She often was severely beaten and poorly treated. As a teenager, she preferred to work in the field, where it was easier to escape the brutality of overbearing mistresses and the unwanted sexual advances of her masters.

Ultimately, field work did not provide Tubman with enough protection from the cruelty of slavery. Between the years of 1834 and 1836, she suffered trauma to her head as a result of being struck by a metal weight. The weight was thrown at an escaping slave by the overseer, and Tubman jumped in the way, attempting to prevent the escapee's capture. The impact of the two-pound metal weight against her head nearly killed her. Her skull was badly crushed, resulting in sleeping spells, headaches, and dizziness that she endured for the rest of her life. However, Tubman claimed that the injury also left her with heightened dreams and prophecies. She said that these visions showed her the future and led her on journeys in which she liberated slaves from the South. Her visions were nurtured by her exposure to evangelical teachings and African-influenced cultural traditions.

After Tubman's injury, no buyer was interested in purchasing or renting her services because she was considered damaged property. Tubman's fear that she might one day be sold to a more abusive master because of her injury fueled her desire to escape. Her first flight took place in 1849. At the time, she was being rented from her master by a man called Doctor Thompson. She had lived on his property for two years with her husband, John Tubman, whom she married in 1844. Although John was a free man, he lived with Tubman in the slave quarters. Even though Tubman did her best to convince her husband to accompany her on the journey, he refused.

*Harriet Tubman.* (Library of Congress)

## LIFE'S WORK

In 1849, Tubman escaped to freedom. She traveled by night, guided only by the North Star, until she reached Philadelphia, a free state. She was aided by abolitionists on the Underground Railroad, who helped her evade capture and identify who would help along the journey. Upon arriving in Philadelphia, however, Tubman found herself confused and saddened. The success of reaching the so-called Promised Land was complicated by a painful realization. She was alone in a strange land without family, friends, or community. While she understood that most of the people she knew did not possess the courage to attempt what she had done, her loneliness prompted her to return and secure the freedom of her family members. She constructed a plan that led her to being called the Moses of her people.

---

### TUBMAN AND THE UNDERGROUND RAILROAD

The Underground Railroad was the name given to the loose network of abolitionists who helped slaves escape to freedom in the North. The Underground Railroad provided protection and guidance for fugitives from the South. "Conducting" the railroad was a dangerous feat that required strength, endurance, and ingenuity; Harriet Tubman possessed all these qualities, and as a result, she enjoyed great success. Frequently, the journey was so treacherous that fugitives would tire and plead to turn back. In cases such as these, Tubman would reveal a shotgun tied to her waist and say, "You gon' be free or you gon' die." She never lost a single passenger.

Song was an important tool in Tubman's work. She used spirituals to communicate danger or safety to her followers while she scouted surroundings or secured supplies and rations. It was a useful form of subterfuge, because many slave owners believed that singing was an indication of a happy slave.

Each person who traveled the Underground Railroad was prepared to risk his or her life for freedom, and no conductor was as eagerly hunted by slave catchers as Tubman. At times, the price on her head reached forty thousand dollars. Despite the danger, she made some nineteen trips into slave territory, and some historians estimate that she led as many as three hundred slaves to freedom.

---

First, Tubman secured employment as a domestic laborer, cooking and cleaning house for northern white women. The money she earned cleaning houses was equally divided between her living expenses and a return trip to Baltimore, Maryland, where she rescued her enslaved sister and her two children. In December of 1850, Tubman, her sister Mary Ann Bowley, and Mary Ann's husband and two children arrived in Philadelphia. Tubman's success in her first venture set the stage for a return a few months later in which she safely delivered her brother and two other men to safety. It was not until the fall of 1851 that she returned to free her husband, John. However, John had remarried and still refused to travel with her. Eager to continue her mission, Tubman abandoned thoughts of helping him and quickly identified a group of slaves who were willing to flee. She also brought this group safely to Philadelphia. Almost from the beginning, Tubman's mission to free slaves reached beyond her own family. From 1851 to 1857, she made at least eleven trips into slave country, and she eventually freed all of her brothers and sisters and her parents during the ten years that she conducted the Underground Railroad.

Tubman viewed the problems facing African Americans, women, and humanity as indelibly intertwined, and her life's work began to reflect this belief. Tubman set about developing relationships with women involved in the suffrage movement, such as Susan B. Anthony, and intensified her relationships with staunch abolitionists such as William Grant Still and John Brown. She believed that the nation could take its greatest strides toward liberation and equality when people—no matter their creed, color, or gender—worked in concert.

It was this belief that led to Tubman's decision to assist the Union Army in the Civil War. She worked for the Army for four years as a nurse and spy, without any recognition or financial compensation. She was deployed by the governor of Massachusetts to the South at the beginning of the Civil War in the position of spy and scout and under the direction of Colonel James Montgomery. Tubman organized a group of black men to scout the inland waterways of South Carolina for Union raids. She also nursed wounded soldiers back to health and taught newly freed African Americans strategies for survival and sustenance. Although efforts were made by Secretary of State William H. Seward to secure a pension for her years of service, she was unsuccessful.

After a period of about four years, Tubman left the Army to continue her work, giving speeches on slavery, abolition, and suffrage. Through her powerful oratory, Tubman urged many slaves to find their way to freedom by educating them about the abolition movement. In December of 1860, Tubman was invited to Boston by Gerrit Smith to speak at a large antislavery meeting. Although

Tubman was illiterate, people in attendance were startled by her eloquence at the podium. However, her oratory was merely an outgrowth of the shrewd critical thinking faculties upon which she had to rely greatly as the most successful conductor of the Underground Railroad.

Near the end of her life, Tubman transformed her New York home into a boardinghouse to providing care for old and disabled African Americans. Tubman died of pneumonia on March 10, 1913, after a two-year residence in the Harriet Tubman Home for Aged and Indigent Colored People. Booker T. Washington was a featured speaker at her funeral service.

## SIGNIFICANCE

During her lifetime Tubman was internationally renowned as a conductor on the Underground Railroad, abolitionist, Civil War spy, nurse, suffragist, and humanitarian. Tubman accomplished a great deal during a time of intense racial, social, political, and economic upheaval. Her primary goal was to secure the freedom of enslaved people and to end the institution of slavery. Her deep commitment to this goal led her to associate with all types of people regardless of race, gender, or class. As the debate over slavery intensified, Tubman was a respected spokesperson for the abolitionist movement.

—*Kidogo A. Kennedy*

## FURTHER READING

Bordewich, Fergus M. *Bound for Canaan: The Epic Story of the Underground Railroad, America's First Civil Rights Movement*. Boston: HarperCollins, 2006. Details the history of the Underground Railroad, emphasizing the real lives and stories of participants.

Bradford, Sarah E. H. *Harriet Tubman: The Moses of Her People*. Introduction by Butler A. Jones. New York: G. R. Lockwood and Son, 1886. Reprint. New York: Corinth Books, 1961. A republication of the 1886 expanded version of the 1869 original book, this is an important source for information on Tubman's life. Bradford interviewed Tubman and also included comments about her by a number of leading nineteenth century Americans.

Clinton, Catherine. *Harriet Tubman: The Road to Freedom*. Boston: Back Bay Books, 2005. Thorough and well-researched biography of Tubman that fleshes out many of her contemporaries, famous and obscure, and examines Tubman's remarkable lifetime accomplishments.

Humez, Jean M. *Harriet Tubman: The Life and the Life Stories*. Madison: University of Wisconsin Press, 2003. Collection of primary source materials, including letters, diaries, memorials, and speeches, that provide a description of Tubman's life and personality. The materials document Tubman's relationships with abolitionist John Brown, Abraham Lincoln, Frederick Douglass, Sojourner Truth, and others.

Larson, Kate Clifford. *Bound for the Promised Land: Harriet Tubman, Portrait of an American Hero*. New York: Ballantine, 2004. Comprehensive account of Tubman's life, based in part on sources such as court records, contemporary newspapers, wills, and letters.

Petry, Ann. *Harriet Tubman: Conductor on the Underground Railroad*. New York: Amistad, 1996. Children's book whose narrative provides a compelling biography of Tubman and history of the Underground Railroad.

**SEE ALSO:** William Craft and Ellen Craft; Martin Robison Delany; Frederick Douglass; James Forten; Henry Highland Garnet; Frances Ellen Watkins Harper; Dred Scott; Maria Stewart; Sojourner Truth; David Walker.

# C. DeLores Tucker
## Activist and politician

*Best known for her outspokenness against the gangsta rap musical genre, Tucker also was a civil rights activist, politician, and champion of equal rights for women. She held a number of posts within the Democratic Party, served as Pennsylvania's first African American woman secretary of state, and chaired the National Political Congress of Black Women.*

**BORN:** October 4, 1927; Philadelphia, Pennsylvania
**DIED:** October 12, 2005; Philadelphia, Pennsylvania
**ALSO KNOWN AS:** Cynthia DeLores Nottage Tucker; Cynthia DeLores Nottage (birth name)
**AREAS OF ACHIEVEMENT:** Government and politics; Social issues; Women's rights

### EARLY LIFE

Cynthia DeLores Nottage Tucker was born on October 4, 1927, in Philadelphia, Pennsylvania. She was the second of eleven children born to the Reverend Whitfield and Captilda Nottage. Tucker was raised in a deeply religious household in which dancing, listening to and playing music, and dating were prohibited until the Nottage children reached the age of twenty-one.

The Reverend Nottage believed deeply in his faith and refused to accept payment for his pastoral work. As a result, Captilda launched several entrepreneurial ventures to raise money. She owned and operated a grocery store and an employment agency for southern African Americans who migrated North in search of employment opportunities, and served as landlord for several properties.

Tucker attended the Philadelphia High School for Girls, where her outspokenness and leadership abilities were evident at a young age. When she was sixteen, she spoke out against a hotel in Philadelphia that refused entry to a group of African Americans. She graduated from high school in 1947. Tucker joined the Philadelphia chapter of the National Association for the Advancement of Colored People (NAACP) and became one of its top fund-raisers. She attended Temple University, Pennsylvania State University, and Wharton College of Business at the University of Pennsylvania. In 1951, she married William A. Tucker, whom she had met in 1947.

### LIFE'S WORK

Tucker continued to work with the NAACP and was an active participant in several marches for equal rights, including the historic Selma-to-Montgomery, Alabama,

march led by Martin Luther King, Jr., in 1965. Tucker also actively campaigned and raised money for African American political candidates. She was appointed Pennsylvania's secretary of state in 1971, earning her the distinction of being the first African American woman to hold this position and the highest ranking African American in state government.

Tucker's achievements as secretary of state included ratifying the Equal Rights Amendment to lower the voting age from twenty-one to eighteen, working to ensure that women were represented at all levels within the Democratic Party and state government, and championing affirmative action, equality in education, and welfare reform. In 1984, Tucker founded the National Political Congress of Black Women. In addition to the work she did on behalf of her organization, Tucker was the first African American woman elected to serve as president of the National Federation of Democratic Women.

Tucker's commitment to equality continued after her political career ended. In 1991, she founded the Bethune-Dubois Institute, an organization dedicated to promoting cultural awareness and education to African American youth. She initiated the campaign to have Sojourner Truth memorialized with other leaders of the women's suffrage movement in 1992. The Sojourner Truth memorial bust was completed and unveiled in 2009 and joined the busts of white suffrage leaders Elizabeth Cady Stanton, Lucretia Mott, and Susan B. Anthony in the United States Capitol building in Washington, D.C.

Tucker's fervor in the fight for equality and respect for African Americans and women carried over to the music industry. Outraged by the sexually explicit lyrics of some rap artists, Tucker partnered with Republican leader William Bennett to organize protests against Time Warner Music and several music stores that sold "gansta" rap.

Tucker received various awards and honorary doctoral degrees, including the NAACP Freedom Fund and Thurgood Marshall awards for her work in the fight for civil rights. After she died on October 12, 2005, she was posthumously honored by the state of Pennsylvania with a portrait at the Pennsylvania State Museum and a historical marker in the North Building of the state capitol.

### SIGNIFICANCE

Tucker was a champion of civil rights and equality for African Americans and women. She was a pioneering leader, politician, and activist whose legacy lives on through the National Political Congress of Black Women and the Bethune-Dubois Institute.

—*Tamela N. Chambers*

### FURTHER READING

"C. DeLores Tucker, Civil Rights Activist, Political Leader, Dies in Philadelphia" *Jet* 108, no. 18 (October 31, 2005): 18-19, 52. Obituary offers a summary of Tucker's career and influence on other civil rights leaders.

Lamb, Yvonne Shinhoster. "C. DeLores Tucker Dies at 78; Rights and Anti-Rap Activist." *The Washington Post*, October 13, 2005. Obituary detailing Tucker's campaign against explicit gangsta rap lyrics.

Mayo, Kierna. "Caught Up in the (Gangsta) Rapture: Dr. C. Delores Tucker's Crusade Against 'Gangsta' Rap." In *And It Don't Stop? The Best American Hip-Hop Journalism of the Last Twenty-five Years*, edited by Raquel Cepeda. New York: Faber & Faber, 2004. Critical examination of Tucker's condemnation of gangsta rap by a writer from the hip-hop magazine *The Source*.

**SEE ALSO:** Daisy Bates; Shirley Chisholm; Myrlie Evers-Williams; Dorothy Height; Barbara Jordan; Pauli Murray; Diane Nash; Eleanor Holmes Norton; Jo Ann Gibson Robinson.

# BIG JOE TURNER
## Blues singer

*Turner was one of the most beloved blues singers of the twentieth century. His music bridged the gap between jazz and blues, and he was respected and admired by musicians and listeners of both musical traditions.*

**BORN:** May 18, 1911; Kansas City, Missouri
**DIED:** November 24, 1985; Inglewood, California
**ALSO KNOWN AS:** Joseph Vernon Turner, Jr.; the Boss of the Blues
**AREAS OF ACHIEVEMENT:** Music: blues; Music: jazz

### EARLY LIFE

Joseph Vernon Turner, Jr., was born in Kansas City, Missouri. His father died in a railroad accident when Turner was barely three years old, and he was raised by his mother and grandmother. He reached his maturity during Prohibition. In the 1920's, Kansas City was run by a corrupt "boss" named Pendergast, and the downtown area was filled with illegal alcohol vendors known as speakeasies. Turner shined shoes and ran errands but gravitated toward the Backbiter Club, a speakeasy where piano player Pete Johnson worked. The teenage Turner was too young to enter, so he drew on a false mustache with eyeliner to get past the doorman and asked Johnson if he could sing with him. Johnson agreed, and Turner made a good impression, singing without a microphone or amplification.

Turner and Johnson became a performing team and later formed a quartet that performed around Kansas City through the end of Prohibition in 1933. The quartet toured the Midwest, but upon Prohibition's repeal they returned to Kansas City. There, they landed a position at the Sunset Club, a prestigious venue where Count Basie also played. Their act eventually grew into a seven-piece group, and they were given the opportunity to broadcast from the club. One of these broadcasts was heard by New York producer and talent scout John Hammond, who came to Kansas City to lure the Basie orchestra to New York. He was impressed by Turner and asked him to come along with the Basie group, but Turner declined. In 1938, Hammond sent Johnson and Turner a telegram asking them to appear at his newly organized "Spirituals to Swing" concert in Carnegie Hall.

### LIFE'S WORK

At the Carnegie Hall concert, Turner and Johnson were teamed with piano players Albert Ammons and Meade Lux Lewis. The resulting quartet was a sensation, and the four quickly found a job playing at the prestigious Café Society in New York. Turner and Johnson also won a recording contract with Vocalion Records and soon afterward recorded for Decca Records. Turner became a very popular performer and recording artist. He appeared in the Duke Ellington stage musical *Jump for Joy* (1941) and, during World War II, sang in Hollywood nightclubs.

Turner was known as "Big Joe" to differentiate him from a jazz piano player of the same name; he was over six feet tall and had become rotund after years of good eating. At the age of twelve, he had escaped a fire by jumping from a second-story window, breaking both of his legs. The legs gave him trouble into his adulthood, and for decades he performed while sitting.

Turner sang up-tempo songs almost exclusively. He said that slow blues tunes made no sense to him, and that the faster numbers suited him. His Kansas City upbringing trained him to sing blues tunes with top jazz musicians, and the intersection of these two musical idioms gave Turner the ability to work with some of the most accomplished names in jazz. In 1954, he recorded "Shake, Rattle and Roll," which was quickly remade by white rock-and-roll pioneer Bill Haley. This song was a huge nationwide hit, and it introduced Turner to a new generation of listeners. He spent the balance of the 1950's as a rock-and-roll star on Atlantic Records, then during the 1960's and 1970's, he returned to singing with small jazz combos.

For the last two decades of his life, Turner remained a celebrated singer, appearing at festivals and winning awards in America and Europe. He died on November 24, 1985, in Inglewood, California.

*Big Joe Turner.* (Redferns/Getty Images)

## SIGNIFICANCE

Turner's style of blues singing, aggressive yet smooth, was a sound he held to throughout his fifty-year career, allowing successive generations to regard it as blues, jazz, rock and roll, then soul. Personable and strong of voice, with or without a microphone, Turner became the model for how a blues singer should sound and act.

*—Jeffrey Daniel Jones*

## FURTHER READING

Balliett, Whitney. *American Singers*. New York: Oxford University Press, 1979. Balliett's section on Turner describes an interview with the singer in a New York nightclub, when Turner was working with another musical legend, piano player Lloyd Glenn.

Guralnuck, Peter. *Lost Highway: Journeys and Arrivals of American Musicians*. Edinburgh, Scotland: Canongate Books, 2002. The section on Turner in this source also is based upon an interesting visit with the singer. Includes some interesting anecdotes about Turner's career.

Kempton, Murray, and Arthur Kempton. "Big Joe Turner: The Holler of a Mountain Jack." In *Bluesland: Portraits of Twelve Major American Blues Masters*, edited by Pete Welding and Toby Byron. New York: Dutton, 1991. This interesting chapter on Turner focuses on his years working for Atlantic Records during the 1950's.

Tosches, Nick. *Unsung Heroes of Rock 'n' Roll: The Birth of Rock in the Wild Years Before Elvis*. New York: Da Capo Press, 1999. Offers an absorbing and detailed account of Turner's career.

**SEE ALSO:** Big Boy Crudup; Willie Dixon; W. C. Handy; John Lee Hooker; Ma Rainey; Muddy Waters.

# HENRY MCNEAL TURNER
## Religious leader and activist

*As a writer, orator, and religious leader, Turner worked to empower African Americans and combat racism. His frustration with the racial climate in the United States led him to embrace Black Nationalism and advocate for emigration to Africa.*

**BORN:** February 1, 1834; Newberry Courthouse, South Carolina

**DIED:** May 8, 1915; Windsor, Ontario, Canada

**AREAS OF ACHIEVEMENT:** Religion and theology; Social issues

### EARLY LIFE

Henry McNeal Turner was born on February 1, 1834, in Newberry Courthouse, South Carolina, to Hardy and Sarah Greer Turner. Although he was not a slave, Turner still experienced the harsh reality of prejudice and racism. He worked in cotton fields alongside slaves and in a blacksmith shop under harsh overseers. When Turner was eight or nine years old, he had a dream in which he stood before a large crowd of African Americans and whites who looked to him for instruction. He interpreted the dream as God preparing him to do great things.

At the age of fifteen, Turner found employment at a law office in Abbeville. The lawyers took notice of his quick mind and eagerness to learn and began teaching him other subjects, such as arithmetic, history, law, and theology. While living in Abbeville, Turner joined the Methodist church and soon thereafter began to preach.

After gaining a license to preach in the southern Methodist Church at the age of nineteen, Turner delivered sermons to large, integrated audiences. However, he found it frustrating that the southern Methodist Church would not ordain him and that he had already achieved the highest level an African American could attain in the denomination. This frustration led Turner to join the all-black African Methodist Episcopal (AME) church in 1858.

### LIFE'S WORK

Turner was ordained an AME minister and, in 1862, he became pastor of Israel AME Church in Washington, D.C. During the Civil War, President Abraham Lincoln commissioned Turner to the office of chaplain in the Union Army, making him the first African American chaplain in any branch of the military. In this capacity, he also became a war correspondent for the AME newspaper, *The Christian Recorder*. When the Civil War ended, Turner was assigned to the Freedmen's Bureau in Georgia as an Army chaplain.

After leaving the military, Turner turned his attention to politics. He was elected to the Georgia legislature in 1868 and believed that change had finally come. However, any excitement that Turner or African Americans in general had for ushering in a new day after the Civil War disappeared quickly when white members of the state legislature voted to disqualify African Americans from holding elected office. After his ouster from the legislature, Turner became the first African American United States postmaster in Macon, Georgia. After leaving that position, he turned his attention to building the AME Church in the South by recruiting African Americans away from the primarily white southern Methodist Church.

In 1876, Turner became publications manager for the AME Church, a position that opened the door for him to become a bishop. As bishop, Turner had a national platform for his ideas on race, politics, lynching, and other issues. However, as racism became more of an issue for African Americans, Turner increasingly became a proponent of emigration to Africa.

In the latter part of the nineteenth century, after several failed attempts at an emigration plan and with the rise of Booker T. Washington and W. E. B. Du Bois as leaders in the black community, Turner's influence waned. However, Turner remained active. He edited two newspapers, *Voice of Missions* (1893-1900) and *Voice of the People* (1901-1904); served as chairman of the board of Morris Brown College from 1896 to 1908; and kept a busy schedule until the end of his life. In May, 1915, while he was in Windsor, Ontario, Canada, for the General Conference of the AME Church, he suffered a massive stroke. Turner died a few hours later at a Windsor hospital.

### SIGNIFICANCE

Turner was widely popular during his career and produced many articles, essays, and editorials. He wrote introductions to several books and published pamphlets, speeches, the hymnal for the African Methodist Episcopal Church, and a polity manual for the denomination. However, despite this ample body of work, Turner has not received the same scholarly attention paid to some of his contemporaries. While his rhetoric was at times harsh—even crude—it anticipated many of the social movements in African American culture during the twentieth century. Du Bois's idea of "cultural nationalism," Marcus Garvey's "Back to Africa" movement, the Civil Rights and Black Power movements, James H. Cone's black liberation theology, and even some elements of hip-hop culture owe a debt to Turner's progressive insights.

Turner also offered an alternative viewpoint in African American rhetorical discourse in the late nineteenth and early twentieth centuries. He rejected accommodation and integration—goals pursued by many other black leaders of the time—and instead offered emigration as a possible solution to the problems African Americans faced.

*—Andre E. Johnson*

### FURTHER READING

Angell, Stephen Ward. *Bishop Henry McNeal Turner and African American Religion in the South.* Knoxville: University of Tennessee Press, 1992. A biogra-

phy that chronicles Turner's life and rise within the AME Church.

Johnson, Robert, Jr. "Bishop Henry McNeal Turner and African American Institutional Support for Repatriation." In *Returning Home: A Century of African American Repatriation.* Trenton, N.J.: Africa World Press, 2005. Examines Turner's support for emigration in the context of other black nationalist and "Back to Africa" movements.

Ponton, Mungo M. *Life and Times of Henry McNeal Turner.* New York: Negro Universities Press, 1970. Chronicles Turner's life, emphasizing his early years, political career, and work as a bishop in the AME Church.

Turner, Henry McNeal. *Respect Black: The Writings and Speeches of Henry McNeal Turner.* Compiled and edited by Edwin Redkey. New York: Arno Press, 1971. Contains edited speeches and writings of Turner from 1863 through 1913.

**SEE ALSO:** Richard Allen; Daniel Coker; Paul Cuffe; Marcus Garvey; John Brown Russwurm.

# IKE TURNER
## Musician

*A successful bandleader and instrumentalist whose career spanned six decades, Turner was a pioneering figure in the birth of rock and roll, as well as the longtime husband and collaborator of singer Tina Turner.*

**BORN:** November 5, 1931; Clarksdale, Mississippi
**DIED:** December 12, 2007; San Marcos, California
**ALSO KNOWN AS:** Izear Luster Turner, Jr. (birth name); Isaac Wister Turner
**AREAS OF ACHIEVEMENT:** Music: bandleading; Music: blues; Music: rhythm and blues; Music: rock and roll

### EARLY LIFE

Ike Turner was born in Clarksdale, Mississippi, on November 5, 1931. His parents were Izear Luster Turner, Sr., a Baptist preacher, and Beatrice Cushenberry, a seamstress. Turner's early childhood was marred by exposure to racial violence, including the death of his father at the hands of a gang of white men; details of this incident varied in Turner's telling. Turner also later recalled

seeing a local black man lynched and castrated. After his father's death, his mother remarried, and Turner developed a tempestuous and violent relationship with his stepfather.

Turner's first music lessons came from legendary blues pianist and Clarksdale resident Pinetop Perkins, and in high school he moonlighted as a disc jockey at a local radio station. Around this time, Turner formed the Kings of Rhythm, the band with which he would tour and record professionally throughout the 1950's. By the time Turner finished high school, he and the Kings of Rhythm were playing regularly in Clarksdale and throughout the Delta region.

In 1951, Turner and his band traveled to Memphis to record at Sun Studio. During these sessions, the band recorded "Rocket 88," written and sung by Turner's saxophonist, Jackie Brenston. Released as a single under the group name Jackie Brenston and His Delta Cats, "Rocket 88" became a national hit and gave Turner his first brush with stardom. In the years afterward, "Rocket 88" was deemed by many as the first rock-and-roll record ever made.

### LIFE'S WORK

Turner remained in the South throughout the early 1950's, working as a musician and record company talent scout, a position through which he advanced the careers of B. B. King, Howlin' Wolf, and others. During this period, Turner switched his primary instrument from piano to guitar, and in 1956, he relocated to East St. Louis, where his Kings of Rhythm soon became the top musical attraction in the city. It was there that Turner crossed paths with a young singer named Anna Mae Bullock. He was instantly impressed with her raspy, raw vocal delivery and charisma. Turner invited her to join his band as a backup singer, and by 1958, Turner and Bullock were married and she had taken the first name Tina.

In 1959, the Kings of Rhythm recorded "A Fool in Love," the first single to feature Tina on lead vocal; the record was a smash hit, and soon thereafter Turner rechristened the band the Ike and Tina Turner Revue. By 1962, Turner and Tina had placed four more singles in the rhythm-and-blues Top 10. Along with Turner's

burgeoning fame came an increasingly serious cocaine problem, and by the mid-1960's, the band's record sales had begun to stagnate while Turner's penchant for violence—often directed at his wife—increased. In 1966, Turner and Tina released "River Deep, Mountain High," their iconic collaboration with producer Phil Spector. Although the single was credited to the couple, Spector found Turner so disruptive that he banned him from the studio while recording the song.

In 1969, the Rolling Stones selected the Ike and Tina Turner Revue as the opening act for their American tour, and the experience of playing for massive rock-and-roll crowds revitalized the Turners' music. They released a series of successful cover versions of rock songs and scored a tremendous success with their rendition of Creedence Clearwater Revival's "Proud Mary." "Proud Mary" reached number four on the *Billboard* Pop Charts in 1971 and won a Grammy for Best R&B Vocal Performance by a Duo or Group.

In 1975, Tina left her husband, both personally and professionally; by the 1980's, Turner was in precarious

*Ike Turner.* (AP/Wide World Photos)

financial straits. In 1986, Tina released her autobiography, *I, Tina*, an international best seller that detailed years of abuse at the hands of her former husband and further damaged Turner's reputation.

In 1991, Turner and Tina were inducted into the Rock and Roll Hall of Fame. Later in his life, Turner enjoyed renewed success as a blues musician, winning a Grammy Award in 2007 for *Risin' with the Blues* (2006). On December 12, 2007, Turner died of a cocaine overdose at the age of seventy-six.

## SIGNIFICANCE

Turner is one of the most important and misunderstood musical figures of the rock-and-roll era. A violent and controlling man whose name became synonymous with spousal abuse, his personal failings have overshadowed his remarkable musical accomplishments. However, he also was a pioneering bandleader and instrumentalist who deserves substantial credit for his role in the development of rock-and-roll music, and the sustained success that he achieved alongside his wife is a formidable accomplishment.

*—Jack Hamilton*

## FURTHER READING

Collis, John. *Ike Turner: King of Rhythm*. London: The Do-Not Press, 2004. This is the first full-length biography of Turner that is widely available.

Turner, Ike, and Nigel Cawthorne. *Takin' Back My Name: The Confessions of Ike Turner*. London: Virgin Books, 1999. A self-serving autobiography, portions of which are inconsistent with Turner's previous accounts of his life, this source nonetheless offers insights into Turner's personality and musical career.

Turner, Tina, and Kurt Loder. *I, Tina*. 1986. Reprint. New York: It Books, 2010. Tina Turner's best-selling account of her life and career, including her marriage to Ike Turner.

Ward, Brian. *Just My Soul Responding: Rhythm and Blues, Black Consciousness, and Race Relations*. Berkeley: University of California Press, 1999. A topnotch history of rhythm-and-blues music in the 1960's, including the Ike and Tina Turner Revue.

**SEE ALSO:** James Brown; Marvin Gaye; Jimi Hendrix; Little Richard; Tina Turner.

# NAT TURNER
## Leader of a slave rebellion

*Enraged by a system that enslaved him and guided by religious visions, Turner led a bloody slave rebellion through the Virginia countryside, killing dozens of white plantation owners and their families. Turner's Rebellion was one of the most significant slave revolts in United States history.*

**BORN:** October 2, 1800; Southampton County, Virginia
**DIED:** November 11, 1831; Jerusalem (now Courtland), Virginia
**ALSO KNOWN AS:** Nathaniel Turner; Nat (birth name); General Turner; Captain Nat
**AREA OF ACHIEVEMENT:** Social issues

## EARLY LIFE

Nathaniel Turner, whose birth name was recorded simply as "Nat," was born on Benjamin Turner's Southampton County, Virginia, plantation to Nancy, a slave and domestic servant. Turner's father, whose name is unknown, ran away when Turner was eight or nine years old and left the young boy to be raised by his mother and paternal grandmother, Bridget. Turner learned to read and was raised a Christian. When he was twelve years old, Turner became a field hand, working from sunrise to sunset plowing, hoeing, and tending animals.

As a teenager, Turner began preaching at secret slave meetings and came to believe that he had been appointed to save fellow slaves from oppression. In 1821, he escaped from his master and spent a month in the woods, but he experienced a vision that prompted him to return voluntarily to the plantation. Turner married a fellow slave named Cherry the next year. On May 12, 1828, another vision persuaded Turner that he had been chosen to fight a battle against a serpent. His revelations and role as a lay preacher led Turner to be dubbed "The Prophet" by some of his followers.

Turner's ownership passed from Benjamin Turner to his son Samuel Turner. When Samuel Turner died, Turner was sold to Thomas Moore for four hundred dollars and Cherry was sold to a nearby plantation owned by Giles Reese for forty dollars. Upon Moore's death,

*Contemporary drawing of Nat Turner's capture.* (Library of Congress)

their way. Some of the group disbanded, but Turner continued to seek fresh recruits.

In the meantime, the Virginia state militia and other armed citizens began to unite. A frenzy resulted; church bells rang, and people in the South were filled with panic. Two groups of militia were near the James W. Parker farm when Turner's men arrived there. The Battle of Parker's Farm ensued, taking the lives of some of the rebels while some others dispersed. Afterward, Turner turned south with his remaining followers to seek more recruits at the large plantation of Thomas Ridley. The militia awaited them there and at the Harris Farm, their final stop, as well.

These counterattacks were brutal and equally heinous. The militiamen managed to capture or kill the majority of Turner's group, as well as many others who were innocent of wrongdoing. The remainder of Turner's band retreated; Turner escaped initial capture and survived in the woods for six weeks. On September 17, 1831, Virginia governor John Floyd delivered a proclamation that described Turner and offered a five-hundred-dollar reward. A slave named Nelson reported seeing Turner on October 15. Fifteen days later, Turner was caught by Benjamin Phipps. On November 1, 1831, Turner's lawyer, slave owner Thomas Gray, recorded the *Confessions of Nat Turner*. Four days later, Tuner was tried, convicted, and sentenced to hang for his role in the rebellion. After his execution on November 11, Turner's body was dismembered. Joseph Travis's heirs were paid $375 for the loss of his "property."

Turner became the property of nine-year-old Putnam Moore. When Moore's mother remarried, Turner fell under the control of her new husband, Joseph Travis.

### LIFE'S WORK
In February, 1831, a solar eclipse provided Turner with a sign that God wanted him to direct a rebellion against slave owners. Initially planned for the Fourth of July but suspended when Turner became sick, the revolt was rescheduled after yet another astronomical event. The sun appeared to be a bluish-green color on August 13; Turner accepted this as an indication that he should pursue his earlier plans. On August 21, Turner, Hark Travis, Nelson Williams, Henry Porter, Sam Francis, Will Francis, and Jack Reese met at Giles Reese's nearby Cabin Pond. In the early hours of the next day, Turner and his followers murdered Joseph Travis, his wife, and their family; they then traveled to other plantations and repeated their actions. They killed many of the white men, women, and children they encountered. As they proceeded under the guidance of Turner, the slaves moved toward Jerusalem, Virginia, the county seat, and other slaves joined them. After nearly two days had passed, they had slain between fifty-five and sixty-five white people. The band of slaves was weary, and some among them were under the influence of alcoholic beverages that they had found along

### SIGNIFICANCE
Tuner's rebellion sent shock waves through the South. The hysteria that ensued resulted in the murder of many innocent people. The event led several southern states to pass tougher slave laws and more strictly enforce existing statutes. Abolitionists faced increased hostility. Over time, the details of the rebellion have become more difficult to verify. Literary and fictional treatments of the rebellion have created stereotypes and misconceptions that have further compounded the mysteries that surround Turner.

*—Cynthia J. W. Svoboda*

**FURTHER READING**

Bisson, Terry. *Nat Turner*. New York: Chelsea House, 1988. Part of the Black Americans of Achievement Series. Describes Nat Turner as a slave revolt leader.

French, Scott. *The Rebellious Slave: Nat Turner in American Memory*. Boston: Houghton Mifflin, 2004. Examines the various depictions of Turner's legacy in American culture, including his *Confessions* and the controversial novel by William Styron, *The Confessions of Nat Turner* (1967).

Greenberg, Kenneth S., ed. *Nat Turner: A Slave Rebellion in History and Memory*. New York: Oxford University Press, 2003. A series of essays that includes an examination of who Turner was, a review of his confessions, stories of the rebellion, and observations of how he is remembered.

**SEE ALSO:** William Craft and Ellen Craft; Frederick Douglass; Dred Scott; Denmark Vesey.

# TINA TURNER
## Singer

*Known for her electric stage presence and robust vocals, Turner is one of the most accomplished rock-and-roll singers of all time. After first ascending to stardom in the 1960's, she survived a turbulent marriage and returned to prominence as a solo artist in the 1980's. During a career spanning some five decades, Turner has sold more than sixty million records.*

**BORN:** November 29, 1939; Nutbush, Tennessee
**ALSO KNOWN AS:** Anna Mae Bullock (birth name); Queen of Rock and Roll
**AREAS OF ACHIEVEMENT:** Film: acting; Music: crossover; Music: pop; Music: rhythm and blues; Music: rock and roll

### EARLY LIFE

Anna Mae Bullock was born in Nutbush, near Brownsville, Tennessee, and raised in a plantation shack in the segregated town. She was the younger of two daughters born to Zelma and Floyd Richard Bullock; her sister, Alline, was three years her senior. Turner's mother was a spirited woman of Native American heritage, while her father was a farmer and church deacon. The couple fought bitterly throughout her childhood; Turner was largely treated as an unwanted child—the product of a stormy marriage—and afforded very little attention.

Turner's early life was turbulent and unstable. When she was only a small child, her family was split apart: Alline went to live with their mother's family, and Turner was sent to live with her father's relatives. Deeply religious and strict, they were ill prepared to handle the feisty young Turner, who often found herself in trouble and was generally unhappy under their care. Turner was

briefly reunited with her family in Knoxville before her parents separated, deserting both daughters, who were left in the care of an aunt. After this point, neither Turner nor Alline had any meaningful contact with their parents for some time, and both were forced to take jobs to support themselves.

In 1956, the children's aunt died, and both Turner and Alline were reunited with their mother, who took them both to St. Louis to reside with her. A talented singer with experience in church music, Turner frequented the nightclubs of St. Louis with her sister and their friends in search of further musical opportunities. At the age of seventeen, she visited the Club D'Lisa to see a rising rhythm-and-blues group, Ike Turner and the Kings of Rhythm. Ike was a charismatic, talented young man who reveled in his newfound celebrity status and the financial benefits it entailed. Turner later recalled of the singer-guitarist: "I almost went into a trance just watching him." After weeks of watching the Kings of Rhythm perform, Turner was invited onstage to sing with the band. The crowd responded enthusiastically, and Ike was thoroughly impressed. Soon thereafter, he offered Turner a permanent spot singing backup vocals with his band.

### LIFE'S WORK

Turner soon became Ike's sidekick in the band, serving as lead vocalist and becoming the main draw in all his live performances; the relationship cemented what would come to be known as the Ike and Tina Turner Revue. Their first hit on the rhythm-and-blues charts, "A Fool in Love" (1960), also crossed over to reach the Top 30 on the U.S. pop charts. In the wake of the song's success, Turner adopted the stage name Tina Turner, although she did not formally wed Ike until 1962. The song was followed by the Grammy-nominated "It's Gonna Work Out Fine," recorded with the pop duo Mickey and Sylvia, which reached number fourteen on the *Billboard* Top 100. Despite their inability to score a number one single on the pop charts, Turner and Ike became renowned as a live act, performing on national television and receiving praise from a host of famed rock artists.

In 1966, Ike and Turner embarked upon a collaboration with producer Phil Spector that would seal their reputation as a musical act: the iconic single "River Deep, Mountain High." Although the song—which Spector considered the pinnacle of his artistic achievement—was credited to both Turners, in reality, Spector had bribed Ike to leave the recording sessions; thus, Turner and Spector ultimately worked alone together on the track.

*Tina Turner.* (Michael Ochs Archives/Getty Images)

The song, which employs Spector's famous "Wall of Sound" production technique, reached number three on the British charts but was overlooked during its initial release in the United States. Nonetheless, the song became one of Turner's most celebrated works and a staple of her live shows.

After the success of "River Deep, Mountain High" in the United Kingdom, the Ike and Tina Turner Revue became an international phenomenon. The pair opened for the Rolling Stones in 1966 and 1969 and kept to an active performance schedule in the United States. In 1968, their album *Outta Season* stirred controversy: Its cover depicted the Turners in whiteface, eating watermelon. The image was intended to express the idea that African American musicians needed to appear "more white" to be commercially accepted in the music industry. Their 1969 album, *The Hunter*, earned Turner a Grammy nomination for Best Female R&B Vocal Performance for the bluesy song "Bold Soul Sister."

In 1970, Ike and Turner covered Sly and the Family Stone's psychedelic single "I Want to Take You Higher." Their version outperformed the original song on the U.S. pop charts. That year, the Turners also debuted their cover of Creedence Clearwater Revival's "Proud Mary" on *The Ed Sullivan Show*. The song, which reached number four on the U.S. charts, represents the height of the Ike and Tina Turner Revue's success as pop artists and earned them a Grammy the next year for Best R&B Vocal Performance by a Duo or Group. The group next released *Nutbush City Limits* (1973)—named for Turner's hometown in Tennessee—and *The Gospel According to Ike and Tina* (1974).

In 1975, Turner starred in the musical film *Tommy*, based on the Who's 1969 rock opera of the same name. Turner played the role of the Acid Queen, an LSD-dealing gypsy who sells drugs to the troubled Tommy. She performed the Pete Townshend song "Acid Queen" for the film's sound track. Critics hailed Turner's performance as an actor and singer.

By this time, the Ike and Tina Turner Revue's commercial success had begun to decline, and the couple's marriage was becoming increasingly rocky. Ike was a controlling perfectionist in the studio, and his demands led to bitter disputes between the couple; Turner later accused him of drug use and physical abuse. After a fight with Ike during a tour, Turner abruptly left the group and fled to a Ramada Inn with only the change in her pocket. She subsequently filed for divorce, relinquishing her financial stake in the band in return for the continued use of her stage name.

Turner went on to mixed success as a solo artist, faring far better in Europe than in the United States before making a comeback in the 1980's. In 1986, she released her autobiography, *I, Tina*, which detailed her rise to stardom and her turbulent marriage to Ike. The book was adapted into the film *What's Love Got to Do with It* (1993). Angela Bassett and Laurence Fishburne both were nominated for Academy Awards for their portrayals of Turner and Ike. Turner's work on the film's sound track was well received.

Throughout the 1990's and 2000's, Turner continued to record and tour. In 2005, she received a Kennedy Center Honor from President George W. Bush. Bush famously commented that, in addition to being one of the most talented singers in history, Turner also possessed "the most famous legs in show business."

## SIGNIFICANCE

Turner is a music legend who made a name for herself in rhythm and blues and rock and roll. By 2010, she had won eight Grammy Awards, and her recordings of "River Deep, Mountain High" and "Proud Mary" with the Ike and Tina Turner Revue have been inducted into the Grammy Hall of Fame. The Ike and Tina Turner Revue was inducted into the Rock and Roll Hall of Fame in 1991. Famous for her high-energy performances, Turner scored hits with original songs as well as innovative covers. She collaborated with some of the most celebrated artists of the era, including Elton John, Cher, Eric Clapton, Phil Collins, David Bowie, and Carlos Santana, and remained one of the most popular touring artists into her sixties, a testament to her ageless star power.

—*Erica K. Argyropoulos*

---

## TURNER'S COMEBACK

By 1978, Tina Turner's career had dramatically declined. Her first two albums after her separation from Ike Turner, *Rough* (1978) and *Love Explosion* (1979), failed to make an impact on the charts. Despite these setbacks, Turner continued to draw crowds at her concerts in both the United States and Europe, and her 1983 cover of Al Green's "Let's Stay Together" enjoyed moderate success on both the British and American charts. Based on that success, Turner managed to secure a record contract with Capitol Records, which released her breakthrough multiplatinum album *Private Dancer* (1984). The record, lauded by critics worldwide, yielded the blockbuster hit "What's Love Got to Do With It," which solidified Turner's credibility as a solo artist. The single reached number one in the United States and Australia and number three in the United Kingdom. At the 1985 Grammy Awards, Turner won Best Female Pop Vocal Performance, Record of the Year, and Song of the Year.

After the success of *Private Dancer*, Turner released the platinum album *Break Every Rule* (1986). By the end of the decade, she had released yet another successful album, *Foreign Affair* (1989). In 1995, she recorded the theme song for the James Bond film *Goldeneye*, which enjoyed success on the European charts. The next year, her album *Wildest Dreams* also was well received. *Foreign Affair*, *Wildest Dreams*, and her next album, *Twenty Four Seven* (2000), all reached gold status in the United States.

---

## FURTHER READING

Armani, Eddy. *My Twenty-two Years with Tina Turner.* London: John Blake, 1999. A friend and business associate of Turner relates incidents from the artist's life, beginning with her relationship with Ike and covering the years following their divorce and the rebuilding of her career. The account is generally flattering and considered by some reviewers to be biased, although it does present inside information.

Bego, Mark. *Tina Turner: Break Every Rule.* New York: Taylor, 2005. Named after her album of the same title, this book addresses Turner's early years with Ike, the couple's tumultuous breakup, her solo career, and her career as a superstar. It features several personal stories and carefully researched behind-the-scenes-information on her life in and out of the spotlight.

Brackett, Nathan, and Christian Hoard, eds. *The New Rolling Stone Album Guide.* 4th ed. New York: Simon & Schuster, 2004. This fourth edition guide lists all of Ike and Tina Turner's key studio releases and Turner's solo projects through 2000. Includes detailed reviews of albums.

Campbell, Michael, and James Brody. *Rock and Roll: An Introduction.* New York: Schirmer Books, 1999. This historical account of rock and roll includes references to Turner, particularly during her resurgence in the 1980's.

Shaw, Arnold. *Black Popular Music in America: The Singers, Songwriters, and Musicians Who Pioneered the Sounds of American Music.* New York: Schirmer Books, 1986. A highlight of this resource is a discussion of how Turner transcended racial boundaries to become a successful crossover star.

Turner, Tina, with Kurt Loder. *I, Tina.* New York: William Morrow, 1986. This autobiography was the inspiration for the feature film about her life, *What's Love Got to Do With It.* The text candidly traces all facets of her relationship with Ike and how she survived their split.

**SEE ALSO:** Angela Bassett; James Brown; Aretha Franklin; Patti LaBelle; Diana Ross; Ike Turner; Leslie Uggams.

# MCCOY TYNER
## Jazz musician

*Tyner ranks among the best-known jazz pianists, with a career that began in the early 1960's (as member of the first John Coltrane Quartet). He belongs to the generation of Herbie Hancock, Chick Corea, and Keith Jarrett but has a distinctly different style. Over the years, he has performed in various settings and roles, from soloist to head of his own big band.*

**BORN:** December 11, 1938; Philadelphia, Pennsylvania

**ALSO KNOWN AS:** Alfred McCoy Tyner; Sulaimon Saud

**AREAS OF ACHIEVEMENT:** Music: bandleading; Music: composition; Music: jazz

### EARLY LIFE

Alfred McCoy Tyner was born in 1938 to parents who had roots in North Carolina. He grew up in a musical environment: His mother was a pianist, and his neighbors were the jazz pianist brothers Bud and Richie Powell. They, Art Tatum, and Thelonious Monk were Tyner's first influences when he formally took up the piano at the age of thirteen. He received theory lessons from the Granoff School of Music.

In 1953, while attending West Philadelphia High School, Tyner began leading his first band and played in informal jam sessions with trumpeter Lee Morgan, pianist Bobby Timmons, and bassist Reggie Workman. Two years later, Tyner met John Coltrane at Philadelphia's Red Rooster Club. He converted to Islam through the Ahmadiyya Muslim Community around the same time, adopting the Muslim name Sulaimon Saud. In his native city, Tyner worked with Coltrane, Jimmy Garrison, Cal Massey, Albert "Tootie" Heath, and Benny Golson, who took him to San Francisco for a three-week stand at the Jazz Workshop with Curtis Fuller, Leroy Vinnegar, and Lennie McBrowne in 1959. Later in the same year, Tyner moved to New York and joined the Benny Golson-Art Farmer Jazztet, with whom he recorded the album *Meet the Jazztet* (1960).

### LIFE'S WORK

Tyner's international career began in June of 1960 when he joined Coltrane's legendary Classic Quartet (with Garrison on bass and Elvin Jones on drums). Tyner recorded with the quartet the landmark albums *My Favorite Things* (1960), *Impressions* (1963), and *A Love Supreme* (1965). Between 1962 and 1964, Tyner also appeared as leader on six albums for Impulse! Records, accompanied by such players as Heath, Thad Jones, Art Davis, Henry Grimes, Roy Haynes, and John Gilmore. After leaving Coltrane's quartet in December of 1965, Tyner toured Japan in 1966 and the United States with Art Blakey's Jazz Messengers in 1967, the year he formed his own trio. From 1967 to 1970, Tyner recorded seven albums as leader for Blue Note. His debut album, *The Real McCoy* (1967), is considered the most notable of this series. During the 1960's, Tyner also played as a sideman on more than forty albums for Blue Note.

After a few less successful years, Tyner gained great acclaim at the Newport Jazz Festival in 1972 and the Montreux Jazz Festival in 1973. He also signed a record contract with Milestone in 1972 that resulted in nineteen albums by 1981 and established Tyner as a well-regarded pianist, arranger, and composer. In 1978, he toured and recorded with the Milestone Jazzstars (Sonny Rollins, Ron Carter, and Al Foster), before forming a small group that included saxophonist Garry Bartz and violinist John Blake in the early 1980's. He later assembled the McCoy Tyner Trio with bassist Avery Sharpe (who was replaced by John Lee in 1982) and drummer Louis Hayes.

In his hometown in 1984, Tyner formed a big band that went on to perform in New York nightclubs and win a Grammy Award in 1992. Later in the 1980's, Tyner toured in all-star groups with Freddie Hubbard and Frank Morgan. Through the 1990's, he continued to lead small groups with a wide variety of musicians. Starting in 1995, Tyner led a group he called the Afro-Cuban All Stars, featuring trombonist Steve Turre, tenor saxophonist David Sanchez, and trumpeter Claudio Roditi, with bassist Sharpe and several Cuban and Puerto Rican percussionists. In 1997, he explored new territory by dedicating a tribute album to the music of Burt Bacharach. In 1998, Tyner headed a quartet that included Joshua Redman, Christian McBride, and Brian Blade.

In the 2000's, Tyner continued his prolific recording career and performance schedule. He collaborated with tap dancer Savion Glover in 2005. Two years later, he founded his own label, McCoy Tyner Music, and released its first album, *McCoy Tyner Quartet*, featuring saxophonist Joe Lovano, bassist McBride, and drummer Jeff "Tain" Watts.

## SIGNIFICANCE

With more than eighty albums to his credit, Tyner ranks among the most accomplished jazz pianists from 1960 onward. His vigorous two-handed technique is characterized by a percussive left hand that accentuates the low basses of the piano and a right hand that plays dense block chords in a modal style, with repeated notes, or forceful tremolos, incorporating the whole upper range of the instrument. His dramatic style distinguishes itself through a dense orchestral voicing, unexpected dynamic changes, and an urgent forward motion. Tyner has frequently incorporated African and spiritual elements into his music (for example, in 1972's *Sahara* and 1977's *Inner Voices*). Tyner was named a Steinway Artist in 1977

and has won five Grammys. He received the Jazz Master Award from the National Endowment for the Arts in 2002, the 2003 Hero Award from the Philadelphia Chapter of the BMI Recording Academy, and an honorary doctorate of music from Berklee College in 2005.

—*Michael Baumgartner*

## FURTHER READING

Doerschuk, Robert L. *Eighty-eight: The Giants of Jazz Piano*. San Francisco: Backbeat Books, 2001. Includes a brief biography of Tyner and analysis of his piano style and place in jazz history.

Kahn, Ashley. *The House That Trane Built: The Story of Impulse Records*. New York: W. W. Norton, 2006. Kahn discusses Coltrane's and Tyner's albums as leaders within the context of the label's emerging status in the early 1960's.

Kofsky, Frank. *Black Nationalism and the Revolution in Music*. New York: Pathfinder Press, 1970. Kofsky presents a comprehensive survey of Tyner's activism during the Civil Rights movement of the 1960's.

Lyons, Len. *The Great Jazz Pianists: Speaking of Their Lives and Music*. New York: William Morrow, 1983. Lyons offers an informative interview, with numerous details about Tyner's life and professional career.

Rinzler, Paul. "McCoy Tyner: Style and Syntax." In *Annual Review of Jazz Studies 2*. New Brunswick, N.J.: Transaction Books, 1983. Rinzler provides an excellent analysis with full transcriptions of Tyner's solos in "Blue Monk" (1963), "May Street" (1970), "The Night Has a Thousand Eyes" (1972), "Impressions" (1975), and "Moment's Notice" (1977).

**SEE ALSO:** John Coltrane; Earl Hines; Ellis Marsalis, Jr.; Thelonious Monk; Little Brother Montgomery; Jelly Roll Morton; Herbie Nichols; Professor Longhair; Horace Silver; Fats Waller.

# CICELY TYSON
## Actor and activist

*Tyson is an award-winning actor and advocate for educational, civic, and humanitarian causes. Her commitment to portraying positive African American characters resulted in many memorable performances.*

**BORN:** December 19, 1933; Harlem, New York
**ALSO KNOWN AS:** Cicely L. Tyson
**AREAS OF ACHIEVEMENT:** Fashion; Film: acting; Social issues

### EARLY LIFE
Cicely L. Tyson (SIH-suh-lee TI-suhn) was born in Harlem to a family struggling for economic survival. Her parents, William and Theodosia Tyson, had immigrated to the United States from Nevis, a small Caribbean island. William was a carpenter and sold fruit from a

*Cicely Tyson.* (Hulton Archive/Getty Images)

pushcart. Theodosia worked as a domestic. Tyson, the youngest of three siblings, sold shopping bags on the streets. Even so, the family needed welfare to keep food on the table and a roof over their heads. They moved frequently from one Harlem tenement to another, and Tyson's parents' divorce introduced more instability into her childhood. Tyson found solace in the church, although she resented the restrictions placed on her by her deeply religious mother. She was not allowed to socialize outside church or date until she was seventeen.

Tyson grew up restless and curious, and she found ways to break through her physical and emotional boundaries. While in high school, she would ride the bus across the city and contemplate a better future. Working as a typist for the Red Cross after graduation, she declared that she would not spend her life "banging on a typewriter." Although she was unsure of what she wanted to do, Tyson felt destined for a life more significant than the one she was living.

The opportunity for that different life came when Tyson modeled in a hair show. Her striking features, high cheekbones, small frame, and ebony skin drew notice, and she was encouraged to pursue fashion modeling. She became one of the top ten African American models in the country. However, she grew tired of being seen simply as a pretty face in designer clothes. Encouraged by Freda DeKnight, an editor at *Ebony*, Tyson auditioned for a role in an independent film, *Caribe Gold*. The film was never completed, but the experience introduced her to the thrill of acting. Despite her mother's strong objections, Tyson enrolled in classes at the Actors Studio. She had to leave home, but she began making money and drawing praise as an actor.

### LIFE'S WORK
Tyson garnered favorable reviews for her first stage role in *Dark of the Moon* (1958-1959), but it was in Jean Genet's *The Blacks* (1961) that Tyson became a nationally recognized artist. Her comedic performance as a prostitute named Virtue earned Tyson her first Drama Desk Award.

In her first major film role, in Carson McCullers's *The Heart Is a Lonely Hunter* (1968), and on television, Tyson wore her hair in a short Afro. She drew criticism from some, black and white, for her "natural" hair and dark skin, and for not conforming to the image of a middle-class African American woman. Others, however, considered her looks revolutionary; she was the embodiment of the slogan Black Is Beautiful. In 1963, she became the first female African American actor to appear regularly in a dramatic series, in the acclaimed *East Side, West Side*. More television appearances in programs as diverse as the Western *Gunsmoke* and the soap opera *The Guiding Light* followed. Her film roles, however, were few during the 1960's and 1970's because she refused to play the hypersexual characters of the blaxploitation era. Tyson insisted on roles that cast black women in a positive light, and her career is distinguished by her portrayals of multidimensional characters who do not fit into any popular stereotype.

One of Tyson's most notable film roles was in *Sounder* (1972) as a defiant, smart, and deeply loving woman. Reviewers hailed the character, Rebecca Morgan, as the first black heroine of film. Tyson received an Oscar nomination as Best Actress. In 1974, she won more plaudits for her starring role in the television film *The Autobiography of Miss Jane Pittman* as a fictional 110-year-old woman whose life encompasses slavery and the Civil Rights era. Other female heroine roles followed: Tyson played Kunta Kinte's mother Binta in the historic television miniseries *Roots* (1977); Coretta Scott King in *King* (1978); Harriet Tubman in *A Woman Called Moses* (1978), for which she was also a producer; and educator Marva Collins in *The Marva Collins Story* (1981). Having established herself as a dramatic actor, Tyson also triumphed in comedic roles, such as *Bustin' Loose* with Richard Pryor (1981), and in three films by writer-producer-actor Tyler Perry: *Diary of a Mad Black Woman* (2005), *Madea's Family Reunion* (2006), and *Why Did I Get Married Too?* (2010).

With hundreds of performances to her credit, Tyson also is recognized as an energetic advocate for education, women's rights, and human rights. Well into her sixties and seventies, she traveled to schools and colleges across the country to educate students about history and race. She served as a world ambassador for United Nations Children's Fund (UNICEF) and an advocate for Save the

---

### THE AUTOBIOGRAPHY OF MISS JANE PITTMAN

If the film *Sounder* (1972) introduced Cicely Tyson as a talented African American actor, *The Autobiography of Miss Jane Pittman* two years later sealed her reputation as a superb performer regardless of race. She received top billing and two Emmy Awards, a first for a black woman, for her portrayal of the title character, a 110-year-old former slave who takes a defiant stand during the Civil Rights movement. Tyson, then forty-one, endured hours of makeup to transform from the young, newly freed Jane to the old, frail Miss Jane. Tyson earned widespread praise for transforming the symbolic character into a witty, smart, deeply wounded, and yet triumphant human being. Miss Jane, Tyson said, was one of three positive roles she had longed to play; Rebecca Morgan of *Sounder* and Harriet Tubman in *A Woman Called Moses* (1978) were the other two. In the decades after the television film's debut, Miss Jane Pittman remained an iconic character.

---

Children, and in 2005, she traveled to Phuket, Thailand, to help rebuild schools after the devastation of the 2004 Indian Ocean tsunami. A vegetarian who observes a strict regimen of diet and exercise, she also has lectured about health issues.

As of 2010, Tyson had received two Emmy Awards, twelve Image Awards from the National Association for the Advancement of Colored People (NAACP), and numerous honorary degrees. She is the namesake of the Cicely L. Tyson Community School for the Performing and Fine Arts, in East Orange, New Jersey. The school provides prekindergarten through high school education for future writers, musicians, dancers, and actors.

**SIGNIFICANCE**

Over her six-decade career, Tyson has made hundreds of appearances on film, on television, and on stage. She also has contributed to humanitarian efforts worldwide. While she suffered setbacks in her personal life, including a brief marriage to jazz great Miles Davis, Tyson won acclaim for her insistence on portraying positive images of African American women.

—*Joyce A. Barnes*

**FURTHER READING**

Bogle, Donald. *Brown Sugar: Over One Hundred Years of America's Black Female Superstars*. New York: Continuum, 2007. Discusses Tyson's many roles and her career in the context of female African American entertainers.

Mapp, Edward. "1972 Cicely Tyson." In *African Americans and the Oscar: Seven Decades of Struggle and*

*Achievement*. Lanham, Md.: Scarecrow Press, 2003. Describes Tyson's role in *Sounder* and the critical and social reaction to it. Places the film and Tyson's Oscar nomination in historical context.

Sanders, Charles L. "Cicely Tyson: She Can Smile Again After a Three-Year Ordeal." *Ebony* 34, no. 3 (January, 1979): 27-36. Tyson discusses her return to acting after a period of depression following her mother's death.

Schleier, Curt. "Cicely Tyson Takes the High Road." *The Detroit News*, January 24, 1996. In this profile and interview, Tyson discusses the lack of quality film roles for African American women and the discrimination she has faced in her career.

**SEE ALSO:** Diahann Carroll; Ruby Dee; Coretta Scott King; Eartha Kitt; Hattie McDaniel; Tyler Perry; Harriet Tubman; Leslie Uggams.

# MIKE TYSON
## Boxer

*In the late 1980's, Tyson was the most feared heavyweight boxer in the world. Storming into the sport at the age of eighteen, he won most of his early bouts convincingly. A shocking defeat in 1990 changed Tyson's life, however, and started a downward spiral in his personal and professional lives.*

**BORN:** June 30, 1966; Brooklyn, New York
**ALSO KNOWN AS:** Michael Gerard Tyson; Iron Mike; Kid Dynamite; the Baddest Man on the Planet; Malik Adbul Aziz
**AREA OF ACHIEVEMENT:** Sports: boxing

### EARLY LIFE
Michael Gerard Tyson was born in Brooklyn, New York, to Jimmy Kirkpatrick and Lorna Smith Tyson. He had a

brother, Rodney, and a sister, Denise. By the time Tyson was two years old, his father had left the family. His mother was later forced to move the family to Brownsville, Brooklyn, one of the more troubled areas in the city.

Because of his high voice, lisp, and small stature, Tyson was often a target for bullies. He learned to fight at a young age and fell in with a crowd that committed petty crimes. By the time Tyson was thirteen, he had been arrested thirty-eight times. His subsequent remand to the Tryon School for Boys marked a turning point in his life. Tyson's counselor at the facility, Bob Stewart, was a former amateur boxing champion and helped to shape Tyson's early forays into boxing. Despite some initial reluctance about the boy, Stewart later tried to teach Tyson everything he knew. Tyson took to boxing with a focused gusto, reading books on the sport and often sneaking out after curfew to work on his punches.

Stewart, sensing that Tyson was ready for more advanced training, introduced the young fighter to Cus D'Amato, a well-known boxing trainer. D'Amato became Tyson's surrogate father, taking custody of the boy when he was fourteen. With a rigorous training schedule, Tyson honed his skills and began fighting in amateur bouts. Just when he was beginning to develop a more stable life, however, his mother died of cancer in 1982. Tyson later described her death as emotionally crushing. Around this time, he also was expelled from Catskill High School.

*Mike Tyson.* (Archive Photos/Getty Images)

## LIFE'S WORK

Rather than return to a conventional high school, Tyson finished his schooling with tutors as he prepared for the 1984 Olympic trials. He did not earn a spot in the Olympic Games and instead turned professional at the age of eighteen. On March 6, 1985, Tyson made his professional debut in Albany, New York, against Hector Mercedes, whom he knocked out in the first round.

In November, 1985, Tyson was felled by the death of D'Amato. Observers have speculated that D'Amato's death haunted Tyson throughout his career. Kevin Rooney took over training Tyson, who achieved his thirteenth knockout in his next fight.

By the age of twenty, Tyson had accumulated a 22-0 record, with 21 of those victories coming by knockout. He became the youngest championship fighter in history when he beat Trevor Berbick for the World Boxing Council (WBC) title on November 22, 1986. He added the World Boxing Association (WBA) championship belt when he beat James Smith on March 7, 1987. Tyson beat Tony Tucker for the International Boxing Federation belt on August 1 of that same year, becoming the first boxer to hold all three major boxing championships.

With his boxing success came the trappings of fame, and Tyson relished them. He had a brief, ill-fated marriage to actor Robin Givens, from February, 1988, to February, 1989. His behavior became erratic and violent. In addition, his boxing began to falter as he sought flashy one-punch knockouts, disregarding the training that had made him a champion.

These problems came to a head on February 11, 1990, in Tokyo. Despite being heavily favored against Buster Douglas, Tyson was knocked out in the tenth round. Tyson not only had never lost a professional fight, but he also had never been knocked out. In 1991, Tyson was arrested on charges of raping an eighteen-year-old woman. He was later convicted and served three years of a six-year prison sentence. After his release, Tyson vowed to return to his boxing form.

Tyson won a few bouts during this comeback bid, but when he faced Evander Holyfield in 1996, he was thwarted in the eleventh round. Feeling that Holyfield had repeatedly head-butted him during the fight, Tyson

---

## TYSON'S CONVICTION AND PRISON SENTENCE

In July, 1991, Mike Tyson was arrested on charges of raping Desiree Washington, Miss Black Rhode Island, in an Indianapolis hotel. Because of Tyson's stature, the case generated widespread media attention and intense scrutiny. Washington asserted that Tyson had raped her on July 19, 1991, and statements from Tyson's chauffeur and the emergency room doctor who treated her corroborated her story. Tyson maintained his innocence, claiming that his and Washington's encounter had been consensual.

During the trial the next year, Tyson might have sealed his fate when he appeared hostile during his cross-examination. After ten hours of jury deliberations, Tyson was convicted of rape. He received a sentence of six years of prison and four years of probation. The boxer struggled to adapt to prison and had fifteen days added to his sentence for threatening a guard. In addition, Tyson's father died while he was incarcerated; Tyson did not ask to attend the funeral. After his initial troubles, however, Tyson became a model inmate and converted to Islam, adopting the name Malik Abdul Aziz. On March 25, 1995, after serving three years of his sentence, Tyson was released from prison and looked to resume his boxing career. He never regained the form that had made him the world's best heavyweight in the late 1980's.

---

sought and received a rematch. The second fight, in 1998, was marred by an infamous incident in which Tyson bit off part of Holyfield's ear. Tyson's boxing license was suspended. When it was reinstated, Tyson mounted another comeback attempt. In 2002, he had the opportunity to face Lennox Lewis, the World Boxing Organization (WBO), International Boxing Federation (IBF), and International Boxing Organization (IBO) champion. In a then record-setting pay-per-view event, Lewis dominated Tyson, scoring an eighth-round knockout. The fight was the last major bout of Tyson's career.

Tyson's life after boxing was fraught with legal and financial troubles. He filed for bankruptcy in 2003, despite earning some $400 million during his career. He sought treatment for drug addiction after arrests for drug possession and driving under the influence. In the late 2000's, he worked primarily as a pitchman for various products. He also made a brief appearance as himself in the hit comedy film *The Hangover* (2009).

## SIGNIFICANCE

In his prime, Tyson was one of the most fearsome heavyweight fighters of all time. He was the youngest heavyweight champion in history. Tyson's early success, however, led to a precipitous decline. With celebrity came poor training habits, troubles with the law, and financial irresponsibility. After his retirement, Tyson's outrageous behavior, legal woes, and film and television appearances cemented his status as a major figure in pop culture.

—*P. Huston Ladner*

**FURTHER READING**

Cashmore, Ellis. *Tyson: Nurture of the Beast.* Malden, Mass.: Polity Press, 2005. Accessible source that explores Tyson's psyche and examines his influence on American culture.

Layden, Joe. *The Last Great Fight: The Extraordinary Tale of Two Men and How One Fight Changed Their Lives Forever.* New York: St. Martin's Press, 2007. Detailed examination of the Tyson-Douglas bout and

its ramifications for both parties and the sport of boxing.

O'Connor, Danial, ed. *Iron Mike: A Mike Tyson Reader.* New York City: Thunder's Mouth Press, 2002. Collection of essays on Tyson by various writers, some close to him. Provides a wide-ranging look at his life.

Shaw, Mark. *Down for the Count: The Shocking Truth Behind the Mike Tyson Rape Trial.* Champaign, Ill.: Sagamore, 1993. Details the trial that, in effect, was the catalyst for Tyson's career slide. It explores the strategies used by both parties and analyzes whether Tyson received a fair trial.

**SEE ALSO:** Muhammad Ali; Ezzard Charles; George Foreman; Joe Frazier; Evander Holyfield; Jack Johnson; Joe Louis; Floyd Patterson; Jersey Joe Walcott.

# NEIL DEGRASSE TYSON
## Astrophysicist and writer

*Tyson, an accomplished astrophysicist, became one of the most visible and respected scientists of the early twenty-first century. Through his numerous books, television appearances, public lectures, and radio shows, he has done much to popularize astronomy.*

**BORN:** October 5, 1958; New York, New York
**AREA OF ACHIEVEMENT:** Science and technology

**EARLY LIFE**

Neil deGrasse Tyson (deh-GRASS TI-suhn) was born in New York City to Sunchita and Cyril Tyson. As a child, he often climbed to the top floor of the Skyview Apartments where he lived to gaze at the night sky through binoculars. His parents encouraged his interest in astronomy with regular trips to the Hayden Planetarium. In 1970, Tyson's father bought him a telescope for his twelfth birthday, and his interest in the cosmos grew into an obsession.

Tyson attended the Bronx High School of Science from 1972 to 1976 and also took after-school astronomy classes at the planetarium. He was an outstanding student and captain of the wrestling team. When he was fourteen years old, Tyson attended an astronomy camp in the Mojave Desert, and when he was fifteen, he began to make a name for himself by giving astronomy lectures. Stories about him piqued the interest of Cornell Univer-

sity astronomer Carl Sagan, who energetically recruited Tyson for the Cornell astronomy program. Tyson, however, attended Harvard University, where he majored in physics, was a member of the wrestling team, and earned his bachelor's degree in 1980.

For graduate school, Tyson attended the University of Texas, Austin, where he earned his master's degree in astronomy in 1983. He also was a member of a dance company. In 1985, he won a gold medal at a national ballroom dancing tournament in the International Latin style. In 1988, Tyson transferred to Columbia University, where he earned his doctorate in astrophysics in 1991.

**LIFE'S WORK**

After graduate school, Tyson worked as a postdoctoral research associate at Princeton University for three years. In May, 1996, he was made director of New York's Hayden Planetarium.

In 2001, President George W. Bush appointed Tyson to the Commission on the Future of the United States Aerospace Industry. In 2004, President Bush appointed him to serve on the President's Commission on Implementation of United States Space Exploration Policy. For his work on these commissions, the National Aeronautics and Space Administration (NASA) awarded Tyson its Distinguished Public Service Medal, the highest honor given by NASA to nongovernmental civilians.

Although Tyson has published dozens of technical

papers, he is most famous as a popular communicator of science. While he was in graduate school, Tyson wrote his first popular book on astronomy, *Merlin's Tour of the Universe* (1989). In this book, a fictional character from another galaxy (Merlin) answers common astronomical questions. This book was the first of many that Tyson has written to present astronomy to the public. He also has written the "Universe" column for *Natural History* magazine.

Tyson also became a very public media figure. His wit and theatrical flair make him engaging and effective at explaining science to general audiences. In 2004, he hosted the four-part *Origins* miniseries for PBS's *Nova* program. In the fall of 2006, Tyson became the host of PBS's *Nova ScienceNow*. In 2009, with funding from the National Science Foundation, Tyson and comedian Lynn Koplitz started a commercial radio program called *Star-Talk*, which helps nonprofessionals engage with modern science.

Tyson has been honored extensively for his efforts to expand public knowledge of science. *Time* magazine named him one of the One Hundred Most Influential People of 2007. In December, 2008, *Discover* magazine listed him among the Fifty Best Brains in Science. His fellow astronomers honored him by naming the asteroid 13123 Tyson for him.

## SIGNIFICANCE

When astronomer Carl Sagan, the famous popularizer of science, died in 1996, Tyson quickly took Sagan's place as one of the most famous communicators of astronomical science to the public. His fluency with his subject and immensely likable demeanor endeared him to all kinds of viewers. His childlike fascination and awe for the universe inspired many people, even those with little formal education, to learn more about astronomy.

Tyson had to overcome racial stereotypes to become an astrophysicist, but he said that he was so "deeply in love" with his subject that no one could stand in his way. He is truly a role model for any aspiring scientist, regardless of their skin hue.

*—Michael A. Buratovich*

## FURTHER READING

Mirsky, Steve. "When the Sky Is Not the Limit." *Scientific American* 282, no. 2 (February, 2000): 28. Profile of Tyson covering his work with the Hayden Planetarium and role in educating the general public about astronomy.

Tyson, Neil deGrasse. *Death by Black Hole and Other Cosmic Quandaries*. New York: W. W. Norton, 2007. A collection of Tyson's lively "Universe" columns from *Natural History*.

_____. *The Pluto Files: The Rise and Fall of America's Favorite Planet*. New York: W. W. Norton, 2009. A chronicle of Pluto's discovery, classification as a planet, and later reclassification as a dwarf planet and the reactions it generated, including strongly worded letters from schoolchildren.

_____. *The Sky Is Not the Limit: Adventures of an Urban Astrophysicist*. New York: Doubleday, 2000. Tyson's autobiography describes his early yearning to study the universe and the obstacles he had to surmount to become an astrophysicist.

Tyson, Neil deGrasse, and Donald Goldsmith. *Origins: Fourteen Billion Years of Cosmic Evolution*. New York: W. W. Norton, 2004. This companion book to the PBS miniseries *Origins* traces the development of the universe from its first three seconds through the formation of stars, galaxies, and solar systems.

**SEE ALSO:** Benjamin Banneker; Guion Bluford; Frederick Drew Gregory; Mae C. Jemison; Robert H. Lawrence, Jr.; Ronald E. McNair.

# WYOMIA TYUS
## Track-and-field athlete

*Tyus was the first runner, male or female, to win gold medals for the 100-meter event in back-to-back Olympic Games. Tyus not only successfully defended her Olympic 100-meter championship in 1968 but also set new world and Olympic records for the event while doing so.*

**BORN:** August 29, 1945; Griffin, Georgia
**ALSO KNOWN AS:** Wyomia Tyus-Tillman
**AREAS OF ACHIEVEMENT:** Sports: Olympics; Sports: track and field

### EARLY LIFE
Wyomia Tyus (WI-oh-mee-uh TI-uhs) was born in Griffin, Georgia, on August 29, 1945, to Willie Tyus, a dairy farmer, and Marie Tyus, a laundry worker. The only girl and the youngest of four children, Wyomia Tyus was inspired to run at an early age to keep up with her older brothers. Tyus's father encouraged her to play sports and compete, even against boys. Tyus's mother and other female relatives, however, strongly disapproved of her participating in sports, claiming that it was unfeminine and unladylike.

Although an elementary school was within walking distance of Tyus's home, the school was for whites only. Segregation laws in the South forced Tyus to ride a bus one hour each morning to Annie Shockley Elementary School, a school for African Americans. Tyus idolized Olympic champion Jesse Owens, and by the time she entered Griffin's Fairmont High School, Tyus's goal had become to compete in the track-and-field high jump competition. Unsuccessful as a high jumper, Tyus nonetheless discovered, while sprinting before jumps, her natural talent for running. After she won a Georgia high school sprinting competition in 1959, at the age of fourteen, Tyus was invited by Tennessee State University (TSU) women's track-and-field coach Ed Temple to attend the summer TSU Track-and-Field Clinic. Tyus spent the next two summers at TSU, training with Temple's Tigerbelles, women runners who included Olympic champion Wilma Rudolph, who was five years older than Tyus. In 1960, Tyus's father, her great supporter, died, and Temple became a surrogate father to Tyus as well as her coach. After training for two years with Temple, in 1962 Tyus won the 50-yard, 75-yard, and 100-yard dashes at the Amateur Athletic Union (AAU) National Championships, setting two new American records, and in 1963, she won the 75-yard and 100-yard races at the AAU National Championships again.

### LIFE'S WORK
In fall, 1963, Tyus entered TSU and trained intensively with Temple as a Tennessee Tigerbelle. After winning the 100-yard dash for the third year in a row at the 1964 AAU National Championships, Tyus competed at the 1964 Olympic Games in Tokyo, where she won a gold medal in the 100 meters, with a world-record time of 11.49 seconds, and won a silver medal in the 4-by-100-meter relay. After her Olympic victory, Georgia governor Lester Maddox proclaimed November 21, 1964, as "Wyomia Tyus Day." In 1965, Tyus set a world record for the 100 meters at the U.S.A.-U.S.S.R. Competition in Kiev. In 1966, after winning the 100 at the AAU Championships, the Southeastern Track and Field Meet, the All-American Track-and-Field Meet, and the U.S.S.R.-British Commonwealth Track-and-Field Meet, Tyus was requested by the U.S. State Department, along with 1964 Olympic teammate Edith McGuire and Temple, to go on a goodwill tour of Africa. The group traveled to Malawi, Kenya, Uganda, and Ethiopia, demonstrating proper running techniques.

In 1967, Tyus won the 200 meters at the Pan-American Games and the 100 at the Europe-America Track-and-Field Meet. Racial tension in 1968 in the United States led some African American athletes to boycott the 1968 Olympic Games in Mexico City, but Tyus ran, winning a gold medal in the 100 meters and setting a new world record of 11.08 seconds, plus winning a second gold medal for the 4-by-100-meter relay. After Olympic runners Tommie Smith and John Carlos raised their black-gloved fists in a Black Power salute on the winners' podium and later were ousted from the Olympic Village for doing so, Tyus dedicated her 100-meter gold medal to them and wore black shorts to show her support for their protest of racism.

Tyus retired from track in 1968 and graduated with a bachelor's degree in recreation from TSU. Tyus married and divorced Albert Simberg, with whom she had a daughter, Simone; later, she married Duane Tillman, with whom she had a son, Tyus. In 1973, Tyus began competing again, winning all twenty-two races she ran in 1974 for the International Track Association, afterward again retiring from track. Tyus moved to Los Angeles, where she began to teach physical education and to coach at Beverly Hills High School. Tyus was inducted into the Track and Field Hall of Fame in 1980 and the Olympic Hall of Fame in 1985.

### SIGNIFICANCE

Tyus removed perceived age limitations for Olympic runners by winning the 100 meters twice. Prior to Tyus winning Olympic gold medals in the event at the 1964 and 1968 Olympic Games, no runner ever had repeated in the event, leading to assumptions that four years was simply too long a time period for a sprinter to remain in top form. Tyus also forever changed the manner in which Olympic runners prepare themselves in their lanes shortly before an Olympic race. Prior to 1968, runners were historically formal and reserved in their lanes, focused, looking straight ahead. When Tyus suddenly began gyrating in her lane to loosen up, performing the moves to a 1968 dance and song called "The Tighten Up," her fans went wild. Years later, Tyus's Olympic running competitors confessed that her dancing had shocked and intimidated them, breaking their concentration and throwing them off their game.

—*Mary E. Markland*

*Wyomia Tyus.* (AP/Wide World Photos)

### FURTHER READING

Bass, Amy. *Not the Triumph but the Struggle: The 1968 Olympics and the Making of the Black Athlete.* Minneapolis: University of Minnesota Press, 2002. Describes the racism and sexism faced by Tyus at the 1968 Olympic Games, where Tyus remembers women being secondary.

Sears, Edward S. *Running Through the Ages.* Jefferson, N.C.: McFarland, 2001. Profiles Tyus's training as a Tennessee Tigerbelle with Temple, leading to her winning back-to-back Olympic gold medals.

Tyus, Wyomia. *Inside Jogging for Women.* Chicago: Contemporary Books, 1978. Tyus explains her philosophy of running, describes her training techniques, and gives advice on how to avoid running pitfalls and injuries.

**SEE ALSO:** John Carlos; Florence Griffith-Joyner; Jackie Joyner-Kersee; Jesse Owens; Wilma Rudolph; Tommie Smith.

# LESLIE UGGAMS
## Actor

*Uggams's success and versatility as an actor and singer enabled her to attain many breakthroughs for African Americans in entertainment. During the 1960's and 1970's, she became a major television star, achieving national and international recognition. At the height of her fame and popularity, Uggams presented an image of African American womanhood that emphasized beauty, grace, and class.*

**BORN:** May 25, 1943; New York, New York
**ALSO KNOWN AS:** Leslie Marian Uggams
**AREAS OF ACHIEVEMENT:** Film: acting; Music: pop; Radio and television

### EARLY LIFE

Leslie Marian Uggams (UHG-guhmz) was born on May 25, 1943, in the Washington Heights section of New York City. She was the second daughter born to Harold Uggams, an elevator operator and floor waxer, and Juanita Smith Uggams, a former chorus girl and waitress. Uggams knew from an early age that she wanted to be a performer, an ambition that her parents encouraged. She developed and exhibited her vocal talents early by singing along with records.

Uggams made her first appearance on television at the age of six, when she appeared as Ethel Waters's niece in the television sitcom *Beulah*. At the age of eight, she made an appearance on *Paul Whiteman's TV Teen Club*. She also expanded her performance repertoire by taking lessons in tap dance. After she completed the third grade at her local public school, she enrolled in the prestigious New York Professional Children's School.

By the time she was nine years old, Uggams was opening as a singer, dancer, and impressionist at the legendary Apollo Theater for a number of show business luminaries, such as Louis Armstrong, Ella Fitzgerald, and Dinah Washington. She also appeared on a number of variety shows, including *The Milton Berle Show* and *The Arthur Godfrey Show*. At the age of fifteen, she was a contestant on the television quiz show *Name That Tune*. Her performance of the song "He's Got the Whole World

---

### ROOTS

Although she already had built a long career in a variety of entertainment genres, it was Uggams's role in *Roots* in 1977 that made her an international star. The television miniseries, which aired on ABC for eight consecutive nights and attracted record ratings, was adapted from Alex Haley's book *Roots: The Saga of an American Family* (1976). While both the book and television series were cultural milestones, the show was particularly revolutionary in that it depicted the African American experience of slavery and its aftermath. It spurred greater interest in genealogical research and expanded dominant conceptions of history. Uggams's portrayal of the young slave girl Kizzy Reynolds enabled viewers to see the brutality of everyday life for those forced into servitude. In recognition of her performance, Uggams was nominated for a Golden Globe and an Emmy Award. In 1978, she won the Critics Choice Award for Best Supporting Actress.

in His Hands" not only won her a $12,500 college scholarship but also caught the attention of Columbia Records producer Mitch Miller. Miller signed Uggams to a recording contract and released her first album in 1959. Although her career was taking off, Uggams remained in high school and graduated in 1961. She attended the prestigious Juilliard School to study music composition and theory before finally leaving in 1963 to pursue her career full time.

## LIFE'S WORK

Miller starred in his own television show, *Sing Along with Mitch*, and in 1961 he invited Uggams to appear in it, first as a guest vocalist and then as a regular performer. Through her appearances on the show, Uggams became the first African American performer featured in a national primetime television series. During a time when rock and roll was the most popular genre of music, the show's thematic focus on more traditional music enabled Uggams to project a wholesome image more typically associated with white performers of the era. She thus saw her position on the show as one in which she could help earn respect for African Americans.

After the show was canceled in 1964, Uggams performed in nightclubs, on stage, and in variety shows. After appearing in the musical *The Boyfriend* in Berkeley, California, she made her debut on Broadway in 1967 as the lead in *Hallelujah, Baby!* Uggams was offered the role after her idol, Lena Horne, dropped out. Although the show, which chronicled the history of African Americans in show business, received mediocre reviews, Uggams won the 1968 Tony Award for Best Actress in a Musical. Next, she starred as Cleopatra in the musical *Her First Roman*.

In the late 1960's, Uggams decided to return to television. She made guest appearances on a number of popular television series, such as *I Spy* in 1965, and *The Man from U.N.C.L.E.* in 1966. In 1969, she hosted a variety series on CBS, *The Leslie Uggams Show*, becoming the first black female performer to host her own series since Hazel Scott in the 1950's. Although the show was canceled in December of that year, after only six months on the air, it was the first program to feature an African American host and a predominantly African American cast of performers. Uggams also branched out into films, appearing in *Skyjacked* (1972), *Black Girl* (1972), and *Poor Pretty Eddy* (1975).

*Leslie Uggams.* (Archive Photos/Getty Images)

In 1977, Uggams appeared in the groundbreaking television miniseries *Roots*. Her role in the drama garnered a number of award nominations and won her worldwide recognition as a dramatic actor. After *Roots*, she went on to star in many other television series. She won an Emmy Award for *Fantasy* in 1983.

In the years that followed, Uggams focused her attention on the theater. She returned to Broadway in the late 1980's, starring in *Blues in the Night, Jerry's Girls, Thoroughly Modern Millie*, and *Anything Goes*. She also starred in musicals in regional theaters across the United States. In 2009, she starred as Horne in *Stormy Weather* at the Pasadena Playhouse, near Los Angeles. She also released several music albums and performed in concert tours throughout her career.

## SIGNIFICANCE

Uggams was a television pioneer whose vocal talents and affable stage presence enabled her to appeal to diverse audiences. Such broad appeal was crucial in an era when few black performers achieved mainstream popular success. Her performances in *Sing Along with Mitch*, *The Leslie Uggams Show*, and *Roots* helped demonstrate the marketability of African American entertainers. In these performances and others, Uggams brought many different aspects of African American life to the light on the screen and stage. Her achievements in television during the 1950's, 1960's, and 1970's are especially notable, given that roles for African American actors at the time were rigidly circumscribed.

—*Patricia G. Davis*

**FURTHER READING**

Bogle, Donald. *Primetime Blues: African Americans on Network Television*. New York: Farrar, Straus and Giroux, 2002. A scholarly yet accessible history of African Americans in television, this book provides important context for the conditions that gave rise to Uggams's remarkable achievements in entertainment.

Davidson, Telly. *TV's Grooviest Variety Shows of the '60s and '70s*. Nashville, Tenn.: Cumberland House, 2006. This history of American variety shows includes detailed coverage of *The Leslie Uggams Show*.

*Ebony*. "She Sings Along with Mitch." 17, no. 5 (March, 1962): 40-46. Well-illustrated profile from early in Uggams's career describes her role on *Sing Along with Mitch*, her work as a child actor, and her thoughts on the Civil Rights movement.

**SEE ALSO:** Irene Cara; Diahann Carroll; Nell Carter; Phylicia Rashad; Cicely Tyson; Vanessa Williams; Alfre Woodard.

# BLAIR UNDERWOOD
## Actor

*Underwood is an award-winning television and film actor best known for his roles in* L.A. Law, Rules of Engagement, City of Angels, *and* In Treatment. *He is also a tireless charity worker who has supported organizations such as Artists for a New South Africa, the Muscular Dystrophy Association, and YOUTHaids.*

**BORN:** August 25, 1964; Tacoma, Washington
**AREAS OF ACHIEVEMENT:** Film: acting; Film: direction; Philanthropy; Radio and television

### EARLY LIFE

Blair Underwood was born in Tacoma, Washington, on August 25, 1964, to Marilyn, an interior decorator, and Frank Underwood, a colonel in the U.S. Army. Underwood, along with his parents, brother, and two sisters, moved frequently because of his father's profession, living on several military bases in the United States and Germany. From an early age, Underwood felt great national pride and responsibility because of his father's accomplishments. As he stated in an interview for National Public Radio on September 2, 2003, "All of us as children knew and understood that whenever we walked out of the house—you represent yourself, you represent your father, and you represent your country."

After Underwood graduated from Petersburg High School in Petersburg, Virginia, he attended the Carnegie Mellon School of Drama, where he joined Phi Beta Sigma, the well-known African American fraternity founded at Howard University in 1914. Upon completion of his theatrical training at Carnegie Mellon, Underwood moved to New York to pursue a professional career.

### LIFE'S WORK

Within days of moving to New York in 1985, Underwood landed a guest role on *The Cosby Show*. Months later, he made his film debut in *Krush Groove*, in which he played a fictionalized version of Def Jam records mogul Russell Simmons. In late 1985 and early 1986, Underwood joined the cast of the daytime television program *One Life to Live*.

From 1987 to 1994, Underwood played the role of attorney Jonathan Rollins in the critically acclaimed television series *L.A. Law*, earning a Golden Globe nomination, an Image Award from the National Association for the Advancement of Colored People (NAACP), and widespread national recognition.

During his tenure at *L.A. Law*, Underwood occasionally appeared in motion pictures and made-for-television films. On the big screen, Underwood directed and acted in the contentious film *The Second Coming* (1992), in which he played the role of Jesus Christ. On television, he appeared in *Heat Wave* (1990) and *Murder in Mississippi* (1990), among others.

When *L.A. Law* ended in 1994, Underwood decided against signing on to another long-standing television program. In the second half of the 1990's, Underwood appeared in *Just Cause* (1995), *Set It Off* (1996), *Gattaca* (1997), and *Deep Impact* (1998) on the big screen. Underwood also appeared as Jackie Robinson in the television film *Soul of the Game* in 1996.

As the 2000's began, Underwood continued acting in films but also reentered the world of episodic television. In the film arena, the actor appeared opposite Samuel L. Jackson and Tommy Lee Jones in *Rules of Engagement* (2000), for which Underwood won an NAACP Image Award. He also appeared in *G* (2002), *Full Frontal* (2002), *Malibu's Most Wanted* (2003), *Something New* (2006), and *Madea's Family Reunion* (2006).

Concurrently, in the television domain, Underwood began the 2000's playing Dr. Ben Turner in the short-lived medical drama *City of Angels*, for which he won another NAACP Image Award. In 2003-2004, Underwood appeared in four episodes of the acclaimed HBO series *Sex and the City* as a love interest of Cynthia Nixon's character, Miranda Hobbes. From 2006 to 2008, Underwood portrayed a schoolteacher in the CBS comedy *The New Adventures of Old Christine*. In 2008, he had a role in the HBO drama *In Treatment*, for which he was nominated for a Golden Globe Award. From 2007 to 2009, he played billionaire Simon Elder in ABC's *Dirty Sexy Money*. In 2010, Underwood was cast as the president of the United States on the NBC series *The Event*.

Underwood also has a long history of philanthropic work. He cofounded the nonprofit organization Artists for a New South Africa in 1989. In 1993, his work with the Muscular Dystrophy Association earned him a Humanitarian Award. In 2003, Underwood served as an ambassador for YOUTHaids, a nonprofit organization that asks celebrities to help prevent the spread of AIDS through "life-saving messages, products, services, and care." He also is a trustee for the Robey Theater Company, cofounded by Ben Guillory and Danny Glover, which aims to present new plays and uncover overlooked works by African American playwrights.

Underwood married Desiree DaCosta in 1994. The couple has three children.

## SIGNIFICANCE

Underwood has played complex characters that reflect the strengths and weaknesses of the American male at the turn of the twenty-first century, just as his acting hero, Sidney Poitier, did for the previous generation. Underwood has worked in a wide array of productions, sometimes in predominantly white casts, other times with all-African American casts. Underwood's television and film work is complemented by his humanitarian efforts, and he has drawn accolades for his achievements in both arenas.

*—Eric Novod*

## FURTHER READING

Johnson, Pamela. "Blair Underwood." *Essence* 19, no. 2 (June, 1988): 52. A profile of Underwood written during his second year of *L.A. Law*, just as the actor was receiving increased national attention.

Morrison, Mark. "Sidney Poitier and Blair Underwood." *InStyle* 11, no. 11 (October, 2004): 515-516. Underwood discusses his admiration for Poitier in this feature article.

Underwood, Blair. "A Conversation with Blair Underwood." Interview by Tavis Smiley. National Public Radio, September 2, 2003. http://www.npr.org/templates/story/story.php?storyId=1417849. A detailed radio interview with revealing information on Underwood's childhood, education, and career path.

**SEE ALSO:** Don Cheadle; Omar Epps; Laurence Fishburne; Cuba Gooding, Jr.; Sidney Poitier; Will Smith; Courtney B. Vance; Denzel Washington; Forest Whitaker; Jeffrey Wright.

# GENE UPSHAW
## Football player and executive

*A first-ballot Hall of Fame selection, Upshaw was the first football player to appear in a Super Bowl in three different decades. Many, however, consider his greatest achievement to be maintaining labor peace for the National Football League (NFL) Players Association during the enormous growth of the league.*

**BORN:** August 15, 1945; Robstown, Texas
**DIED:** August 20, 2008; Lake Tahoe, California
**ALSO KNOWN AS:** Eugene Thurman Upshaw, Jr.; the Governor; Uptown Gene; the Pope
**AREA OF ACHIEVEMENT:** Sports: football

### EARLY LIFE

Eugene Thurman Upshaw, Jr., was born on August 15, 1945, in Robstown, Texas, a small town not far from Corpus Christi. He was one of three boys born to Eugene, Sr., and Cora Upshaw. His father worked in the nearby oil fields, while his mother was a maid for white fami-

*Gene Upshaw.* (Getty Images)

lies in the area. Because the family had little money, Upshaw and his brother Marvin started picking cotton at a young age.

Eugene, Sr., sought to instill discipline in his sons. He made sure that they focused on their schoolwork and went to church, but their free time inevitably was devoted to sports, usually baseball. As a youth, Upshaw became a junior deacon, choir singer, and a baseball team captain.

Upshaw continued to play sports throughout high school. When he graduated, he stood 6 feet tall and weighed 200 pounds but had no interest in playing football at a collegiate level. After arriving on campus at the Texas College of Arts and Industries, he stood watching football practice when the coach encouraged him to join the team. Although later he said he never knew why he agreed, Upshaw accepted the offer—a decision that changed his life.

### LIFE'S WORK

Initially a defensive lineman, Upshaw moved to the offensive line and literally grew into the role, reaching 6 feet, 5 inches and 260 pounds. His play at the small school in Texas was spectacular enough that it garnered the attention of the National Football League (NFL) scouts. Upshaw's performance in the Senior Bowl, essentially an audition for the NFL, bumped him from being a possible third-round selection to being a probable first-round choice in the draft. However, when he was selected by the Oakland Raiders, Upshaw's first reaction was disappointment. The Raiders were known as a rowdy bunch, and Upshaw longed for a more stable environment.

Nevertheless, Upshaw thrived in Oakland. In his rookie year, the Raiders reached the Super Bowl, where they lost to the Green Bay Packers. His start with the team was indicative of his career in Oakland; the team fail to make the play-offs only four times while Upshaw was on the roster. Upshaw and Art Shell, who played the left tackle position, formed an impressive tandem that opened holes for their running backs and kept defensive linemen away from their quarterbacks.

Offensive linemen often are overlooked on the football field, their work in the trenches overshadowed by quarterbacks, running backs, and wide receivers, but Upshaw was a standout player. By 1969, only two years into his career, he had cemented himself as one of the foremost guards in the league and become an All-Pro.

Outside of football, Upshaw began to express an interest in other matters, becoming a representative for the NFL Players Association (NFLPA) and winning an appointment to the Alameda County Planning Commission. He sought ways to help people, and these two platforms allowed him to work for his peers and the community in which he lived. Upshaw's work with the union laid the foundation for his second career, which began in 1983 when he retired from the Raiders. By the time of his retirement, Upshaw had played in 217 games, won two Super Bowls, and earned numerous Pro Bowl berths.

Although Upshaw enjoyed a stellar playing career, his work with the players' union would eclipse it. After serving as a player representative for several years, in 1983 he ascended to the head of the organization and built the NFLPA from a weak and financially unstable organization to one that was strong and well funded. Upshaw fought for players' rights and interests, all the while trying to maintain strong ties to the NFL leadership and avoid acrimony that would hinder the profits of both parties.

Upshaw served as the NFLPA's executive director until his death on August 20, 2008. He had intended to lead the union for two more years and then retire but was stricken suddenly with pancreatic cancer. In remembrance of his life, every player in the NFL wore a sticker on his helmet with the letters *GU* for the entire 2008 season.

### SIGNIFICANCE

Upshaw was one of the best offensive linemen in NFL history. From his humble roots in Texas to his NFL career to his leadership in the NFLPA, Upshaw was a unique and complex man. He earned six Pro Bowl trips, and played on two Super Bowl-winning teams and remains the only player to participate in a Super Bowl in three different decades (the 1960's, 1970's, and 1980's). He entered the Pro Football Hall of Fame in his first year of eligibility. Instead of resting on his laurels, however, Upshaw found reward in working for the NFLPA and helping to maintain labor peace that helped the sport grow dramatically.

*—P. Huston Ladner*

---

## UPSHAW AND THE NFLPA

The demands that Gene Upshaw faced as executive director of the National Football League (NFL) Players Association (NFLPA) were numerous, but he always maintained a sense of calm. He was one of the first African Americans and nonlawyers to lead a major union.

His style of management often was criticized, as his quiet demeanor and cordiality led players and outsiders to believe he was too submissive to NFL commissioners Pete Rozelle and Paul Tagliabue. However, the reality of their negotiations told a different story, as Upshaw held his line and won raises for his players in each successive collective bargaining agreement.

Another problem that Upshaw increasingly faced as the head of the NFLPA involved retired players. These players, who toiled during years when salaries were low and safety equipment was rudimentary at best, began to face costly medical bills and received little assistance from the union. Upshaw answered their criticism by saying that he did not work for the retirees and that his focus was on the players currently active in the union. Although accurate as to his duties as union chief, these comments were poorly received. Before his sudden death, Upshaw was seeking ways to help these former players.

---

### FURTHER READING

Battista, Judy. "Gene Upshaw, Union Chief, Dies at 63." *The New York Times*, August 22, 2008. This comprehensive obituary offers a sweeping biography of Upshaw.

Richmond, Peter. *Badasses: The Legend of Snake, Foo, Dr. Death, and John Madden's Oakland Raiders.* New York: Harper, 2010. Details the teams and the environment in which Upshaw spent his football career. His quiet demeanor served as a calming force in a rather wild atmosphere.

Smith, Gary. "Bitter Battle for the Old Guard." *Sports Illustrated* 108, no. 4 (February 4, 2008): 64-75. This profile of Upshaw provides an excellent snapshot of the trials of being the labor head for the NFLPA while also offering biographical information.

Upshaw, Gene, et al. "Sports Law." In *Counseling Clients in the Entertainment Industry, 2004: Television, Interactive Software, Entertainment, Film, Sports Law, Music Publishing, Sound Recordings, Ethics, and the Development of an Entertainment Law Practice,* compiled by James I. Charne et al. New York: Publishing Law Institute, 2004. Upshaw provides insight on how he helped keep labor peace in the NFL.

SEE ALSO: Marcus Allen; Earl Campbell; Bo Jackson; Willie Lanier; Deion Sanders; Art Shell; O. J. Simpson.

# USHER
## Singer and actor

*Usher emerged in the late 1990's as one of the preeminent rhythm-and-blues singers of his generation, his silky tenor accentuated by vibrant rhythms that made his songs dance-club standards.*

**BORN:** October 14, 1978; Dallas, Texas
**ALSO KNOWN AS:** Usher Terry Raymond IV (birth name)
**AREAS OF ACHIEVEMENT:** Film: acting; Music: hip-hop; Music: pop; Music: rhythm and blues

### EARLY LIFE
Usher was born Usher Terry Raymond IV on October 14, 1978, in Dallas, Texas. After his father abandoned the family, his mother relocated to Chattanooga, Tennessee, to be near her family. Early in his life, Usher demonstrated a remarkable proclivity for music, picking out

*Usher.* (NY Daily News via Getty Images)

hymn melodies in church when he was only five. By nine, he was singing in the local Baptist church choir. However, he and his family had bigger dreams.

In 1991, the family moved to Atlanta in the hopes of securing Usher entrance into the music industry. He earned a spot in the nationally syndicated talent show *Star Search*. With his confident stage presence and accomplished voice, Usher easily won the Teen Male Vocalist category. His performance drew the attention of a studio executive who signed the twelve-year-old to a recording contract.

Usher moved to New York, where he recorded his first CD, *Usher* (1994), which sold respectably. Usher was packaged as a new Marvin Gaye and, despite his relatively young age, the songs emphasized smoldering sexuality. His good looks and easy charisma gave Usher the chance, in 1997, to expand his range of talents to acting—initially in a recurring role in the cable sitcom *Moesha* and then on the CBS soap opera *The Bold and the Beautiful*.

### LIFE'S WORK
Usher's sophomore recording effort, 1997's *My Way*, launched him to superstardom. With three number-one dance tracks, including "You Make Me Wanna," the CD sold more than nine million copies and Usher's music dominated the club scene. The album title's allusion to Frank Sinatra did not go unnoticed by music critics—it was a measure of Usher's self-assurance and his own sense of his stardom. Usher sold out arenas, and his concerts became known for impeccably choreographed hip-hop numbers and stunning spectacle effects. Critics found Usher's third studio release, originally titled *All About You* but later reissued as *8701* (2001), uneven; however, two of its tracks, "U Remind Me" and "U Don't Have to Call," secured Usher back-to-back Grammys for Best Male R&B Performance. *Billboard* named Usher its artist of the year in 1998. For the next two years, the singer was ubiquitous—his romances covered by the tabloid media and his talents featured in a string of films, most prominently 1998's *The Faculty* and 1999's *She's All That*.

Usher's 2004 album, *Confessions*, cemented his international star status, ultimately selling more than twenty-five million units. The album's four signature singles—"Yeah," "Burn," "Confessions II," and "My Boo" featuring Alicia Keys—dominated both rhythm-

and-blues and adult pop formats. Usher became only the third recording artist (joining the Beatles and the Bee Gees) to have three songs in the Top 10 simultaneously. He won three Grammy Awards (he was nominated for eight) and was again named *Billboard*'s artist of the year.

In 2008, Usher released *Here I Stand*, which enjoyed similar international success, as did the 2010 release *Raymond v. Raymond*. Many of the songs on the latter album revealed a more adult perspective. Usher tackled his recent divorce, his infidelities, and his relationship with his two children. That evolution continued with the August, 2010, release of the extended play *Versus*, which featured songs about being a parent and about his difficult relationship with his mother (whom he had replaced as his manager) and his father, who died in 2008. *Versus* debuted at number one on both the pop and rhythm-and-blues charts.

In addition to his performing career, Usher started his record company, US Records, and became a mentor to young artists such as teenage phenomenon Justin Bieber. He also served as chief executive officer of a chain of exclusive restaurants and took an ownership stake in the Cleveland Cavaliers professional basketball team. That entrepreneurial savvy as much as his recording success positioned Usher, still in his thirties, as one of the most influential—and wealthiest—stars in the entertainment industry.

## SIGNIFICANCE

Emerging at a time when hip-hop was dominated by "gangsta" rap artists, Usher offered a striking alternative.

Maintaining the vigorous dance rhythms and vocal pyrotechnics of hip-hop, Usher infused the club sound with a sense of cool and a smoldering sexuality that recalled greats such as Marvin Gaye and Smokey Robinson. Enjoying phenomenal record sales and international concert success at a remarkably young age, Usher came to define the club scene of the new millennium.

—*Joseph Dewey*

## FURTHER READING

Chang, Jeff. *Can't Stop Won't Stop: A History of the Hip Hop Generation*. New York: Picador, 2005. Exhaustive but very readable look at the controversial musical context within which Usher emerged, written by one of the movement's most accomplished and respected chroniclers.

Grigoriadis, Vanessa. "Usher's Wild Ride: So Many Girls, So Little Time." *Rolling Stone* 948 (May 13, 2004): 56-60. Probing interview that emphasizes Usher's player image, including extensive commentary on his private life and his relationship with his family.

Usher. "After Years of Chasing Fame, R&B Star Usher Is Taking Stock." Interview by Brian McCollum. *The Detroit Free Press*, December 2, 2010. Usher discusses the next phase of his career and his evolution from teenage sensation to seasoned star, mentor, and father.

**SEE ALSO:** Babyface; Toni Braxton; Mariah Carey; Alicia Keys; Beyoncé Knowles; Rihanna.

# COURTNEY B. VANCE
## Actor

*Classically trained in acting, Vance is one of those rare actors able to define a successful career in three media—stage, film, and television—bringing to a variety of distinguished roles—whether leading or supporting, comic or dramatic—a signature gravitas that imbues those characters with depth and nuance.*

**BORN:** March 12, 1960; Detroit, Michigan
**ALSO KNOWN AS:** Courtney Bernard Vance
**AREAS OF ACHIEVEMENT:** Film: acting; Radio and television; Theater

### EARLY LIFE

Courtney Bernard Vance was born on March 12, 1960, into a comfortable middle-class family in the suburbs of Detroit, Michigan. His father was a manager of a franchise grocery store, his mother a librarian. Distinguishing himself early in the classroom, Vance matriculated at a private prep school for gifted students. He was accepted for study at Harvard University. While working on his degree in history, Vance was introduced to the theater. He first joined the university's acting troupe and then a regional repertory company, the Boston Shakespeare Company, where he learned the craft of acting.

Determined to pursue acting as a career after graduation, Vance was accepted for graduate study at the prestigious Yale School of Drama. It was there that he received his first critical plaudits in 1987, starring alongside James Earl Jones in the Broadway production of August Wilson's *Fences*, which won the Pulitzer Prize. Vance played the troubled son, Cory Maxson, a gifted athlete who struggles with his domineering father (Jones). The play won that year's Tony Award for Best Drama, and

Vance was nominated for Best Featured Actor. The performance won Vance the Clarence Derwent Award for Most Promising Actor, an award presented by Broadway actors themselves. The performance cemented Vance's position among the most sought-after young stage actors.

### LIFE'S WORK

In 1990, Vance enjoyed critical praise for his role as the clever con artist pretending to be actor Sidney Poitier's illegitimate son in John Guare's biting postmodern satire *Six Degrees of Separation*. The play won the Tony for Best Drama, and Vance once again was nominated for Best Featured Actor. In 1990, he won an Off-Broadway Obie Award for his work as a teacher in Athol Fugard's inspirational and poignant play about a black girl who befriends a white boy in South Africa in the 1980's, *My Children! My Africa!*

Although committed to stage work and by this time one of the most recognized and respected actors in New York, Vance found several attractive supporting roles in feature films, often in ensemble films, testing a wide variety of genres and refusing to be typecast. He appeared in the searing war drama *Hamburger Hill* (1987); the political thriller *The Hunt for Red October* (1990); the psychological police drama *Beyond the Law* (1992); the politically charged drawing-room satire *The Last Supper* (1995); and as Jim, the runaway slave, in *The Adventures of Huck Finn* (1993). However, it was his role in Penny Marshall's sentimental romantic comedy *The Preacher's Wife* (1996) that established Vance with a wide audience. He was cast as an inner-city preacher who struggles with growing doubts until an angel (Denzel Washington) intervenes. Although playing a supporting role alongside screen heavyweights Washington and Whitney Houston (as his titular wife), Vance played the role with conviction—the project was filmed in the difficult aftermath of the suicide of Vance's father and Vance's own return to his Christian faith—and audiences found him a sympathetic character. Although a critical flop, the film was a box-office hit. At the same time, Vance began a romance with Oscar-nominated actor Angela Bassett. They married and, in 2006, became parents of twins.

Although Vance continued appearing in films—most notably in Robert Altman's comedy *Cookie's Fortune* (1999) and Clint Eastwood's *Space Cowboys* (2000)—he increasingly turned his focus on television. Initially, he appeared in films made for television distribution, most notably the 1997 remake of the 1950's classic *Twelve Angry Men* and *Blind Faith* (1999), in which Vance played an attorney in 1950's Chicago who defends a gay black man accused of killing his white lover. Vance was nominated for an Independent Spirit Award for the role. In addition, Vance played a recurring role alongside Bassett on the long-running medical series *ER*. From 2001 to 2006, he costarred in NBC's *Law & Order: Criminal Intent* as assistant district attorney Ron Carver. In 2009, he joined the cast of ABC's mystery series *FlashForward*, then the next year took a role on TNT crime drama *The Closer*.

### SIGNIFICANCE

Unlike other African American actors of his generation who gave voice to the incendiary anger of the black com-

munity, Vance pursued acting in its purest expression, selecting roles that created the opportunity for him to explore the range of his own acting skills. With his impeccable sense of dramatic timing, the gravitas of his screen presence, and his command of a wide range of dramatic emotions, Vance defined himself among the preeminent (and most honored) character actors of stage, screen, and television.

*—Joseph Dewey*

### FURTHER READING

Bassett, Angela, and Courtney Vance. *Friends: A Love Story.* Atlanta, Ga.: Kimani, 2009. Husband and wife trade chapters in this touching—if sentimental—record of a successful Hollywood relationship that balances work, family, and Christian faith.

Jewel, Don, and Karen Brailsford. "Vance Fever." *People* 47, no. 2 (January 20, 1997): 96. Profile of Vance upon the opening of *The Preacher's Wife*, one of his best-known roles. Discusses his faith and relationship with Bassett.

Vance, Courtney B. "Speaking into Our Lives." In *A Hand to Guide Me*, compiled by Denzel Washington and Daniel Paisner. Des Moines, Iowa: Meredith Books, 2006. Vance describes an influential teacher from his youth and how his upbringing prepared him for success.

**SEE ALSO:** Angela Bassett; Laurence Fishburne; James Earl Jones; Blair Underwood; Denzel Washington; Jeffrey Wright.

# JAMES VAN DER ZEE
## Photographer

*Van Der Zee is best known for his more than 100,000 photographs of life in Harlem, New York, during the early to mid-twentieth century. These photographs include sensitive portraits and photographs of weddings, funerals, schools, and persons in the street that captured the essence of the neighborhood.*

**BORN:** June 29, 1886; Lenox, Massachusetts
**DIED:** May 15, 1983; Washington, D.C.
**ALSO KNOWN AS:** James Augustus Joseph Van Der Zee (birth name)
**AREA OF ACHIEVEMENT:** Art and photography

### EARLY LIFE

James Augustus Joseph Van Der Zee was born in 1886, the second of six children born to John and Susan Van Der Zee. His parents were servants or waiters for the rich in Lenox, Massachusetts, a summer haven for the wealthy. The family lived in a house with enough outside space to grow a garden and raise livestock. There always was enough food to eat and enough money for small luxuries, such as a bicycle. The children also did odd jobs during the summer to earn spending money.

Van Der Zee's parents encouraged their children to do their best in school; Van Der Zee enjoyed art and music

## VAN DER ZEE'S IMAGES OF BLACK NEW YORKERS

James Van Der Zee was Harlem's most important photographer, especially during the period from 1920 to 1945. He took thousands of portraits and many group photographs of families, schools, funerals, weddings, and persons in the street. Before 1920, he had few props for portraits, but he soon began to use backdrops and studio props, such as garden scenes, columns, and a variety of furniture. Also available was a variety of clothing and costumes. He photographed everyone willing to pay his fee, so most of his portraits are of the common citizens of Harlem. However, he also photographed many notable African American actors and musicians. It was his practice to retouch his photographs, removing skin blemishes, reducing his subjects' wrinkles, brightening their eyes, and straightening their teeth. Consequently, most of his subjects look better in their portraits than they did in real life.

Much of his business was dedicated, however, to taking photographs of groups of people outside of his studio. One large assignment, for example, was to photograph the activities of the Universal Negro Improvement Association (UNIA), a group that was dedicated to improving the rights of persons of African ancestry. Van Der Zee made several thousands of photographs of the UNIA in 1924, including many from the organization's national convention. One photograph, for example, shows the founder of the UNIA, Marcus Garvey, standing on a platform watching a UNIA parade.

the most. He played the violin and piano quite well, and he enjoyed looking at pictures. He obtained his first camera by selling sachet powder, but he ruined the film while trying to develop it himself. In 1900, at the age of fourteen, he obtained a second camera with which he produced a number of successful photographs.

Van Der Zee quit school at the age of fourteen and worked as a waiter with his father at a luxury hotel in Lenox. From 1900 to 1904, he developed his photographic skills by taking pictures of people and friends around town.

In 1905, Van Der Zee went to New York City to join his father, who had gone ahead to work in the dining room of the Knickerbocker Trust Bank. Van Der Zee worked as a waiter and an elevator operator, and he also played his violin and piano in a variety of settings.

Van Der Zee met his future wife, Kate Brown, in New York City; they were married in 1907. The couple temporarily moved back to Lenox when she was ready to deliver their baby. They then visited Kate's parents in Virginia, where Van Der Zee took many photographs. Many of these pictures began to approach the sensitivity of his later photographs. He found work in a luxury hotel and took some classes in a music school, but he felt that he was more talented than the music faculty, so he began to teach music.

In 1908, the family left for New York City because Van Der Zee could not tolerate the segregation in Virginia. However, he had learned that he could succeed as a photographer and musician.

### LIFE'S WORK

The Van Der Zee family moved into an apartment in Harlem in 1908. Initially, Van Der Zee worked as a waiter, elevator operator, and musician to obtain a steady income. Eventually, he became a darkroom assistant for portrait photographer Charles Gertz in 1911. Van Der Zee soon graduated to taking portraits when Gertz and the customers soon recognized that he was the better photographer.

From 1912 to 1915, Van Der Zee took portraits and taught music at the Toussaint Conservatory of Art and Music. Usually, he took portraits in the subject's surroundings or in his studio to evoke the subject's personality. For example, one portrait shows a soldier sitting in a chair looking down at a small dog—the photograph was titled "The Last Goodbye."

Kate was never persuaded that Van Der Zee could make a living taking photographs. Because of this and other problems, she left him in 1916. Van Der Zee soon became acquainted with Gaynella Greenlee, a white woman who worked as a telephone operator in the building where he worked. He and Gaynella married in 1917.

Van Der Zee and Gaynella opened a photo studio together in 1917. The studio was quite successful, as many organizations and people in Harlem wanted photographs taken. Many of the African American men going off to fight in Europe during World War I had their portraits taken before leaving. This turned out to be a good advertisement for their studio, as many members of the soldiers' families also wanted their pictures taken.

The Depression years of the 1930's were difficult for Van Der Zee, but his photography business continued to make money. He did have to move his studio several times, however. Van Der Zee also operated several other businesses, most under Gaynella's direction, such as renting rooms and gardening. Van Der Zee's photographs from the Depression era were among his best.

The income from Van Der Zee's photographic business dropped during World War II. To make ends meet, he took photographs wherever he could—including identification photos, autopsy photos, and even photos of car accidents for insurance use. After World War II, his photography studio suffered even more, partially because many people could take their own photographs more cheaply and some people viewed his portraits as old fashioned. Harlem had a large middle class before World War II, but the middle class moved out after the war, leaving many low-income residents behind. Van Der Zee partially made up for the drop in his portrait income by restoring old photographs. Nevertheless, he could not pay his mortgage. The family became destitute as his portrait income disappeared during the 1960's.

A photographer, Reginald McGhee, discovered Van Der Zee's photographs in 1967 (Van Der Zee was eighty-one years old at the time) while looking for photographs for a Metropolitan Museum of Art exhibit called "Harlem on My Mind," documenting the history of Harlem. Van Der Zee's photographs became the nucleus of the exhibition. He eventually received $3,500 for his work and instant national recognition. Nevertheless, soon after the exhibit, the Van Der Zees were evicted from their home.

During the 1970's, Van Der Zee's fame helped return him to financial stability. Many African American celebrities, such as Bill Cosby, Muhammed Ali, and Ossie Davis, had their portraits taken by Van Der Zee. He received many awards during his later years, including several honorary doctoral degrees and the Living Legacy Award, presented by President Jimmy Carter. Van Der Zee died on May 15, 1983, in Washington, D.C.

## SIGNIFICANCE

Van Der Zee was one of the few photographers to document the lives of the African Americans living in Harlem during the early to mid-twentieth century. This was a time when African Americans in the white popular media typically were caricatured and stereotyped. His tens of thousands of photographs illustrated the pride and dignity of African Americans and offered a more realistic depiction of black culture. Some experts in photography rank Van Der Zee among the greatest American photographers, alongside artists such as Gordon Parks, Alfred Stieglitz, and Edward Steichen.

—*Robert L. Cullers*

## FURTHER READING

Driskell, David, David Lewis, and Deborah Ryan. *Harlem Renaissance Art of Black America*. New York: Harry N. Abrams, 1987. Contains a chapter on Van Der Zee's career and significance to African American arts and culture.

Sandler, Martin W. *America Through the Lens*. New York: Henry Holt, 2005. Includes a chapter examining Van Der Zee's style and body of work.

Van Der Zee, James, and Reginald McGhee. *The World of James Van Der Zee: A Visual Record of Black Americans*. New York: Grove Press, 1969. Contains an interview with Van Der Zee along with many of his photographs.

Westerbeck, Colin, James Van Der Zee, and Dewoud Bey. *The James Van Der Zee Studio*. Chicago: Art Institute of Chicago, 2004. Summarizes information and some photographs from the studio of Van Der Zee.

Willis-Braithwaite, Deborah, and Rodger C. Birt. *Van Der Zee: Photographer, 1886-1983*. New York: Harry N. Abrams, 1993. Contains a detailed biography along with many of Van Der Zee's photographs.

SEE ALSO: James Presley Ball; Roy DeCarava; Austin Hansen; Milt Hinton; Gordon Parks, Sr.; Ernest Withers.

# MARIO VAN PEEBLES
## Actor and filmmaker

*Van Peebles has made important artistic contributions in film and television as an actor and a director. He works for social change in creating films that address issues of importance to the African American community.*

**BORN:** January 15, 1957; Mexico City, Mexico
**ALSO KNOWN AS:** Mario Cain Van Peebles; Chip
**AREAS OF ACHIEVEMENT:** Film: acting; Film: direction

### EARLY LIFE

Mario Cain Van Peebles was born in Mexico City, Mexico, on January 15, 1957. He is the son of director, writer, and actor Melvin Van Peebles and photographer Maria Magdalena Marx. Shortly after Mario Van Peebles was born, his parents moved to San Francisco. When he was two years old, the family moved to Holland, and later Van Peebles lived for short periods in Paris and Morocco. When his parents divorced, his mother moved to San Francisco with the children. In 1967, his father returned to San Francisco. An amiable relationship between his parents allowed him to spend time with both. In 1971, Van Peebles appeared in his father's film, *Sweet Sweetback's Baadasssss Song.*

After graduating from high school, Van Peebles was interested in becoming an actor and asked his father to help him get a start in the profession. His father refused, insisting that his son accomplish his goals on his own and emphasizing the importance of having business expertise in order to succeed in filmmaking and acting. Thus, Van Peebles enrolled at Columbia University and earned a B.S. in economics in 1978. In 1979, he accepted a position as a budget analyst with New York City. In 1981, he appeared with his father in *Waltz of the Stork*, a Broadway play written and directed by his father. Van Peebles studied acting with Stella Adler and worked as a model.

### LIFE'S WORK

Van Peebles obtained a small part in *The Cotton Club* (1984), played X, a villain, in *Exterminator Two* (1984), and appeared in the television soap opera *One Life to Live*. In 1986, Van Peebles was cast in the role of "Stitch" Jones in the Clint Eastwood film *Heartbreak Ridge*. He received an Image Award for outstanding supporting actor. He also had a recurring role on *L.A. Law* and played an unusual scientist in the film *Jaws: The Revenge* (1987). In 1987, he starred in the television comedy-drama *Sonny Spoon*, about an African American detective in a large city. While portraying Sonny Spoon, Van Peebles also directed several episodes of *Wiseguys* and *Twenty-One Jump Street* and *Malcolm Takes a Shot*, a children's special on the Columbia Broadcasting Service (CBS).

Like his father, Van Peebles was interested in acting and directing, prepared to act in any film he was directing. In 1990, Warner Bros. gave him the opportunity to do that when the studio hired him to direct *New Jack City*, in which he cast himself as a policeman. The film about drug dealing in Harlem grossed more than ten million dollars its first weekend. This was

*Mario Van Peebles, left, and Melvin Van Peebles.* (Getty Images)

the beginning of a successful career as actor-director for Van Peebles. He followed *New Jack City* with *Posse* (1993), a Western film from an African American perspective; a collaboration with his father, *Panther* (1995), about the Black Panther Party; and *Gang in Blue* (1996), addressing police brutality and corruption.

In 2003, Van Peebles produced, directed, and starred in a film tribute to his father, *Baadasssss!* (also known as *How to Get the Man's Foot Out of Your Ass*). The film chronicles his father's experiences making *Sweet Sweetback's Baadasssss Song*. Portraying his father in the film, Van Peebles recounts the film's making with sensitivity and admiration. *Baadasssss!* was well received by critics and filmgoers; it earned Van Peebles twelve award nominations and the 2004 Philadelphia Film Festival Best Feature Film Award and the 2005 Black Reel Awards for Best Director and Best Screenplay. Van Peebles has continued to play an active role in the film industry, as an actor and a director, with roles in *Carlito's Way: Rise to Power* (2005), *Hard Luck* (2006), and *Kerosene Cowboys* (2009), which he directed.

Van Peebles has also continued to work in television. In 2007, he appeared in *Law & Order* and directed the episode "Sweetie" in 2008. He also played in *All My Children* and acted in and directed *Damages*. In 2009, Van Peebles and his family—wife Chitra, their five children, and his parents—became involved in the green movement and appeared in a reality show called *Mario's Green House*. The first episode of the show aired on September 27, 2009, on TVOne, a station that targets the African American audience. The episodes depicted the importance of green living and the problems encountered in changing to such a lifestyle. In 2010, he directed the seventh episode, "Dr. Linus," of the sixth season of the popular series *Lost*.

## SIGNIFICANCE

Through his work as an actor-director, Van Peebles has made an important contribution to the craft of filmmaking and to the artistic representation of African American culture and life experiences. His films, like those of his father, depict African Americans as complex individuals and emphasize their individuality. With his accurate portrayal of African American culture and experience, he has helped to eliminate the African American stereotypes of past films. In collaboration with his father, he has brought African American culture into the mainstream of filmmaking and created films that realistically depict the issues and conflicts that African Americans face.

—*Shawncey Webb*

## FURTHER READING

Donalson, Melvin. *Black Directors in Hollywood*. Austin: University Press of Texas, 2003. Traces the history of African American filmmakers in Hollywood. Discusses their social and cultural impact and their contribution to presenting an authentic portrayal of the African American experience.

Massood, Paula J. *Black City Cinema: African American Urban Experiences in Film*. Philadelphia: Temple University Press, 2003. Discusses the role of the "hood" and other urban themes in African American films. Treats *New Jack City* and *Posse*.

Van Peebles, Melvin, and Mario Van Peebles. *No Identity Crisis: A Father and Son's Story of Working Together*. New York: Fireside, 1990. Explores the cultural and social importance of their films and their relationship as filmmakers.

**SEE ALSO:** Spike Lee; John Singleton; Robert Townsend; Melvin Van Peebles.

# MELVIN VAN PEEBLES
## Filmmaker

*An artist in diverse media, Van Peebles has pushed the boundaries of art in film, music, and theater, earning many honors and awards. Although he is best known for his contributions to cinema, his career extends beyond pop culture to the world of finance.*

**BORN:** August 21, 1932; Chicago, Illinois
**ALSO KNOWN AS:** Melvin Peebles (birth name)
**AREAS OF ACHIEVEMENT:** Film: acting; Film: direction

### EARLY LIFE

Melvin Van Peebles was born in Chicago, Illinois, on August 21, 1932, and grew up on the South Side in an area first settled by runaway slaves. His father was a tailor. As a child, his interest in film began with triple-features at a theater the locals called "National Rat Alley." At age twelve, Van Peebles became aware of the power of imagery when he realized the African Americans on screen filled him with shame. The characters were unlike any of the individuals he knew in a neighborhood of self-sufficient African Americans who, despite the pressures of discriminatory housing restrictions, were interested in building lives.

The first in his family to go to college, Van Peebles joined the Reserve Officers' Training Corps at Ohio Wesleyan University. At age twenty-one, he graduated with a degree in literature as an officer in the U.S. Air Force.

### LIFE'S WORK

Van Peebles served well beyond his eighteen-month commitment as a celestial and radar navigator and bombardier, during which time he married a white woman whose father had taught at Harvard. They had three children: Megan, Max, and Mario. After his discharge, he was excluded from jobs in his field because the airlines barred African Americans from the cockpit. After a brief stint in Mexico painting portraits, Van Peebles moved to San Francisco, where he found work driving cable cars. He also altered his name, giving it gravitas by adding "Van" to Peebles.

Van Peebles published his first book, *The Big Heart* (1957), a mix of his personal experiences and cable car photographs by Ruth Bernhard. He taught himself filmmaking after a passenger commented that his book was like a film. He made three short films and took them to

Hollywood, hoping for a director's assignment, without success. In 1959, he took a boat to the Netherlands to enter graduate school in astronomy.

Soon, Van Peebles began working with Dutch theater before receiving an invitation to screen his films at the Cinémathèque Française in Paris. Auteurs such as Jean-Luc Godard frequented screenings at this noted film archive. Van Peebles stayed to make films but lacked the proper documentation to work in France. He became a street entertainer and spent nights in jail for performing without a license. He discovered that writers were given temporary residence, so he became a journalist for *L'Observateur*. The Harlem Renaissance by now had relocated to Paris, and Van Peebles became acquainted with a sizable community of African American writers and artists; at one point, he interviewed novelist Chester Himes.

Van Peebles published five novels in French. One, *La Permission* (1967; *The Story of a Three-Day Pass*), won him admission to the French Cinema Center as a director, with a grant to adapt it as a film. In 1968, it was entered as a French film in the San Francisco International Film Festival and won the Craft of Cinema Award, drawing the attention of Hollywood moguls who had no idea that Van Peebles was an African American.

Van Peebles found himself in Hollywood at last. African American directors had never worked there, and it had been years since the southern black cinema of directors such as Oscar Micheaux had lost venues for their work. He made *Watermelon Man* (1970) for Columbia Pictures, then sought a project with which he could counter the paternalistic, demeaning depictions of African Americans in mainstream white cinema.

On his own and with few resources, Van Peebles left the studio system to almost single-handedly make the high-grossing, groundbreaking film *Sweet Sweetback's Baadasssss Song* in 1971. He pretended to be making a pornographic film in order to evade industry and union regulations. In the film, a coming-of-age story about black rebellion against white oppression, the eponymous hero's decision to protect a fellow African American man from police brutality launches him on a journey of self-discovery and newfound awareness of his potential. The film resists white structure in every mode, from film language to music and production. *Sweet Sweetback's Baadasssss Song* began a new era in film history in which Hollywood churned out blaxploitation films that distorted Van Peebles's revolutionary message of individual empowerment.

Van Peebles went on to write, direct, and act in many more films over the subsequent decades. He also recorded several albums and wrote two plays that were staged on Broadway. He has won awards in a range of media, including a Daytime Emmy for a CBS children's special. He also became the first African American trader on Wall Street and wrote a financial self-help book, *Bold Money* (1986).

## SIGNIFICANCE

While America was in racial turmoil, Van Peebles made his stand against stereotypical Hollywood images of African Americans by making a film celebrating black passion and power for black audiences. Van Peebles's innovative creative works speak to African Americans with the traits his life has demonstrated: resourcefulness and a drive for the power to define oneself.

*—Cristine Soliz*

## FURTHER READING

Chaffin-Quiray, Garrett. "'You Bled My Mother, You Bled My Father, But You Won't Bleed Me': The Underground Trio of Melvin Van Peebles." In *Underground U.S.A.: Filmmaking Beyond the Hollywood Canon*, edited by Xavier Mendik and Steven Jay Schneider. New York: Wallflower, 2002. Examines the ways Van Peebles resists and reacts to traditional mainstream filmmaking styles and themes.

Hartmann, Jonathan. "From Chicago to Watts by Way of Paris and Hollywood: Art-Film Influence on Melvin Van Peebles' Early Features." In *Cinema Inferno: Celluloid Explosions from the Cultural Margins*, edited by Robert G. Weiner and John Cline. Lanham, Md.: Scarecrow Press, 2010. Describes Van Peebles's film influences and the cultural context for his early work.

Van Peebles, Melvin. "Lights, Camera, and the Black Role in Movies." *Ebony* 61, no. 1 (November, 2005): 92-98. Van Peebles offers a biting critique of Hollywood's historical treatment of African Americans and analyzes the strides black filmmakers have made over time.

_____. *Panther: A Novel*. New York: Thunder's Mouth Press, 1995. Van Peebles chronicles the Oakland, California, beginnings of the Black Panther Party in this book, which also was filmed as a documentary.

_____. *Sweet Sweetback's Baadasssss Song: A Guerilla Filmmaking Manifesto*. New York: Thunder's Mouth Press, 2004. Van Peebles describes his low-budget, largely nonprofessional film shoot for his signature work.

**SEE ALSO:** Julie Dash; Ossie Davis; Spike Lee; Oscar Micheaux; John Singleton; Robert Townsend; Mario Van Peebles.

# SARAH VAUGHAN
## Jazz singer

*The first jazz singer to incorporate bop styling and phraseology into her vocals, Vaughan was one of the most influential artists in jazz over her forty-five-year career. Her recordings were prolific and diverse, encompassing a variety of styles, although she never strayed far from her jazz roots.*

**BORN:** March 27, 1924; Newark, New Jersey
**DIED:** April 3, 1990; Hidden Hills, California
**ALSO KNOWN AS:** Sarah Lois Vaughan; Sassy; the Divine One
**AREAS OF ACHIEVEMENT:** Music: jazz; Music: pop

## EARLY LIFE

Sarah Lois Vaughan (vahn) was born into a musical family in Newark, New Jersey, on March 27, 1924. Vaughan's father, Asbury, was a carpenter who supplemented the family income by playing guitar. Her mother, Ada, was a laundress who sang in Newark's Mount Zion Baptist church choir. As a child, Vaughan played the piano. By the mid-1930's, she was singing and playing organ for the church.

Vaughan's interest in music was not confined to church. By her teenage years, she had begun visiting and performing in a number of Newark's nightclubs despite being underage. Her popularity at the Piccadilly Club led her to strive for a career in music. She dropped out of Newark's Arts High School in 1940 to follow this dream.

Although Vaughan found singing engagements in Newark, her friend Doris Robinson persuaded her to go to New York. In 1942, Vaughan sang at Amateur Night at the Apollo Theater in Harlem. She won the contest, and with it the chance to open the next spring for Ella Fitzgerald. At that engagement, Billy Eckstine, a singer in Earl

*Sarah Vaughan.* (Michael Ochs Archives/Getty Images)

Hines's band, saw Vaughan and recommended her to Hines. After her audition, she was hired and went on tour. This was Vaughan's big break, gaining her national exposure and valuable experience. Although she never recorded with Hines because of a recording strike, she spent most of her off hours with fellow band members Eckstine, Dizzy Gillespie, and Charlie Parker "incubating" what developed into bop music. Vaughan did with her voice what innovative jazz instrumentalists were doing with melodies—breaking them down, rearranging them, and creating unique presentations without losing the heart of the song. By the time Vaughan left Hines in 1944 to join Eckstine's new band, she had a sound all her own.

## LIFE'S WORK

In 1945, Vaughan left Eckstine's band and became a solo artist. While she typically performed with her own trios over the next four decades, Vaughan's popularity and unique style made her an in-demand guest vocalist for many other bands, including those led by Gillespie, Stuff Smith, and Quincy Jones, with whom Vaughan recorded one of her biggest hits in 1957, "Misty."

During the 1950's and 1960's, Vaughan began to perform pop music, although she never completely left the realm of jazz. For example, during a stint with Mercury Records from 1954 to 1959, she cut popular records for the main label and pure jazz sides for Mercury subsidiary EmArcy. In all, Vaughan released more than one hundred long-playing albums during her career, while touring regularly.

Vaughan had three failed marriages and one long-term living arrangement. In her marital and business affairs, she was a strange contradiction. She actively sought to separate herself from the business side of her career to concentrate on her singing. Vaughan deferred all business dealings to her husbands, who alternately helped and hurt her career and financial stability. Although determined to delegate authority in business, Vaughan also had a very strong and often mercurial personality that balked at being controlled or manipulated. This combination led to frequent arguments, controversies, and perhaps even physical altercations.

Vaughan ceased recording and limited touring between 1967 and 1971 as a result of changing musical tastes, but her boundless energy could not be stifled for long. In 1971, Vaughan's career picked up again, resulting in more than two dozen recordings in fifteen years, both her own records and guest vocals on other releases. The highlight of this phase of Vaughan's career was her collaboration with Michael Tilson-Thomas and the Los Angeles Philharmonic Orchestra on first a series of live performances, followed by a Public Broadcasting System special and a recording, *Gershwin Live!* (1982), for which she won a Grammy Award for Best Female Jazz Vocal Performance. In 1988, Vaughan was inducted into the American Jazz Hall of Fame.

Although Vaughan continued to tour, in 1989 her health declined and began to affect her performances. Shortness of breath and fatigue led her to cancel a European tour. After a few months' rest, Vaughn returned to performing in New York but soon received a diagnosis of lung cancer. She returned to California and began chemotherapy treatments, but with little improvement and her voice growing weaker, Vaughan eventually decided to cease treatment. She died on April 3, 1990, at the age of sixty-six.

## SIGNIFICANCE

Vaughan was a musical force in American music for more than four decades. Contemporaries Mel Torme and Betty Carter said that she had the greatest voice in jazz. In 1997, the New Jersey Performing Arts Center in Newark opened at Center Street and Sarah Vaughan Way, about two miles from where Vaughan grew up and three miles from Mount Zion Baptist Church, where she made her singing debut.

—*Michael V. Kennedy*

**FURTHER READING**

Crowther, Bruce, and Mike Pinfold. *Singing Jazz: The Singers and Their Styles.* San Francisco: Miller Freeman Books, 1997. An enlightening discussion of jazz singing styles and personalities. Discusses Vaughan's career in detail, her influence on other singers, and the potential conflict between jazz and commercial singing.

Feather, Leonard. *The Jazz Years: Earwitness to an Era.* New York: Da Capo Press, 1987. Jazz promoter, critic, historian, and educator Feather's memoir includes an account of his helping Vaughan obtain her first recording dates.

Gates, Henry Louis, Jr., and Cornel West. *The African American Century: How Black Americans Have Shaped Our Country.* New York: Free Press, 2000. The authors present a decade-by-decade look at the twentieth century through the lives of prominent African Americans. Vaughan is included as an influence on the decade 1950-1959.

Gillespie, Dizzy, with Al Fraser. *To Be or Not . . . to Bop.* New York: Doubleday, 1979. In this autobiography, Gillespie discusses his relationship with many of the musical personalities of his era. Includes comments by and about Vaughan.

Gourse, Leslie. *Sassy: The Life of Sarah Vaughan.* New York: Charles Scribner's Sons, 1993. Authoritative biography of Vaughan covers information from interviews with many people who knew and worked with her. Includes extensive discography.

Williams, Martin. *The Jazz Tradition.* 2d rev. ed. New York: Oxford University Press, 1993. A series of essays presents the evolution of jazz through the contributions of two dozen major figures, including Vaughan.

**SEE ALSO:** Billy Eckstine; Ella Fitzgerald; Dizzy Gillespie; Earl Hines; Billie Holiday; Lena Horne; Etta James; Charlie Parker; Nina Simone.

# BEN VEREEN
## Entertainer

*Vereen is an actor, singer, and dancer who won a Tony Award for his role in Broadway's* Pippin *and became a household name for playing Chicken George in the landmark 1977 television miniseries* Roots.

**BORN:** October 10, 1946; Laurinburg, North Carolina
**ALSO KNOWN AS:** Benjamin Augustus Middleton (birth name)
**AREAS OF ACHIEVEMENT:** Dance; Film: acting; Music: pop; Radio and television

**EARLY LIFE**

Ben Vereen (vuh-REEN) was born Benjamin Augustus Middleton in Laurinburg, North Carolina, on October 10, 1946, to Essie Middleton, also known as Essie May Pearson. Vereen was adopted as a young child and did not learn his biological mother's identity until much later in life.

When Vereen was eight years old, a recruiter for Star Time Dance School visited his parents to urge them to enroll the child in tap-dance lessons. Vereen's mother, Pauline, was persuaded and began saving her earnings to pay for his education. The experience at the dance school instilled in Vereen a passion for the stage. His training taught him the importance of discipline, dedication, and hard work. Further education at Manhattan's High School of Performing Arts strengthened his desire to become an entertainer.

**LIFE'S WORK**

In 1972, Vereen was nominated for a Tony Award for his role as Judas Iscariot in the Broadway musical *Jesus Christ Superstar.* The next year, he won a Tony for his performance in *Pippin.* Vereen's other Broadway credits include *Hair* in 1968, *Grind* in 1985, *Jelly's Last Jam* in 1992, *Fosse* in 2001, and *Wicked* in 2005.

Vereen's reputation as a veteran Broadway star led him into film and television. He came to national fame as Chicken George in the landmark 1977 miniseries *Roots,* based on Alex Haley's novel of the same name. He also played song-and-dance men in the feature films *Funny Lady* (1975) and *All That Jazz* (1979). In 1980, Vereen

*Ben Vereen.* (Ron Galella/WireImage/Getty Images)

In 2007, Vereen received a diagnosis of type 2 diabetes. He became a spokesman for the disease and founded Celebrities for a Drug-Free America, which raises funds to assist drug-rehabilitation centers, community-based programs, and education centers. He continued to perform in one-man shows, nightclubs, and as a lecturer on African American history.

### SIGNIFICANCE

Vereen is a multitalented entertainer whose success in a variety of genres paved the way for younger singers, dancers, and actors. His godson is the rhythm-and-blues star Usher Raymond, who followed Vereen's footsteps to become a successful singer and dancer. His social engagement also has been influential.

—*Willette F. Stinson*

### FURTHER READING

McWaters, Debra. *The Fosse Style.* Gainesville: University Press of Florida, 2008. This book vividly illustrates Broadway choreographer Bob Fosse's dance style and includes Vereen's commentary on performing it.

Moore, Marat. "Vereen to ASHA Members: 'You Are My Angels.'" *The ASHA Leader*, December 15, 2009. Recaps Vereen's keynote address to members of the American Speech-Language Association during their convention's opening general session on November 19, 2009.

Vereen, Ben. "Ben Vereen." Interview by Rose Eichenbaum. In *The Dancer Within: Intimate Conversations with Great Dancers*, edited by Aron Hirt-Manheimer. Middletown, Conn.: Wesleyan University Press, 2008. In a candid interview, Vereen discusses his lifelong love of dance and the people who have influenced him throughout his career.

_____. "Ben Vereen." http://benvereen.com. Vereen's official Web site includes a biography, photo archive, and news about his activities.

SEE ALSO: Debbie Allen; LeVar Burton; Danny Glover; Savion Glover; Gregory Hines; Brian Stokes Mitchell; Phylicia Rashad.

costarred with Jeff Goldblum in the television series *Tenspeed and Brown Shoe*, playing the role of a parolee turned private investigator. Eight years later, Vereen reprised the character in the series *J. J. Starbuck.*

In 1989, Vereen was devastated by the death of his sixteen-year-old daughter, Naja, in a car accident. He struggled with drug addiction. In 1992, while walking along Pacific Coast Highway in Malibu, Vereen was hit by a truck. He suffered head and internal injuries and a broken leg. When physicians said he would have to consider an alternative career, he turned to a speech pathologist and voice trainer to help him return to performing. The next year, Vereen returned to the Broadway stage in a leading role in *Jelly's Last Jam.*

# DENMARK VESEY
## Slave-revolt leader

*Vesey, a former slave who became a carpenter, is credited with leading one of the most significant slave rebellions in the United States. The 1822 South Carolina revolt that bears his name became the largest slave uprising in North America since the 1739 Stono Rebellion, although it quickly failed.*

**BORN:** c. 1767; St. Thomas, Virgin Islands
**DIED:** July 2, 1822; Charleston, South Carolina
**ALSO KNOWN AS:** Telemaque Vesey
**AREA OF ACHIEVEMENT:** Social issues

### EARLY LIFE

Denmark Vesey (VEE-see) is a shadowy figure. Not much is known about his early life, and the events of his adult life are disputed by historians. Vesey was probably born into slavery on the Danish Caribbean sugar island of St. Thomas around 1767. In 1781, he was purchased by Captain Joseph Vesey, a slave trader, who trained him as cabin boy. Vesey renamed the boy Telemaque, after the mythical son of Odysseus. In time, he became known as Denmark after the island of his birth.

In 1783, Joseph Vesey settled in Charleston, South Carolina. Denmark, literate and multilingual, lived with the Vesey family and worked in the family's imported-goods business as an office clerk and trader. He married a slave woman, Beck, who gave birth to at least three of his children. Any children born to a slave mother were legally slaves from birth, so Vesey had very limited control over his own children, whose names and fates are unknown. Since whites did not recognize the marriages of slaves, Vesey and Beck never lived together and were separated when Vesey's owner moved his household to an Ashley River plantation. The children remained with their mother. When Vesey won fifteen hundred dollars in a lottery, he purchased his freedom and returned to Charleston, possibly to be closer to his children and Beck. He became a carpenter.

### LIFE'S WORK

After his relationship with Beck ended, Vesey married Susan and became one of the first members of the African Methodist Episcopal (AME) Church, commonly known as the African Church, in Charleston. Embittered by the continuing enslavement of Beck and their children, Vesey eventually turned his back on the New Testament and what he regarded as Christianity's false promise of universal brotherhood.

Vesey began to plan to lead his children and friends to freedom in Haiti. This small Caribbean island nation stood as a beacon of liberty to enslaved African Americans because Haitian slaves had overthrown their French masters in a bloody revolution that concluded in 1804. What made Vesey's conspiracy unique was both his advanced age of fifty-four and that he planned a mass exodus of black families out of Charleston. The plot called for slaves in the vicinity of the Ashley and Cooper rivers to slay their masters on the morning of Sunday, July 14, 1822, and fight their way toward the city docks. Although Vesey employed several black men to make weapons, the leading conspirators, including Gullah Jack in Pritchard, decided that they would not risk stockpiling weapons or recruiting soldiers before July. Vesey believed that once the revolt began, men would flock to his side.

Despite efforts to maintain secrecy, conspirator William Paul told of the planned revolt to Peter, a slave, on May 22. At about the same time, another slave, George Wilson, gave information about the plan to his master. Exactly one month later, Vesey was arrested. Found guilty, he was hanged on July 2, 1822, along with five other conspirators as an immense crowd of African Americans and whites watched. Charleston courts eventually arrested 131 slaves and free African Americans, executing 35 and transporting 37 to Spanish Cuba. A total of 23 African Americans were acquitted, 2 died in custody, 3 were found not guilty but whipped, and 1 free black was released on condition that he permanently leave the state. The African Church was razed, possibly as an attack by whites on black independence and autonomy. It was rebuilt in 1865 at the end of the Civil War.

### SIGNIFICANCE

In 2001, Michael Johnson, professor of history at Johns Hopkins University, presented evidence that Vesey did not organize the rebellion that bears his name. Johnson argued that Vesey was simply one of many black victims of a conspiracy engineered by the white power structure of 1822 Charleston. The passage of time has made it impossible to know what really happened. However, it is clear that slaves and former slaves did fight back against oppression; they did not passively accept their fate. Whether or not Vesey led the rebellion, he is significant as a symbol of fierce black resistance to slavery.

*—Caryn E. Neumann*

**FURTHER READING**

Egerton, Douglas R. *He Shall Go Out Free: The Lives of Denmark Vesey.* Lanham, Md.: Rowman & Little-field, 2004. This readable book re-creates the Caribbean and South Carolina of the 1700's and early 1800's to explore Vesey's life as an emigrant, a slave, and a freedman.

Paquette, Robert L., and Douglas R. Egerton. "Of Facts and Fables: New Light on the Denmark Vesey Affair." *South Carolina Historical Magazine* 105, no. 1 (January, 2004): 8-48. A good account of what is known and what is rumored about Vesey's Rebellion.

Robertson, David M. *Denmark Vesey: The Buried Story of America's Largest Slave Rebellion and the Man Who Led It.* New York: Vintage, 2000. This is a solid biography of Vesey and his impact.

Vesey, Denmark, et al. *The Trial Record of Denmark Vesey.* Reprint. Boston: Beacon Press, 1970. This old work is useful because it reprints the transcript of Vesey's trial.

**SEE ALSO:** William Craft and Ellen Craft; Frederick Douglass; James Forten; Sally Hemings; Absalom Jones; John Brown Russwurm; Dred Scott; Robert Smalls; Nat Turner; David Walker.

# C. T. VIVIAN
## Activist and religious leader

*An associate of Martin Luther King, Jr., Vivian was instrumental in bringing to the Civil Rights movement the tactic of nonviolent direct action. An ordained minister, Vivian also helped organize Christian church support of the movement's goals and wrote the first insider's reflection on the movement's successes, failures, and future.*

**BORN:** July 28 or 30, 1924; Boonville, Missouri
**ALSO KNOWN AS:** Cordy Tindell Vivian
**AREAS OF ACHIEVEMENT:** Civil rights; Religion and theology; Social issues

### EARLY LIFE

Cordy Tindell Vivian was born in Howard County, Missouri, the only child of Robert Cordie and Euzetta Tindell Vivian. After setbacks early in the Great Depression, Euzetta and her mother, Annie Woods Tindell, moved to Macomb, Illinois, with Tindell when he was six.

In the community and as a student, Vivian experienced discrimination. African Americans were prohibited from swimming in a local pool and he recalled a schoolmate sending him a card with a racist comment. However, as an adolescent, Vivian became active in the African Methodist Episcopal (AME) Church, in which he taught Sunday school and unsuccessfully tried to organize African Americans in local Baptist and Church of God in Christ congregations to worship together.

After graduating from high school, Vivian attended Western Illinois State Teachers College in Macomb. There, he struggled with faculty he considered bigoted and worked for the student newspaper, *The Western Courier*, where he won an award for sports writing. He dropped out before graduation and moved to nearby Peoria, where he worked as assistant director at a community center and met his future wife, Octavia Geans.

In Peoria in the late 1940's, Vivian participated in his first protests, attempting to integrate a restaurant and the city's major employer, Caterpillar Tractor Co. After working at the Young Men's Christian Association (YMCA) in Chicago, Vivian returned to Peoria to work at the Foster and Gallagher mail-order company. There, he felt a calling to the ministry, and company owner Helen Gallagher helped him enroll in a seminary.

### LIFE'S WORK

At the American Baptist Theological Seminary in Nashville, Tennessee, in 1955, Vivian served as pastor at churches in Nashville and Chattanooga. While studying in Nashville, he met James Lawson, a minister and acolyte of Mahatma Gandhi who was teaching nonviolent direct action strategies to a local student group. Among Vivian's fellow students were young people from Fisk and Tennessee State universities, and his classmates included James Bevel, Bernard LaFayette, Diane Nash, and John Robert Lewis. Lewis became a Georgia congressman; Nash helped found the Student Nonviolent Coordinating Committee (SNCC); LaFayette was active with the Quakers' American Friends Service Committee; and Bevel was involved with civil rights for decades, including helping to organize 1995's Million Man March.

Vivian helped organize the first sit-ins for social justice in Nashville in 1960. On April 19 of that year, 4,000 demonstrators marched on Nashville's City Hall, where Vivian and Nash challenged Nashville mayor Ben West to agree that racial discrimination was morally wrong. He did so, publicly. Many of the students involved in that demonstration became involved with SNCC.

A year later, Vivian was one of the few members of the clergy who joined the bus integration Freedom Rides through the segregated South, replacing injured members of the Congress of Racial Equality (CORE) after mobs had assaulted participants. He rode on the first Freedom Bus to enter Jackson, Mississippi.

In 1963, Vivian was appointed to the executive staff of the Southern Christian Leadership Conference (SCLC), where Martin Luther King, Jr., named him national director of affiliates. In that capacity through 1966, Vivian was one of that select group known as King's lieutenants. He was the liaison between headquarters and SCLC chapters throughout the South, along with a few in the North. He also worked as a sort of front man, going into cities whose residents had asked for King's and the SCLC's help, gathering information to take back to headquarters, where King and his staff would analyze the situation and decide how to proceed. Throughout, Vivian helped with grassroots organizing and teaching nonviolent strategies.

During this time, Vivian was beaten, repeatedly jailed, and narrowly escaped being drowned, shot, and blown up. For example, Vivian later wrote, 1963's Birmingham campaign—which SCLC leaders dubbed "Project C"—was the first widespread use of nonviolent direct action. The city that had closed public parks rather than integrate them and that had seventeen unsolved bombings of African American churches saw multiple mass protests until almost twenty-five hundred demonstrators were in jail at one time.

"There were the joys of those who had never before stood up and defied the ancient cruelties," Vivian said in his book *Black Power and the American Myth* (1970). "But there were terrors, too. Two blocks away [from their church headquarters] at the edge of the ghetto were the barricades where we were attacked by Bull Connor's police and firemen with dogs, clubs and high-pressure hoses."

In 1965, Vivian confronted Sheriff Jim Clark on the steps of the Selma, Alabama, courthouse during a voter registration drive. After an impassioned speech by Vivian, Clark—one of the local officials responsible for the arrests of civil rights protestors during the three important Selma-to-Montgomery marches—struck Vivian

*C. T. Vivian.* (AP/Wide World Photos)

on the mouth, an incident that made national news. The following summer, Vivian conceived of and directed an educational program, Vision, and sent more than seven hundred Alabama students to college with scholarships. The program later became Upward Bound.

Vivian in 1969 wrote *Black Power and the American Myth*, an insider's analysis of the Civil Rights movement. Published by Fortress Press in 1970, the paperback explains five goals the movement had in the 1950's and 1960's: creating a new condition, bringing the black middle class into the struggle, changing the values of the whole United States, considering new methods of social action to cement citizen involvement and to create a more effective force, and using nonviolence. The book also seemed to predict, if not advocate, an armed insurrection should nonviolence continue to fall short of its goals.

In his later years, Vivian led the Black Strategy Center think tank and organized and chaired the National Anti-Klan Network. Later renamed the Center for Democratic Renewal and affiliated with Political Research Associates and the Policy Action Network, it is a multiracial group that promotes the vision of a democratic, just society free of racism and bigotry.

Vivian also established the Atlanta-based Black Action Strategies and Information Center (BASIC), which consults employers on race relations and multicultural training.

## SIGNIFICANCE

Whether working for civil rights in the 1960's, speaking about racism, nonviolence, and King, or appearing on television programs and documentaries, Vivian dedicated several decades to the fight for social justice. Throughout, he has embraced and promoted the ethics and effectiveness of nonviolence.

*—Bill Knight*

## FURTHER READING

Adams, Pam. "Changing the Nation." *Peoria Journal Star*, October 24, 1999. An exhaustive profile of Vivian accompanied by a time line and an interview.

Fitzgerald, David. "C. T. Vivian Earns His Way." *The Western Courier*, September 29, 2003. A news story on Vivian's visit to his hometown and first college on the occasion of the community celebrating C. T. Vivian Day and naming a street in his honor.

Vivian, C. T. *Black Power and the American Myth*. Philadelphia: Fortress Press, 1970. The first look at the U.S. Civil Rights movement from an insider's perspective, this book outlines its methods and warns of dire consequences should reform not take place.

Walker, Lydia. *Challenge and Change: The Story of Civil Rights Activist C. T. Vivian*. Alpharetta, Ga.: Dreamkeeper Press, 1993. A biography of Vivian aimed at young readers.

Williams, Juan. *Eyes on the Prize*. New York: Penguin, 1988. Written as a companion to the PBS television series of the same name, this book benefits from the author's insights into the Civil Rights movement and period photos that together effectively summarize the time.

**SEE ALSO:** James Bevel; James Forman; Martin Luther King, Jr.; James Lawson; Diane Nash; Bayard Rustin; Hosea Williams; Whitney Young.

# JERSEY JOE WALCOTT
## Boxer

*Like many athletes of his era, Walcott was born poor and turned to boxing as a means to lift himself out of poverty. In a career spanning twenty-three years, he forged a respectable career—often interrupted by the need to find outside work—that culminated in a world championship.*

**BORN:** January 31, 1914; Merchantville, New Jersey
**DIED:** February 25, 1994; Camden, New Jersey
**ALSO KNOWN AS:** Arnold Raymond Cream (birth name)
**AREA OF ACHIEVEMENT:** Sports: boxing

### EARLY LIFE

Jersey Joe Walcott was born Arnold Raymond Cream. He was one of twelve children born to Joseph Cream, an immigrant from Barbados who had come to America as a boy. Walcott attended school until age thirteen, when his father died. He dropped out to help support his family by working at the Camden factory of Campbell Soup. Within a short time, he began training as a boxer at nearby Battling Mac's Gym. After a few amateur bouts, he debuted as a professional in 1930, fighting locally as a lightweight on the club circuit. Competing for as little as seven dollars and fifty cents per match, he won his first six bouts—all by knockout or technical knockout—before losing on points in 1933. Early in his career, he adopted the professional name "Jersey Joe Walcott," in honor of Joe Walcott, a British Guyana-born welterweight champion known as "the Barbados Demon," who grew up on the Caribbean island before relocating to Boston late in the nineteenth century.

Jersey Joe, however, had a difficulty making a living as a boxer. During the Depression, matches were scarce (he fought just three times in 1930, once in 1931, three times in 1933, and not at all in 1932 or 1934) and purses were meager. In the early 1930's, Walcott had to accept public assistance to afford room and board. After marrying—he eventually would father six children—he worked at a succession of menial jobs to make ends meet.

In the mid-1930's, Walcott connected with trainer Jack Blackburn, who greatly improved the young boxer's skills and worked him into fighting shape. Walcott started his comeback with five straight knockouts in 1935, and went 19-6 in twenty-five professional fights staged in New Jersey, Pennsylvania, and New York between 1935 and 1938. Then Blackburn was lured to Chicago to train amateur boxer and future world champion Joe Louis. Blackburn invited Walcott to join the stable of boxers under Louis's managers, but Walcott was ill with typhoid. Upon recovery, he briefly served as Louis's sparring partner but was fired after knocking down the "Brown Bomber."

Without proper management, Walcott's boxing career faltered. From 1939 to 1943, he fought just five times (going 4-1), with no matches in 1942 or 1943. Walcott took a full-time job as a dockworker and gave up his dream of becoming champion.

### LIFE'S WORK

The dream was revived in the mid-1940's, when local sports promoter and gambler Felix Bocchicchio coaxed Walcott out of retirement. His second comeback was launched in the summer of 1944. A heavyweight now, he went 15-1 through mid-1946, with ten fights ending in knockouts or technical knockouts. In December, 1947, after two straight victories over Joey Maxim and one over Elmer "Violent" Ray (both had earlier beaten Walcott), he was given a shot at world heavyweight champion Louis. During the fifteen-round bout, Walcott twice knocked Louis down and to spectators was the clear victor, but ring judges awarded the fight to Louis.

Walcott and Louis met at a rematch in mid-1948. This time the champion dominated, knocking out Walcott in the eleventh round. A year later, Louis retired after an eleven-year reign as champion, and Walcott was pitted against Ezzard Charles for the vacant title. After a tough fifteen-round loss on points, Walcott announced his retirement.

The retirement was short-lived. Once again, Bocchicchio persuaded Walcott to keep fighting. Walcott returned to the ring in August, 1949, and rattled off five straight wins, setting him up for another chance at the championship. In March, 1951, Charles once again won on points over fifteen rounds. In his third try against Charles later that year, Walcott knocked out the champion in the seventh round to claim the heavyweight crown. At age thirty-seven, he was the oldest boxer ever to win the championship, a distinction that stood until 1994, when George Foreman won the title at age forty-five. In celebration, Camden declared "Jersey Joe Walcott Day," and the whole city turned out to welcome the new champion.

Early in 1952, Walcott embarked on a succession of exhibition matches against boxer Jackie Burke. Mid-year, he successfully defended his world title, out-pointing Charles in fifteen rounds. His second title defense, in September, 1952, did not go as well: In a hard-fought battle, he became the first fighter to knock down unbeaten Rocky Marciano before being knocked out in the thirteenth round. By the rematch in Chicago on May 15, 1953, time had caught up with thirty-nine-year-old Walcott. Marciano knocked him out in the first round. Soon afterward, Walcott retired from boxing for good, with a record of fifty-one wins (thirty-two by knockout), eighteen losses, and two draws in seventy-one official professional fights.

After retirement, Walcott remained a popular figure in the Camden area. For a time, he served with the Cam-

---

### WALCOTT'S ROLE IN THE FILM *THE HARDER THEY FALL*

A hard-hitting film dealing with boxing corruption, *The Harder They Fall* (1956) featured Humphrey Bogart in his final film role before his death from cancer. The story was loosely based on the career of Italian boxer Primo Carnera, a huge man (6 feet, 6 inches, 284 pounds) whose bouts allegedly were fixed to make him world champion so that gamblers could bet against him when he attempted to defend his title. In his losing 1934 title match against Max Baer, Carnera was knocked down eleven times, giving credence to the rumors that earlier fights had been rigged.

Jersey Joe Walcott has a small but memorable role in *The Harder They Fall*. Just four years removed from his reign as world champion, he portrayed George, an ex-boxer who serves as trainer to a Carnera-like Argentine fighter named Toro Moreno. In a pivotal scene before a title bout (against a challenger played by Max Baer), worldly wise George easily penetrates Moreno's defenses and drops him repeatedly to the canvas, demonstrating that the Argentine is not as skilled as he thinks he is; Moreno fights anyway and is brutally beaten. Despite Walcott's convincing, sympathetic performance as a former pugilist, he never again appeared on film.

---

den Police Department as a parole officer for juvenile offenders. In 1963, he tried competing in a boxing-wrestling match: Although he felled champion grappler Lou Thesz with a punch, the semiconscious wrestler grabbed Walcott and pinned him. Walcott served for a short time as a boxing referee, but controversy over his handling of the second Muhammad Ali-Sonny Liston fight in 1965 ended his officiating career. That same year, Walcott was named Camden assistant director of public safety. In 1971, Walcott was elected sheriff of Camden County, a post he held for three years. Between 1975 and 1984, when he reached mandatory retirement, he was chairman of the New Jersey State Athletic Commission, although his time as a commissioner was tainted by allegations that he accepted monetary gifts. Walcott died on February 25, 1994, of complications from diabetes.

### SIGNIFICANCE

A solid, persistent fighter, Walcott picked up weight, muscle, and pugilistic skills as he matured. He grew into a hard hitter with either hand, equally skilled at offense and defense, by the time he retired from the sport. Walcott fought some of the most experienced boxers of the time, including Al Ettore, Tiger Jack Fox, Joe Baksi, Jimmy Bivins, Tommy Gomez, Joey Maxim, Elmer Ray, and Harold Johnson. Late in his career, he held his own against some of the greatest all-time heavyweight champions: Ezzard Charles, Joe Louis, and Rocky Marciano. Walcott's title-winning bout against Charles in 1951 earned him fighter of the year honors. He was inducted into the Ring Hall of Fame in 1969, and into the International Boxing Hall of Fame in 1990.

—*Jack Ewing*

## FURTHER READING

Callis, Tracy, Chuck Hasson, and Michael Delisa. *Philadelphia's Boxing Heritage: 1876-1976*. Mount Pleasant, S.C.: Arcadia, 2002. This illustrated historical overview covers a century of boxing in the Philadelphia-Camden metropolitan area, where Walcott lived during his entire career.

Roberts, James, and Alexander Skutt. *The Boxing Register: International Boxing Hall of Fame Official Record Book*. Ithaca, N.Y.: McBooks Press, 2006. This illustrated reference contains biographies and official fight records for Joe Walcott and nearly 200 other boxers.

Sugar, Bert Randolph. *Boxing's Greatest Fighters*. Guilford, Conn.: Lyons Press, 2006. Written by the former *Ring* magazine editor, this book discusses some of the greatest all-time fighters—including Walcott—and their most challenging matches.

SEE ALSO: Muhammad Ali; Ezzard Charles; George Foreman; Jack Johnson; Sonny Liston; Joe Louis.

# ALICE WALKER
## Writer

*Walker is best known for her novel* The Color Purple *(1982), which won the Pulitzer Prize and an American Book Award. She also wrote several other novels, volumes of poetry, and collections of essays and short stories.*

**BORN:** February 9, 1944; Eatonton, Georgia
**ALSO KNOWN AS:** Alice Malsenior Walker
**AREAS OF ACHIEVEMENT:** Literature; Poetry; Women's rights

## EARLY LIFE

Alice Malsenior Walker was the youngest child of Willie Lee and Minnie Tallulah Walker, Georgia sharecroppers. Both parents were skilled storytellers. Walker was a beautiful child and doted upon by her family. At the age of eight, however, an accident caused a major change in her life. Walker's brother shot her in the face with a BB gun, costing her the use of her right eye and leaving an obvious scar. She withdrew, becoming more of an observer and less of a participant in events.

Walker remained an excellent student. The valedictorian of her high school class, she won a scholarship to Spelman College in 1961. There, she became involved in the Civil Rights movement. In 1963, she transferred to Sarah Lawrence College, where she wrote poetry for the school's literary journal. She was one of only six African American students at Sarah Lawrence. During the summer of 1964, Walker traveled to Kenya. When she returned, she was pregnant. Despondent, she considered suicide, and her poetry reflected her emotional

*Alice Walker.* (Jeff Reinking/Picture Group)

## THE COLOR PURPLE

Alice Walker's third novel, one which she had planned to spend five years writing, was finished in just under a year. Its main character, Celie, was based on Walker's great-great-grandmother, a slave who was raped at the age of eleven by her white master. In *The Color Purple* (1982), Celie is born into poverty and suffers emotional and physical abuse. She is raped by her stepfather and gives birth to two children, who are taken away from her. Her stepfather later gives her in marriage to a man who does not love her. Albert, Celie's husband, treats her as a servant and abuses her, saving his love for Shug Avery, an itinerant blues singer. Over the course of the novel, Celie grows spiritually, intellectually, and sexually, going from oppressed and downtrodden to independent and empowered. Her transformation illustrates a rejection of patriarchy and racist repression.

*The Color Purple* was a literary sensation in 1983, winning a Pulitzer Prize and an American Book Award. In 1985, director Steven Spielberg adapted the novel into a film, although he rejected Walker's own screenplay for it. In December, 2005, a musical adaptation of *The Color Purple* opened on Broadway. It ran until February, 2008.

struggles. She decided to have an abortion in 1965. A children's story she wrote around the time, *To Hell with Dying* (1988), represented Walker's decision to reject suicide. Her first book of poetry, *Once: Poems* (1968), contained material written at Spelman, in Kenya, and at Sarah Lawrence.

After graduating from college Walker moved to Mississippi to teach and to continue her political activism. She met Melvyn Leventhal, a Jewish civil rights lawyer, and they married in early 1967. One of the few interracial married couples in the state of Mississippi, Walker and Leventhal had a daughter, Rebecca, before divorcing in 1976. During this time, Walker taught at Jackson State College and Tougaloo College and was involved in the Head Start program in the state. In 1970, she published her first novel, *The Third Life of Grange Copeland*, about an African American man who suffers under racist oppression, internalizes it, and ultimately conquers it. One of Walker's best-received volumes of poetry, *Revolutionary Petunias, and Other Poems*, was published in 1973. This work was nominated for the National Book Award.

### LIFE'S WORK

Seven years in Mississippi and a failed marriage left Walker depressed. Her second novel, *Meridian*, published in 1976, was largely autobiographical. Based on Walker's experiences, the story follows a student at a black women's college in the South who is caught up in

the Civil Rights movement. *Meridian* is a character study, a snapshot of a young woman caught up in the transition of a people and a country. Although the novel was not a critical success, it helped Walker define her "womanist" ideas, defining for herself what it meant to be a black feminist.

After brief stints teaching at Yale and working as an editor at *Ms.* magazine, Walker moved to San Francisco with Robert Allen, a writer. She soon moved to Mendocino County, California, seeking isolation in order to dedicate more energy to her novel *The Color Purple* (1982). The early 1980's were a highly creative and productive time for Walker. In addition to *The Color Purple*, she published the nonfiction work *In Search of Our Mothers' Gardens: Womanist Prose* (1983) and cofounded Wild Trees Press with Allen in 1984.

*The Color Purple* was in many ways the apex of Walker's career. In a journal entry written in 1984, she wrote, "Next month I will be forty. In some ways, I feel my early life's work is done, and done completely. The books that I have produced already carry forward the thoughts that I feel the ancestors were trying to help me pass on." Walker began to come to terms with her ancestors, embracing her African American heritage but also accepting the presence of a white slave owner and a part-Cherokee great-grandmother in her lineage. Her fourth published volume of poetry, *Horses Make a Landscape Look More Beautiful* (1984), and her second collection of essays, *Living by the Word: Selected Writings, 1973-1987* (1988), mark Walker's attempts to make sense of these diverse elements of her identity.

Seven years after *The Color Purple*, Walker's fourth novel was published. *The Temple of My Familiar* (1989) revisited themes from earlier novels, building on the development of female characters. Walker characterized this novel as a romance spanning five hundred thousand years, from precolonial Africa to 1980's San Francisco. Although the novel featured the granddaughter of *The Color Purple*'s Celie, it suffered from comparisons to its predecessor. Walker's fifth novel, *Possessing the Secret of Joy* (1992), also continues themes from her two previous novels. Tashi, a character from *The Color Purple*, appears as a character who has undergone ritual female circumcision. The practice, also known as female genital mutilation, sparked Walker's outrage. She collaborated on the documentary film *Warrior Marks: Female Genital Mutilation and the Sexual Blinding of Women* (1993) with Pratibha Parmar, an Indian woman raised in Africa.

In 2003, after some years of inactivity, Walker published her fifth collection of poetry, *Absolute Trust in the Goodness of the Earth: New Poems*. Her 2004 novel, *Now Is the Time to Open Your Heart*, was a memorial to her paternal grandmother, who was murdered when Walker's father was young.

## SIGNIFICANCE

A major author of fiction, nonfiction, and poetry from the 1960's into the twenty-first century, Walker emphasized the often-overlooked perspectives of women, African Americans, and especially African American women in her work. She famously characterized the African American woman as "the mule of the world," carrying on her back all the troubles no one else will carry. Beyond writing, Walker participated in voter-registration drives in the South and campaigned for African tribes to end the practice of female circumcision. She taught at Yale, Brandeis University, and the Univer-sity of California at Berkeley and served as a member of the board of trustees at Sarah Lawrence College, her alma mater.

*—Randy L. Abbott*

## FURTHER READING

Robinson, Cynthia Cole. "The Evolution of Alice Walker." *Women's Studies* 38, no. 3 (2009): 293-311. Traces the life of the author from her roots in the Deep South and the influence of her poor upbringing on her literary work, especially *The Color Purple*.

Walker, Alice. *In Search of Our Mothers' Gardens: Womanist Prose*. San Diego, Calif.: Harcourt Brace Jovanovich, 1983. In this collection of essays, Walker discusses influences on her writing, especially Zora Neale Hurston.

White, Evelyn C. *Alice Walker: A Life*. New York: W. W. Norton, 2004. Based on letters, journals, and interviews with Walker, her friends and family, this work examines Walker's life and writing.

SEE ALSO: Maya Angelou; Toni Cade Bambara; Barbara Chase-Riboud; Michelle Cliff; Zora Neale Hurston; Jamaica Kincaid; Toni Morrison; Margaret Walker.

# DAVID WALKER
## Abolitionist and writer

*Walker's work, commonly known as the* Appeal to the Colored Citizens of the World *(1829), broke new ground in the abolition movement in the United States and had a major impact on the long-term struggle for civil rights in the years that lay ahead.*

BORN: September 28, 1785; Wilmington, North Carolina
DIED: June 28, 1830; Boston, Massachusetts
AREAS OF ACHIEVEMENT: Abolitionism; Civil rights; Social issues

## EARLY LIFE

David Walker was born in Wilmington, North Carolina, on September 28, 1785. His father was a slave, but his mother was free, and under North Carolina law at the time, Walker was granted his mother's free status. Little is known of his early life, but it is clear that he had ample opportunity to witness the institution of slavery during his formative years. He learned to read and write in his youth and eventually acquired considerable knowledge in the fields of politics, history, and religion.

In his early twenties, Walker moved to Charleston, South Carolina, drawn by the rich cultural life and economic opportunities of that city. However, after a few years there—and especially in the period of suppression after the Denmark Vesey slave-revolt conspiracy in 1822—his bitter hatred of slavery caused him to leave the South. After spending some time traveling to other parts of the country, he eventually settled in Boston in the mid-1820's.

In Boston, Walker established himself in a second-hand clothing business. In February of 1826, he married Eliza Butler, a member of a well-known local African American family. His marriage brought him into the highest levels of Boston's free black society and he became increasingly involved in the abolition movement. He was a strong supporter of the New York abolitionist newspaper *Freedom's Journal* and an early member of the Massachusetts General Colored Association, an abolitionist group that later merged with the New England Anti-Slavery Society. It was in September of 1829, however, with the publication of *Walker's Appeal, in Four Articles; Together with a Preamble, to the Colored Citizens of the World, but in Particular, and Very Expressly, to Those of the United States of America*, that he made his greatest impact as a writer and abolitionist.

## LIFE'S WORK

Walker's famous work, better known as the *Appeal to the Colored Citizens of the World*, broke new ground in the growing struggle against slavery. Addressed to African Americans (both free and enslaved) as well as whites, it took a more militant tone than previous writings on the subject. Its four sections discussed the nature of slavery in the United States, how black potential was undermined by the withholding of education, religious views regarding slavery, and why Walker believed African colonization was not a practical solution to the slavery problem. In the minds of many whites, especially in the South, Walker's fiery writing was capable of inciting those who read it to violence. The work's structure—a preamble followed by a series of articles—paralleled the U.S. Constitution. In its conclusion, the author wrote eloquently of the basic incongruity of slavery with the ideals set forth in the Declaration of Independence.

Following the publication of the pamphlet, Walker worked personally to disseminate it. He used the mail, distributed copies to friends and acquaintances traveling to other parts of the country, and engaged black sailors to smuggle copies into southern ports. By the end of the year, the *Appeal to the Colored Citizens of the World* had reached most of the major cities of the South, setting off a firestorm of reaction. In December of 1829, the mayor of Savannah, Georgia, informed the governor of the state of the work's presence in his city. He also wrote to the mayor of Boston, asking him to take steps to suppress the work; the Boston mayor, stating that no law had been broken, took no action. Eventually, word circulated in the South that a bounty had been placed on Walker: three thousand dollars for his death or ten thousand dollars for his capture.

In the midst of the outcry, on June 28, 1830, Walker died suddenly. Rumors circulated that he had been murdered, but no evidence to support that claim was discovered. Despite Walker's untimely death, the controversy surrounding his work continued. The slave revolt led by Nat Turner in Virginia two years after the pamphlet's publication has sometimes been attributed to its influence, but no direct evidence supports this claim, either.

## SIGNIFICANCE

Walker's *Appeal to the Colored Citizens of the World* was one of the most controversial abolitionist writings of its time. Even white abolitionists of the period—William Lloyd Garrison and Benjamin Lundy among them—thought its views extreme, but its influence cannot be underestimated. In the short term, it served to increase the fears and paranoia of the South in regard to slave resistance, while in the long term it was an important source of inspiration for the militancy of later generations of civil rights leaders from W. E. B. Du Bois to Malcolm X.

—*Scott Wright*

## FURTHER READING

Aptheker, Herbert. *"One Continual Cry": David Walker's Appeal to the Colored Citizens of the World (1829-1830): Its Setting, Its Meaning*. New York: Humanities Press, 1965. Places Walker and his work in the larger context of the antislavery movement in U.S. history; also contains the full text of the 1830 edition of the *Appeal*.

Crockett, Hasan. "The Incendiary Pamphlet: David Walker's *Appeal* in Georgia." *The Journal of Negro History* 86, no. 3 (Summer, 2001): 305-318. Examines the response to Walker's work in one southern state.

Hinks, Peter P. *To Awaken My Afflicted Brethren: David Walker and the Problem of Antebellum Slave Resistance*. University Park: Pennsylvania State University Press, 1997. The definitive Walker biography, offering a detailed analysis of the *Appeal to the Colored Citizens of the World* and a full history of its impact.

Walker, David. *David Walker's Appeal to the Colored Citizens of the World*. Rev. ed. Edited by Peter P. Hinks. University Park: Pennsylvania State University Press, 2000. The 1830 edition of the *Appeal*, edited and with useful introductory material by Hinks.

**SEE ALSO:** Martin Robison Delany; Frederick Douglass; James Forten; Henry Highland Garnet; Absalom Jones; John Brown Russwurm; Maria Stewart; Sojourner Truth.

# GEORGE WALKER
## Musician and educator

*Walker was the first African American composer to win the Pulitzer Prize in music. He was one of the most significant American composers of the twentieth and early twenty-first centuries.*

**BORN:** June 27, 1922; Washington, D.C.
**ALSO KNOWN AS:** George Theophilus Walker
**AREAS OF ACHIEVEMENT:** Education; Music: classical and operatic; Music: composition

### EARLY LIFE

George Theophilus Walker was born in Washington, D.C., to Rosa King Walker and Artmelle George Theophilus Walker. Neither of Walker's parents had any musical training. His mother worked at the Government Printing Office in Washington, and his father was a respected physician who owned his own medical practice. His parents believed in the importance of education. During the summers, Walker's mother organized math and English lessons for the children in their neighborhood. On occasion, Walker's parents provided financial support for students at Howard University who were faced with financial difficulties.

Walker started his first music lessons at the age of five. He learned the piano from Mary L. Henry, who taught children in the neighborhood. When Henry organized piano recitals, they were held at the Walkers' home because the family had an upright piano in the parlor. Walker's piano skills were so advanced by the time he reached junior high school that Henry was unable to continue teaching him. His mother enrolled him into the Junior Department of Music at Howard University, where classical music was the focus. Walker was assigned to study classical piano with Lillian Mitchell, who so emphasized playing the correct notes and rhythms of a composition that Walker never had the opportunity to perform an entire piano piece from beginning to end.

While attending the segregated Dunbar High School in Washington, D.C., Walker had the opportunity to perform at school assemblies. He played piano pieces such as "Majesty of the Deep" by George Hamer and "Juba Dance" by Nathaniel Dett. His classmates responded to his energetic performances with enthusiasm.

Walker first realized he wanted to pursue a career in music when he began to consider colleges. His piano instructor, Mitchell, suggested that he apply to Oberlin College. He won a four-year scholarship to Oberlin, covering tuition, room, and board. He was the only African American in his conservatory class and the youngest student in the entire school. While attending Oberlin, Walker had to adjust to practicing four hours a day instead of the half hour he was accustomed to during high school. His minor concentration was organ, an instrument he had never studied before. During his junior year, he served as the organist for the Oberlin Theological Seminary. Walker also studied composition for one semester with Normand Lockwood. After discontinuing his composition lessons, he composed his first solo piano work, "Danse Exotique," which was retitled "Caprice" before its publication.

Upon graduating from Oberlin College in 1941 with the highest honors in his conservatory class, Walker sought a career as a concert pianist. He was sure that the Curtis Institute of Music would prepare him for such a career. In 1941, Walker was accepted into the Curtis Institute, where he studied piano with Rudolf Serkin and composition with Rosario Scalero. In 1944, Walker had enough credits to graduate but decided to remain at the Curtis Institute another year to continue studying repertoire with Serkin. In 1945, Walker made his concert debut in a recital at Town Hall in New York.

After graduating from the Curtis Institute, Walker traveled to Europe to study and perform. He studied in France with Robert Casadesus at the American School in Fontainebleu in the summer of 1947. Later that year, he returned to Washington, D.C., with hopes of performing in the United States. In 1953, Walker presented two poorly received recitals at Town Hall. Because black classical singers had more opportunities in Europe than they did in the United States, Walker desired to present a concert tour of Europe. His concerts in cities such as Stockholm, Amsterdam, Milan, and London were well received. However, he had to discontinue his concert tour when he developed an ulcer.

### LIFE'S WORK

Walker began teaching piano and theory at Dillard University in New Orleans in 1953. He taught at Dillard for one year before leaving to pursue a doctoral degree from the Eastman School of Music. He completed his degree in December of 1956 and was the first black student to receive a doctorate of music arts and an arts diploma in piano. Shortly thereafter, he traveled to Paris to study composition with Nadia Boulanger. Over the subsequent decades, Walker held faculty positions at Dalcroze School of Music, the New School for Social Research, Smith College in Massachusetts, the University of Colorado, Rutgers University (where he served as department chair), the Peabody Institute of Johns Hopkins University, and the University of Delaware, where he was awarded their first Minority Chair.

Walker composed several major pieces and released a number of albums. His best known work, however, was the Pulitzer Prize-winning *Lilacs* (1996). Commissioned by the Boston Symphony Orchestra to compose a piece in honor of the African American tenor Roland Hayes, Walker set to music Walt Whitman's poem *When Lilacs Last in the Dooryard Bloom'd*, about the assassination of President Abraham Lincoln. The piece, written for voice and orchestra, was Walker's seventieth published work.

### SIGNIFICANCE

Walker received several awards, including a Fulbright Fellowship, two Rockefeller Fellowships, and a John Hay Whitney Fellowship. He also was awarded honorary doctoral degrees from universities such as the Curtis Institute of Music (1997), Oberlin College (1983), and Spelman College (2001). Walker was the first black composer to win the Pulitzer Prize. In 2000, he became the first living composer to be inducted into the American Classical Music Hall of Fame.

—*Monica T. Tripp-Roberson*

### FURTHER READING

Baker, David N., Linda M. Belt, and Herman C. Hundson, eds. *The Black Composer Speaks*. Metuchen, N.J.: Scarecrow Press, 1978. Contains an interview with Walker and information on his life, beliefs, inspirations, and thoughts on his work.

Floyd, Samuel A. *The Power of Black Music: Interpreting Its Music from Africa to the United States*. New York: Oxford University Press, 1996. Examines the development of African American music and its contributions to American culture. Walker's work in the 1950's is discussed in detail.

Walker, George. *Reminiscences of an American Composer and Pianist*. Lanham, Md.: Scarecrow Press, 2009. Provides a detailed account of Walker's life and accomplishments.

**SEE ALSO:** Blind Tom Bethune; James Bland; Margaret Allison Bonds; Anthony Braxton; Harry T. Burleigh; R. Nathaniel Dett; Father Divine; Ulysses Kay; George Russell.

# JIMMIE WALKER
## Actor and comedian

*As the central character in* Good Times, *the groundbreaking 1970's situation comedy, Walker shaped his generation's conception of the hip black teenager, at once cocky and assertive, becoming in the process one of the decade's most recognized African American entertainers.*

**BORN:** June 25, 1947; Bronx, New York
**ALSO KNOWN AS:** James Carter Walker
**AREAS OF ACHIEVEMENT:** Entertainment: comedy; Radio and television

### EARLY LIFE

James Carter Walker was born in the impoverished housing projects of the south Bronx, New York, on June 25, 1947. Given his lanky frame and love of athletics, Walker dreamed of a professional basketball career and paid little attention at school. When it became clear that he was not destined for basketball stardom, Walker abandoned high school a year before graduation. He worked delivery jobs in his neighborhood but soon realized that he needed to return to school. Under the aegis of a federally funded program, Search for Education, Evaluation, and Knowledge (SEEK), Walker completed his high school equivalency. In a writing class that involved reading aloud his own essay, Walker discovered that his writing (and his delivery) could make people laugh.

Walker studied radio engineering technology at the RCA Technical Institute. A year later, having earned his engineering license, he secured work at a small radio station as a part-time engineer. Walker still toyed with the idea of doing stand-up comedy on the side. With the help of a friend, he got the chance to open for the Last Poets, a group of street poets whose incendiary political verse, delivered with passion, had stirred black audiences in the theaters of Harlem. Walker agreed to warm up the audiences with five minutes of original material. He was a hit and stayed with the group for a year and a half.

*Jimmie Walker poses with a doll modeled after his* Good Times *character.* (Hulton Archive/Getty Images)

Norman Lear, then the producer of ground-breaking sitcoms (most notably *All in the Family* and *Sanford and Son*) that had redefined television comedy by introducing social and political issues into prime time television. Lear was developing a sitcom, tentatively titled *Good Times*, that would be a spinoff of his hugely successful *Maude*. *Good Times* would be based on Maude's black housekeeper and her family's struggles in the ghetto of Chicago. Walker, although by then in his late twenties, was offered the role of J. J. Evans, the high school-age son who dreams of being an artist. The role was intended to be a supporting character, but Walker's easy charm, smart-aleck swagger, and broad smile immediately engaged audiences. Over the six years of the show's run, Walker became a bona-fide crossover star—both black and white audiences loved the character.

The show quickly came to center on J. J., whose catchphrase, "Dyn-o-mite!," entered the vocabulary of popular culture on bumper stickers, posters, and T-shirts—a line of dolls even uttered the phrase. Walker's presentation of the character was not entirely admired by the cast, however. John Amos, who played his father, and Esther Rolle, who played his mother, both objected to the image of J. J. as a minstrel-show stereotype—wide-grinning, not terribly bright, perpetually interested in sex, and easily coaxed into foolish get-rich-quick schemes—that distracted from the show's higher purpose, a gritty depiction of a family working together amid economic hard times. Regardless, the show was regularly at the top of the Nielsen ratings, and Walker a national phenomenon—he released a comedy album and regularly appeared on game shows, variety shows, and late-night talk shows. Indeed, he was named the first recipient of the National Association for the Advancement of Colored People (NAACP) Image Award, and *Time* magazine named him the Comedian of the Decade.

After *Good Times* ended in 1979, Walker's popularity waned. His attempts to move into other television shows and films foundered, restricted largely to cameo roles in which he played J. J. Evans-style characters (most notably, Walker appeared in a dozen episodes of *The Love Boat*). He tested a number of sitcoms in the 1980's (*B.A.D.*

## LIFE'S WORK

Walker worked other New York area nightclubs, developing material centered on his own street experiences. In 1969, David Brenner, a nightclub and television comedian, saw Walker's show and arranged for him to move up to bigger venues. Walker performed at the Improv, known for launching young comedians, and had a weeklong gig as master of ceremonies at the legendary Apollo Theater. However, television was the key to any breakthrough. In 1972, at the urging of Brenner and other friends of Walker (among them singer Bette Midler), Walker got his chance on *The Jack Paar Show*. His routine was a ratings bonanza and Walker was flown to Los Angeles, where, after a guest appearance on the edgy comedy variety show *Laugh-In*, CBS signed him to warm up audiences for *Carlucci's Department*, a sitcom that was filmed live.

Walker drew the attention of a casting director for

*Cats*; *At Ease*; *Bustin' Loose*), although none survived more than a season. However, Walker never abandoned his nightclub act. He worked steadily, eventually using his celebrity as J. J. Evans as fodder for his comedy routines. In the early 2000's, his sitcom now a classic, Walker found himself once again in demand for appearances on late-night talk shows and cameos in cable sitcoms. Over sixty, Walker continued to perform more than thirty weeks a year in nightclubs across the country.

## SIGNIFICANCE

In the 1970's, Walker became the first African American entertainer to find crossover celebrity through television. The character of J. J. Evans achieved rare iconic status. Although Walker weathered criticism from the black community, who feared the character played into entrenched (and racist) depictions of black youths, the easygoing confidence and wisecracking optimism of Walker's character was a critical counterpoint to the image of the angry black young men of the 1960's.

—*Joseph Dewey*

## FURTHER READING

Campbell, Sean. *The Sitcoms of Norman Lear*. Jefferson, N.C.: McFarland, 2006. Comprehensive survey of the uncompromising creative vision of the television producer who created the sitcom that launched Walker's television career.

Gregory, Adamo. *African Americans in Television*. New York: Peter Lang, 2010. Provocative study of how portrayals of black characters affect social and cultural perceptions of African Americans, with particular emphasis on the emerging role of African Americans in behind-the-scenes television production.

Pegg, Robert. "Jimmy Walker: 'J. J.' Evans on *Good Times*." In *Comical Co-Stars of Television Sitcoms: From Ed Norton to Kramer*. Jefferson, N.C.: McFarland, 2002. Discusses Walker's famous role in terms of comedy and television history.

**SEE ALSO:** Godfrey Cambridge; Bill Cosby; Cleavon Little; Eddie Murphy; Richard Pryor; Tim Reid; Paul Winfield.

# MADAM C. J. WALKER
## Entrepreneur and inventor

*Founder of the Madam C. J. Walker Manufacturing Company, Walker not only created products that boosted the self-esteem of African American women but also became the first American female self-made millionaire. She provided economic opportunity for thousands of African American women and contributed to the community as a social activist.*

**BORN:** December 23, 1867; Delta, Louisiana
**DIED:** May 25, 1919; Irvington-on-Hudson, New York
**ALSO KNOWN AS:** Sarah Breedlove McWilliams Walker; Sarah Breedlove (birth name); Madam Charles Joseph Walker; Sarah Breedlove McWilliams Davis
**AREAS OF ACHIEVEMENT:** Business; Invention

## EARLY LIFE

Sarah Breedlove McWilliams Walker was born on December 23, 1867, to Owen and Minerva Breedlove in Delta, Louisiana. Former slaves, the Breedloves worked on a cotton plantation owned by Robert W. Burney. Walker later estimated that she had only three months of formal schooling. Orphaned by the age of seven, she moved to Vicksburg with her sister Louvinia and brother-in-law and worked as a laundress. In order to escape her abusive brother-in-law, Walker began a relationship with Moses McWilliams at the age of fourteen and gave birth to her daughter and only child, Lelia (later called A'Lelia), in 1885. Approximately three years later, Moses died and Walker and Lelia moved to St. Louis to stay with Walker's brothers. As barbers, they were among the city's largest group of black entrepreneurs. Known as Sallie McWilliams at the time, Walker supported herself by working as a laundress and was befriended by the women of the St. Louis Colored Orphans Home. Determined that Lelia would not have to engage in the drudgery of laundry work, she enrolled the child in first grade at Dessalines Elementary School, which was maintained by the organization.

After the death of her oldest brother, Alexander, in 1894, Walker began a relationship with a man named John Davis and eventually married him. Davis proved to be an alcoholic who rarely worked and physically abused Walker. Nevertheless, she managed to save enough money to enroll Lelia in Knoxville College in 1902. Before Walker and Davis separated in 1903, she began to see a man named Charles Joseph (C. J.) Walker. He was a light-skinned newspaperman who had built a reputation as a successful salesman.

### LIFE'S WORK

During the mid-1890's, Walker's hair began to fall out, and she feared going bald. This was not an unusual situation for poor women and resulted from a variety of conditions: poor diet, infrequent washing, scalp disease, damaging hair treatments, and stress. She later claimed to have prayed for guidance. Her prayer was answered in the form of a dream in which a large black man instructed her as to how to concoct a treatment. Although she said the remedy originated in Africa, the secret ingredient might have been coconut oil, which was mixed with other substances to produce a scalp ointment. It remains disputed whether Walker's invention was entirely her own. Walker had become acquainted with Annie Turnbo Malone, who had her own line of scalp treatments and hair-growing products and a distribution system throughout the South. As one of Malone's earliest sales agents, Walker recognized the business as a way to improve her economic status and take advantage of a growing market among the urban black population.

In 1905, Walker traveled to Denver, Colorado, to stay with her sister-in-law, Lucy Crockett Breedlove, and her nieces. Supplementing her income by working as a cook, she continued to sell the products shipped to her by what was then known as the Pope-Turnbo Company. Since she had to add ingredients to the products, she eventually began to experiment with the mixtures and ultimately came up with her own formula. She married C. J. in 1906 and took his name despite the fact that she had never officially divorced Davis. C. J.'s promotional abilities and Walker's drive for self-improvement made their fledgling business immediately successful. She severed connections with Pope-Turnbo and began marketing her products under the name Madam C. J. Walker.

The Walkers turned their attention south, where they held classes, sold products door to door, and hired agents. In late 1907 or early 1908, they made Pittsburgh their temporary headquarters and Walker began to make plans for a Madam C. J. Walker Manufacturing Company stock offering. In 1910, the couple moved their company to Indianapolis. She solicited well-known African Americans such as Booker T. Washington for support and made the rounds of black fraternal organizations

*Madam C. J. Walker.* (Michael Ochs Archives/Getty Images)

and businesses. She also took in boarders at her house (a common practice at the time), two of whom—attorneys Freeman Briley Ransom and Robert Lee Brokenburr—became not only her legal advisers but also her lifelong friends and leaders in the community.

As her business grew, Walker contributed to black causes and campaigns. Her one-thousand-dollar donation to a Young Men's Christian Association building drew headlines. Against the wishes of Washington, she persisted in an appearance at the 1912 Negro Farmers' Conference, going to Tuskegee and giving "demonstrative treatments" of her hair-care method. Her relationship with Washington was never good, possibly because he was threatened by the very notion of a successful businesswoman. In addition, Washington may have been among the critics who accused Walker of trying to make black women conform to white standards of beauty by straightening their hair. Around this time, Walker and C. J. divorced.

By the end of 1920, the Walker Manufacturing Company claimed to have trained twenty thousand agents who worked in the burgeoning hair-care business. In the meantime, her rivalry with Malone (whose company was now known as the Poro System) continued. As her wealth grew, Walker spent much of 1917 constructing an opulent thirty-four-room mansion in Westchester County, New York, that was named Villa Lewaro (a partial anagram of Lelia Walker Robinson) by Enrico Caruso. It became a gathering place for a wide range of artists and personalities, including those associated with the Harlem Renaissance.

In 1918, Walker died after a long struggle with hypertension. She had amassed a fortune that would lead others to label her the first American woman—black or white—to become a self-made millionaire. She credited her success to perseverance, hard work, faith in herself and in God, honest business dealings, and quality products. Her daughter succeeded her as president of the Madam C. J. Walker Manufacturing Company.

## SIGNIFICANCE

As a self-made black woman entrepreneur, Madam Walker influenced the advancement of women's rights as well as the prospects of African Americans. By improving the hygiene practices of thousands of women, she contributed to the creation of a black hair-care industry. Although biographers have focused on her invention of the metal hot comb for straightening hair, she denounced that claim and insisted that her interest was with growing rather than straightening hair. As an African American philanthropist, she contributed to groups such as the National Association for the Advancement of Colored People (NAACP), the National Association of Colored Women (NACW), and black colleges and churches. In addition, she contributed large amounts of time and money to the NAACP's antilynching campaign. Thousands of women who graduated from the Walker College of Hair Culture sold products, opened their own shops, and improved their economic prospects.

—*Jayne R. Beilke*

---

### WALKER'S PRODUCTS

Madam C. J. Walker initially sold five products. The most popular product was Madam Walker's Wonderful Hair Grower, a scalp treatment. This product was paired with Madam Walker's Vegetable Shampoo. Glossine was a moisturizing ointment that was used in combination with the heated metal pressing comb. Temple Salve was used for dandruff and scalp itch, while Tetter Salve treated the more serious conditions of psoriasis and eczema. Although she often is mistakenly credited with inventing the hot comb, it was the use of her products along with the hot comb that proved successful. An employee of Madam Walker, Marjorie Joyner, invented an improved permanent wave machine that made the wave last longer and was patented in 1928. Walker also manufactured a skin cream. She is credited with popularizing the idea of beauty as an escape from poverty and drudgery; her products offered ways for women to improve their appearances, and in turn, their self-esteem.

---

## FURTHER READING

Bundles, A'Lelia. *On Her Own Ground: The Life and Times of Madam C. J. Walker.* New York: Charles Scribner's Sons, 2001. The definitive biography, written by a descendant of Walker.

Gates, Henry Louis, Jr., and Evelyn Brooks Higginbotham, eds. "Madam C. J. Walker." In *Harlem Renaissance Lives from the African American National Biography.* New York: Oxford University Press, 2009. Detailed biography that puts Walker's achievements in the context of contemporary African American culture and entrepreneurship. This resource also includes a biography of Walker's daughter and successor.

Lasky, Kathryn. *Visions of Beauty: The Story of Sarah Breedlove Walker.* Cambridge, Mass.: Candlewick Press, 2000. Accessible biography aimed at younger readers.

Peiss, Kathy L. *Hope in a Jar: The Making of America's Beauty Culture.* New York: Henry Holt, 1998. A cultural history of the cosmetics industry, including the contributions of Annie Turnbo Malone and Walker.

SEE ALSO: Paul Cuffe; Amos Fortune; Arthur George Gaston; Berry Gordy, Jr.; John H. Johnson; Robert L. Johnson.

# MARGARET WALKER
## Poet, novelist, and professor

*Walker is best known for* Jubilee *(1966), a neo-slave narrative depicting the everyday lives of slaves, and* For My People *(1942), her first volume of poetry, which propelled her to national prominence. She was the founder of the Margaret Walker Alexander National Research Center.*

**BORN:** July 7, 1915; Birmingham, Alabama
**DIED:** November 30, 1998; Chicago, Illinois
**ALSO KNOWN AS:** Margaret Abigail Walker; Margaret Walker Alexander
**AREAS OF ACHIEVEMENT:** Education; Literature; Poetry

### EARLY LIFE

Margaret Abigail Walker was born in Birmingham, Alabama, to Sigismund C. and Marion Dozier Walker. Walker, the oldest of five children, grew up in a home where education and literature were emphasized. Her Jamaican father was a Methodist minister and linguistics professor, and her mother was a music professor. The family moved frequently because of her father's position as a minister. Walker's maternal grandmother, the storyteller Elvira Ware Dozier, lived with the family.

The family moved to New Orleans when Walker was ten years old. By the time she completed high school at Gilbert Academy at the age of fourteen, she had written several poems. She attended Dillard University, and during her sophomore year, Walker became acquainted with Langston Hughes, who saw her talent and encouraged her parents to send her north to school to ensure the development of her talents. In 1932, she transferred to Northwestern University, where she received her bachelor's degree in 1935 in English. In 1936, Walker moved to Chicago to work for the Federal Writers' Project and worked with several up-and-coming writers, including Richard Wright, Gwendolyn Brooks, and Frank Yerby. Walker received her master's degree in 1940 from the University of Iowa.

Walker turned to teaching to help support her family. She taught at Livingston College in 1941 and at West Virginia State College in 1942. In 1943, Walker married Firnist James Alexander, an interior designer and disabled veteran. The couple and their three children moved to Jackson, Mississippi, in 1949, and she began teaching at Jackson State College. Walker returned to the University of Iowa and completed her Ph.D. in English in 1965.

### LIFE'S WORK

As a preteen, Walker had recorded her poems and conversations with her grandmother in her journal. Early exposure to great literature and poetry, listening to her grandmother's stories, and support from her parents influenced her ambition to become a writer.

By the age of eighteen, Walker had completed 365 pages of poetry in her journal. Her poetry reflects her father's advice to always include images, rhythm, and meaning. Walker's first poem was published in *The Crisis* in 1934. Her first volume of poetry, her master's thesis *For My People* (1942), won the Yale Series of Younger Poets Award in 1942. Walker was the first black woman in the American literary arena to be so honored. She published many more volumes of poetry, including *The Ballad of the Free* (1966), *Prophets for a New Day* (1970), *October Journey* (1973), *Farish Street Green* (1986), and *This Is My Century: New and Collected Poems* (1989).

Walker's sole novel, *Jubilee* (1966), took thirty years to complete, although she wrote several hundred pages of it while she was at Northwestern. The novel was the result of the stories told to her by her maternal grandmother about the slave life of Walker's maternal great-grandmother, Margaret Duggins. Walker's other literary contributions include numerous essays and a controversial biography, *Richard Wright, Daemonic Genius: A Portrait of the Man, a Critical Look at His Work* (1988).

Walker received numerous awards, including the Rosenwald Fellowship (1944), a Ford Fellowship for study at Yale (1954), a Houghton Mifflin Literary Fellowship (1966), a Fulbright Fellowship (1971), a National Endowment for the Humanities Fellowship (1972), the Living Legacy Award (1992), and the Lifetime Achievement Award for Excellence in the Arts, presented by the governor of Mississippi (1992). She was inducted into the African American Literary Hall of Fame in 1998. She also received honorary doctorates from several colleges and universities. July 12, 1980, was proclaimed Margaret Walker Day in Jackson, Mississippi. She died of cancer on November 30, 1998.

### SIGNIFICANCE

In *Jubilee*, Walker combined thoroughly researched history with folklore to create the first neo-slave narrative that chronicles the antebellum South, the Civil War, and Reconstruction. The novel provides a humanistic vision of the everyday lives of slaves from the viewpoint of her great-grandmother. Very few novels about slavery had been written before *Jubilee*. Walker provided subject matter and form that influenced African American novels for several decades after *Jubilee*.

—*Joyce K. Thornton*

**FURTHER READING**

Rushdy, Ashraf H. A. "The Neo-slave Narrative." In *The Cambridge Companion to the African American Novel*, edited by Maryemma Graham. Cambridge, England: Cambridge University Press, 2004. Describes and analyzes the genre of neo-slave narrative, with particular focus on Walker's *Jubilee*.

Walker, Margaret. *Conversations with Margaret Walker.*

Edited by Maryemma Graham. Jackson: University Press of Mississippi, 2002. A compilation of fourteen interviews and conversations with Walker covering her life, her works, and her worldview.

_____. *How I Wrote "Jubilee" and Other Essays on Life and Literature*. Edited by Maryemma Graham. New York: Feminist Press at the City University of New York, 1990. Collection of essays and speeches from 1930 to 1980 providing a basic introduction to Walker's thought and vision.

**SEE ALSO:** Maya Angelou; Alice Childress; Ernest J. Gaines; Alex Haley; Gayl Jones; Paule Marshall; Toni Morrison; Ann Petry; Alice Walker; Richard Wright.

# FATS WALLER
## Jazz musician, composer, and entertainer

*Waller, although perhaps best known for his comic entertainment style, was a gifted jazz musician whose greatest contribution to music lay in his virtuosic Harlem stride piano compositions.*

**BORN:** May 21, 1904; Waverley, New York
**DIED:** December 15, 1943; Kansas City, Missouri
**ALSO KNOWN AS:** Thomas Wright Waller
**AREAS OF ACHIEVEMENT:** Entertainment: vaudeville; Music: composition; Music: jazz; Music: swing; Radio and television

**EARLY LIFE**

Thomas Wright Waller (WAH-luhr) was born on May 21, 1904, in New York near Harlem—a city that was on its way to becoming the largest and most significant urban community of African Americans in the Northeast. In Harlem, Waller and other artists would launch one of the major cultural movements in American history, the Harlem Renaissance.

Waller's parents—Edward, a Baptist lay preacher, and Adeline—migrated to New York from Virginia in 1888, and by 1902 had permanently settled in Harlem. Waller, who came to be known as "Fats" in his youth, was the youngest of the couple's five children. Edward and Adeline were devout churchgoers and intensely musical; indeed, religious music was part of their everyday lives. This reverence for music had a tremendous impact on Waller. By the age of six, he was playing the harmonium to accompany his father's sermons.

Waller's musical education and professional growth intensified in his teenage years. In 1918, he won a talent contest for his rendition of James P. Johnson's "Carolina

*Fats Waller.* (Archive Photos/Getty Images)

Shout," which was considered to be the barometer by which all budding stride pianists were measured. By 1920, he was studying with Johnson, the father of the Harlem stride piano style. Around that time, Waller also began to perform regularly at Harlem's Lincoln and Lafayette theaters. During the next few years, as a result of his increasingly frequent public appearances, Waller came to be acknowledged as one of the most inventive and virtuosic of the younger generation of stride practitioners. He made his debut recording, "Birmingham Blues" and "Muscle Shoals Blues," in October of 1922; other early performance activity included accompanying blues singers, such as Bessie Smith, on recordings and cutting numerous piano rolls in 1923 for the Victor, QRS, and Okeh labels. During the early 1920's, he continued to play for rent parties, engaged in cutting contests, was an organist at movie theaters, and served as an accompanist for various vaudeville acts.

### LIFE'S WORK

While still in his early twenties, Waller composed dozens of songs (although some were not published) and began critical collaborations with songwriters such as Spencer Williams and, most important, Andy Razaf.

In 1927, Waller recorded his own composition, "Whiteman Stomp," with Fletcher Henderson's orchestra, one of the pioneering African American bands of the swing era. Henderson used other compositions by Waller as vehicles for his arrangements and improvisations, including "I'm Crazy 'bout My Baby" and "Stealin' Apples."

In 1928, along with Razaf, Waller contributed much of the music for Johnson's all-black Broadway musical *Keep Shufflin'*. He also made his Carnegie Hall debut on April 27, 1928, when he was the piano soloist in a version of Johnson's *Yamekraw, a Negro Rhapsody* for piano and orchestra.

Waller's star rose rapidly in 1929; in that year alone, he was involved in numerous extensive recording sessions that documented some of his finest songs, including "Ain't Misbehavin'," "I've Got a Feeling I'm Falling," "Honeysuckle Rose," "(What Did I Do to Be So) Black and Blue?," "The Minor Drag," and "Numb Fumblin'." This exposure gained him cachet with record

---

> ## WALLER AND THE MUSICAL REVUE *HOT CHOCOLATES*
>
> *Hot Feet*, an all-African American musical revue with lyrics by Andy Razaf and music by Fats Waller, opened at Connie's Inn in February of 1929. Connie's Inn, a Harlem nightclub owned by brothers George and Connie Immerman, was the primary competitor of the famous Cotton Club and had similar elaborate floor shows, restrictive admission policies, and purported ties to organized crime.
>
> *Hot Feet* was considered one of the best floor shows to emerge from a Harlem nightclub, and its success prompted the Immerman brothers to move it to Broadway, where the show opened at the Hudson Theater in June of 1929. They had renamed the revue *Connie's Hot Chocolates* and asked Waller and Razaf to compose a few more numbers for the revamped show; these songs included "(What Did I Do to Be So) Black and Blue?" "Can't We Get Together," and the show's most popular tune, "Ain't Misbehavin'."
>
> Despite the critical and commercial success of "Ain't Misbehavin'," it was the racially charged "Black and Blue" that served as an anthem of the burgeoning cultural pride of the African American community.

---

executives and he was permitted to use an interracial band, one of the earliest in recording history.

In 1930, Waller appeared on radio as one of the earliest African Americans hosts. From 1932 to 1934, he broadcast his own show for WLW in Cincinnati, *Fats Waller's Rhythm Club*. When the WLW contract concluded in early 1934, Waller returned to New York, where he broadcast the *Rhythm Club* show over the CBS network to a larger audience. This experience would prove to be invaluable as it offered an unparalleled opportunity to sing, satirize, and provide commentary while he was playing—all traits for which he would become widely known.

Waller's success on CBS persuaded Victor to sign him to his first recording contract; Waller decided upon a six-piece band format similar in organization to a typical Dixieland band ensemble: clarinet, trombone, trumpet, piano, bass, and drums. Maintaining the association with the *Rhythm Club* name, Waller dubbed the band Fats Waller and His Rhythm. Between 1934 and 1942, the group recorded about four hundred sides, well over half of Waller's lifetime recorded output. Many critics consider the band's best work the records issued in 1935 and 1936, and many of these releases sold millions of copies. In February, 1938, Victor extended Waller's contract through May, 1944.

In 1938, Waller undertook a European tour and recorded in London with his group Continental Rhythm and made solo organ recordings for the HMV (His Master's Voice) label. His second European tour, the following year, was terminated by the outbreak of World War II, but while in Great Britain, he recorded his *London Suite*, an extended series of six related pieces for solo piano: "Piccadilly," "Chelsea," "Soho," "Bond Street," "Limehouse," and "Whitechapel." It became Waller's greatest composition in scale and magnitude and is indicative of his aspirations to be a composer of concert works, along the lines of his mentor, Johnson.

The final years of Waller's life involved frequent recordings and extensive tours of the United States. In early 1943, he traveled to Hollywood to make the film *Stormy Weather* with Lena Horne and Bill "Bojangles" Robinson, in which he led an all-star band. His professional responsibilities intensified in that year with more touring as well as collaborating with the lyricist George Marion for the stage show *Early to Bed*.

This exhausting schedule along with constant overindulgence in food and alcohol irrevocably damaged Waller's health. He died of pneumonia in December, 1943, while returning to New York by train with his manager, Ed Kirkeby.

### SIGNIFICANCE

Waller, in his short life, served as an ebullient champion of African Americans' contributions to the cultural fabric of the United States. Whether it was through his jubilant and virtuosic musical performances, his comedic antics, or his dapper sartorial taste, Waller was determined to celebrate his community and transcend the racial barriers put before him.

—*Michael Conklin*

### FURTHER READING

Kirkeby, Ed. *Ain't Misbehavin': The Story of Fats Waller.* New York: Dodd, Mead, 1966. Reprint. New York: Da Capo Press, 1975. This informal narrative of Waller's life and music serves as a moving memoir of the musical genius as told by Waller's personal manager, Kirkeby.

Machlin, Paul S. *Stride: The Music of Fats Waller.* Boston: Twayne, 1985. The first in-depth, scholarly examination of the work of this major jazz figure whose talents as an entertainer often overshadowed his considerable artistic contributions. It includes musical analysis of Waller's idiomatic style and delves into some obscure Waller compositions, such as his works for pipe organ.

Shipton, Alyn. *Fats Waller: The Cheerful Little Earful.* Rev. ed. New York: Continuum, 2002. In this fully revised and updated biography of Waller, Shipton argues that Waller's talents as a songwriter, composer, and recording and broadcasting artist have not been fully appreciated. Includes a comprehensive discography of Waller's recordings as they have been reissued on compact disc.

Taylor, Stephen. *Fats Waller on the Air.* Lanham, Md.: Scarecrow Press, 2006. Examines the often overlooked aspect of Waller's career—his years as a radio personality. The broadcasts, including tributes to Waller after his death, are covered in detail, featuring dates, times, songs played, and other artists who appeared on the program.

Waller, Maurice, and Anthony Calabrese. *Fats Waller.* New York: Schirmer Books, 1977. An exploration of Waller's life as seen through the eyes of his son, Maurice.

**SEE ALSO:** Earl Hines; Scott Joplin; Ellis Marsalis, Jr.; Thelonious Monk; Little Brother Montgomery; Jelly Roll Morton; Herbie Nichols; Professor Longhair; Horace Silver; McCoy Tyner.

# ERIC WALROND
## Writer

*Although he spent only ten years of his life in the United States, Walrond's writing was pivotal to the Harlem Renaissance and African American literature. His most famous work,* Tropic Death, *was a collection of vivid and poetic short stories about the Caribbean. Walrond also was involved with the influential journalist and activist Marcus Garvey and the National Urban League.*

**BORN:** December 18, 1898; Georgetown, British Guiana (now Guyana)
**DIED:** August 8, 1966; London, England
**ALSO KNOWN AS:** Eric Derwent Walrond
**AREAS OF ACHIEVEMENT:** Journalism and publishing; Literature

### EARLY LIFE

Eric Derwent Walrond was born on December 18, 1898, in Georgetown, British Guiana (now Guyana). His father was from British Guinea, his mother from Barbados; Walrond's father left early in the boy's life to work in Panama, and the family moved to Barbados in 1906 to stay with his mother's relatives. Walrond attended St. Stephen's Boys' School until 1911, when his destitute family sold their possessions and moved to Colón, Panama.

In Colón, Walrond faced harsh discrimination and prejudice from Spanish-speaking whites. This racism—the likes of which Walrond had not previously experienced—had a profound impact on him and was reflected in much of his later writings about the area. In the course of his education, he learned to speak Spanish fluently.

### LIFE'S WORK

In 1916, Walrond found work as a reporter at the Spanish-language newspaper *The Panama Star and Herald*. An American colleague described the United States to him, and Walrond was sufficiently intrigued by the country to leave Colón in 1918. When he arrived in the United States, he was shocked at the treatment he received from New Yorkers, both white and black. Walrond encountered American whites whose racism was more vitriolic than that of Panamanian whites; he also met southern African Americans who disliked West Indian immigrants such as himself.

After being forced to work menial jobs to support himself, Walrond was able to leverage his journalism experience to secure a job at *The Weekly Review*, a magazine published by civil rights campaigner and fellow West Indian immigrant Marcus Garvey. Walrond caught Garvey's eye after winning a writing contest held by Garvey's Universal Negro Improvement Association with a short story that lavished praise on Garvey himself. It was published in Garvey's magazine *The Negro World*, on which Walrond became an associate editor.

Despite his initial high opinion of Garvey, by 1923 Walrond had grown disillusioned with *The Negro World*. Chief among his disagreements with editorial policy was his insistence that aesthetic quality was more essential to literary art than political propaganda. During this period, Walrond also published a series of essays titled "On Being Black" in *The New Republic*; they described the racist attitudes Walrond had witnessed in the Caribbean and New York. In a radical 1923 essay for *Current History*, "The New Negro Faces America," Walrond criticized such eminent African American leaders as W. E. B. Du Bois and Booker T. Washington, calling for a "New Negro" who behaves differently from white Americans, and has no desire to return to Africa. In addition to dismissing a major tenet of Garvey's politics—emigration to Africa—Walrond criticized Garvey directly; he was dropped from the staff of *The Negro World* soon after its publication.

Walrond began writing fiction for the magazine *Opportunity*, a left-leaning publication run by Charles Spurgeon Johnson's National Urban League. *Opportunity* is considered one of the original inspirations for the Harlem Renaissance, and Walrond made significant contributions while politically aligning himself with the New Negro movement. In keeping with his literary philosophy, Walrond's stories aimed for poetic effect rather than racial uplift. From 1925 to 1927, he worked as *Opportunity*'s business manager and was instrumental in encouraging the magazine to feature more young African American writers.

In 1926, Walrond published his masterpiece, a collection of short stories about the Caribbean titled *Tropic Death*. One of the most acclaimed works in all of Caribbean literature, it examines the region's mix of European and African identities in a harsh, unromantic light. The book is often praised for Walrond's pervasive use of dialect, which lends the stories verisimilitude. Despite

*Tropic Death*'s depiction of violence, racism, and despair, it is written in a poetic style that upholds classic aesthetic standards.

Walrond published another acclaimed short story, "City Love," in 1927. He left the United States the next year to visit Panama and begin a follow-up to *Tropic Death*. However, he never finished the planned novel. Walrond moved to Paris in 1929. While he went on to produce short fiction and journalistic articles for Garvey's later periodical *The Black Man*, none of his output received the acclaim of his Harlem writings. He moved to England in 1932 and remained there for the rest of his life.

Walrond suffered from health problems throughout his adult life. He died of a massive coronary—his fifth heart attack—on August 8, 1966.

### SIGNIFICANCE

Walrond had a major influence on the nascent Harlem Renaissance and won major accolades for his writing: a Zona Gale scholarship at the University of Wisconsin, a Harmon Award, and a Guggenheim Fellowship, which financed his trip to Panama. Although he is chiefly remembered for *Tropic Death*, many academics consider his work essential to the canon of Caribbean and African American literature.

*—C. Breault*

### FURTHER READING

Niblett, Michael. "The Arc of the 'Other America': Landscape, Nature, and Region in Eric Walrond's *Tropic Death*." In *Perspectives on the "Other America": Comparative Approaches to Caribbean and Latin American Culture*, edited by Michael Niblett and Kerstin Oloff. New York: Rodopi, 2009. Examines Walrond's depiction of the Caribbean's assortment of races, nationalities, religions, and cultures, and how he experienced them during his travels throughout the region.

Pederson, Carl. "The Caribbean Voices of Claude McKay and Eric Walrond." In *The Cambridge Companion to the Harlem Renaissance*, edited by George Hutchinson. New York: Cambridge University Press, 2007. Useful essay describing the influence of Caribbean immigrants—in particular McKay and Walrond—on African American art and culture during the Harlem Renaissance.

Walrond, Eric. *Winds Can Wake Up the Dead: An Eric Walrond Reader*. Edited by Louis Parascandola. Detroit: Wayne State University Press, 1998. The introduction to this volume of Walrond's fiction provides a thorough biographical sketch.

SEE ALSO: Arna Bontemps; Sterling A. Brown; Paul Laurence Dunbar; Marcus Garvey; Alain Locke; Claude McKay.

# ALEXANDER WALTERS
## Religious leader and activist

*An energetic African Methodist Episcopal bishop, Walters was the leading force in the National Afro-American Council, one of the first major civil rights organizations for African Americans in the United States.*

BORN: August 1, 1858; Bardstown, Kentucky
DIED: February 2, 1917; Brooklyn, New York
AREAS OF ACHIEVEMENT: Civil rights; Religion and theology; Social issues

### EARLY LIFE

Alexander Walters was born a slave on August 1, 1858, in Bardstown, Kentucky. His parents, Henry Walters and Harriet Mathers, also were slaves; Henry was the son of a slave owner. Harriet was a devout Methodist of strong character. Alexander Walters was the fifth of eight children.

Walters was well educated in private schools. He was an outstanding student and was selected by the local African Methodist Episcopal (AME) Zion Church for training for the ministry. AME Zion was a progressive denomination that had branches throughout the United States. Walters graduated from school in 1875. In 1877, he married his first wife, Katie Knox. They would have five children before Katie died in 1896. In 1877, Walters was licensed as a preacher in the Kentucky AME Zion Churches. The next year, he was appointed pastor of AME Zion churches in Corydon and Smith, Kentucky.

Recognizing his capabilities, the AME Zion Conferences elected Walters to successively higher positions in the denomination. With great energy, he set about reviving numerous churches in Kentucky. In 1883, he was appointed pastor of the Stockton Street Church in San Francisco, a historic church that had fallen on hard times and that Walters helped revive. In 1886, he was briefly pastor of the Chattanooga Church before being appointed to the Mother AME Zion Church in New York City, where the denomination had been founded in October, 1796. On May 4, 1892, Walters was elected by the AME Zion General Conference as a bishop of the church; at thirty-four years of age, he was one of the youngest bishops ever appointed by that denomination. His Episcopal district included Kentucky, Missouri, Arkansas, California, West Tennessee, Mississippi, and Oregon. AME Zion was a socially oriented denomination that emphasized education, progress in society, and civil rights. In 1896, Walters's wife died, and he married Emeline Virginia Bird. They would have one child before Emeline's death in 1902. Walters later married Lelia Coleman.

## LIFE'S WORK

As Walters advanced through the ranks of the church, he became more active in working for the benefit of the African American community. He was dismayed by the plight of African Americans and began to organize efforts to win civil rights. He placed blame on the Republican Party for the political compromise of 1877, in which the Republicans agreed to end Reconstruction in return for securing the presidency for Rutherford B. Hayes. Walters wrote that the Republican Party had "sold out" African Americans. In March, 1896, he spoke out against white labor unions for excluding African Americans from industrial jobs.

Alarmed in 1898 by the increase of violence against African Americans, Walters assisted the journalist T. Thomas Fortune in reestablishing the National Afro-American Council as the leading civil rights organization in the country. Many leaders of the African American community joined the council. Walters was elected president, and the group immediately spoke out against lynching, the convict-lease system, railroad segregation, and discrimination in the workplace as the greatest evils facing African Americans. He served as the council's president from 1898 to 1904 and again from 1906 to 1907. In addition to Walters and Fortune, Booker T. Washington and Congressman George White were mainstays of the council. As president, Walters advocated for the use of the term "Afro-American" in place of "colored" or "Negro." However, because of rifts in the National Afro-American Council, Walters launched the National Independent Political League in 1907. For the

rest of his life, Walters was a strong advocate of literacy, industrial work, and accumulation of resources as the surest path to civil rights.

In 1900, Walters was elected president of the Pan-African Association, which was dedicated to assisting people of African descent throughout the world. He grew increasingly interested in African affairs and served as the nonresident AME Zion bishop of Africa from 1904 to 1908, visiting Africa and the West Indies in furtherance of his duties. In 1908, Walters denounced the traditional allegiance of African Americans to the Republican Party and became an ardent Democrat. As head of the National Colored Democratic League, he made several speeches describing how the party of Abraham Lincoln had betrayed African Americans. In this manner, Walters anticipated one of the seismic shifts of American political history: the switch of allegiance of African Americans from the Republican to the Democratic Party over the course of the twentieth century.

Walters originally was an ally of Booker T. Washington and a supporter of his gradualist approach to civil rights. By 1906, however, his sympathies had shifted toward the more activist perspective of W. E. B. Du Bois. In light of the rise of racial violence against African Americans, Walters became an outspoken critic of Washington's pacifist approach. He threw his considerable influence behind Du Bois and the newly founded National Association for the Advancement of Colored People (NAACP), serving on its first national committee. As an ardent Democrat, Walters was disappointed when Woodrow Wilson's election as president in 1912 did not bring appointments of African Americans to federal positions, but he apparently did not object to Wilson's segregationist policies. Walters died in Brooklyn, New York, on February 2, 1917.

## SIGNIFICANCE

Walters's work as a bishop for the AME Zion Church led him into civil rights work for the African American community. He was appalled by the conditions of African American life he saw in his pastoral travels, and he was alarmed by the upsurge of violence against African Americans in the waning years of the nineteenth century. As a result, Walters helped launch one of the first major civil rights organizations for African Americans in American history, the National Afro-American Council. In its major goals, the National Afro-American Council was not a success, but it paved the way for the founding of the NAACP and the National Urban League. Walters's work in the National Afro-American Council reflects his prescience in civil rights matters. He foreshadowed much of the future Civil Rights movement in its leadership by African American clergy, the transition of the bulk of African Americans from supporters of the Republican Party to mainstays of the Democratic Party, his insistence on integration of industrial labor, and even his advocacy of the term "Afro-American" as a more accurate appellation for African Americans.

—*Howard Bromberg*

**FURTHER READING**

Justesen, Benjamin. *Broken Brotherhood: The Rise and Fall of the National Afro-American Council.* Carbondale: Southern Illinois University Press, 2008. History of the National Afro-American Council as the first national civil rights organization in the United States and as predecessor to the NAACP and the National Urban League. Illustrated.

Norrell, Robert. *Up from History: The Life of Booker T. Washington.* Cambridge, Mass.: Belknap Press of Harvard University, 2009. A comprehensive biography of the multidimensional Booker T. Washington, who advocated an accommodationist approach to uplifting African Americans. The author describes how Walters's increasing activism turned him from an ally of Washington to a critic.

Walters, Alexander. *My Life and Work.* New York: Fleming H. Revell, 1917. Walters's memoirs include lengthy quotations from the resolutions of the various religious and civil rights groups in which he was involved. He also explains his views on racial equality and civil rights.

**SEE ALSO:** W. E. B. Du Bois; Henry McNeal Turner; Booker T. Washington; Walter White.

# DIONNE WARWICK

## Pop singer

*With her subtle alto voice and mastery of the intricate rhythms of songs written by Burt Bacharach and Hal David, Warwick was one of the first African American female singers to appeal to a pop audience.*

**BORN:** December 12, 1940; East Orange, New Jersey
**ALSO KNOWN AS:** Marie Dionne Warrick (birth name); Marie Dionne Warwick; Dionne Warwicke
**AREAS OF ACHIEVEMENT:** Music: pop; Radio and television

### EARLY LIFE

Marie Dionne Warwick (DEE-ahn WOHR-wihk) was the oldest of three children of Mancel Warrick, a train porter and chef, and Lee Drinkard, a member of the gospel singing group the Drinkard Sisters. Music was part of Warwick's background, and at age six, at the request of her grandfather, the Reverend Elzae Warrick, Warwick made her singing debut at the New Hope Methodist Church. She learned to play the piano and occasionally sang with the Drinkard Sisters. One of the sisters, her Aunt Emily, nicknamed Cissy, became the mother of Whitney Houston. When they were teens, Warwick and her sister Delia, nicknamed Dee Dee, formed a singing group, the Gospelaires. When visiting the Apollo Theater in Harlem to see the Drinkard Sisters in concert,

Warwick heard that a producer was looking for a group to provide background singing for saxophone player Sam "The Man" Taylor; she jumped at the chance. The next night the Gospelaires sang backup for Taylor.

Other opportunities followed. During weekends and school breaks, the Gospelaires sang background for a number of stars, including Dinah Washington, Ray Charles, and Brook Benton. Warwick's earnings and a scholarship financed college. In 1958, she enrolled at the Hartt School of Music, at the University of Hartford, in Connecticut, intending to become a music teacher. During one of her backup stints for the Drifters in 1961, her voice caught the attention of songwriters Burt Bacharach and his partner Bob Hilliard. Bacharach needed a vocalist for "Move It on the Backbeat," a single he was recording, and he contacted Warwick. Bacharach and his new lyricist, Hal David, began using Warwick as their main vocalist for demonstration records. When a demonstration of their song "It's Love That Really Counts" was presented to Florence Greenberg, owner of Scepter Records, Greenberg said she hated the song but loved the singer, and she offered Warwick a contract.

### LIFE'S WORK

Warwick's recording debut as a solo artist was in August, 1962, singing "Don't Make Me Over." Her last name

(Warrick) was misprinted on the record label as Warwick. The record was a hit. In 1963, Bacharach persuaded actor Marlene Dietrich, then starring in a show at the Olympia Theater in Paris, to invite Warwick to perform. Warwick left college and went to Paris. There, with Dietrich's help, Warwick learned how to dress and move on stage. She was so successful in Paris that the French press called her "The Black Pearl." Warwick was the first African American female contemporary music artist to achieve stardom in Europe.

Back in the states, Warwick began to record hit after hit. Singing the songs of Bacharach and David, Warwick had a sound that appealed to both pop and rhythm-and-blues audiences. "Anyone Who Had a Heart" (1963) was number eight on the Top Ten pop hits chart. Her next record, "Walk on By" (1964), sold more than a million copies and made her a star. Between the mid-1960's and the early 1970's, she had a string of hit songs, including "You'll Never Get to Heaven (If You Break My Heart)" (1964); "Message to Michael" (1966); "Alfie" (1967); "I Say a Little Prayer" (1967); "Do You Know the Way to San Jose?" (1968), which earned Warwick her first Grammy Award; "Promises, Promises" (1968); and "I'll Never Fall in Love Again" (1969). Warwick did not want to record "Alfie," since a number of artists already had recorded the song, but her version hit number fifteen on *Billboard*'s Hot 100, and she sang it at the Academy Awards ceremony in 1967.

Warwick married Bill Elliott, an actor and musician, in 1963; they divorced in 1964 and remarried in 1965. They had two sons and divorced again in 1975. In 1971, Warwick left Scepter Records and signed a five-million-dollar contract with Warner Bros. Records. It was the most money a female vocalist had earned up to that time. She was contracted for albums, and Bacharach and David were to write the songs and produce the records. Her first, *Dionne* (1972), peaked at number fifty-seven on the *Billboard* hot album chart, but Bacharach and David had a major falling out, and their breakup affected Warwick. Without them as songwriters, Warwick's career slumped. When her contract expired in 1977, she left Warner Bros. and moved to Arista Records. Her song "I'll Never Love This Way Again" (1979) sold a million copies and regenerated her career. The album *Dionne* (1979) was certified

*Dionne Warwick.* (Hulton Archive/Getty Images)

platinum, having sold more than one million copies. Her next release, "Déja Vu," hit number one on the adult contemporary chart. In 1980, Warwick won a Grammy Award for Best Pop Vocal Performance, Female, for "I'll Never Love This Way Again" and another Grammy Award for Best Rhythm and Blues Performance, Female, for "Déja Vu." She was the first female artist in the history of the awards to win in both categories in the same year.

During the 1980's Warwick became increasingly involved with charities. She was one of the singers on the single "We Are the World" in 1984, a record that raised money for famine relief in Africa, and in 1985 she persuaded Stevie Wonder, Gladys Knight, and Elton John to record "That's What Friends Are For." The song, written by Bacharach and Carole Bayer Sager, raised more than two million dollars for research into acquired immunodeficiency syndrome (AIDS). Warwick has been involved in supporting other health causes, including sudden infant death syndrome (SIDS) and sickle cell anemia. When Warwick traveled to Brazil in the 1960's, she became fascinated by the people. She adopted a favela (shanty town), recorded *Aquarela do Brasil* (*Watercolor of Brazil*) in 1994, and purchased a home in Rio de Janeiro.

In addition to recording, Warwick has had some success in television. Her first special was for the Columbia Broadcasting System (CBS) in 1969, *The Dionne Warwick Chevy Special*. She hosted a two-hour special, *Solid Gold '79*, that was later adapted into a weekly one-hour show, *Solid Gold*, which she hosted in 1980 and 1981 and for the 1985-1986 season. Warwick tried acting as well, appearing in the film *Slaves* (1969); *Rent-A-Cop* (1988); and the documentary *The Making and Meaning of "We Are Family"* (2002). Over the years she has acted in episodes of various television series and was in the television film *Divas II* (2008). In 2011 she appeared in the reality series *Celebrity Apprentice*. Warwick has continued to record and tour. In 2002 she cofounded the Dionne Warwick Design Group, which redesigns private estates and hotels. She has also written books: *My Point of View* (2003) and *My Life, As I See It* (2010).

### SIGNIFICANCE

Known for her distinctive smooth voice, Warwick has won five Grammy Awards and recorded forty-five albums. In the mid-1960's and into the 1970's, her songs hit the top of the charts. During a career spanning more than four decades, she finished college and became an honorary trustee of the Hartt School of Music. She has

---

### WARWICK'S AMBASSADORSHIPS

Like many celebrities, Dionne Warwick has done a lot of work to support charities. Her particular interest is acquired immunodeficiency syndrome (AIDS). In 1987, she and Stevie Wonder, Elton John, and Gladys Knight recorded "That's What Friends Are For," which became a theme song for the fight against AIDS. It went to number one on the charts and raised millions for AIDS research. In recognition of her work, President Ronald Reagan named her the U.S. Ambassador of Health. Her mission was to educate people on AIDS prevention, and she has traveled around the world to do so. In 1988, she started the Dionne Warwick Foundation to benefit AIDS research and sufferers, and in 1989 she organized a four-day benefit to raise funds for AIDS education and pediatric AIDS care. Friends who attended the black-tie dinner included Sammy Davis, Jr., Frank Sinatra, Cyndi Lauper, and Warwick's cousin, Whitney Houston. Over the years, Warwick has given concerts to benefit AIDS research, and in 2006 she was honored for her work by the Black AIDS Institute. In 2002, Warwick was named Goodwill Ambassador for the United Nations' Food and Agricultural Organization.

---

continually worked to benefit others, particularly those suffering from hunger and AIDS.

—*Marcia B. Dinneen*

### FURTHER READING

Nathan, David. "Dionne Warwick." In *The Soulful Divas*. New York: Billboard Books, 1999. The chapter includes information on Warwick's life and career.

Shuler, Deardra. "Dionne Warwick: Rising to Her Blessings." *New York Amsterdam News*, December 22, 2005, p. 22. Discusses Warwick's career and her efforts for charities.

Warwick, Dionne, and David Freeman Wooley. *My Life, as I See It*. New York: Atria Books, 2010. In her autobiography Warwick reflects on her fifty years in show business and her personal life.

SEE ALSO: Macy Gray; Gladys Knight; Beyoncé Knowles; Patti LaBelle; Stevie Wonder.

# BOOKER T. WASHINGTON
## Educator and activist

*Born into slavery on a tobacco farm, Washington became a famous educator and spokesman for African Americans during the trying period after the end of Reconstruction in the South. From 1890 to 1915, he was the best-known African American in the United States. He was able to raise significant educational funds from wealthy white supporters because of his belief that African Americans should temporarily accept institutional racism while developing their farming and industrial skills.*

**BORN:** April 15, 1856; near Hale's Ford, Virginia
**DIED:** November 14, 1915; Tuskegee, Alabama
**ALSO KNOWN AS:** Booker Taliaferro Washington
**AREAS OF ACHIEVEMENT:** Education; Social issues

### EARLY LIFE

Booker Taliaferro Washington spent his first nine years as a slave on the small tobacco-producing Burroughs plantation. He grew up in a one-room log cabin with a dirt floor and slept on a bed of old rags. His mother, Jane, was the cook for the Burroughs family and their one room also served as the plantation's kitchen. All that Washington ever revealed about his father was that he was a white plantation owner.

In April, 1865, a proclamation was read on the Burroughs Plantation announcing that slavery was at an end. Soon Washington left with his family for Maiden, West Virginia, to join his stepfather. The family moved into another rundown shack. Washington later said that he was thankful that slaves learned how to do many things on the plantation, and he pitied the former slave owners and their families who had not mastered the skills necessary for survival.

Life in Maiden for the nine-year-old Washington meant work in the salt furnace and coal mines, often starting early in the morning. He received some schooling in the afternoons, whenever possible. It was at school that he made up the name Washington, since he was the only student in the class who did not have a surname. An opportunity for some improvement came when he was selected as a houseboy for a wealthy local woman who encouraged Washington to further his education. According to Washington, this experience also pro-

vided him with the values of frugality, cleanliness, and personal morality, which he would carry with him for the rest of his life. In 1872, he left for a new school for black students, the Hampton Institute, one of the earliest freedmen's schools focusing on industrial education. Like many Hampton students, he paid his tuition by working, mostly as a janitor.

### LIFE'S WORK

After graduating with honors in 1875, Washington taught school in Maiden for two years and then attended Wayland Seminary in Washington, D.C. He returned to Hampton in 1879 as an instructor and organized a night program to train seventy-five American Indian students. This program was used as a model for his founding of the Tuskegee Institute in Tuskegee, Alabama, in 1881. The

*Booker T. Washington.* (Library of Congress)

## UP FROM SLAVERY

After its publication in 1901, Booker T. Washington's autobiography, *Up from Slavery*, quickly became the most influential book ever published by an African American. Washington's memoirs provide a vivid account of his life as a slave and cite education as the main driver of his career. His early education came from working in various capacities on the farm, and to this experience he attributes his unshakable belief in hard work and self-reliance.

Although slaves were uneducated, Washington wrote that they were remarkably well informed about national developments. Frequent reports were passed along in whispers about the latest developments in the Civil War, picked up from the post office or from overheard conversations in the "big houses." Washington recalled that he had never met a slave who did not want freedom, nor did he ever meet an African American who wanted a return to slavery.

*Up from Slavery* also details Washington's transition from student to teacher and outlines his development as an educator and founder of the Tuskegee Institute in Alabama. Washington tells the story of Tuskegee's growth from humble beginnings to a two-thousand-acre campus with modern buildings. In the final chapters of the book, Washington describes his career as a public speaker and fund-raiser, and how he pursued African American betterment in the racial climate of the times. Since his "accommodationist" approach was the subject of much controversy, Washington's autobiography is an invaluable source for understanding his motivations and perspective on African Americans' place in American society.

state legislature gave Washington two thousand dollars a year for the school. He started holding classes in an old church and a run-down building. When it rained, one of the taller students would hold an umbrella over the teacher's head to keep him dry. Washington led Tuskegee Institute for the final thirty-four years of his life. At the time of his death in 1915, the institution's endowment was two million dollars.

The school reflected the Washington credo of self-reliance born of hard work. His students made the brick and built most of the buildings on the original campus. The school, which stressed industrial training rather than traditional academic learning, also embodied Washington's willingness to accommodate segregationist policies. For Washington, freedom from economic servitude was the first step before later civil rights could be achieved. He stated his position in his "Atlanta Compromise" address of 1895, which accepted temporary segregation and voting-rights restrictions if whites would

support African American economic and educational advancement: "In all things that are purely social we can be as separate as the fingers, yet one as the hand in all things essential to mutual progress." Washington was a handsome man and a dynamic speaker, and this speech at the Cotton States and International Exposition in Atlanta catapulted him into the national spotlight and gained him fame as the leading spokesperson for African Americans.

Few whites were threatened by Washington's "accommodationist" attitudes, and most African Americans were highly respectful of his rising national prestige. He was able to gain financial support from powerful white supporters such as John D. Rockefeller, Andrew Carnegie, and Henry H. Rogers, a particularly close friend who was also one of the richest men in the United States. Their philanthropy helped Washington establish thousands of small community schools and institutes for African Americans. The Tuskegee Institute grew from two undersupplied buildings to more than one hundred well-equipped buildings. He was a celebrated dinner guest of President Theodore Roosevelt in 1901, becoming the first African American invited into the White House. That same year, Washington's autobiography, *Up from Slavery*, became a widely read work. Soon, he became a political adviser to Roosevelt and President William H. Taft, influencing a multitude of political patronage positions. He also served on the board of trustees for both Fisk and Howard universities. Washington helped found the National Negro Business League in 1900 with the support of Carnegie. Tuskegee Institute, under his guidance, emerged as a national center for industrial and agricultural training as well as a center for training black teachers.

As new African American leadership came to the fore in the Niagara Movement (1905-1909) and under the auspices of the National Association for the Advancement of Colored People (NAACP), beginning in 1909, Washington's ideas were openly challenged. A chief critic was the Harvard sociologist and writer W. E. B. Du Bois, who found Washington's silence on racial oppression and disenfranchisement to be reprehensible. The Washington-Du Bois clash of ideas became one of the great debates in American political life. In his later years, Washington denounced the increasing number of lynchings in the South and advocated making "separate but equal" facilities more equal. He also wrote under assumed names to denounce Jim Crow laws and racial violence directed toward African Americans. However, his central belief was that once African Americans developed needed skills and proved to be responsible citizens, fuller participation in American life would follow. Patience, industry, thrift, and usefulness were the qualities that he felt would lead to eventual equality.

Washington died at Tuskegee on November 14, 1915, at the beginning of both the Great Migration from the rural South to the urban North and World War I, two events that would transform the remainder of the twentieth century. An autopsy performed in 2006 confirmed that the fifty-nine-year-old Washington had died of hypertension. His third wife, Margaret J. Murray, whom he married in 1893 following the deaths of his first two wives, outlived him by ten years. She was instrumental in raising Washington's two sons from his previous marriages.

## SIGNIFICANCE

Washington rose from slavery to become the nation's most influential African American and remains a pioneer on the long journey toward racial equality. He was one of America's great self-made men, and his theme of self-reliance would be repeated for many succeeding generations. However, critics found fault with his acceptance of racial segregation and emphasis on vocational merit as a substitute for political and social equality. His undeniable legacy, though, is as one of America's foremost educators. His birthplace in Franklin County, Virginia, was designated a national monument in 1956.

—*Irwin Halfond*

## FURTHER READING

Bontemps, Arna W. *Young Booker: Booker T. Washington's Early Days*. New York: Dodd and Mead, 1972. Traces the events of Washington's youth and early career that led to his emergence as a famous educator.

Harlan, Louis R. *Booker T. Washington: The Making of a Black Leader, 1856-1901*. New York: Oxford University Press, 1972. A scholarly study of Washington's life and his rise to a national leadership position.

Smock, Raymond W. *Black Leadership in the Age of Jim Crow*. Chicago: Ivan R. Dee, 2009. An analysis of Washington's life and works within the context of the time in which he lived. Written by the editor of fourteen volumes of Washington's private papers.

Thornbrough, Emma. *Booker T. Washington*. Englewood Cliffs, N.J.: Prentice Hall, 1969. A standard biography of Washington.

Verney, Kevern. *Booker T. Washington and Black Leadership in the United States, 1881-1925*. New York: Palgrave Macmillan, 2009. A study of the subtle ways in which Washington tried to undermine the foundations of white supremacy.

Washington, Booker T. *Up from Slavery: An Autobiography*. 1901. Reprint. Mineola, N.Y.: Dover, 1995. Washington's landmark autobiography details his life experiences and philosophies.

**SEE ALSO:** Mary McLeod Bethune; Charlotte Hawkins Brown; Septima Poinsette Clark; Alexander Crummell; W. E. B. Du Bois; James Carmichael Evans; Charlotte L. Forten Grimké; John Hope.

# DENZEL WASHINGTON
## Actor

*In the late twentieth and early twenty-first centuries, Washington distinguished himself as a versatile, critically acclaimed, and popular actor across many genres in film, television, and theater. He won Academy Awards in lead and supporting roles. Financial and artistic success made it possible for Washington to add producing and directing to his repertoire.*

**BORN:** December 28, 1954; Mount Vernon, New York
**ALSO KNOWN AS:** Denzel Hayes Washington, Jr.
**AREAS OF ACHIEVEMENT:** Film: acting; Film: direction

## EARLY LIFE

Denzel Hayes Washington, Jr. (dehn-ZEHL), was born and raised in Mount Vernon, New York. His father was a Pentecostal minister and his mother, who was originally from Georgia, owned and operated a beauty parlor. Washington was a high school basketball star at a private military academy in New York and at a public school in Florida. He played basketball for Fordham University during his first year of college but soon turned his attention to acting. After graduating from Fordham with majors in drama and journalism, Washington was awarded a scholarship to the American Conservatory Theater in San Francisco. He returned to New York City after one year to begin acting on stage and in television.

One of Washington's first important theater roles was playing Malcolm X in the Negro Ensemble Company's Off-Broadway production of *When the Chickens Come Home to Roost* (1981). The handsome young actor next spent six seasons (1982-1988) on the popular television series *St. Elsewhere.*

## LIFE'S WORK

In 1989, Washington had one of his first major film roles as a defiant former slave and Union soldier in *Glory.* He won an Oscar for Best Supporting Actor for his searing performance. Washington next moved into leading roles in independent films, then big-budget films. By the mid-1990's, he had become a Hollywood star.

During the 1990's, Washington appeared in eighteen films, demonstrating tremendous versatility in productions ranging from Shakespearean comedy (*Much Ado About Nothing,* 1993) to science fiction (*Virtuosity,* 1995). He was equally successful as a homophobic lawyer in the

*Denzel Washington in* St. Elsewhere. (AP/Wide World Photos)

celebrated AIDS drama *Philadelphia* (1993), a playful angel in the romance *The Preacher's Wife* (1996), and an investigative journalist in the mystery thriller *The Pelican Brief* (1993). He frequently appeared (often in military or police uniform) in male-dominated thrillers (many directed by Tony Scott), appealingly balancing his athletic grace with a virile intensity. Although perennially named among *People* magazine's Sexiest Men Alive, Washington avoided sexually explicit scenes onscreen, especially with white costars. Four films—*Mo' Better Blues* (1990), *Mississippi Masala* (1991), *Devil in a Blue Dress* (1995), and *He Got Game* (1998), each directed by a person of color—were exceptions to this rule.

Among Washington's many critically acclaimed performances in the 1990's, two major biographical roles earned Academy Award nominations: the title character in Spike Lee's *Malcolm X* (1992) and boxer Rubin Carter in *The Hurricane* (1999). The sense of justified rage that characterized many of Washington's performances particularly suited his portrayals of these two famous men. Meticulously prepared and known for his determination to stay in character, the actor used no stand-in for the grueling fight scenes in *The Hurricane.* Washington brought a special dedication to the complex role of Malcolm X. Not only did the actor build on his earlier stage interpretation of the African American leader and devote himself to extensive research, but Washington also observed Islamic practices, fasting, abstaining from alcohol, and reading the Qur'ān during the long production period. He collaborated with director Lee on the script and became familiar with all aspects of the production. The resulting performance was hailed as a major acting achievement and ranked seventeenth in *Premiere* magazine's 2006 list of the one hundred best performances of the all time.

Washington has played a broad range of real and fictional Africans and African Americans—from a murderous private first class in *A Soldier's Story* (1984) and South African antiapartheid leader Steve Biko in *Cry Freedom* (1987) to a demanding debate coach in *The Great Debaters* (2007) and a suave hoodlum in *American Gangster* (2007)—with grace, intensity, and skill. The actor also lobbied successfully for leading roles that were not race-specific in films such as *Much Ado About Nothing, The Pelican Brief, Philadelphia, Crimson Tide* (1995), *Courage Under Fire* (1996), *The Manchurian Candidate* (2004), and *The Taking of Pelham 123* (2009). In doing so, Washington not only created opportunities for himself but also stood as an example for race-blind casting.

In 2001, Washington became the second African American (after Sidney Poitier) to win an Oscar for Best Actor for his performance as a rogue cop in *Training Day*. Washington was the first African American to win two Academy Awards. In 1990, Washington launched his own production company, Mundy Lane Entertainment. He added directing to his repertoire with *Antwone Fisher* (2002) and *The Great Debaters*, both based on real-life achievements of African Americans, continuing his career-long association with biographical films.

Washington was one of the producers of the postapocalyptic drama *The Book of Eli* (2010), in which he starred as a survivor who travels a devastated world, clutching the only surviving Bible. Returning to the theater intermittently throughout his career, Washington played Brutus in a 2005 Public Theater production of *Julius Caesar* and the working-class protagonist in a Broadway revival of August Wilson's Pulitzer Prize-winning drama *Fences* in 2010. In preparing for his role in *Fences* as a former star athlete trapped in a demeaning job as a garbage collector, Washington recalled his experience of going backstage to see James Earl Jones, who originated the role. In 1983, when Washington was studying drama at Fordham University, seeing the magnetic Jones onstage inspired the younger actor to follow his dream to act on Broadway.

In 2006, Washington published *A Hand to Guide Me*, a book of recollections of the influences of mentoring on the lives of seventy people, many of them famous, including himself. The actor traces much of his success to the guidance of his mentor from the Boys and Girls Club of Mount Vernon, New York. A grateful alumnus, Washington became a spokesman for the Boys and Girls Club of America, and his book was issued to coincide with the centennial of the organization. The actor supports many civic groups and is known for his religious commitment. A devout Pentecostal, he said that he reads the Bible daily. In 1983, he married Pauletta Pearson Washington, a professional singer and the daughter of the president of a historically black university in North Carolina. They have four children. In 1995, the couple renewed their wedding vows in South Africa before Archbishop Desmond Tutu.

---

## WASHINGTON ON *ST. ELSEWHERE*

When the hospital drama series *St. Elsewhere* was first broadcast on NBC in October, 1982, Denzel Washington, who played the sincere young surgeon Dr. Philip Chandler, was unfamiliar to most Americans. When the celebrated series ended in 1988, Washington had demonstrated his broad audience appeal and was on the brink of major stardom. Although he appeared in all 137 episodes, Washington was a supporting player on the series, a position that afforded him the dual advantage of regular audience exposure and the freedom to accept roles in films shot during the series's production period.

Set in a dilapidated Boston teaching hospital, St. Eligius, *St. Elsewhere* focused on the personal lives of the overworked staff, all of whom were portrayed as fallible, even quirky, individuals. With its overlapping storylines, a dark sense of humor, and sometimes depressing outcomes, the show never gained a large audience; however, it did draw a small, devoted, and upscale following that pleased advertisers. Produced by MTM Enterprises, *St. Elsewhere* earned sixty-three Emmy nominations and won thirteen awards. The ensemble cast on the long-running series featured three African Americans: Washington; Eric Laneuville, who played the orderly Luther Hawkins; and Alfre Woodard, who appeared on thirteen episodes between 1985 and 1987 as gynecologist Roxanne Turner. Drs. Chandler and Turner added some intrigue to the series with an on-and-off romance. In the course of the show's six seasons, the character Chandler evolved from an idealistic young doctor, worried that he might not meet the high standards expected of a surgeon, to an experienced physician who hated his chosen profession.

---

### SIGNIFICANCE

The most decorated African American actor of his generation, Washington drew critical acclaim for the intensity and depth of his screen and stage performances. Both admirers and detractors characterized Washington as the Sidney Poitier of his generation: a handsome leading man who exudes intelligence, dignity, and a sense of controlled power, and who appeals to both male and female viewers of all races. Although Washington appeared in films of various genres between 1987 and 2009, he played more biographical roles than any other film star, bringing a sense of authenticity to the lives of many diverse men. One of his most popular biographical roles was Herman Boone, a football coach at a newly integrated Virginia high school. In the family film *Remember the Titans* (2000), the authoritarian Boone forms a remarkably successful team from racially divided and suspicious players of both races. In this influential role and many others, Washington simultaneously embodies a strong pride in his race and supports a project of integration and mutual understanding. As the twenty-first century began, the celebrated actor continued to be highly regarded. He was named America's Favorite Actor three years in a row by a national Harris poll and commanded a salary of twenty million dollars for each film role.

—*Carolyn Anderson*

**FURTHER READING**

Brode, Douglas. *Denzel Washington: His Films and Career.* Secaucus, N.J.: Carol, 1997. A general biographical introduction precedes nineteen chapters, each devoted to a single film. Black-and-white and color photographs.

Guerrero, Ed. *Framing Blackness: The African American Image in Film.* Philadelphia: Temple University Press, 1993. Important survey and analysis of how African Americans have been portrayed in American cinema, with considerable attention to Washington's career. Black-and-white photographs.

Lee, Spike, and Kaleem Aftab. *That's My Story and I'm Sticking to It.* New York: W. W. Norton, 2005. Career biography of Lee, with attention to his many film collaborations with Washington. Black-and-white photographs.

Samuels, Allison. *Off the Record: A Reporter Unveils the Celebrity Worlds of Hollywood, Hip-Hop, and Sports.* New York: Amistad/HarperCollins, 2007. Admiring profiles of dozens of famous African Americans, including Washington.

Washington, Denzel, with Daniel Paisner. *A Hand to Guide Me: Legends and Leaders Celebrate the People Who Shaped Their Lives.* Des Moines, Iowa: Meredith Books, 2006. Compilation of personal stories, including Washington's, about the importance of mentoring.

**SEE ALSO:** Halle Berry; Don Cheadle; Laurence Fishburne; Jamie Foxx; Spike Lee; Malcolm X; Sidney Poitier; Will Smith; Alfre Woodard.

# HAROLD WASHINGTON
## Politician and lawyer

*Washington mobilized the overwhelming support of African American voters to defy Chicago's long-entrenched Democratic political machine and become the city's first black mayor.*

**BORN:** April 15, 1922; Chicago, Illinois
**DIED:** November 25, 1987; Chicago, Illinois
**ALSO KNOWN AS:** Harold Lee Washington
**AREAS OF ACHIEVEMENT:** Government and politics; Law

### EARLY LIFE

Harold Lee Washington was one of four sons born to Roy and Bertha Washington. Roy, a lawyer, was one of the first Democratic precinct captains in Chicago, and he worked to solicit votes in the Third Ward, a predominantly African American area on the city's South Side. Harold Washington learned about politics at an early age, helping his father campaign for Franklin D. Roosevelt in 1932 and meeting some of Chicago's mayors and aldermen (city council members). Washington was a member of the first graduating class of segregated Du Sable High School. In 1942, he was drafted into the armed forces and sent to the Philippines, where he was assigned to a segregated engineering unit of the Army Air Force.

In 1946, Washington enrolled at Roosevelt College (now Roosevelt University), one of the few Chicago-area universities to accept black students. He was an active member of the student council and eventually was elected student body president. After graduating in 1949, Washington attended Northwestern University Law School, where he was the only black student in his class. He earned his law degree in 1952 and went to work the next year in his father's law practice.

### LIFE'S WORK

Washington never enjoyed practicing law. His first love was politics, and he launched his political career by working as a precinct captain for Ralph Metcalfe, an alderman representing Chicago's Third Ward. Metcalfe became Washington's mentor, and he assigned Washington to organize and advise the Young Democrats group in his ward.

It is impossible to appreciate Washington's achievements without understanding Chicago's peculiar political culture. When Washington was embarking upon a political career, the most powerful organization in the city was the Cook County Democratic Committee, whose fifty members doled out patronage, granted contracts and other favors, and worked to elect committee-endorsed

*Harold Washington.* (AP/Wide World Photos)

candidates. The Democratic machine reached the height of its power during the administration of Mayor Richard J. Daley, who was in office from 1955 until his death in December, 1976. Under Daley's leadership, the machine severely restricted the aspirations of African American politicians, limiting its support only to candidates who ran for office in a few predominantly black districts.

Washington resented the machine's stranglehold on politics and believed it was an obstacle to civil rights, but he initially worked with it in order to establish his political career. In 1964, with the machine's backing, he successfully ran for a seat in the Illinois House of Representatives, in which he served from 1965 through 1976. Washington similarly obtained machine support in his 1975 bid for the Illinois Senate, in which he served from 1976 through 1980. As a state lawmaker he walked a tightrope, voting with the machine on some issues while defying it on others, particularly in his staunch advocacy of civil rights. His accomplishments include organizing a

black legislative caucus and sponsoring fair housing legislation, a human rights act, and a measure declaring Martin Luther King, Jr.'s birthday a state holiday.

In the early 1970's, however, Washington suffered two blows to his career. In 1970, the Chicago Bar Association suspended his law license for one year after it received complaints that Washington had cheated clients out of $205. The next year, the Internal Revenue Service charged him with failing to file income tax returns for four years; although he paid his taxes in these years, he owed the government $508. Washington was sentenced to forty days in jail, three years' probation, and a $1,000 fine; to fulfill his sentence, he spent thirty-six days in the Cook County Jail.

After Daley's death, Washington broke with the machine and ran as an independent candidate in the 1977 special mayoral election. His entered the race too late, ran a poorly organized campaign, and obtained only 11 percent of the vote. He had better luck in 1979, when he ran as an independent candidate for the U.S. House of Representatives, in which he served from 1980 until he became mayor. He was one of the Democratic congressional leaders who worked to extend the Voting Rights Act.

While Washington was in Congress, Chicago's African American community was engaged in its own efforts to extend voting power. In June, 1982, a coalition of community organizations, African American churches, and African American businesses organized a voter registration drive that added more than 127,000 African Americans to the voting rolls.

The success of this campaign was one of the reasons that Washington announced his intention to run as an independent candidate in the February, 1983, Democratic mayoral primary. His opponents in this race were Mayor Jane Byrne, who was backed by the machine, and Richard M. Daley, the Illinois attorney general and son of the former mayor. The election galvanized the city's African Americans, who saw Washington's candidacy as a crusade for political liberation; one commentator remarked that his campaign rallies were more like religious revivals than political gatherings. Washington won the primary with 37 percent of the vote, compared with 33 percent for Byrne and 30 percent for Daley; more than 90 percent of Washington's votes came from African Americans, who turned out in unprecedented numbers and formed a solid bloc of support.

Normally, the winner in the Democratic primary was backed by the party's machine and easily defeated the Republican opponent in the general election. Washington, however, did not receive the machine's endorsement, and only a few of its members supported him; many more either publically opposed him or privately supported his Republican opponent, Bernard Epton. While the primary generally was free of racism, the general election was an ugly brawl in which Epton and his supporters stoked white voters' fears of an African American mayor who would allow African Americans to move into their neighborhoods and would control the public schools and police department. Epton also attacked Washington for, among other things, failing to pay his income taxes.

The election on April 12, 1983, was the closest Chicago mayoral race since 1919, with the majority of voters selecting candidates solely on the basis of their race. Washington won with 52 percent of the vote, compared with 48 percent for Epton; once again, Washington received solid support from African Americans and also polled well among Latinos, while the majority of whites voted for Epton. On April 29, 1983, Washington became Chicago's forty-second mayor—and its first African American mayor.

Despite his victory, Washington continued to encounter machine opposition during his early years in office. Twenty-nine of the city's fifty aldermen were machine supporters who refused to adopt his proposed legislation. During these so-called Council Wars, Washington typically would introduce a bill, which would be defeated by a vote of twenty-nine to twenty-one aldermen; the machine majority would then revise his proposal and adopt its own bill; Washington, in turn, would veto the revised bill, knowing the machine lacked sufficient support to overturn his veto.

The battle continued until early 1986, when a federal judge ruled that Chicago's wards violated the federal Voting Rights Act by denying adequate representation to African Americans and Latinos; the judge ordered that special elections be held in seven wards concurrently with the March, 1986, primary. As a result of these elections, Washington obtained the support of twenty-five alderman, and as chairman of the city council he could break a tie vote to enact his proposals, including a tenant's bill of rights and a political ethics ordinance.

By the time Washington was reelected in 1987, some of the city's white voters had softened their opposition to him, and the primary and general elections lacked the fervent racism of the 1983 race. However, Washington's victory was short-lived. On November 25, 1987, he suffered a massive heart attack while in his office, and he died at the age of sixty-five.

**SIGNIFICANCE**

Washington's election in 1983 reversed the trend of declining African American participation in electoral politics; Chicago's African American community mobilized and asserted their rights as citizens to vote and take control of the city's institutions. This political empowerment would have been significant in any city, but it was particularly important in Chicago, where an all-powerful Democratic machine had a political stranglehold. Washington's victory dealt a serious blow to the machine and in so doing created opportunities for other independents, including African Americans and Latinos, to play a greater role in Chicago politics.

*—Rebecca Kuzins*

**FURTHER READING**

Kleppner, Paul. *Chicago Divided: The Making of a Black Mayor.* De Kalb: Northern Illinois University Press,

1985. A history of Chicago's politics and changing demographics from 1870 until the 1983 mayoral election.

Levinsohn, Florence Hamlish. *Harold Washington: A Political Biography.* Chicago: Chicago Review Press, 1983. Levinsohn, a Chicagoan and friend of Washington, brings her knowledge of the city to her coverage of his political career, culminating in the 1983 election.

Muwakkil, Salim. *Harold! Photographs from the Harold Washington Years.* Photographs by Antonio Dickey and Marc PoKempner. Evanston, Ill.: Northwestern

University Press, 2007. Collection of photographs documenting Washington's mayoral campaign and tenure.

Rivlin, Gary. *Fire on the Prairie: Chicago's Harold Washington and the Politics of Race.* New York: Henry Holt, 1992. The best coverage of Washington's career, describing the people and sociopolitical developments that led to his mayoral victory.

**SEE ALSO:** Tom Bradley; Willie Brown; David Dinkins; Maynard Jackson; Dutch Morial; Andrew Young; Coleman Young.

# KENNY WASHINGTON
## Football player

*Washington was a star football player at the University of California at Los Angeles. After many years of being denied the opportunity to play professionally because of his race, in 1946 he broke the color line in the National Football League when the Los Angeles Rams signed him to a contract.*

**BORN:** August 31, 1918; Los Angeles, California
**DIED:** June 24, 1971; Los Angeles, California
**ALSO KNOWN AS:** Kenneth S. Washington; Kingfish
**AREAS OF ACHIEVEMENT:** Sports: baseball; Sports: football

### EARLY LIFE

Kenneth S. Washington, often called Kenny, was born on August 31, 1918, in Los Angeles. His father, Edgar, and his mother, Marione Lanone, married while both were teenagers. When Edgar left Marione, Washington moved in with his grandparents. Washington did not see much of his father while growing up. Edgar Washington had small parts in several films, including *Gone with the Wind* (1939), and played baseball with several Negro League teams. The Washingtons were the only black family in the predominantly Italian neighborhood of Lincoln Heights. Washington's grandmother, Susie Washington, worked as a janitor for a local grammar school. He was raised mostly by his grandmother and his uncle Rocky, a lieutenant with the Los Angeles Police Department. Rocky attended Washington's football games, advised him, and was a strong presence throughout his life.

Washington was a talented all-around athlete. He played football, baseball, and basketball and also partici-

pated in track and boxing at the Downey Avenue Playground. Washington played baseball and football at Lincoln High School, graduating in 1936.

When his top college choices, Notre Dame and the University of Southern California, would not accept him because of his race, Washington decided to attend the University of California at Los Angeles (UCLA) because it admitted African Americans and had a national reputation in sports. He had already developed a local following in high school, and his fans followed his college career.

### LIFE'S WORK

In the late 1930's, UCLA became one of the first colleges to recruit black players. When Washington enrolled at the university, tens of thousands of fans came to watch him play football, many of them African American. Washington began attending UCLA in the fall of 1936 and played on the freshman football team as a single-wing tailback. His teammates included longtime friend Woody Strode and, two years later, Jackie Robinson. When the team traveled, the African American players had to endure racist taunts, punishing blows, and other dirty tactics from opposing players. In 1939, Washington was the first player from UCLA to be named a consensus All-American. That year, he led the nation in total offense. Nevertheless, he was not picked to play in the postseason East-West Shrine Game, an honor given to the nation's best players.

The National Football League (NFL) had not started out segregated. Fritz Pollard, an African American, had been one of the league's first stars in the 1920's and its first black coach. However, after the 1932 season, the NFL owners had agreed to an informal ban on African American players. Thus, in 1940, Washington and Strode signed contracts with the semiprofessional football team the Hollywood Bears, a charter member of the Pacific Coast Football League, which was essentially a high-level minor league. In the spring of 1940, Washington earned his bachelor's degree from UCLA. The following September, he married June Bradley. Semiprofessional football was not a full-time job, so Washington became a police officer. He played for the Hollywood Bears during the 1940-1941 season and again in 1945. In 1944, he played for the San Francisco Clippers. Washington spent 1942-1943 touring with the United Service Organizations (USO). A knee injury prevented him from active duty during World War II.

The Los Angeles Rams of the NFL signed Washington to a professional contract on March 21, 1946. The Rams had moved from Cleveland and petitioned the Los Angeles Coliseum Commission to use the Coliseum, a venue previously reserved for amateur sports. At the meeting to hear the petition, three African American journalists, Edward "Abie" Robinson, Halley Harding, and Herman Hill, objected to segregated teams using the public stadium. The commission passed a measure prohibiting segregation. Shortly after, the Rams signed Washington, followed by Strode in mid-May. Segregation prevented Washington and others from playing professional football during their peak physical years, but they did play well when given the chance.

In 1948, Washington retired after three seasons with the Rams. In 1956, he was inducted into the National Football Foundation's College Hall of Fame. UCLA retired his number, thirteen, making Washington the first player to receive that honor. After football, Washington worked as a public relations executive for a liquor company and baseball scout for the Los Angeles Dodgers. He had a son, Kenny Washington, Jr. Washington died June 24, 1971, in Los Angeles after battling congestive heart and lung illnesses.

## SIGNIFICANCE

Washington reintegrated the National Football League after twelve seasons of segregation. When he signed with the Los Angeles Rams in 1946, Washington helped usher in a new era of integration in sports after World War II. In the late 1930's and early 1940's, he was considered one of the greatest football players ever to play the game. Denied the opportunity to attend the college of his choice or pursue a professional career during his prime because of his race, Washington eventually made his mark on an integrated college team, semiprofessional team, and professional football team.

*—Amy Essington*

## FURTHER READING

Levy, Alan H. *Tackling Jim Crow: Racial Segregation in Professional Football.* Jefferson, N.C.: McFarland, 2003. An overview of the development of segregation in football and the move to reintegrate the sport.

Ross, Charles K. *Outside the Lines: African Americans and the Integration of the National Football League.* New York: New York University Press, 1999. Gives the history of the integration of the National Football League while raising questions about the participation of African American athletes in social change.

Smith, Thomas G. "Outside the Pale: The Exclusion of Blacks from the National Football League, 1934-1946." *Journal of Sport History* 15, no. 3 (Winter, 1988): 225-281. An article about the period of segregation in professional football from the falling of the color line to the reintegration of the sport.

Strode, Woody, and Sam Young. *Goal Dust, an Autobiography: The Warm and Candid Memoirs of a Pioneer Black Athlete and Actor.* Lanham, Md.: Madison Books, 1990. An autobiography by Washington's longtime friend and teammate, athlete and movie star Woody Strode.

Wolff, Alexander. "The NFL's Jackie Robinson." *Sports Illustrated*, October 12, 2009. Compelling chronicle of Washington's life and career, with emphasis on the events surrounding his 1946 reintegration of the NFL, especially the role of Los Angeles journalist Harding in pushing the Rams to sign Washington.

**SEE ALSO:** Marcus Allen; Jim Brown; Bob Hayes; Walter Payton; Jackie Robinson; Art Shell; O. J. Simpson; Woody Strode.

# MAXINE WATERS
## Politician

*As one of the longest-serving African American women in the U.S. Congress, Waters demonstrated her dedication to civil rights, improving communities, health care, global issues, and economic incentives, while also serving as a role model for women and minorities interested in greater political or other public involvement.*

**BORN:** August 15, 1938; St. Louis, Missouri
**ALSO KNOWN AS:** Maxine Moore Waters; Maxine Moore (birth name)
**AREAS OF ACHIEVEMENT:** Government and politics; Social issues

### EARLY LIFE

Born on August 15, 1938, in St. Louis, Missouri, to Remus Moore and Velma Lee Carr Moore, Maxine Moore Waters had twelve siblings. Beginning at age thirteen, she found employment in factories and restaurants. At age eighteen, Waters married Edward Waters. The couple had two children, Edward and Karen, before divorcing in 1972.

Waters moved to Los Angeles in 1961 with her husband and children. She worked in a garment factory and later became a telephone operator, but her life changed when she joined the federally funded Head Start program in Watts as an assistant teacher. This experience inspired her to earn a bachelor's degree in sociology from California State University, Los Angeles, from which she graduated in 1970.

Waters's work with Head Start launched her political career. She worked with the children's parents to ask for additional funding for the young program. As part of these efforts, Waters and the parents contacted legislators and asked for additional resources for their economically disadvantaged community. Moving from the classroom to city government, Waters became the chief deputy for City Councilman David Cunningham, Jr., in 1973.

### LIFE'S WORK

Waters's life experience led her to align herself with the Democratic Party, and she left city government in 1976 to run for election to the California State Assembly. Elected on her first attempt, Waters spent fourteen years in state government and dedicated her efforts to improving economic opportunities and living conditions for women and minorities. She wrote bills concerning the awarding of public contracts to qualified minority applicants and protections for tenants. Thinking globally, Waters persuaded her fellow assembly members to divest state pension funds from companies invested in South Africa, which was then a practitioner of apartheid.

While in the Assembly, Waters continued to champion Head Start at Democratic National Conventions from 1972 through 1988. She also helped create the Child Abuse Prevention Training Program, one of the first programs of its type in the country.

In 1977, Waters married former professional football player Sidney Williams. Williams was later appointed a United States ambassador to the Commonwealth of the Bahamas by President Bill Clinton.

In 1991, Waters moved into national politics with her election to the U.S. Congress. She began with a seat in the Twenty-ninth Congressional District but successfully ran for the larger Thirty-fifth District seat in 1992. Waters's new district included South Central Los Angeles, among other areas, en-

*Maxine Waters.* (Roll Call/Getty Images)

couraging her to concentrate on creative solutions for a variety of issues such as helping single-parent families.

Waters served on the House Committee on Financial Services and was chairwoman of the Financial Services Subcommittee on Housing and Community Opportunity, which fit well with her emphasis on community development. She also served as a member of the Committee on the Judiciary and was a member of the Congressional Black Caucus.

Waters became known for her focus on welfare reform and affirmative action. She also advanced discussion of women's health and other health issues, including legislation addressing the needs of patients with common illnesses such as diabetes, cancer, and Alzheimer's disease. While lamenting the effects of illegal drugs on communities, Waters argued against mandatory minimum sentences for drug offenders because these regulations did not allow judges leniency. During the presidential campaigns of fellow Democrat Jesse Jackson in 1984 and 1988, Waters offered substantial support in speeches and public arenas, hoping to help elect an African American president. Regarding foreign policy, Waters spoke out against the Iraq War during the early twenty-first century, voting against the resolution that formally started the war.

Demonstrating her interest in helping minorities in other countries, Waters took an active role in Congress regarding debt relief. After the devastating earthquake in Haiti in January, 2010, Waters visited the small country and sponsored a successful bill titled Debt Relief for Earthquake Recovery, freeing Haiti from its earlier international debts and allowing the country to focus on rebuilding its infrastructure and economy.

In 2010, Waters faced allegations of ethical violations. It was alleged that, during the crisis that led to the massive federal bailout of the banking industry, Waters had attempted to steer funds to a bank in which her husband held stock. Waters denied the charges, saying she had sought to aid minority-owned banks in general. A trial scheduled to begin late in the year was postponed indefinitely in November.

## SIGNIFICANCE

While representing some of California's most economically disadvantaged districts, Waters drew on her own experiences to promote legislation in the United States House of Representatives that she believed would directly benefit economically disadvantaged Americans. She also actively pursued justice in cases of international or corporate misuses of power and had a passion for engaging in foreign policy debates.

—*Bonnye Busbice Good*

## FURTHER READING

Bullard, Robert, ed. *The Quest for Environmental Justice: Human Rights and the Politics of Pollution.* Foreword by Maxine Waters. San Francisco: Sierra Club Books, 2005. Waters's foreword spells out her own beliefs concerning the corporate abuses of the natural environment and communities.

Gill, Laverne McCain. *African American Women in Congress: Forming and Transforming History.* Piscataway, N.J.: Rutgers University Press, 1997. Gill examines Waters's political stances on poverty and empowering the disadvantaged in her district.

Waters, Maxine. "Youth and the Political Process." In *Say It Loud: Great Speeches on Civil Rights and African American Identity*, edited by Catherine Ellis and Stephen Drury Smith. New York: New Press, 2010. Waters's speech focuses on getting children and young adults involved in politics, noting that governmental decisions directly affect young people.

**SEE ALSO:** Shirley Chisholm; Jesse Jackson; Sheila Jackson Lee; Barbara Jordan; Eleanor Holmes Norton.

# MUDDY WATERS
## Blues musician

*Waters is best known as the pioneer of postwar electric Chicago blues. His band, the premier electric blues combo in the 1950's, became the archetype of the genre.*

**BORN:** April 4, 1913; Jug's Corner, Issaquena County, near Rolling Fork, Mississippi
**DIED:** April 30, 1983; Westmont, Illinois
**ALSO KNOWN AS:** McKinley A. Morganfield
**AREAS OF ACHIEVEMENT:** Music: blues; Music: rock and roll

### EARLY LIFE

McKinley A. Morganfield was born in Jug's Corner, Mississippi, and grew up on Stovall's Plantation outside Clarksdale. After he lost his mother early, he was raised by his grandmother, who gave him his nickname for playing in the muddy puddles near the Mississippi River.

Waters bought his first guitar, a popular and affordable instrument at the time, in 1930, when he was about seventeen. He learned slide guitar techniques from legendary Delta blues performer Son House.

While working on the plantation, Waters performed at juke joints and house parties. In the summer of 1941, he was visited by African American musicologist John Work III of Fisk University and folklorist Alan Lomax of the Library of Congress, who were working on the Coahoma County Study. They returned to Waters the following summer and recorded his performances, including "Country Blues" and "I Be's Troubled." Hearing his own performances for the first time gave Waters the confidence to become a professional musician. In the summer of 1943, after a fight with his plantation owner, Waters moved to Chicago, which became home base for the rest of his life.

### LIFE'S WORK

Waters pursued a musical career in Chicago while working a day job. After having made commercially unsuccessful records for 20th Century Records and Columbia Records in 1946, he got another chance from Aristocrat Records (later Chess Records) in 1947. His record from the third session in 1948, "I Can't Be Satisfied" coupled with "I Feel Like Going Home" (reworkings of "I Be's Troubled" and "Country Blues," respectively), was an unexpected hit both for Waters and the company.

With the new sounds of electric slide guitar, Waters's lyrical descriptions of frustration in a new environment

and nostalgia for the South fascinated audiences, who, like Waters himself, had recently moved from the rural South to the big city. Another salient theme in his early songs was womanizing, particularly illicit affairs, heard in songs such as "Rollin' Stone" and "She Moves Me."

Waters had different ensembles for recordings and live performances. In the studio, he had a small ensemble consisting only of his own electric guitar supported by a standup bass. For crowded club gigs, on the other hand, Waters played with electric guitarist Jimmy Rogers, amplified harmonica player Little Walter, and drummer "Baby Face Leroy" Foster. Waters's recording producer Leonard Chess was initially reluctant to change Waters's small ensemble, but he gradually allowed Waters to bring in his band members. In 1951, Foster was replaced by Elgin Evans, and in 1953, pianist Otis Spann became a regular member of Waters's recording ensemble. With the extended combo, Waters explored his musical potential and dynamism. He was no longer playing amplified Delta blues but was defining the new sounds of electric Chicago blues.

In 1954, Willie Dixon, a house songwriter at Chess

*Muddy Waters.* (Michael Ochs Archives/Getty Images)

Records, offered Waters "Hoochie Coochie Man." This song, which combined an urban sound with a secularized myth of a powerful figure coming out of the Delta, became Waters's signature. For Waters, Dixon's compositions, such as "I Just Want to Make Love to You," "I'm Ready," "Don't Go No Further," "I Love the Life I Live, I Live the Life I Love," and "Close to You," were indispensable parts of his repertoire.

Around the end of the 1950's Waters started to gain fame outside African American communities. In 1958, he was invited to perform in England. While his performance with electric guitar stunned some audience members who expected he would play acoustic, it appealed to the musicians who later took part in the British Invasion. Also in the United States, Waters won new white fans with his enthusiastic performance, especially "Got My Mojo Working," at the Newport Jazz Festival in July, 1960.

In 1976, after Chess Records closed down, Waters signed with Blue Sky Records, a Columbia Records subsidiary. He made several recordings there with guitarist Johnny Winter. Their collaboration resulted in three Grammy-winning records. Waters played throughout the United States, Europe, and Japan until his death in 1983. In 1987, he was inducted into the Rock and Roll Hall of Fame as one of the genre's "early influences."

### SIGNIFICANCE

Waters's influence is best shown by his iconic early recording "Rollin' Stone," which inspired the name of the famous rock-and-roll band, Bob Dylan's song "Like a Rolling Stone," and the name of the legendary music magazine. Many of his band members also had successful solo careers, such as harmonica players Junior Wells and James Cotton and guitarists Bob Margolin and Luther Johnson, as well as the members of Waters's classic band in the 1950's.

—*Mitsutoshi Inaba*

### FURTHER READING

Gordon, Robert. *Can't Be Satisfied: The Life and Times of Muddy Waters*. Boston: Little, Brown, 2002. A biography based on interviews with family members and close associates. Includes an appendix covering Gordon's research in the archives of the Coahoma County Study.

O'Neal, Jim, and Amy van Singel. "Muddy Waters." In *The Voice of the Blues: Classic Interviews from "Living Blues" Magazine*. New York: Routledge, 2002. Collection of Waters's interviews from 1974, 1980, and 1981.

Tooze, Sandra B. *Muddy Waters: The Mojo Man*. Toronto: ECW Press, 1997. The author captures Waters's personality through interviews of Waters and his bandmates. Includes a detailed discography.

SEE ALSO: Bobby Blue Bland; Big Boy Crudup; Willie Dixon; W. C. Handy; John Lee Hooker; B. B. King; Little Walter; Ma Rainey; Big Joe Turner.

# FAYE WATTLETON
## Activist

*Wattleton made history when she became the first black woman to head the Planned Parenthood Federation of America. The organization, which provides comprehensive reproductive health care and information, serves as one of the world's largest and most visible advocacy organizations for women's health. Wattleton, who also was the youngest person and first woman to head Planned Parenthood since its founder, served as the group's president until 1992. She used her position to campaign for women's reproductive rights, including access to legal abortions and comprehensive sex education.*

BORN: July 8, 1943; St. Louis, Missouri
ALSO KNOWN AS: Alyce Faye Wattleton
AREAS OF ACHIEVEMENT: Medicine; Women's rights

### EARLY LIFE

Alyce Faye Wattleton (WAH-tul-tuhn) was born on July 8, 1943, in St. Louis, Missouri, to George Wattleton, a laborer, and Ozie Garrett Wattleton, an itinerant preacher. An only child, she often accompanied her parents to church camp meetings all over the country. At other times, she was sent to stay with various church members or relatives in St. Louis and Mississippi. Wattleton later credited her strength of will and conviction, as well as her commitment to public service, to her mother's influence. She finished high school outside Houston, Texas, and decided to pursue a career in nursing. In 1960, nursing was one of the few professions open to black women, and offered a way for Wattleton to fulfill her childhood dream of caring for sick people.

Also during 1960, Wattleton entered the nursing program at Ohio State University. It was during her clinical training that Wattleton found her calling in obstetrics. Upon her graduation in June of 1964, she briefly taught labor-and-delivery nursing near Dayton, Ohio, before entering a graduate program in maternal and infant care at Columbia University. There, she received training in midwifery. Her experiences as a nurse and midwife enabled her to witness firsthand the life-threatening complications that often resulted from women's attempts to end unwanted pregnancies themselves at a time when abortion was illegal in most states. Wattleton viewed these conditions as a consequence of the poverty she observed in the surrounding Harlem neighborhood, and decided to focus her career on public health.

Upon earning a master's degree, Wattleton returned to Dayton to work for the local health department, setting up the first prenatal clinics in two urban neighborhoods. Wattleton's work in maternal health care, which attuned her to the problems of teenagers and poor women, informed her inclination to fight for the reproductive rights of all women. In September of 1970, she became executive director of the Planned Parenthood affiliate in Dayton. More than two years later, on January 22, 1973, the Supreme Court handed down its landmark decision in *Roe v. Wade*, invalidating most federal and state restrictions on abortion. The ensuing backlash prompted Planned Parenthood to expand its focus to reproductive rights advocacy.

## LIFE'S WORK

On January 28, 1978, Wattleton was appointed the president of the Planned Parenthood Federation of America. In this position, she played a prominent role in defining national debates over reproductive rights, women's health, and family planning. Her professionalism, honed from her years of experience as a nurse-midwife, enabled her to present a knowledgeable image during the contentious public battles over reproductive rights during the 1980's and 1990's. The presidencies of both Ronald Reagan and George H. W. Bush, combined with the growing influence of a number of conservative and religious organizations formed in response to *Roe v. Wade*, brought about a series of legislative and judicial challenges to the rights established by the decision. Most of these challenges centered on minors' and poor women's access to family planning programs and legal abortions. Wattleton helped mold Planned Parenthood into a crucial lobbying operation and, in numerous public appearances, demonstrated her fierce dedication to preserving women's reproductive rights in the face of highly contentious challenges.

Additionally, Planned Parenthood had served as an institutional provider of family planning services overseas since 1971, linking population policies with economic development. As the president of Planned Parenthood, Wattleton became the public face of the organization's legislative battles on behalf of women both in the United States and in the developing world.

During her tenure at Planned Parenthood, Wattleton wrote and lectured frequently in support of comprehensive sex education in schools as a means of reducing the rates of teenage pregnancy, arguing that these interventions improved young women's chances for leading independent and productive lives. She served as the organization's leader until 1992.

Wattleton's activist work for women's rights earned her numerous honors and awards. She was inducted into the National Women's Hall of Fame in 1993, and she has received the American Public Health Association's Award of Excellence, the Congressional Black Caucus Foundation Humanitarian Award, and the Women's Honors in Public Service Award from the American Nurses Association, among other distinctions. She also has been awarded many honorary degrees and has served on the boards of directors of numerous nonprofit organizations, as well as both private and public corporations.

## SIGNIFICANCE

Wattleton devoted her career to securing reproductive rights for all women. After her retirement from Planned Parenthood, she continued her advocacy work on behalf of women, cofounding the nonprofit Center for Gender Equality in 1995 (later renamed the Center for the Advancement of Women). The center is a nonprofit institution committed to research, education, and advocacy of women's rights and other progressive health and social issues. Wattleton continued to write and lecture on the centrality of reproductive rights to broader struggles for gender equality and social justice.

—*Patricia G. Davis*

## FURTHER READING

Carr, Pamela, and Faye Wattleton. "Which Way Black America? Anti-Abortion/Pro-Choice." *Ebony* 44, no. 12 (October 1, 1989): 134-138. Wattleton and anti-abortion activist Carr outline their opposing views on the issue of abortion and its implications for the African American community.

Hull, N. E. H., and Peter Charles Hoffer. *Roe v. Wade: The Abortion Rights Controversy in American History*. Lawrence: University Press of Kansas, 2001. Provides a complete legal history of abortion in the United States from colonial times to the early twenty-first century.

Janosik, Robert J. "*Roe v. Wade*." In *U.S. Court Cases*, edited by Thomas Tandy Lewis. 2d ed. Pasadena, Calif.: Salem Press, 2011. Analysis of the Supreme Court's landmark ruling on abortion with attention to the social impact of the ruling.

Wattleton, Faye. *Life on the Line*. New York: Random House, 1998. In her autobiography, Wattleton recounts the childhood and early career experiences that influenced her later activist work and the challenges she faced as head of Planned Parenthood.

_____. "Unfinished Agenda: Reproductive Rights." In *Sisterhood Is Forever*, edited by Robin Morgan. New York: Washington Square Press, 2003. An essay in which Wattleton links reproductive rights to the broader issue of social equality.

**SEE ALSO:** Carol E. Moseley Braun; Marian Wright Edelman; Bell Hooks; Barbara Smith.

# J. C. WATTS
## Politician and football player

*Born into a poor, industrious family in rural Oklahoma, Watts gained national attention as the quarterback of the University of Oklahoma football team and later regained attention nationally as a congressman, an orator, a leader in the Republican Party, and a champion of African American conservatism.*

**BORN:** November 18, 1957; Eufaula, Oklahoma
**ALSO KNOWN AS:** Julius Caesar Watts, Jr.
**AREAS OF ACHIEVEMENT:** Government and politics; Sports: football

### EARLY LIFE
Julius Caesar Watts, Jr., was born on November 18, 1957, in Eufaula, Oklahoma. He was the fifth of six children of Julius Caesar "Buddy" Watts, Sr., and Helen Pierce Watts. Living in an African American neighborhood, the Watts family was poor but independent. Watts's father spent long hours at various jobs, while his mother often skipped supper with the family and ate only what the others left on their plates. As a youth, Watts contributed what he could to keep the family off public assistance.

Watts finished first grade at an all-black school but then became one of the first African American pupils at a previously white school. Gifted in athletics, Watts had a life-changing experience on Thanksgiving Day, 1971, when he watched the nationally televised football game between top-ranked Nebraska and second-ranked Oklahoma and saw his older friend Lucious Selmon play a prominent part in the Oklahoma effort. It was then that Watts began to think about playing college football and earning a degree. At Eufaula High School, he defied racial stereotypes by starting nearly three full seasons at quarterback and attracted national attention with his performance. Recruited widely, he decided in his senior year, 1975-1976, to accept a scholarship from the University of Oklahoma (OU). In that school year, however, he also fathered two daughters with two young women. Frankie Jones, one of the women, kept her child, and Watts's uncle and aunt, Wade and Betty Watts, raised the other.

### LIFE'S WORK
Watts had a difficult transition from a small high school to a large university. He played little his first semester, and the following semester, he almost quit the football team. His father, however, reminded him that starting for OU was a goal he would have to work hard to reach, and Coach Barry Switzer promised that he would become a starter after one season as a redshirt and another as a reserve. Watts stayed with the team and married Frankie in the summer of 1977. During the 1979 and 1980 seasons, he played as OU's first-team quarterback and was voted most valuable player in the 1980 and 1981 Orange Bowls. In May, 1981, Watts earned a bachelor's degree in journalism.

Disappointed by his low position in the National Football League's 1981 draft and believing his chance to play quarterback professionally would improve in Canada, Watts signed with the Ottawa Rough Riders of the Canadian Football League (CFL). He played several seasons in the CFL with Ottawa and the Toronto Argonauts.

After his playing career ended, he became youth director in 1987 at Sunnylane Baptist Church in suburban Oklahoma City. While low-paying, the job proved spiritually rewarding and strengthened his Christian faith. In 1989, after long thought and business experience, he decided to switch his voter registration from Democrat to Republican.

Helped in politics by his football fame, his talent as a speaker, and his outgoing personality, Watts in 1990 won election to the Oklahoma Corporation Commission. Then, in 1994, he was elected to the U.S. House of Representatives from Oklahoma's Fourth District for the first of four consecutive terms. Watts became a nationally prominent conservative. Two years later, he spoke at the Republican National Convention and, in 1997, delivered the Republican response to President Bill Clinton's State of the Union address. In 1998, his colleagues elected him chair of the House Republican Conference, thus making him one of the top members of his party.

In 2002, Watts decided not to run for reelection to Congress, opting to end his weekly commute between Norman, Oklahoma, and Washington, D.C., and spend more time with his wife and their five children. He returned to business, chairing the J. C. Watts Companies and writing a semimonthly newspaper column through the 2000's.

### SIGNIFICANCE

Watts was the first African American to serve on the Oklahoma Corporation Commission, as an Oklahoma congressman, and as chair of the House Republican Conference. A generally conservative Republican, he quickly rose to prominence in the House but alienated some of his colleagues by refusing to oppose affirmative action and intimating that he might support Democrat Barack Obama in the 2008 presidential election. Nevertheless, he was one of black conservatism's most visible figures in the late 1990's and 2000's.

—*Victor Lindsey*

*J. C. Watts.* (AP/Wide World Photos)

### FURTHER READING

Coates, Ta-Nehisi. "House Negro." *Washington Monthly* 34, no. 12 (December, 2002): 49-50. Reviews Watts's autobiography, attacking its author for ignorance of the systemic nature of American racism and comparing him unfavorably to Louis Farrakhan.

Lutz, Norma Jean. *J. C. Watts.* Philadelphia: Chelsea House, 2000. Tells an admiring story of Watts up to 1999 and includes many photographs, a chronology, his college football statistics, and a bibliography.

Switzer, Barry, with Bud Shrake. *Bootlegger's Boy.* New York: William Morrow, 1990. Includes the former Oklahoma football coach's thoughts on Watts as a college quarterback and notes his personal loyalty.

Watts, J. C., Jr., with Chriss Winston. *What Color Is a Conservative? My Life and My Politics.* New York: HarperCollins, 2002. Starts with Watts's decision not to run again for Congress in 2002 and fills in his life and his political thinking until then.

**SEE ALSO:** Jesse Jackson, Jr.; Sheila Jackson Lee; Alan Keyes; John McWhorter; Rodney Peete; Michael Steele; Maxine Waters.

# ROBERT C. WEAVER
## Politician and activist

*From the New Deal era, when he served as a member of President Franklin D. Roosevelt's "Black Cabinet," to the time of his service as a trail-blazing member of President Lyndon B. Johnson's cabinet and as a university professor, educator, and civil rights leader, Weaver enjoyed an active career that spanned forty-five years.*

**BORN:** December 29, 1907; Washington, D.C.
**DIED:** July 17, 1997; New York, New York
**ALSO KNOWN AS:** Robert Clifton Weaver
**AREAS OF ACHIEVEMENT:** Government and politics; Social issues

### EARLY LIFE

Robert Clifton Weaver was born into a modestly prosperous family environment. His father, Mortimer Grover Weaver, was a Washington, D.C., postal employee; his mother, Florence Freeman, was a schoolteacher. Upon graduating in 1925 from what is now Paul Laurence Dunbar High School, Robert C. Weaver entered Harvard, earning a B.A. in 1929, an M.A. in 1931, and a Ph.D. in economics in 1934. The sudden death of his gifted older brother, Mortimer Grover, Jr., in 1929 affected Weaver deeply, motivating him to advance his education.

### LIFE'S WORK

In 1933, Weaver began work as associate adviser to the secretary of the interior. His vast knowledge of urban issues, his interpersonal skills, his attention to administrative detail, and his capacity for hard and methodical work propelled him, in spite of his young age, to the top ranks of the Federal Council of Negro Affairs (better known as the "Black Cabinet"). This was a loosely organized group of about forty-five African American academics, civil servants, and community activists, which was patched together by First Lady Eleanor Roosevelt and Mary McLeod Bethune to advise President Franklin D. Roosevelt on matters pertaining to the African American community. Weaver was instrumental in helping to engineer the "Great Switchover" of the African American vote to the Democratic Party. In July, 1935, Weaver married Ella V. Haith. The couple adopted a son in 1942 and named him Robert Clifton Weaver, Jr.

During the 1930's, Robert C. Weaver undertook various projects. In 1938, he went from the Department of the Interior to be special assistant in the U.S. Housing Authority. In 1940, he worked for the National Defense Advisory Commission, then as chair, in succession from 1942 to 1944, of the Negro Employment and Training Branch of the War Production Board and the Negro Manpower Service. Disillusioned by the slow pace of progress against racial discrimination in government, Weaver left his position as head of the Negro Manpower Service on February 1, 1944, and went to work for the Chicago mayor's office as head of its Committee on Race Relations. From 1945 to 1955, he had short-term university lecturing positions and a six-month stint in 1946 as acting deputy chief of the United Nations Relief and Rehabilitation Administration's initiative in war-ravaged areas of the Soviet Union. From 1955 to 1959, he served the state of New York as deputy housing commissioner and rent administrator; then from 1959 to 1960 he chaired the board of the National Association for the Advancement of Colored People (NAACP).

On February 11, 1961, Weaver returned to government service as President John F. Kennedy's appointee to head the Bureau of Housing and Home Finance, declining the cabinet position as secretary of health, education, and welfare. It then became Kennedy's intent to elevate Weaver to secretary of a proposed cabinet-level Department of Housing and Urban Development, but the proposal was stymied in Congress in 1961 and 1962 by Republicans and Southern Democrats because of the likelihood of a black man's appointment to the position. It would not be until the administration of President Lyndon B. Johnson that Congress passed the Housing and Urban Development Act of 1965, and on January 13, 1966, Weaver was sworn in as the department's first secretary and the first African American to attain a presidential cabinet post. After Weaver left the cabinet in 1969, he served for a year as president of Baruch University and rounded off his career as Distinguished Professor for Urban Studies at Hunter College from 1971 to 1978. He wrote four books: *Negro Labor: A National Problem* (1946), *The Negro Ghetto* (1948), *The Urban Complex: Human Values in Urban Life* (1964), and *Dilemmas of Urban America* (1965).

On November 6, 1962, the Weaver family suffered a devastating blow when Robert, Jr., died of a gunshot to the head, self-inflicted while playing Russian roulette. In 1997, Weaver died at home at the age of eighty-nine.

## SIGNIFICANCE

Because of his preference for working behind the scenes in a low-key style and for avoiding confrontation and publicity, Weaver is a much-overlooked figure. This has obscured public perception of his effectiveness as a groundbreaker and an agent for change and the enduring and pivotal role he played in the field of civil rights. His efforts formed the foundation and conceptualization of urban renewal as it has moved into the twenty-first century. Weaver was among the early New Deal reformers to tie economics to racial discrimination.

—*Raymond Pierre Hylton*

## FURTHER READING

Bowser, Benjamin P., Louis Kushnick, and Paul Grant. *Against the Odds: Scholars Who Challenged Racism in the Twentieth Century.* Amherst: University of Massachusetts Press, 2004. A series of short individual autobiographical studies, using the subject's own words to demonstrate his or her lifelong struggles against racism. Weaver is studied in chapter 6: "Blending Scholarship with Public Service: Robert C. Weaver."

Pritchett, Wendell E. *Robert C. Weaver and the American City: The Life and Times of an Urban Reformer.* Chicago: University of Chicago Press, 2008. As the first definitive biography of Weaver, this volume is indispensable for anyone who wants to understand his role and his significance. It is clearly written and highly detailed.

Taylor, Henry Louis, Jr., and Walter Hill, eds. *Historical Roots of the Urban Crisis: African Americans in the Industrial City, 1900-1950.* New York: Garland, 2000. Sigmund Shipp's contributing article (chapter 8), "Building Bricks Without Straw: Robert Weaver and Industrial Employment, 1934-1944," sheds some light on the crucial nature of Weaver's published research and intragovernmental lobbying efforts in bringing about racial labor and housing reforms.

SEE ALSO: Patricia Roberts Harris; Samuel R. Pierce, Jr.

# CHICK WEBB
## Jazz musician

*Webb is among the most famous drummers and bandleaders of the big band era. He was renowned for winning famous drum battles at Harlem's Savoy Ballroom and for introducing singer Ella Fitzgerald.*

BORN: February 10, 1909; Baltimore, Maryland
DIED: June 16, 1939; Baltimore, Maryland
ALSO KNOWN AS: William Henry Webb
AREAS OF ACHIEVEMENT: Music: bandleading; Music: jazz; Music: swing

## EARLY LIFE

William Henry Webb was born to William Henry and Marie Johnson Webb on February 10, 1909, in Baltimore, Maryland. He got his nickname because of his short stature. The well-known story that Webb was dropped as a child and severely injured is probably untrue. It is more likely that Webb suffered from tuberculosis, which caused his lifelong health problems and deformed spine.

After beginning on homemade instruments, Webb acquired a drum set around age twelve. It has been reported that he took up drumming as therapy for the joint stiffness associated with tuberculosis. Later, during his teen years, Webb joined the local Jazzola Orchestra. Around 1925, Webb moved to New York with Jazzola member John Trueheart. There, in 1926, Webb formed his own five-piece group, which spent five months at the Black Bottom Club. He then led an eight-piece group at the Paddock Club before taking his group, the Harlem Stompers, to the Savoy Ballroom in January, 1927. During the rest of the 1920's, Webb and his band played in the New York area; Webb made his first recordings in June, 1929, under the name the Jungle Band.

## LIFE'S WORK

In 1931, Webb and his Harlem Stompers began playing regular seasons at Harlem's Savoy Ballroom. When not at the Savoy, they toured. In 1932, they played a series of theater dates accompanying Louis Armstrong. The band's sound and Webb's showmanship quickly attracted a large following, and the group changed its name to the Chick Webb Orchestra.

The first of numerous residencies at the Savoy Ballroom marked Webb's emergence as one of the outstanding bandleaders of the swing period. Webb's band remained the resident group at the Savoy from 1933 until Webb's death in 1939. Although the group had only a

*Chick Webb.* (Archive Photos/Getty Images)

few prominent soloists, including Taft Jordan and Sandy Williams, during its years of prolific recording activity it developed a distinctive style. That sound was characterized by Webb's forceful drumming and the compositions and arrangements provided by Edgar Sampson. In April, 1935, Webb engaged Ella Fitzgerald as the band's singer. She helped Webb and the band achieve popular success with performances and recordings of songs such as "A Tisket, a Tasket" (1938). Fitzgerald was an orphan and Webb came to regard her as his own daughter, legally adopting her soon after she joined the band. Webb and his band achieved national prominence through the recordings featuring Fitzgerald.

Throughout his career, Webb was widely admired by drummers for his forceful sense of swing, precise technique, control of dynamics, and imaginative breaks and fills. Although he was unable to read music, he led the band's arrangements by giving memorized cues with his drumming while playing on a raised platform in the center of the band. Unlike earlier drummers of the 1920's, Webb used the woodblocks and cowbells only for momentary effects and varied his playing with rim shots, temple-block sounds, and cymbal crashes.

Webb and his band regularly defeated rival bands in the Savoy Ballroom's famous cutting contests. One of Webb's most famous battles was with Benny Goodman's band on May 11, 1937. Webb's victory over Goodman's band and drummer Gene Krupa enhanced his reputation as a showman and bandleader. Webb's success also led to an exhausting schedule, which was partly responsible for a serious decline in his health. In June, 1939, Webb was hospitalized in Baltimore and died after surgery. After Webb's death, Fitzgerald led the band for several years.

### SIGNIFICANCE

Webb's unique big band drumming style included both the timekeeping and soloistic qualities that had previously been separate. In addition to displaying remarkable clarity of technique, Webb excelled as an improviser. His drumming was an inspiration to many of the famous big band drummers who followed in the 1940's. In spite of his challenging health problems, Webb was admired for his consistent excellence.

—*David Steffens*

### FURTHER READING

Charters, Samuel B., and Leonard Kunstadt. *Jazz: A History of the New York Scene*. New York: Doubleday, 1962. A section on Webb includes biography and a short but detailed analysis of his career and place in the history of the Savoy Ballroom.

Korall, Burt. "Chick Webb." In *Drummin' Men: The Heartbeat of Jazz, the Swing Era*. New York: Schirmer Books, 2002. Includes analysis of Webb's career, style, and personality with many firsthand accounts of Webb's playing.

McCarthy, Albert. *Big Band Jazz*. New York: G. P. Putnam, 1974. Includes a general history of Webb's career and detailed readings of Webb's recordings.

Schuller, Gunther. "The Great Black Bands." In *The Swing Era: The Development of Jazz, 1930-1945*. New York: Oxford University Press, 1989. Includes a detailed history of Webb's band and analysis of Webb's drumming style.

Tumpak, John R. "Chick Webb and Mario Bauza." In *When Swing Was the Thing: Personality Profiles of the Big Band Era*. Milwaukee, Wis.: Marquette University Press, 2009. Offers a detailed profile of Webb in the context of his big band contemporaries. Also provides historical and cultural context.

SEE ALSO: Louis Armstrong; Edward Blackwell; James Reese Europe; Ella Fitzgerald; Jelly Roll Morton; King Oliver.

# IDA B. WELLS-BARNETT
## Activist and journalist

*Wells-Barnett applied investigative journalism to the pervasive crime of lynching, publishing statistical and anecdotal evidence that showed the brutality and injustice of racial violence. She was a vocal proponent of African American civil rights and women's rights throughout her career.*

**BORN:** July 16, 1862; Holly Springs, Mississippi
**DIED:** March 25, 1931; Chicago, Illinois
**ALSO KNOWN AS:** Ida Bell Wells (birth name); Iola
**AREAS OF ACHIEVEMENT:** Civil rights; Journalism and publishing; Women's rights

### EARLY LIFE

Ida B. Wells-Barnett was born in Holly Springs, Mississippi, on July 16, 1862, to slaves James Wells and Elizabeth Warrenton. Her father, the only son of his former master, received training and became a skilled carpenter long before his freedom. Well respected as a free wage-earner after the Civil War, he also achieved the rank of Master Mason in the Freemasons.

As a young girl, Wells-Barnett received basic education from the Freedmen's Aid Society of the Episcopal Church. At age sixteen, after both her parents' deaths, she earned a teaching certificate in order to support her five siblings. Because of her father's Masonic rank, the local Masons helped her obtain a teaching position. Wells-Barnett first became aware of the injustice of Jim Crow segregation when she was forcibly removed from a first-class rail car despite having a valid ticket.

Wells-Barnett's teaching career took her to Memphis, where she discovered new opportunities in journalism. She found writing more fulfilling than teaching and soon dedicated herself to an antilynching campaign.

### LIFE'S WORK

Writing for *The American Baptist* and other newspapers under the pen name Iola, Wells-Barnett attracted a national audience. She became known as "The Princess of the Press." By 1889, she had acquired one-third ownership in a Memphis newspaper, *Free Speech*. Af-

ter a local school refused to renew her teaching contract because of an article she had written, she turned to journalism and newspaper ownership full time.

Wells-Barnett increased *Free Speech*'s subscriber base by nearly 40 percent. Her involvement as owner, editor, and writer turned the paper into a force in the fight for racial justice. In 1891, three Memphis businessmen—one of whom was a close friend of Wells-Barnett—were targeted by a white mob because their grocery store was competing with a nearby white-owned store. After the businessmen fought back, injuring some of the attackers, they were lynched. The murders deeply affected Wells-Barnett and drove her to shift her focus from civil rights in general to lynching specifically.

Wells-Barnett's militant articles about lynching stirred controversy in Memphis. After her newspaper's offices were destroyed by a mob, she left the city for New York. She took a job with *The New York Age*, an African American weekly publication that also had broad white readership. She launched a public-speaking career in October, 1892, as well. That year, Wells-Barnett wrote an article for *The New York Age* in which she attacked the myth that lynching was a form of vigilante justice for black men who raped white women; she used data to expose the attitudes toward race and sexuality that underlay

---

### WELLS AND THE ANTILYNCHING MOVEMENT

Ida B. Wells-Barnett was an outspoken, independent activist who was driven to expose the brutality and injustice of lynching. Through her groundbreaking journalism, she brought international attention to racial violence. In particular, Wells-Barnett sought to dispel the myth that only African American men who raped white women were lynched. Her first published pamphlet, *Southern Horrors: Lynch Law in All Its Phases* (1892), based on an article she wrote for the *Free Speech* newspaper in Memphis, suggested that consensual sexual relationships between white women and black men often were misconstrued and offered anecdotes about women who lied about rape to cover up interracial affairs. These claims raised the ire of many whites in Memphis, and Wells-Barnett was forced to leave the city. In 1895, she published a report titled *The Red Record: Tabulated Statistics and Alleged Causes of Lynching in the United States*, the first documented statistical report on lynching. Her meticulously documented report showed that lynching was much more frequent and far reaching than commonly thought, and that the crime was closely tied to entrenched attitudes about race, gender, and sexuality in the United States. It described in detail many cases in which men were lynched "for anything or nothing."

the southern culture of racial violence. The article became the pamphlet *Southern Horrors: Lynch Law in All Its Phases*, published by the end of 1892. The speaking tour that followed took her across the United States and to the United Kingdom. She became an international figure in the campaign against lynching.

In 1893, Wells-Barnett helped to organize a boycott of the World's Columbian Exhibition in Chicago and contributed to a pamphlet titled *The Reason Why the Colored American Is Not in the World's Columbian Exhibition*, which was distributed at the event. The trip culminated in her decision to move to Chicago, where she spent the remainder of her life. In Chicago, she began writing for newspaper owner and attorney Ferdinand Barnett's *The Chicago Conservator*. In 1895, she and Barnett were married. They had four children. Although she remained active in the national antilynching campaign, of which she was a founding member, she scaled back her activism to focus on her family.

Over the subsequent decades, Wells-Barnett balanced activism with motherhood. She provided the means and the leadership for the creation of the National Association of Colored Women (NACW). She also canvassed the state to promote suffrage for women and establish the first suffrage association for African American women in Chicago. Her political interests eventually led her to run for a state senate seat in the 1930's. An active champion of social justice, she developed strategies for the antilynching campaign that would be used by activists generations later.

Wells-Barnett died in Chicago, still actively pursuing the cause of justice for all. Her bid for political office, a campaign to prevent the appointment of a North Carolina judge to the U.S. Supreme Court, and work on her autobiography filled the last days of her life.

## SIGNIFICANCE

Wells-Barnett's investigative reporting and forceful editorials forced her readers—black and white—to confront the cruelty and injustice of lynching. She devoted her career to disproving the myths about race and gender that contributed to the prevalence of lynching in the South. She also worked more generally for African American civil rights and women's rights and suffrage.

—*Kay J. Blalock*

## FURTHER READING

Bay, Mia. *To Tell the Truth Freely: The Life of Ida B. Wells*. New York: Hill and Wang, 2009. This thorough biography offers insight into the life and times of Wells-Barnett and analysis of her impact.

Giddings, Paula J. *Ida, a Sword Among Lions: Ida B. Wells and the Campaign Against Lynching*. New York: Amistad, 2008. Drawing on Wells-Barnett's words and several published and unpublished works, this biography presents a well-researched look at her role in the African American reform movements.

Schechter, Patricia A. *Ida B. Wells-Barnett and American Reform, 1880-1930*. Chapel Hill: University of North Carolina Press, 2001. Examines and analyzes Wells-Barnett's ideas and activism in terms of gender and race.

Schraff, Anne. *Ida B. Wells-Barnett: "Strike a Blow Against a Glaring Evil."* Berkeley Heights, N.J.: Enslow, 2008. Biography for younger readers, offering an accessible overview of Wells-Barnett's life's work.

Wells-Barnett, Ida B. *Crusade for Justice: The Autobiography of Ida B. Wells*. Edited by Alfreda M. Duster. Chicago: University of Chicago Press, 1970. This posthumously published autobiography was edited by Wells-Barnett's daughter.

_____. *The Memphis Diary of Ida B. Wells*. Edited by Miriam Decosta-Willis. Boston: Beacon Press, 1995. Wells-Barnett's diary offers an intimate look at the antilynching crusader as a young woman.

SEE ALSO: Robert S. Abbott; Charlotta Spears Bass; John E. Bruce; Henrietta Vinton Davis; W. E. B. Du Bois; Angelina Weld Grimké; Maria Stewart; Mary Church Terrell; Emmett Till; Sojourner Truth.

# CORNEL WEST
## Scholar and activist

*Best known for his cultural critiques, youth advocacy, and academic works, West has had a prolific career as a public intellectual, lecturer, writer, recording artist, and actor. In his writings, he dissects race and religion, democracy, and the need to empower youths through education.*

**BORN:** June 2, 1953; Tulsa, Oklahoma
**ALSO KNOWN AS:** Cornel Ronald West
**AREAS OF ACHIEVEMENT:** Education; Scholarship;
   Social issues

### EARLY LIFE
Cornel Ronald West was born June 2, 1953, in Tulsa, Oklahoma, to Clinton and Irene West. His father, a civilian contractor for the Air Force, and mother, an educator, moved the family several times before settling in a working-class segregated community in Sacramento, California, during the late 1960's. The Sacramento chapter of the Black Panther Party provided West with early exposure to the necessity for struggle and activism. His burgeoning activism was tempered with lessons of love from the local Baptist church and from his grandfather, Baptist minister Clinton West, Sr. Although West was profoundly shaped by the views of the Panthers, he never joined the party, citing its hostility toward religion. West, an adamant church attendee, found the black Christian liberation philosophies of James Cone equally influential in his development as the community programs implemented by the Black Panther Party.

In 1970, at the age of seventeen, West received a scholarship to attend Harvard University. He recalled his mind-set upon first reaching the university: "I arrived at Harvard unashamed of my African, Christian, and militant de-colonized outlooks." His outlook was further expanded through the teaching of Stanley Cavell and Robert Nozick. West graduated three years later magna cum laude with a bachelor of arts degree in Middle Eastern languages and literature. He then entered graduate school at Princeton University and received his doctoral degree in 1980. West's studies were informed and influenced by the sociological perspectives of Karl Marx. His dissertation, *Black Theology and Marxist Thought*, later was published as *The Ethical Dimensions of Marxist Thought* (1991).

In his mid-twenties, West accepted a W. E. B. Du Bois Fellowship and returned to Harvard University. For the next decade, he taught at the Union Theological Seminary in New York, as an assistant professor; Princeton, as the director of African American studies; and Harvard, where he had a joint appointment in African American studies and divinity. In 1987, while serving as a professor of American studies at Yale, he was arrested at a protest urging divestment from apartheid South Africa. He was reprimanded by the university, which canceled his leave the next semester, forcing West to commute between Yale and the University of Paris. In 1989, West was awarded the Alphonse Fletcher Chair, the highest distinction given to a faculty member at Harvard University. This honor gave West the freedom to teach in multiple disciplines, and he elected to teach in the areas of divinity, religion, African American studies, and philosophy.

*Cornel West.* (WireImage/Getty Images)

In 2001, West was embroiled in what he called "a monumental conflict" with Harvard president Lawrence Summers. According to West, Summers accused him of frequently canceling classes to campaign for Democratic presidential hopefuls Bill Bradley and Al Sharpton. Summers also reportedly accused West of grade inflation and shirking his academic responsibilities in favor of personal projects such as a rap album. The confrontation sparked public debate and led West to leave Harvard for a tenured position at Princeton in 2002. In the book *Democracy Matters: Winning the Fight Against Imperialism* (2004), West writes about the disagreement in relation to the state of academia: "A market-driven technocratic culture has infiltrated university life with the narrow pursuit of academic trophies and the business of generating income from grants and business partnerships taking precedence over the fundamental responsibility of nurturing young minds."

### LIFE'S WORK

West's first several books and articles reflect his lifelong interest in Marxism and religion. *Prophesy Deliverance! An Afro-American Revolutionary Christianity* (1982), *Prophetic Fragments* (1988), and *The Ethical Dimensions of Marxist Thought* all discuss the social responsibility of the black church to the black community. One of his most popular works, the essay collection *Race Matters* (1993), was published to coincide with the one-year anniversary of the Rodney King beating and Los Angeles riots. In this work, West shifts his focus to race relations and nihilism among African Americans. He criticizes many African American leaders for being short-sighted and self-serving.

West was very critical of President George W. Bush and his administration during the Iraq War, often calling them "evangelical nihilists." In 2004, West supported Ralph Nader's campaign for president, although he declined to be Nader's running mate, citing his political support for Democratic Party hopeful Al Sharpton. In 2008, West supported Barack Obama's campaign for president. He was critical, however, when Obama accepted the Nobel Peace Prize, calling him "a war president with a peace prize."

West also became a pop-culture figure later in his career, appearing in the 2003 philosophical science-fiction films *The Matrix Reloaded* and *The Matrix Revolutions* as Councilor West. West appeared on countless television talk shows; received dozens of awards; and recorded the hip-hop albums *Sketches of My Culture* (2001) and *Never Forget: A Journey of Revelations* (2007). He was a member of Alpha Phi Alpha fraternity and the World Policy Council.

### SIGNIFICANCE

West inspired many young African Americans to pursue scholarship by challenging them to serve their communities. He made it his mission to advocate for the oppressed. In his books, he examines race, culture, class, gender, and religion, encouraging readers to think critically about how these factors affect their lives.

*—Derrick J. Jenkins, Sr.*

### FURTHER READING

Johnson, Clarence Sholé. *Cornel West and Philosophy: The Quest for Social Justice*. New York: Routledge, 2003. Provides brief biography and a detailed examination of West's philosophy, including his views on subjects such as Marxism, Christianity, black-Jewish relations, and affirmative action.

West, Cornel. *Brother West: Living and Loving Out Loud—A Memoir*. New York: SmileyBooks, 2009. West discusses his life, career, and philosophies in this candid memoir.

_____. *The Cornel West Reader*. New York: Basic Civitas Books, 1999. A collection of works divided into eight critical areas exploring the elimination of oppression through democracy.

_____. *Race Matters*. 1993. Reprint. Boston: Beacon Press, 2001. A critical assessment of race in America one year after the Rodney King beating.

_____. *Restoring Hope: Conversations on the Future of Black America*. Edited by Kelvin Shawn Sealey. Boston: Beacon Press, 1997. West interviews prominent African Americans about race relations and sources of hope for the future.

Yancy, George, ed. *Cornel West: A Critical Reader*. Malden, Mass.: Blackwell, 2001. Collection of essays by a diverse group of scholars on West's work.

**SEE ALSO:** Angela Davis; William Thomas Fontaine; Henry Louis Gates, Jr.; Addison Gayle, Jr.; Lewis Gordon.

# DAVID WEST
## Basketball player

*West was a college basketball star at Xavier University who went on to a promising career in the National Basketball Association (NBA) with the New Orleans Hornets. An accomplished power forward, he won the Oscar Robertson Trophy for college player of the year in 2003 and was an NBA All-Star in 2008 and 2009.*

**BORN:** August 29, 1980; Teaneck, New Jersey
**ALSO KNOWN AS:** David Moorer West
**AREA OF ACHIEVEMENT:** Sports: basketball

### EARLY LIFE
David Moorer West was born on August 29, 1980, in Teaneck, New Jersey, to Amos and Harriet West. From a young age, West was a risk-taker: At age four, he climbed to the top of a utility pole, emulating a worker he had seen perform the feat. When his mother chastised him, West merely responded that he wanted to see if he could reach the top.

West's basketball record in high school provided little evidence that a lucrative career in the sport lay ahead. While living in New Jersey, he did not get much playing experience because he was neither the quickest nor the strongest player. When West moved to Garner, North Carolina, before his junior year of high school, he initially wanted to give up basketball. However, his coach at Garner Magnet High School saw his abilities—as well as his 6-foot, 8-inch height—and persuaded him to try out for the team.

After graduating from high school, West received a basketball scholarship to Xavier University in Cincinnati, Ohio. During his impressive college career, the power forward led his team to a national top-ten ranking; Xavier also received a number-three seed in the National Collegiate Athletic Association (NCAA) Tournament. Although West struggled academically at times, he stayed in school to complete his communications degree in 2003.

In 2003, West won the Oscar Robertson Trophy, which honors the best college basketball player of the year. That year, West was selected by the New Orleans Hornets with the eighteenth pick in the National Basketball Association (NBA) draft.

### LIFE'S WORK
West's NBA career started quietly; he averaged 3.8 points in 13.1 minutes per game as a rookie. During his second season, he improved his averages to 6.2 points in 18.4 minutes of playing time. However, it was the 2005-2006 season that proved that West could be the powerhouse player he had been in college. His scoring average increased dramatically—to 17.1 points per game—and he was second in voting for the NBA's most improved player award.

As the 6-foot-9, 240-pound player began getting more and more playing time, his national profile also increased. While his main position was still that of power forward, he also played as a center for the team in a few situations. Despite injuries that kept him out of some games during the 2006-2007 season, West continued to improve his scoring and rebounding. West and point guard Chris Paul led an exciting young Hornets team that lifted the spirits of New Orleans in the aftermath of 2005's Hurricane Katrina. In 2007-2008, West had one of his best years. The Hornets secured a play-off berth, and he was voted into the NBA All-Star Game as a reserve. This honor was especially significant because New Orleans hosted the All-Star Game in the Superdome, which had been rebuilt after suffering significant hurricane damage. He was an All-Star again the next seaon.

In the 2009-2010 season, West recorded averages of 19 points and 7.5 rebounds per game—down slightly from the previous two years, but strong numbers nonetheless. Over the first seven years of his professional career, he averaged 16 points and 7.2 rebounds per game.

### SIGNIFICANCE
Although West's basketball career got off to a slow start in high school, he grew into a dominant college player and consistent contributor in the NBA. In 2007, *Sports Illustrated* named him to its NCAA All-Decade team for the 2000's.

—*Jill E. Disis*

### FURTHER READING
Nance, Roscoe. "Xavier's West on Waiting List." *USA Today*, June 25, 2003, p. 3C. This profile summarizes West's college career and captures the nervousness that he experienced during the days leading up to the NBA draft.

NBA.com. "David West." http://www.nba.com/player file/david_west/index.html. The official NBA Web site lists West's career statistics and a brief biography.

Wahl, Grant. "It Says Here West Is Best." *Sports Illustrated* 98, no. 11 (March 17, 2003). Profiles West after he won the Oscar Robertson Trophy at Xavier University.

Weir, Tom. "West Enjoys Last Laugh with Xavier." *USA Today*, March 18, 2003, p. 1C. Examines West's personal life and family relationships near the end of his career at Xavier.

**SEE ALSO:** Tim Duncan; Kevin Garnett; Dwight Howard; Kenyon Martin; Chris Paul.

# DOROTHY WEST
## Writer

*West was a writer of the Harlem Renaissance and the period after it whose first novel,* The Living Is Easy, *was published in 1948. She also was a short-story writer, editor, and journalist who published two short-lived literary magazines highlighting the work of black writers.*

**BORN:** June 2, 1907; Boston, Massachusetts
**DIED:** August 16, 1998; Oak Bluffs, Martha's Vineyard, Massachusetts
**ALSO KNOWN AS:** Mary Christopher
**AREAS OF ACHIEVEMENT:** Journalism and publishing; Literature

### EARLY LIFE

Dorothy West was born in Boston, Massachusetts, in 1907 to Rachel Pease Benson and Isaac Christopher West. Her father, a man of great ambition, was a former slave from Virginia who saved until he could start his own business. His success eventually made the Wests one of the wealthiest African American families in Boston. West enjoyed a privileged upbringing and ample education. At the age of two, she began her formal education with a tutor, Bessie Trotter. At four, she became a student at the Farragut School; she was capable of doing second-grade work. She completed elementary school at the Matin School in the Mission District of Boston.

By the time West was seven, she had decided that she wanted to become a writer. Her father wanted her to become a businesswoman, while her mother wanted her to be a musician. However, her precocious writing talent was evidenced when, at the age of fourteen, her short story "Promise and Fulfillment" was published in *The Boston Post*. She became a regular contributor to the paper and a recipient of several of its literary awards. West completed her high school education at the prestigious Girl's Latin School in Boston, where she graduated in 1923 before continuing her studies at Boston University and at Columbia University, where she studied journalism.

In 1926, West's short story "The Typewriter" tied for second place in an *Opportunity* magazine contest with a story by Zora Neale Hurston. West and her cousin, Helene Johnson, traveled to New York for the magazine's awards ceremony, a move that began West's long association with Harlem.

### LIFE'S WORK

The early years of West's writing career were difficult. She struggled to get her work published and to attract readers, black or white. She did, however, contribute to *The Martha's Vineyard Gazette*, and two stories she wrote during the late 1920's were published in *The Saturday Evening Quill*, a black publication. To supplement her income, West took a job as an extra in the original production of George Gershwin's *Porgy and Bess*, performing both on Broadway and in London. The Great Depression was taking its toll on many Americans, and in 1932, West traveled with a group of some twenty African American intellectuals to Russia with the intention of producing a film on the subject of racism in the United States. When they arrived, they discovered that the film had been canceled. Although she was disappointed, West liked Russia and remained there for more than a year, returning after she learned of her father's death.

On her return, West took the bold step of using her savings to found the literary magazine *The Challenge*. The Harlem Renaissance was fading amid the Depression, and West sought to rekindle some of the excitement of that era. Her goal was to publish works by established writers and to introduce new and younger ones. In the six issues of the magazine, the first goal was met, but most of the submissions by new writers did not meet the magazine's standards, and publication ceased in 1937. Later that year, West and Richard Wright cofounded *The New Challenge*, but it lasted only one issue.

After the magazines failed, West became a welfare relief worker in Harlem. Accustomed to affluence, she was shocked at the living conditions she found. Her short story "Mammy" reflected this experience. In 1940, West got a job with the Works Progress Administration's Writers' Project. During this time, she wrote a number of stories and began a long association with *The New York Daily News*, publishing more than two dozen stories. She also contributed to several other magazines. Her first novel, *The Living Is Easy*, about the life of an upper-class African American family, was published in 1948.

West spent the next several decades working as a journalist on Martha's Vineyard. Thanks in part to the encouragement of Jacqueline Kennedy Onassis, West's second novel, *The Wedding*, was published in 1995 when she was eighty-five. West died on August 16, 1998, at the age of ninety-one.

## SIGNIFICANCE

While West's identification with the Harlem Renaissance provided visibility and important connections, her first novel, published in 1948 after the decline of the Harlem Renaissance, helped renew interest in the work of black writers. When *The Living Is Easy* was reissued in 1982, the novel drew the interest of a new generation of readers who interpreted her work from a feminist perspective.

*—Victoria Price*

## FURTHER READING

Jones, Sharon L. *Rereading the Harlem Renaissance: Race, Class, and Gender in the Fiction of Jessie Fauset, Zora Neale Hurston, and Dorothy West*. Contributions in Afro-American and African Studies 207. Westport, Conn.: Greenwood Press, 2002. Examines the work of West, Hurston, and Fauset and contends that all three writers challenged racial, gender, and class repression.

Kramer, Victor A., ed. *The Harlem Renaissance Reexamined*. New York: AMS Press, 1987. Contains a section dealing with the cultural context of the Harlem Renaissance and a section of essays on the art of specific writers, including West.

Russell, Sandi. *Render Me My Songs: African-American Women Writers from Slavery to the Present*. New York: St. Martin's Press, 1991. Includes a profile of West covering her biography, writings, and their cultural impact.

West, Dorothy. *The Richer, The Poorer: Stories, Sketches, and Reminiscences*. New York: Doubleday, 1995. Offers an interesting look at West's writing and life in her own words.

*Dorothy West.* (AP/Wide World Photos)

**SEE ALSO:** Charlotta Spears Bass; Daisy Bates; Jessie Redmon Fauset; Zora Neale Hurston; Nella Larsen; Ann Petry; Margaret Walker.

# KANYE WEST
## Hip-hop musician

*Best known for his outspoken and controversial public persona, West is also a groundbreaking hip-hop artist, label executive, and producer.*

**BORN:** June 8, 1977; Atlanta, Georgia
**ALSO KNOWN AS:** Kanye Omari West
**AREAS OF ACHIEVEMENT:** Business; Music: hip-hop; Music: production; Philanthropy

### EARLY LIFE
Kanye Omari West (KAHN-yay oh-MAHR-ee) was born June 8, 1977, in Atlanta, Georgia, to Ray West and Donda Williams West. He moved with his mother to Chicago at age three following his parents' divorce. As a child, West was known for his outspokenness and often found himself in trouble for refusing to obey rules with which he did not agree. He wrote and recorded his first rap, "Green Eggs and Ham," while attending Vanderpoel Elementary. Later, he saved his allowance and bought his first keyboard at the age of fourteen. West formed a group with some high school friends in which he wrote rhymes, created beats, and made up dance routines.

After graduating from high school, West enrolled in Chicago State University, where his mother worked as an English professor. As his interest in music grew, his interest in academia declined. After a year of study, West decided to take time off to work on his music, much to the chagrin of his mother. When it became apparent that he would not be returning to college, West's mother asked him to move out of the house. At the age of twenty, he moved to New Jersey to pursue music production full time.

West achieved some limited success at first, earning production credit for work on lesser-known artists' albums. His first real break came when he was given the opportunity to contribute four tracks to multiplatinum hip-hop artist Jay-Z's *The Blueprint* album in 2001. However, West faced an uphill battle to be taken seriously as a solo artist.

### LIFE'S WORK
West sustained serious injuries in a car accident in October, 2002, when he fell asleep at the wheel on his way home from a recording session. He underwent surgery to reconstruct his face. Not wanting to miss the opportunity to be regarded as a serious recording artist, West recorded the song "Through the Wire," rhyming the lyrics through jaws that had been wired shut. This song became the first single from West's debut album, *The College Dropout* (2004), which was released to much critical acclaim. Praised for its self-aware and intelligent content, a rarity in mainstream hip-hop, *The College Dropout* achieved platinum status and garnered West several Grammy Award nominations, including Album of the Year. While he did not win that award, West won awards for Best Rap Album of the Year and Best Rap Song. In 2005, West was featured on the cover of *Time* magazine. *College Dropout* was followed by *Late Registration* (2005), *Graduation* (2007), *808s and Heartbreak* (2008), and *My Beautiful Dark Twisted Fantasy* (2010)—all of which were well received by critics and fans.

As West's success grew, so did his larger-than-life persona. His notoriety spiked when he made unscripted comments criticizing President George W. Bush during a televised telethon to aid victims of Hurricane Katrina. Praised and condemned for his opinionated outbursts,

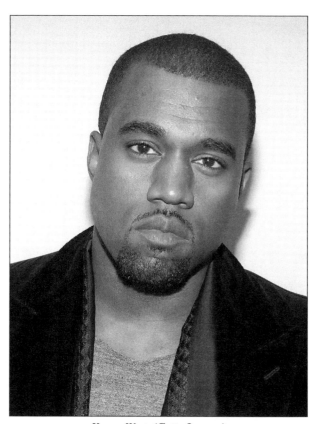

*Kanye West.* (Getty Images)

West is as well known for his off-the-cuff remarks as for his acclaimed music.

In November, 2007, West's mother died suddenly of complications from cosmetic surgery. West was profoundly affected by her loss. In 2010, the state of California passed the Donda West Law, which requires that patients receive medical clearance before undergoing elective cosmetic surgery.

West has used hip-hop as a platform to draw attention to issues he believes in. He has spoken out against homophobia in hip-hop, a genre known for unbridled machismo. In addition to producing music for artists through his G.O.O.D. (Getting Out Our Dreams) Music label, West established the Kanye West Foundation. The foundation's initiatives include Loop Dreams, which teaches at-risk youths how to write and produce music; and the College Drop In Program, in association with the Dr. Ralph Bunche Center for African American Studies at the University of California at Los Angeles (UCLA), which introduces local middle school students to college courses, faculty, and campus life.

## SIGNIFICANCE

West's introspective lyrics, fashion sense, and middle-class background set him apart from other popular hip-hop artists whose work was largely influenced by inner-city "gangsta" culture. His work has broached subjects largely untouched in mainstream hip-hop, such as religion, homophobia, and family relationships. Although he is notorious for his often controversial comments, West has built his reputation through musical talent and philanthropy.

—*Tamela N. Chambers*

## FURTHER READING

Tyrangiel, Josh. "Why You Can't Ignore Kanye." *Time*, August 29, 2005: 54-61. Profile written after the success of *The College Dropout*. Explores West's meteoric rise to fame and the significance of his music.

Weicker, Gretchen. *Kanye West*. Berkeley Heights, N.J.: Enslow, 2009. Presents biographical information in a simple, easy-to-read format.

West, Donda. *Raising Kanye: Life Lessons from the Mother of a Hip-Hop Superstar*. New York: Pocket Books, 2007. West's mother recounts her life and shares her views on her famous son and the people and events that helped shape him.

SEE ALSO: Dr. Dre; 50 Cent; Ice Cube; Jay-Z; Wyclef Jean; L. L. Cool J.; Puff Daddy; Snoop Dogg.

# TOGO WEST
## Government official and lawyer

*West held two senior-level posts in President Bill Clinton's administration. In 1993, he became the second African American to hold the post of secretary of the Army; from 1998 to 2000, he served as secretary of the Department of Veterans Affairs.*

BORN: June 21, 1942; Winston-Salem, North Carolina
ALSO KNOWN AS: Togo Dennis West, Jr.; Togo D. West, Jr.
AREAS OF ACHIEVEMENT: Government and politics; Law; Military

## EARLY LIFE

Togo Dennis West, Jr. (TOH-goh) was born on June 21, 1942, in Winston-Salem, North Carolina, the son of Togo D. West, Sr. and Evelyn Carter. Some reports say that West's grandmother named his father "Togo" in honor of Admiral Heihachiro Togo, the Japanese naval hero of the Russo-Japanese War.

West was an outstanding student, and in his senior year, he earned medals for the highest four-year averages in five subjects: English, social studies, mathematics, foreign languages, and the sciences. His stellar academic record also earned him the honor of being named valedictorian of the class of 1959 at Atkins High School, where his mother taught and his father was the principal. West went on to attend Howard University in Washington, D.C., graduating in 1965 with a B.S. degree in electrical engineering. A year later, he married his Howard University classmate Gail Estelle Berry, an attorney. The couple had two daughters, Tiffany Berry and Hilary Carter, who also became lawyers.

West worked briefly as an engineer for the Duquesne Light and Power Company before returning to Howard to attend law school. While pursuing his law degree, he worked as a legal intern at the Equal Employment Opportunity Commission, as a clerk at the Covington & Burling law firm, and as editor of the *Howard Law Jour-*

*nal.* West received his law degree in 1968, graduating cum laude and first in a class of 130. He spent the year after graduation as a clerk for Judge Harold R. Tyler, Jr., of the U.S. District Court for the Southern District of New York.

## LIFE'S WORK

In 1965, West was commissioned as a second lieutenant in the Army Field Artillery Corps; he entered active service in 1969 as a captain in the Judge Advocate General's Corps. West spent the first of his four years on active duty working in the Military Justice Division and the remaining three years, from 1970 to 1973, as the attorney-adviser to the assistant secretary of the Army for manpower and reserve affairs. In 1973, West left military service and briefly rejoined Covington & Burling before being appointed the associate deputy attorney general in 1975 by President Gerald Ford. Two years later, he began serving in President Jimmy Carter's administration, first as general counsel for the Department of the Navy (1977 to 1979), then as the special assistant to the secretary and deputy secretary of defense, and, from 1980 to 1981, as the general counsel for the Department of Defense.

In 1981, West left government service and returned to the private sector to manage the Washington office of the New York law firm Patterson Belknap Webb & Tyler. He remained there until 1990, when he left to serve as the senior vice president for government relations for the Northrop Corporation, a military aircraft manufacturer.

In 1993, West was nominated by President Bill Clinton to serve as secretary of the Army. Although he was confirmed in November, 1993, West's tenure was clouded by accusations of discrimination and sexual harassment in the ranks. The most widely reported was in 1996 when the Army charged higher-ranking male officers with assaulting female soldiers at the Aberdeen Proving Ground military base in Aberdeen, Maryland. West's response to the scandal was swift and decisive. He instituted a zero-tolerance policy toward sexual harassment and ordered all soldiers to undergo sexual harassment training.

In 1998, during his second term, Clinton named West the acting secretary of veterans affairs. West was confirmed despite intense scrutiny over allegations that the Clinton administration had given burial space in Arlington National Cemetery to Democratic Party donors. In 2000, facing allegations of overspending and mismanagement, West resigned from the agency. West returned to the Covington & Burling law firm and remained there until 2004, when he was named president and chief executive officer of the Joint Center for Political and Eco-

nomic Studies, a Washington, D.C.-based think tank. West left the center in 2006 and founded the TLI Leadership Group, a strategic consulting firm.

Although retired from public service, West has been called upon to share his advice and expertise on a number of issues. In 2007, for example, he was appointed by the Pentagon to cochair the Department of Defense's Independent Review Group on conditions at Walter Reed Army Medical Center and the National Naval Medical Center. In early 2010, he was selected as one of the leaders in the Pentagon's investigation of shootings at Fort Hood, Texas. Later that year, Mayor Adrian Fenty tapped him to serve as chairman of the D.C. Board of Elections and Ethics.

West has been the recipient of numerous honors and awards. His military decorations include the Meritorious Service Medal and the Legion of Merit. As a public servant, he received distinguished service medals from the departments of Defense, Army, Air Force, Navy, and Veterans Affairs. West has served on the board of visitors of the Wake Forest School of Law and the North Carolina School of the Arts, as an adjunct faculty member at the Duke University School of Law, and on the boards of several corporations and organizations. He pledged the Alpha Phi Omega fraternity in college and also became a member of the Omega Psi Phi Fraternity.

## SIGNIFICANCE

West has had a long and distinguished career—though controversial—as a lawyer, military officer, and public servant. As Secretary of the Army, he managed a budget of $60 billion and provided leadership to over one million soldiers and 270,000 civilian employees. Upon his confirmation as secretary of veterans affairs, he became the third person to hold the office and head of the second largest department in the federal government, responsible for health care services, benefits and programs, and national cemeteries for 26 million veterans.

—*V. Tessa Perry*

## FURTHER READING

Bell, William Gardner. "Togo Dennis West, Jr." In *Secretaries of War and Secretaries of the Army: Portraits and Biographical Sketches.* Rev. ed. Washington, D.C.: Center of Military History, United States Army, 2005. This book provides a portrait and brief biographical sketch of West.

U.S. Congress. Senate. Committee on Veterans' Affairs. *Nomination of Hon. Togo D. West, Jr., to Be Secretary of Veterans' Affairs: Hearing Before the Committee on Veterans' Affairs, United States Senate*. 105th Congress, 2d Session, 1998. Washington, D.C.: U.S. Government Printing Office, 1999. The official account of the confirmation hearing on West's nomination to secretary of Veterans Affairs.

West, Togo. "Q&A: Togo Dennis West, Jr., the New Joint Center President." Interview by Joe Davidson. *FO-CUS* (January/February, 2005): 3-4. Interview with West shortly after he was named president and chief executive officer of the Joint Center for Political and Economic Studies.

**SEE ALSO:** Eric Holder; Vernon Jordan; Hazel R. O'Leary; Colin Powell; Larry D. Thompson.

# CLIFTON REGINALD WHARTON, JR.
## Educator

*Wharton accomplished many firsts for African Americans, including being the first black president of a major university. He began his career as an international development economist and adviser on human resources, became a leading businessman and academic administrator, and then was named the deputy secretary of state under President Bill Clinton.*

**BORN:** September 13, 1926; Boston, Massachusetts
**AREAS OF ACHIEVEMENT:** Diplomacy; Education; Government and politics; Social sciences

### EARLY LIFE

Clifton Reginald Wharton, Jr., the oldest of four children, was born in Boston, Massachusetts, on September 13, 1926. His father, Clifton R. Wharton, Sr., was a lawyer and ambassador, while his mother, Harriet Banks, was a chemistry professor and social worker. Because he and his family resided in the Canary Islands in Spain during his formative years, Wharton's mother was his teacher, and she taught him through correspondence courses from the Baltimore schools. Later, Wharton moved to Boston and lived with his grandmother while he attended Boston Latin School. While at the school, he became a track star and worked at a local spool factory.

Wharton entered Harvard University at the age of sixteen and became an announcer on the college radio station and a founder of the National Student Association lobbying group. At the age of nineteen, Wharton was trained as an Air Force pilot in Tuskegee, Alabama, but because it was the end of the war, his service was brief. After earning his bachelor of arts degree in history in 1947, he became the first African American to receive a master of arts degree from the School of Advanced International Studies of Johns Hopkins University.

From 1948 to 1953, Wharton worked for Nelson A. Rockefeller's American International Association for Economic and Social Development, serving mostly Latin American countries. On April 15, 1950, he married Dolores Duncan. They had two sons, Clifton III and Bruce. In 1953, Wharton enrolled in the graduate school of economics at the University of Chicago. While Wharton studied, he worked first as a research assistant and then as a research associate in economics. He became the first African American to earn his Ph.D. in economics at the University of Chicago in 1958.

### LIFE'S WORK

Wharton accepted a position with the Agricultural Development Council (ADC), a nonprofit organization founded by John D. Rockefeller III, and directed council programs in Asia for six years. During this period, he guest lectured at the University of Singapore (1958-1960) and the University of Malaysia (1960-1964). Wharton took a sabbatical and spent a year teaching economic development at Stanford University in 1964. Later that year, he directed the American University Research Program for the ADC. In 1966, he was named the executive director of ADC, served as a member of the president's Task Force on Agriculture in Vietnam, and was a member of the Advisory Panel on East Africa for the U.S. Department of State. Wharton became the vice president of ADC in 1967. He edited *Subsistence Agriculture and Economic Development* in 1969. His experiences, excellent reputation, leadership, and speaking skills earned him memberships on many prestigious commissions and advisory boards. He also served on boards of directors for numerous companies and organizations, including the Equitable Life Assurance Society of the United State, Ford Motor Company, Time Warner, Harcourt General, Burroughs Corporation, Public Broadcasting Service, Carnegie Foundation, Rockefeller Foundation, and the New York Stock Exchange.

On January 2, 1970, during a period of social unrest

on many campuses, Wharton began an eight-year term as president of Michigan State University, a predominantly white university, in East Lansing. Gaining this position made Wharton the first African American president of a major research university. He taught courses in economics there, too. Wharton published *Continuity and Change: Academic Greatness Under Stress* (1971) and cowrote *Patterns for Lifelong Learning: A Report of Explorations Supported by the W. K. Kellogg Foundation* (1973). Beginning in 1976, Wharton served a seven-year term as chairman of the Board for International Food and Agricultural Development for the U.S. State Department. In 1978, he became the first African American chancellor of the State University of New York (SUNY). He also was named to the Presidential Commission on Hunger that year.

After resigning from SUNY, Wharton was selected as the chief executive officer and chairman of the Teachers Insurance and Annuity Association and College Retirement Equities Fund (TIAA-CREF). This made him the first African American to head a *Fortune* 100 company. He served on the U.S. Advisory Commission on Trade Policy and Negotiations in 1991. In January, 1993, President Bill Clinton named Wharton the deputy secretary of state; Wharton served in this capacity—as second in command of the State Department—until November, when he returned to TIAA-CREF as an overseer. In 1996, TIAA-CREF named the auditorium at its headquarters in his honor.

## SIGNIFICANCE

Wharton's distinguished career included foreign economic development, business, and education. He has re-ceived more than sixty honorary degrees, many awards, trusteeships, directorships, chair positions, and commissions. Michigan State University opened the Clifton and Dolores Wharton Center for Performing Arts in 1982, and SUNY opened the Clifton and Dolores Wharton Economics Research Center in 1987. Wharton's legacy rests on his strong interest in Third World development issues, support of universal education, and many historic firsts for African Americans.

—*Cynthia J. W. Svoboda*

## FURTHER READING

Clarke, Caroline V. *Take a Lesson: Today's Black Achievers on How They Made It and What They Learned Along the Way.* New York: John Wiley & Sons, 2001. Provides biographical information on successful African American executives, including Wharton.

Metcalf, George R. "Alvin F. Poussaint." In *Up from Within: Today's New Black Leaders.* New York: McGraw-Hill, 1971. Includes fairly in-depth coverage of Wharton's life up to the beginning of his presidency at Michigan State University.

Quartey, Koko A. *A Critical Analysis of the Contributions of Notable Black Economists.* Burlington, Vt.: Ashgate, 2003. An introduction to several prominent black economists that describes Wharton as a "trailblazer."

**SEE ALSO:** Andrew Felton Brimmer; Kenneth Chenault; Mellody Hobson; Vernon Jordan; Ruth Simmons; Thomas Sowell.

# PHILLIS WHEATLEY
## Poet

*Wheatley is known as the mother of African American literature. Kidnapped from her West African home as a child and sold into slavery in America, she was the first woman of African descent to earn a living as a writer in pre-Revolutionary America. She is often heralded as an example of the literary achievements and importance of African Americans in the history of American literature.*

**BORN:** possibly 1753 (?); west coast of Africa
    (possibly the Senegal-Gambia region)
**DIED:** December 5, 1784; Boston, Massachusetts
**AREAS OF ACHIEVEMENT:** Literature; Poetry

### EARLY LIFE

Phillis Wheatley (FIH-lihs WEET-lee) was born approximately in the year 1753 and sold into slavery when she was seven or eight years old. She arrived in America at a

*Phillis Wheatley.* (Library of Congress)

Boston harbor on July 11, 1761, aboard the ship *Phillis*, for which she was renamed. A Boston merchant named John Wheatley and his wife, Susanna, bought the small girl at a bargain rate because she appeared sickly and weak. She was purchased for domestic work but proved too frail to be of much use as a physical laborer.

At a young age, Wheatley exhibited an intellectual curiosity; her owners' daughter, Mary, taught her how to read English and Latin. Wheatley also read the Bible. She was a quick study, mastering the English language in less than two years, according to her master in an introductory letter attached to her one and only published volume of poetry. The family encouraged Wheatley's intellectual development, supplying her with books and writing material. She wrote her first poem as a young teen. The poem, "On Messrs. Hussey and Coffin," was a reflection on the near-death experience of two family friends of the Wheatleys and appeared in a Rhode Island newspaper on December 21, 1767. One of her most famous poems, published in 1770, is an elegy occasioned by the death of the Reverend George Whitefield, the famous English Methodist evangelist.

### LIFE'S WORK

By her late teens, Wheatley had become an accomplished poet. Her poetry fused classic Greek and Latin structures, styles, and classical allusions. Her themes were often patriotic, familial, and religious, veering into the sociopolitical. Despite her growing popularity, Wheatley, guided by her mistress, struggled to publish her first book of poetry in 1772. Potential subscribers hesitated to fund the book because they doubted that she had produced the work herself. Few believed a person of African descent had the intellectual and literary ability to write poetry. To prove her authorship, Wheatley underwent an intense examination before eighteen of Boston's most elite white citizens, including the colony's governor Thomas Hutchinson.

Even after examiners vouched for her poetic abilities, Wheatley still could not find a publisher in America. Her mistress then shipped off the volume to England. There, with the help of an English philanthropist named Selina Hastings, Countess of Huntingdon, Wheatley found a publisher. In 1773, Wheatley traveled with her master's son Nathaniel to England to oversee publication of her volume of poetry, *Poems on Various Subjects, Religious and Moral*. The book was a success and garnered her fame in both England and America. She was treated as a kind of novelty, an African genius. Her company was sought by prominent Americans and Englishmen such as Benjamin Franklin, who was in England during the time of her visit, Benjamin Rush, and English abolitionist Granville Sharp. Even King George requested her audience, an invitation Wheatley was forced to decline because her mistress's poor health called her back to Boston prematurely.

Shortly after the book was published in September of 1773, Wheatley's owners freed her. Despite acclaim after her first book, though, she struggled to maintain her success. With the outbreak of the Revolutionary War, it became even more difficult for her to find patrons. The nascent nation's attention was consumed by American freedom and nationhood. In 1778, Wheatley married John Peters, who owned a small grocery store. Together, they had three children, none of whom lived into adulthood. In 1779, Wheatley tried to publish a second volume of poetry but failed. She and her husband continued to struggle financially. She died on December 5, 1784, at approximately thirty-one years old. She was never able to publish a second book but did publish several individual poems in the months before her death.

---

## WHEATLEY'S VOLUME OF POETRY

Phillis Wheatley's only published volume of poetry covers a range of topics and poetic styles. The volume contains odes and elegies for famous figures such as the Reverend George Whitefield. Some poems are personal addresses to English royalty. Some are patriotic and reverent. Others hint of sentimentality, mourning the death of children. One of her most frequently anthologized poems is "On Being Brought from Africa," which muses about Wheatley's own Christian conversion experience. She constructs herself as the model convert, a self-avowed African heathen who finds religion in America. She reminds her readers that salvation is accessible to African Americans and whites alike. Written in iambic pentameter, complete with heroic couplets, the poem harkens back to classical poetry, which gives Wheatley authority as a poet, showing that she is well-versed in traditional forms.

Not everybody recognized Wheatley's poetic genius. Shortly after Wheatley's death, Thomas Jefferson, in his *Notes on the State of Virginia*, denied her the label of poet, dismissing her work as unimaginative, unworthy even of criticism. Jefferson's perspective echoed a common assumption of the time that African Americans were incapable of literary production. He shifted the terms of the debate, however, so that it was no longer about whether African Americans could produce art (clearly Wheatley was an example that they could) but whether they could produce quality art. To emphasize Wheatley's genius, her master carefully packaged the volume by including his own letter in which he characterizes her as a prodigy. He also included the names of elite Bostonians who had all interrogated Wheatley and vouched for her authenticity. Thus, the volume derived its meaning not only from Wheatley's own literary genius but also from a white patriarchal system that hovered over the text as a validity shield.

---

beings or part of a subhuman species related to apes. She stood as living proof of African Americans' intellectual capabilities and equality.

—*Cassander L. Smith*

## SIGNIFICANCE

As a poet, Wheatley was one of the first people of African descent to participate in the larger American literary tradition. She did not just participate, however; she manipulated the tradition to give voice to an African American presence and consciousness. Furthermore, she made the public more comfortable with the idea of African Americans as literary, as artistically gifted, figures. Her religious-themed poetry made it impossible for African Americans to be dismissed as savages; she argued that salvation was accessible to all humanity. Wheatley proclaimed African American humanity at a time when race theorists and philosophers, such as Immanuel Kant, were contemplating whether African Americans were human

## FURTHER READING

Gates, Henry Louis, Jr. *The Trials of Phillis Wheatley: America's First Black Poet and Her Encounters with the Founding Fathers*. New York: Basic Civitas Books, 2003. Explores Wheatley's central role in the development of African American literature.

Mason, Julian D., Jr., ed. *The Poems of Phillis Wheatley*. Rev. ed. Chapel Hill: University of North Carolina Press, 1989. Includes Wheatley's poetry, letters, and biographical information that provides a good overview of her life.

May, Cedrick. "Phillis Wheatley and the Charge Toward Progressive Black Theologies." In *Evangelism and Resistance in the Black Atlantic, 1760-1835*. Athens:

University of Georgia Press, 2008. Examines Wheatley's use of Christian rhetoric as a form of resistance and cultural critique.

Zafar, Rafia. "Sable Patriots and Modern Egyptians: Phillis Wheatley, Joel Barlow, Ann Eliza Bleecker." In *We Wear the Mask: African-Americans Write American Literature, 1760-1870*. New York: Columbia University Press, 1997. Argues that early African American writers such as Wheatley appropriated mainstream genres and techniques to construct identities.

**SEE ALSO:** James Madison Bell; Paul Laurence Dunbar; Alice Dunbar-Nelson; Charlotte L. Forten Grimké; Frances Ellen Watkins Harper; James Weldon Johnson.

# TYRONE WHEATLEY
## Football player and coach

*One of the most talented athletes ever to come out of metropolitan Detroit, Wheatley was a standout in high school before playing football at the University of Michigan. After playing professionally for ten years, he began a new career in coaching.*

**BORN:** January 19, 1972; Inkster, Michigan
**ALSO KNOWN AS:** Tyrone Anthony Wheatley
**AREAS OF ACHIEVEMENT:** Sports: football; Sports: track and field

### EARLY LIFE

Tyrone Anthony Wheatley (ti-ROHN) was born on January 19, 1972, in Inkster, Michigan, in metropolitan Detroit. Wheatley struggled through considerable hardships while he was growing up. When he was just two years old, his father, Tyrone, died of a gunshot wound to the head. His mother, Patricia, remarried, and Wheatley's stepfather died of a heart attack when Wheatley was thirteen. After his stepfather's death, Wheatley's mother lost her job and became an alcoholic. At the age of fourteen, Wheatley was almost entirely responsible for his sister and half brother. The neighborhood where Wheatley grew up was plagued by drugs and gang violence, and this, coupled with his mother'sd rinking problem, motivated him to leave home with his younger siblings. He moved into his aunt's home, where he lived with his siblings for the remainder of his childhood.

Despite the difficulties of his youth, Wheatley developed into an outstanding athlete. He attended Hamilton J. Robi-chaud High School in Dearborn Heights, Michigan, where he excelled in track and field, football, and basketball. Considered the best Michigan high school athlete in history, he set many records in track and field, football, and basketball.

### LIFE'S WORK

After graduating from high school in 1991, Wheatley accepted an athletic scholarship from the University of Michigan, where he played running back on the football team for four years and ran track for three. As he did in high school, Wheatley excelled as an athlete. In 1992, he was named the Big Ten player of the year; in 1993, he led the Wolverines to the Rose Bowl, where he was named most valuable player (MVP). He also was named MVP of the 1994 Hall of Fame Bowl. He was a three-time All-

*Tyrone Wheatley.* (Getty Images)

Big Ten selection for football and a three-time All-Big Ten honoree as a sprinter on the track team.

In the university's athletic history, Wheatley ranks fourth in career rushing yards and second in career rushing touchdowns as of 2010. He set a record at the university for single-season yards per carry and recorded twenty 100-yard rushing games. After leaving the university in 1995, he entered the National Football League (NFL) draft and was the seventeenth overall pick. He played professionally for ten years, with the New York Giants from 1995 to 1998 and with the Oakland Raiders from 1999 to 2004.

After ending his professional career in 2004, Wheatley began pursuing a career in coaching, a field in which always had been interested. He got coaching experience by serving minority coaching fellowships with the Pittsburgh Steelers and the Tampa Bay Buccaneers. In 2006 and 2007, he served as the head football coach and boys track coach at his alma mater, Robichaud High School. He got his first experience coaching at the collegiate level during the 2009 season, when he was running backs coach at Eastern Michigan University. In the winter of 2010, he was hired as the running backs coach at Syracuse University in New York.

In 2008, Wheately returned to Ann Arbor to complete his bachelor's degree at the University of Michigan. He graduated that year with a degree in sport management. He and his wife, Kim, have five children.

### SIGNIFICANCE

Wheatley is a major figure in Michigan sports history. During his high school career, he earned recognition as one of the state's most talented high school athletes ever. He went on to become a star for the powerhouse University of Michigan. Despite a turbulent professional career, Wheatley generally was well regarded by coaches and teammates. His love of athletics led him to pursue coaching after his playing days were finished.

*—Sarah Grace Small*

### FURTHER READING

Blackman, Frank. "Wheatley's Hit Man for Inside Jobs." *The San Francisco Chronicle*, September 17, 2000. Report on what Wheatley's signing with Oakland might mean to the Raiders, with many details about Wheatley's playing career to that point.

Curtis, Dave. "Where Do Football Players Go When They Retire? Back to School." *Sporting News*, May 10, 2010, p. 70. Brief article on Wheatley's return to the University of Michigan to complete his education after retiring from the NFL.

Freeman, Mike. "Wheatley's Problems with Giants Did Not Start at Michigan." *The New York Times*, December 15, 1996. Critical discussion of Wheatley's difficulties adjusting to the New York Giants, with extensive comments on his earlier career.

Pennington, Bill. "The Two Sides of the Giants' Biggest Enigma." *The New York Times*, July 6, 1998. Another extended discussion of Wheatley's problems fitting in with the Giants.

SEE ALSO: Marcus Allen; Jim Brown; Earl Campbell; Bob Hayes; Walter Payton; Deion Sanders; O. J. Simpson.

# FOREST WHITAKER
## Actor and director

*Whitaker is a versatile actor whose devastating portrayal of Ugandan dictator Idi Amin in* The Last King of Scotland *(2006) earned him the Academy Award for Best Actor.*

BORN: July 15, 1961; Longview, Texas
ALSO KNOWN AS: Forest Steven Whitaker
AREAS OF ACHIEVEMENT: Film: acting; Film: direction; Philanthropy

### EARLY LIFE

Forest Steven Whitaker (WIH-tah-kuhr) was born in Longview, Texas, in 1961, to Forest Whitaker, Jr., an insurance salesman, and Laura Francis, a schoolteacher with two graduate degrees. The family relocated to South Central Los Angeles when the younger Forest Whitaker was a child. After ten years, the family moved to the Carson section of Los Angeles, where the teenage Whitaker lived until leaving for college at age seventeen. Whitaker grew up with an older sister, Deborah, and two younger brothers, Kenn and Damon.

Whitaker's mother, aware of the top public schools in the area, insisted on sending her son to Palisades High School, which required a two-hour daily commute. Whitaker was a superior student, a defensive tackle on the football team, and a promising singer and actor.

Upon graduating in 1979, Whitaker chose to attend California State Polytechnic Institute, Pomona, on a football scholarship. When he was sidelined by a serious back injury, he decided to change both his school and career path. Whitaker was accepted by the University of Southern California (USC), first as a voice student (an operatic tenor) and then as a student in the school's Drama Conservatory. An exceedingly focused student, Whitaker continued his studies at the Drama Studio London in Berkeley, California, upon his graduation from USC in 1982.

## LIFE'S WORK

Whitaker's professional career began shortly after he relocated to Berkeley in the early 1980's. Beginning in television, he guest-starred in episodes of *Cagney and Lacey* (1983), *Hill Street Blues* (1984), and *Diff'rent Strokes* (1985). Upon auditioning for feature film work, Whitaker promptly received supporting roles in major motion pictures, including Cameron Crowe's *Fast Times at Ridgemont High* (1982), Martin Scorsese's *The Color of Money* (1986), Oliver Stone's *Platoon* (1986), and Barry Levinson's *Good Morning, Vietnam* (1987).

While Whitaker had already garnered industry attention from these notable supporting roles, it was his memorable portrayal of Charlie "Bird" Parker in Clint Eastwood's *Bird* (1988) that made the young character actor into an award-winning leading man. His legendary preparation for this role, which included extensive research into jazz and intensive saxophone lessons, solidified his reputation as one of film's most dedicated craftsmen. For his depiction of Parker, Whitaker won the best actor award at the 1988 Cannes Film Festival, and he was nominated for a Golden Globe award.

Whitaker continued working consistently throughout the 1990's, varying the occasional leading role with several well-received supporting parts. Notable roles from this period include those in Neil Jordan's *The Crying Game* (1992), in Stephen Hopkins's *Blown Away* (1994), in Robert Altman's *Prêt-à-Porter* (1994), in Jon Turteltaub's *Phenomenon* (1996), and the title role in Jim Jarmusch's *Ghost Dog: The Way of the Samurai* (1999).

Whitaker began directing films in the 1990's, debuting with a Home Box Office (HBO) film about inner-city violence, *Strapped*, in 1993. He then directed a successful romantic comedy, *Waiting to Exhale* (1995), starring Angela Bassett and Whitney Houston, and *Hope Floats* (1998), a drama starring Harry Connick, Jr., and Sandra Bullock.

Steady work continued for Whitaker throughout the 2000's. The decade began with his role as Ker in *Battlefield Earth* (2000), a film that met with minimal box office sales and universally poor reviews. Rebounding from an atypical disappointment, Whitaker next appeared in David Fincher's *Panic Room* (2002); in Joel Schumacher's *Phone Booth* (2002); in Aric Avelino's *American Gun* (2002), for which he was nominated for an Independent Spirit Award; and in *First Daughter* (2004), which he also directed.

In 2006, Whitaker delivered his second award-winning, career-defining role with his portrayal of Ugandan dictator Idi Amin in Kevin Macdonald's *The Last King of Scotland*. Whitaker won nearly every major acting award for this role, including the Academy Award, Golden Globe, Screen Actors Guild Award, and the British Academy of Film and Television Arts Award.

After his Oscar win, Whitaker balanced appearances in big-budget films, including Denzel Washington's *The Great Debaters* (2007) and Peter Travis's *Vantage Point* (2008), with roles in small independent pictures, including *Winged Creatures* (2009) and *My Own Love Song* (2010). Whitaker appeared in television shows more frequently throughout the 2000's, participating in six episodes of the NBC hospital drama *ER*, from 2006 to 2007, and seasons five and six of the FX Network police drama *The Shield*.

Whitaker met his wife, actor Keisha Nash, on the set of *Blown Away* (1994), and the couple married in 1996. They have two daughters, Sonnet and True, and a son and a daughter from previous relationships, Ocean and Autumn.

## SIGNIFICANCE

Willing to learn a new instrument, language, or cultural tradition and to change his physical appearance for any role, Whitaker has set an industry standard for commitment to his professional craft. Aside from his on-screen legacy, Whitaker is a deeply peaceful, spiritual, and philanthropic man who has benefited from karate and kundalini yoga, has contributed to People for the Ethical Treatment of Animals (PETA), and has supported Hope North, a boarding school for Ugandan children.

*—Eric Novod*

## FURTHER READING

Gabbard, Krin. *Jammin' at the Margins: Jazz and the American Cinema*. Chicago: University of Chicago Press, 1996. Includes a discussion of the authenticity of Whitaker's portrayal of Charlie Parker in Clint Eastwood's *Bird* (1988).

Mapp, Edward. *African Americans and the Oscar: Decades of Struggle and Achievement.* Lanham, Md.: Scarecrow Press, 2008. A discussion of the African American men who have won the Academy Award for Best Actor, and the roles for which they were honored.

Sternbergh, Adam. "Out of the Woods: How Forest Whitaker Escaped His Career Slump." *New York Magazine* (January 9, 2006). A discussion of how Whitaker's Academy Award-winning performance in *The Last King of Scotland* (2006) positively altered his career.

**SEE ALSO:** Don Cheadle; Laurence Fishburne; Samuel L. Jackson; Sidney Poitier; Denzel Washington.

# BILL WHITE
## Baseball player, broadcaster, and executive

*White was an All-Star first baseman who spent much of his distinguished career with the St. Louis Cardinals. After his playing days were over, he became a respected broadcaster and then served as president of the National League, making him the highest-ranking African American executive in American professional sports.*

**BORN:** January 28, 1934; Lakewood, Florida
**ALSO KNOWN AS:** William DeKova White
**AREAS OF ACHIEVEMENT:** Radio and television; Sports: baseball

### EARLY LIFE
William DeKova White was born on January 28, 1934, in Lakewood, Florida, but grew up in Warren, Ohio. He never had a relationship with his father and was left in the care of his grandmother and aunt while his mother, Edna Mae Young, worked as a secretary on military bases from Pennsylvania to Oklahoma.

In 1953, White signed with the New York Giants to earn money to finance his premedical studies at Hiram College in Hiram, Ohio. He was assigned to a minor league team in Danville, Virginia. His determination to obtain an education came from his mother, who had been denied a chance to attend the college of her choice even though she had been her high school valedictorian.

As one of the first African Americans in the Carolina League, White experienced segregation for the first time. African Americans were barred from restaurants, hotels, and movie theaters. He ate his meals on team buses, boarded with African American families on the road, and was subjected to racial epithets during games. When White made an obscene gesture at his hecklers in Burlington, North Carolina, he found himself surrounded after the game by a large crowd of angry whites. Armed with bats, White and his teammates made their way through the mob, which stoned their bus as they departed.

### LIFE'S WORK
As a first baseman, White compiled a .304 batting average over four seasons in the minor leagues before being called up by the Giants early in 1956. He batted .259 as a rookie and hit twenty-two home runs. After missing all of 1957 and most of 1958 because of military service, White was traded to the St. Louis Cardinals. He hit .302 in his first season with the Cardinals and quickly established himself as a slick fielder and a consistent hitter. He hit at least 20 home runs for six straight seasons beginning in 1961, drove in more than 100 runs in four of those seasons, and batted over .300 in three. White's best season came in 1963, when he had career highs with 106 runs scored, 200 hits, 27 home runs, and 109 runs batted in, while hitting .304. His highest batting average was .324 in 1962.

Along with other African American stars such as Curt Flood and Bob Gibson, White helped lead the Cardinals to a World Series victory over the New York Yankees in 1964. He was traded to the Philadelphia Phillies after the 1965 season. After a solid year in 1966 he was a part-timer for the Phillies in 1967-1968 and with the Cardinals again in 1969.

White was an outspoken opponent of racism throughout his playing career. When no black players were invited to a breakfast at a yacht club during the Cardinals' spring training in St. Petersburg, Florida, in 1960, an angry White leaked the story to an Associated Press reporter. An African American newspaper in St. Louis called for a boycott of Anheuser-Busch, the brewery that owned the team, and black players on other teams joined the chorus of protests. When the company threatened to move the Cardinals' spring training camp out of Florida, local businesses bought two motels in a prominent section of St. Petersburg for the use of the Cardinal players and their families. The two biggest Cardinal stars, Stan Musial and Ken Boyer, gave up their private beachfront houses and moved into the motels. The players' wives then created an integrated day school and kindergarten. All these actions prompted a breakdown of segregated practices to which African American players had been subjected during spring training in Florida. Ironically, White told *The New York Times* that if he had been invited to the breakfast, he would not have attended because he did not get up that early.

After his playing career, White became a broadcaster covering New York Yankees games on New York television station WPIX. From 1971 to 1988, White was teamed with former Yankee shortstop and longtime broadcaster Phil Rizzuto. White distinguished himself by the ease with which he conveyed his knowledge of baseball and with his good humor toward the eccentric Rizzuto, famous for his malapropisms, who once began a broadcast by introducing himself as Bill Rizzuto and his partner as Phil White. During White's tenure with the Yankees, he was approached about the possibility of becoming the team's general manager but declined to be considered.

Before the 1989 season began, White was asked to interview for the position of president of the National League, soon to be vacated by newly appointed baseball commissioner A. Bartlett Giamatti. White, by then the divorced father of five adult children, initially declined because he was working only a handful of games each season and devoting more of his time to fishing. Peter O'Malley, owner of the Los Angeles Dodgers, convinced White to agree to an interview, and the former star was persuaded to accept the position. Former Dodger executive Al Campanis had created an uproar in 1987 by claiming that African Americans lacked the qualities necessary to be baseball executives, and the sport felt pressured to prove otherwise. White remained in the post until 1994, when he was replaced by another African American, business executive Leonard Coleman. In 1999, commissioner Bud Selig discontinued league presidencies.

---

## WHITE'S PRESIDENCY OF THE NATIONAL LEAGUE

During his five-year tenure as National League president, Bill White hoped to restore a sense of fun to a sport that had lost some of its former camaraderie, primarily because of labor disputes both players and umpires had with the team owners. Instead, White found himself under attack for being too blunt and outspoken in his criticism of what he perceived as the game's deficiencies. Conversely, White also was criticized for keeping a low profile. Reluctant to be perceived as a one-issue president, White worked behind the scenes to encourage affirmative-action hiring practices. In 1991, he became outraged when the expansion team the Colorado Rockies filled six front-office positions without interviewing a single African American or Hispanic candidate after promising they would do so. This failure came after white men had been hired for all but one of twenty-two executive openings during the previous year. White became increasingly frustrated by his inability to effect change in the game he loved and by his responsibility to be diplomatic during times when he felt he should be expressing his anger. He clashed with Richie Phillips, head of the umpires' union, and seemed aloof toward the owners and defensive with the news media. Feeling handcuffed by Fay Vincent and Bud Selig, the baseball commissioners during most of his time as league president, White found that he had little real power beyond fining players for misbehavior.

---

### SIGNIFICANCE

In addition to being a steady offensive threat for most of his career, White was considered one of the most graceful first basemen ever in the major leagues. He was selected to the National League All-Star team five times and was awarded a Gold Glove as the league's best fielder at his position for seven straight seasons, 1960 through 1966. White also was one of the most intelligent players of his era, adept at knowing how opposing pitchers would approach particular situations. After his playing days, White distinguished himself throughout his long broadcasting career before becoming the first African American league president and the highest ranking black executive in professional sports in the United States.

—*Michael Adams*

### FURTHER READING

*Ebony.* "Bill White, the National League's New Boss: Baseball Selects the First Black to Head a Major-League Sports Organization." 44, no. 7 (May, 1989): 44-45. Summarizes White's career and his qualifications to be National League president.

Randolph, Laura B. "Bill White: National League President." *Ebony* 47, no. 8 (August, 1992): Considers White's achievements in the context of African American history.

Smith, Claire. "Baseball's Angry Man." *The New York Times Magazine* (October 13, 1991): 28-31, 53, 56. In-depth look at White's early life, his playing career, and his time as National League president.

Zoss, Joel, and John Stewart Bowman. *Diamonds in the Rough: The Untold History of Baseball.* Lincoln: University of Nebraska Press, 2004. Includes a sec-tion describing White's hiring as National League president and his reputation for fighting for equality for African American players.

**SEE ALSO:** Hank Aaron; Ernie Banks; Lou Brock; Roberto Clemente; Curt Flood; Bob Gibson; Willie Mays; Frank Robinson.

# WALTER WHITE
## Activist and writer

*White headed the National Association for the Advancement of Colored People (NAACP) from 1929 until his death in 1955. During that time, he championed a sweeping array of civil rights proposals and was the author of several books that highlighted the plight of African Americans.*

**BORN:** July 1, 1893; Atlanta, Georgia
**DIED:** March 21, 1955; New York, New York
**ALSO KNOWN AS:** Walter Francis White; Mr. NAACP
**AREAS OF ACHIEVEMENT:** Civil rights; Social issues

### EARLY LIFE

Walter Francis White was one of seven children born to Madeline and George White. All members of the family appeared, at least on the surface, to have European features. Even as an adult, White's blond hair and blue eyes led most to believe him white at first glance. White was unsure of the composition of his racial ancestry but he recognized that he had a small percentage of African American blood. In the age of Jim Crow, however, one drop of black blood made a person black and thus subject to all manner of discrimination.

Although they were members of Atlanta's black upper class, White's family still experienced the violence and intimidation confronted by all African Americans in this period of southern history. In his autobiography, White recognized that, despite outward appearances, he was an African American, a point painfully brought home during the race riots that engulfed his Atlanta home in 1906. White thus had firsthand knowledge of the terror built into the Jim Crow structure that was then in its infancy. Although the height of lynching incidents in America had passed by the time White reached maturity, racial violence and the crime itself still occurred. The violence he witnessed left an indelible mark on White and would forever shape his identity.

White attended the all-black Atlanta Preparatory School and Atlanta University, from which he graduated in 1916. After college, White started a promising career as an insurance salesman with Standard Life, while also revealing his activist tendencies. During this period, he became one of the founding members of the Atlanta chapter of the National Association for the Advancement of Colored People (NAACP). He proved an active cru-

*Walter White.* (Archive Photos/Getty Images)

sader, attracting the attention of the national NAACP with a successful effort to block the Atlanta Board of Education's efforts to cut the seventh grade from area African American schools. NAACP secretary James Weldon Johnson was so impressed with White's organizational talents that he invited White to join the national organization's staff in New York. In 1918, White took the job. It was a decision that would place him at the forefront of the battle against racial prejudice. When White returned to the South, he did so as an agent of the NAACP.

## LIFE'S WORK

White's early work with the NAACP was as an undercover agent investigating episodes of racial violence across the nation. White estimated that he investigated eight race riots and forty-one lynchings while masquerading as a journalist. His fair complexion led many people to speak openly with him about the reasoning behind the attacks. White's reports were then widely circulated by the NAACP, a fact that increasingly placed White's identity, and his life, at risk. Several times, White recounted episodes in which his cover was blown and he barely escaped harm. At the end of his work as an undercover operative, White wrote his 1929 book *Rope and Faggot: A Biography of Judge Lynch*, in which he explored the causal factors that produced southern lynchings. *Rope and Faggot* represented White's first nonfiction work. Earlier, he had produced two fictional books rooted in the reality of black life in the 1920's, *The Fire in the Flint* (1924) and *Flight* (1926). White's literary output clearly placed him in the spirit of the cultural explosion known as the Harlem Renaissance that emanated from the Manhattan community where he lived.

The 1929 retirement of Johnson opened the way for White to assume control of the NAACP, a position he would hold until his 1955 death. As NAACP executive secretary, White worked for congressional passage of legislation to make lynching a federal crime, to abolish the poll tax, and to fight discrimination in public life. In the 1930's, no civil rights issue loomed as large in Washington as did the antilynching cause. White placed himself and the organization that he led at the forefront of the struggle. Enlisting the help of Washington elites, in-

---

### A MAN CALLED WHITE

Walter White's 1948 autobiography placed before the nation the unique perspective of America's preeminent civil rights leader. In it, White reveals the pain of discrimination he first encountered in Atlanta, Georgia, and how his family, despite their respectable middle-class status, was treated poorly solely because of their race. From that point forward, he knew that race mattered a great deal in the American South and in the nation as a whole. He devoted his career to battling the prejudices that produced the violence he had witnessed. *A Man Called White* traces White's rise to prominence, including harrowing accounts from his days infiltrating racist mobs, to his efforts to convince Washington politicians that equality should be their cause. Especially insightful are his discussions of the many failed battles with segregationists on Capitol Hill. Despite one defeat after another, White refused to give up the cause in which he so deeply believed. He concludes his account with a heartfelt plea for his readers to embrace a color-blind world in which "black is white and white is black." *A Man Called White* offers the reader a glimpse of life on the front lines of the struggle for racial justice in America, from the perspective of a man who often placed himself in great jeopardy to get his point across.

---

cluding Eleanor Roosevelt, White began an aggressive campaign for the enactment of federal legislation on the subject.

In 1938, the Wagner-Van Nuys Anti-Lynching bill appeared on the verge of success. A canvass of the Senate's membership revealed that an overwhelming majority favored its passage. On the Senate floor, however, the bill faced a well-orchestrated filibuster that drained momentum from its supporters. Every day, White sat in the Senate gallery watching the debate, only to once again face disappointment as the Senate failed to invoke cloture against the filibuster. Despite this and other legislative failures, White always believed that any public airing of grievances would benefit the movement in the long term, even if its goals were not achieved in the short term. Under White's leadership, the NAACP targeted politicians with large African American constituencies, threatening ousters if the politicians failed to support the organization's agenda. The threat demonstrated that the organization expected more than mere lip service from politicians.

After war broke out in Europe in 1939, America commenced a massive rearmament campaign that did much to heal the wounds of the Great Depression. Factories sprang up across the nation, and the federal government poured billions into defense spending, thereby ending the economic malaise that had plagued the nation for a decade. As jobs became available, African

Americans often found that discrimination barred their access to employment. White joined forces with labor leader and civil rights activist A. Philip Randolph and threatened a march on Washington to secure equal employment opportunities in the burgeoning defense industry.

Randolph and White played a crucial role in President Franklin D. Roosevelt's issuing of an executive order creating the Fair Employment Practices Commission. During World War II, White shifted the focus of the NAACP from antilynching laws to legislation outlawing poll taxes. Although they came close on several occasions, the votes necessary to enact the proposals never materialized. White also visited African American units serving overseas, sending reports back to American newspapers describing the discrimination these units faced. After the war, White proved influential in convincing President Harry S. Truman that he should desegregate the nation's military and become a champion of civil rights legislation in Washington. White also served as an adviser to the American delegation sent to participate in the founding session of the United Nations in 1945.

White lived long enough to see the landmark *Brown v. Board of Education* decision in 1954. Although the Supreme Court ruling did not end segregation, it served as a pivotal precedent in the fight for equality. White died the following year.

## SIGNIFICANCE

White's ability to place the issues of African Americans on the national agenda represented his most important contribution. Before White assumed command of the NAACP and began aggressively pushing reform, Congress was largely indifferent to the cause of racial equality. Tireless in his efforts, White believed deeply in the concept of equality. Later in his career, White faced challenges to his leadership but always remained on top. A major reason for his success was his ability to cultivate relationships with prominent Americans such as Eleanor Roosevelt, who contributed greatly to the organization after her husband's death. Under White's leadership, the NAACP's massive legal campaign against discrimination ultimately toppled the established system of segregation in America.

*—Keith M. Finley*

## FURTHER READING

Berg, Manfred. *The Ticket to Freedom: The NAACP and the Struggle for Black Integration*. Gainesville: University Press of Florida, 2005. Important study of the evolution of the NAACP's strategy before, during, and after the secretaryship of White. Offers valuable insight into the evolution of America's foremost civil rights organization.

Dyja, Thomas. *Walter White: The Dilemma of Black Identity in America*. Chicago: Ivan R. Dee, 2008. Brief biography of White that places special emphasis on the vagaries and shifting meaning of race in early twentieth century America.

Finley, Keith M. *Delaying the Dream: Southern Senators and the Fight Against Civil Rights, 1938-1965*. Baton Rouge: Louisiana State University Press, 2008. Focuses on the legislative struggle over civil rights in the twentieth century. In this work, special attention is given to the antilynching and anti-poll tax campaigns in which White prominently figured.

Janken, Kenneth Robert. *White: The Biography of Walter White, Mr. NAACP*. New York: New Press, 2003. The first full-length biography of the NAACP head, this work remains the standard interpretation of White's life and career, covering everything from the personal to the political.

White, Walter F. *A Man Called White: The Autobiography of Walter White*. New York: Viking Press, 1948. White's powerful account captures the triumphs and tragedies of his life and career as a crusader for racial justice. This work is essential for understanding the man.

**SEE ALSO:** Cyril V. Briggs; Septima Poinsette Clark; Clarence M. Mitchell, Jr.; E. D. Nixon; A. Philip Randolph; Alexander Walters; Roy Wilkins; Robert Franklin Williams.

# JOHN EDGAR WIDEMAN
## Writer and educator

*Wideman is a critically acclaimed writer, Rhodes Scholar, and university professor. He is best known for his novels, short stories, essays, and social critiques that are closely related to his formal upbringing in Homewood, a predominantly African American neighborhood in Pittsburgh, Pennsylvania. His writings speak to the plight of the black family, specifically broken relationships between black fathers and sons.*

**BORN:** June 14, 1941; Washington, D.C.
**AREAS OF ACHIEVEMENT:** Education; Literature

### EARLY LIFE

John Edgar Wideman was born in Washington, D.C., to Edgar and Betty Wideman. Shortly after Wideman's birth, the family moved to Homewood, a predominantly black neighborhood in Pittsburgh, Pennsylvania. After residing in Homewood from 1941 to 1951, the family moved to Shadyside, an all-white, upper-middle-class suburb in Pittsburgh. There, Wideman attended Peabody High School, where he was one of the few African American students to excel academically and athletically. In 1959, Wideman graduated as class valedictorian and was awarded the Benjamin Franklin Scholarship to attend the University of Pennsylvania (Penn).

At Penn, Wideman majored in English, became a member of Phi Beta Kappa, and was an all-star athlete in basketball and track. During his undergraduate years (1959-1963), Wideman was an excellent student. In his senior year, 1963, Wideman was awarded a Rhodes Scholarship to study at Oxford University. That same year, *Look*, a general-interest magazine based in Des Moines, Iowa, did a profile on Wideman's Rhodes Scholarship titled "The Astonishing John Wideman." Wideman became the second African American to receive the Rhodes Scholarship; Alain Locke, a Harvard graduate, pivotal contributor to the Harlem Renaissance, and author of *The New Negro* (1902), was the first. In 1963, Wideman received his bachelor's degree in English and decided to become a writer.

In 1965, Wideman married Judith Ann Goldman and accepted a summer teaching position at Howard University, a historically black university in Washington, D.C. The couple had three chil-

dren: Daniel Jerome, Jacob Edgar, and Jamila Ann. In 1966, following his teaching stint, Wideman returned to Oxford University and earned a bachelor's degree in philosophy. After completing his studies at Oxford in 1966, Wideman moved back to the United States and was awarded the Kent Fellowship at the University of Iowa's Writer's Workshop. At the University of Iowa, Wideman completed his first novel, *A Glance Away*, in 1967.

### LIFE'S WORK

Wideman continued to write and work in academia. In the fall of 1967, he accepted a teaching position at his alma mater, the University of Pennsylvania. Between 1967 and 1972, Wideman held two major positions at Penn: creative writing instructor and assistant basketball coach. During the rise of the Civil Rights movement in the 1960's, demand surged for African American literature courses. In 1968, Wideman agreed to teach such a course. Not long after, in 1970, he published his second novel, *Hurry Home*. In 1971, he founded the African

*John Edgar Wideman.* (University of Wyoming)

American studies program at Penn and served as its director for two years.

In 1973, Wideman published his third novel, *The Lynchers*, which explores the conflicting issues of race, class, and identity in American life and literature. The novel is about a group of young black men who unsuccessfully plan to lynch a police officer in the rural South. *The Lynchers* won acclaim for Wideman in academic and literary circles across the country. In 1974, Wideman was named professor of English at the University of Pennsylvania and was inducted into the Philadelphia Big Five Basketball Hall of Fame. Following his success at Penn, Wideman accepted a professorship at the University of Wyoming and remained there for eleven years.

Despite Wideman's success as a writer and academic, however, he experienced much turmoil in his personal life. In 1976, his brother Robby was sentenced to life in prison for murder and armed robbery. Ten years later, his eighteen-year-old son Jacob confessed to murdering his roommate at summer camp and was sentenced to life in prison. Jacob's story is echoed in Wideman's widely read novel *Philadelphia Fire*, published in 1990.

In 1986, Wideman accepted a professorship in the University of Massachusetts at Amherst's master of fine arts program. He continued to teach at the university until the mid-1990's. During that time, Wideman published four more books: a novel, *Reuben* (1987); a short-story collection, "Fever" (1989); the novel *Philadelphia Fire*, for which he won a PEN/Faulkner Award (1990); and another short-story collection, *All Stories Are True* (1993). His novels *Sent for You Yesterday* (1983) and *Philadelphia Fire* made Wideman the first writer to receive two PEN/Faulkner Awards. *Philadelphia Fire* is a fictionalized version of the 1985 bombing of the African American MOVE Organization that killed five adults and six children in West Philadelphia. In Wideman's fictionalized version, the protagonist, Cudjoe, returns to his neighborhood to document the bombing. He tackles the issues of the bombing through interviews with citizens from the neighborhood. As Cudjoe unearths these previously suppressed horror stories, he begins to understand that other pressing issues related to the bombing are affecting the community: socioeconomic struggles, family tensions, and lack of education.

---

### *FATHERALONG*

John Edgar Wideman's memoir *Fatheralong: A Meditation on Fathers and Sons, Race and Society* (1994) is a thought-provoking work that describes how Wideman mended his relationship with his father, Edgar, during a road trip to Promise Land, South Carolina, where many of their family members once lived. The book weaves in Wideman's advice on how black fathers and their sons can heal broken relationships. He describes the social disadvantages that black men endure because of racial discrimination. These discussions go beyond the obvious racial issues that drive each of his texts; Wideman is much more interested in examining deeper issues plaguing the contemporary African American community: posttraumatic stress disorder, economics, intraracial relationships and education. Wideman's memoir brings these topics to the forefront, using his personal experiences to engage readers and urging them to work for solutions.

---

Wideman's literary career has spanned more than half a decade. In 2000, his short story "Weight," published by the *Callaloo* journal, won the O. Henry Award. He went on to serve as a professor of Africana studies and English at Brown University.

### SIGNIFICANCE

Wideman has published more than a dozen books and has edited many African American literary anthologies. His work is reflective of and relevant to the African American experience, covering time periods from slavery to the twenty-first century. Wideman's writings also set an example for future African American authors to continue to speak about the state of the black community.

—*Casarae L. Gibson*

### FURTHER READING

Coleman, James W. *Writing Blackness: John Edgar Wideman's Art and Experimentation*. Baton Rouge: Louisiana State University Press, 2010. Scholarly examination of the techniques and themes of Wideman's work.

TuSmith, Bonnie, ed. *Conversations with John Edgar Wideman*. Jackson: University Press of Mississippi, 1998. Collection of personal and public interviews covering Wideman's career from 1967 to 1997.

TuSmith, Bonnie, and Keith Byerman, eds. *Critical Essays on John Edgar Wideman*. Knoxville: University of Tennessee Press, 2006. Collection of literary criticism on Wideman's novels, essays, short stories, and nonfiction. A recommended text for students and scholars who want to know more about Wideman's work from a academic standpoint.

Wideman, John Edgar. *Fatheralong: A Meditation on Fathers and Sons, Race and Society.* New York: Pantheon Books, 1994. Wideman's memoir discusses his personal relationship with his father and a trip to his ancestral hometown in South Carolina.

_____. *Philadelphia Fire.* New York: Holt, 1990. Wideman's acclaimed novel centers on the 1985 MOVE bombing that killed eleven African Americans in West Philadelphia, Pennsylvania.

**SEE ALSO:** Steven Barnes; David Bradley; Leon Forrest; Ernest J. Gaines; William Melvin Kelley; Walter Mosley; Walter Dean Myers; Ishmael Reed; Al Young.

# L. DOUGLAS WILDER
## Politician

*Wilder created new opportunities for black politicians by becoming the first African American elected governor in the nation's history. His commitment to public service led him to become a candidate for the Democratic nomination during the 1992 presidential election.*

**BORN:** January 17, 1931; Richmond, Virginia
**ALSO KNOWN AS:** Lawrence Douglas Wilder
**AREA OF ACHIEVEMENT:** Government and politics

### EARLY LIFE

Lawrence Douglas Wilder was born in Richmond, Virginia, on January 17, 1931, during the Great Depression. He was named for the African American poet Paul Laurence Dunbar and abolitionist Frederick Douglass. His father, Robert, worked for an insurance company as a supervisor, while his mother, Beulah, raised Wilder and his seven siblings.

Wilder experienced racism first hand at George Mason Elementary School and Armstrong High School, both segregated institutions. He earned a bachelor's degree in chemistry from Virginia Union University in Richmond in 1951. After college, Wilder was drafted into the newly desegregated U.S. Army and was awarded the Bronze Star for his heroism in combat in the Korean War. After the war, he attended law school at Howard University in Washington, D.C. (at the time, no Virginia law school admitted African Americans), receiving his degree in 1959. He also married Eunice Montgomery, whom he divorced in 1978. Wilder returned to Virginia, passed the bar exam, and opened a law office specializing in criminal defense and personal injury cases.

A decade later, Wilder decided to enter state politics. He won a special election for a seat in the Virginia Senate in 1969 as a Democrat, becoming the first African American to sit in that body since the end of the Civil War. Reelected for four additional terms, Wilder wielded considerable influence in the senate, serving on committees that dealt with political appointments and transportation, among other issues.

In 1985, Wilder was elected lieutenant governor under Governor Gerald Baliles. When Baliles's term ended, Wilder decided to run for the governorship in 1989. He narrowly won the election against Marshall Coleman by approximately sixty-seven hundred votes.

### LIFE'S WORK

Wilder became Virginia's sixty-sixth governor when he was sworn into office on January 13, 1990. He was the first African American in the nation's history to be elected governor of a state. As governor, Wilder quickly gained a reputation as a fiscally conservative Democrat. He made difficult decisions concerning state spending, reduced the number of state employees, and balanced the state's budget even as the country went through a recession.

Wilder also earned a reputation as a "law and order" governor, pursuing legislation that would require drug testing for college students and allowing a series of criminals to be executed. This reputation was somewhat damaged when he issued a pardon for basketball player Allen Iverson, at the time a high school student, after Iverson's conviction for assault.

As the 1992 presidential election approached, Wilder officially entered the race for the Democratic nomination in September, 1991. Although his candidacy drew media attention, he was unable to generate campaign donations and dropped out of the race in January, 1992, citing the need to focus on the fiscal problems facing Virginia. He finished his term as governor two years later and was succeeded by Republican George Allen.

After he left office, Wilder ran for the U.S. Senate in 1994 as an independent but later withdrew from the race. By 2004, Wilder was ready to return to elective office, running for the position of mayor of Richmond. He easily won, garnering nearly four-fifths of the vote, and served a single term as mayor, working to end corruption in city government and to reduce the spread of firearms. He chose not to run for reelection in 2008. Wilder became an adjunct professor at Virginia Commonwealth University in the School of Government and Public Affairs, which bears his name.

### SIGNIFICANCE

Wilder's career in Virginia politics, as well as briefly on the national stage, demonstrated an ability to rise above racial divisions to become a successful public figure. By pursuing the highest elective offices, Wilder created new opportunities for other African American politicians to aim for positions previously held only by whites. His bid for the presidency in 1992 also was important for the Democratic Party itself, as Wilder demonstrated that a more moderate Democrat could appeal to independent voters.

—*David Smailes*

### FURTHER READING

Bacon, Lisa. "Famous Mayor Under Fire in Virginia." *The New York Times*, October 21, 2007, p. A25. A general account of some of the difficult decisions Wilder made as mayor of Richmond, with emphasis on his power to force changes.

Baker, Donald. *Wilder: Hold Fast to Dreams—A Biography of L. Douglas Wilder.* Santa Ana, Calif.: Seven Locks Press, 1990. A good introduction to Wilder's early career, based largely on interviews with the Wilder himself. The book ends before Wilder takes office as governor, however.

Cooper, Matthew. "The Call of the Wilder." *U.S. News and World Report* 110, no. 18 (May, 1991): 32-33. Profile written in the run-up to Wilder's presidential campaign, with particular emphasis on his formative experiences as well as his years as governor.

Jeffries, Judson. *Virginia's Native Son: The Election and Administration of Governor L. Douglas Wilder.* West Lafayette, Ind.: Purdue University Press, 2000. An excellent general description of Wilder's experience as governor, with a focus on the role of racism in his election and administration, and his legacy as governor.

**SEE ALSO:** David A. Paterson; Deval Patrick; P. B. S. Pinchback.

# LENNY WILKENS
## Basketball player and coach

*Wilkens has enjoyed success as a professional basketball player and coach. His work ethic and perseverance have won him several awards and honors. After his retirement from basketball, Wilkens continues to make a positive impact on young people and the community.*

**BORN:** October 28, 1937; Brooklyn, New York
**ALSO KNOWN AS:** Leonard Randolph Wilkens, Jr.
**AREA OF ACHIEVEMENT:** Sports: basketball

### EARLY LIFE

Leonard Randolph Wilkens, Jr., was born on October 28, 1937, in Brooklyn, New York. His father was African American, his mother Irish. The oldest of four children, Wilkens played basketball in Catholic Youth Organization (CYO) leagues. He made the varsity team at Boys High School as a junior but quit to play CYO basketball because his coach did not give him enough playing time. He was the starter until he graduated from high school in January, 1956.

Wilkens attended Providence College in Rhode Island. One of six African American students at the college, he majored in economics and made the dean's list. For the Friars, he averaged 14.9 points per game as a starter in his three years. He was named the most valuable player in the National Invitational Tournament in 1960 and awarded All-American honors.

### LIFE'S WORK

Wilkens was the sixth pick in the first round of the 1960 National Basketball Association (NBA) draft. He signed with the St. Louis Hawks for eight thousand dollars. In his first season, he averaged 11.9 points per game. During the 1961-1962 season, Wilkens played in only twenty games because he was called to active duty in the U.S. Army. He returned for the 1962-1963 season and made the Eastern Conference All-Star team. Wilkens was traded in the 1968-1969 season to the Seattle SuperSonics, where he was the team's leading scorer with 22.4 points per game and 8.2 assists per game.

In 1969, Wilkens became the second African American NBA head coach (after Bill Russell), when he served as a player-coach of the SuperSonics. In the 1970-1971 season, the team's record was 38-44, and Wilkens was named the most valuable player at the All-Star game. The next season, he led his team to a winning record (47-35) for the first time in franchise history. However, because the team failed to make the play-offs, Wilkens was replaced as head coach. He was traded to the Cleveland Cavaliers before the start of the 1972-1973 season. With the Cavaliers, Wilkens averaged 8.4 assists per game in 1972-1973 and 7.1 assists per game in 1973-1974.

In 1974, Wilkens was traded to the Portland Trail Blazers, where he was a player-coach. He retired from playing basketball in 1975, but continued to coach the Trail Blazers for another season. In 1977, Wilkens returned to the SuperSonics as director of player personnel and took over as coach after they lost 17 of 22 games. The team went 42-18 under Wilkens. The next season, the SuperSonics went 52-30 and won the NBA championship over the Washington Bullets. Wilkens stayed with the SuperSonics until 1986, when he became head coach of the Cleveland Cavaliers. During the 1988-1989 season, Wilkens coached the team to 57 regular-season wins. In 1989, he was inducted into the Naismith Memorial Basketball Hall of Fame. In 1993, he became the head coach of the Atlanta Hawks. He led the Hawks with a 57-25 record, tied for the best record in the Eastern Conference, and was named NBA coach of the year. Wilkens won his 1,000th regular-season game in 1996 against the Indiana Pacers. He also won a gold medal as coach of the 1996 U.S. Olympic basketball team. He also coached the Toronto Raptors and New York Knicks before retiring from coaching in 2005.

Wilkens holds honorary doctoral degrees from Providence College, Seattle University, and St. Francis College. He founded the Lenny Wilkens Foundation, a nonprofit organization dedicated to health care and education for young people. He and his wife, Marilyn, have three children: Leesha, Jamee, and Leonard III.

## SIGNIFICANCE

Despite a journeyman career, Wilkens persevered to become a Hall of Fame player and coach. Although he was not a prolific scorer, his passing and tempo-setting play created opportunities for teammates. He was the NBA's second African American coach (a role he took on while still playing) and built a thirty-five-year career in the profession. At the time of his retirement, Wilkens was the winningest coach in NBA history.

*—Tina Chan*

*Lenny Wilkens holds the trophy after his Supersonics won the NBA championship in 1979.* (AP/Wide World Photos)

## FURTHER READING

Evans, Jayda. "Wilkens a Sonic Again—as Vice Chairman." *The Seattle Times*, December 1, 2006. Describes Wilkens's ties to the SuperSonics franchise and long basketball career.

Thomas, Ron. "Black Coaches Extend Integration Beyond the Sidelines." In *They Cleared the Lane: The NBA's Black Pioneers*. Lincoln: University of Nebraska Press, 2002. Includes a long section on Wilkens's career and approach to dealing with racism.

Wilkens, Lenny. *The Lenny Wilkens Story*. New York: Eriksson, 1974. Wilkens recounts his early life in his first autobiography.

Wilkens, Lenny, and Terry Pluto. *Unguarded: My Forty Years Surviving in the NBA*. New York: Simon & Schuster, 2000. Wilkens's second autobiography chronicles his long career as a player and coach.

SEE ALSO: Elgin Baylor; Wilt Chamberlain; Walt Frazier; Oscar Robertson; Bill Russell.

# ROY WILKINS
## Activist

*Wilkins was involved in the National Association for the Advancement of Colored People (NAACP) for fifty years, twenty-two as the organization's influential executive secretary. He helped to secure passage of most of the major civil rights bills of the twentieth century and orchestrated the legal campaign that culminated with the landmark 1954* Brown v. Board of Education *decision.*

**BORN:** August 30, 1901; St. Louis, Missouri
**DIED:** September 8, 1981; New York, New York
**ALSO KNOWN AS:** Mr. Civil Rights
**AREAS OF ACHIEVEMENT:** Civil rights; Government and politics; Law; Social issues

### EARLY LIFE
Roy Wilkins was born on August 30, 1901, to William and Mayfield Wilkins in St. Louis, Missouri. When Wilkins was four years old, his mother died of tuberculosis, and his father sent him and his younger siblings to

*Roy Wilkins.* (Library of Congress)

live with their aunt and uncle in St. Paul, Minnesota. The move proved fortuitous for Wilkins as it afforded him a chance to grow up in amid considerable ethnic diversity in community in which race was not paramount. As a high school student, he edited the school newspaper, and he remembered facing little overt discrimination.

Wilkins's experience in Minnesota gave him a glimpse of the benefits afforded in a color-blind society. He would remain a champion of integration for the rest of his life. In 1919, Wilkins enrolled in the University of Minnesota, where he majored in sociology and minored in journalism. He worked low-paying odd jobs in order to subsidize his education.

Upon graduating in 1923, Wilkins found employment with the prominent black newspaper *The Kansas City Call*, which enjoyed statewide circulation. While in Missouri, he felt the sting of racial prejudice for the first time. Segregation governed social interaction in the city as well as the state, a fact that compelled the young Wilkins to join the local chapter of the National Association for the Advancement of Colored People (NAACP), thus beginning his decades-long affiliation with the group. Wilkins wrote increasingly assertive editorials for *The Call* that urged African Americans to exercise their right to vote and challenge the entrenched authority that upheld Missouri's segregation statutes. The 1930 defeat of staunch segregationist U.S. Senator Henry Allen was considered a direct result of Wilkins's campaign. Wilkins's effectiveness brought him to the attention of the head of the NAACP, Walter White. He was about to set out on a career path that would make him one of the most important civil rights leaders of the twentieth century, placing him at the forefront of the drive for racial equality.

In 1931, Wilkins found himself working directly with White at the NAACP headquarters in New York. His first major assignment required him to travel to Mississippi, where he served as an undercover operative, earning ten cents a day constructing federally subsidized levees, risking his life in pursuit of justice. The eye-opening experience prompted Wilkins to write a 1932 report titled "Mississippi Slave Labor," in which he revealed the brutal oppression faced by the project's employees. Wilkins's report reached Washington, D.C., prompting Congress to help the levee workers suffering under the brutal conditions typically experienced by African Americans in the South.

## WILKINS AND THE MARCH ON WASHINGTON

On August 28, 1963, an estimated 250,000 people descended on the nation's capital to demand racial justice in America. The March on Washington often is considered the high point of the Civil Rights movement, coming as it did after the shocking racial violence in Birmingham, Alabama, earlier the same year and President John F. Kennedy's vow to end segregation in America. National media attention focused on the demonstration's message of hope. Martin Luther King, Jr., delivered his famous "I Have a Dream" speech, which captured the spirit of the event and galvanized the forces dedicated to ending oppression.

Often overlooked is a man who played a prominent role in bringing about the historic march, Roy Wilkins. It was Wilkins who, in the face of much doubt, kept faith that an impressive crowd would attend. History proved him right. Although King held the spotlight at the event, Wilkins was more focused on its success than on who received the accolades. His approach to the event underscored how he approached the civil rights fight in general—nothing mattered but the end result.

### LIFE'S WORK

In 1934, Wilkins became the editor of the NAACP's national news magazine, *The Crisis*. He also continued his active work on behalf of the NAACP, keeping a busy speaking schedule and championing the group's numerous causes. When White fell ill in 1949, Wilkins temporarily filled his post until White's return. After White's death in 1955, the NAACP's board of directors made Wilkins the group's executive secretary. The organization that Wilkins now commanded had made itself the voice of black America. Wilkins, like White before him, believed in bringing about racial equality through well-established channels. The organization challenged the constitutionality of segregation and all of its satellite institutions through the legal system, hoping that the Supreme Court would rule such laws unconstitutional and Congress would enact legislation to right historic wrongs against African Americans.

During the 1920's and 1930's, the NAACP sought legislation to make lynching a federal crime. Wilkins was at the center of the campaign that culminated in legislative defeat. Despite the failure, he had faith in the long-term success of the movement to thwart lynching, for although a bill never passed, the publicity that the NAACP brought to the crime fostered national outrage and encouraged southern states to work toward curtailing the crime. Lynchings decreased dramatically even without the passage of federal legislation.

For Wilkins, the message was clear: Slow and steady effort produced victory. This lesson was reinforced in 1954 when the Supreme Court issued its verdict in *Brown v. Board of Education*, which represented the culmination of an ongoing legal challenge orchestrated by the NAACP. Much to Wilkins's delight, the court ruled that segregated public schools were unconstitutional, thus establishing a precedent that undermined the sanctity of the 1896 *Plessy v. Ferguson* ruling upon which all segregation statutes rested. It was a major victory for the organization and for the cause of racial justice, but it did not produce change overnight. Instead, many white southerners embraced the doctrine of "massive resistance," vowing to fight the *Brown* ruling with all lawful means at their disposal. The backlash set the stage for a showdown over segregation; Wilkins and the NAACP found themselves in the middle of a firestorm.

The slow process of school integration and the continued injustices perpetrated in the name of segregation prompted the emergence of the Civil Rights movement. Across the South, African Americans took to the streets in protest. New leaders such as Martin Luther King, Jr., and his Southern Christian Leadership Conference emerged and took some of the spotlight away from the NAACP. Wilkins supported the endeavors of rival organizations and often orchestrated activities in concert with them. The famous 1963 March on Washington, for example, was brought about in part by the efforts of Wilkins.

Aware of the power of propaganda from his earliest days with the NAACP, Wilkins recognized that anything that shed light on the horrors of segregation was a positive, whether he received credit for it or not. Behind the scenes, Wilkins pressed the fight against segregation on both the state and national levels. His calm, moderate approach to the nation's racial problems made him a favorite of politicians, who regularly called on him to use his influence in the African American community to urge restraint among the demonstrators. Wilkins figured prominently in all of the major legislative battles over civil rights during the 1950's and 1960's, from the unsatisfactory Civil Rights Act of 1957 to the sweeping Civil Rights Act of 1964 to the deeply fulfilling Voting Rights Act of 1965.

As legislative victories mounted, some African Americans rallied to the Black Nationalist movement, a development that Wilkins, who had always championed an integrated America, could not bear and often criticized. This stance led some to condemn Wilkins as being out of touch with the movement. As the 1970's dawned, membership in the NAACP fell, as did support for Wilkins's leadership. In 1977, Wilkins officially stepped down as the head of the NAACP, but he remained active in the cause of racial justice until his death in 1981.

## SIGNIFICANCE

Wilkins was one of America's preeminent civil rights leaders in the twentieth century, despite being overshadowed by more outspoken members of the movement. He adopted a behind-the-scenes approach that might have garnered less attention, but still brought about many important advances for African Americans. A longtime member and leader of the NAACP, he was involved in the antilynching crusade of the 1930's, the anti-poll-tax battles of the 1940's, and the drive for the eradication of all forms of discrimination during the 1950's and 1960's. His patient strategy brought success with the landmark *Brown v. Board of Education* decision and the equally significant civil rights legislation in the subsequent decade.

Wilkins's impressive credentials, coupled with his tone of moderation, made him a trusted adviser for many politicians as they attempted to grapple with the civil rights crusade. During the 1970's, Wilkins criticized the administrations of presidents Richard M. Nixon and Gerald Ford for threatening to turn back the clock on the advances made in previous decades. He continued the fight for an integrated America, including supporting controversial busing programs as a means of redressing racial imbalances in public schools.

*—Keith M. Finley*

## FURTHER READING

Finley, Keith M. *Delaying the Dream: Southern Senators and the Fight Against Civil Rights, 1938-1965.* Baton Rouge: Louisiana State University Press, 2008. Chronicles the legislative battle over civil rights to which Wilkins devoted much of his career as a member of the NAACP.

Gilmore, Glenda. *Defying Dixie: The Radical Roots of Civil Rights, 1919-1950.* New York: W. W. Norton, 2009. Offers key context for Wilkins's earlier career by exploring the wide array of interests that made up the modern civil rights crusade that he joined and helped to shape.

Sugrue, Thomas J. *Sweet Land of Liberty: The Forgotten Struggle for Civil Rights in the North.* New York: Random House Trade Paperbacks, 2009. Explores the battle for racial justice above the Mason-Dixon Line and highlights the schism within the civil rights community that ultimately threatened Wilkins's leadership.

Sullivan, Patricia. *Lift Every Voice: The NAACP and the Making of the Civil Rights Movement.* New York: New Press, 2009. This is the first major history of the NAACP. It covers the organization before, during, and after Wilkins's tenure.

Wilkins, Roy, and Tom Matthews. *Standing Tall: The Autobiography of Roy Wilkins.* New York: Da Capo Press, 1994. First-person account of the political strategy and internal workings of the NAACP under the leadership of Wilkins.

**SEE ALSO:** Ralph David Abernathy; Myrlie Evers-Williams; Martin Luther King, Jr.; Clarence M. Mitchell, Jr.; A. Philip Randolph; Bayard Rustin; Walter White; Robert Franklin Williams.

# BERT WILLIAMS
## Entertainer

*During the early years of the twentieth century, Williams became the first African American comedian to attain superstar status. Forced to perform in blackface, Williams, along with his partner George Walker, starred in Broadway shows that transcended the minstrelsy that was popular during the era. His critical and popular successes helped create future opportunities for African Americans in musical theater.*

**BORN:** November 12, 1874; Antigua, West Indies
**DIED:** March 4, 1922; New York, New York
**ALSO KNOWN AS:** Egbert Austin Williams
**AREAS OF ACHIEVEMENT:** Entertainment: comedy; Entertainment: minstrelsy; Entertainment: vaudeville

### EARLY LIFE

Egbert Austin Williams was born November 12, 1874, on the West Indies island of Antigua, to Frederick and Julia Monceur Williams. His family led a fairly comfortable life, as his paternal grandfather was a high-ranking government official and successful rum exporter. Nevertheless, the family migrated to the United States in 1885, living briefly in Florida before finally settling in Riverside, California. His father found work as a farmer in the booming citrus industry, while his mother worked as a laundress. Williams eventually enrolled in high school there.

Williams's true desires lay not in academics but in entertainment. An only child, Williams adapted to his solitary environment by developing a keen sense of imagination and creativity. At the age of sixteen, he dropped out of school and left home to become a barker in one of the popular medicine shows traveling through Riverside and other rural towns in California. His father soon found him and, although intrigued by his son's performance, persuaded him to return home. Williams further honed his talents in storytelling and mimicry by continuing to perform in the medicine shows and by working as a singing waiter at an exclusive hotel. Eventually, he decided that his goals of becoming a professional entertainer exceeded the opportunities available in small-town Southern California. In 1893, Williams headed to San Francisco.

### LIFE'S WORK

Williams arrived in San Francisco as a member of a performing troupe called Martin and Selig's Mastodon Min-

strels. Minstrelsy, which had existed since the 1820's, was the first distinctly American theatrical form. Although the genre relied on prevailing stereotypes of African Americans, in Williams's era it provided an avenue for black entertainers to enter theatrical performance. Ironically, because Williams had a very light complexion, he had to apply burnt cork to his skin for the performances, which were in blackface.

Williams's performances with the group represented the key turning point in his career. It was through his association with the Mastodon Minstrels that he met George Walker, who became his partner. The Walker and Williams duo performed song-and-dance numbers, dialogues, and comedic skits. In addition to their initial appearances with the Mastodon Minstrels, they performed at various venues along the California coast, including the San Francisco Midwinter Exposition in 1894. The theatrical circuit had provided many occasions for the men to meet other black performers, who spoke enthusiastically about the greater opportunities available in the East. After a brief stop in Los Angeles, the pair headed to Chicago and then Detroit. These performances, in which Williams's gift for comedy stood out, signaled a switch in the balance of the act, with Walker playing the role of the straight man and Williams the comedian. With this switch, they changed their act's name to Williams and Walker. Finally, during a performance in West Baden, Indiana, the team got their first big break when they were invited to perform in a musical opening in New York.

Williams and Walker made their New York debut in a show called *The Gold Bug*. Although their performance was well received by critics and theatergoers, the production was a failure and soon closed. After appearances in a few more variety shows, the pair made their vaudeville debut in November of 1896. Vaudeville, a genre of live variety performance, was the major American theater form at the time. Thus, Williams and Walker's entrance into the circuit marked their entrance into mainstream entertainment.

By 1898, Williams and Walker had incorporated the cakewalk into their act and were thereafter recognized as uniquely skilled at it. Over the next few years, the duo performed in a series of musical comedies, including *Senegambian Carnival*, *A Lucky Coon*, *The Policy Players*, and *Sons of Ham*, in which they established themselves as the leading African American comedians in show business. In September of 1902, the duo debuted in

*In Dahomey*, the production that made Williams an international star. The musical, which signaled a break from stereotypical images, represented the first full-length, major Broadway musical written and performed by African Americans. After successful runs in New York, London, and other cities, the show closed in 1905. Williams and Walker continued to enjoy exceptional success in vaudeville until Walker, in ill health, retired from performing in 1909. He died in January of 1911.

Now a solo act, Williams continued to perform successfully in vaudeville. In April of 1910, he received an offer to appear in the *Ziegfeld Follies*, the leading revue on Broadway. His appearance with the show made him the first African American entertainer to appear in a regular, full-length Broadway show. In June, Williams made his debut in *Ziegfeld Follies* to good reviews. He continued to perform as one of the biggest stars, and the only African American, in the show from 1910 to 1919. Williams, who had become a naturalized American citizen on June 14, 1918, used his celebrity to speak out against the segregated accommodations he had to endure while on tour with the revue, and against racism in general.

After leaving *Ziegfeld Follies*, Williams returned to recording music and performing on Broadway. In early 1922, he became ill while starring in a musical called *Under the Bamboo Tree*. Despite feeling ill, he insisted on performing in the shows. On February 27, his performance had to be cut short when he was unable to continue. The next day, Williams was transported home to New York City where, on the evening of March 4, 1922, he died of pneumonia complicated by heart disease.

### SIGNIFICANCE

As both a solo performer and a member of the Williams and Walker team, Williams used his exceptional commercial appeal to present a more realistic depiction of African American life. During an era in which black entertainers faced severe limitations, Williams managed to attain international celebrity as a comedian. His success as an entertainer during an era of pervasive racism led to a number of pioneering efforts and achievements. In addition to his groundbreaking accomplishments in vaude-

---

## WILLIAMS AND THE CAKEWALK CRAZE

One of the distinguishing features of the early vaudeville routines of Bert Williams and George Walker was their performance of a dance called the cakewalk. The cakewalk was a dance style that had its origins in both West African traditional dance ceremonies and plantation slave culture. The performance of the cakewalk enabled the slaves to maintain African cultural traditions while mocking the pretensions of the aristocratic southern whites they often observed at ballroom dances. By the 1870's, it had become part of minstrelsy and musicals, and during the 1890's, it was a very common dance form. The popular form of the dance emphasized its more satiric aspects, which evolved into what has been described as a "prancing strut." By integrating the cakewalk into their shows, Williams and Walker were instrumental in making it a national dance craze. Williams, in particular, was seen as having mastered a unique interpretation of the cakewalk. Williams and Walker's role in popularizing the dance soon caused it to be closely associated with their names.

---

ville and on Broadway, in 1901, he became the first African American recording artist. Moreover, he and Walker also were the first major stars to do business with a black-owned music publisher.

*—Patricia G. Davis*

### FURTHER READING

Forbes, Camille F. *Introducing Bert Williams: Burnt Cork, Broadway, and America's First Black Star.* New York: Perseus Books, 2008. Biographical treatment of Williams emphasizing his importance to early black musical theater and his appeal to both black and white audiences.

Krasner, David. *Resistance, Parody, and Double Consciousness in African American Theatre, 1895-19.* New York: Palgrave Macmillan, 1997. Provides important historical context to the difficult social conditions under which Williams worked and succeeded as an entertainer.

Smith, Eric Ledell. *Bert Williams: A Biography of the Pioneer Black Comedian.* London: McFarland, 1992. Offers a detailed account of Williams's life and career, with particular attention to critical reviews of his performances in vaudeville and on Broadway.

**SEE ALSO:** Louise Beavers; Stepin Fetchit; Moms Mabley; Hattie McDaniel; Florence Mills; Bill Robinson.

# BILLY DEE WILLIAMS
## Actor

*Williams earned major roles in Broadway productions, television, and films. He is noted for his appearances as Lando Calrissian in George Lucas's* Star Wars *series.*

**BORN:** April 6, 1937; Harlem, New York
**ALSO KNOWN AS:** William December Williams, Jr.
**AREAS OF ACHIEVEMENT:** Art and photography; Film: acting; Radio and television

### EARLY LIFE

Billy Dee Williams and his twin sister Loretta were born to William December Williams, Sr., a caretaker who was born in Texas, and his wife Loretta, an elevator operator at Broadway's Lyceum Theatre who was born in the West Indies. Billy Dee Williams's maternal grandmother helped in his rearing. Williams attended the Fiorello H.

*Billy Dee Williams.* (Michael Ochs Archives/Getty Images)

LaGuardia High School of Music and Art and Performing Arts in New York. His preparation in art and performance was at New York City's National Academy School of Fine Arts and Design. He studied also with Sidney Poitier in the Actor's Workshop in Harlem.

Williams's first role was at age seven as a page in the Broadway musical *The Firebrand of Florence* (1945). Other early stage roles were in *Take a Giant Step* (1956), *A Taste of Honey* (1960), *The Cool World* (1961), and *The African Americans* (1962). After his initial stage success, he began to pursue film and television roles on the West Coast.

Williams made his film debut as a juvenile delinquent in the 1959 film *The Last Angry Man.* In the 1950's and 1960's, he secured roles in such television series as *Hawk, The Mod Squad,* and *Another World.*

In addition to performing in the film *The Out-of-Towners* (1970), Williams played Chicago Bears star Gale Sayers in the television film *Brian's Song* (1971). Williams received an Emmy Award nomination for his performance as Sayers, a close friend of Brian Piccolo, who died of cancer.

### LIFE'S WORK

In the 1970's, Williams appeared in such films as *Lady Sings the Blues* (1972), *Mahogany* (1975), and *The Bingo Long Traveling All-Stars and Motor Kings* (1976); the last—about a traveling African American baseball team during the time of the Negro leagues—featured James Earl Jones and Richard Pryor. Williams earned the starring role in Universal's *Scott Joplin* (1978). His performances in eleven films by 1980 established his image as a leading man.

Two of Williams's major roles in the 1980's were as Lando Calrissian in George Lucas's *Star Wars, Episode V: The Empire Strikes Back* (1980) and *Star Wars, Episode VI: Return of the Jedi* (1983). In the mid-1980's he performed in the prime-time soap opera *Dynasty.*

During the decades of the 1980's and 1990's, he appeared in eight television series, in eight television films, and in fourteen films. Williams earned induction into the African American Filmmakers Hall of Fame (1984), recognition on the Hollywood Walk of Fame (1985), and the Phoenix Award (1988) from the Black American Cinema Society.

Williams began to pursue art seriously. Beginning in 1990, Williams created the covers for the yearly programs of the Thelonius Monk Competitions. In 1993, New York's Schomburg Center for Research in Black Culture sponsored Williams's exhibit. His works appear also in the National Portrait Gallery and the Smithsonian Institution; all received good reviews.

By 2002, Williams had written three books, including *Just/In Time* (2000), *PSI/Net* (1999) with Rob Mac-Gregor, and *Twilight: A Novel* (2002) with Elizabeth Atkins Bowman. Williams participated in various videos, provided the voice and visual effects for some video games, and toured with Robin Givens in 2004 in the play *If These Hips Could Talk* (2003). Williams's roles from 2000 to 2010 have included parts in nine television series, a play, ten films, many videos, and a television film.

Williams has been married three times. His first wife—Audrey Sellars—gave birth to their son, Corey; Williams and Sellars divorced in 1963. In the late 1960's, Williams married actor Marlene Clark; they divorced in 1971. In 1972, he married Teruko Nakagami, and they had a daughter Hanako. Williams is also the father of a daughter named Camera.

### SIGNIFICANCE

Williams has had success in all aspects of the arts: painting, writing, and performing in films, plays, and televi-

sion. He has appeared in more than thirty films. He has been honored widely for his accomplishments, and he has portrayed African American characters—such as Joplin; Louis McKay, the husband of Billie Holiday; and an African American baseball player in the Negro Leagues—with great power and sensitivity.

　　　　　　　　　　　　　　　　　　*—Anita Price Davis*

### FURTHER READING

Boston, Lloyd. *Men of Color: Fashion, History, Fundamentals.* New York: Artisan, 2000. Boston profiles Williams and his screen achievements. Williams states that his role and his attire in *Lady Sings the Blues* transformed him into a matinee idol.

Brown, Dennis. *Actors Talk: Profiles and Stories from the Acting Trade.* New York: Proscenium, 1999. Williams shares anecdotes about his acting experiences, especially when he worked as a child.

Falkner, David. "The Actor as Athlete: Subtle and Complex Portrait." *The New York Times*, February 7, 1988. Praises Williams's ability to portray athletes on stage and on screen.

**SEE ALSO:** James Earl Jones; Thelonious Monk; Sidney Poitier; Richard Pryor.

# COOTIE WILLIAMS
## Jazz musician

*Williams was a well-known trumpeter who performed with several high-profile jazzmen, including Benny Goodman and Duke Ellington. His collaboration with Ellington produced some of Williams's most famous work, including several albums and compositions of his own using members of Ellington's orchestra.*

**BORN:** July 24, 1910; Mobile, Alabama
**DIED:** September 15, 1985; Queens, New York
**ALSO KNOWN AS:** Charles Melvin Williams
**AREAS OF ACHIEVEMENT:** Music: bandleading; Music: jazz; Music: swing

### EARLY LIFE

Charles Melvin Williams was born on July 24, 1910, in Mobile, Alabama. He began performing music at an early age, and when he was fourteen, he began playing professionally with the Young Family Band. The band included esteemed saxophonist and clarinetist Lester

Willis Young, a popular jazz musician who reached the height of his fame in the 1930's through the 1950's. Williams also performed with Johnny Pope and Holman's Jazz Band. When Williams was fifteen, he moved to Pensacola, Florida, where he joined a jazz group led by Calvin Shields.

Williams's career began to take off when he moved to New York City in 1928. In New York, he recorded with pianist James P. Johnson, a jazz composer, and performed in bands with Chick Webb and Fletcher Henderson. Webb was a bandleader and swing drummer, while Henderson was a pianist and composer who led one of the most influential African American orchestras of the time.

### LIFE'S WORK

Williams's work with these composers and bandleaders brought him acclaim. In 1929, he began performing with legendary bandleader Duke Ellington, replacing Ellington's previous saxophonist, Bubber Miley. Williams continued to perform with Ellington for eleven years. Ellington was so impressed with his work that he allowed Williams to use members of the band in his own recordings. These recordings were released under the names Cootie Williams and His Rug Cutters or the Cootie Williams Orchestra. Williams also did freelance work outside Ellington's big band.

In 1940, Williams left Ellington to join Benny Goodman's orchestra. Two years earlier, in 1938, Williams had played with Goodman in a concert at Carnegie Hall in New York. The stint with Goodman was short, however; Williams soon asked to go back to Ellington's band, but he eventually was persuaded to start his own band. The move was a success, as Williams was able to gather talented musicians such as Charlie Parker and Eddie "Lockjaw" Davis in his group. The orchestra held its first performance in Chicago in 1942.

When the big band era began to wane around the end of the decade, however, so did Williams's career. He scaled down his full orchestra to a sextet and began concentrating on rhythm and blues instead of swing. In 1952, Williams reunited with Ellington. He remained with the band through Ellington's death in 1974 and continued to perform, even making an appearance at the Super Bowl IX halftime show the next year. Williams died on September 15, 1985, in Queens, New York.

## SIGNIFICANCE

Williams was known for playing in a distinctive, fierce "jungle" style and for his use of the plunger mute. He also sang on some of Ellington's recordings, such as "Echoes of the Jungle." Although he is best remembered as a member of Ellington's famous band, he also was a noted artist in his own right. In 1991, Williams was posthumously inducted into the Alabama Jazz Hall of Fame.

—*Jill E. Disis*

## FURTHER READING

Barnhart, Scotty. *The World of Jazz Trumpet: A Comprehensive History and Practical Philosophy.* Milwaukee, Wis.: Hal Leonard, 2005. Offers an overview and analysis of Williams's musical style and career.

Duffy, Timothy. "Cootie Williams." In *Music Makers: Portraits and Songs of the Roots of America.* Athens, Ga.: Hill Street Press, 2002. Profile of Williams in the context of jazz history. Illustrated, with a compact disc.

Hasse, John Edward. *Beyond Category: The Life and Genius of Duke Ellington.* Cambridge, Mass.: Da Capo Press, March 22, 1995. Because Williams was such an integral part of Ellington's orchestra, this source provides insight into his environment and influences.

**SEE ALSO:** Louis Armstrong; Benny Carter; Duke Ellington; Dizzy Gillespie; Charlie Parker; Chick Webb.

# DANIEL HALE WILLIAMS
## Physician, surgeon, and educator

*In 1893, only fifty-six years after James McCune Smith became the first African American physician and only forty-six after David Jones Peck became the first African American to graduate from a regular American medical school, Williams performed the world's first successful open-heart surgical operation. It would be seventy years before open-heart surgery became routine.*

**BORN:** January 18, 1856; Hollidaysburg, Pennsylvania
**DIED:** August 4, 1931; Idlewild, Michigan
**ALSO KNOWN AS:** Doctor Dan
**AREAS OF ACHIEVEMENT:** Education; Medicine

## EARLY LIFE

Daniel Hale Williams was born in Hollidaysburg, Pennsylvania, on January 18, 1856, the fifth of seven children of Daniel Williams, a prosperous free mulatto, and his wife Sarah, a free woman of African, white, and Native American ancestry. Williams began his education in Annapolis, Maryland. Family fortunes declined after his father died of tuberculosis in 1867. His desperate mother broke up the family, leaving some of her children with relatives in Baltimore and taking others to her new home in Rockford, Illinois.

Williams quit his shoemaker's apprenticeship in Baltimore and traveled west to rejoin his mother and younger siblings in Janesville, Wisconsin, where he found work in a barbershop. With financial and tutorial support from his landlord and employer, Harry Anderson, and his mentor, Orrin Guernsey, he received a secondary school diploma from Janesville Classical Academy in 1878. Eager for more education and a professional career, he apprenticed to Henry Palmer, a physician in Janesville. He entered the Chicago Medical College of Northwestern University in 1880 and earned his M.D. in 1883.

### LIFE'S WORK

"Doctor Dan," as Williams was known, interned at Mercy Hospital in Chicago before starting a private surgical practice in 1884, when he was also named surgeon to the South Side Dispensary. Until 1887, he taught anatomy at Northwestern. In 1889, he became a member of the Illinois State Board of Health. Disturbed that he was one of only three black physicians in Chicago and eager to try to overcome the effects of discrimination and prejudice, he proposed founding a new hospital and nursing school with race-blind policies. The board accepted his proposal, which led directly to the opening in 1891 of the Provident Hospital and Nursing Training School, one of the nation's earliest interracial health care facilities. By 1896, it had sixty-five beds.

On the night of July 9, 1893, James Cornish, a victim of a bar fight, was brought to Provident Hospital with a stab wound between the fourth and fifth ribs on his left side. As is typical of puncture wounds, there was little bleeding. Without any of the sophisticated diagnostic equipment that would become common in the twentieth century, Williams was at first unable to determine the extent, severity, or prognosis of the wound, but he saw that Cornish was in shock and fading rapidly. He decided to use an unprecedented procedure to try to save the young man's life.

Williams insisted that he and his staff be familiar with the latest and best medical technology, medical science, and surgical techniques. At the time, only two of the three conditions necessary for complicated modern surgery had been met. John Collins Warren had introduced anesthesia in 1846, but anesthesiology was still an undeveloped science. Ignaz Semmelweis, Oliver Wendell Holmes, James Marion Sims, and Joseph Lister had pioneered antisepsis in the 1840's, 1850's, and 1860's, but it too was still unreliable and not even fully accepted. George Washington Crile would not publish his results on the control of surgical shock and hemorrhage until 1899. Thus, in Williams's operating room, however careful and knowledgable he and his colleagues were, not much existed to prevent patients from suffering pain, developing infections, or bleeding to death.

Williams was aware of these risks and deficiencies when he decided to open Cornish's chest. He had no device to prevent Cornish's lung from collapsing or to safeguard his heart. Williams went ahead anyway, dealing

*Daniel Hale Williams.* (NLM)

with the dangers as best he could. Upon cutting a hinged opening in the chest above the heart, Williams noticed damage to the left internal mammary artery and the pericardium. He repaired both, irrigated the chest with saline solution, and closed the chest. Cornish survived for fifty years.

Williams became instantly famous, not only in local medical and surgical circles but also in the popular press. He was in demand nationwide for prestigious positions. From 1894 to 1898, he was chief of surgery at Freedmen's Hospital in Washington, D.C., and a member of the medical faculty of Howard University. In 1898, he married Alice Johnson and returned to Chicago, where he served at the Provident until 1912. Beginning in 1900, he was occasionally a visiting professor of surgery at Meharry Medical College in Nashville, Tennessee. From 1912 to 1926, he was senior staff surgeon at St. Luke's Hospital in Chicago.

Williams retired after suffering a stroke in 1926. He died of another stroke on August 4, 1931, at his home in Idlewild, Michigan.

### SIGNIFICANCE

In 1895, because the American Medical Association (AMA) would not yet admit people of color as members,

Williams and five other African American physicians—Robert F. Boyd, Daniel L. Martin, David H. C. Scott, H. R. Butler, and Miles V. Lynk—founded a parallel organization, the National Medical Association (NMA), to represent their professional interests. Boyd was its first president and Williams its first vice president. By 2009, NMA membership comprised more than thirty thousand African American physicians.

Williams's lasting importance to the history of medicine was not primarily based on his skill and innovation as a first-rate operative surgeon, but rather on his demonstration to a skeptical world that African Americans could achieve and maintain the highest standards of medicine and surgery. He was the only African American among the founders of the American College of Surgeons in 1913.

*—Eric v.d. Luft*

**FURTHER READING**

Buckler, Helen. *Daniel Hale Williams: Negro Surgeon.* Rev. ed. New York: Pitman, 1968. The standard biography of Williams, revised from its first publication in 1954 as *Doctor Dan: Pioneer in American Surgery.*

Byrd, W. Michael, and Linda A. Clayton. *An American Health Dilemma: A Medical History of African Americans and the Problem of Race: Beginnings to 1900.* New York: Routledge, 2000. Discusses the unique dilemmas of nineteenth century African Americans as both patients and caregivers.

Leavitt, Judith Walzer, and Ronald L. Numbers, eds. *Sickness and Health in America: Readings in the History of Medicine and Public Health.* 3d ed. Madison: University of Wisconsin Press, 1997. Describes the sociological, political, and historical context of Williams's achievements.

Moxsey, Mary E. "Daniel Hale Williams." In *Rising Above Color,* edited by Philip Henry Lotz. New York: Girvin, 2007. A hagiographic and didactic sketch aimed at younger readers.

Shumacker, Harris B. *The Evolution of Cardiac Surgery.* Bloomington: Indiana University Press, 1992. Presents the scientific and medical context of Williams's work.

Williams, Daniel Hale. "Stab Wound of the Heart and Pericardium, Suture of the Pericardium, Recovery, Patient Alive Three Years Afterward." *Medical Record* 51 (1897): 437-439. Williams's own professional account of his groundbreaking feat.

**SEE ALSO:** Dorothy Lavinia Brown; Charles R. Drew; Vance Hunter Marchbanks; Vivien Thomas; Louis T. Wright.

# GUS WILLIAMS
## Basketball player

*One of the best players in the history of the Seattle SuperSonics franchise, Williams was a standout performer throughout his twelve-year career. He often is remembered by his nickname, "The Wizard," which reflects his versatility and acrobatic ability on the court. Williams was one of the stars of the 1979 SuperSonics team that won the National Basketball Association (NBA) title, the only championship in Seattle's NBA history.*

**BORN:** October 10, 1953; Mount Vernon, New York
**ALSO KNOWN AS:** The Wizard
**AREA OF ACHIEVEMENT:** Sports: basketball

**EARLY LIFE**

Gus Williams was born October 10, 1953, in Mount Vernon, New York, a community that has produced a number of basketball stars. Williams's brother Ray also played in the National Basketball Association (NBA), and local brothers Rodney and Scooter McCray did the same about a decade later. Williams grew up playing basketball in this competitive environment and excelled as a player for the Mount Vernon High School basketball team. In 1971, the New York Sportswriters Association picked Williams as the state player of the year. After graduating from Mount Vernon, Williams received an athletic scholarship from the University of Southern California, where he became one of the stars of the Trojans' basketball team.

**LIFE'S WORK**

The Golden State Warriors selected Williams in the second round of the 1975 NBA draft. He had a solid first season, averaging 11.7 points per game and earning a place on the NBA All-Rookie Team. However, in his second year with Golden State, Williams's performance declined, and he managed only 9.3 points per game. After the 1976-1977 season, Williams left Golden State over a contract dispute and signed with the Seattle Super-Sonics.

The years Williams spent with the SuperSonics were the best of his career. Williams was known for his hustle, which earned him the nickname "The Wizard": he moved swiftly across the court and applied constant defensive pressure. He was called a "one-man fast break" by an admiring Jack Ramsay, coach of the Portland Trail Blazers. (He also was known for his stubbornness: After Nike ended its sponsorship contract with him, Williams cut their logos off his sneakers.) Williams had his greatest triumph in 1979, when he helped lead the SuperSonics to the NBA Finals, where they defeated the Washington Bullets to win the championship. This title was only the second in Seattle professional sports history, after a 1917 Stanley Cup win by Seattle's hockey team, the Metropolitans. Williams's teammate Dennis Johnson was named most valuable player (MVP) of the series, but Williams was the top scorer, averaging a stellar 28.6 points per game.

The next year, the SuperSonics underwent many roster changes and suffered through a losing season. Johnson was traded for Paul Westphal, who sat out most of the season, and several other players had suffered serious injuries or retired. Williams reached the end of his three-year contract and tried to leave the team for Portland. However, after sitting out the entire season, Williams returned as a starter for the SuperSonics in 1981-1982 and was named to the All-NBA First Team. During the 1983-1984 season, Williams signed with the Washington Bullets, where he played for two years. He spent his last season in the NBA playing for the Atlanta Hawks, recording a lackluster average of 4.2 points per game.

After his retirement from the NBA, Williams worked as an entrepreneur and investor. He assisted Howard Graves in the creation of Champions for Families, a Florida charity focused on helping victims of domestic abuse, and recruited other star athletes to help publicize the group. Williams also became involved with the charity organization Boys and Girls Club of Mount Vernon.

## SIGNIFICANCE

Despite missing a year at the height of his career, Williams was one of the NBA's most skilled players in the late 1970's and early 1980's. Over the course of his twelve-year career, Williams maintained a scoring average of 17.1 points per game and often was the leading scorer for the SuperSonics. In 2004, the SuperSonics retired his jersey number.

*—C. Breault*

## FURTHER READING

Johnson, Roy S. "No Gus, No Glory: With Its Star Gus Williams Sidelined by a Contract Dispute, Seattle Is Sub-Sonic." *Sports Illustrated* 54, no. 5 (February 2, 1981). Written during Williams's contract dispute with the SuperSonics, this article discusses his role as the team's major star.

NBA.com. "Gus Williams." http://www.nba.com/history/ players/guswilliams_stats .html. The NBA's official Web site contains a page listing Williams's career statistics.

Williams, Gus. "Gus Williams Group." http://www .guswilliams.com. Williams's official Web site provides a brief biography and details about his charity work.

Wu, Sunny. "Gus Williams, Super Sonic." *Sports Illustrated* 94, no. 24 (June 11, 2001). Short, colorful piece about Williams's work with charities after the end of his NBA career.

**SEE ALSO:** Kareem Abdul-Jabbar; Darryl Dawkins; Julius Erving; Magic Johnson; Oscar Robertson.

# HOSEA WILLIAMS
## Activist and politician

*Williams led a direct-action movement that desegregated public facilities in Savannah, Georgia. He served on the Southern Christian Leadership Conference's board and led the 1965 Summer Community Organization and Political Education (SCOPE) project. In the 1970's, he became a politician and founded a charity, Hosea Feeds the Hungry and Homeless.*

**BORN:** January 5, 1926; Attapulgus, Georgia
**DIED:** November 16, 2000; Atlanta, Georgia
**ALSO KNOWN AS:** Hosea Lorenzo Williams
**AREAS OF ACHIEVEMENT:** Civil rights; Education; Government and politics

### EARLY LIFE
Hosea Lorenzo Williams (ho-ZAY-ah loh-REHN-zoh WIHL-yuhms) was the illegitimate son of a blind woman who died shortly after his birth. Brought up by his grandfather in Attapulgus, Georgia, Williams left home when he was twelve years old after a lynch mob attacked him for dating a white girl. After working as a hustler, he joined the U.S. Army during World War II. He was the sole survivor when a shell exploded near his platoon in France. He believed that God had saved him so that he could serve a higher purpose.

After leaving the Army in 1947, Williams took advantage of the G.I. Bill to complete high school and went on to earn bachelor's and master's degrees in chemistry from Morris Brown College in Atlanta. He moved to Savannah to begin work as a chemist for the U.S. Department of Agriculture.

Williams traced his growing consciousness of racial injustice, and his subsequent involvement in the Civil Rights movement, to several incidents in his early life. After being unable to buy his children a soda at a segregated lunch counter, he became involved in Savannah's local branch of the National Association for the Advancement of Colored People (NAACP). He became branch membership chairman in 1955 and vice president in 1960. Williams took part in various activities, including desegregating the city's public library and joining with several other parents to sue for school desegregation.

### LIFE'S WORK
On March 17, 1960, three members of Savannah's NAACP Youth Council sat down at a segregated lunch counter in a downtown department store and refused to leave when they were refused service. Before the demonstration, they had asked the local NAACP president, W. W. Law, for support. Law asked Williams to train them in nonviolent methods, and Williams subsequently led the direct-action campaign. Believing that social change also required political action, Williams founded a voter registration committee, the Chatham County Crusade for Voters (CCCV), the following month. In the fall of 1960, Williams also cooperated with Septima Poinsette Clark of Highlander Folk School to open a number of "citizenship schools." The schools, which trained lo-

*Hosea Williams, right, meets with Student Nonviolent Coordinating Committee chairman John Lewis in 1965.* (Library of Congress)

cal African Americans to read and write so that they could pass the state's literacy test and register to vote, also encouraged Afrincan Americans to join the city's direct-action movement. In the summer of 1963, Savannah's direct-action campaign escalated, and Williams spent thirty-four days in jail. In order to quell racial protest, Mayor Malcolm Maclean appointed a racially mixed committee of businessmen and NAACP representatives to desegregate the city's stores and lunch counters.

In 1964, Williams moved to Atlanta to join the Southern Christian Leadership Conference (SCLC) as a full-time staff member. The following year, he designed the Summer Community Organization and Political Education (SCOPE) project, in which three hundred northern white students worked to register African American voters in fifty-one counties in the South. As a result, some counties saw a significant increase in the number of African American voters; for example, in Hale County, the number of voters rose from 235 to 3,242 in a month. Williams regularly participated in SCLC demonstrations, including the 1968 Memphis sanitation workers' strike. He was with Martin Luther King, Jr., when the SCLC leader was assassinated in 1968 at the Lorraine Motel.

After King's death, Williams remained on SCLC's staff until 1979. However, during the 1970's, he turned his attention to other social and charity work. In 1971, he founded Hosea Feeds the Hungry and Homeless (HFTH) in Atlanta, which has since distributed more than three billion dollars' worth of aid to people in need. In 1987, he organized a march against racism in Forsyth County, Georgia. Williams also entered politics, serving in the Georgia House of Representatives from 1974 to 1985, on the Atlanta City Council from 1985 to 1990, and on the DeKalb County Commission from 1985 to 1990. He ran unsuccessfully for mayor of Atlanta in 1989. Williams died of cancer on November 16, 2000, in Atlanta.

## SIGNIFICANCE

Williams led a campaign in Savannah that resulted in the desegregation of the city's facilities a year before the 1964 Civil Rights Act. When King visited Savannah in January, 1964, he lauded it as "the most integrated city south of the Mason-Dixon line." Williams supported voter registration drives and citizenship schools that not empowered and educated African Americans. He re-

mained committed to the Civil Rights movement and voter registration throughout the 1960's, including leading the SCOPE project. His legacy continues through HFTH, which was particularly active in New Orleans, Louisiana, during the aftermath of Hurricane Katrina in 2005. After Williams's death, his daughter Elizabeth Omilami took over as the charity's leader.

*—Clare Russell*

## FURTHER READING

Branch, Taylor. *Pillar of Fire: America in the King Years, 1963-65*. New York: Simon & Schuster, 1998. Critically appraises Williams's role in the SCOPE program, noting controversies over his financial administration.

Gillespie, Deanna M. "They Walk, Talk, and Act Like New People: Citizenship Schools in Southeastern Georgia, 1960-1975." In *Teach Freedom: Education for Liberation in the African American Tradition*, edited by Charles M. Payne and Carol Sills Strickland. New York: Teachers College Press, 2008. Gillespie discusses the development of citizenship schools in Savannah and surrounding areas and the contributions that the schools made to the local direct-action movement.

Tuck, Stephen G. N. *Beyond Atlanta: The Struggle for Racial Equality in Georgia, 1940-1980*. Athens: University of Georgia Press, 2001. Presents a detailed history of the Civil Rights movement in the state, including behind-the-scenes maneuvering and tensions among and within the various organizations working for equality.

_____. "A City Too Dignified to Hate: Civic Pride, Civil Rights, and Savannah in Comparative Perspective." *Georgia Historical Quarterly* 79 (October, 1995): 533-559. In his extensive account of the Civil Rights movement in Georgia, Tuck critically assesses Williams's early life, his activism in Savannah, and the SCOPE project.

SEE ALSO: James Bevel; Septima Poinsette Clark; Myrlie Evers-Williams; James Forman; Jesse Jackson; Martin Luther King, Jr.; James Lawson; C. T. Vivian; Whitney Young.

# JUAN WILLIAMS
## Journalist

*Williams is a fixture in American political journalism who has worked in radio, television, and print media. He was a columnist and White House reporter for* The Washington Post *and served as host of* Talk of the Nation *on National Public Radio (NPR). Williams has been featured frequently on Fox News as a political analyst. He also has written extensively about African American history, including the books* Eyes on the Prize: America's Civil Rights Years, 1954-1965 *(1987) and* Thurgood Marshall: American Revolutionary *(1998).*

**BORN:** April 10, 1954; Colón, Panama
**AREAS OF ACHIEVEMENT:** Journalism and publishing; Radio and television

### EARLY LIFE

Juan Williams was born to Rogelio and Alma Geraldine Williams on April 10, 1954, in Colón, Panama. His family moved to New York when he was a child and he later won a scholarship to Oakwood Friends School in Poughkeepsie, New York. Although he was one of very few black students, he was active in student government and sports and wrote for the school paper.

Williams attended Haverford College in Philadelphia, where he majored in philosophy. He graduated in 1976 and began his journalism career that year as an intern at *The Washington Post.*

### LIFE'S WORK

Over the course of a twenty-three-year career at *The Washington Post*, Williams served as a national correspondent, columnist, and White House reporter. He covered every national election between 1980 and 2000. *The Washingtonian* named him Columnist of the Year in 1982, and he also won awards for his investigative reports on Washington, D.C., mayor Marion Barry. Williams's career was struck by controversy when, in 1995, he publicly defended Supreme Court nominee Clarence Thomas, who had been accused of sexual harassment. Williams soon found himself accused of sexual harassment by female employees of *The Washington Post*. He was disciplined by the newspaper and apologized.

While covering the White House during the administration of President Ronald Reagan, Williams developed an interest in the Civil Rights movement. He interviewed prominent figures from the movement and incorporated

his research into *Eyes on the Prize: America's Civil Rights Years, 1954-1965* (1987). The book, along with a companion television series, has been used in universities and schools across the nation. In 1997, he joined the Fox News network as a political contributor. He has since been featured on a number of television news shows, including CNN's *Crossfire* (which he often cohosted), ABC's *Nightline*, and PBS's *Washington Week in Review*. In 2000-2001, Williams worked for National Public Radio (NPR) hosting *Talk of the Nation*.

In October, 2010, Williams was fired by NPR after making comments critical of Muslims. The incident created a controversy; Williams was criticized for his remarks, but NPR also drew fire for what was seen as an attempt to limit Williams's freedom of speech because of his conservative views. Williams was quickly offered a new contract at Fox News.

Beyond his journalistic work, Williams has published books. Besides *Eyes on the Prize*, he is the author of the biography *Thurgood Marshall: American Revolutionary* (1998), which was selected as a notable book of the year

*Juan Williams.* (AP/Wide World Photos)

by *The New York Times*. In 2006, he published, *Enough: The Phony Leaders, Dead-End Movements, and Culture of Failure That Are Undermining Black America—and What We Can Do About It*. He has contributed to other books and documentaries as well, including the Emmy-winning *From Riot to Recovery* (1989).

Williams married Susan Delise in 1978. The couple has two children, Antonio and Regan.

## SIGNIFICANCE

Williams is a well-known figure in American political journalism. He has worked with news organizations on both sides of the political divide in NPR and Fox News, engaging audiences regardless of his medium. As an author, Williams also has contributed to preserving African American history and the legacy of the Civil Rights movement.

*—Kim M. LeDuff*

## FURTHER READING

Phillips, Lisa A. "The Outsider Inside: Juan Williams." In *Public Radio: Behind the Voices*. New York: CDS Books, 2006. Profile describing Williams's upbringing, education, and philosophical approach to journalism.

Williams, Juan. *Enough: The Phony Leaders, Dead-End Movements, and Culture of Failure That Are Undermining Black America—and What We Can Do About It*. New York: Three Rivers Press, 2006. In response to Bill Cosby's criticism of black America, Williams looks at the politics surrounding the current social and economic status of African Americans.

_____. *Eyes on the Prize: America's Civil Rights Years, 1954-1965*. New York: Viking, 1987. A companion book to the PBS series of the same name, chronicling the history of the Civil Rights movement in the United States.

_____. *Thurgood Marshall: American Revolutionary*. New York: Three Rivers Press, 1998. Biography of Marshall detailing his civil rights work and his involvement in the landmark case *Brown v. Board of Education*.

Williams, Juan, and Dwayne Ashley. *I'll Find a Way or Make One: A Tribute to Historically Black Colleges and Universities*. New York: Amistad Press, 2004. A reflection on the importance and impact of historically black colleges and universities in the African American community and in American society.

Williams, Juan, and Quinton Dixie. *This Far by Faith: Stories from the African American Religious Experience*. New York: HarperCollins, 2003. A companion book to the PBS documentary of the same name, detailing the importance of religion in African American history and culture.

**SEE ALSO:** Marion Barry; Bryant Gumbel; Gwen Ifill; Thurgood Marshall; Clarence E. Page; Leonard Pitts; Tavis Smiley; Clarence Thomas.

# MARY LOU WILLIAMS
## Jazz musician and composer

*Williams was best known as a jazz pianist whose style evolved with the times. She also was a composer and arranger who is credited with more than three hundred original compositions and countless arrangements. She endeavored to help struggling jazz musicians in need and grew deeply involved in the Roman Catholic Church, even composing three jazz masses and other religious anthems.*

**BORN:** May 8, 1910; Atlanta, Georgia
**DIED:** May 28, 1981; Durham, North Carolina
**ALSO KNOWN AS:** Mary Elfrieda Scruggs (birth name); Mary Lou Burley; Mary Lou Winn
**AREAS OF ACHIEVEMENT:** Entertainment: vaudeville; Music: boogie-woogie; Music: composition; Music: jazz; Religion and theology

## EARLY LIFE

Mary Lou Williams was born on May 8, 1910, in Atlanta, Georgia, to Virginia Riser and Joseph Scruggs. Confusion over Williams's surname during the early years is attributed to her mother's brief marriage to Mose Winn shortly before Williams's birth and then to Fletcher Burley sometime before 1915; Williams herself did not discover the identity of her biological father until the 1930's. In 1915, Williams migrated with her family (stepfather, mother, and sister Mamie) to Pittsburgh, Pennsylvania, in search of opportunity and prosperity.

Williams's prowess as a musician was evident very early. As a small child, she often sat on her mother's lap as Virginia played the organ at church. On one occasion, the young girl reproduced, note for note, what she had just heard her mother play. Once in Pittsburgh, Williams developed her talents through exposure to the many musical groups that came through the city. In addition, her stepfather (an important early influence) purchased a player piano on which Williams could learn the piano techniques of jazz greats such as Jelly Roll Morton and James P. Johnson. While her mother and stepfather worked long hours to make ends meet, Williams entertained neighbors' families with her piano playing and even earned a little money doing so. By the age of six, she was known as "The Little Piano Girl," playing for parties and teas throughout the city.

She first experienced life on the road in 1922 as a member of a traveling musical group called Buzzin' Harris and his Hits and Bit. This first experience was limited to eight weeks, but two years later she was back on the road with the group, traveling the black vaudeville circuit and earning thirty dollars per week.

### LIFE'S WORK

Williams became the pianist for a popular dance team called Seymour and Jeanette after the Hits and Bits show folded in 1925. The next year, she married the saxophonist in the group, John Williams. When the dance act fell apart, Williams and her husband moved to Memphis, where they started a group called the Syncopators. A short time later, John accepted a job with a band based in Oklahoma City known as the Clouds of Joy, while Williams stayed in Memphis with the Syncopators. In 1928, Williams rejoined her husband; however, she was not given a role in Clouds of Joy until 1929, after it had reorganized and relocated to Kansas City.

Williams became the band's pianist as well as its chief composer and arranger. Led by Andy Kirk, the Clouds of Joy hustled to make a living, routinely traveling hundreds of miles overnight after one engagement had ended in order to get to the next. Williams's reputation in the music world grew quickly, and she turned down a number of opportunities to join other bands. Philosophical differences between Kirk and Williams over their preferred musical styles and other factors converged in 1942, and she finally left the band and relocated to New York.

Williams spent the next decade as a freelance musician. She was at the peak of her musical career, both as a performer and as a writer. She supplied arrangements to

---

### RELIGIOUS INFLUENCES IN WILLIAMS'S MUSIC

Mary Lou Williams's professional struggles in Paris and her inability to get back to America precipitated a crisis in her career. She reached a breaking point during a gig at a Paris club and walked off the bandstand. Always a spiritual person, Williams found comfort in reading the Psalms and praying daily. On her return to New York in 1954, she began attending a nearby Roman Catholic church, spending hours praying there each day in addition to attending weekly mass. Once she resumed her music career, she referred to her piano playing as praying through her fingertips, and in the early 1960's, she began composing hymns and anthems such as "St. Martin de Porres," "The Devil," and "Animi Christi." At the urging of the priests Williams had befriended, she composed three settings of the Catholic mass: *Mass* (1967), *Mass for Lenten Season* (1968), and *Music for Peace* (1969).

---

numerous bands, including those led by Benny Goodman and Duke Ellington. Williams also remained a highly regarded performer, regularly fronting trios and larger combos. She found her greatest job security with a steady engagement at the Café Society in New York, especially during the first half of the decade.

By the end of the 1940's, Williams's debts had begun to mount, and she devoted much of her time corresponding with recording companies, attempting to collect royalties. During the fall of 1952, she traveled to England for a nine-day performing engagement, but this trip was disastrous. Although her financial woes persisted, she stayed active in London and earned the respect of many fans who proclaimed her the "Grande Dame of Jazz." In 1953, Williams moved to Paris to be near friends and to take advantage of the active jazz scene there, but this move did not translate into the artistic or fiscal success she had expected. She could not afford a ticket home, and it was not until friends arranged for her passage back to New York in late 1954 that the trip finally came to an end.

By this time, Williams had experienced a profound spiritual awakening and turned to Roman Catholicism for comfort and strength. She ceased nearly all musical endeavors and instead began assisting jazz musicians suffering with substance abuse, providing them with food, clothing, and shelter and helping them find gigs. Her apartment served as a makeshift boardinghouse for musicians in need. She established the nonprofit Bel Canto Foundation with the hope of purchasing and maintaining a staffed addiction recovery center with music facilities to allow its patients to continue playing during their stays. This center never materialized. Williams resumed her performance career with an appearance at the 1957 Newport Jazz Festival, persuaded by her priests that she could help people the most by using her natural talents. Searching for ways to raise funding for her foundation, she opened the first of a series of thrift shops in 1958. By the early 1960's, she had begun focusing her compositional energies on sacred music written in a jazz idiom. The result was a body of music for the church that included not only sacred songs and anthems, but also three settings of the Catholic mass.

Williams maintained an active performing and recording career during the 1970's, even embracing the rhythms of rock and roll and integrating them with the jazz and blues of her musical heritage. She taught and performed as an artist-in-residence at Duke University from 1977 until she died of cancer in 1981.

### SIGNIFICANCE
Williams's prodigious talents as a jazz pianist helped her to break down stereotypes of both gender and race. She was a versatile performer whose style changed with the times from stride and boogie-woogie to swing, bebop, and rock and roll. Ultimately, however, her style remained infused with the blues and spiritual influences that she believed formed the essence of jazz. As a jazz composer and arranger, Williams managed to assimilate the styles around her while pushing the conventions of

the day in new directions, a quality that Ellington described as her ability to be "perpetually contemporary." Her focus on writing sacred music in the jazz idiom places her (along with Ellington) among the first to write music for the church in this style.

—*Ted Buehrer*

### FURTHER READING

Dahl, Linda. *Morning Glory: A Biography of Mary Lou Williams*. New York: Pantheon Books, 2000. The first complete biography of Williams, including several useful bibliographic and discographic appendixes.

Kernodle, Tammy. *Soul on Soul: The Life and Music of Mary Lou Williams*. Boston: Northeastern University Press, 2004. Another significant biography on Williams, this one with a more scholarly tone.

Williams, Mary Lou. "Mary Lou Williams." In *Reading Jazz: A Gathering of Autobiography, Reportage, and Criticism from 1919 to Now*, edited by Robert Gottlieb. New York: Pantheon Books, 1996. Lengthy autobiographical essay by Williams first published in *Melody Maker* in 1954.

**SEE ALSO:** Margaret Allison Bonds; Duke Ellington; Thelonious Monk; Jelly Roll Morton; Herbie Nichols.

# MONTEL WILLIAMS
### Entertainer and writer

*Best known for his military career, his long-running talk show* The Montel Williams Show, *and his battle with multiple sclerosis, Williams has had an impact in many diverse fields because of his leadership and rhetorical skills.*

**BORN:** July 3, 1956; Baltimore, Maryland
**ALSO KNOWN AS:** Montel Brian Anthony Williams
**AREAS OF ACHIEVEMENT:** Military; Radio and television

### EARLY LIFE
Montel Brian Anthony Williams was born July 3, 1956, in Baltimore, Maryland. His father, Herman Williams, was a firefighter and the city's first African American fire chief. At Andover High School, Williams excelled in academics and athletics. He was elected class president in his junior and senior years.

After graduating from high school in 1974, Williams

enlisted in the Marine Corps and was selected for the Naval Academy Preparatory School. The following year, he was admitted to the U.S. Naval Academy in Annapolis, Maryland. In 1980, Williams became the first African American to graduate from both the U.S. Navy's prep school and Annapolis. In addition to studying Chinese, he majored in general engineering and minored in international security affairs. Shortly thereafter, he joined the Navy as an ensign.

While serving upon the USS *Sampson* as an intelligence officer with a specialization in cryptology, Williams earned a degree in Russian. He also was awarded numerous medals. After a dozen years of service, Williams was honorably discharged from the Navy as a lieutenant commander.

### LIFE'S WORK
In 1988, Williams began counseling families of servicemen and -women under his command. Because of his

*Montel Williams.* (AP/Wide World Photos)

rhetorical gifts and interpersonal skills, he was commissioned by the Navy to travel around the country speaking about leadership and overcoming obstacles.

Three years later, in 1991, Williams debuted *The Montel Williams Show.* The popular talk show, which tackled a wide array of issues, earned him a Daytime Emmy Award for Outstanding Talk Show Host in 1996. He was later nominated for Outstanding Talk Show in 2001 and 2002 and Outstanding Talk Show Host in 2002. After a seventeen-year run, the television show ended in 2008.

Williams received a diagnosis of multiple sclerosis (MS) in 1999. He publicly disclosed his battle with the disease, contacted experts at Harvard University, traveled to Sweden and was treated at the Karolinska Institute, and dedicated his life to finding a cure. He later created the Montel Williams MS Foundation to raise awareness of the disease.

Also in 1999, Williams received the Larry Stewart Leadership and Inspiration Award from the Entertainment Industries Council. A year later, in 2000, Williams created Mountain Movers Press, a publishing company focusing on progressive works and health issues. He has written several bestselling books, including *Life Lessons and Reflections* (2000), *Mountain, Get Out of My Way* (1996), and *Climbing Higher* (2004). His work has touched upon various aspects of inspiration, leading a purpose-filled and healthy life, and finding a cure for MS.

Williams received the Beacon Award in 2002 from the New York State Psychological Association for his self-help books and television show. The organization honored his "commitment to bringing psychological information to a large audience of real people." In 2003, he was presented with the American Federation of Television and Radio Artists' Disability Awareness Award for awareness and being an encouraging role model to the masses. Williams also continued to act in and direct television shows, films, and plays.

### SIGNIFICANCE

Williams's career has been diverse and prolific. As a young man, he became the first African American to graduate from both the Naval Academy Prep School and the U.S. Naval Academy. He left the military as a highly decorated officer. In later years, he received accolades for his work on *The Montel Williams Show* and wrote several bestselling books. He used his multiple sclerosis diagnosis to raise awareness of the debilitating disease and search for a cure.

—*Natalie M. Dorfeld*

### FURTHER READING

Lowney, Kathleen S. *Baring Our Souls: TV Talk Shows and the Religion of Recovery.* New York: Aldine de Gruyter, 1999. Examines the format and content of Williams's eponymous talk show and its cultural implications.

Williams, Montel, and William Doyle. *Living Well Emotionally: Break Through to a Life of Happiness.* New York: New American Library, 2010. Williams shares personal stories of inspiration and advice. He also includes a wellness program detailing a daily plan for healthy diet and exercise.

Williams, Montel, and Lawrence Grobel. *Climbing*

*Higher.* New York: New American Library, 2004. Williams recounts his initial shock, anger, and denial when he received the MS diagnosis. This deeply personal narrative discusses living with and coming to terms with the illness.

Williams, Montel, and Daniel Paisner. *Mountain, Get Out of My Way: Life Lessons and Learned Truths.*

New York: Warner Books, 1996. Williams discusses contentious issues such as discrimination, race, and prayer in schools in this somewhat controversial text.

**SEE ALSO:** Ed Gordon; Bryant Gumbel; Arsenio Hall; Al Roker; Tavis Smiley; Juan Williams; Oprah Winfrey.

# ROBERT FRANKLIN WILLIAMS
## Activist and writer

*Williams was an influential author and social activist who advocated armed resistance in the fight for desegregation and equality during the Civil Rights and Black Power movements. Wrongfully accused of crimes, he was forced to flee the United States and live in exile for nearly a decade.*

**BORN:** February 26, 1925; Monroe, North Carolina
**DIED:** October 15, 1996; Grand Rapids, Michigan
**AREAS OF ACHIEVEMENT:** Civil rights; Literature

### EARLY LIFE
Robert Franklin Williams was the son of John L. Williams and Emma Carter Williams. He was the grandson of a slave, Sikes Williams, who became a teacher, political activist, and newspaper publisher. He was raised in the home of his grandmother, another former slave, who gave her grandson his first rifle. As a boy growing up in North Carolina, Williams was profoundly affected by an event he witnessed: police officer Jesse Helms (father of longtime U.S. Senator Jesse Helms) brutally beating and humiliating a black woman in the course of arresting her.

Williams became a machinist and, in 1942, moved to Detroit, Michigan, to work at Ford Motor Company. The next year, he experienced race riots in the city. Drafted into military service in 1944, he served with a segregated Army unit before his discharge in 1946. Williams returned to Detroit, where he worked at Cadillac Motors. In 1947, he married Mabel Robinson, with whom he fathered two sons.

During the late 1940's and early 1950's, Williams wrote poetry and articles for periodicals, including *The Daily Worker*, the newspaper of the American Communist Party. With the assistance of the G.I. Bill, he studied psychology and literature at a number of African American colleges, including West Virginia State University, Johnson C. Smith University, and North Carolina Cen-

tral University. In 1953, he enlisted in the U.S. Marines but violently resisted the corps' racial discrimination and was given an undesirable discharge in 1955. He returned to his North Carolina hometown.

### LIFE'S WORK
In 1955, Williams joined the Monroe chapter of the National Association for the Advancement of Colored People (NAACP) as a community organizer and was later elected president. He came to national attention in 1958 during the notorious "Kissing Case," in which two local young black boys, ages seven and nine, were charged with rape after allowing a young white girl to kiss them. The boys faced fourteen-year terms in reform school for the alleged offense. Williams unleashed a barrage of protest, publicity, and outright ridicule that eventually led white authorities to drop all charges and free the boys.

During the decade, Williams began an anti-discrimination newsletter, *The Crusader*, and led retail store sit-ins. He campaigned successfully to integrate the town library but failed in his attempts to integrate the public swimming pool. In response to regular Ku Klux Klan-led violence against African Americans, he organized and trained a cadre of residents in self-defense; the well-armed Black Guards drove off several racist assaults. When Williams publicly spoke of meeting violence with violence, he was suspended from the NAACP, which supported a policy of nonviolence.

In 1961, Freedom Riders arrived in Monroe to help protest racism, which raised tensions in the community and led to confrontations between whites and African Americans. During the height of the demonstrations, an angry mob of African Americans surrounded a white couple in a black neighborhood, thinking they were advance scouts for the KKK. To protect the couple from harm, Williams sheltered them in his home. He was subsequently charged with kidnapping. Not wishing to be subjected to southern justice, Williams fled to Canada with his family. The Federal Bureau of Investigation (FBI) put him on its Ten Most Wanted list.

Williams made his way to Cuba, where he lived from 1962 to 1965. While there, he wrote—he completed his best-known work, *Negroes with Guns* (1962), in Havana—sold subscriptions to *The Crusader*, and hosted a revolutionary radio program of music and political commentary, *Radio Free Dixie*. Between 1965 and 1969, the Williams family resided in China. There, Williams's *Radio Free Dixie* broadcasts were aimed at African American military personnel serving in Vietnam, to discourage them from participating in an unjust war.

Williams returned to the United States in 1969, settling in Michigan. Working as a lecturer and human rights consultant, he fought extradition to North Carolina to face trial. In the mid-1970's, the kidnapping charges were dropped. Afterward, Williams continued to write, speak, and act for equality. He founded the People's Association for Human Rights and served as an officer with the NAACP in Michigan. Williams also completed his autobiography, which was not published. He died of Hodgkin's disease on October 15, 1996.

## SIGNIFICANCE

Williams's aggressive opposition to racism and discrimination stood in stark contrast to the nonviolent methods of Martin Luther King, Jr., and other Civil Rights movement leaders. As such, Williams's philosophy attracted revolutionaries willing to explore alternatives to stoic persistence. *Negroes with Guns* was a major influence on such young radicals as Huey Newton, founder of the Black Panther Party. In 1969, Williams was proclaimed president of the Republic of New Afrika, a social movement proposed to create an African American country within the United States. Although he only achieved mainstream recognition of his efforts late in life, Williams ultimately was accorded such honors as the Malcolm X Black Manhood Award (1989), the John Brown Society's Gold Medal (1991), and the NAACP Black Image Award (1992).

—*Jack Ewing*

## FURTHER READING

Cohen, Robert Carl. *Black Crusader: A Biography of Robert Franklin Williams*. Rev. ed. Charleston, S.C.: CreateSpace, 2008. An updated, illustrated edition of the radical's life story first published in 1972.

Tyson, Timothy B. *Radio Free Dixie: Robert F. Williams and the Roots of Black Power*. Chapel Hill: University of North Carolina Press, 2001. This work includes interviews and excerpts from Williams's broadcasts while focusing on his years in exile.

Williams, Robert Franklin. *Negroes with Guns*. Reprint. Detroit: Wayne State University Press, 1998. Williams's landmark work describes the events that led to his community's armed resistance to racism.

**SEE ALSO:** Stokely Carmichael; Eldridge Cleaver; Malcolm X; Huey P. Newton; Bobby Seale.

# SERENA WILLIAMS
## Tennis player

*Williams reached the top of the professional tennis world in singles and doubles with her sister Venus. She also branched out into fashion design and entertainment. As African Americans excelling at a sport historically dominated by upper-class whites, the Williams sisters attracted much attention throughout their careers.*

**BORN:** September 26, 1981; Saginaw, Michigan
**ALSO KNOWN AS:** Serena Jameka Ross Evelyn Williams
**AREAS OF ACHIEVEMENT:** Fashion; Sports: golf and tennis; Sports: Olympics

## EARLY LIFE

Serena Jameka Ross Evelyn Williams was born in Saginaw, Michigan, the youngest of five daughters of Richard, part-owner of a security business, and Oracene Price Williams, a nurse. The family soon moved to Compton, California, a poor and crime-ridden suburb of Los Angeles. Richard coached Williams and her sister Venus on the local public tennis courts and entered Williams in her first tournament when she was four years old. Over the next five years, Williams gained national attention for her performance in the junior tournament circuit.

By 1991, Williams had become the highest ranked

*Serena Williams, left, and Venus Williams celebrate after winning a doubles match at the 2010 French Open.* (AP/Wide World Photos)

ten-year-old tennis player in Southern California. Her father removed his daughters from the circuit and enrolled them in Rick Macci's tennis academy in Florida. This move was controversial at the time, as the tournament circuit was considered to be the best venue for success in the sport. The girls were homeschooled while they attended Macci's academy. In 1995, Richard returned to coaching his two daughters in tennis and also published newsletters on their progress. In October, 1995, at the Bell Challenge in Vanier, Quebec, fourteen-year-old Williams debuted as a professional tennis player. Over the next couple of years, she was overshadowed by her sister's abilities, but in 1997, she went from being ranked number 453 to number 99. She placed well at the Ameritech Cup tournament later that year.

### LIFE'S WORK
Williams participated in the Australian Open, her first Grand Slam tournament, in January, 1998. She lost to her sister Venus in the second round. Six months later, Williams paired with Max Mirnyi of Belarus and won the

mixed double tournament at Wimbledon. Her ranking soon jumped to number 21 and garnered her a twelve-million-dollar contract with Puma. Williams won her first Women's Tennis Association (WTA) championship at the Open Gaz de France in 1999 and her second one at the U.S. Open later that year. She and her sister also won the doubles championship at the U.S. Open. After several injuries and illnesses forced her out of competitions in 1999 and 2000, Williams had a string of wins. She was bested by her sister in March at the Lipton Championships in Florida, but still earned a top-ten ranking. The duo won the doubles title at Wimbledon in 2000; Williams won in singles at the Faber Grand Prix; and then the sisters earned a gold medal at the Summer Olympics in Sydney.

The 2001 tennis season brought mixed results for Williams. After her sister withdrew, Williams won the singles title at Indian Wells, California. She lost in the Australian Open, but the sisters won the doubles championship. Williams then was bested at the French Open, Wimbledon, and the U.S. Open. In 2002, a sprained ankle forced Williams to withdraw from the Australian Open. Later that year, Williams earned the number-one ranking in women's tennis. She won the singles title at Wimbledon in 2003, but a knee injury at the U.S. Open forced Williams to skip the rest of the year's major tournaments. That year, she signed a forty-million-dollar contract with Nike that included her own signature clothing line, Aneres.

When she returned to the WTA circuit, Williams won the 2004 NASDAQ-100 Open, the 2005 China Open, and the 2006 Australian Open. After a six-month hiatus, Williams won the singles titles at the 2007 Australian Open, the 2007 Sony Ericsson Open, the 2008 Hopman Cup, and the 2008 U.S. Open. She and her sister also won the doubles title at Wimbledon and a second Olympic gold medal at the Beijing Olympics. In 2009, Williams overpowered Venus for the singles title at Wimbledon and accompanied her in the doubles title. At the U.S. Open in 2009, Williams's angry outburst against a line judge resulted in a fine and two years' probation. Despite this incident, Williams and her sister won the tournament's doubles crown. In November, Williams won the Sony Ericcson Championship. In December, 2009, Williams was named Associate Press Female Athlete of the Year, and the International Tennis Federation named her a world champion in singles and doubles. She continued her dominance of women's tennis in 2010, winning Wimbledon and the Australian Open.

Williams's other interests include fashion designing and entertainment. She attended the Art Institute of Fort Lauderdale and designed her own clothing line. In 2005, she debuted in a television series, *Venus and Serena: For Real*; she also made guest appearances on many talk shows and television programs. Williams became part-owner of the Miami Dolphins football team in 2009.

## SIGNIFICANCE

Williams rose from humble beginnings to become top-ranked in the WTA. While at times she was overshadowed by her sister, Williams became a champion through talent and determination. She also used her success to promote outreach to inner-city youths. She supported middle school and high school mentoring programs and helped found the Venus and Serena Williams Tutorial/Tennis Academy and the Serena Williams Secondary School in Matooni, Kenya.

—*Cynthia J. W. Svoboda*

## FURTHER READING

Rodgers, R. Pierre, and Ellen B. Brogin Rodgers. "'Ghetto Cinderellas': Venus and Serena Williams and the Discourse of Racism." In *Out of the Shadows: A Biographical History of African American Athletes.* Fayetteville: University of Arkansas Press, 2006. Examines the Williams sisters' careers, public image, and how their race affects the ways they are portrayed and perceived.

Williams, Serena, and Daniel Paisner. *On the Line.* New York: Grand Central Publishing, 2009. Provides insight into Williams's childhood and life as a tennis professional.

Williams, Venus, Serena Williams, and Hilary Beard. *Venus and Serena: Serving from the Hip—Ten Rules for Living, Loving, and Winning.* Boston: Houghton Mifflin Harcourt, 2005. The Williams sisters provide advice to teenagers on best practices in everyday life.

SEE ALSO: Arthur Ashe; Althea Gibson; Venus Williams.

# VANESSA WILLIAMS
## Actor and singer

*Williams has forged a long and successful career in music, film, and theater. The first African American woman to be crowned Miss America, she later lost the title amid scandal but redeemed herself and became a major force in entertainment.*

BORN: March 18, 1963; Tarrytown, New York
ALSO KNOWN AS: Vanessa Lynn Wiliams; Vanessa L. Williams
AREAS OF ACHIEVEMENT: Film: acting; Music: pop; Music: rhythm and blues

## EARLY LIFE

Vanessa Lynn Williams was born on March 18, 1963, in Tarrytown, New York. Her parents, Milton and Helen, both were music teachers, and the arts had a prominent role in the Williams household. Raised in mostly white Millwood, New York, Williams often was the only African American student in her classes and was pressured to excel to combat prejudice. She and her brother, Christopher, were encouraged to play musical instruments, and Williams chose to learn piano and French horn. She also studied various forms of dance, such as ballet, tap, and jazz, and dreamed of performing on Broadway.

Williams began attending Syracuse University in 1981. At the school, she discovered beauty pageants. Although she was reluctant, she was drawn to the scholarships they offered and entered the Miss Greater Syracuse Pageant in 1983. Williams won the title and went on to win the Miss New York title later the same year. The victory allowed her to represent New York in the Miss America pageant, where she became the first African American to be crowned Miss America.

## LIFE'S WORK

After winning the Miss America pageant, Williams was beset by scandal. In 1984, nude photographs of Williams were published in *Penthouse* magazine. The photos had been taken before Williams entered the Miss America pageant, and she had not authorized their release, but she was forced to give up her crown.

With the help of her publicist, Ramon Hervey, Williams was able to redeem herself and begin a career in the entertainment industry. In 1988, she released her first al-

*Vanessa Williams as Miss America in 1983.* (AP/Wide World Photos)

bum, *The Right Stuff*. The album peaked at number thirty-eight on the *Billboard* charts and produced hit songs "The Right Stuff" and "Dreamin'." The album earned three Grammy nominations in 1988 and was certified gold. In 1991, Williams released her second album, *The Comfort Zone*, which peaked at number seventeen and spent more than ninety weeks on the *Billboard* charts. Her single "Save the Best for Last" reached number one. By 2011, Williams had released eight albums and recorded numerous songs for various film and television sound tracks. Her recording of "Colors of the Wind" for the Disney animated film *Pocahontas* (1995) won an Academy Award.

Williams also achieved success onstage, starting with her first acting role in the Off-Broadway production of the musical *One Man Band* in 1985. Williams's breakout performance on Broadway came in 1994 when she replaced Chita Rivera in the leading role in the musical

*Kiss of the Spider Woman*. She also starred in the musical *Into the Woods*, for which she was nominated for a Tony Award in 2002.

In 1986, Williams won her first film role in *Under the Gun*. She went on to appear in *Another You* and *Harley Davidson and the Marlboro Man*, both released in 1991. Her first major role was in the 1996 thriller *Eraser*, costarring Arnold Schwarzenegger. A year later, in 1997, Williams costarred in the African American family drama *Soul Food*. While building a film career, she also made several television appearances in sitcoms such as *The Fresh Prince of Bel-Air* in television movies such as *The Jacksons: An American Dream* (1992), *The Odyssey* (1997), and *A Diva's Christmas Carol* (2000). In the late 2000's, she costarred as a devious fashion magazine editor in the ABC series *Ugly Betty*. The role made Williams a style icon and drew several award nominations. In the fall of 2010, Williams began a new television role on the ABC drama *Desperate Housewives*.

### SIGNIFICANCE

Despite an early scandal that marred her triumph as the first African American Miss America, Williams has built a successful career in music and entertainment. In 2008, she completed her undergraduate degree in theater arts from Syracuse University, more than twenty years after she left the school to focus on her pageant pursuits. Williams's victory in the Miss America pageant was seen as an inspirational achievement for African American young women, and her longevity in the industry is a testament to the power of perseverance.

—*Quentin D. Washington*

### FURTHER READING

Freedman, Suzanne. *Vanessa Williams*. Philadelphia: Chelsea House, 2000. Basic biography of Williams written for younger readers.

Fried, Joseph P. "Following Up." *The New York Times*, May 23, 2004. Describes the 1984 scandal involving Williams's nude photos and its aftermath.

Morgan-Murray, Joan. "The Season of Her Content." *Essence* (July, 2000). Profile of Williams written early in her marriage to basketball player Rick Fox. Discusses Williams's redemption as an entertainer and her longevity in the industry.

**SEE ALSO:** Halle Berry; Toni Braxton; Mariah Carey; Suzette Charles; Natalie Cole; Whitney Houston.

# VENUS WILLIAMS
## Tennis player

*Williams is a professional women's tennis player who spent time at the top of the sport's rankings and also had success in acting, interior decorating, and fashion design. She has won singles, doubles, and mixed doubles titles and three Olympic gold medals.*

**BORN:** June 17, 1980; Lynwood, California
**ALSO KNOWN AS:** Venus Ebone Starr Williams
**AREAS OF ACHIEVEMENT:** Fashion; Sports: golf and tennis; Sports: Olympics

### EARLY LIFE

Venus Ebone Starr Williams was born in Lynwood, California, to Richard and Oracene Price Williams. The family settled in Compton, a poor and crime-ridden suburb of Los Angeles, where Richard coached Williams and her younger sister, Serena, on the local public tennis courts. Williams competed in her first tennis tournament when she was four years old. By the time she was seven, her talents were making news.

As a ten-year-old, Williams became the top-ranked tennis player in the under-twelve division in Southern California. She excelled at other sports, too, particularly sprinting and middle-distance running, but her parents encouraged her to focus on tennis. In 1991, the family moved to Florida, where Williams and her sister were enrolled in Rick Macci's tennis academy. Because she was not actively competing during this time, many observers wondered if the lack of tournament experience would adversely affect her tennis career.

At age fourteen, Williams participated in her first professional match at the Bank of the West Classic in Oakland, California. The next year, Reebok offered her a twelve-million-dollar endorsement agreement that included the creation of her own sportswear line.

### LIFE'S WORK

Williams waited until 1997 to join the Women's Tennis Association (WTA) full time. In 1997-1998, she participated in the singles tournaments at the Grand Slam events—Wimbledon and the French, U.S., and Australian Opens. She won a mixed doubles title that year in Australia. In March, 1998, Williams won her first WTA tournament, the IGA Tennis Classic in Oklahoma City. She won her second title at the Lipton Championships in Key Biscayne, Florida. In 1999, she won the singles title at the U.S. Open and, together with her sister, took the

doubles titles at the U.S. and French Opens. The next year, Williams won the U.S. Open and Wimbledon, then earned a gold medal at the Summer Olympics in Sydney, Australia. She and her sister won women's doubles at both events and at the Olympics, too. Williams was chosen as the Sportswoman of the Year by *Sports Illustrated*. The next year, she signed a forty-million-dollar contract with Reebok. Williams became the top-ranked player in the WTA in 2002.

A stomach muscle injury prevented Williams from participating in the 2003 U.S. Open, but she won two tournaments in 2004. Williams and her sister pursued other interests in 2005. They starred in a six-episode television show and published a book, *Venus and Serena: Serving from the Hip—Ten Rules for Living, Loving, and Winning*. The year 2006 was a challenging one for Williams, but she battled back and won at Wimbledon in 2007 and 2008. She and her sister earned a gold medal at the 2008 Beijing Olympics. In 2009, Williams won singles titles at tournaments in Dubai and Acapulco, Mexico. She also won the Billie Jean King Cup—an exhibition competition among the year's four Grand Slam tournament winners—in March, 2010.

### SIGNIFICANCE

By 2010, Williams had won more than forty WTA titles. She and her sister have used their celebrity to reach out to inner-city youths, founding the Venus and Serena Williams Tutorial/Tennis Academy of Los Angeles. Williams also helped fund the OWL Foundation, a program begun by her mother that helps students struggling with learning problems. In 2006, she was named ambassador of gender equality for the WTA Tour Gender Equity Program, a campaign for equal prize money. Williams also served as a spokeswoman for the Center of Disease Control's Verb Campaign, which encourages youths to be physically active. In 2009, Williams was named to All-Stars Helping Kids' Dream Team for Public Service in recognition of her service to the community.

In December, 2007, Williams earned an associate degree in fashion design from the Art Institute of Florida. She also became a certified interior designer and opened V Starr Interiors. Her fashion lines include the Venus Williams Collection for Wilson's Leather and EleVen for the retailer Steve and Barry's. Williams also endorsed Reebok, American Express, and Avon.

—*Cynthia J. W. Svoboda*

## FURTHER READING

Rodgers, R. Pierre, and Ellen B. Brogin Rodgers. "'Ghetto Cinderellas': Venus and Serena Williams and the Discourse of Racism." In *Out of the Shadows: A Biographical History of African American Athletes.* Fayetteville: University of Arkansas Press, 2006. Examines how the Williams sisters' race affected how they were portrayed in the media and received within the white-dominated tennis community.

Watson, Galadriel Findlay. *Venus and Serena Williams: A Biography.* Westport, Conn.: Greenwood Press, 2005. Outlines the sisters' lives, careers, and their relationship.

Williams, Venus, Serena Williams, and Hilary Beard. *Venus and Serena: Serving from the Hip: Ten Rules for Living, Loving, and Winning.* Boston: Houghton Mifflin Harcourt, 2005. The Williams sisters provide advice to teenagers on best practices in everyday life.

**SEE ALSO:** Arthur Ashe; Althea Gibson; Serena Williams.

# WILLIE L. WILLIAMS
## Law enforcement official

*Williams was instrumental in developing new approaches to policing, including community involvement and emphasis on service to and protection of all segments of the community.*

**BORN:** October 1, 1943; Philadelphia, Pennsylvania
**ALSO KNOWN AS:** Willie Lawrence Williams
**AREA OF ACHIEVEMENT:** Law

### EARLY LIFE

Willie Lawrence Williams was born in Philadelphia, Pennsylvania, on October 1, 1943, one of seven children of Willie, a meat cutter, and Helen Williams. Willie L. Williams suffered from attacks of asthma as a child. He graduated from Overbrook High School in 1960, and he worked briefly as a meat cutter with his father; after Williams severely injured his hand, he sought other work. In 1964, he became a patrolman with the Fairmount Park Guards, a special police force patrolling the expansive Fairmount Park area of Philadelphia, and later he advanced to the position of sergeant. In 1967, he married Evelina, and they had three children. In 1972, the Fairmount Park Guards became part of the Philadelphia City Police Department, and Williams joined the city police as a detective.

### LIFE'S WORK

Williams was a member of the Philadelphia City Police for twenty years (1972 to 1992). He served under two police commissioners, Frank Rizzo (to 1985) and Kevin Tucker (1985 to 1988), and then Williams became police commissioner in June, 1988. During his employment with the Philadelphia City Police, Williams attended the Philadelphia College of Textiles and Science and received an A.A. in 1982. He also took courses in management at St. Joseph's University and at Harvard University. Williams, who sensed a strong current of racism in the department under Rizzo's leadership, had difficulties with Rizzo's hard-line methods. When Williams was promoted to captain in 1984 and assigned to the North Philadelphia district, he initiated an open-door policy, even though the area was one of the heaviest crime districts in the city. Williams's policies and ideas did not make him a candidate for further advancement under Rizzo. Beginning in the mid-1970's, the department began to draw public attention for its policies, which included a United States Justice Department investigation for brutality, a narcotics scandal, and in 1985 the use of a bomb to quell the activities of the African American liberation group MOVE, which resulted in the death of eleven MOVE members and the destruction of about sixty row houses. As a result, Tucker replaced Rizzo as commissioner in 1985. Tucker's appointment enabled Williams to advance rapidly in his career. In 1986, he was promoted to inspector and in 1988 to deputy commissioner.

In June of 1988, Williams was appointed commissioner of the Philadelphia City Police Department. He began putting his ideas of community policing into practice. By opening, in the most dangerous districts of Philadelphia, mini-police stations, where residents could report crimes and seek help, he made the services of the police force more readily available. Williams rode along on patrols, participated in arrests, and increased the number of promotions of minority employees. He made it a policy to investigate all accusations of police brutality and fired any officer proven guilty of such conduct.

When the beating of Rodney King by Los Angeles police officers and the subsequent investigations and riots brought about the resignation of Police Chief Darryl F. Gates, Williams's reputation for working well with minority communities within Philadelphia, his openness to reform, and his experience as police commissioner of Philadelphia brought him an invitation to apply for the position of Los Angeles's police chief. On July 1, 1992, Williams was sworn in as chief of police. While Williams's appointment was welcomed by the residents of Los Angeles, the vast majority of officers in the Los Angeles Police Department (LAPD) were not enthusiastic about working for Williams. He was the first African American police chief of the LAPD and the first chief from outside the department in more than twenty years. Williams set goals of improving morale in the city's population, retraining the police force to use methods other than force and instilling fear, and using techniques of community policing to involve residents in cooperative efforts with the police. He established an office of community policing, community police advisory boards throughout Los Angeles, and a Commitment to Action Plan. The LAPD received a $607,000 grant from the Department of Justice to revitalize and improve the police force. The funding enabled the department to build a Recruit Training Center (1995), to begin construction of an Emergency Vehicle Operations Center (1996), and to open three new stations. Because of lack of support within the department and in the city, Williams was not reappointed as chief and left the LAPD in May of 1997. In 2002, Williams became federal security director for Hartsfield Atlanta International Airport.

## SIGNIFICANCE

During his career as a city police department employee, Williams exercised a positive influence on improving the relationship between law enforcement officials and the community, particularly ethnic communities. He was a strong proponent of reform and insisted upon law enforcement departments taking responsibility for the conduct of their officers. His ideas and beliefs continue to inform concepts of effective policing techniques. Williams is also a role model for the African American community, exemplifying the success of an individual who, through effort and determination, succeeded in his career choice.

*—Shawncey Webb*

## FURTHER READING

Skogan, Wesley G. *Community Policing: Can It Work?* Belmont, Calif.: Wadsworth, 2003. Good for understanding Williams's approach to police work and common problems encountered in relationships between ethnic and minority communities and law enforcement.

Tervalan, Jervey, and Ceitian A. Sierra, eds. *Geography of Rage: Remembering the Los Angeles Riots of 1992.* Los Angeles: Really Great Books, 2002. Examines the rage and resentment that Williams faced as LAPD police chief.

Weitzner, Ronald, and Steven A. Tuch. *Race and Policing in America: Conflict and Reform.* New York: Cambridge University Press, 2006. In-depth study of issues that Williams addressed during his career in law enforcement.

Williams, Willie L., and Bruce Henderson. *Taking Back Our Streets: Fighting Crime in America.* New York: Scribner's, 1996. Williams presents his ideas about community policing and recounts his retraining of the LAPD officers.

**SEE ALSO:** Tom Bradley.

# MAURY WILLS
## Baseball player

*Wills helped revolutionize baseball by becoming the record-breaking base stealer of his era.*

**BORN:** October 2, 1932; Washington, D.C.
**ALSO KNOWN AS:** Maurice Morning Wills
**AREA OF ACHIEVEMENT:** Sports: baseball

### EARLY LIFE

Maury Wills was born Maurice Morning Wills on October 2, 1932, in Washington, D.C., one of thirteen children. His father, Guy Wills, was a machinist in the Washington Navy Yard and also an ordained Baptist minister. At Cardoza High School, Wills pitched on the baseball team and was quarterback on the football team. He received nine football scholarship offers but was determined to make a name for himself in baseball. Wills tried out for the New York Giants as a pitcher but was rejected because of his small size, 5 feet, 10 inches and 155 pounds.

At a later tryout with the Brooklyn Dodgers, scout Rex Bowen was more impressed by Wills's running

*Maury Wills.* (AP/Wide World Photos)

speed than his pitching and signed him as an infielder in 1951. Wills's progress through the Dodger minor league system was slow because he his path to the major leagues was blocked by future Hall of Fame shortstop Pee Wee Reese.

### LIFE'S WORK

Discouraged, Wills slumped to an uncharacteristically low batting average of .202 in 1955 and considered quitting. He eventually convinced himself that if he could have a good season in 1956 he would finally make it to the major leagues. Wills lived up his promise to himself with a career-high .302 average and 34 stolen bases. In 1958 at Spokane, manager Bobby Bragan converted him into a switch hitter because being able to bat both right-handed and left-handed would increase his chances of making the Dodgers, and hitting left-handed would also take advantage of his speed by being a step closer to first base.

When Wills hit only .253, however, the Dodgers, who had moved to Los Angeles in 1958, sold his contract conditionally to the Detroit Tigers. Unimpressed with his spring training performance in 1959, the Tigers sent him back to Los Angeles. In Spokane Wills batted .313 and stole 25 bases in 48 games before being called up by the Dodgers, where he at first alternated with Don Zimmer as replacements for the retired Reese but soon became the full-time shortstop. He helped the Dodgers defeat the Chicago White Sox in the World Series.

Luis Aparicio, the shortstop of the White Sox, had brought new attention to the art of stealing bases in the 1950's, but Wills took these advancements to a new level. Wills had 50 stolen bases in 1960, the first time a National Leaguer had attained this level since 1923, and 35 in 1961. The following season Wills accumulated an amazing 104 stolen bases, breaking the modern stolen base record set by Ty Cobb with 96 in 1915. Wills batted .299, with career highs of 130 runs and 208 hits, and also led the league with ten triples. He was named the league's most valuable player and was chosen athlete of the year by the Associated Press. Wills's stolen base record lasted until 1974 when Lou Brock of the St. Louis Cardinals had 118. Brock's mark was broken by Rickey Henderson of the Oakland Athletics with 130 in 1982.

In 1963 Wills's legs were still sore from his exertions the previous year, and he stole only 40 bases. However, he batted a career high .302 and helped lead the Dodgers to a four-game sweep of the New York Yankees in the World Series. His stolen bases increased to 53 in 1964 and 94 in 1965, when he led the league for the sixth straight season. He then batted .367 as the Dodgers defeated the Minnesota Twins in the World Series. The following season the Dodgers were swept in the World Series by the Baltimore Orioles. Wills had been bothered by a leg injury during 1966, and when he declined to participate in a postseason tour of Japan, he was traded to the Pittsburgh Pirates.

Switching to third base Wills again batted .302 in 1967 and stole 52 bases the following season. He was chosen by the Montreal Expos in the 1969 expansion draft and then traded back to the Dodgers than June. Will performed ably as the Los Angeles shortstop in 1969-1971 but was a part-time player by 1972, when he hit only .129 and was released, ending his playing career.

Wills returned to the spotlight briefly in 1980-1981 when he managed the Seattle Mariners, but he was fired after winning only twenty-six of eighty-two games over parts of two seasons. Wills's tenure was notable for his erratic behavior, the result of addictions to alcohol and cocaine which lasted until 1989. His son, Bump Wills, was second baseman for the Texas Rangers and Chicago Cubs from 1977 through 1982.

### SIGNIFICANCE

Wills demonstrated perseverance by playing nine seasons in the minors while waiting for his chance to prove himself. His greatest accomplishment was proving that the stolen base could be as dominant a weapon as the home run. Despite his late start, Wills accumulated 586 stolen bases, 2,134 hits, and 1,067 runs to go with his .281 lifetime batting average. He was selected to the National League all-star team five times and won the Gold Glove as the league's best fielding shortstop twice. Wills was the dominant shortstop and base stealer of his era, leading the Dodgers to victories in three of four World Series.

*—Michael Adams*

### FURTHER READING

Leahy, Michael. "Dodgers' Man of Steal Seeks a Gold Plaque." *The Washington Post*, October 4, 2009, p. D1. Considers Wills's qualifications for the Baseball Hall of Fame.

Wills, Maury, and Mike Celizic. *On the Run: The Never Dull and Often Shocking Life of Maury Wills*. New York: Carroll & Graf, 1991. Wills discusses his baseball career, his chaotic family life, his many affairs, and his struggle to overcome his addiction to drugs.

Wills, Maury, and Don Freeman. *How to Steal a Pennant*. New York: Putnam, 1976. Wills explains his philosophy of managing a baseball team.

**SEE ALSO:** Hank Aaron; Ernie Banks; Barry Bonds; Lou Brock; Roberto Clemente; Larry Doby; Willie Mays; Frank Robinson; Jackie Robinson; Bill White.

# AUGUST WILSON
## Playwright

*A celebrated playwright, Wilson received critical acclaim for his ambitious cycle of works about African American life in the twentieth century. One of the few playwrights to win two Pulitzer Prizes, Wilson also was the first African American to have two plays running simultaneously on Broadway.*

**BORN:** April 27, 1945; Pittsburgh, Pennsylvania
**DIED:** October 2, 2005; Seattle, Washington
**ALSO KNOWN AS:** Frederick August Kittel (birth name)
**AREAS OF ACHIEVEMENT:** Literature; Theater

### EARLY LIFE

August Wilson was born Frederick August Kittel in Pittsburgh to Frederick August Kittel, a German baker, and Daisy Wilson, an African American cleaner. The fourth of six children, he grew up in a poor household. Wilson had little contact with his biological father and as an adult he adopted his mother's maiden name. After his parents divorced, Wilson was raised by his African American stepfather, David Bedford. The family moved to a predominantly white suburb where Wilson experienced racism at school. He dropped out after ninth grade and continued his education in the local public library, where books by Langston Hughes, James Baldwin, and Richard Wright inspired him to become a writer. While working at odd jobs, he spent time in Pittsburgh's Hill District, a predominantly black neighborhood. This area would later provide inspiration for the characters and dialogue in his plays.

In 1963, Wilson enlisted in the Army but managed to have himself discharged after a year. He bought his first typewriter in 1965 and began to write poems, some of which were published in small magazines. Wilson was active in the Black Power movement. Along with Rob Penny, a playwright and teacher, he founded the Black Horizon Theater in Pittsburgh, where he directed plays by the writer and activist Amiri Baraka. Wilson married Brenda Burton, a member of the Nation of Islam, in 1969. They had one daughter but were divorced in 1972.

### LIFE'S WORK

Never very successful as a poet, Wilson was encouraged to write plays by his friend Claude Purdy from the Playwrights Center in Minneapolis. Wilson's early attempts at drama were very poetic and he found it hard to write convincing dialogue. Purdy encouraged Wilson to give his characters voices he recalled from conversations in the Hill District of Pittsburgh.

*August Wilson.* (David Cooper/Courtesy, Yale Repertory Theatre)

Wilson's first play, *Recycle* (1973), examines the breakup of a marriage. His second, *The Homecoming* (1976), based on the mysterious death of the blues guitarist Blind Lemon Jefferson, prefigured some of the themes of his later work *Ma Rainey's Black Bottom* (1984). In interviews, Wilson cited as influences for his plays the "four *b*'s"—the blues, the writers Baraka and Jorge Luis Borges, and the painter Romare Bearden. Baraka stressed that all art is political and can be used in the struggle for equality, while the scenes of black life depicted in Bearden's work provided the inspiration for some of Wilson's plays. The fiction of Argentinean writer Borges taught Wilson that writing could be specific to a time and place yet still reflect universal themes. The influence of the blues is evident in the ideas and characters in Wilson's plays.

Wilson moved to St. Paul, Minnesota, in 1978 to work as scriptwriter at the Science Museum. He wrote a draft of *Jitney*, a play about life in a gypsy cab station. *Jitney* and his next play, *Fullerton Street*, were both produced in Pittsburgh in 1982. It was only after Wilson submitted *Jitney* to the Playwrights Center in Minneapolis and won a fellowship that he began to consider himself a serious playwright. With the support of his second wife, Judy Oliver, a social worker whom he married in 1981, he was able to quit his job and concentrate on writing plays.

Another important figure in his career was Lloyd Richards, the director and dean of the Yale University School of Drama. Wilson submitted *Ma Rainey's Black Bottom* to the National Playwrights Conference, where it came to Richards's attention. Recognizing Wilson's talent, Richards helped him refine the play, which was produced in 1984 in New Haven. Later the same year, it opened on Broadway, where it was enthusiastically received by the critics. This launched Wilson's chronicle of twentieth century African American life; ten plays, each set in a different decade, which became known as the Pittsburgh Cycle. *Gem of the Ocean* (2003) is set in 1904, *Joe Turner's Come and Gone* (1986) in 1911, *Ma Rainey's Black Bottom* (1984) in 1927, *The Piano Lesson* (1987) in 1936, *Seven Guitars* (1995) in 1948, *Fences* (1985) in 1957, *Two Trains Running* (1990) in 1969, *Jitney* (1982) in 1977, *King Hedley II* (1999) in 1985, and *Radio Golf* (2005) in 1997. Each play explores issues the daily lives of African Americans at a particular time and place as well as universal themes such as love, honor, betrayal, and duty. His characters are ordinary people and the plots grow out of the characterization.

Wilson followed up the success of *Ma Rainey* with two more plays, both of which won Pulitzer Prizes. *Joe Turner's Come and Gone*, set in a black boardinghouse in 1911, deals with the uncertainty of newly freed African American migrants from the South, like Wilson's grandmother. *Fences'* main character is a trash collector and former Negro League baseball player who is prevented from playing professional baseball by white racism. The character is loosely based on Wilson's stepfather. The play opened on Broadway in 1987 with James Earl Jones in the starring role and won a Tony Award.

In 1994, Wilson moved to Seattle with his third wife, Constanza Romero, a costume designer with whom he had a daughter. He continued to set his plays in his hometown, Pittsburgh. An autobiographical play, *How I Learned What I Learned*, in which Wilson starred, was produced in 2003. During preparations for the premiere of his last play, *Radio Golf*, Wilson's health began to decline. He died at age sixty of liver cancer.

## SIGNIFICANCE

Wilson was a champion of independent black theater and race-specific casting, but he brought African American themes and what he described as an African consciousness to mainstream theater. His plays present a history of America from an African American viewpoint, exploring how ordinary individuals cope with racism and the legacy of slavery. Although he dramatizes tensions within the black community, rather than simply being works of protest Wilson's plays reveal the dignity of individuals struggling to overcome their past. The plays won many awards, including two Pulitzer Prizes, a Tony Award, seven New York Drama Critics Circle Awards, and a Laurence Olivier Award for *Jitney* in London in 2001.

—*Christine Ayorinde*

---

### MA RAINEY'S BLACK BOTTOM

One of the plays in August Wilson's series on African American life in the twentieth century, *Ma Rainey's Black Bottom* is based on an imagined day in the life of blues singer Gertrude "Ma" Rainey. The play, part musical and part drama, is set in a Chicago recording studio in the 1920's. It opens with Rainey arriving late to the studio because a racist cabdriver refused to pick up the band after their car broke down. The police then attempt to arrest them for arguing with the driver. The story revolves around the tension between Rainey and Levee, a trumpeter in her band. Levee has a new arrangement of a dance called the Black Bottom, but in the recording session, Rainey insists on singing the usual version. The potential for trouble escalates when Levee flirts with Ma's young lesbian lover, Dussie Mae. Levee's frustration reaches a peak when a white producer offers him a paltry sum for his songs, telling him they are no good. Rather than attacking the white man, Levee vents his frustration by stabbing a fellow musician who has unintentionally stepped on his shoes. The play explores themes such as the impact of racism, white disrespect for black art, and black-on-black violence. As in Wilson's other plays, the dialogue is infused with poetry, and the blues are sung at key moments.

---

### FURTHER READING

Bigsby, Christopher. *The Cambridge Companion to August Wilson*. New York: Cambridge University Press, 2007. Examines Wilson's life and career and the wider context of his plays. A chapter is devoted to each play in the Pittsburgh Cycle.

Bryer, Jackson R., and Mary C. Hartig, eds. *Conversations with August Wilson*. Jackson: University Press of Mississippi, 2006. A selection of interviews Wilson gave from 1984 to 2004 in which the playwright discusses his plays and his background.

Elkins, Marilyn, ed. *August Wilson: A Casebook*. New York: Routledge, 2000. This collection of essays and interviews with the playwright covers Wilson's influences, politics, folklore, Africa, gender, and the blues.

Snodgrass, Mary Ellen. *August Wilson: A Literary Companion*. Jefferson, N.C.: McFarland, 2004. Examines the characters, dates, events, and themes from Wilson's theatrical output and includes an annotated chronology of his life and works.

**SEE ALSO:** Amiri Baraka; Ed Bullins; Ossie Davis; Charles Fuller; Lorraine Hansberry; Tyler Perry; Lloyd Richards; Ntozake Shange; Anna Deavere Smith; George C. Wolfe.

# FLIP WILSON
## Actor

*Wilson was the first African American to have a successful weekly hourlong variety show. He demonstrated that a black performer could not only carry a series but also be extremely popular with all segments of the television audience. Wilson undoubtedly paved the way for several other black entertainers to be awarded their own series.*

**BORN:** December 8, 1933; Jersey City, New Jersey
**DIED:** November 25, 1998; Malibu, California
**ALSO KNOWN AS:** Clerow Wilson, Jr. (birth name)
**AREAS OF ACHIEVEMENT:** Entertainment: comedy; Radio and television

### EARLY LIFE
Flip Wilson was born Clerow Wilson, Jr., in Jersey City, New Jersey, in 1933, one of at least eighteen children from a poor family. He grew up in foster homes and might have spent time in a reform school before joining the U.S. Air Force in 1950. Only sixteen years old at the time, he had to lie about his age to enlist. During his four years in the Air Force, he gained the nickname "Flip,"

*Flip Wilson as Geraldine Jones on* The Flip Wilson Show. *(AP/Wide World Photos)*

supposedly for his manic or "flipped out" personality.

Upon his discharge, Wilson found work as a bellhop and part-time entertainer at a San Francisco hotel. He worked for little pay in small clubs throughout the country, finally appearing at the famous Apollo Theater in Harlem, New York. His initial comic persona relied heavily on African American stereotypes.

### LIFE'S WORK
Wilson's regular appearances at the Apollo helped him build a national reputation, and he began performing on such television series as *The Ed Sullivan Show*, *Rowan & Martin's Laugh-In*, and *Love, American Style*. He was a guest several times on *The Tonight Show*, then became a substitute host.

After a successful television special in 1969, Wilson was offered his own series; With *The Flip Wilson Show*, which debuted in 1970, he became the first African American to have a successful hourlong weekly variety show. Other black performers, including Nat King Cole, Leslie Uggams, and Sammy Davis, Jr., had preceded him on television, but none was nearly as successful. Wilson's show earned two Emmys in 1971, for Outstanding Writing and Outstanding Variety Musical Show. Overall, it was nominated for eleven Emmys.

That same year, Wilson won a Golden Globe for the Best Television Actor in the musical and comedy category and a Grammy Award for Best Comedy Album for *The Devil Made Me Buy this Dress*. An earlier album, *Cowboys and Colored People* (1967) is credited with bringing him to Hollywood's attention. By 1972, *The Flip Wilson Show* was rated television's most popular variety hour and ranked in the top five shows overall. Wilson was paid more than $1 million a year. The series ended in 1974; reports conflict as to whether Wilson voluntarily departed or the show was canceled. His career declined thereafter, although he made many guest appearances on other series. His new shows, a 1984 remake of *People Are Funny* and *Charlie and Company*, which aired in 1985 and 1986, were unsuccessful, and Wilson made few television appearances after 1990.

While never completely eschewing the stereotypical caricatures of his early career, Wilson developed a style of deadpan stand-up comedy that relied more on storytelling than on throwaway gags. However, his humor was controversial, and some African Americans believed that it cast them in an unfavorable light.

Wilson created some wildly popular characters, particularly Geraldine Jones, a sassy, liberated black woman. Her much-repeated sayings included "What you see is what you get," "When you're hot, you're hot," and "The devil made me do it." Other recurring characters in his act included the slick Reverend Leroy; Sonny, the wise White House janitor; and Freddy the playboy. Wilson invariably greeted the guests on his show with his patented "handshake," consisting of multiple hand slaps and hip and elbow bumps.

Among Wilson's few films were *Uptown Saturday Night* (1974), *Skatetown U.S.A.* (1979), and *The Fish That Saved Pittsburgh* (1979). He also appeared in the made-for-television movie *Pinocchio* (1976). Wilson was married twice, to Lovenia "Peaches" Wilson and "Cookie" MacKenzie, and had five children. Both marriages ended in divorce. Wilson died on November 25, 1998, in Malibu, California.

## SIGNIFICANCE

Along with such performers as Bill Cosby, Dick Gregory, Redd Foxx, and Nipsey Russell, Wilson brought African American comedy to the forefront of popular culture in the late 1960's and 1970's. Their irreverent humor was a revelation to white audiences who were used to the stereotypical black characters previously seen on television in such shows as *Amos 'n' Andy* and *Beulah*. Wilson seemed particularly intent on presenting strong, positive images of African American women. He was a perfec-

tionist who was involved in all aspects of his show, doing much of the writing himself and closely supervising his writing team and guest stars. The success of his series helped pave the way for other shows featuring African Americans, such as *Good Times*, *The Jeffersons*, and ultimately *The Cosby Show*. Featured on the cover of *Time* magazine in early 1972, Wilson was dubbed "TV's First Black Superstar."

*—Roy Liebman*

## FURTHER READING

Acham, Christine. *Revolution Televised: Prime Time and the Struggle for Black Power*. Minneapolis: University of Minnesota Press, 2004. Examines African American performers and images on television; contains a section on Wilson's career, particularly his variety series.

Braun, Thomas. *On Stage, Flip Wilson*. Danbury, Conn.: Children's Press, 1976. A brief biography intended for young readers.

Haggins, Bambi. *Laughing Mad: The Black Comic Persona in Post-Soul America*. New Brunswick, N.J.: Rutgers University Press, 2007. Informative analysis of Wilson's comedy routines and variety show, including his unprecedented level of creative control.

Sutherland, Megan. *The Flip Wilson Show*. Detroit, Mich.: Wayne State University Press, 2008. Scholarly analysis of *The Flip Wilson Show* in social and political contexts.

**SEE ALSO:** Bill Cosby; Redd Foxx; Dick Gregory; Cleavon Little; Leslie Uggams; Paul Winfield.

# JACKIE WILSON
## Singer

*Wilson's electrifying live performances and extraordinary vocal range made him one of the greatest American rhythm and blues singers. He influenced singers from Elvis Presley to Michael Jackson to Van Morrison and helped black music cross over into the mainstream.*

**BORN:** June 9, 1934; Detroit, Michigan
**DIED:** January 21, 1984; Mount Holly, New Jersey
**ALSO KNOWN AS:** Jack Leroy Wilson, Jr.; Sonny Wilson; Mr. Excitement
**AREAS OF ACHIEVEMENT:** Music: crossover; Music: rhythm and blues; Music: soul; Sports: boxing

### EARLY LIFE

Jack Leroy Wilson, Jr., was born in Detroit, Michigan, on June 9, 1934, to an alcoholic father and a doting mother. Introduced to alcohol by his father before his ninth birthday, Wilson was alcohol- and drug-dependent for most of his life. By 1944, Jack, Sr., had abandoned the family. At twelve, Wilson joined the Ever Ready Gospel Singers, singing at churches and neighborhood events and gaining a large local following.

Wilson began associating with the Shakers, a local gang. He would entertain them by singing and they would protect him from other gangs. He rarely attended school and had numerous brushes with the law. He was twice sent to Lansing Correctional Institute, where he took up boxing. He entered the Golden Gloves program, but his mother made him quit and promise never to box again because it was too dangerous. Wilson dropped out of school at the age of sixteen, never having passed the ninth grade.

In 1951, Wilson married his pregnant girlfriend, Freda Hood. With a new family to support, he pursued his singing career more seriously.

### LIFE'S WORK

In 1951, Wilson and his cousin Levi Stubbs formed the Falcons. Then a local talent promoter, Johnny Otis, arranged for Wilson to join the Thrillers, a rhythm-and-blues group. They dropped Wilson just before signing a record deal as the Royals. In 1952, Wilson sang with Dizzy Gillespie, recording "Danny Boy." This song, which Wilson rerecorded years later, was nothing like the material for which he was popular. However, his love for all music styles, ranging from opera to rock and roll, often led to eccentric recording choices.

In 1953, Wilson joined Billy Ward's Dominoes as a backup singer for Clyde McPhatter. When McPhatter left a few months later, Wilson began singing lead. This relationship earned Wilson his first modest success with "You Can't Keep a Good Man Down." In 1956, he charted again with "St. Therese of the Roses."

Wilson went solo in 1957; Nat Tarnopol signed him to Brunswick Records, a Decca subsidiary, and became his manager. Tarnopol introduced Wilson to Berry Gordy, Jr., and Roquel "Billy" Davis, with whom he produced nine hits including "Reet Petit" and "Lonely Teardrops," one of his signature songs. Gordy and Davis broke up the partnership in 1958 because of problems with Tarnopol.

After the split, Wilson did not fare as well as the other producers. Many blame Tarnopol for mismanaging Wilson's career and for producing poor records. Many of Wilson's Brunswick albums used old-fashioned arrangements and were unsuccessful. A 1961 tribute album to Al Jolson, Wilson's favorite singer, was a marked failure. However, he also recorded some hits from 1958 to 1964, including "Doggin' Around," "Alone at Last," "Night" (a number-one hit), and another signature song, "Baby Workout."

In 1961, while juggling extramarital affairs, Wilson was shot twice by Juanita Jones. He lost a kidney and lived the rest of his life with a bullet embedded near his spine. Other tragedies followed. Freda divorced him, and his son and daughter died, plunging him into depression and exacerbating his alcohol and drug abuse. He was audited by the Internal Revenue Service and lost his home. Despite making $260,000 a year, he found himself broke. In 1967, he married Harlean Harris, with whom he had three children; that marriage also failed. In 1967, he was arrested in South Carolina on a morals charge for being with a white woman.

Despite these problems, Wilson continued to record and perform. In the late 1960's, he teamed with Chicago producer Carl Davis and released "Whispers (Gettin' Louder)" and his international hit "(Your Love Keeps Lifting Me) Higher and Higher."

Although he continued to make records, Wilson was relegated to performing in oldies shows. During a performance on September 29, 1975, he suffered a heart attack, fell, and hit his head. He spent more than eight years in a coma. On January 21, 1984, Wilson died of pneumonia in a nursing home in Mount Holly, New Jersey. He was buried in an unmarked grave. In 1987, he was inducted into the Rock and Roll Hall of Fame. In 1990, Wilson's body was exhumed and reburied alongside his mother in Wayne, Michigan, in a mausoleum donated by fans.

## SIGNIFICANCE

Wilson was a leading soul performer for more than twenty years, producing twenty-four Top 40 singles, six number-one hits, and fifty-five Top 100 records. He was an international star whose perfect tenor and falsetto gave him a unique singing range. He was famous for his live performances, during which he danced around the stage in a frenzy, driving fans wild. His dancing style, which he said he stole from Elvis Presley, influenced James Brown, Michael Jackson, and Presley himself, among many others. Although his career was cut short, Wilson had a lasting influence on rhythm and blues.

—*Leslie Neilan*

## FURTHER READING

Carter, Doug. *The Black Elvis: Jackie Wilson.* Berkeley, Calif.: Heydey Books, 1998. Compares the musical and performance styles of the two seminal singers.

Douglas, Tony. *Jackie Wilson: Lonely Teardrops.* New York: Routledge, 2005. This biography is based on interviews with Wilson's colleagues, family, and friends.

_____. *Jackie Wilson: The Man, the Music, the Mob.* Edinburgh, Scotland: Mainstream, 2001. Suggests that Wilson was cheated and mismanaged by Tarnopol. This source also details Wilson's womanizing and addictions.

Pruter, Robert. *Chicago Soul.* Music in American Life. Chicago: University of Chicago Press, 1992. This comprehensive look at Chicago-based soul music contains information about Wilson's work with Carl Davis.

**SEE ALSO:** James Brown; Sam Cooke; Bo Diddley; Fats Domino; Marvin Gaye; Berry Gordy, Jr.; Clyde McPhatter.

# WILLIAM JULIUS WILSON
## Educator, sociologist, and writer

*Wilson's work as an educator, researcher, scholar, and writer has generated spirited discussions of racism and urban poverty that have raised widespread awareness of these issues. His ideas have energized and expanded research efforts to better understand these complex social phenomena.*

**BORN:** December 20, 1935; Derry Township, Pennsylvania

**AREAS OF ACHIEVEMENT:** Education; Scholarship; Social sciences

## EARLY LIFE

William Julius Wilson was born in Derry Township, Pennsylvania, on December 20, 1935, to Pauline and Esco Wilson. He spent his early childhood there before moving to Blairsville, Pennsylvania, near Pittsburgh. Wilson's family was of very modest means, and he grew up in a small house in which he and his five siblings shared one bedroom. His parents were high school dropouts who instilled the values of hard work and education in their children, all of whom earned college degrees. Esco Wilson was a coal miner and steelworker, and when Wilson was twelve, his father's death from black lung disease plunged the family into abject poverty, forcing them to live on public assistance until his mother found relatively stable work cleaning houses. Wilson later characterized his childhood as having been happy with no real sense of deprivation, in spite of his family's economic hardships.

Wilson's aunt Janice Wardlaw, a psychiatric social worker in New York City, was an important influence and mentor. During the summers that Wilson spent with her, she introduced him to New York's cultural amenities and insisted that he be well-read and excel academically. She also assisted him financially when he attended Wilberforce University in Ohio on a scholarship. Wilson earned a bachelor's degree in sociology at Wilberforce in 1958. After spending two years in the military, he earned a master's degree in sociology from Bowling Green State University in 1961 and a Ph.D. in sociology and anthropology from Washington State University in 1966.

## LIFE'S WORK

Wilson had developed an interest in race relations and poverty at Wilberforce, but neither his master's thesis nor his doctoral dissertation dealt with these topics. He joined the University of Massachusetts faculty after earning his Ph.D. in 1966; by 1971, when he left to teach at the University of Chicago, race had become the focus of his work. At Chicago, he advanced quickly and became chair of the sociology department in 1978. Based on his Urban Poverty and Family Life Survey in 1987, Wilson established and became the director of the Center for the Study of Urban Inequality in 1990. His teaching and research-based publications examined race, urban poverty, and social stratification.

Wilson's numerous books and articles have been widely read and influential within and outside of academia. He was critical of the methodology and conclusions of much of the race-oriented research done in the 1960's and 1970's, and his studies, which employed an empirical data-analysis approach, sometimes produced controversial findings. One of Wilson's most controversial books, *The Declining Significance of Race: Blacks and Changing American Institutions* (1978), concluded that African Americans' life chances were affected more by class than race, leaving poor African Americans in a nearly hopeless cycle of impoverishment, while their middle-class counterparts' prospects were good. Wilson openly resented conservative academics and politicians using these findings, and even his own life, to support their assertions that government poverty-assistance programs should be eliminated. In a 1987 publication, Wilson disavowed any conservative connections by proposing that large-scale race-neutral government programs were needed to provide assistance and create educational and career opportunities for the impoverished. In subsequent publications, he expanded these proposals to include calls for universal health care and New Deal-style public job programs instead of welfare stipends.

In 1996, Wilson joined the faculty of the John F. Kennedy School of Government at Harvard University, where he became the director of the Joblessness and Urban Poverty Research Program. He also became a member of the Department of African and African American Studies. Wilson has earned the highest honors and awards in his field, including being elected to the National Academy of Sciences in 1991 and receiving the National Medal of Science in 1998, and has testified before congressional committees and advised powerful political leaders.

**SIGNIFICANCE**

Through his career as a teacher, author, public speaker, and political activist, Wilson has shown that sociology can provide valuable insights into social problems and uncover ways to address them. By challenging various ideological positions regarding the causes and possible solutions for poverty, Wilson has shown that scientific evidence belongs in the public forum and the political arena. His work has pushed studies of race and poverty to the forefront of sociology's research agenda and has been a major force in directing the work of a new generation of scholars in these areas.

*—Jack Carter*

**FURTHER READING**

Waldinger, Roger David. *Still the Promised City? African-Americans and New Immigrants in Postindustrial New York*. Cambridge, Mass.: Harvard University Press, 1999. Examines Wilson's theories on urban African Americans' economic malaise and offers some alternative sociological explanations.

Wilson, Frank Harold. *Race, Class, and the Postindustrial City: William Julius Wilson and the Promise of Sociology*. New York: New York State University Press, 2004. An examination and critical analysis of Wilson's theories on race relations and politics.

Wilson, William Julius. *The Bridge over the Racial Divide: Rising Inequality and Coalition Politics*. Berkeley: University of California Press, 2001. Wilson calls for working- and middle-class Americans to overcome their racial biases to form a political alliance to counteract the elitist policies that have exacerbated the problems of nonwealthy citizens.

_____. *More than Just Race: Being Black and Poor in the Inner City*. New York: W. W. Norton, 2009. Wilson examines the ways in which institutional factors and the perceptions and attitudes of whites, African Americans, and social scientists have contributed to continuing high rates of poverty among urban African Americans.

**SEE ALSO:** Kenneth Clark; Patricia Hill Collins; Asa Grant Hilliard III; Charles S. Johnson; Claude M. Steele.

# PAUL WINFIELD
## Actor

*Best known for his commanding role in the film*
Sounder *(1972), Winfield was a prolific and versatile actor who found success in theater, film, and television. He was the third African American actor nominated for an Academy Award for Best Actor and performed in more than 125 films and television shows.*

**BORN:** May 22, 1939; Los Angeles, California
**DIED:** March 7, 2004; Los Angeles, California
**ALSO KNOWN AS:** Paul Edward Winfield
**AREAS OF ACHIEVEMENT:** Film: acting; Radio and
  television

### EARLY LIFE
Paul Edward Winfield was born in Los Angeles in 1939 to a single mother, Lois Beatrice Edwards, a garment worker and labor organizer. She married Clarence Winfield, a construction worker and garbage collector, when Winfield was eight years old. The Winfields and their four children moved to Portland, Oregon, where he spent his early years. After a series of moves, the family finally settled in the Watts section of Los Angeles during the neighborhood's transition from all white to predominantly black. Winfield's life was influenced greatly by his mother and by an older woman with whom he had an affair.

Winfield was bused to Manual Arts High School, at that time a predominantly white school, where he was the first student to be selected as the best actor in the Southern California Speech and Drama Teachers Association Drama Festival competition for three consecutive years. Winfield, who tended to be a loner, was an excellent student and a talented violinist and cellist.

Winfield turned down a scholarship to Yale University, fearful of not fitting in, and instead accepted a two-year drama scholarship at the University of Portland in Oregon. He left the university after two years and briefly attended Stanford, then Los Angeles City College and the University of California at Los Angeles (UCLA). He left UCLA six credits shy of earning a degree to make his first stage appearance. Winfield was an artist-in-residence at Stanford University from 1964 to 1965 and at the University of Hawaii in 1965.

### LIFE'S WORK
Winfield was first inspired to become an actor when he watched James Edwards in the film *Home of the Brave*

(1949). Edwards's role as Private Peter Moss impressed upon Winfield that African Americans could play roles other than jesters, chauffeurs, and servants. Although most of his appearances were character roles, Winfield's versatility allowed him to make a successful career on the stage, in film, television, and in voice-overs.

Performing onstage was Winfield's first love. He landed his first stage roles in 1964 in two plays by LeRoi Jones (later known as Amiri Baraka), *Dutchman* and *The Toilet*, directed by Burgess Meredith. Winfield's performance was noted by Sidney Poitier. Winfield joined the Stanford Repertory Theater and, as a member of the Inner City Cultural Center Theater, helped produce professional plays for high school students. He had a fondness for Shakespearean plays. His Shakespearean performances included *A Midsummer Night's Dream*, *The Merry Wives of Windsor*, and the title role in *Othello*. Other stage performances included Anton Chekhov's

*Paul Winfield.* (AP/Wide World Photos)

---

### WINFIELD'S ROLE IN *SOUNDER*

Paul Winfield's emotional portrayal of Nathan Lee Morgan, a share-cropper trying to provide for his family during the Depression, in *Sounder* (1972) earned the actor an Academy Award nomination for Best Actor. *Sounder* appeared during the period when African Americans were mostly cast in subservient roles in mainstream films, while the "blaxsploitation" genre cast its African American heroes as hyperviolent and hypersexual. Winfield's dignified performance thus was a refreshing change and demonstrated that African American actors could movingly express warmth, love, and humanity. A great deal of the film's success can be attributed to Winfield making the character so believable, perhaps because Winfield saw so much of his father in Nathan and conceivably because Winfield himself and Nathan had a lot in common: love for the land, love of work, and a gentle side. His brilliant performance was instrumental in the film's appeal to mainstream audiences.

---

*The Seagull*, Henrik Ibsen's *Enemy of the People*, and A. R. Gurney's *Love Letters*. He performed in many plays at the Los Angeles Mark Taper Forum and appeared in the Broadway play *Checkmates*.

Winfield's first film role was in *The Lost Man* (1969), directed by Poitier. Although roles for African American actors were sparse during the early 1970's, Winfield had boycotted many films because he viewed them as exploitative. However, he ended his boycott for a role in *Trouble Man* (1972) because it opened craft unions to African Americans. In 1972, Winfield was selected for the role of Nathan Lee in *Sounder*, the film for which he gained international recognition. After *Sounder*, most of his film roles were as a supporting actor. His credits included *A Hero Ain't Nothin' but a Sandwich* (1978) and *Star Trek II: The Wrath of Khan* (1982). His most notable films in the 1990's included *Presumed Innocent* (1990), *Catfish in Black Bean Sauce* (1999), and *Second to Die* (2002).

Winfield made his television debut in 1965 in the series *Perry Mason*. Television provided steady work for him throughout his career, and he had an impressive list of television roles. He appeared in *Julia* (1968-1970) with Diahann Carroll, *227* (1988-1990), and *Touched by an Angel* (1995-2003). Winfield's television career also included several made-for-television films and miniseries, including *It's Good to Be Alive* (1974), portraying Martin Luther King, Jr., in *King* (1978), and *Roots: The Next Generations* (1979); the latter two earned him Emmy nominations. During the mid-1980's, he often played more authoritative figures in television films and series such as *The Sophisticated Gents* (1982), *For Us*

the *Living: The Medgar Evers Story* (1983), *The Women of Brewster Place* (1989), *Tyson* (1995), and *Strange Justice* (1999).

Because one of Winfield's greatest assets was his powerful voice, he was sought after for voice-over and narration roles. He narrated the PBS documentary *Baseball* in 1994; appeared in several episodes of *The Magic School Bus*, *Spider-Man* (1994-1998), and *The Simpsons*; and is best known for his highly melodramatic narration of *City Confidential* from 1998 to 2004.

Winfield's honors include an Image Award from the National Association for the Advancement of Colored People (NAACP) for Best Actor in 1982 for the television film *The Sophisticated Gents*, induction into the Black Filmmakers Hall of Fame in 1991, an Emmy for Outstanding Guest Actor in a Drama Series for *Picket Fences* in 1995, and the St. Louis International Film Festival's Lifetime Achievement Award in 1999.

Winfield was romantically involved with Cicely Tyson for almost two years. He later had a thirty-year relationship with his partner Charles Gillian, Jr., although he was discreet about their relationship. He battled obesity and diabetes for a number of years and served as a spokesman to raise awareness of diabetes. Winfield died of a heart attack on March 7, 2004.

### SIGNIFICANCE

Winfield was the third African American to be nominated for an Academy Award for Best Actor. He also was nominated for three Emmy Awards, winning once. A socially conscious performer, Winfield sought roles that elevated the status of African Americans during a period when roles for black actors were sparse. His role on *Julia* was noted for creating more opportunities for African Americans in the entertainment industry.

—*Joyce K. Thornton*

### FURTHER READING

Bogle, Donald. *Toms, Coons, Mulattoes, Mammies, and Bucks: An Interpretive History of Blacks in American Film*. 4th ed. New York: Continuum, 2001. Puts Winfield's work and achievements into cultural and racial context.

Elbert, Albert. "Paul Winfield: A Man unto Himself." *Essence* 4 (June, 1973): 27. Provides excellent information on Winfield's early childhood, relationships, points of view, and the influences that shaped his career.

Mapp, Edward. "1972: Paul Winfield." In *African Americans and the Oscar: Seven Decades of Struggle and Achievement*. Lanham, Md.: Scarecrow Press, 2003. Brief examination of the controversy over *Sounder*

and Winfield's performance that includes quotations from the actor himself about the significance of the role.

**SEE ALSO:** Diahann Carroll; Bill Cosby; Morgan Freeman; Louis Gossett, Jr.; Robert Guillaume; James Earl Jones; Cicely Tyson.

# OPRAH WINFREY

## Talk-show host, entertainer, and entrepreneur

*A television icon, Winfrey is one of the wealthiest and most successful entertainers in the world. Her long-running talk show,* The Oprah Winfrey Show, *became a powerful forum that is credited with launching the careers of other media personalities, turning books into best sellers, and drawing major attention to charitable causes. Winfrey also has produced several films and won praise for her acting in films such as* The Color Purple *(1985) and* Beloved *(1998).*

**BORN:** January 29, 1954; Kosciusko, Mississippi
**ALSO KNOWN AS:** Oprah Gail Winfrey; Oprah; Queen of Daytime TV; First Lady of Talk Shows
**AREAS OF ACHIEVEMENT:** Business; Film: acting; Film: production; Philanthropy; Radio and television

### EARLY LIFE

Oprah Gail Winfrey (OH-pruh gayl WIHN-free) was born to Vernon Winfrey and Vernita Lee in the winter of 1954 in the small southern town of Kosciusko, Mississippi. Vernon and Vernita were young and unmarried; Vernon soon relocated to Nashville, Tennessee, while Vernita moved to Milwaukee, Wisconsin, to find work. Winfrey was left in the care of her grandparents, Earlist and Hattie Mae Lee, on their farm. She spent her early years in poverty but well loved by her strict grandmother, who taught Winfrey to read at age three and took her to church to recite scripture. Winfrey's natural speaking ability would prove to be an asset to her as an adult.

At age six, Winfrey moved to Milwaukee to live with her mother and half sister, Patricia. Vernita worked long hours as a housekeeper and had little time for her children. The conditions pushed Winfrey into independence at an early age, but her life was painful and unstable. At age nine, she was molested by her mother's nineteen-

year-old cousin. Other abuses followed, leaving Winfrey with deep emotional scars.

Winfrey found her escape in education, where she excelled. An avid reader, she especially enjoyed books about African Americans such as Harriet Tubman and Sojourner Truth. Winfrey's abilities were noted by her teachers at Lincoln Middle School. One caring teacher helped her secure a scholarship to Nicolet High School in Glendale, a suburb of Milwaukee, where she could participate in the progressive Upward Bound program. She was the only African American student at the school.

Winfrey continued to struggle at home, however. After running away from her mother's home at age fourteen, Winfrey moved to Nashville to live with her father, Vernon, a barber with a strong work ethic, and stepmother, Zelma. This disciplined environment provided Winfrey with much-needed stability. Her father stressed the importance of education and work and held Winfrey to high standards. Zelma also was supportive and encouraged Winfrey to excel. Winfrey's life began to change for the better. One of her favorite books, Maya Angelou's *I Know Why the Caged Bird Sings* (1969), helped inspire her to believe in her own innate worth. She represented her high school at the White House Conference on Youth held in Colorado and won an Elks Club oratorical contest that provided her a four-year college scholarship.

During Winfrey's senior year in high school, she needed a business sponsor for the March of Dimes Walkathon. She contacted a local radio station, WVOL, and met acting director Joe Heidelberg, an African American disc jockey. He liked her voice and offered her part-time work reading the news on the radio. In 1971, at age seventeen, Winfrey represented the radio station in a local beauty pageant run by the Nashville Fire Department; she won the title of Miss Fire Prevention.

### LIFE'S WORK

In 1972, Winfrey entered college at Tennessee State University in Nashville, focusing on speech, English, and drama. That same year, she was crowned Miss Black Tennessee. Her sophomore year, 1973, she took a job as a news anchor at WTVF-TV, a CBS affiliate. At nineteen, she was the youngest person and the first African American woman to anchor the news at the station.

After college, Winfrey moved to Baltimore to work at WJZ-TV. She was assigned local morning news updates and progressed to a morning talk show. High ratings brought her the opportunity to audition for WLS-TV, an ABC affiliate in Chicago, where she became the first African American female anchor for *A.M. Chicago* in 1983. Winfrey tailored her show to include controversial issues and current events; the show was renamed *The Oprah Winfrey Show* in 1985. The popularity of *The Oprah Winfrey Show* quickly led to national syndication, and it immediately displaced *Donahue* as the country's highest-rated talk show. The show eventually expanded into more than one hundred other countries and won numerous Emmy Awards. Because she holds an ownership stake in the show, Winfrey became a millionaire when it began airing nationally in 1986.

In 1985, Winfrey was cast as Sofia in Steven Spielberg's film *The Color Purple*, based on Alice Walker's 1982 novel of the same name. In 1986, she received an Academy Award nomination for Best Supporting Actress. Winfrey's only previous acting credit was in the 1978 one-woman show *The History of Black Women Through Drama and Song*. In 1988, she founded Harpo Productions and produced and costarred in a miniseries, *The Women of Brewster Place*, based on Gloria Naylor's 1982 novel, which aired in early 1989; the follow-up series, *Brewster Place*, was shown in 1990. She has produced several other film adaptations of books by African American women authors, including a 1998 feature version of Toni Morrison's *Beloved* (1987) and a 2005 television movie based on Zora Neale Hurston's *Their Eyes Were Watching God* (1937).

In 1996, Winfrey used her national stature to launch a reading initiative, Oprah's Book Club. Drawing on her love of books and her belief in the power of reading, Winfrey initiated monthly discussions that sent each

*Oprah Winfrey.* (Getty Images)

book she selected to the top of the best-seller lists. In 2000, she launched *O, The Oprah Magazine*, a lifestyle publication that targets affluent and middle-class women.

Winfrey also used her influence to address social-justice issues and political concerns. In 1998, she testified on behalf of the National Child Protection Act, also known as the "Oprah Bill," which ultimately was signed into law by President Bill Clinton. In 2005, "Oprah's Child Predator Watch List" targeted child predators and offered rewards of $100,000 to apprehend fugitives wanted by the Federal Bureau of Investigation (FBI). In 2008, Winfrey asked her viewers to support U.S. Senate Bill 1738, dubbed the "Protect Our Children Act" which addressed child pornography on the Internet; the bill passed in the fall of 2008. That year, she also made headlines by endorsing Barack Obama's presidential campaign, a major test of her influence.

In 2009, Winfrey announced that she would end her talk show in 2011, at the end of its twenty-fifth season. She turned her attention to launching her own cable network, OWN: The Oprah Winfrey Network, which debuted on January 1, 2011.

Because of her success in many different media, Winfrey became the first black woman billionaire. According to *Forbes*, her net worth topped $1 billion in 2003 and had risen to $2.7 billion by September, 2010. Winfrey has been called the greatest philanthropic African American of all time. In 2005, *BusinessWeek* listed her among its top fifty philanthropists with an estimated $303 million in donations; she was the first African American to be included on the list. In 1998 Winfrey started Oprah's Angel Network, which raised more than fifty million dollars before Winfrey dissolved it in 2010. The Angel Network raised eleven million dollars in 2005 to aid victims of hurricanes Katrina and Rita; Winfrey added ten million dollars of her own to the cause. In 2007, Winfrey donated forty million dollars to open the Oprah Winfrey Leadership Academy for Girls in South Africa.

## SIGNIFICANCE

Winfrey's rags-to-riches story remains a powerful testament to the power of self-reliance and perseverance. She

## OPRAH WINFREY'S COMMERCIAL ENTERPRISES

For more than twenty years, Oprah Winfrey has built a wide array of commercial enterprises with her ingenuity, creativity, and marketing acumen. In 1986, Winfrey established Harpo, Inc. In 1988, her Harpo Productions assumed control of *The Oprah Winfrey Show*, which was watched by an estimated 42 million viewers per week in the United States. Winfrey was the first woman to own her own talk show as well as produce it. Harpo Productions later diversified to include Harpo Studios, Harpo Films, and Harpo Radio. Harpo Studios produces television talk shows such as *The Dr. Oz Show*, *Dr. Phil*, *Rachael Ray*, and *The Nate Berkus Show*. In 2010, Harpo Studios launched Harpo Creative Works, a team of writers, designers, and producers who specialize in advertising campaigns. By 2010, Harpo Films had produced several television films, including *Tuesdays with Morrie* (1999) and *Their Eyes Were Watching God* (2005), and the feature film *Beloved* (1998). Her *O: The Oprah Magazine* launched in 2000 and remained a strong seller despite a general downturn for print publications in the late 2000's. Winfrey produced radio programming for satellite radio and other media and expanded into cable in 2011 with the launch of OWN: The Oprah Winfrey Network, a partnership with Discovery Communications.

built on her speaking ability and innate empathy to become a television icon, media mogul, and powerful tastemaker. She has built a business empire whose reach extends throughout popular culture. Although the scope of her influence has drawn criticism at times, and she has promoted controversial products and people, her power as a trendsetter is unquestionable. Among her numerous awards and honors are an Emmy Lifetime Achievement Award (1998), a Global Humanitarian Action Award (2004), a George Foster Peabody Individual Achievement Award (1995), and induction into the Broadcasting Hall of Fame and National Association for the Advancement of Colored People (NAACP) Hall of Fame.

—*Marylane Wade Koch*

## FURTHER READING

Cotten, Trystan T., and Kimberly Springer, eds. *Stories of Oprah: Oprahfication of American Culture*. Jackson: University Press of Mississippi, 2009. Collection of essays focusing on Winfrey's influence over American culture.

Farr, Cecilia Konchar. *Reading Oprah: How Oprah's Book Club Changed the Way America Reads*. Albany: State University of New York Press, 2004. Describes how Winfrey influenced reading comprehension and popularized the concept of reading for pleasure.

Harris, Jennifer, and Elwood Watson, eds. *The Oprah Phenomenon*. Lexington: University Press of Kentucky, 2007. Collection of essays examining the economics and power of Winfrey over American culture through her influence on entertainment, politics, and national opinions.

Noel, Jennifer. "Lights! Camera! Oprah!" *Ebony* 40, no. 6 (April, 1985):100-105. Detailed, well-illustrated profile of Winfrey written when she anchored *A.M. Chicago*.

Paprocki, Sherry Beck. *Oprah Winfrey: Talk Show and Media Magnate*. New York: Chelsea House, 2006. Written for young-adult readers, this biography offers a concise overview of Winfrey's life and accomplishments.

Stone, Tanya Lee. *Oprah Winfrey: Success with an Open Heart*. Minneapolis, Minn.: Milbrook Press, 2001. Written for younger students, this biography provides insight into Winfrey's life challenges and successes.

Winfrey, Oprah. "Oprah Winfrey's Official Biography." http://www.oprah.com/pressroom/Oprah-Winfreys -Official-Biography. Winfrey's official Web site includes this detailed, illustrated biography as well as information on her many business and charitable interests.

**SEE ALSO:** Bryant Gumbel; Arsenio Hall; John H. Johnson; Robert L. Johnson; Montel Williams.

# JAMES WINKFIELD
## Jockey

*An international celebrity at the beginning of the twentieth century, Winkfield accomplished the rare feat of winning the Kentucky Derby in consecutive years. His career spanned thirty years and more than twenty-six hundred wins. After his racing days were over, he became an owner and trainer of horses.*

**BORN:** April 12, 1882; Chilesburg, Kentucky
**DIED:** March 23, 1974; Maisons-Laffitte, France
**AREA OF ACHIEVEMENT:** Sports: miscellaneous

### EARLY LIFE

James Winkfield was born on April 12, 1882, in Chilesburg, Kentucky, near Lexington. He was the youngest of his parents' seventeen children, and he was raised on the farm where his father worked as a sharecropper. Winkfield dropped out of school before completing his high school education but rode horses from an early age; by 1898, he was racing horses professionally for a monthly salary of $8.

### LIFE'S WORK

In one of Winkfield's first races, he was involved in a four-horse collision at the starting line and received a brief suspension from the sport. However, his talent was such that he soon found himself back on the track, making increasingly large sums. In 1900, he finished third in the Kentucky Derby while riding Thrive. In 1901, Winkfield won the Derby riding His Eminence, then repeated the feat on Alan-a-Dale in 1902. Few jockeys ever have won the Kentucky Derby in consecutive years. In

1903, Winkfield finished second in the Derby with the horse Early.

That year, Winkfield allegedly accepted a late offer of $3,000 from a rival owner to switch camps, racing a different horse than he originally had promised in the Futurity Stakes event. Although the details were disputed, Winkfield's reputation plummeted; after enduring racism within the racing community and outright threats on his life from the Ku Klux Klan, Winkfield decided to move to Europe, where racing was more lucrative. He became an international celebrity, racing in events with much larger purses than the Kentucky Derby. He won the Emperor's Purse and the Moscow, St. Petersburg, and Warsaw races (the so-called "Tsarist Triple Crown"). Winkfield bounced around Europe, moving to Germany to race there in 1909, then moving back to Russia in 1913.

The Russian Revolution brought an end to aristocratic patronage of horse racing in Russia in 1919, and Winkfield took part in the daring transport of 150 horses out of the country and into Poland. Winkfield returned to Paris destitute in 1920 and began to race again. He soon found renewed success, winning both the Prix du Président de la République and Grand Prix de Deauville in 1922. In 1930, Winkfield retired as a jockey and began directing his energy toward his own stable of horses.

Although Winkfield's career as an owner lasted throughout the 1930's, the oubreak of World War II brought an end to his business; in 1940, he was evacuated to the United States. Virtually unknown in the United States and penniless once again, Winkfield became a construction worker for the federal Works Progress Administration and eventually found work at a stable. He returned to France in 1953 and again became an owner and trainer of horses. In 1961, he visited Louisville, Kentucky, for an event commemorating his victories at the Kentucky Derby sixty years earlier.

Winkfield died near Paris on March 23, 1974, at the age of ninety-one. He was interred at Maisons-Laffitte, near his home.

## SIGNIFICANCE

Although his accomplishments were long overlooked, Winkfield ranks among the best jockeys of all time. Over a thirty-year span, he won many of the major racing prizes of his day; his contributions to the sport continued even after his career as a jockey ended, through his successful ventures as an owner and trainer. In 2003, an exhibition at the Kentucky Derby Museum brought him back into the public eye, and in 2004, he was inducted into the National Museum of Racing and Hall of Fame. He also was recognized in a 2005 Congressional resolution, passed shortly before the 131st Kentucky Derby. A race in his honor, the Jimmy Winkfield Stakes, has been run annually at the Aqueduct Racetrack in New York since 1985.

—*C. Breault*

## FURTHER READING

Drape, Joe. *Black Maestro: The Epic Life of an American Legend*. New York: HarperCollins, 2007. Drape's account of Winkfield's life is the best full biography of the athlete available, providing a well-researched account of his career written in an accessible manner.

"'A Feeling of a Lifetime': St. Julien Will Be First Black Jockey in Seventy-nine Years at Derby." The Associated Press, May 4, 2000. Provides a concise summary of the history of African Americans at the Kentucky Derby.

Hotaling, Ed. *Wink: The Incredible Life and Epic Journey of Jimmy Winkfield*. New York: McGraw-Hill, 2005. This entertaining full-length popular biography, written in a readable style by a racing insider, is a good source for details on Winkfield's life.

Winkler, Lisa K. "The Kentucky Derby's Forgotten Jockeys." Smithsonian.com, April 24, 2009. http://www.smithsonianmag.com/history-archaeology/The-Kentucky-Derbys-Forgotten-Jockeys.html. A statistics-filled history of African American jockeys in the United States, with a focus on the Kentucky Derby.

**SEE ALSO:** Isaac Burns Murphy; Bill Pickett; Willie Simms.

# ERNEST WITHERS
## Photographer

*Withers took photographs of some of the most important events of the Civil Rights movement during the 1950's and 1960's. He captured famous images of the Emmett Till murder trial and Martin Luther King, Jr., among other major figures. After his death, it was revealed that he had worked covertly for the U.S. government, helping to monitor civil rights activists.*

**BORN:** August 7, 1922; Memphis, Tennessee
**DIED:** October 15, 2007; Memphis, Tennessee
**AREAS OF ACHIEVEMENT:** Art and photography; Civil rights

## EARLY LIFE

Ernest Withers was born on August 7, 1922, in Memphis, Tennessee. Little is known about his mother; his father was a postal worker. Withers grew up with an interest in cameras, starting with his very first as a teenager. He borrowed a Brownie camera from his sister's boyfriend and took pictures around his hometown. One of his first pictures was of acclaimed boxer Joe Louis's wife, who visited his school.

Withers's interest in photography was interrupted by the onset of World War II. Even though Withers entered the Army, however, he was not deterred from his passion for long. The Army had set up a school of photography that Withers was able to attend. He began to take even more pictures, including ones of his fellow soldiers that they were able to send home to their families.

When the war ended, Withers's experience in civil and military service enabled him to become a policeman in the Memphis area. However, he soon realized that what he really wanted to pursue in life was photography.

## LIFE'S WORK

Withers's early jobs as a photographer were modest. He started taking photos of events and happenings in his community, from baseball games to weddings. One of

*Ernest Withers revisits the Lorraine Motel, site of Martin Luther King, Jr.'s assassination, in 1989.* (Time & Life Pictures/Getty Images)

Withers's biggest projects at this time was taking pictures of Negro American League baseball players such as Jackie Robinson and Willie Mays. Withers also took pictures of famous musicians such as Elvis Presley, B. B. King, Ray Charles, and Aretha Franklin.

Withers's legacy rests on his images of the Civil Rights movement. His work in this field began in late 1955 when Emmett Till, an African American teenager from Chicago, was killed in Mississippi. Withers took photos of Till's battered face and his mother crying after Till's killers were acquitted. The striking photographs helped bring the lynching to national attention at the same time it helped Withers become more visible as a photojournalist.

Withers's most prominent assignments came when he worked closely with Martin Luther King, Jr., at the height of the Civil Rights movement. Withers traveled with King and became close with several African American activists. He took photographs of King riding integrated buses in Montgomery, the enrollment of the first

African American student at the University of Mississippi, and many other landmark events. Many of his photographs were iconic, bringing the people and issues of the Civil Rights movement to audiences nationwide. Withers died in October 15, 2007, of complications from a stroke.

In 2010, it was also revealed that Withers had worked as a confidential informant for the Federal Bureau of Investigation (FBI) during the 1950's and 1960's. Withers reported on the movements and activities of the civil rights leaders he photographed, including King.

### SIGNIFICANCE

Withers occupied a lofty position as the unofficial photographer of the Civil Rights movement. Enjoying unparalleled access to the leaders and major events of that tumultuous era, Withers captured images that became symbolic of the movement itself. His extensive work has been published in several books. The revelations that Withers also reported on civil rights activities to the FBI demonstrates the government's wariness of African American activism and the reach of its domestic intelligence activities. Withers was a respected confidant of leaders such as King, and his unmasking as an FBI informer years after his death came as a shock to many of his contemporaries.

*—Jill E. Disis*

**FURTHER READING**

"Ernest Withers: Photographer Who in Documenting the Civil Rights Movement Contributed to Its Success." *The Times* of London, October 27, 2007. This obituary goes into great detail about Withers's photographs of the Emmett Till murder trial and Martin Luther King, Jr.

Hurley, Jack F., Brooks Johnson, Ernest Withers, and Daniel Wolff. *Pictures Tell the Story: Ernest C. Withers Reflections in History.* Norfolk, Va.: Chrysler Museum of Art, 2000. Collection of many photographs taken by Withers throughout his life, including pictures of baseball players and jazz musicians in addition to the images of the Civil Rights movement.

Perrusquia, Marc. "Photographer Ernest Withers Doubled as FBI Informant to Spy on Civil Rights Movement." *The Memphis Commercial Appeal*, September 12, 2010. This investigative report reveals details of Withers's work for the FBI.

Till-Mobley, Mamie, and Christopher Benson. *Death of Innocence: The Story of the Hate Crime That Changed America.* New York: Random House, 2003. This memoir by Emmett Till's mother includes discussion of Withers's role in photographing the trial of Till's killers.

**SEE ALSO:** Roy DeCarava; Austin Hansen; Milt Hinton; Martin Luther King, Jr.; Gordon Parks, Sr.; Emmett Till.

# GEORGE C. WOLFE
## Playwright, director, and producer

*An award-winning playwright and director, Wolfe uses his skills to shatter the constraints of stereotypes in the theater.*

**BORN:** September 23, 1954; Frankfort, Kentucky
**ALSO KNOWN AS:** George Costello Wolfe
**AREA OF ACHIEVEMENT:** Theater

**EARLY LIFE**

One of four siblings, George Costello Wolfe grew up in the small state capital Frankfort, Kentucky. His father, Costello, worked as an officer for the Kentucky Department of Corrections, and his mother, Anna, was a teacher and principal of the all-black private school that Wolfe attended. His interest in drama was sparked early as a participant in a theatrical production as a kindergartner. Wolfe went on to attend Frankfort High School, where he wrote poetry and prose for the school literary journal and became involved with school theatrical productions.

Wolfe spent his first year of college at historically black Kentucky State University before transferring to Pomona College, in Claremont, California, where he studied acting and design. He also wrote his first play, *Up for Grabs* (1975), which earned an American College Theater Festival Award. After earning his B.A. from Pomona, Wolfe moved from Claremont to Los Angeles, where he worked as a teacher for the Inner City Cultural Center. Soon thereafter, Wolfe began to feel the pull of Broadway, and in 1979 he moved to New York City to pursue an M.F.A. at New York University's Tisch School of the Arts. He also worked for a brief time as an instructor of acting at City College New York (CUNY) and at the Richard Allen Center for Cultural Art.

**LIFE'S WORK**

Wolfe's Off-Broadway career got off to a rocky start. His musical *Paradise* (1985) was a commercial flop, and his controversial play *The Colored Museum* (1986) created debate over African American stereotypes among actors and other Broadway professionals. Nevertheless, *The Colored Museum* opened to rave reviews and served as a catharsis for the playwright. Wolfe described the play as an "exorcism and a party"; he was able to confront the archetypes that caged his creative energy, and his career began to skyrocket.

In 1989, his adaptation of three Zora Neale Hurston tales, *Spunk*, earned an Obie Award for direction. His musical *Jelly's Last Jam* (1992) earned eleven Tony Award nominations, receiving three Tony Awards and six Drama Desk Awards. He was a Tony Award winner for directing part one of Tony Kushner's *Angels in America* (1991) and was nominated for another for the second installment. Wolfe is recognized by many authorities as the first African American director to have great success on Broadway with a play that is not about the African diaspora. One of Wolfe's aspirations as an artist was to bring color to the main stage without being limited by the label of "black dramatist."

In 1993, Wolfe assumed the post of artistic director-producer of the New York Shakespearean Festival and Joseph Papp Public Theater, where he continued to practice his artistic philosophy of inclusion. In an interview with Charles Rowell for *Callaloo*, Wolfe said, "Much of what I think is what's happening in American culture now is that those who once upon a time were considered 'other' are sort of bored with the little cracks and crevices and corners that have been allotted to them and are beginning to claim their rightful space, center-stage, because in many respects those are the stories of what America is and what America is becoming." During his stint at the Public Theater, Wolfe produced the smash hit musical *Bring in 'da Noise, Bring in 'da Funk* (1996), which earned him his second Tony Award.

Wolfe stepped down from his position at the Public Theater after a tumultuous tenure, which produced a few failures and many successes. He earned several awards and nominations during his eleven years there, solidifying his legacy in the Broadway community. Seeking a challenge, Wolfe moved on to feature film direction and was awarded a Black Reel for Best Director in Television and the Outstanding Directorial Achievement Award in Movies for Television from the Directors Guild of America for the his first effort, the Home Box Office film *Lackawanna Blues* (2005). He continued to direct films and shows for the Public Theater. He also directed the Pulitzer Prize-winning Broadway show *Topdog/Underdog* (2001) by Suzan-Lori Parks.

## SIGNIFICANCE

Wolfe has garnered international fame for his work in drama. His plays have been produced in several countries; his plays and musicals are collected in several drama anthologies; and he is counted among the greatest directors of drama by several authorities. He is also credited with cultivating the careers of numerous Asian, African American, and Latino playwrights, such as Diana Son, Suzan-Lori Parks, José Rivera, and Nilo Cruz. This was not his intention; Wolfe said in a 2005 interview with *The New York Times*, "I get incredibly annoyed when the work that I've done gets reduced to, 'And he did plays that brought colored people to the theater.'" As an artist, Wolfe has worked to eliminate the constraints of stereotypes, in order to encourage artists of all races and creeds to create without color consciousness.

*—J. Jehriko Turner*

## FURTHER READING

Elam, Harry J. "Signifyin(g) on African-American Theatre: *The Colored Museum* by George Wolfe." *Theatre Journal* 44, no. 3 (1992): 291-303. Wolfe discusses the impact of his work on the perception of African American theater.

Gerard, Jeremy. "*Colored Museum*'s Author's Exorcism." *The New York Times*, November 6, 1986, p. 16. Wolfe discusses his controversial play and its effect on him as an artist.

Keene, John. "George C. Wolfe: A Brief Biography." *Callaloo* 16, no. 3 (1993): 593-594. A short snapshot of Wolfe's accomplishments.

McKinley, Jesse. "Exiting the Public Stage." *The New York Times*, May 29, 2005. A great article that highlights Wolfe's success and his graceful exit from Joseph Papp's Public Theater.

Rowell, Charles H. " I Just Want to Keep Telling Stories": An Interview with George C. Wolfe." *Callaloo* 16, no. 3 (1993): 602-623. Wolfe discusses the impact of his work as the African American director of *Angels in America*, a play by acclaimed Jewish playwright Kushner.

SEE ALSO: Amiri Baraka; Savion Glover; Zora Neale Hurston; Jelly Roll Morton; Ntozake Shange; Anna Deavere Smith.

# STEVIE WONDER
## Singer and musician

*Wonder is well known for his contributions to rhythm-and-blues and pop music as a singer-songwriter and record producer. By 2010, he had won twenty-two Grammy Awards, more than any other male solo artist. In 2009, he performed at the inauguration of President Barack Obama. The same year, Wonder was named a United Nations Messenger of Peace.*

**BORN:** May 13, 1950; Saginaw, Michigan
**ALSO KNOWN AS:** Steveland Hardaway Judkins (birth name); Steveland Morris
**AREAS OF ACHIEVEMENT:** Business; Music: pop; Music: production; Music: rhythm and blues

### EARLY LIFE
Stevie Wonder was born Steveland Hardaway Judkins in Saginaw, Michigan, on May 13, 1950. He was the third of six children born to Calvin and Lula Mae Judkins.

Wonder was born prematurely and suffered from an eye condition known as retinopathy of prematurity, which rendered him completely blind. Wonder's parents divorced a few years later; his mother returned to her maiden name, Morris, and changed Wonder's last name to Morris as well. After the divorce, Wonder's mother moved him and his siblings to Detroit.

In Detroit, Wonder became interested in music; by the age of nine, he had already learned how to play the drums, harmonica, and piano. He also sang in local church choirs. It was not long before Wonder's talents were noticed by the local record label, Motown, which signed him at the age of twelve. Under the guidance of Motown founder Berry Gordy, Jr. Wonder made his debut under the stage name Little Stevie Wonder.

Wonder's first few records drew little attention; however, at thirteen years old, he recorded his first hit single, "Fingertips (Pt. 2)." The song appeared on Wonder's

*Stevie Wonder.* (Getty Images)

## WONDER AT PRESIDENT OBAMA'S INAUGURATION

On January 18, 2009, a public celebration to commemorate the inauguration of the President Barack Obama was held on the National Mall in Washington, D.C. The event, "We Are One: The Obama Inaugural Celebration at the Lincoln Memorial," was attended by an estimated 400,000 people. It included performances by numerous influential musicians, actors, and writers. As Stevie Wonder had been an ardent supporter of Obama's presidential campaign, he was among the performers. Wonder, accompanied by pop musicians Usher and Shakira, performed his 1973 hit song "Higher Ground." During the musical performance, Obama, his wife, Michelle, and daughters Sasha and Malia could be seen dancing.

third album, *Recorded Live: The Twelve-Year-Old Genius* (1963), and topped both the rhythm-and-blues and *Billboard* Hot 100 chart.

### LIFE'S WORK

Wonder's success in 1963 soon led to a series of hit singles under his shortened stage name, Stevie Wonder. The 1966 song "Uptight (Everything's Alright)" marked the first time Wonder received a cowriting credit. He began working in Motown's songwriting department and cowrote the song "The Tears of a Clown," which was recorded by Smokey Robinson and the Miracles. The song debuted in 1967 and quickly became an international hit. The next year, 1968, Wonder recorded the hit "For Once in My Life." In 2002, "The Tears of a Clown" was inducted into the Grammy Hall of Fame.

After resolving a contract dispute in 1972, Wonder returned to the Motown label to release his album *Talking Book*. The album was a success, and Wonder joined the Rolling Stones on their American tour. The album contained two of Wonder's best-known songs, "Superstition" and "You Are the Sunshine of My Life." Shortly after the release of *Talking Book*, Wonder released his next album, *Innervisions* (1973). The album was another success and contained several well-known Wonder compositions such as "Higher Ground" and "Living for the City." Between the *Talking Book* and *Innervisions* albums, Wonder was nominated for seven Grammys in 1973. He won awards for Album of the Year and Best Engineered Recording for *Innervisions*, Pop Male Vocalist for "You Are the Sunshine of My Life," and Best Rhythm and Blues Male Vocal Performance and Best Rhythm and Blues Song for "Superstition." By 2010, Wonder had won twenty-two Grammy Awards, more than any other male pop artist since the award's inception in 1958. He

also received the prestigious Grammy Lifetime Achievement Award.

In the early 1970's, Wonder began to express his political opinions by criticizing President Richard M. Nixon and his administration. Two such attacks come in the form of Wonder's compositions "He's Misstra Know It All" and "You Haven't Done Nothin'." Politics would become a recurring theme in his musical career. Wonder supported the campaign to make Martin Luther King, Jr.'s birthday a federal holiday, played benefit concerts for the needy, did substantial work with the United Negro College Fund, and lent his support to the Democratic Party for Barack Obama's 2008 presidential bid. After Obama's election, Wonder performed at an inaugural concert at the Lincoln Memorial. In 2009, Wonder was named a United Nations Messenger of Peace—a title awarded every three years to an outstanding individual in sports or the arts who has helped raise awareness of U.N. peace efforts.

Wonder's album *Songs in the Key of Life* (1976) is considered one of his most influential releases. It debuted at number one on the *Billboard* Album Chart, the first time that an album by an American artist had achieved that feat. The album contained number-one singles such as "I Wish" and "Sir Duke," and in 1977, the album was certified diamond (more than ten million units sold).

After the *Songs in the Key of Life* album, Wonder continued to release commercially and critically successful albums and singles but was unable to return to the number-one position on the charts. However, his 1982 duet with Paul McCartney, "Ebony and Ivory," returned him to number one for seven straight weeks. "Ebony and Ivory" also marked the first time in Wonder's career that he reached number one on the British charts. His only other British number-one single was "I Just Called to Say I Love You." The song was featured in the motion picture *The Woman in Red* (1984) and earned Wonder an Academy Award for Best Original Song.

### SIGNIFICANCE

Wonder has been an influential figure in rhythm-and-blues and pop music for more than four decades. He has received numerous accolades, including being inducted into the Songwriters Hall of Fame and the Rock and Roll Hall of Fame. His music career includes more than 100 million albums sold and dozens of Grammy nominations. Wonder also has shown dedication to many social and political causes.

—*Delbert S. Bowers*

**FURTHER READING**

Brown, Stacy, and Dennis Love. *Blind Faith: The Miraculous Journey of Lula Hardaway, Stevie Wonder's Mother.* New York: Simon & Schuster, 2002. Biography inspired by various interview and print sources about Wonder's family, life, and musical career.

Davis, Sharon. *Stevie Wonder: Rhythms of Wonder.* London: Robson, 2006. Memoir of Wonder's career and influence on pop music written by his former publicist.

Hull, Ted, and Paula L. Stahel. *The Wonder Years: My Life and Times with Stevie Wonder.* Tampa, Fla.: Author, 2002. Wonder's former teacher writes about his time educating Wonder at the Michigan School for the Blind.

Lodder, Steve. *Stevie Wonder: A Musical Guide to the Classic Albums.* San Francisco: Backbeat Books, 2005. Examines the musical influences and styles of Wonder's 1970's and 1980's albums.

Ribowsky, Mark. *Signed, Sealed, and Delivered: The Soulful Journey of Stevie Wonder.* Hoboken, N.J.: John Wiley & Sons, 2010. An essential source, offering a detailed look at Wonder's life and career.

**SEE ALSO:** Solomon Burke; Al Green; Gladys Knight; Patti LaBelle; Aaron Neville; Lionel Richie; Smokey Robinson; Usher; Dionne Warwick; Jackie Wilson.

# ALFRE WOODARD
## Actor

*Recognized for her intense, often gritty portrayals of troubled African American women, Woodard has made an unforgettable mark on the stage, on film, and on television in a wide variety of powerful roles.*

**BORN:** November 8, 1953; Tulsa, Oklahoma
**ALSO KNOWN AS:** Alfre Ette Woodard
**AREAS OF ACHIEVEMENT:** Film: acting; Radio and television

### EARLY LIFE

Alfre Ette Woodard (AL-free WOOD-urd) was born on November 8, 1953, to Marion and Constance Woodard in Tulsa, Oklahoma. The youngest of three children, Alfre Woodard graduated from Bishop Kelley High School, a Catholic school, where she was a cheerleader and ran track. At the suggestion of a nun, she auditioned for a school play and quickly decided to pursue an acting career. In 1974, Woodard earned a B.F.A. from Boston University and headed to Hollywood by way of Broadway.

Hollywood, however, was not prepared for Woodard. Her unconventional "African look" did not fit the standard mold expected of actors on film or in television. Facing repeated rejection, Woodard was tenacious, never doubting herself or her talent. She attributes her confidence and positive self-esteem to the unconditional love of her close-knit family, who supported her emotionally and financially as she struggled to gain recognition. Finally, in 1978, after playing several nondescript parts, Woodard was cast in a feature film called *Remember My Name* (1978). After that performance, her name became a leading one in Hollywood.

That role led to a series of projects, including *Freedom Road* (1979), *H.E.A.L.T.H.* (1979), and *For Colored Girls Who Have Considered Suicide* (1982). In 1983, Alfre married Roderick Spencer, a teacher of screenwriting and directing at Emerson College. A happily married interracial couple, they adopted two biracial children: a son, Duncan, and a daughter, Mavis, who was named Miss Golden Globe 2010.

When Woodard traveled to Zimbabwe in 1986 to film *Mandela*, she was struck by the similarity of her facial features to those of the South African women. For Woodard, their natural beauty validated the looks of African American women so often rejected in the entertainment industry. She returned to the United States eager to embark upon new humanitarian projects and dramatic roles that expressed her political and moral views.

### LIFE'S WORK

Having already completed segments of the television series *Hill Street Blues*, Woodard continued to accept diverse roles in television and film. *L.A. Law, Unnatural Causes* (1986), *The Child Saver* (1988), *A Mother's Courage: The Mary Thomas Story* (1989), and other well-known productions kept her busy, and award nominations began pouring in.

*Alfre Woodard.* (Getty Images)

In 1989, Woodard, her husband, actor Danny Glover, and others cofounded Artists for a New South Africa. By 2010, the nonprofit organization had raised more than nine million dollars and shipped tons of food, medical supplies, and books to impoverished African villages. Every year, Woodard speaks to students and hosts fundraising events to promote saving the environment, to help eradicate poverty, and to raise awareness about human immunodeficiency virus (HIV) and acquired immunodeficiency syndrome (AIDS). She also helped raise money for the Martin Luther King, Jr., national memorial. Meanwhile, her prolific body of work expanded to include *Crooklyn* (1994), *The Piano Lesson* (1995), *Miss Evers' Boys* (1997), *Down in the Delta* (1998), *Funny Valentines* (1999), and television series *The Practice*.

In 2007, she received the Pathfinders to Peace Award for her AIDS initiatives. She is a member of the National Film Preservation Foundation Board and the Academy of Motion Picture Arts and Sciences International Outreach Committee. An active member of the Democratic Party, she crisscrossed the United States to speak in support of Barack Obama, and in 2009 she was appointed to the President's Committee on the Arts and Humanities.

Nevertheless, her acting career has been unceasing. Woodard appeared in the films *Holiday Heart* (2000), *Love and Basketball* (2000), *Beauty Shop* (2005), *Tyler*

*Perry's The Family That Preys* (2008), *American Violet* (2008), and the television series *Desperate Housewives* and *Memphis Beat*. Her labors have been rewarded with seven Image Awards from the National Association for the Advancement of Colored People (NAACP), four Emmy Awards, a Golden Globe, two Screen Actors Guild Awards, the Black Reel Award, and twenty-four other award nominations. In 2008, Woodard produced and directed the audiobook *Nelson Mandela's Favorite African Folktales*, created to assist children affected by AIDS. It was lauded as the best multivoiced performance at the audiobook awards. In 2009, she and other actors represented the Academy of Motion Picture Arts and Sciences in an exchange of creative ideas with Iranian film students in Tehran and Esfahan. Finally, confirming her stance that being a wife and mother supersedes being an actor, she received the Outstanding Mother Award from the National Mother's Day Committee in May, 2010, for her ability to balance her career and family life.

## SIGNIFICANCE

Determination, diligence, and creativity have allowed this award-winning performer to produce exceptionally emotional and entertaining performances year after year. Surprisingly, the large round eyes, glowing brown skin, and full lips that had kept African American actors from reaching their full potential in Hollywood earned Alfre recognition as one of *People* magazine's most beautiful people in 1994. She has used her celebrity, her voice, and her spirit to make the world a better place in which to live. Through her outstanding performances, she passionately inspires viewers to make a difference in their world.

—*Shirlita K. McFarland*

## FURTHER READING

Belichick, Bill. "Honorary Degree Recipients." *B.U. Bridge* 7, no. 30 (May, 2004). Includes profile of Woodard as she receives an honorary Doctor of Fine Arts degree from her alma mater.

Clancy, Frank. "From St. Elsewhere to South Africa." *Mother Jones Magazine* 12, no. 7 (October, 1987): 35. Woodard describes her experience in South Africa when she traveled there to film *Mandela*.

Collier, Aldore. "Alfre Woodard: A Triumph of Talent." *Ebony* 45, no. 9 (July, 1990): 51-54. Woodard speaks about her family and the difficulties she faced trying to break into Hollywood.

**SEE ALSO:** Angela Bassett; Halle Berry; Ruby Dee; Danny Glover; Phylicia Rashad; Cicely Tyson.

# LYNETTE WOODARD
## Basketball player

*In 1985, Woodard became the first woman to play on the legendary Harlem Globetrotters basketball team. A four-time All-America selection and Olympic gold medalist, she used her celebrity to promote women's sports and urged the formation of a women's professional basketball league.*

**BORN:** August 12, 1959; Wichita, Kansas
**AREAS OF ACHIEVEMENT:** Sports: basketball; Sports: Olympics

### EARLY LIFE

Lynette Woodard was born August 12, 1959, in Wichita, Kansas, the third of four siblings. Her father, Lugene, was a firefighter, and her mother, Dorothy, a homemaker. Woodard became interested in basketball as a child, shooting a balled-up sock into a basket hanging over a door with her older brother Darrell.

Woodard later spent many hours honing her skills on a basketball court near her home. After declining an invitation to play on her high school's junior varsity girls team as a freshman, she joined the varsity team as a sophomore. She helped Wichita North High School win two state championships in 1975 and 1977, amassing an astounding 59-3 record. In just 62 high school games, Woodard scored 1,678 points and had 1,030 rebounds. She was named a high-school All-American and heavily recruited by colleges throughout the country. Despite the opportunity to leave home, she accepted a basketball scholarship from the University of Kansas (KU), in large part because of the bond she felt with Coach Marian Washington. She graduated from Kansas in 1981 with a degree in speech communications.

### LIFE'S WORK

Arguably one of the best female basketball players ever, Woodard had a career that earned her numerous honors and audiences with four presidents and Pope John Paul II. As point guard at the University of Kansas, she became the all-time leading scorer for Division I women's collegiate basketball and second only to "Pistol Pete" Maravich as the all-time leading scorer in college basketball. Woodard scored a total of 3,649 points over her career—an average of more than 26 points per game—and was a four-time All-American (1978-1981). She also was the first female student-athlete to be given the Top Five Award by the National Collegiate Athletic Association (NCAA).

A versatile player, Woodard led the nation in rebounding in 1978, scoring in 1979, and steals in 1979, 1980, and 1981. She was on the 1980 U.S. Olympic women's basketball team, but the United States boycotted the Moscow Olympics that year. Four years later, Woodard was captain of the gold medal-winning U.S. team at the Los Angeles Olympic Games.

Because of the lack of professional basketball opportunities for U.S. women, after graduating from college, Woodard signed with UFO Schio, a team in Vicenza, Italy. She received an excellent wage and played only one game a week, on Sundays. The down time allowed her time to read, write, and learn Italian. However, although she enjoyed her experience abroad, Woodard felt homesick for the United States. She recalled that her cousin Herb "Geese" Ausbie, a member of the Harlem Globetrotters, had entertained her and her siblings with basketball tricks whenever he visited. The Globetrotters happened to be considering recruiting a woman to boost their sagging attendance. Even though Woodard was the oldest woman to try out, she made the team.

In 1985, at the age of twenty-six, Woodard became the first woman ever to play for the famous Globetrotters. That year, the team opened its sixtieth season in Brisbane, Australia. Woodard played with the Globetrotters for two years. She rejoined UFO Schio from 1987 to 1990 and led her team to the Italian league championship in 1989. In 1991, she played for Daiwa Securities in Japan.

In 1997, the Women's National Basketball Association (WNBA) was formed, realizing Woodard's dream of playing professionally in the United States. Although she was past her peak athletically, she played for the Cleveland Rockers that year and then with the Detroit Shock the next year before retiring.

Although Woodard is best known for her feats on the basketball court, she has been very productive off the court as well. She was the athletic director for the Kansas City, Missouri, School District from 1993 to 1995 and served on the board of directors for the U.S. Olympic Committee from 1996 to 2000. Woodard also returned to her alma mater as an assistant coach from 1999 to 2003 and served as interim head coach for KU in 2004 during the illness of her former coach, Marian Washington. Woodard has worked as a stockbroker and was president of marketing for Magna Securities Corporation in New York City during the WNBA offseason. She continues to work in finance as a registered investment adviser, coach basketball, and give motivational speeches. In her hometown of Wichita, a recreation center bears her name. At the fourteenth annual Amelia Earhart Festival in 2010, Woodard was honored with the Pioneering Achievement Award, given to a person who carries on Earhart's spirit.

## SIGNIFICANCE

Woodard achieved a number of milestones during her basketball career. She was selected to the first ever *Parade* High School All-American Team for girls' basketball in 1977 and was the first woman to have her jersey retired at the University of Kansas. These feats as well as her play in the 1984 Olympics helped raise the profile of women's basketball in the United States. Not long after Title IX created new opportunities for women athletes, Woodard showed that they could be dominant, versatile, and flashy. She paved the way for many college and WNBA players who followed her. Woodard has been named one of *Sports Illustrated*'s one hundred greatest women athletes of the century. She was inducted into the Basketball Hall of Fame as a member of the Globetrotters in 2002 and individually in 2004. In 2005, Woodard was enshrined in the Women's Basketball Hall of Fame in Nashville, Tennessee, and in 2006, she was inducted into the African American Sports Hall of Fame.

—*Sheree D. White*

## FURTHER READING

Newman, Matt. *Lynette Woodward.* New York: Crestwood Press, 1986. Written just after Woodard's selection to the Globetrotters, this biography focuses on her record-setting exploits at KU and early professional career.

Rosenthal, Bert. *Lynette Woodard: The First Female Globetrotter.* Danbury, Conn.: Children's Press, 1986. Biography aimed at young readers, chronicling Woodard's basketball career and role on the Globetrotters.

Woodard, Lynette. "This Is Our Game: Lynette Woodard." Interview by Jennifer Pottheiser. WNBA.com. November 26, 2010. http://www.wnba.com/features/tiog_woodard_2005.html. Brief biography and interview in which Woodard discusses her love of basketball and career in the financial industry.

Woolum, Janet. "Lynette Woodard (Basketball Player)." In *Outstanding Women Athletes: Who They Are and How They Influenced Sports in America.* 2d ed. Phoenix, Ariz.: Oryx Press, 1998. Chronicles Woodard's career and her place in basketball history.

**SEE ALSO:** Meadowlark Lemon; Lisa Leslie; Cheryl Miller.

# GRANVILLE T. WOODS
## Inventor, engineer, and businessman

*Woods was one of the first major African American inventors, greatly contributing to the technological and scientific advances that followed the American Civil War. Because of his ingenuity with electricity, he became known as the "Black Thomas Edison." By 1887, he was widely considered to be the greatest electrician in the world.*

**BORN:** April 23, 1856; Columbus, Ohio
**DIED:** January 30, 1910; New York, New York
**ALSO KNOWN AS:** Granville Trey Woods; the Black Thomas Edison
**AREAS OF ACHIEVEMENT:** Invention; Science and technology

## EARLY LIFE

Granville Trey Woods was born in Columbus, Ohio, on April 23, 1856, to Tailer and Martha Woods. Because of

the Northwest Ordinance of 1787, which banned slavery from the future state of Ohio, his birth into freedom was a matter of luck.

Woods also was considered fortunate for his short-lived formal education, because most African American children of the nineteenth century fell victim to the "Black Codes." These laws excluded African Americans from public education, state militias, and most civil liberties. However, severe bylaws and segregation would force Woods to leave school at the age of ten. Subsequently, he began working with his father as an apprentice, learning the blacksmith trade while repairing railroad equipment and machinery.

While working with his father, Woods was very observant and took in as much knowledge as he could. He often used his earnings to compensate the master mechanic, to whom his father reported, for private lessons. Woods realized early that education was indispensable.

When he was sixteen, he was ready to begin his own journey and headed West. He secured his first position as a firefighter at the Iron Mountain Railroad in Missouri. In his ample spare time, Woods taught himself the principles of electricity. His friends helped by checking out library books for him. He soon became an engineer at the railroad company. In December, 1874, he moved to Springfield, Illinois, where he got a job in a rolling mill.

In early 1876, Woods moved back East. His applied knowledge of mechanics and electricity qualified him for classes at an engineering college, although the name of the school is unknown. For approximately two years, he attended school at night. During the day, he was employed at a New York City machine shop, where he worked six half-days each week. He left school in 1878 and on February 6 went to sea aboard the *Ironsides*, a British steamer on which he worked as an engineer and visited many countries around the world. Two years later, he returned to Ohio and found work as a steam locomotive engineer for the Danville and Southern Railroad in Cincinnati.

## LIFE'S WORK

Woods received his first patent on June 3, 1884, for an improved steam boiler furnace. His ensuing efforts, however, involved electrical applications. He and his brother Lyates Woods formed the Woods Electric Company in Cincinnati later that year. There, they developed, manufactured, and sold electrical machinery, including telephone and telegraph equipment.

These efforts led to the invention of the "telephone transmitter," patented in December, 1884. Woods's telephone transmitter carried distinct sound over an electrical current, exceeding all telephonic devices in use during that time. However, he never profited from this invention. His means of manufacturing the device were deemed insufficient, and his patent was soon assigned to the American Bell Telephone Company.

Woods obtained his next patent approximately four months later. His "apparatus for transmission of messages by electricity," which he frequently referred to as "telegraphony," was a merger of the telegraph and telephone that enabled operators on both ends to communicate messages in Morse code and articulate speech over a single wire. Aware of the legalities of patent guidelines this time around, Woods managed to sell his patent to American Bell and was generously compensated. The sale enabled him to become a full-time inventor.

In 1887, Woods invented "mutliplex telegraph," also known as the induction telegraph or block system, which enhanced railway travel through electromagnetic induction. By allowing telegraphic messages to be sent and received without interruption, the invention helped dramatically decrease railway casualties. While this achievement placed Woods among science's elite, he also fell victim to Thomas Edison, who filed a lawsuit claiming that he was the device's true inventor. Woods eventually defeated Edison's lawsuit and subsequently turned down a lucrative offer to partner in one of Edison's businesses. Woods was then known as the "Black Thomas Edison." In 1887, the *American Catholic Tribune* declared that Woods was the greatest electrician in the world.

Unfortunately, Woods's legal troubles did not end with Edison. Woods was sued for criminal libel in 1892 for claiming that James S. Zerbe, a manager at the American Engineering Company, stole his patent for the "multiple distributing station system." By then, Woods's assets had been drained by legal fees related to patent disputes. Because he was unable to post money for bail, he served a short jail sentence.

Many of Woods's inventions were ahead of their time. While his vision of implementing his multiple distributing station system faltered, the mechanism is strikingly similar to linear induction railroad propulsion systems that came approximately a century later. Modern telephones utilize the physical properties of Woods's telephone transmitter, and his induction telegraph system was actually a forerunner to local area networking (LAN) systems. Woods died on January 30, 1910.

## SIGNIFICANCE

Woods's innovation and entrepreneurship helped him overcome the racial challenges of his time. At the time of his death, he held at least sixty patents. He was famous for solving problems through invention. In 1969, Brooklyn, New York's elementary public school number 335 was named in his honor. On October 11, 1974, a decree recognizing Woods's scientific achievements was issued by Ohio governor John J. Gilligan.

—*Thomas D. Hubbard*

## FURTHER READING

Fouché, Rayvon, ed. *Black Inventors in the Age of Segregation: Granville T. Woods, Lewis H. Latimer, and Shelby J. Davidson.* Baltimore: Johns Hopkins University Press, 2005. Exposes the myths linked to the legacies of three major African American inventors and offers a candid study of their lives and historical significance.

Haskins, James. "Electrifying Inventors: Lewis Latimer

and Granville T. Woods." In *Outward Dreams: Black Inventors and Their Inventions*. New York: Walker, 1992. Highlights the accomplishments of Woods and Latimer, two of the first major African American inventors in electrical engineering.

Sluby, Patricia Carter. *The Inventive Spirit of African Americans: Patented Ingenuity*. Westport, Conn.: Praeger, 2004. Details the history of African American inventors from the point of view of a former U.S. patent examiner. Includes bibliography, index, and appendix listing inventions, inventors, and patent numbers.

Sullivan, Otha Richard. "The Civil War Years and Reconstruction." In *Black Stars: African American Inventors*, edited by James Haskins. New York: John Wiley & Sons, 1998. A brief look at the life of Woods, highlighting his most notable accomplishments and inventions in the post-Civil War years.

**SEE ALSO:** George Edward Alcorn; Andrew Jackson Beard; Henry Blair; Lewis Howard Latimer; Jan Ernst Matzeliger; Garrett Augustus Morgan; Norbert Rillieux; John Brooks Slaughter.

# TIGER WOODS
## Golfer

*Known for his extraordinary career as a professional golfer and for breaking racial barriers in the game, Woods also enjoyed success as one of the most prolific celebrity endorsers in history. With ninety-five tournament wins and more than one billion dollars in earnings by the year 2011, Woods ranked as one of the best professional golfers ever and the highest paid athlete of all time.*

**BORN:** December 30, 1975; Cypress, California
**ALSO KNOWN AS:** Eldrick Tont Woods (birth name)
**AREAS OF ACHIEVEMENT:** Business; Philanthropy; Sports: golf and tennis

### EARLY LIFE
Born on December 30, 1975, in Cypress, California, Tiger Woods was the only child of Earl, an African American Army officer, and Kultida Woods, a native of Thailand. His father began calling Woods by the nickname "Tiger" in honor of a fellow soldier. Woods displayed athletic ability as early as nine months, when he picked up a club and hit his first golf ball. At eighteen months, Woods was accompanying his father to the local Navy golf course. At age three, he appeared on CBS News and *The Mike Douglas Show*. When he was five, he scored his first birdie on a regulation golf course, an achievement that was noted in an article in *Golf Digest*. By age ten, Woods had won two Junior World Championships. His talent was clear, and with the help of his father and a cadre of coaches dubbed "Team Tiger," he worked hard to cultivate that talent. Golf was his passion and supplanted all other extracurricular activities. His parents financed his training and competition in tournaments by taking out equity loans on their home.

By the time Woods was a teenager, he had become extremely proficient, showing off his skills on television shows such as *Good Morning America*. At age fourteen, he was playing varsity golf and had collected more than two hundred trophies. Woods was profiled for the first time by *Sports Illustrated* in 1990 after becoming the youngest golfer to win the Insurance Youth Golf Classic. As a result, he was recruited by several colleges and universities that were as impressed by his golf swing as his academic achievements. In 1994, Woods enrolled at Stanford University as a business major on a golf scholarship and was named Man of the Year by *Golf World*. He dominated collegiate tournaments, won his third consecutive U.S. Amateur Championship, and ultimately left school in 1996 to join the Professional Golfers' Association (PGA) Tour.

### LIFE'S WORK
Woods took the professional golf world by storm, signing a record forty-million-dollar contract from Nike and being named *Sports Illustrated*'s sportsman of the year. That year, he and his father founded the charitable Tiger Woods Foundation. Woods and his father traveled the country holding junior golf clinics and encouraging kids to follow their dreams. From its inception in 1996 to 2010, more than ten million youths were affiliated with the foundation's character development programs, scholarships, grants, junior golf teams, and Tiger Woods Learning Center.

In 1997, at the age of twenty-one, Woods became the

youngest person to win the Masters Tournament, setting records for score and margin of victory. Despite his accolades and accomplishments, however, early in his career, more attention was paid to Woods's race than to his game. Although he was used to curiosity about his mixed-race background, the media's heightened focus on Woods's racial identity greatly concerned him, particularly after two incidents. The first was an article in *GQ* magazine that revealed his politically incorrect sense of humor. The second was a racially insensitive comment made by professional golfer Frank "Fuzzy" Zoeller, who referred to Woods as "that little boy" who would serve either "fried chicken . . . or collard greens or whatever the hell they serve" at the Masters Champions Dinner, for which the reigning champion selects the menu. These incidents made Woods rethink and reposition his public image. When asked directly about his racial identity and experiences later that year by Oprah Winfrey, Woods coined the term "Cablinasian"—an abbreviation combining the terms "Caucasian," "black," "Indian," and "Asian"—to reflect his racial identity. This drew even more media attention. Woods stated that he did not just want to be the best African American player or the best Asian player. He wanted to be the best golfer ever.

Woods was intent on reaching his goal, and the press was still watching closely. Later that year, Woods was named Male Athlete of the Year by both the Associated Press and ESPN's ESPY Awards. He reached the sport's number one ranking in June, 1997, after winning the Masters with a record score of 270. At the age of twenty-one, he was not only the youngest player ever to win the Masters, but also the first champion of Asian or African American descent. Woods brought many new fans to the sport. Ratings for the final round of each of the four major tournaments collectively jumped 56 percent in 1997 and continued to rise. Woods continued winning throughout 1998 and 1999, and on June 19, 2000, won the one-hundredth U.S. Open by a record fifteen-shot margin. For this achievement, ESPN named him the Golfer of the Decade.

By 2002, Woods had become the world's highest paid athlete. The next 2000's brought three U.S. PGA titles,

*Tiger Woods.* (Getty Images)

three U.S. Open wins, three Open Championship wins and three wins at the Masters. In 2004, Woods married Elin Nordegren, a Swedish model. They had two children: Sam Alexis, born on June 18, 2007, and Charlie Axel, born on February 8, 2009.

Returning to dominate the sport after his nuptials, Woods won six championships in 2005 and was voted the PGA Tour Player of Year for the seventh time. He experienced a great personal loss in 2006 when his father died. Woods returned to the PGA Tour shortly thereafter and won several events, including the PGA Championship and the British Open. After taking time off for his daughter's birth in 2007, Woods won the World Golf Championship and U.S. PGA Championship. He also became one of that year's top philanthropists, giving $9.5 million to organizations including the Tiger Woods Learning Center funded by his foundation.

Woods won the U.S. Open on June 16, 2008, in a nineteen-hole play-off, despite intense pain in his left knee from surgery. After the win, Woods announced that he would undergo more surgery and miss the rest of the season. Woods returned in February, 2009, in the Accenture Match Play Championship, where he lost to Tim Clark. He also competed in the 2009 U.S. Open but missed the cut. Although he did not win any majors, he remained the world's highest paid athlete according to *Forbes* magazine. *Forbes* reported in its September, 2009, issue that a ten-million-dollar bonus had nudged Woods's career earnings past one billion dollars. His earnings surge also was the product of his diverse endorsement portfolio, which included Nike, General Motors's Buick division, AT&T, Pepsi, Electronic Arts, Gillette, Upper Deck, and Accenture. Woods also launched a golf course design business and charged three million dollars in appearance fees when he played outside the United States.

However, late in 2009, Woods's image was badly tarnished when reports surfaced that he had engaged in several extramarital affairs. In November, he was injured in a minor car accident outside his Florida home. After weeks of media speculation, Woods offered a public apology for his infidelity and took an extended leave from golf to seek counseling. He lost several endorsement deals worth millions of dollars.

Five months later, Woods returned to golf at the 2010 Masters Tournament in Augusta, Georgia, on April 8. He tied for fourth place in the tournament. He fared poorly in many of his subsequent outings but tied for fourth again at the U.S. Open in June. In August, 2010, Woods and his wife divorced.

### SIGNIFICANCE

As the most successful and best-known golfer in the world over two decades, Woods has done much to change the sport's audience. He also influenced many young people of color to take up the sport. Woods broke ground in the world of celebrity endorsements as the highest paid athlete in history. His insistence on identifying himself as multiracial brought attention to the experiences and perspectives of people from mixed racial backgrounds.

—*Marcia Alesan Dawkins*

### FURTHER READING

Billings, Andrew C. "Portraying Tiger Woods: Characterizations of a 'Black' Athlete in a 'White' Sport." *The Howard Journal of Communications* 14, no. 1 (January, 2003): 29-37. Scholarly collection and evaluation of the ways Woods was described in the media. Results indicate that when Woods won, he was not

---

### WOODS'S GOLFING RECORDS

Tiger Woods's remarkable professional career began in 1996. Arguably the greatest golfer of his time, Woods had won ninety-five tournaments, seventy-one of which were on the Professional Golfers' Association (PGA) Tour, through the summer of 2010. His victories included the 1997, 2001, 2002, and 2005 Masters Tournaments; 1999, 2000, 2006, and 2007 PGA Championships; 2000, 2002, and 2008 U.S. Opens; and 2000, 2005, and 2006 Open Championships. Upon winning his second Masters in 2001, Woods became the first person to hold all four professional championships simultaneously, a feat that was dubbed a "Tiger Slam." By 2010, he was the career victories leader and the career money-list leader among active players on the PGA Tour. His tournament winnings and many lucrative endorsement deals made Woods the first professional athlete to earn more than one billion dollars in his career. Although unprecedented for any golfer, Woods's achievements are even more profound considering that the PGA did not officially welcome African American players until 1961 and many golf courses practiced de facto segregation long after that.

---

portrayed as African American, but when he was not as successful, he was more likely to be characterized using traditional stereotypes of black athletes.

Bissinger, Buzz. "Tiger in the Rough." *Vanity Fair*, February, 2010. Written weeks after the scandal in Woods's personal life, this article contrasts his public image with glimpses of his private personality.

Londino, Lawrence. *Tiger Woods: A Biography*. Westport, Conn.: Greenwood Press, 2006. A concise biography of Woods's early life, family and professional influences, and experiences and global impact.

Woods, Tiger. *How I Play Golf*. New York: Warner Books, 2001. In this how-to manual, Woods writes about his approach to the sport, offering an intimate portrait of his mental and physical game as well as his personality on and off the course.

Yu, Henry. "Tiger Woods Is Not the End of History: Or, Why Sex Across the Color Line Won't Save Us All." *The American Historical Review* 108, no. 5 (December, 2003): 1406-1414. A scholarly discussion of multiracial identity and representation, this thoughtful piece critiques the depiction of multiracial Americans in general, and Woods in particular, as postracial icons.

**SEE ALSO:** Kobe Bryant; Lee Elder; Michael Jordan; Calvin Peete; Serena Williams; Venus Williams.

# CARTER G. WOODSON
## Educator, scholar, and writer

*A career educator and early advocate of the importance of researching African American history, Woodson founded and directed the first and most influential academic association devoted to the study of African American history. He also was instrumental in establishing February as Black History Month.*

**BORN:** December 19, 1875; New Canton, Virginia
**DIED:** April 3, 1950; Washington, D.C.
**ALSO KNOWN AS:** Carter Godwin Woodson
**AREAS OF ACHIEVEMENT:** Education; Scholarship; Social sciences

### EARLY LIFE

Carter Godwin Woodson was born in rural central Virginia, the son of two former slaves. Woodson and his eight siblings worked on the family farm, although Woodson relished the time he could devote to his education at the local one-room schoolhouse, run by two of his uncles. Because the demands of farming made full-time schooling impossible, Woodson taught himself the basics of a high school education in the evenings.

In 1892, Woodson and one of his brothers moved to Huntington, West Virginia, to earn money in the coal mines. At nineteen, he finally was able to continue his education, enrolling in Huntington's segregated high school. His regimen of self-instruction paid off: He graduated in two years (1897). Eager for more education, Woodson immediately enrolled in Kentucky's Berea College, then one of the nation's few integrated colleges (a year after Woodson graduated, a state law outlawed integrated education). While teaching in local high schools, Woodson earned his undergraduate degree in literature, graduating in 1903. He then accepted a position as an English teacher in the Philippines. When he left there four years later because of poor health, he had been promoted to supervisor and was training local teachers. He returned determined to complete his own education—after spending a year in France and a semester at the Sorbonne, Woodson earned a master's degree in European history from the University of Chicago (1908) and then a doctorate in Civil War history from Harvard (1912), making him only the second African American to earn a doctorate.

During his time at Harvard, Woodson became increasingly concerned about the lack of scholarship on the place of African Americans in the nation's history—that four centuries of slavery had relegated their considerable contributions to the margins. Little was known of their culture, their art, their family life, or the considerable adjustments they had been forced to make to the brutal conditions of slavery. African Americans had become a shadow presence in historical investigation. Addressing that neglect through careful historical research and investigative scholarship, Woodson believed, would ultimately be instrumental in bolstering African Americans' sense of self-respect and would also help alleviate the pernicious logic of racism, as white America would learn of the significant achievements of African Americans.

### LIFE'S WORK

Promoting the documentation of black history quickly became Woodson's mission. Even as World War I raged, he began to campaign vociferously for research into the achievements of African Americans in American history, particularly the work of archiving the public record of the generation born after the Emancipation Proclamation. He was concerned that, without such efforts, that record would be lost forever. In 1915, Woodson was among five prominent black academics who established the Association for the Study of African American Life and History (ASALH). It was the first academic association to promote the study of black history; the organization sponsored research projects that gathered original historical data, arranged national conferences for scholars of black history, worked to preserve original documents, and raised funds to promote black history through publications, lectures, and books. In 1916, the association began to publish the *Journal of Negro History*, the first journal devoted to promoting research into African American history. The journal's mission was to shift the dynamic of the telling of American history from the dominant white perspective and to investigate African Americans as a group with distinct cultural, religious, economic, and social signatures.

Even as Woodson found success as an academic (between 1919 and 1922, he taught at Washington's Howard University before accepting a position as academic dean at West Virginia Collegiate Institute), he became the public voice of both the historical association and its increasingly prestigious journal. While at West Virginia, Woodson founded Associated Publishers, which provided a forum for studies of African American history and culture, studies ignored by more mainstream academic presses. At the same time, Woodson published two semi-

## THE MIS-EDUCATION OF THE NEGRO

Given Carter G. Woodson's profound love of learning, his impeccable credentials in education, and his passionate belief in the benefits of the classroom—especially for African Americans—it is no surprise that his most enduring work examines the education system and its effects on race and race perception. *The Mis-education of the Negro* (1933) boldly challenged the assumption that Eurocentric history sufficiently told the narrative history of America. Woodson argues that narrow, white-dominated versions of history had created a crisis in identity among young African Americans, who could not find their culture's story in schoolbooks. Preserving and studying the history and culture of black America, Woodson argues in the book, not only would create a complete and accurate historical record but also would inspire black youths, who are too often made to feel inferior. He calls for a generation's commitment to researching black history and to presenting its story in a new generation of textbooks. That, in turn, would redefine how American history itself is presented in the classroom. Woodson offers a passionate endorsement of the power of learning. In the end, he concludes, white America would benefit as well; he argues that it is the neglect of African American history that led to the entrenched bigotry of white America. Woodson is confident that learning the truth would dramatically alter race relations in America. The work, a clarion call to reform American education by introducing the contributions and impact of African Americans, was well ahead of its time—it came to be recognized as a landmark work in African American studies.

nal works—*The History of the Negro Church* (1921) and *The Negro in Our History* (1922)—the first of what would become more than a dozen such studies over the next three decades.

In 1922, Woodson retired from teaching to devote his energies to shaping the direction of the ASALH. He handled secretarial work; managed the finances; arranged academic conferences; solicited research projects to preserve thousands of artifacts, papers, and artworks; and scrubbed the floors and repaired the bathrooms in the association's headquarters in Washington. He never married—his commitment to his mission was absolute. Woodson poured his own money into the organization and traveled frequently to raise money. Critics found him egocentric and demanding in his near-dictatorial administration of the ASALH, and conservative establishment historians attacked his goal of defining African Americans' history as distinct, even separate, from their place in American history. Despite these attacks, however, Woodson became a prominent and respected voice in promoting the integrity of black history.

It was to that end that he worked to establish Negro History Week. He proposed setting aside a week in February, the month in which both Abraham Lincoln and Frederick Douglass were born, during which schools would pay particular attention to the contributions of African Americans. Decades after his death, the commemoration would become Black History Month. Woodson prepared hundreds of lesson plans for public school curricula centered on black history, and he published scores of articles advocating the need to preserve that history. He edited the speeches of prominent African Americans (notably Douglass and Booker T. Washington). He gathered and edited a wide-ranging sampling of letters written in the decades leading up to the Civil War, which he published as *The Mind of the Negro as Reflected in Letters Written During the Crisis, 1800-1860* (1927). He published several groundbreaking studies on the economics of the South and the labor migrations of its black workers. In 1933, he completed his defining work, *The Mis-education of the Negro*, a sweeping and visionary reappraisal of how to educate African Americans about their own cultural place in their nation.

Beyond his considerable writings or even his work with the ASALH, Woodson inspired a generation of young historians, black and white, to turn their attention and energies to the contributions of African Americans. That inspiration helped provide critical historic context for the Harlem Renaissance of the 1920's. In 1926, Woodson received the Spingarn Medal, the highest award given by the National Association for the Advancement of Colored People (NAACP), in recognition of his crusade to define a history of African American culture. He continued to work with the ASALH and to publish essays on black history until his death in 1950. The association suffered significantly after his death, struggling to raise sufficient operating capital. That it continued to operate into the twenty-first century is a testament to Woodson's pivotal place in American history.

### SIGNIFICANCE

Woodson's impact is difficult to overstate: Before him, there was a tacit assumption by American historians that African American culture did not merit significant investigation. What attention was paid to African Americans was distorted by the biases and, at times, overt racism of the white establishment. Woodson's pioneering efforts forever altered the narrative of American history. He led the call to define African American history and to use education as a means to effect social change, that both white America and black America would benefit from learning the historical truth of African Americans and their contributions. In his zealous lifelong campaign to promote the cause of African American history, Woodson directly addressed the frustrations among black Americans that their history, their culture, and indeed their very identity had been denied expression. For Woodson, once African Americans could study the considerable contributions of black America that gave shape and narrative to their long presence in America, including the brutalities and suffering of the slavery era, they would have cause to celebrate what generations of American histories had largely denied: black intelligence, black achievement, and ultimately black integrity. His monumental body of writings across more than six decades of public service to his race and to his nation testifies to his enduring optimism that racial harmony would come as a result of reeducation of both white and black America.

—*Joseph Dewey*

**FURTHER READING**

Dagbovie, Pero. *The Early Black History Movement: Carter G. Woodson, and Lorenzo Johnston Greene.* Champaign: University of Illinois Press, 2007. Critical examination of Woodson's pivotal role in defining the mission of African American studies, with particular emphasis on the ASALH.

Durden, Robert Franklin. *Carter G. Woodson: Father of African American History.* Berkeley Heights, N.J.: Enslow, 1998. Accessible overview of Woodson's long career, geared to young adults. Centers on his campaign to establish Negro History Week.

Goggin, Jacqueline Anne. *Carter G. Woodson: A Life in Black History.* Baton Rouge: Louisiana State University Press, 1997. Landmark and definitive biography of Woodson that highlights his work with ASALH and his prodigious writings. Handsomely illustrated.

Rojas, Fabio. *From Black Power to Black Studies: How a Radical Social Movement Became an Academic Discipline.* Baltimore: Johns Hopkins University Press, 2007. Although more contemporary in its investigation, this source offers a cogent look at Woodson's seminal influences and the way his vision shaped the initial definition of African American studies as an academic endeavor with profound cultural ramifications.

Woodson, Carter Godwin. *Carter G. Woodson: A Historical Reader.* Vol. 14 in *Crosscurrents in African American History.* New York: Routledge, 2000. Indispensable collection of Woodson's voluminous writings, showcasing his passion and vision. Provides a helpful introduction that covers Woodson's long career.

**SEE ALSO:** Molefi Kete Asante; Mary McLeod Bethune; Charlotte Hawkins Brown; John Henrik Clarke; John Hope Franklin; Asa Grant Hilliard III; John Hope; Maulana Karenga; Benjamin Quarles; Booker T. Washington.

# ROD WOODSON
## Football player

*One of the greatest defensive backs in National Football League (NFL) history, Woodson had a celebrated career playing both cornerback and safety. He played for a decade with the Pittsburgh Steelers, then split the remainder of his seventeen-season career among three other teams. As of the 2009-2010 season, he held the all-time NFL record for interception return yards. He also was one of the few players to appear in Super Bowls with three different teams.*

**BORN:** March 10, 1965; Fort Wayne, Indiana
**ALSO KNOWN AS:** Roderick Kevin Woodson
**AREA OF ACHIEVEMENT:** Sports: football

**EARLY LIFE**

Roderick Kevin Woodson was born March 10, 1965, in Fort Wayne, Indiana, to James and Linda Jo Woodson. He has three siblings. Woodson's upbringing was contentious, as his African American father and white mother often fought about their children's upbringing. During Woodson's childhood, the family moved out of an impoverished neighborhood and into Fort Wayne's middle-class suburbs. However, they were thrust back into poverty after James lost his job.

Woodson began playing football for a Fort Wayne Police Athletic League team at an early age. He later played defensive back, slot back, and tailback at R. Nelson

Snider High School, where he was named all-state during both his junior and senior seasons. Woodson also excelled at track and field, winning four state titles while in high school.

### LIFE'S WORK

Woodson received a full scholarship to Purdue University, where he studied criminal justice (after abandoning an initial plan to study electrical engineering) and played defensive back, running back, and wide receiver. In 1985 and 1986, he was voted an All-American defensive back. He also was named an All-Big Ten Conference player three times during his college career. Woodson set thirteen university records. He is particularly remembered for his final game, played in 1986, against Purdue's traditional rival Indiana University; he led the team to a 17-15 victory, playing tailback and cornerback, returning three punts and two kickoffs, and appearing in 137 plays. As in high school, Woodson also was an accomplished athlete on the track; as of 2010, he still held the Purdue records for the 60- and 100-meter hurdles. He qualified for the Olympic Trials in 1984 but elected instead to focus on working toward a professional football career.

After graduating from Purdue, Woodson was selected by the Pittsburgh Steelers with the tenth pick in the first round of the National Football League (NFL) draft. The Steelers' defensive coordinator, Tony Dungy, was particularly enthusiastic about Woodson's potential. Early in his professional career, Woodson was known for his skill at returning punts and kicks, averaging the most kick-return yards in the league in 1989. His most notable work for the Steelers, however, came as a defensive back.

Woodson spent a decade as one of the leading members of the Steelers' defense. He was named to the 1990's All-Decade Team and the NFL 75th Anniversary Team in 1994, one of only five active players to receive the latter honor. In 1993, he was named the NFL defensive player of the year. In 1995, Woodson tore his anterior cruciate ligament while tackling Detroit Lions running back Barry Sanders in the first game of the season. Despite the injury, Woodson recovered in time to play for the Steelers in Super Bowl XXX at the end of the season. In 1996, however, the effects of the injury lingered,

*Rod Woodson.* (AP/Wide World Photos)

and he was unable to lift weights or get into peak condition. Nevertheless, Woodson finished the season with six interceptions, two of which he returned for touchdowns.

After leaving the Steelers in 1997 over a contract dispute, Woodson played for the San Francisco 49ers and then the Baltimore Ravens from 1998 to 2001. During this time, he also made an unusual switch in position, from cornerback to safety. He won a championship with the Ravens, who defeated the New York Giants in Super Bowl XXXV. Woodson played his last seasons with the Oakland Raiders in 2002 and 2003. In 2002, he led the NFL in interceptions (with eight) for the first time in his career. He also made his third trip to the Super Bowl. After failing a physical in 2004, Woodson was released by the Raiders and retired from football. He went on to work as a commentator on the NFL Network.

### SIGNIFICANCE

Woodson played seventeen seasons in the NFL and is widely considered one of the best defensive players in the history of the sport. He finished his career with a total of seventy-one interceptions and 1,483 interception-return yards. He was selected for the Pro Bowl eleven times and was inducted into the Pro Football Hall of Fame in 2009. In 2007, *USA Today*'s sportswriters voted Woodson the twenty-second best NFL player of all time, citing his durability and defensive skill.

*—C. Breault*

**FURTHER READING**

Attner, Paul. "The Intimidator." *The Sporting News*, November 29, 1993. An insightful profile that examines Woodson's competitive drive and his unlikely fame as a cornerback.

George, Thomas. "Another Veteran, Another Farewell: Rod Woodson, Steelers' Longtime All-Pro Corner, Heads West." *The New York Times*, July 6, 1997. This profile of Woodson, examining his departure from the Steelers after a decade with the team, reviews his NFL record and speculates on his future in the league.

Hayes, Reggie. "Tracing Woodson's Path to Greatness." *The Fort Wayne News-Sentinel*, August 3, 2009. Woodson's hometown newspaper looks back at his career after his induction into the Pro Football Hall of Fame.

**SEE ALSO:** Willie Lanier; Ray Lewis; Deion Sanders; Lawrence Taylor.

# JANE COOKE WRIGHT
## Scientist and physician

*Wright revolutionized the field of chemotherapy. Her research on chemotherapy agents and their administration continued to be used in clinical practice decades later. She also became the highest-ranking African American woman at a medical institution when she was appointed associate dean at New York Medical College.*

**BORN:** November 30, 1919; New York, New York
**ALSO KNOWN AS:** Jane Jones; the Mother of Chemotherapy
**AREAS OF ACHIEVEMENT:** Education; Medicine; Science and technology

### EARLY LIFE

Jane Cooke Wright was born in 1919 to Louis Tompkins Wright, a prominent surgeon who also specialized in venereal disease and cancer research, and Corrine Cooke, an elementary school teacher. Wright was the eldest of two daughters. Her father instilled in her a strong sense of political and social activism, given his own struggles to overcome racial barriers.

Wright completed secondary schooling at the Ethical Culture Fieldston School in New York City. She was awarded a scholarship to Smith College in 1942. She initially took an interest in nonmedical subjects, including art and physics, but eventually decided on a medical career. Wright obtained a full scholarship to New York Medical College and graduated third in her class with honors in 1945. She interned at Bellevue Hospital and completed her residency at Harlem Hospital.

### LIFE'S WORK

Upon completion of residency, Wright accepted a position as a physician with the New York City Public Schools in 1949. After only six months, Wright left the school district for full-time work at Harlem Hospital. She joined her father at the Harlem Hospital Cancer Research Foundation, which he had established. There, Wright focused on clinical trials for chemotherapy, which was considered experimental and not generally accepted as a treatment for cancer at the time. Wright's work concentrated on possible chemotherapeutic agents for treating leukemia as well as breast, skin, and other cancers. Wright studied drug interactions, techniques for administering chemotherapy, and each agent's effect on a tumor. She also documented patients' reactions to chemotherapy drugs. She was the first chemotherapy researcher to assert that chemotherapeutic agents had to be administered in a specific order, over time, rather than all at once. After her father's death, Wright followed in his footsteps and became the foundation's director at only thirty-three years of age.

Similar to her trailblazing father, Wright created a foundation of her own, the American Society of Clinical Oncology, in 1964. That year, President Lyndon B. Johnson appointed her to the Commission on Heart Disease, Cancer, and Stroke. This commission was influential in creating a national network of treatment centers for the diseases, a concept that came to be considered integral to medical practice and research.

Since 1955, Wright had been an associate professor of surgical research at New York University Medical Center and director of cancer chemotherapy research. In 1967, she became a professor of surgery at New York Medical College and was appointed the college's associate dean. She was the first African American woman to hold such a position at a medical program in the United States. Wright held the post from 1967 to 1975. During this time, she also was the first woman elected president of the New York Cancer Society. Wright remained at

New York Medical College for the remainder of her career. In addition to her research responsibilities, she taught physicians the techniques of chemotherapy and how to conduct research in the field.

Wright won numerous awards, including the Albert Einstein College of Medicine Spirit of Achievement Award (1965), the Hadassah Myrtle Wreath award (1967), the Smith College Medal (1968), the American Association for Cancer Research Award (1975), and the Otelia Cromwell Award (1981). She also published more than 130 journal articles on cancer research and chemotherapy and was dubbed the "Mother of Chemotherapy." Wright served on delegations that taught the principles of cancer research worldwide. She retired in 1987 after forty years of research.

In 1947, Wright married David Dallas Jones, Jr., an attorney specializing in advocacy for affirmative action. The couple had two daughters, Jane and Alison. Wright's work and personal papers were compiled into a collection housed at Smith College in 2006.

### SIGNIFICANCE

Wright's groundbreaking research in the field of chemotherapy cannot be overstated. Although it came to be combined with other modes of treatment such as radiation, chemotherapy remains a key component of cancer treatment. Her visionary work regarding the order of agent administration and variety of patient responses continued to be used clinically and studied many decades later. She held prominent positions, created national organizations, and become a role model both nationally and internationally throughout her career.

—*Janet Ober Berman*

### FURTHER READING

Bobonich, Harry M. "Jane Cooke Wright." In *Pathfinders and Pioneers: Women in Science, Math, and Medicine*. West Conshohocken, Pa.: Infinity, 2008. Offers information on Wright's life, accomplishments, and legacy in the medical community.

*Ebony*. "Homecoming for Jane Wright." 23, no. 7 (May, 1968): 72-77. Details Wright's career path that led her to the position of associate dean of New York Medical College. Includes personal information on Wright and her family life.

Russell, Dick. "Ancestors—The Physicians: Louis Tompkins Wright and Jane Cooke Wright." In *Black Genius and the American Experience*. New York: Carroll & Graf, 1998. Examines Wright's and her father's achievements in a cultural and historical context.

SEE ALSO: Dorothy Lavinia Brown; Charles R. Drew; Vance Hunter Marchbanks; Vivien Thomas; Daniel Hale Williams; Louis T. Wright.

# JEFFREY WRIGHT
## Actor

*Wright is a critically acclaimed film, stage, and television actor who has portrayed such notable African American figures as Jean-Michel Basquiat, Muddy Waters, and Martin Luther King, Jr. He won Tony, Emmy, and Golden Globe awards for his appearances in both the stage and television versions of Tony Kushner's play* Angels in America.

BORN: December 7, 1965; Washington, D.C.
AREAS OF ACHIEVEMENT: Film: acting; Radio and television; Theater

### EARLY LIFE

Jeffrey Wright was born in Washington, D.C., on December 7, 1965. His father died when he was an infant, leaving his mother, a retired lawyer for the U.S. Customs Department, and his aunt, a former nurse, to raise him.

Wright attended the respected St. Albans School for Boys in Washington, D.C., during the school year and spent many summers on his grandfather's farm in Tidewater, Virginia.

Upon graduating from St. Albans, Wright earned his bachelor's degree in political science from Amherst College in 1987, intending to follow his mother's footsteps into the legal profession. During college, however, Wright's career aspirations changed as he discovered his passion for acting. He accepted a scholarship to study acting at New York University in the early 1990's but embarked on his professional acting career after only a few months in college.

### LIFE'S WORK

Wright's earliest professional work occurred in Washington, D.C., shortly before he relocated to New York.

He was a cast member of the Folger Shakespeare Theater's production of *All's Well That Ends Well* in 1989 and appeared in multiple productions at the Arena Stage in 1989-1990, including *Les Blancs* and *She Stoops to Conquer.*

Once settled in New York, Wright appeared in the New York Shakespeare Festival's production of *Othello* in 1991. Wright also appeared in his first major feature film, *Presumed Innocent* (1990), in which he played a prosecuting attorney alongside film star Harrison Ford.

After a brief time touring with John Houseman's famed Acting Company in 1991, Wright landed a Broadway role that solidified his reputation as a top-tier American actor. He was cast as Belize, the homosexual nurse who cares for homophobic attorney Roy Cohn in Tony Kushner's Tony Award-winning play *Angels in America.* Wright appeared in both volumes of the play, *Millennium Approaches* and *Perestroika.* For his work as Belize, Wright won the 1994 Tony Award for Best Featured Actor in a Play and the 1994 Drama Desk Award for Outstanding Supporting Actor in a Play.

In the mid- to late 1990's, Wright added to his film credits. His memorable 1996 portrayal of graffiti artist-turned-renowned painter Jean-Michel Basquiat in Julian Schnabel's *Basquiat* was universally lauded, although the film itself received mixed reviews. Other film roles from this period include character work in Woody Allen's *Celebrity* (1998) and Ang Lee's *Ride with the Devil* (1999).

As the 2000's began, Wright continued acting in feature films while also increasing his productivity in both the theater and television worlds. Notable film work included his portrayal of Peoples Hernandez in John Singleton's *Shaft* (2000), *Ali* (2001), *The Manchurian Candidate* (2004), *Syriana* (2005), *Broken Flowers* (2005), and *Casino Royale* (2006). Near decade's end, Wright portrayed two influential African Americans from entirely different spheres of influence: Colin Powell, in Oliver Stone's *W.* (2008), and Muddy Waters, in Darnell Martin's *Cadillac Records* (2008).

For the second straight decade, Wright landed one of Broadway's premier roles with his portrayal of Lincoln in Suzan-Lori Parks's Pulitzer Prize-winning *Topdog/ Underdog.* He performed nightly alongside Don Cheadle in the show's Off-Broadway run in 2001, and with Mos Def when the show opened on Broadway in 2002. Wright was nominated for both the Tony and Drama Desk awards for his performance in the play's Broadway run.

On television, Wright received praise for his perfor-

*Jeffrey Wright.* (Getty Images)

mance as Martin Luther King, Jr., in HBO's 2001 film *Boycott.* Aside from the significance of this historic role, Wright met his wife, Carmen Ejogo, when they costarred in the film. The couple married in 2000.

In 2003, Wright reprised his award-winning role of Belize in the HBO miniseries version of *Angels in America,* directed by Mike Nichols. Playing opposite Al Pacino's award-winning portrayal of Roy Cohn, Wright won the Golden Globe and Emmy awards for his work, making Belize one of the most highly lauded characters in the history of the stage and screen.

In 2006, Wright played a minor role in the HBO film *Lackawanna Blues,* the story of a young man growing up in 1950's-1960's New York with a Puerto Rican father and an African American mother.

## SIGNIFICANCE

Wright has played a wide range of demanding, artistic roles on stage and screen, earning widespread critical praise. His carefully chosen characters explore social issues such as masculinity and sexuality, race and ethnicity, and class and opportunity. Wright has consequently amassed a body of work that is powerfully and fully representative of the African American experience at the turn of the twenty-first century.

*—Eric Novod*

**FURTHER READING**

Hill, Logan. "How Jeffrey Wright Is Ending His Life-Changing Year." *New York Magazine*, December 1, 2008. Wright discusses his *Cadillac Records* role as Muddy Waters, his support for Barack Obama's presidential campaign, and his career path.

Meadows, Bob. "The Talented Mr. Wright." *Essence* 37, no. 3 (July, 2006): 74-75. A brief interview that summarizes the actor's work in the mid-2000's, with additional information about Wright's family background.

Tate, Greg. "The Wright Brother." *Vibe* 8, no. 3 (April, 2000): 133-135. Discusses Wright's craft and his artistic attempts to avoid stereotypical roles. Also includes quotations from John Singleton, Wright's director on the film *Shaft*.

**SEE ALSO:** LeVar Burton; Don Cheadle; Laurence Fishburne; Jamie Foxx; Cuba Gooding, Jr.; Brian Stokes Mitchell; Will Smith; Wesley Snipes; Blair Underwood; Forest Whitaker.

# JEREMIAH WRIGHT
## Religious leader

*Known for his dynamic preaching style, Wright enjoyed a multifaceted career as a musician, author, educator, orator, and preacher. In his work, he professed a philosophy that links African American political and social activism with Christianity.*

**BORN:** September 22, 1941; Philadelphia, Pennsylvania
**ALSO KNOWN AS:** Jeremiah Alvesta Wright, Jr.
**AREAS OF ACHIEVEMENT:** Education; Religion and theology

**EARLY LIFE**

Jeremiah Alvesta Wright, Jr., was born on September 22, 1941, in Philadelphia, Pennsylvania, to the Reverend Jeremiah Wright, Sr., and Dr. Mary Elizabeth Henderson Wright. Jeremiah, Sr., served as a pastor for more than sixty years and was one of the first African Americans to earn a degree from Philadelphia's Lutheran Theological Seminary. Mary was the first black teacher and principal at Philadelphia's Girls High School. Wright's parents emphasized deep religious faith, educational empowerment, and respect for African American culture, politics, and history. This philosophical upbringing became the foundation for Wright's life experiences and ministry.

The Wrights' home was one in which reading and writing were ways of life. As a child and teenager, Wright read a wide range of literature, from ancient Greek philosophers and William Shakespeare to African American authors such as Carter G. Woodson and Sterling A. Brown. In 1959, Wright graduated from Central High School. He attended Virginia Union University for two years, until 1961, when he left to join the U.S. Marine Corps. In 1963, Wright joined the U.S. Navy. Four years later, he enrolled at Howard University, where he earned a bachelor's degree in 1968 and a master's degree in 1969. Wright went on to earn a second master's degree from the University of Chicago. In 1990, he earned a doctor of divinity degree from the United Theological Seminary in Dayton, Ohio. He specialized in African American sacred music and religious history.

**LIFE'S WORK**

Wright served as senior pastor of Trinity United Church of Christ in Chicago, Illinois, from 1972 to 2008. There, he developed outreach programs to address the needs of the community and enrich the lives of church members. Under his guidance, the church adopted the slogan "Unashamedly Black and Unapologetically Christian." The slogan reflected Wright's efforts to make Trinity United one of the nation's most politically active and socially conscious churches. When he retired, the church had more than fifty active ministries, with social justice advocacy at the core of its African American liberation theological perspective. Wright believes that his greatest accomplishment was "helping young people accomplish goals they never dreamed possible by showing them the unlimited potential and possibility God had placed within them when God created them." Wright is married to the Reverend Ramah Wright, with whom he has five children: Janet, Jeri, Nathan, Nikol, and Jamila.

Despite these accomplishments, Wright is best known for a controversy that gained national attention during Barack Obama's historic presidential campaign. Obama and his wife, Michelle, had been married by Wright, and the Obama family were members of Trinity United. In March, 2008, videos surfaced of sermons in which Wright condemned the values and actions of the United States government. Wright claimed that the United States had brought upon itself the terrorist attacks of September 11, 2001, because of its history of violence against American Indians and other countries.

In his "A More Perfect Union" speech, Obama interpreted Wright's comments and motives in terms of contemporary and historical race relations while voicing his disapproval of Wright's specific sentiments. Wright responded to the controversy with comments that further fanned the flames, including some that were criticized as anti-Semitic. At the end of May, 2008, the Obamas withdrew their membership from Trinity United and Wright retired from the church. After his retirement, Wright spent his time preaching, teaching, and leading study tours to Africa, Brazil, and the Caribbean.

## Significance

Wright taught hundreds of aspiring preachers the art of delivering powerful sermons through critical Biblical analysis and references to historical and current events. He wrote numerous articles on his method for academic journals and published four books widely used in seminaries: *What Makes You So Strong? Sermons of Joy and Strength from Jeremiah A. Wright, Jr.* (1993), *Good News: Sermons of Hope for Today's Families* (1995), *Africans Who Shaped Our Faith: A Study of Ten Biblical Personalities* (1995), and *When Black Men Stand Up for God* (1997). Career highlights include a Rockefeller Fellowship, eight honorary doctoral degrees, a prayer at the Million Man March in 1995, participation in the 1998 White House prayer breakfast, and Simpson College's Carver Medal in 2008. Wright's dedication to intellectual rigor, political critique, and social outreach made Trinity United a model for black churches in the United States and worldwide.

—*Marcia Alesan Dawkins*

## Further Reading

Newkirk, Pamela. *Letters from Black America*. New York: Farrar, Straus and Giroux, 2009. This groundbreaking narrative history of African Americans, told through letters, includes the remarks by Wright addressed to Jodi Kantor of *The New York Times* regard-

*Jeremiah Wright.* (AP/Wide World Photos)

ing a feature on Wright's relationship with Barack Obama.

Wright, Jeremiah A., Jr. *Africans Who Shaped Our Faith: A Study of Ten Biblical Personalities*. Chicago: Urban Ministries, 1995. Collection of sermons based on the biblical characters of Asenath, Shuphrah, Puah, Jethro, Zipporah, Ebedmelech, Jesus, Peter, Paul, and the Ethiopian Eunuch. Exemplifying the author's liberation philosophy, pedagogy, and theology, connections are made from these characters to African American history and twentieth century events.

_____. *What Makes You So Strong? Sermons of Joy and Strength from Jeremiah A. Wright, Jr.* Valley Forge, Pa.: Judson Press, 1993. Collection of Wright's sermons preached as part of an annual series commemorating Martin Luther King, Jr. Includes study questions and sections for reader reflection and comment.

**See also:** James H. Cone; Wilton D. Gregory; T. D. Jakes; Barack Obama; Michelle Obama.

# LOUIS T. WRIGHT
## Surgeon, researcher, and activist

*Wright was a successful surgeon and researcher who achieved goals and held positions previously considered unattainable for African American physicians. His efforts at Harlem Hospital to increase the quality of care and raise the bar for residency set standards for hospital care.*

**BORN:** July 23, 1891; LaGrange, Georgia
**DIED:** October 8, 1952; New York, New York
**ALSO KNOWN AS:** Louis Tompkins Wright
**AREAS OF ACHIEVEMENT:** Medicine; Social issues

### EARLY LIFE

Louis Tompkins Wright was one of two children born to Caeh Kentchen Wright, a physician and Episcopalian minister, and Lula Tompkins, a sewing teacher, both of whom were born as slaves. Wright's father died of gastric cancer when Wright was three years old. His mother remarried, to another physician who cultivated Wright's interest in medicine and raised the boy's awareness about racial discrimination.

Lula enrolled Wright in first grade at Thayer Home, where she taught, at the age of four. He excelled throughout secondary education. Wright was valedictorian of his class and graduated with distinction in chemistry from Clark University in Atlanta, Georgia, in 1912. He then enrolled at Harvard University Medical School. Wright insisted on performing his obstetrics rotation with his classmates at Boston Lying-In Hospital, which served white patients, after the university attempted to force him to an all-African American hospital across town. His diligence brought praise from supervisors and broke the racial barrier at the hospital. He graduated fourth in his class in 1915 but was denied membership in the Alpha Omega Alpha honor society because he was African American. Wright also was rejected from several residency programs because of his race, but he did gain acceptance to a one-year internship at Freedmen's Hospital in Washington, D.C.

### LIFE'S WORK

At Freedmen's Hospital, Wright became interested in the Schick test for diphtheria, which researchers claimed could not be used on African American patients because of their dark skin. He published a scientific article demonstrating that the test was equally valuable and reliable for white and black patients. He then returned to Atlanta, where he established a private practice and became treasurer of the local chapter of the National Association for the Advancement of Colored People (NAACP). Wright's stay in Atlanta was short-lived, however. He enlisted in the U.S. Army's Medical Reserve Corps during World War I. Still stateside, he introduced the intradermal vaccination for smallpox.

While in France, Wright was exposed to phosgene from a German gas shell, which resulted in permanent lung damage. Upon returning from France in 1919 with a Purple Heart, he worked at a venereal disease clinic. Wright was the first physician to treat humans with aureomycin for lymphogranuloma inguinale, a sexually transmitted bacterial infection. Soon afterward, he became the first African American surgeon at Harlem Hospital to obtain an attending position, a position he struggled to get after many attempts. He specialized in head injuries. In 1938, Wright was appointed director of surgeons and the medical board. His contribution to the hospital went beyond medical obligations; he attempted to fully integrate Harlem Hospital, improve the poor physical condition of the facility, and improve the staff's overall professional standards. He created the *Harlem Hospital Bulletin*, the hospital's medical library, and a cancer research center. In 1940, he was awarded the NAACP's Spingarn Medal for raising the quality of medical care and residency training for African American medical professionals.

During the time he served at Harlem Hospital, Wright also became the first African American surgeon employed by the New York City Police Department. In 1934, he became the first African American fellow of the American College of Surgeons. He was made chairman of the board for the NAACP in 1935 and an honorary fellow of the International College of Surgeons in 1950 and was awarded the American Cancer Society Medal in 1953. He published more than twenty-five scientific articles in the area of infectious diseases and more than one hundred total articles throughout his career.

Wright met his wife, Corrine M. Cooke, while in the U.S. Army. The couple had two daughters, Jane Cooke Wright and Barbara Wright Pierce, both of whom also became doctors. Wright died of tuberculosis in 1952 at the age of sixty-one.

### SIGNIFICANCE

Wright's inquisitive scientific mind led him from work on venereal diseases through surgery and cancer research. His passion for providing excellent care was evident in all of his medical and social work. Wright never tolerated racial discrimination and proved that African American physicians could perform as well as doctors of any other race.

—*Janet Ober Berman*

**FURTHER READING**

Hayden, Robert. *Mr. Harlem Hospital: Dr. Louis T. Wright, a Biography.* Littleton, Mass.: Tapestry Press, 2003. Biography outlining Wright's major contributions to the medical field. Discusses his accomplishments in the context of being an African American physician during the early twentieth century.

Reynolds, Preston. "Dr. Louis T. Wright and the NAACP: Pioneers in Hospital Racial Integration." *American Journal of Public Health* 90, no. 6 (June, 2000): 883-892. Comprehensive biography that puts Wright's life in historical context. Thoroughly details Wright's accomplishments with the NAACP.

Wright, Louis T. "The Schick Test, with Especial Reference to the Negro." *Journal of Infectious Diseases* 21, no. 1 (July, 1917): 265-268. Wright's scientific paper detailing how the test for diphtheria can be used in African American patients. This article brought Wright his first widespread recognition within the medical research field.

**SEE ALSO:** Dorothy Lavinia Brown; Charles R. Drew; Vance Hunter Marchbanks; Vivien Thomas; Daniel Hale Williams; Jane Cooke Wright.

# RICHARD WRIGHT
## Writer

*An author of fiction, nonfiction, and poetry, Wright defined in his books on racism the oppressed life of African Americans in the 1920's and 1930's.*

**BORN:** September 4, 1908; Roxie, Mississippi
**DIED:** November 28, 1960; Paris, France
**ALSO KNOWN AS:** Richard Nathaniel Wright
**AREA OF ACHIEVEMENT:** Literature

**EARLY LIFE**

Richard Nathaniel Wright, grandson of slaves, was born on a plantation near Natchez, Mississippi, on September 4, 1908. His father, Nathaniel, was an illiterate sharecropper, and his mother, Ella, was a schoolteacher. When Wright was five, his father abandoned the family, and his mother worked various jobs outside the home. For a time, Wright and his brother were placed in an orphanage, and later they were shifted among various relatives in Mississippi and Arkansas. Around 1920, Ella suffered a paralytic stroke, necessitating the family's move to Jackson, Mississippi, to live with Ella's parents. Wright's stern grandmother was a devoted, if fanatical, Seventh-day Adventist who subjected Richard to daily prayer and meditation, all-night revival meetings, and her restrictive belief that all things nonreligious, specifically fictional writings, were "the devil's work." Wright refused to be subdued by her efforts, maintaining throughout his life a hostility toward religion and espousing instead a humanistic philosophy.

The upheaval of Wright's childhood did not allow for much regular schooling. He was enrolled at the Seventh-day Adventist school in Jackson at the age of twelve and attended a public school for a short time. His first short story, "The Voodoo of Hell's Half Acre," written when he was fifteen, was published in 1924 in *The Southern Register*, a local black newspaper. At the age of sixteen, in 1925, he graduated as valedictorian of the ninth grade at Smith Robertson Junior High School. The following year, he went to Memphis. After working numerous menial jobs, Wright in 1927 joined countless other African Americans desperate to escape the fear, frustration, and violence of the South and migrated north to Chicago on the eve of the Great Depression.

Perceiving a connection between his experience as an African American and the plight of other oppressed working-class people in the world, Wright became involved with the Communist Party. In New York, he became the Harlem editor of the party's publication *The Daily Worker* and helped initiate *New Challenge*. Wright's collection of four stories, *Uncle Tom's Children*, won first place in a *Story* magazine contest open to Federal Writers' Project authors and was published in 1938. He received a Guggenheim Fellowship that enabled him to finish *Native Son* (1940), a best seller and the first Book-of-the-Month selection by an African American author. Wealthy and well-respected, Wright was the recipient of the prestigious Spingarn Medal of the National Association for the Advancement of Colored People (NAACP) in 1941.

### LIFE'S WORK

Because of the enormous popularity of *Native Son*, Wright collaborated with Paul Green on its stage adaptation, produced by John Houseman and Orson Welles in the spring of 1941. During this time, Wright's brief first marriage came to an end and he married Ellen Poplar, a white member of the Communist Party. The couple had two daughters: Julia, born in 1942 and Rachel, born in 1949. In 1941, Wright published his pictorial folk history of African Americans in the United States, *Twelve Million Black Voices*, which expressed his view of the capitalistic exploitation of African Americans and ended with a call for a united black and white workers' revolution.

Because of personal and political differences, Wright left the Communist Party in 1944, writing an essay published that same year in *The Atlantic Monthly*, "I Tried to

*Richard Wright.* (Library of Congress)

Be a Communist." The piece was later republished in *The God That Failed* (1949), a collection of essays by former communists. Wright's autobiography, *Black Boy*, appeared in 1945 and also became a best seller and Book-of-the-Month selection. The book recounted Wright's childhood and adolescence in the South; however, the U.S. Senate, aware of Wright's Communist Party affiliation, deemed it "obscene."

In 1946, Wright was invited to France by noted anthropologist Claude Lévi-Strauss, who, along with intellectuals including Gertrude Stein, Simone de Beauvoir, Jean-Paul Sartre, and Albert Camus, welcomed him to Paris. There, Wright enjoyed relief from the racism he could not escape even in New York; he settled permanently in France in 1947. He became interested in existentialism, a philosophy focusing on the plight of the individual in an unfathomable universe, and explored it in his second novel, *The Outsider* (1953), which is considered the first American existential novel. The book concerns a black man who exists in a disintegrating society with essentially no place for him. The following year, Wright published *Savage Holiday*, an unpopular novel whose characters all were white.

During the 1950's, Wright traveled to Africa, Indonesia, and Spain, observing different races and cultures and interviewing individuals about major social concerns. From these travels he wrote sociological and political nonfiction discussions of topics regarding race relations in predominantly nonwhite areas far from America and, through the inclusion of documented sources, advanced factors he believed determined policy in those areas. Although *Black Power* (1954), *The Color Curtain* (1956), and *Pagan Spain* (1957) are accounts of journeys to the Gold Coast, Africa, Indonesia, and Spain, they reflect Wright's growing international concerns and his vision of a rational, unified world. During his travels and activities, Wright was constantly under surveillance by the Central Intelligence Agency (CIA) and the Federal Bureau of Investigation (FBI).

*White Man, Listen!* (1957), a group of essays that originated as lectures Wright gave in Europe between 1950 and 1956, includes "The Literature of the Negro in the United States." In this overview, Wright considers American writings beginning with those of black colonial poet Phillis Wheatley and extending into the 1940's as reflective of the transition from common themes to those of protest. Although poor and ill in his later years, he wrote approximately four hundred English haikus and a novel, *The Long Dream* (1958). The story, set in a middle-class community in Mississippi in the 1940's, concerns Tyree Tucker, a black father, and his son, Fishbelly. Wright intended this novel as the first in a trilogy, and although he completed the second novel, it was not published. Critics were harsh in their evaluation of Wright's novel, insisting he had been away from creative writing too long to write anything meaningful.

While hospitalized in a Paris hospital for amoebic dysentery, contracted during his travels, Wright died suddenly of a heart attack on November 28, 1960, at the age of fifty-two. His wife, Ellen, effected the posthumous publication of *Eight Men* (1961), a second collection of short stories he had finished a few years earlier, which contained a nihilistic existential novella, "The Man Who Lived Underground." Also published posthumously were *Lawd Today* (1963), written in 1934, and *American Hunger* (1977), a treatise on his membership in and disillusionment with the Communist Party that was removed from *Black Boy* before its publication in 1945.

## SIGNIFICANCE

In the years after his death, Wright's status as a writer dwindled, but in the militant 1960's his work was rediscovered. His inability to find sustaining values in his own African American heritage and his insistence that being black was the same as being nothing alienated him from many other black writers, including James Baldwin, who countered with his conception of the richness of the African American experience. However, Wright's early life in the Deep South had permanently shaped his identity. His books drew attention to the corrosive effects of oppressive, violent racism and served to stoke militant rage. A rebellious person, Wright wanted to communicate to white America the anger and hatred that propelled him to speak out about man's injustice to man. His voice continued to compel readers long after his death.

—*Mary Hurd*

## FURTHER READING

Andrews, William L., and Douglas Taylor, eds. *Richard Wright's "Black Boy (American Hunger)": A Casebook*. New York: Oxford University Press, 2003. A collection of critical responses to *Black Boy*. Includes

---

### NATIVE SON

Richard Wright's first novel, *Native Son*, published in 1940, established Wright as a powerful writer and fascinated a nation of readers. The novel follows the actions of Bigger Thomas, a young black man who rebels against racist white society and murders a rich white woman. In "How 'Bigger' Was Born," Wright explains that he had observed several types of "Biggers" in his youth—some of whom were white—and combined them to create levels of anger and hatred that oppression and exclusion can produce.

The novel's first part describes Bigger's crime. As chauffeur to a wealthy white family, Bigger drives Mary Dalton and her friend Jan Erlone to a communist meeting, after which they all get drunk. Bigger attempts to get Mary into her bed quietly, but fear of being found in her bedroom causes him to accidentally suffocate her. He then stuffs her body into the furnace. In the second part, Mary's bones are discovered in the furnace. The third part describes Bigger's trial, which results in a death sentence.

Bigger comes to realize that in killing Mary he felt alive for the first time in his life, having lashed out against a symbol of his oppression. Wright's pointed title suggests that Bigger was born of the oppression and violence rampant in American race relations. The novel serves as a warning to Americans of the dangers inherent in the inhumanity of man to man.

---

various reviews, an interview of Wright in 1945, and essays that examine a wide range of topics.

Brignano, Russell Carl. *Richard Wright: An Introduction to the Man and His Works*. Pittsburgh, Pa.: University of Pittsburgh Press, 1970. Interesting account of Wright's attraction to Marxism, his attempt to exchange Marxism for existentialism, and the writings that were engendered by both. Also addresses Wright's travel books.

Graham, Maryemma, ed. *The Cambridge Companion to the African American Novel*. New York: Cambridge University Press, 2004. Sumptuous history of African American novelists spanning from slave narratives to modern novelists. Contains a significant chapter on Wright and the protest novel.

Rowley, Hazel. *Richard Wright: The Life and Times*. Chicago: University of Chicago Press, 2008. Detailed biography of Wright, including family background, life in the South during the first quarter of the twentieth century, and his lifelong efforts to fight racism.

Wright, Richard. *Uncle Tom's Children*. Reprint. New York: Harper Perennial, 2008. Excellent introduction to Wright's visceral fiction about white racism and oppression in the South. Four novellas first published in 1938.

**SEE ALSO:** James Baldwin; Ralph Ellison; Chester Himes; Claude McKay.

# Y

## FRANK YERBY
### Writer

*Yerby is the best-selling African American author of all time. His thirty-three historical novels have sold more than sixty million copies.*

**BORN:** September 5, 1916; Augusta, Georgia
**DIED:** November 29, 1991; Madrid, Spain
**ALSO KNOWN AS:** Frank Garvin Yerby
**AREA OF ACHIEVEMENT:** Literature

### EARLY LIFE

Frank Gavin Yerby (YUR-bee) was born in Augusta, Georgia, on September 5, 1916, to Rufus and Wilhelmina Smythe Yerby. Rufus was African American; Wilhelmina was of Scotch-Irish ancestry. From an early age, Frank Yerby was absorbed by books and wrote juvenilia. He attended Haines Normal and Industrial Institute and then Paine College, an African American institution in Augusta, Georgia. Meanwhile, he published short stories and verse in college journals and local magazines.

Yerby graduated from Paine in 1937. In 1938, he received a master's degree in English from Fisk University. Over the next few years, Yerby led a peripatetic existence while continuing to write short stories. He began a doctoral program in English at the University of Chicago. He worked for the Federal Writers' Project, a New Deal program that employed writers to document the cultural life of the United States. He taught English at several African American institutions, including Florida Agricultural and Mechanical College and Southern University. After the United States entered World War II, Yerby worked in defense factories in Dearborn, Michigan, and Queens, New York. In 1941, he married Flora Williams, with whom he would have four children.

### LIFE'S WORK

In 1944, Yerby gained his first critical recognition when he won the O. Henry Memorial Award for his short story "Health Card," which dealt with race relations in the military. Other short stories he published early in

*Frank Yerby.* (Library of Congress)

1628

## *THE DAHOMEAN: AN HISTORICAL NOVEL*

*The Dahomean: An Historical Novel* (1971) generally is considered Frank Yerby's finest novel. It is recognized for its dramatic story, realistic portrayal of a decadent African tribe, unflinching depiction of human evil, and harrowing account of the trans-Atlantic slave trade. Nyasanu Dosu Agausu Hwesu Gbokau Kesu (known as Hwesu) is the son of the king of the empire of Dahomey, a powerful West African kingdom in the eighteenth and nineteenth centuries. Valiant in battle, passionate in love, and revered by his subjects, Prince Hwesu is treacherously betrayed by his envious brother. He is sold into slavery and transported by slave ship to the New World, where he is purchased by two Maryland farmers and given the name Wesley Parks. Yerby's language is heightened by the tragic and even horrific elements of the story. The opportunity to write about African history spurred Yerby to explore the anthropology of an African empire. The barbaric practices of the African tribes and the slave trade are graphically depicted. *A Darkness at Ingraham's Crest* (1979) is Yerby's sequel to *The Dahomean*. Hwesu, now the slave Wesley Parks, calls on all of his talents and shrewdness to confound and resist his white masters. In a common dilemma facing Yerby's protagonists, Parks has to triumph over a merciless society though his superior wit.

his career include "Young Man Afraid" (1937), "Love Story" (1937), "White Magnolias" (1944), "Homecoming" (1946), and "My Brother Went to College" (1946). To support his growing family, Yerby made the decision to write a novel accessible to the general reading public and capable of mass sales. He succeeded on his first try. In 1946, he published the novel *The Foxes of Harrow*. The story is set in New Orleans in 1825 and opens with the arrival of the white protagonist, gambler Stephen Fox. To the dismay of the feudal plantation owners who dominate the South, Fox wins a fortune, as well as the love of several women. With his winnings, Fox builds Harrow, the largest mansion in Louisiana. *The Foxes of Harrow* became an immediate best seller, the first such mass success by an African American novelist. Within a year, more than one million copies had been sold. In 1947, the book was made into a Hollywood feature film starring Rex Harrison and Maureen O'Hara and nominated for an Academy Award, although Yerby did not approve of the screen adaptation. In the decades following its publication, *The Foxes of Harrow* is estimated to have sold about twelve million copies.

Yerby had found a formula for literary success to which he remained faithful. His novels were set in romantically perceived historical periods, usually the antebellum South. Yerby, who had a talent for historical research, re-created period details. His plots were overwrought with heroic characters triumphing in a world

of melodramatic encounters, sensual relationships, and raw power. Yerby became known as the "King of the Costume Novel." Many writers tried to duplicate this formula, but few could match Yerby's success. In 1947, he published *The Vixens*, a sequel to *The Foxes of Harrow*. *The Golden Hawk* (1948) is set among pirates and *Pride's Castle* (1949) in the age of the American robber barons. *Judas, My Brother* (1968) is a tale of early Christianity. *The Girl from Storyville* (1972) is set in the notorious red-light district of New Orleans. His twenty-sixth novel, *The Voyage Unplanned* (1974), is set in Nazi-occupied France. His last novel, *McKenzie's Hundred* (1985), takes place during the Civil War.

By 2011, Yerby's thirty-three novels had sold more than sixty million copies in eighty-two countries and had been translated into more than thirty languages. Twelve of his novels were best sellers; three were made into films. In his essay "How and Why I Write the Costume Novel," published in the October, 1959, edition of *Harper's* magazine, Yerby compared his popular success with canonical writers who also wrote best sellers, such as Charles Dickens, William Thackeray, and Alexandre Dumas. Nevertheless, he was scorned on two counts. His costume novels were called shallow and hackneyed. With the rise of the Civil Rights movement, he was criticized for neglecting the plight of African Americans. Almost all of the protagonists in his novels are white men engaged in adventure and romance. Historical depictions of race relations were included more for local color than for sociological perspective.

Partly in response to this criticism, Yerby wrote his first African American protagonist in *Speak Now* (1969). However, the novel still followed his "costume" formula. He did write a protest novel, *The Tent of Shem* (1963), but it was never published. His most critically acclaimed work, *The Dahomean: An Historical Novel* (1971), is a story of a valiant African prince betrayed into slavery and transported in the trans-Atlantic slave trade. In addition to his historical novels, Yerby wrote well-received short stories such as "The Homecoming" and poems such as "The Fishes and the Poet's Hands."

Yerby left the United States to move to France in 1952

and Spain in 1955. He divorced Flora and married Blanca Calle-Perez in 1956. Blanca served as his literary helpmate for the rest of his life. Yerby lived reclusively in Spain until his death in 1991 from congestive heart failure. In 2004, Yerby's childhood home was moved to the campus of Paine College to serve as a memorial.

## SIGNIFICANCE

Yerby is the best-selling African American author in history, having sold more than sixty million copies of his romance novels. His major themes are tensions between the sexes, people's capacity for heroism or exploitation, and material success that is seized by superior wits and valor. Although most of his novels are set in the antebellum South, he depicted historical periods ranging from the Peloponnesian War to twentieth century Latin America. Other historical periods and events that Yerby recreated in his fiction include the Crusades, Caribbean piracy, the French Revolution, the California gold rush, the American Civil War, the American Gilded Age, the Spanish Civil War, and World War II. Although his talent for historical research rendered each period authentic and elaborate, his plots have been described as melodramatic and conventional. Nevertheless, Yerby's novels reimagine history, revising notions of the Old South, the Confederacy, and glorified notions of other cultures. Because his protagonists mostly are white aristocrats engaged in torrid romances and fighting for fortunes and dynasties, Yerby was criticized for not writing novels of social protest or addressing issues of racial justice. However, his millions of fans enjoyed his picaresque plots, soaked in period detail, and his distinctive rendering of human nature's good and bad sides throughout history.

—*Howard Bromberg*

## FURTHER READING

Glasrud, Bruce, and Laurie Champion. "'The Fishes and the Poet's Hands': Frank Yerby, a Black Author in White America." *Journal of American and Comparative Cultures* 23, no. 4 (Winter, 2000): 15-21. Explores the stages of Yerby's literary career in which he wrestled with the role of race in his writing.

Hill, James. "Yerby, Frank." In *The Concise Oxford Companion to African American Literature*, edited by William Andrews, Francis Foster, and Trudier Harris. New York: Oxford University Press, 2001. Argues that Yerby's significance lies in his unyielding critique of the romanticized views of the Old South, planter aristocracy, and the Confederacy, as well as myths of other cultures.

Jarrett, Gene. "'For Endless Generations': Myth, Dynasty, and Frank Yerby's *The Foxes of Harrow*." *The Southern Literary Journal* 39, no. 1 (Fall, 2006): 54-70. Compares the southern dynasty created by Stephen Fox, the hero of *The Foxes of Harrow*, with that of Sutpen in William Faulkner's *Absalom, Absalom!* (1936).

_____. "The Race Problem Was *Not* a Theme for Me." In *Deans and Truants: Race and Realism in African American Literature*. Philadelphia: University of Pennsylvania Press, 2007. Explores Yerby's novels, especially *The Foxes of Harrow*, in the context of Yerby's predilection to not write about "the race problem."

Moore, Jack. "The Guilt of the Victim: Racial Themes in Some Frank Yerby Novels." *Journal of Popular Culture* 8, no. 4 (Spring, 1975): 746-756. Discusses the treatment in Yerby's fiction of the complicity of African Americans in their own victimization.

Stovall, Eugene. *Frank Yerby: A Victim's Guilt—A Transformative Novel*. Oakland, Calif.: Regent Press, 2006. A novel in which Yerby mixes with the characters of his novels, allowing for a sustained conversation about many of the themes of Yerby's novels, including that of racial victimization.

SEE ALSO: Barbara Chase-Riboud; Alex Haley; Terry McMillan; Alice Walker; Margaret Walker.

# AL YOUNG
## Writer

*Young has written in many genres but is best known for his poetry, memoirs, and fiction. All his works show his appreciation for music, as he sees a connection between the beats and rhythms of everyday life and musical compositions. His writing is infused with themes found in jazz, blues, and contemporary songs.*

**BORN:** May 31, 1939; Ocean Springs, Mississippi
**ALSO KNOWN AS:** Albert James Young, Jr.
**AREAS OF ACHIEVEMENT:** Literature; Poetry; Theater

### EARLY LIFE

Albert James Young, Jr., was born in Ocean Springs, Mississippi, on May 31, 1939, to Albert James Young, Sr., a professional musician and auto worker, and Mary Campbell Young. He grew up in the rural, segregated South but considers himself lucky to have been placed in a special classroom in the second grade. The Kingston School for Colored in the 1940's placed a heavy emphasis on African American literature and culture. Young memorized poems by Langston Hughes and Paul Laurence Dunbar and became well acquainted with black history and creative arts.

Upon his father's discharge from the Navy, the family moved to Detroit. From 1957 to 1960, Young attended the University of Michigan. In 1961, he moved to Berkeley, California, and picked up a wide assortment of jobs, including folk singer, lab aide, disc jockey, medical photographer, clerk typist, and employment counselor. On October 8, 1963, he married Arline Belck, a freelance artist, technical writer, and editor; in 1971, they had a son, Michael James.

Young earned a bachelor of arts degree with honors from the University of California at Berkeley in 1969. From 1969 to 1976, he was the Edward B. Jones Lecturer in creative writing at Stanford University.

### LIFE'S WORK

Young has said that he began writing poetry to "make out the sound of his own background." That he sees a clear relationship between music and everyday living is most evident in two volumes of his five autobiographies: *Kinds of Blue: Musical Memoirs* (1984) and *Drowning in the Sea of Love: Musical Memoirs* (1995). In each, Young etches significant life events through the songs that were popular at that time.

For example, Young recounts an experience he had at age three, watching a fly caught in a spider web, still fluttering its wings as it was devoured head first. Young sees all of life in this tiny moment and wonders at its horrible beauty. The music he associates with the incident is the Ink Spots' 1943 rendition of "Java Jive" and the Andrew Sisters' "They've Got an Awful Lot of Coffee in Brazil." He also links these songs to memories of his aunt Ethel, a coffee lover he describes in poetic detail. Young's musical memoirs are not written chronologically but in a stream-of-consciousness style, with one memory leading to another and music summoning long-ago associations.

Most of Young's poetry is autobiographical, often upbeat and hopeful, although he also shows concern about the growing disconnectedness that comes with the increasing reliance on technology. He also has written tributes to musicians such as Charles Mingus, John Coltrane, Sarah Vaughan, George Gershwin, James Brown, and Janis Joplin. He brings the musical past into focus for contemporary readers.

During the 1970's, Young wrote and collaborated on screenplays for Richard Pryor, Sidney Poitier, and Bill Cosby. By 2010, Young had published nearly twenty works of fiction, memoir, and poetry, and edited several literary anthologies. He also had taught at a number of universities, including the University of Washington, University of Michigan, and Davidson College. From 2005 to 2007, he was the poet laureate of California.

Throughout his academic years, Young received numerous awards, including a Guggenheim Fellowship (1974), three National Endowment for the Humanities fellowships (1968, 1969, 1975), a Fulbright Fellowship (1969), and two American Book Awards, for *Bodies and Soul: Musical Memoirs* (1981) and *The Sound of Dreams Remembered: Poems, 1990-2000* (2001). His work is widely anthologized and has been translated into more than one dozen languages. He has won awards for fiction and nonfiction and is a highly sought-after public reader, performer, and lecturer, covering topics in literature, music, creativity, the arts, and African American culture.

### SIGNIFICANCE

Young is important for the universality of his writings. He has never attempted to conform the subjects or style of his work to the expectations of whites or African Americans. He eschews stereotypes and creates unique characterizations; for example, the poem "A Dance for Militant Dilettantes" criticizes whites for stereotypical thinking while also indicting black militants.

*—Gay Pitman Zieger*

**FURTHER READING**

Battaglia, Joseph F. "Al Young." *Critical Survey of Long Fiction*, edited by Carl Rollyson. 4th ed. 10 vols. Pasadena, Calif.: Salem Press, 2010. Lengthy survey of Young's career with detailed analysis of many of his works.

Chapman, Abraham, ed. *New Black Voices: An Anthology of Contemporary Afro-American Literature*. New York: New American Library, 1972. This valuable anthology contains a section on Young and places his work in the context of African American literature.

Young, Al. *Kind of Blue: Musical Memoirs*. San Francisco, Calif.: Ecco Press, 1984. Young's first autobiography discusses his childhood and introduces his fascination with music.

_____. *Drowning in a Sea of Love: Musical Memoirs*. San Francisco, Calif.: Ecco Press, 1995. This later memoir includes some of Young's earlier essays and continues in its tributes to legendary musicians.

**SEE ALSO:** Maya Angelou; Claude Brown; Wanda Coleman; Leon Forrest; Langston Hughes; William Melvin Kelley; Walter Mosley; Ishmael Reed.

# ANDREW YOUNG
## Activist and politician

*Young became a leader in the Civil Rights movement in 1961, working with Martin Luther King, Jr., for seven years. In 1972, Young was elected to the U.S. Congress, and he later served as a representative to the United Nations and as the mayor of Atlanta.*

**BORN:** March 12, 1932; New Orleans, Louisiana
**ALSO KNOWN AS:** Andrew Jackson Young, Jr.
**AREAS OF ACHIEVEMENT:** Diplomacy; Government and politics; Social issues

**EARLY LIFE**

Andrew Jackson Young, Jr., was born in New Orleans, Louisiana, on March 12, 1932, the eldest son of Andrew and Daisy Young. The junior Young grew up in a comfortable Cleveland Street home, raised primarily by his mother, who had been a teacher. His father, a dentist, provided a solid middle-class living. The family emphasized education and religion, attending a Congregational church. Young's neighborhood was diverse, racially and ethnically, providing him the experience of multiculturalism at an early age. At six, Young enrolled at Valena C. Jones Elementary School, jumping to third grade because he could read. Since public schools in New Orleans offered no eighth grade to African Americans, Young entered the ninth grade at the prestigious Gilbert Academy when he was only eleven, and he graduated at fifteen.

Young's father took his sons on trips into rural areas of Louisiana, which was dangerous for African American men in the 1930's. The father taught his boys that racism was a sickness, and that the best approach was to remain calm and always try to have compassion for those who were rude. He first attempted to have his sons trained in boxing, but when the boys did not embrace that sport he arranged for former Olympic star Ralph Metcalfe to teach them how to run.

After high school, Young attended local Dillard University for one year before transferring to Howard University in Washington, D.C. Earning a bachelor's degree in biology in May, 1951, Young found work in Connecticut and enrolled at Hartford Theological Seminary that fall. During the summer of 1952, Young interned at a church in Marion, Alabama, where he met Jean Childs, who lived in Marion but attended Manchester College in Indiana. The young couple fell in love, and after Childs won a prestigious fellowship they spent six weeks in Austria, working with refugees during the summer of 1953. In 1954, Young and Childs were married, and Young completed his bachelor's degree in divinity in January, 1955. The newlyweds moved to Thomasville, Georgia, to minister to a congregation.

**LIFE'S WORK**

The couple lived in Thomasville for two years. In August, 1957, the family moved to New York, where Young took a job with the Youth Division of the National Council of Churches. As one of only two African Americans working among several hundred employees, Young considered it his duty to teach about racism. Living and working in a multicultural metropolis during the late 1950's was an exciting opportunity for the Young family. Nonetheless, in August, 1961, they moved to Atlanta, where Young began working for the Citizenship Education Program.

During his first year in Atlanta, Young increasingly came into contact with Martin Luther King, Jr., and his Southern Christian Leadership Conference (SCLC). In late 1962, during the protests in Albany, Georgia, Young began working directly for the SCLC. In the spring of 1963, the SCLC organized a major civil rights event in Birmingham, Alabama, and King asked Young to represent the SCLC in negotiations with white business leaders. His ability to serve as an intermediary between the black and white communities helped bring about a successful settlement in Birmingham.

The dramatic events in Alabama caught the attention of President John F. Kennedy, who asked the U.S. Congress to pass an effective civil rights bill. Kennedy was assassinated in November, 1963, but his successor, Lyndon B. Johnson, made the legislation a top priority. In April, 1964, Young became executive director of the SCLC and persuaded King to organize demonstrations in St. Augustine, Florida. While leading a march there in June, Young was badly beaten by the Ku Klux Klan, a racist group. This violence in Florida was the final showdown before Congress passed the landmark Civil Rights Act of 1964, which Johnson signed into law on July 2.

The Civil Rights Act brought tremendous progress in the fight to end segregation and to open jobs to people of color and women, but it did not address the disfranchisement of African Americans that had been rampant throughout the South since the end of Reconstruction. In the hope of drawing attention to this, the SCLC decided to organize demonstrations in Selma, Alabama. Young knew the area well, because it was near the home of his wife, so he went to Selma in January, 1965, to begin planning the protests.

Young was on the scene when the first attempt to cross the Edmund Pettus Bridge on March 7 was beaten back by Alabama state troopers. He worked with King to coordinate the SCLC response to this attack, which resulted in a successful five-day march from Selma to Montgomery later in the month. This watershed event galvanized popular opinion across the country in favor of the Voting Rights Act, which Congress passed and Johnson signed into law in August.

In 1966, Young and the SCLC attempted to move the struggle to the urban north and improve the lives of poor African Americans in Chicago, with limited success. In

*Andrew Young.* (AP/Wide World Photos)

1967, King publicly criticized Johnson's escalation of the war in Vietnam, and Young helped King write the "Beyond Vietnam" speech that he delivered in New York in April. Opposing the war resulted in serious criticism of SCLC, and, as executive director, Young tried to respond. Frustration turned to tragedy in April, 1968, when King was killed in Memphis, and a dramatic period of Young's career soon came to a close.

In 1970, Young ran unsuccessfully for the seat in the House of Representatives for Georgia's fifth district, but he tried again in 1972 and joined Barbara Jordan as the first African Americans elected to Congress in former Confederate states since 1901. Young took office in January, 1973, and quickly made a name for himself on Capitol Hill. He was appointed to the House Banking and Currency Committee and joined its Subcommittee on International Trade.

During his four years in Congress, Young became increasingly involved in relations with Africa, proposing a successful amendment that prohibited American support for the Portuguese wars in Angola and Mozambique and attempting to reimpose economic sanctions against Rho-

## THE ANDREW YOUNG FOUNDATION

Launched in 2007 to mark Andrew Young's seventy-fifth birthday, the Andrew Young Foundation supports education, health, and youth leadership through partnerships with organizations such as Dillard University, the Young Men's Christian Association (YMCA), Grady Hospital, and the Jean Childs Young Institute of Youth Leadership. The foundation advocates nonviolent social change and reflects Young's belief that from those to whom much is given, much will be demanded.

The foundation emphasizes positive stories about some of the good things happening in the world, particularly in Africa, by producing a television documentary series entitled *Andrew Young Presents*. The first episode, "Rwanda Rising," premiered in Los Angeles in 2007, and the ninth episode, "Crossing in St. Augustine," aired early in 2010 to honor Black History Month and Martin Luther King, Jr.'s birthday.

desia. He visited South Africa for the first time in 1974, befriending antiapartheid leader Robert Sobukwe and bringing two of Sobukwe's children to live with him in Atlanta. In 1975, he accompanied Coretta Scott King on a trip to Zambia, where they celebrated the opening of the Martin Luther King Library in Lusaka.

In 1976, Young actively supported the presidential campaign of Jimmy Carter. When Carter won, in great part because of the overwhelming vote of African Americans across the South, he appointed Young as his permanent representative to the United Nations. In his position as U.N. ambassador, Young focused primarily on Africa. He persuaded Carter to repeal the Byrd Amendment, thus putting sanctions back into effect against Rhodesia. Young, Carter, and other members of the administration spent significant amounts of time and energy to settle the Rhodesian conflict. Their efforts contributed to the process that produced the Lancaster House Agreement in December, 1979, which brought peace and a new constitution to Rhodesia. In April, 1980, Young attended the independence ceremony, when Rhodesia was renamed Zimbabwe.

By the time of Zimbabwe's celebration, however, Young was no longer the U.N. ambassador. He had been forced to resign because of his unauthorized meeting with a representative of the Palestine Liberation Organization in New York. Returning to Atlanta, he decided to run for mayor and was elected in October, 1981.

In January, 1982, Young followed in the footsteps of Maynard Jackson to become the second African American mayor of Atlanta. Young was reelected in 1985. During his eight years in office, he helped globalize the city, expanding the airport and attracting international busi-

ness. Atlanta hosted the 1988 Democratic Convention, and Young was a key member of the group that successfully lobbied for the 1996 Summer Olympics to be held in Atlanta, in part by emphasizing the city's proud history of racial progress.

After an unsuccessful run for Georgia governor in 1990, Young retired from politics and joined the private sector, with mixed results. He cofounded a consulting firm, GoodWorks, that has carried out successful projects in African nations including Angola. On the other hand, Young's work for companies such as Nike and Wal-Mart has attracted considerable criticism. His personal life also had its sorrows. His wife Jean died of cancer in 1994. On a happier note, a few years later, Young married Carolyn Watson in Cape Town, South Africa. He and Carolyn decided to form the Andrew Young Foundation in honor of his seventy-fifth birthday in 2007. They began to promote the foundation's mission, advocating health and education among disadvantaged populations in the United States, the Caribbean, and Africa.

### SIGNIFICANCE

Young, a Christian minister like his friend and colleague Martin Luther King, Jr., played a major role in the fight for African American civil rights in the United States. His major contributions were mediating between the black and white communities in troubled Birmingham and facilitating the crucial march from Selma to Montgomery.

As a congressman, ambassador, and mayor, Young broadened the playing field of U.S. foreign relations, opening the door for religious groups, women, and people of color to influence international affairs. He increased the attention paid to racial issues in foreign relations, and he made the issues of Africa a high priority in the late 1970's.

—*Andy DeRoche*

### FURTHER READING

DeRoche, Andrew. *Andrew Young: Civil Rights Ambassador*. Wilmington, Del.: Scholarly Resources, 2003. This biography focuses on Young's role in U.S. foreign relations, focusing on policies toward Angola, South Africa, and Zimbabwe. Utilizes many primary sources from the Jimmy Carter Library.

Jones, Bartlett. *Flawed Triumphs: Andy Young at the United Nations*. Lanham, Md.: University Press of America, 1996. This well-researched study details Young's tenure as Carter's ambassador to the United Nations, from 1977 to 1979. Includes impressive array of interviews.

Young, Andrew. *An Easy Burden: The Civil Rights Movement and the Transformation of America*. New York: HarperCollins, 1996. In this autobiography, Young recounts his early life and experiences as one of King's assistants in the Civil Rights movement. A helpful resource for anyone interested in Young.

Young, Andrew, and Kabir Sehgal. *Walk in My Shoes: Conversations Between a Civil Rights Legend and His Godson on the Journey Ahead*. New York: Palgrave Macmillan, 2010. Young passes along life lessons to Sehgal, whom he has been mentoring for decades. Rich with anecdotes and provocative in tone, this book is an intimate look at the mature Young.

**SEE ALSO:** Tom Bradley; James Chaney; Maynard Jackson; Coretta Scott King; Martin Luther King, Jr.; Coleman Young.

# COLEMAN YOUNG
## Politician

*A five-term mayor of Detroit, Young was a controversial figure for his outspoken style and his controversial political decisions.*

**BORN:** May 24, 1918; Tuscaloosa, Alabama
**DIED:** November 29, 1997; Detroit, Michigan
**ALSO KNOWN AS:** Coleman Alexander Young
**AREAS OF ACHIEVEMENT:** Government and politics; Military; Social issues

### EARLY LIFE
Coleman Alexander Young was born May 24, 1918, in Tuscaloosa, Alabama, to William Coleman, a tailor who had attended Alabama Agricultural and Mechanical University to study tailoring, and Ida Reese Young. When Coleman Young was a boy, his family relocated to Michigan and settled in Detroit's Black Bottom, a neighborhood of immigrants known for its rich black soil. During the 1920's, the Black Bottom was integrated by economics and not by race.

At ten years of age, Young started doing odd jobs in the neighborhood to earn pocket change. Sweeping floors, delivering suits, and running errands kept his pockets filled. As the oldest of five children, Young began to assume more responsibilities as his family dynamic changed. Young's father was a hardworking man who often held several jobs at a time to keep his family comfortable; however, he also was an avid gambler who alternated between heavy drinking and long periods of sobriety. As a result, Young was responsible for making sure his father's gambling winnings made it home before they were lost in the next game of poker or whist. His

father had fair skin, and Young knew this permitted his father a seat at poker tables with white news reporters and photographers and made him privy to conversations that white men had in his presence before they under-

*Coleman Young.* (Library of Congress)

stood he was a black man. Once his heritage was discovered, Young's father was fired from his job as a tailor. Undiscouraged, however, the father opened a dry-cleaning and tailoring shop in a building that doubled as the family home. The discrimination that his father endured left an indelible impression on Young that shaped his worldview.

## LIFE'S WORK

During World War II, Young served in the U.S. Army Air Forces, as a navigator and a bombardier, joining the famed group of Tuskegee Airmen. He began to organize his African American soldier-comrades in demanding equal rights. After the war, in 1960, Young became part of a delegation to create a new constitution for the state of Michigan. Four years later, he was elected to the Michigan State Senate, where he served until 1973. During that time, he was also the executive secretary for the National Negro Labor Council. Young had a passion for justice, and he wanted to ensure that Detroit's citizens were represented by someone who had their best interests at heart. Having grown up in Detroit and witnessed at first hand the racial inequality that existed in the city, Young wanted a chance to change the face of politics in the city.

Following the 1967 riots that set the stage for Detroit's economic downward spiral, Young was appointed to a committee that would address affirmative action within the police department. Few African Americans held positions of power in Detroit's municipal departments, and Mayor Jerome Cavanaugh, who created the committee, eventually capitulated to the police unions, which were determined to quash those efforts. To protest the department's failure to hire more African American officers, Young resigned.

In 1974, Young ran for mayor of Detroit and won. However, his tenure was marked by continuing decline of the city. His outspokenness alienated him from government officials, and because of this Detroit was exempted from federal funding. Young's fierce independence often led to explosive engagements with the media and other public representatives.

Young believed that the challenges Detroit faced were

---

## YOUNG AND THE TUSKEGEE AIRMEN

Coleman Young's military career was marked by activism. In 1942, when he entered an informally segregated Army, he observed and endured racial offenses. He bristled at the idea of fighting for a country in which he believed that he was not afforded full citizenship. Still, he moved quickly through the ranks. He was instrumental in organizing efforts among his African American comrades to protest their inequitable treatment in the military. His efforts garnered him the unwanted attention of the commanding officers, who went to great lengths to defuse what they considered subversion. When the Army instituted Public Law 18, which specifically mandated that African Americans be trained as pilots, Young, already serving in the Air Corps, jumped at the opportunity. He applied for paratrooper and pilot training and was accepted into the pilot-training program in Tuskegee, Alabama. It was then that his career as a Tuskegee Airman began.

Young's reputation had preceded him, and upon arrival at the Tuskegee base, he was made aware that communications had been sent warning the commanding officers of Young's subversive tendencies. The correspondence, however, never made it to the intended hands, and Young threw himself into pilot training. To his great disappointment, Young failed to pass the final flight test. He later learned that, despite his skill, his failing the test was retaliation for his activism in promoting equal rights for African American soldiers.

---

larger than one person could solve. It was his contention that the primary problem was an economic one that would require the creation of jobs, and he fought with those who did not make efforts to bring this about. He was also against public policy that excluded his constituents from benefits that could move the city forward. His disdain for injustice often overrode his willingness to communicate his displeasure in a constructive way. The end result was that he alienated the political and governmental organizations that might have assisted in turning around Detroit's economic decline.

In 1993, after serving five terms, Young stepped down as mayor of Detroit. He experienced considerable frustration with a system that could overlook the plight of an entire urban community. In 1997, Young, a lifelong smoker, died of emphysema.

## SIGNIFICANCE

The work of Young was often overshadowed by his larger-than-life personality. He was unapologetic in his delivery, which was often laced with expletives. However abrasive his manner, he fought long and hard to effect change in his community. He was not shy about speaking out against injustice wherever he saw it. For this he endured ridicule and the naysaying of others while struggling to save his city from decline. Young's legacy is one of contending for justice no matter the consequences. From his early years in the armed forces to his nearly twenty years of service as the mayor of the city of Detroit, Young left a model for African Americans to work unceasingly for improvement.

—*Tresalyn S. Murray-Bray*

**FURTHER READING**

Colburn, David R., and Jeffrey S. Adler, eds. *African American Mayors: Race, Politics, and the American City.* Urbana: University of Illinois Press, 2001. A historical look at twentieth century African American mayors, their contributions, and the role race played in politics.

Rich, Wilbur C. *Coleman Young and Detroit Politics: From Social Activist to Power Broker.* Detroit: Wayne State University Press, 1989. A comprehensive biography chronicling Young's life, from his chilhood through his years as mayor of Detroit.

Young, Coleman A., and Lonnie Wheeler. *Hard Stuff: The Autobiography of Coleman A. Young.* New York: Penguin, 1994. Candid and colorful account of the life of Young, told in his own words. A must read for anyone wanting to know Young's perspective on life.

**SEE ALSO:** Tom Bradley; Maynard Jackson; Ray Nagin; Harold Washington; Andrew Young.

# WHITNEY YOUNG
## Civil rights leader and social worker

*Young won the support of influential political leaders and white corporate America to combat employment discrimination and establish equitable access to housing, health care, education, and social opportunities for poor African Americans. Parts of Young's socioeconomic plan, designated the "domestic Marshall Plan," were included in President Lyndon B. Johnson's War on Poverty.*

**BORN:** July 31, 1921; Lincoln Ridge, Kentucky
**DIED:** March 11, 1971; Lagos, Nigeria
**ALSO KNOWN AS:** Whitney Moore Young, Jr.
**AREAS OF ACHIEVEMENT:** Civil rights; Education

**EARLY LIFE**

Whitney Moore Young, Jr., was born in Lincoln Ridge, Kentucky, to Laura Ray and Whitney M. Young, Sr. He grew up on the campus of Lincoln Institute with his two sisters, Arnita (born 1920) and Eleanor (born 1922). An all-black boarding school, Lincoln Institute was established in 1910 by the trustees of previously integrated Berea College in response to Jim Crow laws banning integrated education.

Young's parents, Laura Ray and Whitney, Sr., married in 1914. Young grew up in an intellectual environment, exposed to the work of African American leaders including Booker T. Washington, W. E. B. Du Bois, Mary McLeod Bethune, and Adam Clayton Powell, Sr. He was influenced by the tenacity of his mother, who became an instructor at the Lincoln Institute and was appointed the

first African American postmaster of Lincoln Ridge, Kentucky, in 1945.

After migrating to Detroit, Michigan, where Young's father worked as an engineer for the Detroit United Railway Co., the family returned to Kentucky in 1920. Whitney, Sr., served as an engineering instructor and subsequently as president of Lincoln Institute. He employed strategies reminiscent of Washington, garnering support from white philanthropists for a janitorial degree program for his school when support for an engineering program lagged. Janitorial education required knowledge of electricity, plumbing, and steam boiler systems, thus enabling African Americans trained at the institute to work in factories, office buildings, and power plants.

Young observed his parents' strategies for gaining fair treatment and access for African Americans. The knowledge he gained from them contributed to the interracial mediation skills that he demonstrated throughout his life's work.

**LIFE'S WORK**

After graduating as valedictorian from the Lincoln Institute, Young attended Kentucky State College, graduating with a bachelor of science degree in 1941. In college, he met Margaret Buckner, whom he married in 1944. The couple had two daughters, Marcia Elaine and Lauren Lee.

Young enlisted in the U.S. Army for service in World War II, rising to the rank of first sergeant. Segregation in the U.S. military relegated African American servicemen to menial duties under the command of white officers. Young's pragmatism contributed to his becoming a mediator between disgruntled black servicemen and the white power structure. Finding he liked this role, he changed his career goal from that of doctor to social worker.

Young enrolled at the University of Minnesota, St. Paul, earning a master's degree in social work in 1947. He volunteered with the St. Paul chapter of the National Urban League in 1947 and became president of the Omaha, Nebraska, branch in 1950.

Young was appointed dean of the Atlanta University School of Social Work, where he worked from 1954 to 1961. During this time, he became president of the Georgia National Association for the Advancement of Colored People (NAACP). Although he is best known for his distinguished service as executive director of the National Urban League (1961-1971), Young also served as president of the National Association of Social Workers (1969-1971) and was an adviser on racial issues to Presidents John F. Kennedy, Lyndon B. Johnson, and Richard M. Nixon.

As executive director of the National Urban League, Young persuaded powerful white political, corporate, and philanthropic leaders to support the Civil Rights movement with the assertion that the movement was consistent with their political and economic interests. Outlining his assertions in two books, *To Be Equal* (1964) and *Beyond Racism* (1969), Young anticipated a future in which African Americans would be relegated to inner-city poverty as whites moved into suburban enclaves. In response, he outlined a federal plan based on integration, community organizing, tax incentives for businesses and industry, and abandonment of discriminatory employment, health care, and welfare practices. As an adviser to Presidents Kennedy and Johnson, Young presented a bold plan for eliminating poverty in black America, calling for federal expenditures of $145 billion over ten years. His became known as the "domestic Marshall Plan," and parts were later included in President Johnson's War on Poverty.

While attending a conference in Nigeria, Young drowned on March 11, 1971. President Nixon gave the eulogy at his funeral.

## SIGNIFICANCE

Young grew up amid a confluence of family, social, and political contexts that shaped his renowned ability to negotiate, mediate, organize, strategize, and subsequently to convince those in power that they would benefit from extending opportunities to disenfranchised African Americans. While he supported the 1963 March on Washington and other civil rights efforts, his tendency was to work within the white power structure rather than to march and rally against it. Young earned his place in history as a civil rights leader and social-work pioneer by persuading white leaders to support the Civil Rights movement and by leading the National Urban League to provide socieconomic programs that helped more African Americans become economically and civically productive. In the twenty-first century, numerous schools, bridges, scholarships, and social programs across the U.S. bear his name.

—*Darlene Grant*

## FURTHER READING

Dickerson, Dennis C. *Militant Mediator: Whitney M. Young.* Lexington: University Press of Kentucky, 2004. Examines Young's interracial leadership strategies within the context of the Civil Rights movement. Explores his success at securing white America's support for integration via inner-city renewal and jobs programs.

Weiss, Nancy J. *Whitney M. Young, Jr., and the Struggle for Civil Rights.* Princeton, N.J.: Princeton University Press, 1990. Examines Young's tenuous position negotiating between the power elite and the black community while establishing the previously beleaguered National Urban League as a major force for civil rights.

Wilkins, Pebbles W. "Young, Whitney Moore, Jr." In *Encyclopedia of Social Work*, edited by R. L. Edwards. 19th ed. Washington, D.C.: NASW Press, 1995. Young is of particular importance to the profession of social work as a social worker and civil rights pioneer, former dean of the Atlanta University School of Social Work, and president of the National Association of Social Workers.

Young, Whitney M., Jr. *Beyond Racism: Building an Open Society.* New York: McGraw-Hill, 1969. Anticipating a future that holds limited opportunities for African Americans, Young outlines a federal plan, called the Open Society, for their uplift and empowerment.

**SEE ALSO:** Ralph David Abernathy; Albert Raby; Bayard Rustin; Leon H. Sullivan; C. T. Vivian; Walter White; Roy Wilkins.

# Appendixes

# CHRONOLOGICAL LIST OF ENTRIES

*All personages appearing in this list are the subjects of articles in* Great Lives from History: African Americans. *The arrangement of personages in this list is chronological on the basis of birth years. Subjects of multiperson essays are listed separately.*

## 1701-1800

Amos Fortune (c. 1710)
Crispus Attucks (1723)
Benjamin Banneker (November 9, 1731)
Prince Hall (c. 1735)
Jean Baptiste Pointe du Sable (c. 1745)
Absalom Jones (November 6, 1746)
Phillis Wheatley (possibly 1753?)
Paul Cuffe (January 17, 1759)
Richard Allen (February 14, 1760)
Joshua Johnson (c. 1763)
James Forten (September 2, 1766)

Denmark Vesey (c. 1767)
Sally Hemings (1773)
Daniel Coker (c. 1780)
David Walker (September 28, 1785)
George Washington Bush (c. 1790)
Dred Scott (c. 1795)
Sojourner Truth (c. 1797)
Jim Beckwourth (April 26, 1798)
John Brown Russwurm (October 1, 1799)
Nat Turner (October 2, 1800)

## 1801-1850

Maria Stewart (1803)
Norbert Rillieux (March 17, 1806)
Henry Blair (c. 1807)
Ira Frederick Aldridge (July 24, 1807)
Benjamin Singleton (1809)
Joseph Cinque (c. 1811)
Martin Robison Delany (May 6, 1812)
Henry Highland Garnet (December 23, 1815)
Frederick Douglass (February, 1817?)
Alexander Crummell (March 3, 1819)
Oscar James Dunn (c. 1820)
Harriet Tubman (c. 1820)
Hiram Rhoades Revels (September 27, 1822)
William Craft (1824)
James Presley Ball (1825)
Master Juba (c. 1825)
Frances Ellen Watkins Harper (September 24, 1825)
Ellen Craft (1826)

James Madison Bell (April 3, 1826)
Edward Mitchell Bannister (c. 1828)
Patrick F. Healy (February 27, 1834)
Henry McNeal Turner (February 1, 1834)
Francis Lewis Cardozo (January 1, 1836)
P. B. S. Pinchback (May 10, 1837)
John Lawson (June 16, 1837)
Charlotte L. Forten Grimké (August 17, 1837)
John Willis Menard (April 3, 1838)
Robert Smalls (April 5, 1839)
William H. Carney (February 29, 1840)
Blanche Kelso Bruce (March 1, 1841)
Samuel Ferguson (January 1, 1842)
Allen Allensworth (April 7, 1842)
Edmonia Lewis (July 21, 1845)
Lewis Howard Latimer (September 4, 1848)
Blind Tom Bethune (May 25, 1849)
Andrew Jackson Beard (March 29, 1850)

## 1851-1860

Jan Ernst Matzeliger (September 15, 1852)
James Bland (October 22, 1854)
Daniel Hale Williams (January 18, 1856)

John E. Bruce (February 22, 1856)
Henry Ossian Flipper (March 21, 1856)
Booker T. Washington (April 15, 1856)

Granville T. Woods (April 23, 1856)
Henry Plummer Cheatham (December 27, 1857)
Charles Waddell Chesnutt (June 20, 1858)

Alexander Walters (August 1, 1858)
Henry Ossawa Tanner (June 21, 1859)
Henrietta Vinton Davis (August 15, 1860)

## 1861-1870

Isaac Burns Murphy (April 16, 1861)
George Washington Carver (July 12, 1861?)
Ida B. Wells-Barnett (July 16, 1862)
Mary Church Terrell (September 23, 1863)
Matthew Alexander Henson (August 8, 1866)
Harry T. Burleigh (December 2, 1866)
Madam C. J. Walker (December 23, 1867)

W. E. B. Du Bois (February 23, 1868)
John Hope (June 2, 1868)
Robert S. Abbott (November 24, 1868)
Scott Joplin (November 24, 1868)
Sissieretta Jones (January 5, 1869)
Willie Simms (January 16, 1870)
Bill Pickett (December 5, 1870)

## 1871-1880

Oscar DePriest (March 9, 1871)
James Weldon Johnson (June 17, 1871)
William Monroe Trotter (April 7, 1872)
Paul Laurence Dunbar (June 27, 1872)
W. C. Handy (November 16, 1873)
Arturo Alfonso Schomburg (January 24, 1874)
Charlotta Spears Bass (February 14, 1874)
Bert Williams (November 12, 1874)
Mary McLeod Bethune (July 10, 1875)
Alice Dunbar-Nelson (July 19, 1875)

Carter G. Woodson (December 19, 1875)
Father Divine (May, 1876)
Garrett Augustus Morgan (March 4, 1877)
Benjamin O. Davis, Sr. (July 1, 1877)
Jack Johnson (March 31, 1878)
Bill Robinson (May 25, 1878)
William Stanley Braithwaite (December 6, 1878)
Nannie Helen Burroughs (May 2, 1879)
Angelina Weld Grimké (February 27, 1880)

## 1881-1890

James Reese Europe (February 22, 1881)
James Winkfield (April 12, 1882)
Jessie Redmon Fauset (April 27, 1882)
R. Nathaniel Dett (October 11, 1882)
Charlotte Hawkins Brown (June 11, 1883)
Ernest Everett Just (August 14, 1883)
Oscar Micheaux (January 2, 1884)
King Oliver (December 19, 1885)
Noble Drew Ali (January 8, 1886)
Ma Rainey (April 26, 1886)

James Van Der Zee (June 29, 1886)
Alain Locke (September 13, 1886)
Eubie Blake (February 7, 1887)
Roland Hayes (June 3, 1887)
Marcus Garvey (August 17, 1887)
Cyril V. Briggs (May 28, 1888)
Sargent Johnson (October 7, 1888)
A. Philip Randolph (April 15, 1889)
Claude McKay (September 15, 1890)
Jelly Roll Morton (October 20, 1890)

## 1891-1900

Zora Neale Hurston (January 7, 1891)
Nella Larsen (April 13, 1891)
Louis T. Wright (July 23, 1891)

Bessie Coleman (January 26, 1892)
Augusta Savage (February 29, 1892)
Arthur George Gaston (July 4, 1892)

Perry Bradford (February 14, 1893)
Big Bill Broonzy (June 26, 1893 or 1898)
Walter White (July 1, 1893)
Charles S. Johnson (July 24, 1893)
Fritz Pollard (January 27, 1894)
Moms Mabley (March 19, 1894)
Bessie Smith (April 15, 1894)
Benjamin E. Mays (August 1, 1894)
Eugene Jacques Bullard (October 9, 1894)
Jean Toomer (December 26, 1894)
Florence Mills (January 25, 1895)
George S. Schuyler (February 25, 1895)
William Grant Still (May 11, 1895)
Hattie McDaniel (June 10, 1895)
Charles Hamilton Houston (September 3, 1895)

Hubert Fauntleroy Julian (January 5 or September 20, 1897)
Marian Anderson (February 27, 1897)
Elijah Muhammad (October 7, 1897)
Lillian Hardin Armstrong (February 3, 1898)
Melvin B. Tolson (February 6, 1898)
Paul Robeson (April 9, 1898)
Septima Poinsette Clark (May 3, 1898)
Eric Walrond (December 18, 1898)
Percy Lavon Julian (April 11, 1899)
Duke Ellington (April 29, 1899)
Aaron Douglas (May 26, 1899)
Marita Bonner (June 16, 1899)
Thomas A. Dorsey (July 1, 1899)
E. D. Nixon (July 22, 1899)
James Carmichael Evans (June 1, 1900)

## 1901-1910

Richmond Barthé (January 28, 1901)
William H. Johnson (March 18, 1901)
Sterling A. Brown (May 1, 1901)
Louis Armstrong (August 4, 1901)
Roy Wilkins (August 30, 1901)
Frederick D. Patterson (October 10, 1901)
Langston Hughes (February 1, 1902)
Louise Beavers (March 8, 1902)
Stepin Fetchit (May 30, 1902)
Arna Bontemps (October 13, 1902)
Cool Papa Bell (May 17, 1903)
Countée Cullen (May 30, 1903)
Ralph Bunche (August 7, 1903)
Benjamin J. Davis (September 8, 1903)
Ella Baker (December 13, 1903)
Earl Hines (December 28, 1903)
Benjamin Quarles (January 23, 1904)
Fats Waller (May 21, 1904)
Charles R. Drew (June 3, 1904)
Count Basie (August 21, 1904)
Horace Mann Bond (November 8, 1904)
Vance Hunter Marchbanks (January 12, 1905)
Leroy Carr (March 27, 1905)
Big Boy Crudup (August 24, 1905)
Eddie "Rochester" Anderson (September 18, 1905)
E. Simms Campbell (January 2, 1906)
Little Brother Montgomery (April 18, 1906)

Josephine Baker (June 3, 1906)
Satchel Paige (July 7, 1906)
Canada Lee (March 3, 1907)
Dorothy West (June 2, 1907)
Benny Carter (August 8, 1907)
Charles Alston (November 28, 1907)
Cab Calloway (December 25, 1907)
Robert C. Weaver (December 29, 1907)
Jane Matilda Bolin (April 11, 1908)
Lionel Hampton (April 20, 1908)
Thurgood Marshall (July 2, 1908)
Richard Wright (September 4, 1908)
Ann Petry (October 12, 1908)
Adam Clayton Powell, Jr. (November 29, 1908)
Chick Webb (February 10, 1909)
Katherine Dunham (June 22, 1909)
Chester Himes (July 29, 1909)
William Thomas Fontaine (December 2, 1909)
Austin Hansen (1910)
Bayard Rustin (March 17, 1910)
Harry Carney (April 1, 1910)
Mary Lou Williams (May 8, 1910)
Scatman Crothers (May 23, 1910)
Milt Hinton (June 23, 1910)
Cootie Williams (July 24, 1910)
Vivien Thomas (August 29, 1910)
Pauli Murray (November 20, 1910)

## 1911-1920

Clarence M. Mitchell, Jr. (March 8, 1911)
Honi Coles (April 2, 1911)
Big Joe Turner (May 18, 1911)
Albert Buford Cleage, Jr. (June 13, 1911)
Romare Bearden (September 2, 1911)
Mahalia Jackson (October 26, 1911)
Buck O'Neil (November 13, 1911)
Josh Gibson (December 21, 1911)
Dorothy Height (March 24, 1912)
Jo Ann Gibson Robinson (April 17, 1912)
Gordon Parks, Sr. (November 30, 1912)
Henry Armstrong (December 12, 1912)
Benjamin O. Davis, Jr. (December 18, 1912)
Rosa Parks (February 4, 1913)
Margaret Allison Bonds (March 3, 1913)
Muddy Waters (April 4, 1913)
Jesse Owens (September 12, 1913)
Cholly Atkins (September 30, 1913)
Archie Moore (December 13, 1913 or 1916)
Jersey Joe Walcott (January 31, 1914)
Ralph Ellison (March 1, 1914)
Joe Louis (May 13, 1914)
Sun Ra (May 22, 1914)
Billy Eckstine (July 8, 1914)
Kenneth Clark (July 24, 1914)
Woody Strode (July 28, 1914)
Fayard Nicholas (October 20, 1914)
Daisy Bates (November 11, 1914)
Owen Dodson (November 28, 1914)
John Henrik Clarke (January 1, 1915)
John Hope Franklin (January 2, 1915)
Billie Holiday (April 7, 1915)
John R. Fox (May 18, 1915)
Willie Dixon (July 1, 1915)
Margaret Walker (July 7, 1915)
Hughie Lee-Smith (September 20, 1915)
Albert Murray (May 12, 1916)

Spottswood W. Robinson III (July 26, 1916)
Frank Yerby (September 5, 1916)
Alice Childress (October 12, 1916)
Ulysses Kay (January 7, 1917)
Ella Fitzgerald (April 25, 1917)
Gwendolyn Brooks (June 7, 1917)
Lena Horne (June 30, 1917)
John Lee Hooker (August 22, 1917)
Jacob Lawrence (September 7, 1917)
Fannie Lou Hamer (October 6, 1917)
Thelonious Monk (October 10, 1917)
Dizzy Gillespie (October 21, 1917)
Ossie Davis (December 18, 1917)
Tom Bradley (December 29, 1917)
John H. Johnson (January 19, 1918)
Pearl Bailey (March 29, 1918)
Coleman Young (May 24, 1918)
Katherine G. Johnson (August 26, 1918)
Kenny Washington (August 31, 1918)
Jimmy Blanton (October 5, 1918)
Professor Longhair (December 19, 1918)
Herbie Nichols (January 3, 1919)
Dorothy Lavinia Brown (January 7, 1919)
Jackie Robinson (January 31, 1919)
Nat King Cole (March 17, 1919)
David Harold Blackwell (April 24, 1919)
Lloyd Richards (June 29, 1919)
Art Blakey (October 11, 1919)
Dorie Miller (October 12, 1919)
Edward W. Brooke (October 26, 1919)
Pearl Primus (November 29, 1919)
Jane Cooke Wright (November 30, 1919)
Roy DeCarava (December 9, 1919)
James L. Farmer, Jr. (January 12, 1920)
Otis Boykin (August 29, 1920)
Charlie Parker (August 29, 1920)

## 1921-1930

Harold Nicholas (March 27, 1921)
Sugar Ray Robinson (May 3, 1921)
James A. Emanuel (June 15, 1921)
Ezzard Charles (July 7, 1921)
Whitney Young (July 31, 1921)
Alex Haley (August 11, 1921)
Joseph Lowery (October 6, 1921)

Roy Campanella (November 19, 1921)
Fred Shuttlesworth (March 18, 1922)
Harold Washington (April 15, 1922)
Charles Mingus (April 22, 1922)
George Walker (June 27, 1922)
Ernest Withers (August 7, 1922)
Samuel R. Pierce, Jr. (September 8, 1922)

Charles Evers (September 11, 1922)
Charles Brown (September 13, 1922)
Leon H. Sullivan (October 16, 1922)
Dorothy Dandridge (November 9, 1922)
Redd Foxx (December 9, 1922)
Faye Adams (c. 1923)
Dexter Gordon (February 27, 1923)
Louise Meriwether (May 8, 1923)
George Russell (June 23, 1923)
Mari Evans (July 16, 1923)
Fats Navarro (September 24, 1923)
Alice Coachman (November 9, 1923)
Larry Doby (December 13, 1923)
Max Roach (January 10, 1924)
Sonny Stitt (February 2, 1924)
Sarah Vaughan (March 27, 1924)
Evelyn Boyd Granville (May 1, 1924)
Patricia Roberts Harris (May 31, 1924)
C. Eric Lincoln (July 23, 1924)
C. T. Vivian (July 28 or 30, 1924)
James Baldwin (August 2, 1924)
Ruby Dee (October 27, 1924)
Shirley Chisholm (November 30, 1924)
Benjamin Hooks (January 31, 1925)
Robert Franklin Williams (February 26, 1925)
Gene Ammons (April 14, 1925)
Malcolm X (May 19, 1925)
Medgar Evers (July 2, 1925)
B. B. King (September 16, 1925)
Sammy Davis, Jr. (December 8, 1925)
Hosea Williams (January 5, 1926)
Ralph David Abernathy (March 11, 1926)
Mervyn Dymally (May 12, 1926)
Miles Davis (May 26, 1926)
Julius Wesley Becton, Jr. (June 29, 1926)
Betye Saar (July 30, 1926)
Andrew Felton Brimmer (September 13, 1926)
Clifton Reginald Wharton, Jr. (September 13, 1926)
John Coltrane (September 23, 1926)
Ray Brown (October 13, 1926)

Chuck Berry (October 18, 1926)
Eartha Kitt (January 17, 1927)
Leontyne Price (February 10, 1927)
Sidney Poitier (February 20, 1927)
Harry Belafonte (March 1, 1927)
Coretta Scott King (April 27, 1927)
Brock Peters (July 2, 1927)
David Dinkins (July 10, 1927)
Althea Gibson (August 25, 1927)
C. DeLores Tucker (October 4, 1927)
Robert Guillaume (November 30, 1927)
Fats Domino (February 26, 1928)
Earl Lloyd (April 3, 1928)
Maya Angelou (April 4, 1928)
Johnny Griffin (April 24, 1928)
Horace Silver (September 2, 1928)
Cannonball Adderley (September 15, 1928)
James Lawson (September 22, 1928)
James Forman (October 4, 1928)
Bo Diddley (December 30, 1928)
Sonny Liston (January, 1929, or May 8, 1932)
Martin Luther King, Jr. (January 15, 1929)
Paule Marshall (April 9, 1929)
John Conyers, Jr. (May 16, 1929)
Meredith C. Gourdine (September 26, 1929)
Dutch Morial (October 9, 1929)
Edward Blackwell (October 10, 1929)
Berry Gordy, Jr. (November 28, 1929)
Bobby Blue Bland (January 27, 1930)
Ornette Coleman (March 19, 1930)
Little Walter (May 1, 1930)
Lorraine Hansberry (May 19, 1930)
Charles Rangel (June 11, 1930)
Thomas Sowell (June 30, 1930)
Sonny Rollins (September 7, 1930)
Ray Charles (September 23, 1930)
Faith Ringgold (October 8, 1930)
Clifford Brown (October 30, 1930)
Odetta (December 31, 1930)

## 1931-1940

Alvin Ailey (January 5, 1931)
James Earl Jones (January 17, 1931)
L. Douglas Wilder (January 17, 1931)
Sam Cooke (January 22, 1931)
Ernie Banks (January 31, 1931)
Toni Morrison (February 18, 1931)

Ivan Dixon (April 6, 1931)
Willie Mays (May 6, 1931)
Adrienne Kennedy (September 13, 1931)
Ike Turner (November 5, 1931)
J. California Cooper (November 10, 1931)
Andrew Young (March 12, 1932)

Meadowlark Lemon (April 25, 1932)
Jackie McLean (May 17, 1932)
Addison Gayle, Jr. (June 2, 1932)
Melvin Van Peebles (August 21, 1932)
Maury Wills (October 2, 1932)
Yvonne Brathwaite Burke (October 5, 1932)
Dick Gregory (October 12, 1932)
Alvin Batiste (November 7, 1932)
Clyde McPhatter (November 15, 1932)
James E. Cheek (December 4, 1932)
Little Richard (December 5, 1932)
Nichelle Nichols (December 28, 1932)
Ernest J. Gaines (January 15, 1933)
Albert Raby (February 19, 1933)
Nina Simone (February 21, 1933)
Lee Calhoun (February 23, 1933)
Godfrey Cambridge (February 26, 1933)
Lloyd Price (March 9, 1933)
Quincy Jones (March 14, 1933)
Myrlie Evers-Williams (March 17, 1933)
Tony Brown (April 11, 1933)
James Brown (May 3, 1933)
Louis Farrakhan (May 11, 1933)
Rod Paige (June 17, 1933)
Gerald William Barrax (June 21, 1933)
James Meredith (June 25, 1933)
Joycelyn Elders (August 13, 1933)
Asa Grant Hilliard III (August 22, 1933)
Wayne Shorter (August 25, 1933)
Flip Wilson (December 8, 1933)
Cicely Tyson (December 19, 1933)
Huey "Piano" Smith (January 26, 1934)
Bill White (January 28, 1934)
Hank Aaron (February 5, 1934)
Bill Russell (February 12, 1934)
Audre Lorde (February 18, 1934)
John Brooks Slaughter (March 16, 1934)
Willie Brown (March 20, 1934)
Arthur Mitchell (March 27, 1934)
Alvin Francis Poussaint (May 15, 1934)
Roy Innis (June 6, 1934)
Jackie Wilson (June 9, 1934)
Lee Elder (July 14, 1934)
Henry Dumas (July 20, 1934)
Roberto Clemente (August 18, 1934)
Sonia Sanchez (September 9, 1934)
Elgin Baylor (September 16, 1934)
Amiri Baraka (October 7, 1934)
Ellis Marsalis, Jr. (November 14, 1934)
Floyd Patterson (January 4, 1935)

Earl G. Graves, Sr. (January 9, 1935)
Ed Bullins (July 2, 1935)
Diahann Carroll (July 17, 1935)
Vernon Jordan (August 15, 1935)
Rafer Johnson (August 18, 1935)
Eldridge Cleaver (August 31, 1935)
Frank Robinson (August 31, 1935)
Robert H. Lawrence, Jr. (October 2, 1935)
Bob Gibson (November 9, 1935)
Ron Dellums (November 24, 1935)
William Julius Wilson (December 20, 1935)
Sam Cornish (December 22, 1935)
Jim Brown (February 17, 1936)
Barbara Jordan (February 21, 1936)
Marion Barry (March 6, 1936)
Virginia Hamilton (March 12, 1936)
Jayne Cortez (May 10, 1936)
Louis Gossett, Jr. (May 27, 1936)
Betty Shabazz (May 28, 1936)
Lucille Clifton (June 27, 1936)
Wally Amos (July 1, 1936)
June Jordan (July 9, 1936)
Wilt Chamberlain (August 21, 1936)
Marva Collins (August 31, 1936)
James Bevel (October 19, 1936)
Bobby Seale (October 22, 1936)
Leon Forrest (January 8, 1937)
Leonard Jeffries (January 19, 1937)
Garrett Morris (February 1, 1937)
Claude Brown (February 23, 1937)
Colin Powell (April 5, 1937)
Billy Dee Williams (April 6, 1937)
Hazel R. O'Leary (May 17, 1937)
Archie Shepp (May 24, 1937)
Morgan Freeman (June 1, 1937)
Eleanor Holmes Norton (June 13, 1937)
Bill Cosby (July 12, 1937)
Roland Burris (August 3, 1937)
Walter Dean Myers (August 12, 1937)
Alice Coltrane (August 27, 1937)
Johnnie Cochran (October 2, 1937)
Lenny Wilkens (October 28, 1937)
William Melvin Kelley (November 1, 1937)
Sister Thea Bowman (December 29, 1937)
Curt Flood (January 18, 1938)
Etta James (January 25, 1938)
Ishmael Reed (February 22, 1938)
Michael S. Harper (March 18, 1938)
Charley Pride (March 18, 1938)
Maynard Jackson (March 23, 1938)

James H. Cone (August 5, 1938)
Maxine Waters (August 15, 1938)
Diane Nash (May 15, 1938)
Oscar Robertson (November 24, 1938)
McCoy Tyner (December 11, 1938)
Charles Fuller (March 5, 1939)
Toni Cade Bambara (March 25, 1939)
Marvin Gaye (April 2, 1939)
Max Robinson (May 1, 1939)
Ralph Boston (May 9, 1939)
Paul Winfield (May 22, 1939)
Al Young (May 31, 1939)
Cleavon Little (June 1, 1939)
Marian Wright Edelman (June 6, 1939)
Bernie Casey (June 8, 1939)
Lou Brock (June 18, 1939)
Barbara Chase-Riboud (June 26, 1939)

Tina Turner (November 29, 1939)
Ernie Davis (December 14, 1939)
Julian Bond (January 14, 1940)
Smokey Robinson (February 19, 1940)
John Robert Lewis (February 21, 1940)
Solomon Burke (March 21, 1940)
George Edward Alcorn (March 22, 1940)
Herbie Hancock (April 12, 1940)
Bernard Shaw (May 22, 1940)
Mary Hatwood Futrell (May 24, 1940)
Wilma Rudolph (June 23, 1940)
James E. Clyburn (July 21, 1940)
George Clinton (July 22, 1940)
Pharaoh Sanders (October 13, 1940)
Richard Pryor (December 1, 1940)
Dionne Warwick (December 12, 1940)

# 1941-1950

Frederick Drew Gregory (January 7, 1941)
Aaron Neville (January 24, 1941)
David Satcher (March 2, 1941)
John Edgar Wideman (June 14, 1941)
Ed Bradley (June 22, 1941)
Stokely Carmichael (June 29, 1941)
Randall Robinson (July 6, 1941)
Maulana Karenga (July 14, 1941)
Emmett Till (July 25, 1941)
Ron Brown (August 1, 1941)
William H. Gray III (August 20, 1941)
Otis Redding (September 9, 1941)
Jeremiah Wright (September 22, 1941)
Chubby Checker (October 3, 1941)
Jesse Jackson (October 18, 1941)
Muhammad Ali (January 17, 1942)
Huey P. Newton (February 17, 1942)
Haki R. Madhubuti (February 23, 1942)
Charlayne Hunter-Gault (February 27, 1942)
Aretha Franklin (March 25, 1942)
Samuel R. Delany (April 1, 1942)
Taj Mahal (May 17, 1942)
Togo West (June 21, 1942)
Andraé Crouch (July 1, 1942)
Connie Hawkins (July 17, 1942)
Molefi Kete Asante (August 14, 1942)
Isaac Hayes (August 20, 1942)
Guion Bluford (November 22, 1942)

Jimi Hendrix (November 27, 1942)
Bob Hayes (December 20, 1942)
Elaine Brown (March 2, 1943)
Houston A. Baker, Jr. (March 22, 1943)
Leslie Uggams (May 25, 1943)
James Chaney (May 30, 1943)
Nikki Giovanni (June 7, 1943)
Willie Davenport (June 8, 1943)
Faye Wattleton (July 8, 1943)
Arthur Ashe (July 10, 1943)
Calvin Peete (July 18, 1943)
Mildred D. Taylor (September 13, 1943)
Willie L. Williams (October 1, 1943)
H. Rap Brown (October 4, 1943)
Joe Frazier (January 12, 1944)
Pat Parker (January 20, 1944)
Angela Davis (January 26, 1944)
Alice Walker (February 9, 1944)
Henry Threadgill (February, 15 1944)
Diana Ross (March 26, 1944)
Patti LaBelle (May 24, 1944)
Gladys Knight (May 28, 1944)
Tommie Smith (June 6, 1944)
Tim Reid (December 19, 1944)
Walt Frazier (March 29, 1945)
August Wilson (April 27, 1945)
Anthony Braxton (June 4, 1945)
John Carlos (June 5, 1945)

Ruth Simmons (July 3, 1945)
Gene Upshaw (August 15, 1945)
Willie Lanier (August 21, 1945)
Wyomia Tyus (August 29, 1945)
Jessye Norman (September 15, 1945)
Rod Carew (October 1, 1945)
Donny Hathaway (October 1, 1945)
Larry D. Thompson (November 15, 1945)
Elvin Hayes (November 17, 1945)
Stanley Crouch (December 14, 1945)
Claude M. Steele (January 1, 1946)
Shelby Steele (January 1, 1946)
Gregory Hines (February 14, 1946)
Robert L. Johnson (April 8, 1946)
Al Green (April 13, 1946)
Reggie Jackson (May 18, 1946)
Shirley Ann Jackson (August 5, 1946)
Charles F. Bolden, Jr. (August 19, 1946)
Bob Beamon (August 29, 1946)
Joe Greene (September 24, 1946)
Ben Vereen (October 10, 1946)
Michelle Cliff (November 2, 1946)
Wanda Coleman (November 13, 1946)
Barbara Smith (November 16, 1946)
Art Shell (November 26, 1946)
Lee Evans (February 25, 1947)
Kareem Abdul-Jabbar (April 16, 1947)
Yusef Komunyakaa (April 29, 1947)
Clarence E. Page (June 2, 1947)
Octavia E. Butler (June 22, 1947)
Jimmie Walker (June 25, 1947)
O. J. Simpson (July 9, 1947)
Alexis M. Herman (July 16, 1947)
Danny Glover (July 22, 1947)

Carol E. Moseley Braun (August 16, 1947)
Wilton D. Gregory (December 7, 1947)
Benjamin Chavis (January 22, 1948)
Patricia Hill Collins (May 1, 1948)
Phylicia Rashad (June 19, 1948)
Clarence Thomas (June 23, 1948)
Kathleen Battle (August 13, 1948)
Nell Carter (September 13, 1948)
Bryant Gumbel (September 29, 1948)
Ntozake Shange (October 18, 1948)
Kweisi Mfume (October 24, 1948)
Samuel L. Jackson (December 21, 1948)
Donna Summer (December 31, 1948)
George Foreman (January 10, 1949)
Jamaica Kincaid (May 25, 1949)
Pam Grier (May 26, 1949)
Dusty Baker (June 15, 1949)
Lionel Richie (June 20, 1949)
Vida Blue (July 28, 1949)
Whoopi Goldberg (November 13, 1949)
Gayl Jones (November 23, 1949)
Sheila Jackson Lee (January 12, 1950)
Debbie Allen (January 16, 1950)
Gloria Naylor (January 25, 1950)
Natalie Cole (February 6, 1950)
Bebe Moore Campbell (February 18, 1950)
Julius Erving (February 22, 1950)
Franco Harris (March 7, 1950)
Stevie Wonder (May 13, 1950)
Alan Keyes (August 7, 1950)
David Bradley (September 7, 1950)
Henry Louis Gates, Jr. (September 16, 1950)
Anna Deavere Smith (September 18, 1950)
Ronald E. McNair (October 21, 1950)

## 1951-1960

Eric Holder (January 21, 1951)
Charles S. Dutton (January 30, 1951)
Kenneth Chenault (June 2, 1951)
Terry McMillan (October 18, 1951)
Walter Mosley (January 12, 1952)
Bill T. Jones (February 15, 1952)
Steven Barnes (March 1, 1952)
Sylvia M. Rhone (March 11, 1952)
Rita Dove (August 28, 1952)
Bell Hooks (September 25, 1952)
Anita DeFrantz (October 4, 1952)

Julie Dash (October 22, 1952)
Cornel West (June 2, 1953)
Gus Williams (October 10, 1953)
Alfre Woodard (November 8, 1953)
Mike Espy (November 30, 1953)
Oprah Winfrey (January 29, 1954)
Juan Williams (April 10, 1954)
David A. Paterson (May 20, 1954)
Walter Payton (July 25, 1954)
Al Roker (August 20, 1954)
George C. Wolfe (September 23, 1954)

Al Sharpton (October 3, 1954)
Stephen L. Carter (October 26, 1954)
Condoleezza Rice (November 14, 1954)
Denzel Washington (December 28, 1954)
Earl Campbell (March 29, 1955)
Helene Doris Gayle (August 16, 1955)
Edwin Moses (August 31, 1955)
Gwen Ifill (September 29, 1955)
Kerry James Marshall (October 17, 1955)
Deval Patrick (January 31, 1956)
Arsenio Hall (February 12, 1956)
Clarence Otis, Jr. (April 11, 1956)
Sugar Ray Leonard (May 17, 1956)
Ray Nagin (June 11, 1956)
Montel Williams (July 3, 1956)
Anita Hill (July 30, 1956)
Mae C. Jemison (October 17, 1956)
Lorene Cary (November 29, 1956)
Darryl Dawkins (January 11, 1957)
Mario Van Peebles (January 15, 1957)
Robert Townsend (February 6, 1957)
LeVar Burton (February 16, 1957)
Spike Lee (March 20, 1957)
Evelyn Ashford (April 15, 1957)
T. D. Jakes (June 9, 1957)
Russell Simmons (October 4, 1957)

Bernie Mac (October 5, 1957)
Leonard Pitts (October 11, 1957)
Brian Stokes Mitchell (October 31, 1957)
J. C. Watts (November 18, 1957)
Linda Johnson Rice (March 22, 1958)
Babyface (April 10, 1958)
Prince (June 7, 1958)
Angela Bassett (August 16, 1958)
Michael Jackson (August 29, 1958)
Neil deGrasse Tyson (October 5, 1958)
Mike Singletary (October 9, 1958)
Michael Steele (October 19, 1958)
Annette Gordon-Reed (November 19, 1958)
Rickey Henderson (December 25, 1958)
Kimberlé Williams Crenshaw (1959)
Lawrence Taylor (February 4, 1959)
Irene Cara (March 18, 1959)
Lynette Woodard (August 12, 1959)
Magic Johnson (August 14, 1959)
Florence Griffith-Joyner (December 21, 1959)
Ed Gordon (1960)
Courtney B. Vance (March 12, 1960)
Marcus Allen (March 26, 1960)
Tony Gwynn (May 9, 1960)
Eric Dickerson (September 2, 1960)
Jean-Michel Basquiat (December 22, 1960)

## 1961-1970

Eddie Murphy (April 3, 1961)
Isiah Thomas (April 30, 1961)
Carl Lewis (July 1, 1961)
Forest Whitaker (July 15, 1961)
Laurence Fishburne (July 30, 1961)
Barack Obama (August 4, 1961)
Wynton Marsalis (October 18, 1961)
Jackie Joyner-Kersee (March 3, 1962)
M. C. Hammer (March 30, 1962)
Lewis Gordon (May 12, 1962)
Elizabeth Alexander (May 30, 1962)
Ilyasah Shabazz (July 22, 1962)
Wesley Snipes (July 31, 1962)
Patrick Ewing (August 5, 1962)
Jerry Rice (October 13, 1962)
Evander Holyfield (October 19, 1962)
Bo Jackson (November 30, 1962)
Cyrus Chestnut (January 17, 1963)
Hakeem Olajuwon (January 21, 1963)

Michael Jordan (February 17, 1963)
Charles Barkley (February 20, 1963)
Suzette Charles (March 2, 1963)
Vanessa Williams (March 18, 1963)
Karl Malone (July 24, 1963)
Damon Allen (July 29, 1963)
Whitney Houston (August 9, 1963)
Cheryl Miller (January 3, 1964)
Michelle Obama (January 17, 1964)
Cedric the Entertainer (April 24, 1964)
Barry Bonds (July 24, 1964)
Blair Underwood (August 25, 1964)
Tavis Smiley (September 3, 1964)
Joseph Simmons (November 14, 1964)
Don Cheadle (November 29, 1964)
Dr. Dre (February 18, 1965)
Rod Woodson (March 10, 1965)
Jesse Jackson, Jr. (March 11, 1965)
David Robinson (August 6, 1965)

Viola Davis (August 11, 1965)
Scottie Pippen (September 25, 1965)
John McWhorter (October 6, 1965)
Jeffrey Wright (December 7, 1965)
Chris Rock (February 7, 1966)
Rodney Peete (March 16, 1966)
Darius Rucker (May 13, 1966)
Janet Jackson (May 16, 1966)
Mike Tyson (June 30, 1966)
Tim Brown (July 22, 1966)
Halle Berry (August 14, 1966)
Toni Braxton (October 7, 1966)
Gail Devers (November 19, 1966)
Debi Thomas (March 25, 1967)
Deion Sanders (August 9, 1967)
Macy Gray (September 6, 1967)
Michael Johnson (September 13, 1967)
Jamie Foxx (December 13, 1967)

Cuba Gooding, Jr. (January 2, 1968)
John Singleton (January 6, 1968)
L. L. Cool J. (January 14, 1968)
Frank Thomas (May 27, 1968)
Barry Sanders (July 16, 1968)
Will Smith (September 25, 1968)
Mellody Hobson (April 3, 1969)
Emmitt Smith (May 15, 1969)
Ice Cube (June 15, 1969)
Tyler Perry (September 13, 1969)
Wyclef Jean (October 17, 1969)
Puff Daddy (November 4, 1969)
Ken Griffey, Jr. (November 21, 1969)
Jay-Z (December 4, 1969)
Queen Latifah (March 18, 1970)
Mariah Carey (March 27, 1970)
Audra McDonald (July 3, 1970)
Tyson Beckford (December 19, 1970)

## 1971-1990

Mary J. Blige (January 11, 1971)
Tupac Shakur (June 16, 1971)
Briana Scurry (September 7, 1971)
Snoop Dogg (October 20, 1971)
Tyrone Wheatley (January 19, 1972)
Shaquille O'Neal (March 6, 1972)
Dwayne Johnson (May 2, 1972)
Lisa Leslie (July 7, 1972)
Benjamin T. Jealous (January 18, 1973)
Marshall Faulk (February 26, 1973)
Omar Epps (July 20, 1973)
Dave Chappelle (August 24, 1973)
Savion Glover (November 19, 1973)
Tyra Banks (December 4, 1973)
Terrell Owens (December 7, 1973)
Derek Jeter (June 26, 1974)
Kimora Lee Simmons (May 3, 1975)
Ray Lewis (May 15, 1975)
Lauryn Hill (May 26, 1975)
Allen Iverson (June 7, 1975)
50 Cent (July 6, 1975)
India.Arie (October 3, 1975)
Marion Jones (October 12, 1975)
Tiger Woods (December 30, 1975)
Tim Duncan (April 25, 1976)

Kevin Garnett (May 19, 1976)
Chauncey Billups (September 25, 1976)
Dominique Dawes (November 20, 1976)
Donovan McNabb (November 25, 1976)
Kanye West (June 8, 1977)
Paul Pierce (October 13, 1977)
Kenyon Martin (December 30, 1977)
Kobe Bryant (August 23, 1978)
Ed Reed (September 11, 1978)
Usher (October 14, 1978)
Aaliyah (January 16, 1979)
Chris Owens (March 1, 1979)
Venus Williams (June 17, 1980)
David West (August 29, 1980)
Alicia Keys (January 25, 1981)
Antonio Bryant (March 9, 1981)
Beyoncé Knowles (September 4, 1981)
Jennifer Hudson (September 12, 1981)
Serena Williams (September 26, 1981)
Shani Davis (August 13, 1982)
LeBron James (December 30, 1984)
Chris Paul (May 6, 1985)
Dwight Howard (December 8, 1985)
Rihanna (February 20, 1988)

# MEDIAGRAPHY

*Approximately 92 percent of the following mediagraphy lists videos, with the other 8 percent made up of films and music (compact discs and rare cassettes).* Amistad *and race movies such as* Hi De Ho *and* Reet, Petite, and Gone *are among the films listed; one obvious yet historically important exception is D. W. Griffith's* The Birth of a Nation. *Noteworthy examples of CDs include* Black Folk Music in America *(volumes 1 and 2) and* Voices of the Civil Rights Movement: Black American Freedom Songs, 1960-1966. *These materials not only provide useful supplements to those studying African American biography and history but also, for research and classroom purposes, can be accessed via searches on the titles through WorldCat, http://www.worldcat.org, a free online catalog that allows users to locate copies held in collections of libraries around the world.*

**Title:** *Affirmative Action and Reaction*
**Released:** 1995
**Summary:** Considers how African Americans' and white Americans' understandings of affirmative action differ, whether it was still needed in 1995 as a remedy for the current effects of past discrimination, and what, if any, programmatic changes should be implemented.

**Title:** *African Americans*
**Released:** 1994
**Summary:** Cultural customs are surveyed with the help of three generations of an African family. Reasons for emigration are discussed, and the impact of African migration on the growth of the United States is analyzed.

**Title:** *Africans in America: America's Journey Through Slavery*
**Released:** 1998
**Summary:** Explores the dilemmas faced by persons of African descent in the United States, primarily from the arrival of the first slaves to the end of the Civil War, while tracing the American social compact vis-à-vis slavery.

**Title:** *Alberta Hunter: My Castle's Rockin'*
**Released:** 1992
**Summary:** Alberta Hunter's more than forty-year career as a blues vocalist and nurse is detailed in this video. Includes a performance at the Cookery in New York City and hits such as "Darktown Strutter's Ball" and "Handy Man."

**Title:** *Alice Walker*
**Released:** 1989
**Summary:** Evelyn White interviews Walker, who reads excerpts from *Revolutionary Petunias and Other Poems*, *Horses Make a Landscape Look More Beautiful*, *The Color Purple*, and *The Temple of My Familiar*.

**Title:** *Almos' a Man*
**Released:** 1977
**Summary:** Based on "The Man Who Was Almost a Man" in the 1961 *Eight Men* anthology. Set in the rural South, the short story shows a young African American man's struggles to concretize his identity.

**Title:** *Always for Pleasure*
**Released:** 1978
**Summary:** Documents various aspects of New Orleans culture, such as music, food, and celebrations. Black Indian traditions and the work of the Wild Tchoupitoulas (the Neville brothers, George Porter, Jr., Teddy Royal, and others) are showcased.

**Title:** *American Apartheid*
**Released:** 1996
**Summary:** Sketches the emergence of two societies, black vs. white, poor vs. rich, uneducated vs. educated, not connected vs. connected, living in fear vs. not living in fear, and contains input from Louis Farrakhan, Johnnie Cochran, and Jesse Jackson.

**Title:** *American Passages: Slavery and Freedom,* **volume 7**
**Released:** 2003
**Summary:** Critiques slavery through the rhetorical vehicles found in Frederick Douglass's *Narrative of the Life of Frederick Douglass*, Harriet Jacobs's *Incidents in the Life of a Slave Girl*, and Harriet Beecher Stowe's *Uncle Tom's Cabin*.

**Title:** *Amistad*
**Released:** 1997
**Summary:** This feature film depicts the 1839 uprising on a slave ship in U.S. waters and subsequent legal battles to determine the captives' civil status. The boilerplate

happy ending partially discounts the havoc that slavery wreaked on people's lives.

**Title:** *At the Jazz Band Ball: Early Hot Jazz, Song and Dance, 1925-1933*
**Released:** 1993
**Summary:** Film clips of various musical and dance performances featuring Duke Ellington, Louis Armstrong, Paul Whiteman, the Dorsey Brothers Orchestra, Bill Robinson, Bessie Smith, and Bix Beiderbecke as representative performers from the Harlem Renaissance era.

**Title:** *Berkeley in the Sixties*
**Released:** 1990
**Summary:** Outlines the impact that the nascent Black Panther Party and some of its leaders, such as Huey P. Newton, along with Jimi Hendrix's music, had on Berkeley in the 1960's.

**Title:** *Bill Cosby on Prejudice*
**Released:** 1972
**Summary:** Satiric monologue about a composite bigot that spews hate against all minorities through blunt and brutal language. Targets include "niggers," Mexicans, Jews, the Irish, Scots, whites in general, women, children, religious groups, and senior citizens.

**Title:** *Billboards*
**Released:** 1994
**Summary:** Describes an artistic collaboration between Prince and the Joffrey Ballet, including an extended rendition of "Thunder," "Sometimes It Snows in April," "Baby I'm a Star," "Purple Rain," and "I Wanna Melt with U."

**Title:** *Biography: Frederick Douglass*
**Released:** 2005
**Summary:** Contemplates Douglass's analysis of the Civil War as a moral crusade against slavery, his labors as an abolitionist and Union propagandist, his activities as a recruiter of black military volunteers, and his misgivings about the efficacy of Reconstruction policies. Highlights various lectures.

**Title:** *Black America: The North, or the End of Illusions*
**Released:** 1993
**Summary:** Surveys the hopes and dreams of African Americans living in New York and Chicago, including

the deleterious realities of urban environments and attempts to break this cycle through the creation of positive familial environments.

**Title:** *Black and White*
**Released:** 1993
**Summary:** An African American woman who passed for white details why she made sure that her birth certificate identified her as black. The use of phenotype as a discriminating factor is dramatically depicted.

**Title:** *Black Folk Music in America*, **volumes 1 and 2**
**Released:** 1993
**Summary:** John Sellers samples the rich African American musical space, including "Sometimes I Feel Like a Motherless Child," "Go Down, Moses," "Michael, Row the Boat Ashore," and "Steal Away to Jesus." Volume 2 includes "Free at Last, Free at Last, Thank God Almighty, I'm Free at Last," "We Shall Overcome," "I Wonder When I'll Get to Be Called a Man," "Hallelujah, I'm a-Travelin'," and "Goin' Down the Road Feelin' Bad."

**Title:** *Black History: Lost, Stolen or Strayed*
**Released:** 1968
**Summary:** U.S. historians' ignoring, downplaying, and improper documentation of several African American achievements— such as medical advances made by African American doctors and sacrifices made during the Civil War—are probed, including the film industry's discriminatory practices.

**Title:** *Black History in America*
**Released:** 1988
**Summary:** Series discusses slavery from 1681 to 1860, the last third of the nineteenth century through the Niagara movement, roughly the first five decades of the twentieth century, Black Revolutionary movements, the Montgomery bus boycott and the 1965 Voting Rights Act, and the 1966-1988 period.

**Title:** *Black Is . . . Black Ain't*
**Released:** 1995
**Summary:** Examines questions about the potential damage caused by self-imposed definitions of, and litmus tests for, essential African American "blackness"; "real" African American men; and "true" African American women vis-à-vis white stereotyping of African Americans.

**Title:** *Black, White and Angry*
**Released:** 1995
**Summary:** Within the context of progress made, relates the complicated interactions between African Americans and European Americans at work and in the community, with reference to myths about the two groups and the role of politics and politicians. Ponders how future intergroup relations may evolve.

**Title:** *Bluesland: A Portrait in American Music*
**Released:** 1993
**Summary:** Chronicles the development of the blues as a genre through the work of Son House, William "Leadbelly" Ledbetter, Bill Broonzy, Bessie Smith, Jimmy Rushing, T-Bone Walker, Elmore James, Sonny Boy Williamson, B. B. King, and others.

**Title:** *Brother Outsider: The Life of Bayard Rustin*
**Released:** 2002
**Summary:** Details, through interviews and writings, Rustin's roles as an adviser to Martin Luther King, Jr., and A. Philip Randolph. Rustin was one of the first Freedom Riders and an organizer of the 1963 March on Washington. Considers the impact that being gay had on his standing in the African American community.

**Title:** *Color Adjustment*
**Released:** 1991
**Summary:** Examines American television's treatment of African Americans from 1948 to 1988. The stereotypical and usually incomplete spectrum runs the gamut from unflattering to inaccurate images of African Americans as prosperous beneficiaries of the American Dream.

**Title:** *Countering the Conspiracy to Destroy Black Boys*, volumes 1 and 2
**Released:** 1986
**Summary:** Volume 1 asks and answers questions about the conspiracy. Volume 2 looks at the relationships between African American mothers and sons, and women teachers and male students, documenting the disproportionate number of African American male students in special education classes and programmatic initiatives such as Rites of Passage.

**Title:** *Crown Heights*
**Released:** 2002
**Summary:** The accidental killing of an African American by a Jew triggered racial conflict in Crown Heights, New York. Two protagonists meet to plan the start of a dialogue between the Hasidic and African American communities to reduce tensions.

**Title:** *Dance Black America*
**Released:** 1990
**Summary:** Over four days, dancers and dance companies celebrate the evolution of black dance at the Brooklyn Academy of Music. Parodies such as the cakewalk and the Alvin Ailey American Dance Theater's body of work are explored and showcased.

**Title:** *Dance Theatre of Harlem: Creole Giselle*
**Released:** 1988
**Summary:** In the Louisiana of the early 1840's, social status among freed African Americans was determined by how far the family was removed from slavery. Giselle's heartbreaking rejection by an amorous interest and his family anchors the plot.

**Title:** *Eyes on the Prize: America's Civil Rights Years, 1954-1964*
**Released:** 1987
**Summary:** Surveys the struggle's first ten years through examinations of testimony given at the trial of Emmett Till's murderer; the integration battle at Central High School in Little Rock, Arkansas; the Freedom Rides; Martin Luther King, Jr.'s rise as a visible movement leader; and other milestones of the period.

**Title:** *Eyes on the Prize II: America at the Racial Crossroads, 1965-1985*
**Released:** 1990
**Summary:** Continues the story by considering such developments as the increasingly organic development of the Civil Rights movement's leadership, the devastating Kerner Commission findings, several iterations of Black Power leadership models, King's growing opposition to the Vietnam War, the Southern Christian Leadership Conference's Poor People's Campaign, and Harold Washington's installation as Chicago's first African American mayor.

**Title:** *4 Little Girls*
**Released:** 1998
**Summary:** Contextualizes the deaths of Addie Mae Collins, Denise McNair, Carole Robertson, and Cynthia Wesley resulting from the explosion on September 15, 1963, of dynamite that the Ku Klux Klan placed at the Sixteenth Street Baptist Church in Birmingham, Alabama.

**Title:** *Freedom on My Mind*
**Released:** 1994
**Summary:** Recounts the story of the Mississippi Freedom Movement of the early 1960's and brings the Student Nonviolent Coordinating Committee's voter registration work to life through the stories of poor sharecroppers, maids, and ordinary laborers.

**Title:** *Gifted Hands: The Ben Carson Story*
**Released:** 1992
**Summary:** Profiles Carson and shadows him during rounds at the Johns Hopkins University Hospital as he encourages children to reach for their full potential. Describes his part in the first successful surgical separation of conjoined twins.

**Title:** *Guts, Gumption and Go-Ahead: Annie May Hunt Remembers*
**Released:** 1992
**Summary:** Hunt shares recollections of her grandmother and mother, which are fleshed out through interviews, music, and images as she offers an account of how she overcame racism and sexism and attained economic independence.

**Title:** *Hi De Ho*
**Released:** 1947
**Summary:** Cab Calloway stars as a man pursuing two women and confronting a connected nightclub owner. Calloway performs many of his hits, including "Minnie's a Hepcat Now" and "St. James Infirmary Blues."

**Title:** *A History of Slavery in America*
**Released:** 1994
**Summary:** Describes slavery in the United States from the 1600's through Emancipation and challenges the notion of slavery's passive nature through a tally of slave rebellions and the Underground Railroad's and abolitionists' challenges to the institution.

**Title:** *In Black and White*
**Released:** 1992
**Summary:** Interviews with Charles Johnson, Gloria Naylor, Toni Morrison, Alice Walker, August Wilson, and John Edgar Wideman. Particularly riveting remarks include an argument for a literature that must include African American voices and Johnson's broad novelistic search for the "particulars of the black experience."

**Title:** *James Baldwin: The Price of the Ticket*
**Released:** 1989
**Summary:** Examines James Baldwin's life in the context of his works; incorporates comments from Baldwin's family and friends, including Maya Angelou, William Styron, and Ishmael Reed; and contains footage from public appearances and his funeral.

**Title:** *Jazz*
**Released:** 2000
**Summary:** Jazz's history—from its beginnings in New Orleans's African American community through its continuing importance as a musical genre—is depicted in ten episodes.

**Title:** *Jazz Icons: Thelonious Monk Live in '66*
**Released:** 2006
**Summary:** A rerelease of the 1966 appearances of the Monk quartet in Oslo and Copenhagen. Signature tunes include "Lulu's Back in Town," "Don't Blame Me," "Blue Monk," "Epistrophy," and "'Round Midnight."

**Title:** *Kwanzaa*
**Released:** 1994
**Summary:** Families' celebration of this holiday, including a discussion of the Seven Principles (Unity, Self-Determination, Collective Work, Cooperation, Purpose, Creativity, and Faith in One's Self), are presented. Includes scenes of West African drumming and highllights the importance of clothing, candles, and folktales.

**Title:** *Lady Day: The Many Faces of Billie Holiday*
**Released:** 1991
**Summary:** Documentary features rare television and movie clips, along with commentary by a group of jazz instrumentalists and singers who knew Holiday well. Classic favorites include "St. Louis Blues," "My Man," and "God Bless the Child."

**Title:** *Malcolm X: His Own Story as It Really Happened*
**Released:** 1972
**Summary:** The collaboration with Alex Haley that resulted in *The Autobiography of Malcolm X* informs this film. Considers Elijah Muhammad's impact on Malcolm X and Malcolm X's maturation as a civil rights activist after his release from jail.

**Title:** *Martin Luther King, Jr.: An Amazing Grace*
**Released:** 1991
**Summary:** Chronicles King's antisegregation efforts through newsreel footage and films. Notes his work and sacrifices during the Montgomery, Alabama, bus boycott and the price he paid in terms of incarcerations, harassment, oppression, and ultimately assassination.

**Title:** *Moving North to Chicago*
**Released:** 1999
**Summary:** Depicts the segregation and discrimination faced by African Americans as they migrated to and settled in a rapidly growing Chicago. Complements Isabel Wilkerson's *The Warmth of Other Suns: The Epic Story of America's Great Migration*.

**Title:** *Multicultural Peoples of North America: African Americans*
**Released:** 1993
**Summary:** Forced emigrations, internal migrations away from the South, and the Civil Rights movement frame the concomitant rise of influential leaders (Martin Luther King, Jr., Malcolm X, A. Philip Randolph, and Thurgood Marshall) and tell the story of the easing of discrimination and other societal ills.

**Title:** *Nat Turner: A Troublesome Property*
**Released:** 2002
**Summary:** Examines the context of Thomas R. Gray's *The Confessions of Nat Turner* (1831). Also addresses Alvin Poussaint's and Ossie Davis's outline of Turner's standing in the African American community and the debates engendered by William Styron's *The Confessions of Nat Turner* (1967).

**Title:** *New Orleans*
**Released:** 2000
**Summary:** The protagonist of this film falls in love and loses his Bourbon Street gambling and music establishment. Nick's multiyear effort to revive audiences' appreciation of jazz as an important genre forms a portion of the movie's story line.

**Title:** *Nothing but the Truth*
**Released:** 1998
**Summary:** Depicts the "circus atmosphere" surrounding the wrongful death civil lawsuits against O. J. Simpson won by Ronald Goldman's parents and Nicole Brown Simpson's estate.

**Title:** *Reet, Petite, and Gone*
**Released:** 1947
**Summary:** A dying musician plans to ensure the futures of his son and the daughter of a former lover. The plot revolves around the manipulations concerning the proceeds due the son and daughter from an imperfect will.

**Title:** *Repercussions: A Celebration of African-American Music*
**Released:** 1984
**Summary:** Somewhat diasporic treatment of the United States' African American musical legacy. Segments examine Gambian Mandinka and Ghanaian Dagomba roots, gospel music, the blues, jazz, Jamaica's and the Dominican Republic's musical antecedents, and the West African music scene of the early 1980's.

**Title:** *Rock & Roll: Renegades, Respect, Make It Funky, and The Perfect Beat* (volumes 1, 2, 4, and 5)
**Released:** 1995
**Summary:** In these installments of the ten-part television miniseries, New Orleans, Memphis, Nashville, and Chicago serve as backdrops as Little Richard, Bo Diddley, Chuck Berry, and others are interviewed about the influence of rhythm and blues, country, gospel, and jazz on rock and roll. Signature cuts include "Tutti Frutti," "Maybellene," and "Johnny B. Goode." *Respect* looks at gospel music's importance as an American musical genre; Martha and the Vandellas' "Dancing in the Streets" and Aretha Franklin's "Respect" help flesh out the story. Filmed in New York, San Francisco, and Philadelphia, *Make It Funky* depicts funk's rise through James Brown's "I Got You (I Feel Good)," Donna Summer's "Hot Stuff," Parliament's "Flash Light," and other funk classics. Rap's emergence and contributions to hip-hop are treated in *The Perfect Beat*, which examines Grandmaster Flash and the Furious Five's "The Message," Afrika Bambaataa & Soulsonic Force's "Planet Rock," Run-D.M.C.'s rendition of "Walk This Way," Public Enemy's "Fight the Power," and Michael Jackson's "Billie Jean."

**Title:** *Roll of Thunder, Hear My Cry*
**Released:** 1978
**Summary:** This three-part series details the Logan family's efforts to obtain equitable treatment in Depression-era Mississippi. The spearheading of a boycott against a racist merchant, Mary Logan's firing as a teacher, and foreclosure proceedings round out the story.

**Title:** *Roots*
**Released:** 1977
**Summary:** Based on Alex Haley's *Roots: The Saga of an American Family*, the series begins with Kunta Kinte's abduction by slavers and the three-month journey to colonial America. The epic plot includes Kinte's killing of the ship's first mate, his repeated attempts to escape, and the birth and coming-of-age of his daughter, Kizzy. Haley's narration concludes the last episode by documenting his and Kinte's direct familial relationship.

**Title:** *Roots: The Next Generation*
**Released:** 1979
**Summary:** The saga resumes in 1882 with Kinte's great-grandson as a prominent leader of Henning, Tennessee's black community. Familial milestones include Will Palmer's takeover of a local lumberyard, Bertha Palmer's enrollment in Lane College, and Alex Haley's growing journalistic reputation. The circle closes as Haley hears about Kinte's capture from an African tribal griot.

**Title:** *Roots of Resistance: A Story of the Underground Railroad*
**Released:** 1990
**Summary:** Escaped slaves' accounts form the basis of this history of the Underground Railroad. Interviews with the descendants of slaves and slaveholders from North Carolina's Somerset Place plantation contextualize the dangers involved in slaves' escapes.

**Title:** *Roots of Rhythm*
**Released:** 1997
**Summary:** Three episodes survey the Spanish and African origins of the New World's music. The impact of music from West Africa, the Iberian Peninsula, and Cuba on the United States' popular music culture are cataloged by Harry Belafonte.

**Title:** *Slavery and the Making of America*
**Released:** 2005
**Summary:** This four-part program examines the history of slavery in the United States, the role it played in shaping the country's development, and the paradox of a democracy that enslaved and oppressed African Americans.

**Title:** *Step by Step: A Story of Black Washington*
**Released:** 1983
**Summary:** African American life in the District of Columbia from the 1920's to the 1950's is discussed by Harold Lewis and William Montague Cobb through dialogue, photographs, and film clips.

**Title:** *That Rhythm, Those Blues*
**Released:** 1989
**Summary:** With a performance at the Apollo Theater as an implicit aspirational goal, 1940's and 1950's rhythm-and-blues performances in small Southern towns and rural areas are presented.

**Title:** *That's Black Entertainment*
**Released:** 1997
**Summary:** This visual history of black films features 1940's music and contains archival footage of Lena Horne, Paul Robeson, Bessie Smith, and Sammy Davis, Jr.

**Title:** *Thurgood Marshall: Portrait of an American Hero*
**Released:** 1985
**Summary:** Traces Marshall's career as the first African American U.S. Supreme Court justice and his service from 1967 to 1991, chronicling his preeminence as a role model and civil rights champion.

**Title:** *Toni Morrison: Profile of a Writer*
**Released:** 1987
**Summary:** Morrison discusses slavery and its legacy and the difficulties of writing about those painful subjects in her novel *Beloved*. The work's imagery, characters, and language also are treated.

**Title:** *Troubled Times*
**Released:** 2003
**Summary:** Comments on Jayson Blair's meteoric rise and fall as a reporter at *The New York Times* and the role that race may have played in fueling this management fiasco.

**Title:** *Tryin' to Get Home: A History of African American Song*
**Released:** 1993
**Summary:** From spirituals to rap, Kerrigan Black performs and historically contextualizes songs through monologues, photographs, and film footage. Features "O Freedom," "St. Louis Blues," "In the Still of the Night," "Heat Wave," and "Climbing Higher Mountains."

**Title:** *Upon This Rock*
**Released:** 1983
**Summary:** Addresses the cultural importance of black churches, both as places of worship and as agents of civil rights. Describes the origins, roles, and activities of these institutions and features choir and solo performances.

**Title:** *Voices and Visions: Langston Hughes*
**Released:** 2000
**Summary:** Hughes's celebration of African American life is chronicled through "The Weary Blues" and "The Negro Speaks of Rivers." Interviews with James Baldwin, Gwendolyn Brooks, and others add context and depth to this portrait.

**Title:** *Voices of the Civil Rights Movement: Black American Freedom Songs, 1960-1966*
**Released:** 1997
**Summary:** This tour de force recording contextualizes many of the songs, such as "Governor Wallace," "Freedom Train," "This Little Light of Mine," "Go Tell It on the Mountain," "We Shall Overcome," and "In the Mississippi River" through a booklet.

**Title:** *W. E. B. Du Bois: A Biography in Four Voices*
**Released:** 1995
**Summary:** Describes Du Bois's accomplishments. Addresses how his struggles during the McCarthy era triggered his emigration to Ghana.

—*José Ortal*

# LITERARY BIBLIOGRAPHY

*The works listed below are categorized by genre and offer students and teachers alike some of the best resources for the study of literature by African Americans.*

## ANTHOLOGIES

Brawley, Benjamin. *Early Negro American Writers: Selections with Biographical Introductions.* Salem, N.H.: Ayer, 1987. 305 pp. First published in 1935, this collection offers the principal slave narratives, poetry, autobiographies, and speeches of African American writers from the eighteenth century to the end of the Civil War. Writers include such prominent figures as Phillis Wheatley and Frederick Douglass and such noted writers and poets as Jupiter Hammond, George B. Vashon, and Ida B. Wells. Himself a poet, Brawley asserts that the serious tone in the works of these writers is a reflection of the experiences and the aspirations of slaves, former slaves, and free African Americans during a tumultuous period of American history.

Brown, Sterling, Arthur P. Davis, and Ulysses G. Lee, eds. *The Negro Caravan: Writings by American Negroes.* North Stratford, N.H.: Ayer, 2000. Reprint. 1,082 pp. Selections in this anthology first published in 1941 are grouped by genre. Among them are fiction, poetry, drama, historical essays, biographies, speeches, pamphlets, and letters. Folk stories and work songs are included for the first time in an anthology of African American literature, and the work of previously unanthologized writers, such as Charles Chesnutt, Waters Turpin, and Robert Heyden, appears. Considered the most comprehensive collection of African American writing of its time.

Carretta, Vincent, ed. *Unchained Voices: An Anthology of Black Authors in the English-Speaking World of the Eighteenth Century.* Lexington: University Press of Kentucky, 1996. 386 pp. Praised by reviewers for the breadth of writings and its depths of scholarship, *Unchained Voices* offers a diversity of works and experiences of African Americans in the English-speaking world. The collection includes recognized (for example, New York poet Jupiter Hammond) and unknown (for example, Boston author of slave narratives Briton Hammond, no relation to the former) writers from Bath to Boston, from London to the Caribbean, separated by distance but united by a desire for liberation from physical and spiritual bondage.

Chapman, Abraham, ed. *New Black Voices: An Anthology of Contemporary Afro-American Literature.* New York: Signet Classic, 2001. 720 pp. The forty-four authors represented in this collection, with the exception of Frederick Douglass, wrote during the "modern period" of African American letters, roughly from the 1920's to the 1970's; their works are marked by a mastery of form and craftsmanship. With an emphasis on the varied and contradictory styles and approaches to literature, this chronological arrangement begins with the poetry of Paul Laurence Dunbar and the fiction of Charles Chesnutt and progresses through the Harlem Renaissance to end with Black Arts movement poets such as Mari Evans and Dudley Randall. Genres included are fiction, poetry, autobiography, and literary criticism.

Clarke, John Henrik. *Black American Short Stories: A Century of the Best.* New York: Hill and Wang, 1993. 448 pp. Recognized for his historical writings, Clarke in 1967 edited this collection (then titled *Negro American Short Stories*) of short stories from fiction writers—Charles Chesnutt, Claude McKay, Zora Neale Hurston, and Chester Himes, to name a few—and from writers known for their works in other genres, including W. E. B. Du Bois, Lerone Bennett, Jr., and Clarke himself (this includes his short story "The Boy Who Painted Christ Black"). The paperback edition adds seven new works by such authors as Maya Angelou, Toni Cade Bambara, James Alan McPherson, and Alice Walker and a new introduction written by Clarke.

Gates, Henry Louis, Jr., and Nellie Y. McKay, eds. *The Norton Anthology of African American Literature.* New York: W. W. Norton, 1997. 2,665 pp. A comprehensive collection of African American literature, the Norton anthology reflects the view that the African American literary tradition is part of the American literary mainstream. The book covers six periods of literary history: slavery and freedom; Reconstruction; the Harlem Renaissance; realism, naturalism, and modernism; the Black Arts movement; and the period since the 1970's. It contains not only fiction, poetry, and drama but also spirituals, the blues, work songs, jazz and rap, sermons, folktales, journals, and autobiographies. Eleven works are included in their entirety.

Hill, Patricia Liggins, et al., eds. *Call and Response: The Riverside Anthology of the African American Literary Tradition*. New York: Houghton Mifflin Harcourt, 2003. 2,039 pp. In contrast to the view that African American literary tradition arises from mainstream American culture, this collection of more than 550 canonical and new works asserts an African oral tradition as the root and the enduring motif of African American literature. Opening with African proverbs, folktales, and chants, this anthology also includes rap lyrics, speeches, and poetry from twenty-first century writers. An audio compact disc has music and spoken-word poetry and historic performances from the Archives of Smithsonian/Folkways Records.

Jarrett, Gene Andrew, ed. *African American Literature Beyond Race: An Alternative Reader*. New York: New York University Press, 2006. 496 pp. This anthology is distinguished by the fact that the stories, written by such well-recognized racial realists as Zora Neale Hurston, Richard Wright, James Baldwin, and Toni Morrison, are "not necessarily about race." In most of the stories, the racial identity of the protagonist is unstated. From Frances E. W. Harper's *Sowing and Reaping* (1876) to Octavia Butler's "Blood Child" (1984), the collection exemplifies the editor's assertion that African American literature should be defined as broadly as possible. This "raceless" African American fiction has been mostly ignored, according to Jarrett. Where other anthologies "overdetermine" the theme of race, this collection emphasizes other themes, experiences, and approaches. A selected bibliography provides sources for further reading of the works.

Killens, John Oliver, and Jerry W. Ward, Jr., eds. *Black Southern Voices: An Anthology of Fiction, Poetry, Drama, Nonfiction, and Critical Essays*. New York: New American Library, 2001. 608 pp. Focusing on African American writers from the South, this work features fifty-six authors who mostly have been absent from anthologies of Southern writers. Richard Wright, Frank Yerby, and Maya Angelou share the volume with such relative unknowns as Arthenia B. Millican and Doris Jean Austin. In his introduction, Killens provides context for this particular subset of African American writers, working in a complicated social and historical environment too often ignored by "the magnolia-scented, honey-suckled status quo."

Lee, Valerie, ed. *The Prentice Hall Anthology of African American Women's Literature*. Upper Saddle River, N.J.: Pearson Prentice Hall, 2006. 426 pp. This is the first comprehensive anthology of its kind, covering historical periods from the eighteenth to the twenty-first centuries and including works as diverse as letters, journal entries, spiritual narratives, detective and romance fiction, melodramas, dramatic monologues, and neo-slave narratives, in addition to the expected poetry, short stories, dramas, and critical essays. From those of Lucy Terry to Pearl Cleage, the writings deal with many issues unique to the concerns of African American women, including African Americanness, interracial relationships, slavery, sexual harassment, and violence. Additional features include biographies, a map of the birthplaces of the authors, and a time line.

Patton, Venetria K., and Maureen Honey, eds. *Double-Take: A Revisionist Harlem Renaissance Anthology*. New Brunswick, N.J.: Rutgers University Press, 2001. 619 pp. Expanding the period of the Harlem Renaissance to the decades from 1916 to 1937, the editors further broaden the scope of this important literary period to include artwork and illustrations never before anthologized, along with the fiction, poetry, and drama from the period. This work differs from others in its nearly equal division of contributions from male and female authors and the highlighting of works and authors who focus on gender issues and gay and lesbian themes. The biographical material for each author discusses how gender, class, and sexual orientation influence the writer's work. Essayists include not only Marcus Garvey but also Amy Jacques Garvey, his wife. Creative works offer a similar mix of well-known and little-known literary and visual artists.

Powell, Kevin, ed. *Step into a World: A Global Anthology of the New Black Literature*. New York: John Wiley & Sons, 2000. 496 pp. Considered a groundbreaking anthology of the hip-hop generation of writers and artists, *Step into a World* offers essays and e-mails, rap lyrics and journalistic writings, and poetry, fiction, and essays. Arranged in six sections, it includes 104 contemporary African American writers, ages twenty-three to forty-three, from nine countries and three continents. Edwidge Danticat, Junot Diaz, Christopher John Farley, John Keene, Victor D. La Valle, Phyllis Alesia Perry, and Bernardine Evaristo are some of the young writers featured, and essay subject matter includes Oprah Winfrey and Tiger Woods.

Young, Kevin, ed. *Giant Steps: The New Generation of African American Writers*. New York: Harper Perennial, 2000. 384 pp. The new generation in this collection is a group of post-civil rights era writers. Among them are National Book Award finalists and winners of the National Poetry Series, the O. Henry Award, and the Puschcart Prize. The collection features thirty-five writers under forty at the time of publication. In his introduction, Young makes the claim that these writers—influenced not by the blues of earlier generations but by the rap of contemporary hip-hop artists—are "not getting their due" as the African American canon begins to solidify. With well-recognized talents such as Edwidge Danticat, Kevin Powell, Hilton Als, and Randall Keenan and a host of lesser-known writers, this work is the first multigenre anthology of this period.

## HISTORY AND CRITICISM

Adell, Sandra. *Double-Consciousness/Double Bind: Theoretical Issues in Twentieth-Century Black Literature*. Urbana: University of Illinois Press, 1994. 184 pp. Considered an iconoclastic work by some critics, *Double-Consciousness/Double Bind* is a collection of essays that analyzes and questions some of the central theoretical issues in twentieth century African American literature and literary criticism. Beginning with an analysis of W. E. B. Du Bois's description of "double consciousness," in *The Souls of Black Folk* (1903), Adell also examines the "double bind" of competing claims of Western European and Afrocentric influences on African American literature. Issues discussed include academic feminism and the role of vernacular theory in literary criticism. Adell sets out to prove that African American literature cannot be divorced from European philosophy and Western traditions, and that critics such as Houston Baker, Henry Louis Gates, Jr., and even herself are still caught in the "double consciousness" and "double bind" that Du Bois articulated early in the twentieth century.

Ahad, Badia Sahar. *Freud Upside Down: African American Literature and Psychoananalytic Culture*. Champaign: University of Illinois Press, 2010. 216 pp. Tracing the influence of psychoanalytic theories in the works of several twentieth century African American writers, this addition to literary history and criticism examines the work of Nella Larsen, Richard Wright, Jean Toomer, Ralph Ellison, Adrienne Kennedy, and Danzy Senna. The author examines both the creative works and the personal lives of these authors and comments on the relationship between African American literature and the psychoanalytic movement of the twentieth century.

Brown, Fahamisha Patricia. *Performing the Word: African American Poetry as Vernacular Culture*. Piscataway, N.J.: Rutgers University Press, 1999. 174 pp. Intended for a college undergraduate audience, *Performing the Word* is an introduction to a diverse group of African American poets grouped by the common theme of orality and vernacular language. Brown analyzes the poems of well-known poets, such as Paul Laurence Dunbar, Langston Hughes, Amiri Baraka, and Gwendolyn Brooks, as well as those of lesser-known poets, such as Mona Lisa Saloy and Saul Williams. Brown also summarizes the academic theories about African American English of critics J. L. Dullard, Geneva Smitherman, and others. All of the poems discussed belong to a continuing "expressive culture" that includes not only poetry but also sermons and song lyrics. Brown intends to highlight the inventive language that was forged out of the experience of slavery in America and to provide readers with a better understanding of these works and vernacular theory.

Bruce, Dickson D., Jr. *The Origins of African American Literature, 1680-1865*. Charlottesville: University Press of Virginia, 2001. 384 pp. In this one-volume history of African American literature before 1865, Bruce examines the formative eras of the literature and emphasizes the influences of white and African American writing on the early works of African American writers. Bruce's definition of African American literature expands beyond the borders of North America to include African, Anglo-African (in England), and Creole Atlantic writers. He discusses not only creative writings but also the journalistic output of such publications as William Lloyd Garrison's *The Liberator* and the African American periodical *Freedom's Journal*. While some critics believe Bruce covers major works extensively—Phillis Wheatley's poetry, Frederick Douglass's *Narrative* (1845), Harriet Jacobs's *Incidents in the Life of a Slave Girl* (1861), and Martin Delany's *Blake* (1859)—others complain that with such an ambitious scope of time and content, deep analysis of major writers and works is lacking in this volume.

Christian, Barbara. *New Black Feminist Criticism, 1985-2000*. Edited by Gloria Bowles, M. Giulia Fabi, and Arlene R. Keizer. Urbana: University of Illinois Press, 2007. 272 pp. After the publication of *Black Women Novelists: The Development of a Tradition, 1892-1976* (1980), the first book-length study on the African American female literary tradition, Christian became recognized as one of the "founding mothers" of African American feminist critical theory. This work is a collection of her essays, book reviews, and lectures written between the publication of her landmark book, *Black Feminist Criticism*, in 1985 and her death in 2000. Christian evaluates African American feminist criticism as a discipline and reflects on African American feminism in the university. Included are discussions of writers such as Alice Walker, Gloria Naylor, Toni Morrison, Jayne Cortez, and Audre Lorde.

Davis, Jane. *The White Image in the Black Mind: A Study of African American Literature*. Westport, Conn.: Greenwood Press, 2000. 184 pp. Examining the works of well-known authors such as Richard Wright and James Baldwin, essayists and social commentators from Frederick Douglass to Kenneth Clark, and literary critics such as Bell Hooks, Derrick Bell, and Ellis Cose, Davis reveals some "uncomfortable truths" about African American writers' portrayals of whites in their literary works. She presents a typology of stereotyped images—the bigot, the weakling, the liberal, and the hypocrite, among others—that occur regularly in African American literature. She examines other, more complex imagery that nonetheless illustrates her point that bigotry and racism are not only a matter of behavior but also a manifestation of white identity. The work includes a selected bibliography.

Draper, James P., Jeffrey W. Hunter, and Jerry Moore, eds. *Black Literature Criticism: Excerpts from Criticism of the Most Significant Works of Black Authors over the Past Two Hundred Years*. Detroit, Mich.: Gale Research, 1999. 2,078 pp. The three-volume set introduces readers to criticism about significant African American writers throughout the world, including Chinua Achebe, Toni Morrison, and Wole Soyinka. The award-winning publication provides introductory sketches, biography, a chronology of principal works, major published criticism, seminal articles, and biographical citations. Some author interviews are also included. It is an alphabetical ar-

rangement of 125 prominent authors of the eighteenth to twentieth centuries. Includes *Black Literature Criticism Supplement*, which adds critical reviews of twenty-five additional authors and their works.

Fisch, Audrey A., ed. *The Cambridge Companion to the African American Slave Narrative*. Cambridge, U.K.: Cambridge University Press, 2007. 290 pp. Entries in this work cover the historical, cultural, political, and literary contexts of and critical approaches to the slave narrative. It includes a chronology, essays concerning well-known writers, such as Olaudah Equiano, Harriet Jacobs, and Frederick Douglass, and other, lesser-known figures, as well as studies of the relationships between the slave narratives and international abolitionism, autobiographies, and African American women's experiences. Also includes a guide for further reading.

Gates, Henry Louis, Jr. *The Signifying Monkey: A Theory of Afro-American Literary Criticism*. New York: Oxford University Press, 1988. 290 pp. Tracing a tradition of signifying (variously defined as verbal wordplay, telling by indirection or subterfuge, boasting, exaggerating, and telling lies) from the trickster of African folktales to the vernacular of African American street talk, Gates proposes an approach to literary criticism of African American writing that was considered groundbreaking. Defining and explaining his use of the term "Talking Book," a central conceit of the slave narratives, Gates uses this tool to reexamine several major works of African American writers, including Zora Neale Hurston's *Their Eyes Were Watching God* (1937), Ralph Ellison's *Invisible Man* (1952), Ishmael Reed's *Mumbo Jumbo* (1972), and Alice Walker's *The Color Purple* (1982). Significant analysis is given to Jean Toomer, W. E. B. Du Bois, and Richard Wright.

Graham, Maryemma, and Jerry W. Ward, Jr. *The Cambridge History of African American Literature*. New York: Cambridge University Press, 2011. 824 pp. Heralded as the first major twenty-first century history of four hundred years of African American writing, this work presents a comprehensive overview of African American literary traditions, both oral and print. In addition to tracing the literary history, this work includes critical essays about foundational scholarship, criticism, and theory as well as a discussion of American literature, New World cultures, and emerging writers. Contributors come from the United States and other countries, each examining the work in discussion as art and as a product of American cultural history. It includes a bibliography and suggestions for further reading.

Jarrett, Gene Andrew, ed. *A Companion to African American Literature*. Malden, Mass.: Wiley-Blackwell, 2010. 488 pp. In essays that cover the literature of the African diaspora from the eighteenth century to the twenty-first, the established and emerging literary scholars in this work not only provide an overview of the tradition—the well-examined themes, contexts, genre studies, authors, and critical approaches—but also question some of the assumptions of these traditions. Essay topics include the slave narratives and racial uplift literature of the eighteenth and nineteenth centuries and examinations of African American science fiction, popular African American women's fiction, and "Queer Studies," the last written by James Baldwin. From the antislavery literature to the current electronic cultural media, this work seeks to show the richness and complexity of and to provide a deeper understanding of the literary tradition.

Johnson, Dianne. *Telling Tales: The Pedagogy and Promise of African American Literature for Youth*. Westport, Conn.: Greenwood Press, 1990. 184 pp. A sourcebook for parents and teachers, this is a presentation of the development of African American literature for children. It includes authors from the 1920's to the 1980's, including close readings of various works, from the *Brownies Book* magazine of the 1920's to the poetry of Lucille Clifton.

Joyce, Joyce Ann. *Warriors, Conjurers and Priests: Defining African-Centered Literary Criticism*. Chicago: Third World Press, 1994. 311 pp. An American Book Award winner for literary criticism, this work is the first book-length effort to define the theory and principles of Afrocentric literary criticism. In thirteen essays, Joyce explains her theories and applies them to several authors, including Richard Wright, Nella Larsen, Gwendolyn Brooks, James Baldwin, Sonia Sanchez, Ann Petry, E. Ethelbert Miller, and Terry McMillan. Described by the publisher as a work for all students of African American literature, the audience is primarily upper-level and graduate students, scholars, and critics.

Krstovic, Jelena O., ed. *Black Literature Criticism: Classic and Emerging Authors Since 1950*. Foreword by Howard Dodson. Detroit, Mich.: Gale Cengage, 2008. 544 pp. This includes several authors born after 1950, thereby including works from the early twenty-first century. Each of its eighty-eight entries provides an introduction, a biography, major works, critical reception, criticism, and titles for further reading. Well-established figures—Toni Morrison, James Baldwin, Amiri Baraka, and Alice Walker—share the three-volume work with younger writers such as Edwidge Danticat, Randall Kenan, Tina McElroy Ansa, and Henry Dumas. The focus is not only African American writers but also those from Africa and the African diaspora, Europe, and the Caribbean, all indexed by author, nationality, and title.

Smith, Karen Patricia, ed. *African American Voices in Young Adult Literature: Tradition, Transition, Transformation*. Lanham, Md.: Scarecrow Press, 2002. 437 pp. Intended for educators, librarians, and others working with young adult literature, this collection of fourteen essays about autobiographies, poetry, novels, periodical literature, and online databases for young adult literature includes in-depth discussion of writers such as Virginia Hamilton, Octavia Butler, Walter Dean Myers, and Mildred Taylor. Winner of the American Library Association G. K. Hall Award (1996).

## INTERVIEWS

Carroll, Rebecca. *I Know What the Red Clay Looks Like: The Voice and Vision of Black Women Writers*. New York: Crown, 1994. 246 pp. Just as the young Zora Neale Hurston sat on the porch and listened to the stories told by the men and women of her hometown, the fifteen established and emerging writers interviewed for this collection speak of remembering stories from their youth and being inspired by women writers before them who paved the way. Carroll invites readers to listen again, as people such as Ida B. Wells, Hurston, Toni Morrison, Nikki Giovanni, and Pearl Cleage speak of sisterhood, the experience of being an African American woman, and why they became writers. Each interview is preceded by a brief biography and followed by an excerpt from that writer's works. (See also the companion work on male writers, *Swing Low: Black Men Writing*.)

_____. *Swing Low: Black Men Writing*. New York: Carol Southern Books, 1995. 266 pp. A companion volume to Carroll's *I Know What the Red Clay Looks Like*, this book contains interviews with sixteen African American male authors. With an introduction by Claude Browne, the collection includes critic Henry Louis Gates, Jr., novelist Ishmael Reed, playwright

August Wilson, poet Yusef Komunyakaa, journalist Nathan McCall, and the newer voices of Trey Ellis and Darryl Pinckney. These and other writers talk about the jobs they had before becoming writers, the experiences that helped them become writers, and the writing process. Each entry includes a photograph, an introductory essay, and an excerpt of poetry, fiction, or nonfiction writing from the author.

Golden, Marita, ed. *The Word: Black Writers Talk About the Transformative Power of Reading and Writing.* New York: Broadway Books, 2011. 224 pp. A writer herself, Golden includes conversations with authors as diverse in age, style, and genre as J. California Cooper, Edwidge Danticat, John Hope Franklin, and Ellis Cose.

O'Brien, John. *Interviews with Black Writers.* New York: W. W. Norton, 1973. 274 pp. Expressing a common belief among most of the authors interviewed in this work, Langston Hughes comments that whites remain astonished that "Negroes" had learned to read, let alone write. The men and women in this book are candid and honest about their work and their lives. Among them are writers from the Harlem Renaissance era, such as Hughes and Arna Bontemps, and later voices, such as Ann Petry, Owen Dodson, Amiri Baraka, and Alice Walker, to name only a few. O'Brien is considered a skillful interviewer who invited a serious discussion of the craft and the issues confronting African American writers.

## REFERENCE SOURCES

Andrews, William L., Frances Smith Foster, and Trudier Harris, eds. *The Concise Oxford Companion to African American Literature.* New York: Oxford University Press, 1997. 866 pp. In addition to the biographies and writings of more than four hundred writers, this companion includes essays on iconic and mythic characters such as Br'er Rabbit and Stagolee, genre analysis including television, and the full text of the essay "Literary History." Beginning in the colonial period of American history, the compilation of signed essays, with an introduction by Henry Louis Gates, Jr., is said to give the "full sweep" of African American literary history.

Beaulieu, Elizabeth Ann, ed. *Writing African American Women: An Encyclopedia of Literature by and About Women of Color.* Westport, Conn.: Greenwood Press, 2006. 1,040 pp. This first-of-its-kind work approaches African American literature from a women's studies perspective. The A-Z entries include writers, works, genres, characters, movements, and historical events. Included are women writers and some men who have significant female characters in their works. Each essay is followed by a bibliography of works about the topic. Preceding the encyclopedic entries are contents lists arranged alphabetically and thematically. A time line and selected bibliography follow the listings.

Dickson-Carr, Darryl. *The Columbia Guide to Contemporary African American Fiction.* New York: Columbia University Press, 2005. 280 pp. This volume focuses on fiction writers published in the thirty years before publication. Organized alphabetically, it contains 160 entries that discuss the works, critical reception, ways of reading key works, and a bibliography for further research. The editor also examines critical theories and movements such as Negritude, the Black Arts movement, feminism, and postmodernism as well as themes and ideas, including Oprah's Book Club, that have shaped contemporary African American fiction and broadened its impact. Dickson-Carr discusses the role of African American literature in society and concludes the book with an annotated bibliography of African American fiction and criticism.

Hatch, Shari Dorantes, ed. *Encyclopedia of African American Writing, Five Centuries of Contribution: Trials and Triumphs of Writers, Poets, Publications, and Organizations.* Amenia, N.Y.: Grey House, 2009. 865 pp. This includes more than seven hundred writers, listed alphabetically and by genre, with black-and-white illustrations. The essays discuss honors, awards, family, and associates as well as the writers' works and what inspired them to create. Intended for public, high school, and university libraries, it is considered a comprehensive collection of information and resources about African American culture from the first arrivals in 1620 to the inauguration of President Barack Obama in 2009. Included also are a time line, forty-three primary works (such as the 1787 "Preamble of the Free African Society"), and genre studies of poetry, fiction, drama, newspapers, journals, book publishers, online resources, and illustrators. Other features include an appendix of writers by genre, a chronology of writers, and a chronology of literary firsts.

Joyce, Donald F. *Black Book Publishers in the United States: A Historical Dictionary of the Presses, 1817-1990*. Westport, Conn.: Greenwood Press, 1991. 272 pp. This is a first-of-its-kind book-length dictionary of forty-six African American-owned publishing companies in the United States. Searching bibliographic works, book advertisements, periodical literature, and business directories, and in some cases conducting personal interviews, the author provides publishing histories, titles, libraries where titles can be found, and the officers and addresses of the publishing organization. The introduction provides a historical overview, and the entries are arranged alphabetically by firm. The book also contains name, title, subject, and geographical indexes.

Murphy, Barbara Thrash, and Deborah Murphy. *Black Authors and Illustrators of Books for Children and Young Adults*. 4th ed. New York: Routledge, 2007. 568 pp. This biographical dictionary includes comprehensive information on major authors and illustrators. This edition adds fifty new profiles to the more than two hundred entries from the previous edition and includes in-depth biographical data, photos, and updated information, such as Web sites and e-mail addresses. Appendixes provide lists of African American publishers, distributors, and book dealers for children's literature; photos of book covers and jackets; a list of awards and honor books; and a listing of online resources related to African American children's literature.

Page, Yolanda Williams, ed. *Encyclopedia of African American Women Writers*. Westport, Conn.: Greenwood Press, 2007. 728 pp. This compilation opens with two listings, by author and by date, of the 168 writers, including some Caribbean writers among the African American women. It covers the period from 1746 to 2006 in entries that range from 750 to 5,000 words. Intended for high school through undergraduate students, it also can be useful to graduate students and researchers doing preliminary research. Each entry includes a biographical narrative, major works, critical reception, and a selected biography. An appendix notes major literary award winners, and the work includes a selected general bibliography.

Peterson, Bernard L., Jr. *Profiles of African American Stage Performers and Theatre People, 1816-1960*. Westport, Conn.: Greenwood Press, 2001. 442 pp. In earlier publications, *Contemporary Black American Playwrights and Their Plays* (1988) and *The African American Theatre Directory, 1816-1960: A Comprehensive Guide to Early Black Theatre Organizations, Companies, Theatres, and Performing Groups* (1997), Peterson provided a comprehensive list of his topics. Here is the directory of more than seven hundred performers, playwrights, directors, producers, choreographers, dancers, composers, comedians, and agents from the nineteenth century dawning of African Americans in theater to the Black Arts movement of the 1960's. As in the earlier works, the descriptions, helpful appendixes and indexes, and extensive bibliography provide information and resources for production companies, educators, and scholars.

Rand, Donna, and Toni Trent Parker. *Black Books Galore! Guide to More Great African American Children's Books*. New York: John Wiley & Sons, 2001. 256 pp. The original publication in this series of books grew out of a need to identify and distribute information about works that featured nonstereotyped African American children as characters. This edition has more than six hundred entries, arranged by age group, including profiles of selected authors and descriptions of works. An introduction, an essay from James Comer, and two chapters providing an age-specific guide for encouraging reading and a calendar to match titles with holidays precede the entries. Appendixes provide information on books for parents, award-winning titles, and Web sites. The book concludes with author, illustrator, title, and topic indexes. Other publications in the series feature books about and for African American boys and girls separately. Originally intended as a guide for parents.

Stanley, Tarshia L., ed. *Encyclopedia of Hip-Hop Literature*. Westport, Conn.: Greenwood Press, 2009. 312 pp. Survey of the world of hip-hop literature, or street lit. This encyclopedia has 180 alphabetically arranged entries that include studies of artists, fictional works, and memoirs, as well as studies of postmodernism, the spoken-word movement, magazines, music, popular culture, and films, such as *Boyz N the Hood* (1991) and others of that genre. Included are the musicians, producers, and fashion designers who are part of hip-hop culture. Each entry includes works for further reading. Beginning with a list of entries and a guide to related topics, the book concludes with a selected bibliography.

*—Joyce A. Barnes*

# ORGANIZATIONS AND SOCIETIES

*United States-based organizations of a nonpolitical, nonsectarian nature are included here. Information is provided for national organizations. Entries are arranged into two categories: organizations and professional associations. The professional associations are those that unite people of particular occupations. The organizations included here were identified through Internet searches conducted in October, 2010. Because URLs change, the accuracy of these site listings is not guaranteed.*

## ORGANIZATIONS

**Association for the Study of African American Life and History (ASALH)**
C. B. Powell Building
525 Bryant Street NW, Suite C-142
Washington, DC 20059
Phone: (202) 865-0053
Fax: (202) 265-7920
http://www.asalh.org

The ASALH initiated Black History Month and hosts an annual scholarly conference in the field of African American studies. The group publishes the *Journal of African-American History*, *The Black History Bulletin*, *The Woodson Review*, and *Fire!!! The Multimedia Journal of Black Studies*. Carter G. Woodson, who created Negro History Week, founded the group in 1915.

**Coalition of Black Trade Unionists (CBTU)**
1150 17th Street NW, Suite 300
Washington, DC 20036
Phone: (202) 778-3318
Fax: (202) 293-5308
http://www.cbtu.org

The CBTU works to ensure fair representation of the well over two million African Americans who belong to a union. CBTU also supports the election of black labor leaders to decision-making bodies and rejects the idea that labor union members should benefit from exploitation of overseas labor.

**Congress of Racial Equality (CORE)**
817 Broadway, Third Floor
New York, NY 10003
Phone: (212) 598-4000
Fax: (212) 982-0184
http://www.core-online.org

CORE's principal activities involve education in financial literacy and job training and placement. CORE also is involved in anti-malaria and "poverty eradication" projects in Africa. It was founded in 1942 to fight racism and was heavily involved in the Civil Rights movement, including organizing the Freedom Rides to integrate interstate transportation in the South.

**National Association for the Advancement of Colored People (NAACP)**
4805 Mount Hope Drive
Baltimore, MD 21215
Phone: (877) 622-2798
Fax: (410) 358-1607 (field organization); (410) 602-9310 (fund-raising); (410) 764-6683 (youths and colleges)
http://www.naacp.org

The NAACP's central organization and its branches focus on voter registration, the environment's effect upon the health of African American communities, and media diversity. The legal department of the NAACP pursues equality in education, jobs, and housing through the courts. *The Crisis* magazine, the organization's official publication, is available by subscription. The NAACP's Web site publishes opportunities for fellowships, grants, scholarships, and contests. Since its inception in 1909, the NAACP has been the preeminent African American civil rights group in the United States.

**National Association of Colored Women's Clubs (NACWC)**
1601 R Street NW
Washington, DC 20009
Phone: (202) 667-4080
Fax: (202) 667-4113
http://www.nacwc.org

The NACWC defends the rights of black women and children, with a special focus on health care. The organization offers scholarships and a GrandParents Academy. Established in 1896 as a coordinating organization for African American women's clubs, the NACWC played a major role in antilynching and women's suffrage campaigns.

## National Black Justice Coalition (NBJC)

1638 R Street NW, Suite 300
Washington, DC 20009
Phone: (202) 319-1552
Fax: (202) 319-7365
http://www.nbjc.org

The NBJC's goal is to end bigotry and prejudice directed at homosexual African Americans. To this end, the group investigates and exposes discrimination in the workplace, homophobia at historically black colleges and universities, and illegal discrimination against those with human immunodeficiency virus (HIV) or acquired immune deficiency syndrome (AIDS).

## National Council of Negro Women (NCNW)

633 Pennsylvania Avenue NW
Washington, DC 20004
Phone: (202) 737-0120
Fax: (202) 737-0476
http://www.ncnw.org

The NCNW works to promote educational and entrepreneurial opportunities for women. The group also organizes the Black Family Reunion, a multicultural festival. The group maintains an archive of historical and current published resources for women. Mary McLeod Bethune established the NCNW in 1935 as an organization for black professional women.

## National Pan-Hellenic Council

3951 Snapfinger Parkway, Suite 218
Decatur, GA 30035
Phone: (404) 592-6145
Fax: (404) 806-9943
http://www.nphchq.org

Nine fraternities and sororities of African American students have coordinated campaigns through the National Pan-Hellenic Council since 1930. The confederation offers education on financial management, health awareness, and the hazards of hazing and substance abuse.

## National Urban League

120 Wall Street
New York, NY 10005
Phone: (212) 558-5300
Fax: (212) 344-5332
http://www.nul.org

The National Urban League works toward equal economic opportunity and leadership development among African Americans. Its serial statistical report, *The State of Black America*, has affected public policy in economic and political arenas. Other publications include *Opportunity* magazine, *Urban Influence* magazine, and the book *Empowering Communities, Changing Lives* (2010). The organization was established in 1910 to assist African Americans who migrated from the South to Northern industrial centers.

## One Hundred Black Men of America

141 Auburn Avenue
Atlanta, GA 30303
Phone: (404) 688-5100
Fax: (404) 688-1028
http://www.100blackmen.org

One Hundred Black Men of America is an organization of African American men who provide community leadership and encourage educational and economic development. Members mentor black youths and advocate for family leadership, business integrity, preventive health care, and religious commitment.

## Rainbow PUSH Coalition

930 East Fiftieth Street
Chicago, IL 60615
Phone: (773) 373-3366
Fax: (773) 373-3571
http://www.rainbowpush.org

The Rainbow PUSH Coalition, founded by the Reverend Jesse Jackson in 1996, is a multiracial organization that promotes peace and social justice. The coalition's members mentor youths of many races and ethnicities. The national office researches urban economies and international business opportunities and lobbies for public policy at the federal level.

## Southern Christian Leadership Conference (SCLC)

320 Auburn Avenue
Atlanta, GA 30303
Phone: (404) 522-1420
Fax: (404) 527-4333
http://www.sclcnational.org

The SCLC provides training in nonviolent conflict resolution and resistance to racially motivated violence. The group's particular areas of focus are voter registration, equality in health care, and economic opportunity. Founders and past presidents include Martin Luther King, Jr., Ralph David Abernathy, and Joseph Lowery.

## PROFESSIONAL ASSOCIATIONS

### African American Police League (AAPL)

1403 East 75th Street
Chicago, IL 60619
Phone: (773) 256-2275
http://www.aapoliceleague.org

The AAPL is a national organization that unites and supports black police officers. Founded in 1968, the league is run jointly by civilians, officers, and retired police, and it counsels officers on promotions, lawyers, exams, harassment, lobbying, and other job-related matters.

### Association of Black Women Historians (ABWH)

Howard University Department of History
2441 Sixth Street NW
Washington, DC 20059
Phone: (202) 806-6815
Fax: (202) 806-4471
http://www.abwh.org

The ABWH advances scholarship on the history of African American women and directs members toward job opportunities and financial support. The ABWH was established in 1979 to counter the marginalization of female historians and their work.

### National Association of Black Journalists (NABJ)

University of Maryland, College Park
1100 Knight Hall, Suite 3100
College Park, MD 20742
Phone: (301) 405-0248
Fax: (301) 314-1714
http://www.nabj.org

The NABJ works to increase African American representation in journalism by helping train aspiring African American journalists and monitoring race issues in the media. It provides networking and professional development opportunities for its members.

### National Bar Association (NBA)

1225 Eleventh Street NW
Washington, DC 20001
Phone: (202) 842-3900
Fax: (202) 289-6170
http://www.nationalbar.org

The NBA is a network of African American lawyers and judges that offers education in civil rights legislation and encourages voting among African Americans. For youths, the NBA provides annual contests and a "law camp."

### National Black Nurses Association (NBNA)

8630 Fenton Street, Suite 330
Silver Spring, MD 20910-3803
Phone: (301) 589-3200
Fax: (301) 589-3223
http://www.nbna.org

The NBNA organizes disaster relief and provides continuing education and professional development training for African American nurses. It focuses on geriatrics, obesity, and mammography. The organization also provides scholarships to African-American nursing students.

### National Coalition of One Hundred Black Women

1925 Adam C. Powell, Jr., Boulevard, Suite 1L
New York, NY 10026
Phone: (212) 222-5660
Fax: (212) 222-5675
http://www.nc100bw.org

Black professional women work through the coalition's chapters to assist working mothers, provide models of successful black women for youths, and advocate prevention of unplanned pregnancies among teenagers.

### National Conference of Black Mayors (NCBM)

191 Peachtree Street NE, Suite 849
Atlanta, GA 30303
Phone: (404) 765-6444
Fax: (404) 765-6430
http://ncbm.org

The NCBM addresses issues including health care, educational reforms, management training, and disaster relief campaigns. The group's Web site offers free publications relevant to the practical concerns of African American elected officials. Thirteen African American mayors established the conference in 1974; by 2010, the organization included more than 650 mayors in the United States.

### National Funeral Directors and Morticians Association (NFD&MA)

6290 Shannon Parkway
Union City, GA 30291
Phone: (800) 434-0958
Fax: (404) 286-6573
http://www.nfdma.com

This organization promotes the professional interests of its members and holds them to the highest professional standards. The NFD&MA also offers service and educational programs for the public and assists in disaster relief efforts.

### National Medical Association (NMA)

8403 Colesville Road, Suite 920
Silver Spring, MD 20910
Phone: (202) 347-1895
Fax: (202) 347-0722
http://nmanet.org

The NMA is devoted to the concerns of African Americans regarding health and medical care. The organization of black doctors and health care professionals educates the public on HIV and AIDS, asthma, cancer, immunizations, heart disease and strokes, clinical trials, obesity, diabetes, and kidney disease. The NMA established the Cobb Institute to research and disseminate information about illness. Publications include the *Journal of the National Medical Association* and numerous pamphlets available online.

### National Pharmaceutical Association (NPhA)

107 Kilmayne Drive, Suite C
Cary, NC 27511
Phone: (877) 215-2091
Fax: (919) 469-5870
http://www.npha.net

The NPhA represents and supports minority pharmacists. It counsels members and students about fellowships, geriatrics studies, internships, certification, and financial planning.

### National Society of Black Engineers (NSBE)

205 Daingerfield Road
Alexandria, VA 22314
Phone: (703) 549-2207
Fax: (703) 683-5312
http://www.nsbe.org

The NSBE promotes academic and professional achievement among African Americans in the engineering field. It provides professional development, mentoring, and job placement and promotes community and cultural involvement among members.

*—Chrissy Lutz*

# Research Centers and Libraries

*Included here are libraries and research centers offering extensive primary and secondary resources for African American history and biography. In most cases, the material can be found through the institution's online library catalog, and many of the collections are represented by online finding aids. Most institutions are making a strong effort to provide at least some of their material in a digital format.*

### African American Museum and Library at Oakland

659 14th Street
Oakland, CA 94612
(510) 637-0200
mos@oaklandlibrary.org
http://www.oaklandlibrary.org/AAMLO/

More than 160 collections containing the papers of individuals and organizations document African Americans in California and the West, particularly in Northern California and the Bay Area. The oral-history collection holds interviews with local civil rights activists, educators, writers, and musicians.

### Amistad Research Center

Tilton Hall
6823 St. Charles Avenue
Tulane University
New Orleans, LA 70118
(504) 862-3222
reference@amistadresearchcenter.org
http://www.amistadresearchcenter.org/

The Amistad Research Center provides original materials on the social and cultural history of African Americans. Holdings include the papers of artists, educators, authors, business leaders, clergy, lawyers, factory workers, farmers, and musicians, along with approximately 250,000 photographs and four hundred works of African and African American art.

### Auburn Avenue Research Library on African American Culture and History

Atlanta-Fulton Public Library
101 Auburn Avenue NE
Atlanta, GA 30303-2503
(404) 730-4001, ext. 100
aarl.reference@fultoncountyga.gov
http://www.af.public.lib.ga.us/aarl

Part of the Atlanta-Fulton Public Library System, the Auburn Avenue Research Library offers archival collections related to African American culture and history with a concentration on local Atlanta history, serving the general public, students, and scholars with textual and microform records, including art and artifacts, rare book collections, and textiles.

### Avery Research Center for African American History and Culture

125 Bull Street
College of Charleston
Charleston, SC 29424
(843) 953-7608
AveryResearchCenter@cofc.edu
http://avery.cofc.edu/

The Avery Research Center provides an archive of nearly four thousand primary and secondary source materials documenting the African American experience, focusing on Charleston, the Low Country, and South Carolina. With two hundred manuscript collections, more than five thousand printed items, and four thousand photographs, the holdings are particularly strong in Gullah and Sea Island culture, slavery, and the Civil War and Reconstruction.

### The Black Archives, History and Research Foundation of South Florida, Inc.

5400 Northwest 22d Avenue
Building C, Suite 101
Miami, FL 33142
(305) 636-2390
baf@theblackarchives.org
http://www.theblackarchives.org

This foundation collects, preserves, and disseminates the history and culture of black South Florida from 1896 to the present, with an emphasis on the twentieth century urban South, for the use of students, artists, researchers, the media, and the community.

### Black Archives of Mid-America

2033 Vine
Kansas City, MO 64108
(816) 241-2272

Via form on Web site

http://www.blackarchives.org/

To facilitate both scholarly inquiry and public understanding of African American history, the Black Archives of Mid-America collects and preserves materials documenting African American social, economic, political, and cultural history, with particular emphasis on the Kansas City, Missouri, region.

**Center for Black Studies Research**

4603 South Hall

University of California

Santa Barbara, CA 93106-3140

(805) 893-3914

ctr4blst@cbs.ucsb.edu

http://research.ucsb.edu/cbs/

The Center for Black Studies Research serves as the major Haitian studies center west of the Mississippi. Its academic mission is to support interdisciplinary research on the social, political, historical, cultural, and economic experiences of communities throughout the African diaspora.

**Charles L. Blockson Afro-American Historical Collection**

Sullivan Hall (007-XX)

1330 West Berks Street

Temple University

Philadelphia, PA 19122

(215) 204-6849

ddturner@temple.edu

http://library.temple.edu/collections/blockson

More than 500,000 items on the global black experience form the Charles L. Blockson Afro-American Collection, including rare books, prints, photographs, slave narratives, manuscripts, letters, sheet music, foreign-language publications, and ephemera, as well as holdings in African, African American, and African Caribbean publications dating back to the sixteenth century.

**Daley Library Special Collections and University Archives**

801 South Morgan Street, Room 3-330

University of Illinois at Chicago

Chicago, IL 60607

(312) 996-2742

Via form on Web site

http://www.uic.edu/depts/lib/specialcoll/

The Special Collections Department of the Richard J. Daley Library, University of Illinois at Chicago, holds

assorted archival materials—including audio reels, letters, transcripts, brochures, and clippings—related to African American history. The holdings are particularly strong in papers from twentieth century African American organizations, such as the Associated Negro Press, Black Panthers, National Alliance of Black Feminists, National Black Feminist Organization, Commission on Interracial Cooperation, and local Urban League chapters.

**John Henrik Clarke Africana Library**

Cornell University Africana Studies and Research

　Center

310 Triphammer Road

Cornell University

Ithaca, NY 14850

(607) 255-3822

afrlib@cornell.edu

http://www.library.cornell.edu/africana/

The Cornell University Africana Studies and Research Center houses the John Henrik Clarke Africana Library. Here researchers will find a collection of more than eighteen thousand volumes focusing on the history and cultures of peoples of African descent in their social, economic, and political dimensions.

**John Hope Franklin Research Center for African and African American History and Culture**

Perkins Library

Duke University

Durham, NC 27708

(919) 660-5922

franklin-collection@duke.edu

http://library.duke.edu/specialcollections/franklin/

The John Hope Franklin Research Center provides materials for the history of Africa and people of African descent, focusing on those generated by them, as opposed to being about them. Many of the holdings are available online. The Black Voices Collection groups first-person accounts of preachers, teachers, missionaries, lawyers, physicians, soldiers, politicians, activists, journalists, and entrepreneurs, as well as many former slaves or children of slaves. Features "Jim Crow narratives," texts written by African Americans born after the end of slavery, most between 1860 and 1919.

**Library of Congress**

101 Independence Avenue SE

Washington, DC 20540

(202) 707-5000

Via form on Web site
http://lcweb2.loc.gov/ammem/aaohtml/aohome.html

The Library of Congress provides extensive material, much of it freely available online in digital format. The African-American Odyssey: A Quest for Full Citizenship displays the library's array of books, government documents, manuscripts, maps, musical scores, plays, and films. Major collections include the Frederick Douglass Papers; Slaves and the Courts, 1740-1860; the African American Pamphlet Collection; and more than twenty-three hundred first-person accounts of slavery and five hundred photographs of former slaves.

**Mayme Clayton Library and Museum**
4130 Overland Avenue
Culver City, CA 90230
(310) 202-1647
info@claytonmuseum.org
http://www.claytonmuseum.org

The Mayme A. Clayton Collection comprises more than ten thousand rare and out-of-print books, including a signed copy of a Phillis Wheatley book; about seventeen hundred film titles and film posters; seventy-five thousand photographs; more than one thousand documents, including pre-Civil War material; and three hundred pieces of personal correspondence.

**Moorland-Spingarn Research Center**
Howard University
Washington, DC 20059
(202) 806-7240
Via form on Web site
http://www.founders.howard.edu/moorland-spingarn/

The Moorland-Spingarn Research Center (MARC), one of the largest and most comprehensive collections of material on the history and culture of the African diaspora, collects, preserves, and makes accessible more than 175,000 bound volumes and tens of thousands of journals, periodicals, and newspapers; more than 17,000 feet of manuscript and archival collections; nearly 1,000 audio tapes; hundreds of artifacts; and 100,000 prints, photographs, maps, and other graphic items.

**Neal-Marshall Black Culture Center Library**
Neal-Marshall Center A113
275 North Jordan
Indiana University
Bloomington, IN 47405
(812) 855-3237

Via form on Web site
http://www.libraries.iub.edu/index.php?pageId=75

The NMBCC Library emphasizes the history and culture of African Americans, with a core collection of five thousand monographs on African American history and culture focusing on the performing arts: music, dance, theater, television, and film.

**Ralph J. Bunche Center for African American Studies Library and Media Center**
160 Haines Hall
Box 951545
University of California
Los Angeles, CA 90095-1545
(310) 825-7403
dhunter@bunche.ucla.edu (Librarian Dalena Hunter)
http://www.bunche.ucla.edu

The Ralph J. Bunche Library and Media Center, part of the Center for African American Studies, holds books, journals, multimedia, and archives documenting the African, African American, and Afro-Caribbean experience, with more than eight thousand books, unique items documenting lesser known civil rights struggles, and early data on African American communities.

**Robert W. Woodruff Library**
Atlanta University Center
111 James P. Brawley Drive, SW
Atlanta, GA 30314
(404) 978-2000
askref@auctr.edu
http://www.auctr.edu/rwwl

With a focus on the African, African American, and Caribbean experience, the Woodruff Library's Archives and Special Collections contain rare publications and manuscript holdings that document civil rights, race relations, education, literature, visual and performing arts, religion, politics, and social work. Highlights of the collection include records of the Commission on Interracial Cooperation, Southern Regional Council, and Freedmen's Aid Society.

**Schomburg Center for Research in Black Culture**
New York Public Library
515 Malcolm X Boulevard
New York, NY 10037-1801
(212) 491-2200
scmarbref@nypl.org
http://www.nypl.org/locations/schomburg

The Schomburg Center, a research unit of the New York Public Library, provides access to more than ten million items, including art objects, audio and video tapes, books, manuscripts, films, newspapers, periodicals, photographs, prints, music discs, and sheet music.

### Southeastern Regional Black Archives Research Center and Museum

Carnegie Library
Florida Agricultural and Mechanical University
Tallahassee, FL 32307
(850) 599-3020
http://www.famu.edu/index.cfm?blackarchives

The center holds archival records relating to the history of African American institutions and organizations. Its strengths are in manuscripts, rare books, journals, magazines, maps, newspapers, and photographs.

### Vivian G. Harsh Research Collection of Afro-American History and Literature

Carter G. Woodson Regional Library
Chicago Public Library
9525 South Halsted Street
Chicago, IL 60628
(312) 747-6900

Via form on Web site
http://www.chipublib.org/branch/details/library/woodson-regional/p/FeatHarsh/

As the largest African American history and literature collection in the Midwest, the Vivian G. Harsh Collection, concentrating on African American history in Illinois, includes seventy thousand books, many of them rare; more than five thousand reels of microfilm; and manuscript holdings, such as those of Richard Wright, Langston Hughes, and Arna Bontemps.

### W. E. B. Du Bois Library Special Collections

154 Hicks Way
University of Massachusetts
Amherst, MA 01003
(413) 545-2780
askanarc@library.umass.edu
http://www.library.umass.edu/spcoll/

With approximately thirty-five thousand rare books, nationally significant manuscript collections, and historical maps, the library's Department of Special Collections has substantial holdings in African American history and culture, as well as social and racial justice, including the papers of W. E. B. Du Bois.

—*Jan Voogd*

# BIBLIOGRAPHY

*This bibliography offers resources about African Americans, beginning with general reference and then arranged alphabetically by areas of achievement.*

## CONTENTS

General Reference Works. . . . . . . . . . . . 1673
Art, Architecture, and Photography . . . . . . 1674
Business and Industry . . . . . . . . . . . . . . 1674
Civil Rights and Social Activism . . . . . . . . 1674
Culture and History . . . . . . . . . . . . . . . 1675
Education . . . . . . . . . . . . . . . . . . . . . 1676
Entertainment: Dance, Film, and Television . . . . 1676

Journalism and Publishing . . . . . . . . . . . 1677
Military and War . . . . . . . . . . . . . . . . . 1677
Music . . . . . . . . . . . . . . . . . . . . . . . 1678
Politics, Government, and Leadership . . . . . . 1679
Religion . . . . . . . . . . . . . . . . . . . . . . 1679
Science, Medicine, and Technology . . . . . . . 1680
Sports . . . . . . . . . . . . . . . . . . . . . . . 1680

## GENERAL REFERENCE WORKS

Abdul-Jabbar, Kareem, and Alan Steinberg. *Black Profiles in Courage: A Legacy of African American Achievement.* New York: Perennial, 2000.

Baraka, Amiri, and Larry Neal, eds. *Black Fire: An Anthology of Afro-American Writing.* 1968. Baltimore: Black Classics Press, 2007.

Braithwaite, Kisha, Paula Mitchell, and Veronica G. Thomas. *African American Women: An Annotated Bibliography.* Westport, Conn.: Greenwood Press, 2000.

Burg, Barbara A., et al. *Guide to African American and African Primary Sources at Harvard University.* Westport, Conn.: Greenwood Press, 2000.

Claytor, Constance, and Joan Potter. *African American Firsts: Famous, Little-Known and Unsung Triumphs of Blacks in America.* Elizabethtown, N.Y.: Pinto Press, 1994.

Daley, James. *Great Speeches by African Americans: Frederick Douglass, Sojourner Truth, Dr. Martin Luther King, Jr., Barack Obama, and Others.* Mineola, N.Y.: Dover, 2006.

Davies, Carole E. Boyce. *Encyclopedia of the African Diaspora: Origins, Experiences, and Culture.* 3 vols. Santa Barbara, Calif.: ABC-CLIO, 2008.

Flamming, Douglas. *African Americans in the West.* Santa Barbara, Calif.: ABC-CLIO, 2009.

Gates, Henry Louis, Jr., and Evelyn Brooks Higginbotham. *The African American National Biography.* 8 vols. New York: Oxford University Press, 2008.

Hawkins, Walter L. *African American Biographies, 3: Profiles of 909 Current Men and Women.* Jefferson, N.C.: McFarland, 2009.

Hine, Darlene Clark, and Kathleen Thompson. *Encyclopedia of Black Women in America.* New York: Facts On File, 1997.

Hudson, Wade. *Powerful Words: More than 200 Years of Extraordinary Writing by African Americans.* New York: Scholastic, 2004.

Johnson, Vernon D., and Bill Lyne. *Walkin' the Talk: An Anthology of African American Studies.* Upper Saddle River, N.J.: Prentice Hall, 2002.

Kinshasa, Kwando M. *African American Chronology.* Westport, Conn.: Greenwood Press, 2006.

Mallegg, Kristin B. *Who's Who Among African Americans.* Detroit: Gale, 2010.

Miles, Johnnie H., et al. *Almanac of African American Heritage: A Book of Lists Featuring People, Places, Times, and Events That Shaped Black Culture.* San Francisco, Calif.: Jossey-Bass, 2001.

Mullane, Deirdre. *Crossing the Danger Water: Three Hundred Years of African-American Writing.* New York: Anchor Books, 1993.

Newman, Richard. *Black Access: A Bibliography of Afro-American Bibliographies.* Westport, Conn.: Greenwood Press, 1984.

Rustavo, S. T. *Black American Culture and Society: An Annotated Bibliography.* New York: Nova Science, 1994.

Schomburg Center for Research in Black Culture, New York Public Library. *African American Desk Reference.* New York: John Wiley & Sons, 1999.

Smith, Jessie C. *Black Firsts: Four Thousand Ground-Breaking and Pioneering Historical Events.* Detroit: Visible Ink Press, 2003.

Smith, Jessie C., and Joseph M. Palmisano. *Reference Li-

*brary of Black America.* Farmington Hills, Mich.: Gale Group, 2000.

Stevenson, Rosemary M. *Index to Afro-American Reference Resources.* Westport, Conn.: Greenwood Press, 1988.

Thompson, Kathleen, and Hilary Austin. *The Face of Our Past: Images of Black Women from Colonial America to the Present.* Bloomington: Indiana University Press, 2000.

## ART, ARCHITECTURE, AND PHOTOGRAPHY

Bearden, Romare, and Harry Henderson. *A History of African-American Artists from 1792 to the Present.* New York: Pantheon Books, 1993.

Farris, Phoebe. *Women Artists of Color: A Bio-Critical Sourcebook to 20th Century Artists in the Americas.* Westport, Conn.: Greenwood Press, 1999.

Jegede, Dele. *Encyclopedia of African American Artists.* Westport, Conn.: Greenwood Press, 2009.

Macklin, A. D. *A Biographical History of African-American Artists, A-Z.* Lewiston, N.Y.: Edwin Mellen Press, 2001.

Thomison, Dennis. *The Black Artist in America: An Index to Reproductions.* Metuchen, N.J.: Scarecrow Press, 1991.

Weiss, Ellen B. *An Annotated Bibliography of African-American Architects and Builders.* Philadelphia, Pa.: Society of Architectural Historians, 1993.

Williams, Ora. *American Black Women in the Arts and Social Sciences.* 3d ed. Metuchen, N.J.: Scarecrow Press, 1994.

Willis, Deborah. *Reflections in Black: A History of Black Photographers 1840 to the Present.* New York: W. W. Norton, 2000.

_____, et al. *Let Your Motto Be Resistance: African American Portraits.* Washington, D.C.: National Museum of African American History and Culture, Smithsonian Institute, 2007.

Wilson, Dreck Spurlock. *African-American Architects: A Biographical Dictionary, 1865-1945.* New York: Routledge, 2004.

## BUSINESS AND INDUSTRY

Ballard, Donna. *Doing It for Ourselves: Success Stories of African-American Women in Business.* New York: Berkley Books, 1997.

Bell, Gregory S. *In the Black: A History of African Americans on Wall Street.* New York: John Wiley & Sons, 2002.

Biddle, Stanton F. *The African-American Yellow Pages: A Comprehensive Resource Guide and Directory.* New York: Henry Holt, 1996.

Cobbs, Price M., and Judith L. Turnock. *Cracking the Corporate Code: The Revealing Success Stories of Thirty-two African-American Executives.* New York: Amacom, 2003.

Dingle, Derek T. *Black Enterprise Titans of the B.E. 100's: Black CEOs Who Redefined and Conquered American Business.* New York: John Wiley & Sons, 2002.

Harris, Wendy, and Wendy Beech. *Against All Odds: Ten Entrepreneurs Who Followed Their Hearts and Found Success.* New York: John Wiley & Sons, 2001.

Ingham, John N., and Lynne B. Feldman. *African-American Business Leaders: A Biographical Dictionary.* Westport, Conn.: Greenwood Press, 1994.

Kranz, Rachel. *African-American Business Leaders and Entrepreneurs.* A to Z of African Americans. New York: Facts On File, 2004.

Smith, Jessie C. *Encyclopedia of African American Business.* 2 vols. Westport, Conn.: Greenwood Press, 2006.

Walker, Juliet E. K. *Encyclopedia of African American Business History.* Westport, Conn.: Greenwood Press, 1999.

Woodard, Michael D. *Black Entrepreneurs in America: Stories of Struggle and Success.* New Brunswick, N.J.: Rutgers University Press, 1998.

## CIVIL RIGHTS AND SOCIAL ACTIVISM

Bowser, Benjamin P., and Louis Kushnick. *Against the Odds: Scholars Who Challenged Racism in the Twentieth Century.* Amherst: University of Massachusetts Press, 2002.

Branch, Taylor. *Parting the Waters: America in the King Years, 1954-1963.* New York: Simon & Schuster, 1989.

_____. *Pillar of Fire: America in the King Years 1963-65.* New York: Simon & Schuster, 1999.

_____. *At Canaan's Edge: America in the King Years, 1965-68.* New York: Simon & Schuster, 2006.

Carrier, Jim. *A Traveler's Guide to the Civil Rights Movement.* Orlando, Fla.: Harcourt, 2004.

Carson, Clayborne, et al., eds. *The Eyes on the Prize Civil Rights Reader: Documents, Speeches, and Firsthand Accounts from the Black Freedom Struggle.* New York: Penquin, 1991.

Collier-Thomas, Bettye, and V. P. Franklin. *Sisters in the Struggle: African American Women in the Civil Rights-Black Power Movement.* New York: New York University Press, 2001.

Crawford, Vicki L., Jacqueline Anne Rouse, and Barbara Woods. *Women in the Civil Rights Movement: Trailblazers and Torchbearers, 1941-1965*. Bloomington: Indiana University Press, 1993.

Gore, Dayo F., Jeanne Theoharis, and Komozi Woodard. *Want to Start a Revolution? Radical Women in the Black Freedom Struggle*. New York: New York University Press, 2009.

Hampton, Henry, Steve Fayer, and Sarah Flynn, comps. *Voices of Freedom: An Oral History of the Civil Rights Movement from the 1950's Through the 1980's*. New York: Bantam Books, 1990.

Marable, Manning, and Leith Mullings, eds. *Let Nobody Turn Us Around: Voices of Resistance, Reform, and Renewal: An African American Anthology*. Lanham, Md.: Rowman & Littlefield, 2000.

Murray, Paul T. *The Civil Rights Movement: References and Resources*. New York: G. K. Hall, 1993.

Sargent, Frederic O. *The Civil Rights Revolution: Events and Leaders, 1955-1968*. Jefferson, N.C.: McFarland, 2004.

Sugrue, Thomas J. *Sweet Land of Liberty: The Forgotten Struggle for Civil Rights in the North*. New York: Random House, 2008.

Sullivan, Patricia. *Lift Every Voice: The NAACP and the Making of the Civil Rights Movement*. New York: New Press, 2009.

Williams, Juan. *Eyes on the Prize: America's Civil Rights Years, 1954-1965*. New York: Penguin, 1988.

Wynn, Linda T., and Jessie C. Smith. *Freedom Facts and Firsts: 400 Years of the African American Civil Rights Experience*. Canton, Mich.: Visible Ink Press, 2009.

## CULTURE AND HISTORY

Alexander, Leslie M., and Walter C. Rucker, eds. *Encyclopedia of African American History*. 3 vols. Santa Barbara, Calif.: ABC-CLIO, 2010.

Appiah, Kwame Anthony, and Henry Louis Gates, Jr. *Africana: The Encyclopedia of the African and African American Experience*. New York: Basic Books, 2005.

Arsenault, Raymond. *Freedom Riders: 1961 and the Struggle for Racial Justice*. New York: Oxford University Press, 2006.

Asante, Molefi K., and Mark T. Mattson. *The African-American Atlas: Black History and Culture—An Illustrated Reference*. New York: Macmillan, 1998.

Battle, Thomas C., and Donna M. Wells. *Legacy: Treasures of Black History*. Washington, D.C.: National Geographic, 2006.

Boyd, Herb. *Autobiography of a People: Three Centuries of African American History Told by Those Who Lived It*. New York: Doubleday, 2000.

Brosman, Catharine S. *Dictionary of Twentieth Century Culture: African American Culture*. Detroit, Mich: Gale Cengage, 1996.

Chafe, William H. *Remembering Jim Crow: African Americans Tell About Life in the Segregated South*. New York: New Press, 2001.

Davis, Thomas J., and Michael L. Conniff. *Africans in the Americas: A History of the Black Diaspora*. New York: St. Martin's Press, 1994.

Earle, Jonathan Halperin. *The Routledge Atlas of African American History*. New York: Routledge, 2000.

Finkelman, Paul. *Encyclopedia of African American History, 1619-1895: From the Colonial Period to the Age of Frederick Douglass*. New York: Oxford University Press, 2006.

_____. *Encyclopedia of African American History, 1896 to the Present: From the Age of Segregation to the Twenty-first Century*. New York: Oxford University Press, 2009.

George, Nelson. *Post-Soul Nation: The Explosive, Contradictory, Triumphant, and Tragic 1980's as Experienced by African Americans (Previously Known as Blacks and Before That Negroes)*. New York: Viking, 2004.

Halliburton, Warren J. *Historic Speeches of African Americans*. New York: F. Watts, 1993.

Harley, Sharon. *The Timetables of African-American History: A Chronology of the Most Important People and Events in African-American History*. New York: Simon & Schuster, 1996.

Harris, Robert L., and Rosalyn Terborg-Penn. *The Columbia Guide to African American History Since 1939*. New York: Columbia University Press, 2008.

Higginbotham, Evelyn B., Leon F. Litwack, and Darlene C. Hine. *The Harvard Guide to African-American History*. Cambridge, Mass.: Harvard University Press, 2001.

Hine, Darlene C., and Jacqueline McLeod. *Crossing Boundaries: Comparative History of Black People in Diaspora*. Bloomington: Indiana University Press, 1999.

Holland, Jesse J. *Black Men Built the Capitol: Discovering African-American History in and Around Washington, D.C.* Guilford, Conn.: Globe Pequot Press, 2007.

Hornsby, Alton. *A Companion to African American History*. Malden, Mass.: Blackwell, 2005.

_____. *Milestones in Twentieth Century African-American History*. Detroit: Visible Ink Press, 1993.

Joseph, Peniel E. *Waiting 'Til the Midnight Hour: A Narrative History of Black Power in America*. New York: Henry Holt, 2006.

Katz, William L. *The Black West: A Documentary and Pictorial History of the African American Role in the Westward Expansion of the United States*. New York: Simon & Schuster, 1996.

Kelley, Robin D. G., and Earl Lewis. *To Make Our World Anew: A History of African Americans*. New York: Oxford University Press, 2000.

Laird, Taneshia N., Elihu Bey, and Roland O. Laird. *Still I Rise: A Graphic History of African Americans*. New York: Sterling, 2009.

Maguire, Jack, and Thomas D. Cowan. *Timelines of African-American History: 500 Years of Black Achievement*. New York: Berkley, 1994.

Marable, Manning, Nishani Frazier, and John C. McMillian. *Freedom on My Mind: The Columbia Documentary History of the African American Experience*. New York: Columbia University Press, 2003.

Mullings, Leith, Sophie Spencer-Wood, and Manning Marable. *Freedom: A Photographic History of the African American Struggle*. London: Phaidon Press, 2002.

Painter, Nell I. *Creating Black Americans: African-American History and Its Meanings, 1619 to the Present*. New York: Oxford University Press, 2006.

Palmer, Colin A. *Encyclopedia of African American Culture and History: The Black Experience in the Americas*. 6 vols. Detroit: Macmillan, 2006.

Salzman, Jack, David L. Smith, and Cornel West. *Encyclopedia of African-American Culture and History*. New York: Macmillan, 1996.

Schneider, Mark R. *African Americans in the Jazz Age: A Decade of Struggle and Promise*. Lanham, Md.: Rowman & Littlefield, 2006.

Spivey, Donald. *Fire from the Soul: A History of the African-American Struggle*. Durham, N.C.: Carolina Academic Press, 2003.

Wright, Kai. *The African American Experience: Black History and Culture Through Speeches, Letters, Editorials, Poems, Songs, and Stories*. New York: Black Dog and Leventhal, 2009.

## EDUCATION

Anderson, Noel S., and Haroon Kharem. *Education as Freedom: African American Educational Thought and Activism*. Lanham, Md.: Lexington Books, 2010.

Bower, Beverly L., and Mimi Wolverton. *Answering the Call: African American Women in Higher Education Leadership*. Sterling, Va.: Stylus, 2009.

Cox, Clinton, and James Haskins. *African American Teachers*. New York: John Wiley & Sons, 2000.

Dillihunt, Monica L., and Kenneth Maurice Tyler. *Connecting the Legacies: African American Scholars in Education*. New York: Peter Lang, 2007.

Fairclough, Adam. *A Class of Their Own: Black Teachers in the Segregated South*. Cambridge, Mass.: Belknap Press of Harvard University Press, 2007.

Gasman, Marybeth, and Katherine Sedgwick. *Uplifting a People: African American Philanthropy and Education*. New York: Peter Lang, 2005.

Jenoure, Terry. *Navigators: African American Musicians, Dancers, and Visual Artists in Academe*. Albany: State University of New York Press, 2000.

Wilds, Mary. *I Dare Not Fail: Notable African American Women Educators*. Greensboro, N.C.: Avisson Press, 2004.

## ENTERTAINMENT: DANCE, FILM, AND TELEVISION

Berry, Torriano, and Venise T. Berry. *The A to Z of African American Cinema*. Lanham, Md.: Scarecrow Press, 2009.

_____. *Historical Dictionary of African American Cinema*. Lanham, Md.: Scarecrow Press, 2007.

Bogle, Donald. *Blacks in American Films and Television: An Encyclopedia*. New York: Garland, 1989.

_____. *Bright Boulevards, Bold Dreams: The Story of Black Hollywood*. New York: One World Ballantine Books, 2005.

_____. *Brown Sugar: Over One Hundred Years of America's Black Female Superstars*. New York: Continuum, 2007.

Donalson, Melvin B. *Black Directors in Hollywood*. Austin: University of Texas Press, 2003.

Dreher, Kwakiutl L. *Dancing on the White Page: Black Women Entertainers Writing Autobiography*. Albany: State University of New York Press, 2008.

Fearn-Banks, Kathleen. *The A to Z of African-American Television*. Lanham, Md.: Scarecrow Press, 2009.

Geran, Trish. *Beyond the Glimmering Lights: The Pride and Perseverance of African Americans in Las Vegas*. Las Vegas: Stephens Press, 2006.

Gill, Glenda E. *No Surrender! No Retreat! African-American Pioneer Performers of Twentieth-Century American Theater*. New York: St. Martin's Press, 2000.

Glass, Barbara S. *African American Dance: An Illustrated History*. Jefferson, N.C.: McFarland, 2007.

Hacker, Carlotta. *Great African Americans in the Arts.* Outstanding African Americans. New York: Crabtree, 1997.

Hill, Anthony D. *Pages from the Harlem Renaissance: A Chronicle of Performance.* New York: P. Lang, 1996.

Lotz, Rainer E. *Black People: Entertainers of African Descent in Europe and Germany.* Bonn: Birgit Lotz Verlag, 1997.

MacDonald, Fred J. *Blacks and White TV: African Americans in Television Since 1948.* 2d ed. Florence, Ky.: Wadsworth, 1992.

Magus, Jim. *Magical Heroes: The Lives and Legends of Great African American Magicians.* Marietta, Ga.: Magus Enterprises, 1995.

Manchel, Frank. *Every Step a Struggle: Interviews with Seven Who Shaped the African-American Image in Movies.* Washington, D.C.: New Academia, 2007.

Mapp, Edward. *African Americans and the Oscar: Decades of Struggle and Achievement.* Lanham, Md.: Scarecrow Press, 2008.

Mask, Mia. *Divas on Screen: Black Women in American Film.* Urbana: University of Illinois Press, 2009.

Peterson, Bernard L. *Profiles of African American Stage Performers and Theatre People, 1816-1960.* Westport, Conn.: Greenwood Press, 2001.

Reed, Bill. *Hot from Harlem: Twelve African American Entertainers, 1890-1960.* Jefferson, N.C.: McFarland, 2010.

Regester, Charlene B. *African American Actresses: The Struggle for Visibility, 1900-1960.* Bloomington: Indiana University Press, 2010.

Rennert, Richard S. *Performing Artists. Profiles of Great Black Americans.* New York: Chelsea House, 1994.

Tanner, Jo A. *Dusky Maidens: The Odyssey of the Early Black Dramatic Actress.* Westport, Conn.: Greenwood Press, 1992.

## JOURNALISM AND PUBLISHING

Broussard, Jinx C. *Giving a Voice to the Voiceless: Four Pioneering Black Women Journalists.* New York: Routledge, 2004.

Dawkins, Wayne. *Rugged Waters: Black Journalists Swim the Mainstream.* Newport News, Va.: August Press, 2003.

Jackson, Ronald L., and Sonja M. Brown Givens. *Black Pioneers in Communication Research.* Thousand Oaks, Calif.: Sage Publications, 2006.

Joyce, Donald F. *Black Book Publishers in the United States: A Historical Dictionary of the Presses, 1817-1990.* Westport, Conn.: Greenword Press, 1991.

Potter, Vilma Raskin. *A Reference Guide to Afro-American Publications and Editors, 1827-1946.* Ames: Iowa State University Press, 1993.

Streitmatter, Rodger. *Raising Her Voice: African-American Women Journalists Who Changed History.* Lexington: University Press of Kentucky, 1994.

Terry, Wallace. *Missing Pages: Black Journalists of Modern America—An Oral History.* New York: Carroll and Graf, 2007.

Wolseley, Roland Edgar. *Black Achievers in American Journalism.* Nashville, Tenn.: James C. Winston 1995.

**LITERATURE.** *See* **"LITERARY BIBLIOGRAPHY"** IN THIS VOLUME, PAGES **1658-1664**

## MILITARY AND WAR

Astor, Gerald. *The Right to Fight: A History of African Americans in the Military.* Novato, Calif.: Presidio, 1998.

Brown, Edward. *A Brief History of African Americans in the Military.* De Soto, Tex.: Edward Rose Counseling, 1997.

Buckley, Gail L. *American Patriots: The Story of Blacks in the Military from the Revolution to Desert Storm.* New York: Random House, 2002.

Burbridge, Doris A. D. V., et al. *African-Americans in the Military: World War I and World War II, Selected Biographies.* New York: AAHGS-NY Writers Group, 2008.

Dunklin, Arthur L. *African American Men and Opportunity in the Navy: Personal Histories of Eight Chiefs.* Jefferson, N.C.: McFarland, 2008.

Goff, Stanley, Robert Sanders, and Clark Smith. *Brothers: Black Soldiers in the Nam.* New York: Berkley, 1987.

Hawkins, Walter L. *African American Generals and Flag Officers: Biographies of Over 120 Blacks in the United States Military.* Jefferson, N.C.: McFarland, 1993.

_____. *Black American Military Leaders: A Biographical Dictionary.* Jefferson, N.C.: McFarland, 2007.

Homan, Lynn M., and Thomas Reilly. *Black Knights: The Story of the Tuskegee Airmen.* Gretna, La.: Pelican, 2001.

Latty, Yvonne, comp. *We Were There: Voices of African American Veterans from World War II to the War in Iraq.* New York: Amistad, 2004.

Moore, Christopher P. *Fighting for America: Black Soldiers, the Unsung Heroes of World War II*. New York: One World, 2005.

Reef, Catherine. *African Americans in the Military*. New York: Facts On File, 2004.

Schneller, Robert John. *Breaking the Color Barrier: The U.S. Naval Academy's First Black Midshipmen and the Struggle for Racial Equality*. New York: New York University Press, 2005.

Weir, William. *The Encyclopedia of African American Military History*. Amherst, N.Y.: Prometheus Books, 2004.

Wright, Kai. *Soldiers of Freedom: An Illustrated History of African Americans in the Armed Forces*. New York: Black Dog and Leventhal, 2002.

## Music

Berry, Lemuel J. *Great African American Musicians: From Marian Anderson to Stevie Wonder*. Lewiston, N.Y.: Edwin Mellen Press, 2010.

Bianco, David. *Heat Wave: The Motown Fact Book*. Ann Arbor, Mich.: Pierian Press, 1988.

Camp, Shermanita. *Blacks in the Holocaust: An Untold and Striking Story of Survival of Seven Black Jazz Musicians in Hitler's Concentration Camp*. Hollywood, Calif.: Hallelujah, 2000.

Cheatham, Wallace. *Dialogues on Opera and the African-American Experience*. Lanham, Md.: Scarecrow Press, 1997.

Clifford, Mike, Jon Futrell, Ray Bonds, et al. *The Illustrated Encyclopedia of Black Music*. New York: Random House, 1988.

Crazy Horse, K. *Rip It Up: The Black Experience in Rock'n'Roll*. New York: Palgrave Macmillan, 2004.

Davis, Angela Y. *Blues Legacies and Black Feminism: Gertrude "Ma" Rainey, Bessie Smith, and Billie Holiday*. New York: Pantheon Books, 1999.

Davis, Sharon. *Chinwaggin': The Classic Soul Interviews*. New Romney, Kent, England: Bank House Books, 2006.

Donovan, Richard X. *Black Musicians of America*. Portland, Oreg.: National Book Co., 1991.

Floyd, Samuel A., and Marsha J. Reisser. *Black Music Biography: An Annotated Bibliography*. White Plains, N.Y.: Kraus, 1987.

Foster, Pamela E. *My Country, Too: The Other Black Music*. Nashville, Tenn.: My Country, 2000.

Gambrell-Drayton, Joyce. *Distinguished Church Musicians in the United States*. Philadelphia: Church Musicians Services, 1994.

Greig, Charlotte. *Icons of Black Music*. San Diego, Calif.: Thunder Bay Press, 1999.

Handy, D. A. *Black Women in American Bands and Orchestras*. Metuchen, N.J.: Scarecrow Press, 1999.

Hine, Darlene C., and Kathleen Thompson. *Music*. Vol. 5 in *Facts On File Encyclopedia of Black Women in America*. New York: Facts On File, 1997.

Jasper, Kenji, Ytasha Womack, Robert Johnson, and Mark Allwood. *Beats, Rhymes and Life: What We Love and Hate About Hip-Hop*. New York: Harlem Moon/Broadway Books, 2007.

Mandel, Howard. *Miles, Ornette, Cecil: How Miles Davis, Ornette Coleman, and Cecil Taylor Revolutionized the World of Jazz*. London: Routledge, 2007.

Nash, Elizabeth, comp. *Autobiographical Reminiscences of African-American Classical Singers, 1853-Present: Introducing Their Spiritual Heritage into the Concert Repertoire*. Lewiston, N.Y.: Edwin Mellen Press, 2007.

Neff, Robert, and Anthony Connor. *The Blues: In Images and Interviews*. New York: Cooper Square Press, 1999.

Oliver, Paul. *The Story of the Blues*. Boston: Northeastern University Press, 1998.

Othello, J. *The Soul of Rock 'n Roll: A History of African Americans in Rock Music*. Oakland, Calif.: Regent Press, 2004.

Porter, Eric. *What Is This Thing Called Jazz? African American Musicians as Artists, Critics, and Activists*. Berkeley: University of California Press, 2002.

Price, Emmett George, III, ed. *Encyclopedia of African American Music*. 3 vols. Westport, Conn.: Greenwood Press, 2010.

Ramsey, Frederic, and Charles E. Smith. *Jazzmen*. New York: Limelight, 1985.

Rubin, Dave. *Inside the Blues: 1942 to 1982*. Milwaukee, Wis.: Hal Leonard, 2007.

Rylatt, Keith. *Groovesville USA: The Detroit Soul and R&B Index*. Great Britain: Stuart Russell, 2010.

Smith, Eric L. *Blacks in Opera: An Encyclopedia of People and Companies, 1873-1993*. Jefferson, N.C.: McFarland, 1995.

Spellman, A. B. *Four Jazz Lives*. Ann Arbor: University of Michigan Press, 2004.

Taylor, Art. *Notes and Tones: Musician-to-Musician Interviews*. New York: Da Capo Press, 1993.

Turner, Patricia. *Dictionary of Afro-American Performers: 78 RPM and Cylinder Recordings of Opera, Choral Music, and Song, 1900-1949*. New York: Garland, 1990.

Walker-Hill, Helen. *From Spirituals to Symphonies: African-American Women Composers and Their Music*. Westport, Conn.: Greenwood Press, 2002.

Ward, Andrew. *Dark Midnight When I Rise: The Story of the Fisk Jubilee Singers*. New York: Amistad, 2001.

## POLITICS, GOVERNMENT, AND LEADERSHIP

Amer, Mildred L. *Black Members of the United States Congress with Biographies, 1789-2004*. New York: Novinka Books, 2007.

Clay, William L. *Just Permanent Interests: Black Americans in Congress, 1870-1991*. New York: Amistad Press, 1992.

Elliot, Jeffrey M. *Encyclopedia of African-American Politics*. Santa Barbara, Calif.: ABC-CLIO, 1995.

Farrar, Hayward. *Leaders and Movements: African American Life*. Vero Beach, Fla.: Rourke Press, 1995.

Freedman, Eric, and Stephen A. Jones. *African Americans in Congress: A Documentary History*. Washington, D.C.: CQ Press, 2008.

Hackney, Carrie M., and Arthuree M. L. Wright. *"The Black Church and the Spirituality of Politics": A Bibliography Compiled for the 80th Annual Convocation of the Howard University School of Divinity*. Washington, D.C.: Howard University Libraries, 1996.

Haskins, James. *Distinguished African American Political and Governmental Leaders*. Phoenix, Ariz.: Oryx Press, 1999.

Johnson, Ollie A., and Karin L. Stanford. *Black Political Organizations in the Post-Civil Rights Era*. New Brunswick, N.J.: Rutgers University Press, 2002.

King-Meadows, Tyson, and Thomas F. Schaller. *Devolution and Black State Legislators: Challenges and Choices in the Twenty-first Century*. Albany: State University of New York Press, 2006.

Ragsdale, Bruce A., and Joel D. Treese. *Black Americans in Congress, 1870-1989*. Washington, D.C.: U.S. Government Printing Office, 1990.

Salser, Mark R. *Black Americans in Congress*. Portland, Oreg.: National Book, 1991.

Schultz, Jeffrey D., et al., eds. *Encyclopedia of Minorities in American Politics*. 2 vols. Phoenix, Ariz.: Oryx Press, 2000.

Smith, Robert C. *Encyclopedia of African American Politics*. New York: Facts On File, 2003.

Tate, Katherine. *Black Faces in the Mirror: African Americans and Their Representatives in the U.S. Congress*. Princeton, N.J.: Princeton University Press, 2003.

Thompson, J. P. *Double Trouble: Black Mayors, Black Communities, and the Call for a Deep Democracy. Transgressing Boundaries*. New York: Oxford University Press, 2006.

Uschan, Michael V. *Blacks in Political Office*. Detroit, Mich.: Lucent Books, 2008.

Walters, Ronald W., and Cedric Johnson. *Bibliography of African American Leadership: An Annotated Guide*. Westport, Conn.: Greenwood Press, 2000.

White, John. *Black Leadership in America: From Booker T. Washington to Jesse Jackson*. London: Longman, 1990.

## RELIGION

Aaseng, Nathan. *African-American Religious Leaders: A-Z of African Americans*. New York: Facts On File, 2010.

Best, Felton O. *Black Religious Leadership from the Slave Community to the Million Man March: Flames of Fire*. Lewiston, N.Y.: Edwin Mellen Press, 1998.

DuPree, Sherry Sherrod. *African-American Holiness Pentecostal Movement: An Annotated Bibliography*. New York: Garland, 1996.

Hemesath, Caroline. *Our Black Shepherds: Biographies of the Ten Black Bishops of the United States*. Washington, D.C.: Josephite Pastoral Center, 1987.

Jones, Bobby, and Les Sussman. *Touched by God: America's Black Gospel Greats Share Their Stories of Finding God*. New York: Pocket Books, 1998.

Paris, Peter J. *Black Religious Leaders: Conflict in Unity*. Louisville, Ky.: Westminster John Knox Press, 2004.

Pinn, Anthony B., Stephen C. Finley, and Torin Alexander. *African American Religious Cultures*. Santa Barbara, Calif.: ABC-CLIO, 2009.

Raboteau, Albert J. *Canaan Land: A Religious History of African Americans*. New York: Oxford University Press, 2001.

Ritz, David. *Messengers: Portraits of African American Ministers, Evangelists, Gospel Singers, and Other Messengers of the Word*. New York: Doubleday, 2006.

Sernett, Milton C. *African American Religious History: A Documentary Witness*. 2d ed. Durham, N.C.: Duke University Press, 1999.

Wayman, A. W. *Cyclopædia of African Methodism*. Chapel Hill: University of North Carolina Press, 2000.

Williams, Juan, and Quinton H. Dixie. *This Far by Faith: Stories from the African-American Religious Experience*. New York: William Morrow, 2003.

## SCIENCE, MEDICINE, AND TECHNOLOGY

Barber, John T. *The Black Digital Elite: African American Leaders of the Information Revolution.* Westport, Conn.: Praeger, 2006.

Bellinger-Biggers, Vivian. *African American Science Books for Younger Readers.* Washington, D.C.: Library of Congress, 1994.

Bernstein, Leonard, Alan Winkler, and Linda Zierdt-Warshaw. *African and African American Women of Science.* Maywood, N.J.: Peoples Publishing Group, 1998.

Broadnax, Samuel L. *Blue Skies, Black Wings: African American Pioneers of Aviation.* Westport, Conn.: Praeger, 2007.

Brodie, James Michael. *Created Equal: The Lives and Ideas of Black American Innovators.* North Yorkshire, U.K.: Quill, 1994.

Carey, Charles W., Jr. *African Americans in Science: An Encyclopedia of People and Progress.* 2 vols. Santa Barbara, Calif.: ABC-CLIO, 2008.

Donovan, Richard X. *African-American Scientists.* Portland, Oreg.: National Book, 1999.

Greene, Robert E. *Physicians and Surgeons of Color: Real Image Models for Youth and Adults.* Fort Washington, Md.: R. E. Greene, 1996.

Gubert, Betty Kaplan. *Invisible Wings: An Annotated Bibliography of Blacks in Aviation, 1916-1993.* Westport, Conn.: Greenwood Press, 1994.

Hardesty, Von. *Black Wings: Courageous Stories of African Americans in Aviation and Space History.* New York: HarperCollins, 2008.

Harmon, Marylen E., and Sherry Guertler. *Visions of a Dream: History Makers—Contributions of Africans and African Americans in Science and Mathematics.* Roanoke, Va.: M. E. Harmon, 1994.

Hine, Darlene Clark, and Kathleen Thompson, eds. *Science, Health, and Medicine.* Vol. 11 in *Facts On File Encyclopedia of Black Women in America.* New York: Facts On File, 1997.

Jenkins, Edward Sidney. *To Fathom More: African American Scientists and Inventors.* Lanham, Md.: University Press of America, 1996.

Jordan, Diann. *Sisters in Science: Conversations with Black Women Scientists About Race, Gender, and Their Passion for Science.* West Lafayette, Ind.: Purdue University Press, 2006.

Kessler, James H., et al. *Distinguished African American Scientists of the Twentieth Century.* Phoenix, Ariz.: Oryx Press, 1996.

Krapp, Kristine M. *Notable Black American Scientists.* Detroit: Gale, 1999.

Lang, Mozell P. *Contributions of African American Scientists and Mathematicians.* Orlando, Fla.: Harcourt, 2005.

Marchè, Wina. *African American Achievers in Science, Medicine, and Technology: A Resource Book for Young Learners, Parents, Teachers, and Librarians.* Bloomington, Ind.: 1st Books, 2003.

Sammons, Vivian O. *Blacks in Science and Medicine.* New York: Hemisphere, 1990.

Sluby, Patricia Carter. *The Inventive Spirit of African Americans: Patented Ingenuity.* Westport, Conn.: Praeger, 2008.

Spangenburg, Ray, and Diane Moser. *African Americans in Science, Math, and Invention.* New York: Facts On File, 2003.

Spurlock, Jeanne. *Black Psychiatrists and American Psychiatry.* Washington, D.C.: American Psychiatric Association, 1999.

Sullivan, Otha Richard, and James Haskins. *African American Women Scientists and Inventors.* New York: John Wiley & Sons, 2002.

Warren, Wini. *Black Women Scientists in the United States.* Bloomington: Indiana University Press, 1999.

Webster, Raymond B. *African American Firsts in Science and Technology.* Detroit, Mich.: Gale, 1999.

Williams, Michael, and Djehuti-Ankh-Kheru. *Black Women Scientists and Inventors.* London: BIS, 2007.

Wilson, Donald, and Jane Wilson. *The Pride of African American History: Inventors, Scientists, Physicians, Engineers.* Bloomington, Ind.: 1st Books, 2003.

## SPORTS

Aaseng, Nathan. *African-American Athletes.* New York: Facts On File, 2010.

Ashe, Arthur. *A Hard Road to Glory: A History of the African American Athlete—Boxing.* New York: HarperCollins, 2000.

Bayne, Bijan C. *Sky Kings: Black Pioneers of Professional Basketball.* New York: Franklin Watts, 1998.

Dawkins, Marvin P., and Graham C. Kinloch. *African American Golfers During the Jim Crow Era.* Westport, Conn.: Praeger Press, 2000.

Freedman, Lee. *African American Pioneers of Baseball: A Biographical Encyclopedia.* Westport, Conn.: Greenwood Press, 2007.

Hogan, Lawrence D. *Shades of Glory: The Negro Leagues and the Story of African-American Baseball.*

Washington, D.C.: National Geographic Society, 2006.

Hunter, Shaun. *Great African Americans in the Olympics*. New York: Crabtree, 1997.

Jacobs, Barry. *Across the Line—Profiles in Basketball Courage: Tales of the First Black Players in the ACC and SEC*. Guilford, Conn.: Lyons Press, 2008.

Jacobson, Steve. *Carrying Jackie's Torch: The Players Who Integrated Baseball—and America*. Chicago: Lawrence Hill Books, 2007.

Johnson, M. Mikell. *The African American Woman Golfer: Her Legacy*. Westport, Conn.: Praeger Press, 2007.

Kennedy, John H. *A Course of Their Own: A History of African American Golfers*. Lincoln: University of Nebraska Press, 2005.

Lapchick, Richard Edward. *100 Pioneers: African-Americans Who Broke Color Barriers in Sport*. Morgantown, W.Va.: Fitness Information Technology, 2008.

McNary, Kyle P. *Black Baseball: A History of African-Americans and the National Game*. Canton, Ohio: PRC Publishing, 2006.

Porter, David L. *African-American Sports Greats: A Biographical Dictionary*. Westport, Conn.: Greenwood Press, 1995.

Ross, Charles. *Outside the Lines: African Americans and the Integration of the National Football League*. New York: New York University Press, 2001.

Walter, John C., and Malina Iida. *Better than the Best: Black Athletes Speak, 1920-2007*. Seattle: University of Washington Press, 2010.

Whitaker, Matthew C. *African American Icons of Sport: Triumph, Courage, and Excellence*. Westport, Conn.: Greenwood Press, 2008.

Wiggins, David Kenneth. *Out of the Shadows: A Biographical History of African American Athletes*. Fayetteville: University of Arkansas Press, 2006.

Wiggins, David Kenneth, and Patrick B. Miller. *The Unlevel Playing Field: A Documentary History of the African American Experience in Sport*. Urbana: University of Illinois Press, 2005.

Wigginton, Russell Thomas. *The Strange Career of the Black Athlete: African Americans and Sports*. Westport, Conn.: Praeger, 2006.

*—Joyce A. Barnes*

# Web Site Directory

*Online resources for further study of African Americans are listed below.*

## General Resources

### African American History, University of Washington Libraries

http://www.lib.washington.edu/subject/history/tm/black.html

This information network provides links to many other sites, companions, electronic texts, organizations, and projects via the University of Washington Libraries' Web page. It is divided into the following categories: General History, Civil War and Slavery, Civil Rights, Sites Arranged Chronologically, and Biographies.

### African American History Month

http://www.africanamericanhistorymonth.gov/

Created by the Library of Congress in conjunction with five other government organizations, this extensive resource has as its purpose the acknowledgment of the generations of African Americans who "struggled with adversity to achieve full citizenship in American society." This site includes links to teacher resources, images, audio-video materials, exhibits, and collections.

### African Studies

http://www.columbia.edu/cu/lweb/indiv/africa/cuvl/afroambiog.html

The Columbia University Libraries have compiled this site, which includes links to other Web sites, databases, newspapers, electronic texts, projects (such as Columbia's Malcolm X Project), organizations regarding specific African Americans, and events in history.

### Answer.com: Black Biographies

http://www.answers.com/library/Black%20Biographies-letter-1A

This site was created by About.com and provides biographies of a range of prominent African Americans in history. Also provided are bibliographies for further reading and research purposes.

### Black Collegian: The Career Site for Students of Color

http://www.black-collegian.com/african/aaprofil.shtml

This career site intended for African American undergraduate students provides biographical sketches of well-known African Americans.

### Black Past: Online Reference Guide to African American History

http://www.blackpast.org/?q = view/vignettes&page = 1

This site includes short descriptions of individuals, places, and events that have contributed to the shaping of African American history. This resource is for anyone looking for a starting point or basic introduction to African American history.

### Biography: Celebrate Black History

http://www.biography.com/blackhistory/index.jsp

This Web site corresponds to the Biography Channel and includes videos, a timeline, quizzes, games, a photo gallery, an interactive tour of the historic Apollo Theater in Harlem, and many featured biographies.

### History Channel Online: Black History Month

http://www.history.com/topics/black-history-month

This Web site coincides with the History Channel and includes biographies, videos, information on events, and even quizzes.

### The History Makers

http://www.thehistorymakers.com/

This site is an archival collection of video-recorded interviews of well-known and lesser-known African Americans in fields such as business, entertainment, law, media, medicine, military, religion, sports, and art. Included are the stories of individual African Americans, African American organizations, events, movements, and periods of time that are significant to the African American community. An important part of the American experience, these are "stories of success against the odds, of achievement in the face of adversity, and of inspiration. They are America's missing stories."

**InfoPlease: Famous Firsts by African Americans**

http://www.infoplease.com/spot/bhmfirsts.html

This Web site, created by InfoPlease.com, is an all-inclusive listing of famous firsts by African Americans. The listings link to a biography or description of the person, organization, or event. Also includes an African American history time line.

**Institute for African American Studies**

http://www.uga.edu/iaas/research/history.html

Provided by the Institute for African American Studies of the University of Georgia's Franklin College of Arts and Sciences, this Web site includes brief biographical sketches of several prominent African Americans in history.

**Lawson State Community College (LSCC) Black History Links**

http://www.ls.cc.al.us/blackhistory/blackhistory.html

A compilation resource from Lawson State Community College, this Web site includes information and links to such resources as biographies, obituaries, events, images, and newspaper articles.

**Public Broadcasting Service: *Africans in America***

http://www.pbs.org/wgbh/aia/home.html

The Africans in America Web site is the companion to the *Africans in America* public television series. The Web site archives the history of racial slavery in the United States from the sixteenth century to the end of the American Civil War in 1865. This site investigates the inconsistency of the American story that all men are equal. The site also outlines the intellectual and economic fundamentals of slavery in America and how the global economy prospered from it, while revealing how the presence of African people and their struggle for freedom had a major impact on America. The site is divided into four parts that coincide with the four periods covered in the television series. Each part includes Narrative, Resource Bank, People and Places, Historical Documents, Modern Voices (interviews from the television series), and a Teacher's Guide.

## THE ARTS

**Artcyclopedia: African American Artists**

http://www.artcyclopedia.com/nationalities/African-American.html

This site is a search tool to find African American artists and their artwork. Artist listings may include images, articles, museums, galleries, Web sites, and multimedia links.

**Black Classic Films**

http://www.blackclassicmovies.com/index.html

This site is a great resource for film information. There is a Top 100 list with carefully selected films. The selection criteria include release date, award winners, milestone films, and highly acclaimed films. Includes film database, artist database, film feature, artist profile, and featured DVD.

**Black Gospel**

http://www.blackgospel.com/

This Web site was created to provide resources and information for participants in and supporters of the ministry of gospel music. The site supplies news, a Top 10 list, links to gospel radio stations, reviews, and interviews.

**Carnegie Hall Presents Honor! A Celebration of the African American Cultural Legacy: A History of African American Music**

http://www.carnegiehall.org/honor/history/index.aspx

Originally an online companion to the festival with the same name, this interactive resource pays tribute to the legendary African American performers throughout history who have made appearances at Carnegie Hall. The timeline allows access to audio and biographical information of artists from each genre.

**Center for Black Music Research**

http://www.colum.edu/cbmr/

This site, founded at Columbia College Chicago in 1983, provides materials and information that document the "black music experience across Africa and the diaspora" and "illuminate the significant role that black music plays in world culture."

**Smithsonian Institution: America's Jazz Heritage**

http://www.si.edu/ajazzh/default.htm

"America's Jazz Heritage" is an initiative to research, preserve, and present the history of jazz through exhibitions, performances, recordings, radio, publications, and educational programs at the Smithsonian Institution and across the nation. Included are recordings and interviews.

## CIVIL RIGHTS

**InfoPlease: Civil Rights Movement Time Line**

http://www.infoplease.com/spot/civilrights
timeline1.html

This site provides a chronology of the civil rights era, starting in 1948, to the present. It lists the milestones in the modern Civil Rights movement and includes links to biographies, events, places, organizations, and images.

**Television News of the Civil Rights Era, 1950-1970**

http://www2.vcdh.virginia.edu/civilrightstv/

This Web site is a project in progress that provides streaming video of network television news footage from the civil rights era. Some of the footage included in this project, such as full speeches of Martin Luther King,

Jr., and presidents of this era, is rare. Included also is original footage of debates, interviews of citizens, public meetings, and school desegregation.

**Voices of Civil Rights**

http://www.voicesofcivilrights.org/

This site includes a timeline, a video, and other resources for anyone interested in the personal accounts of the struggle to execute the promise of equality for all. The American Association of Retired Persons, the Leadership Conference on Civil Rights, and the Library of Congress have teamed up to collect and preserve these personal accounts.

## MILITARY

**The History Place: African Americans in World War II**

http://www.historyplace.com/unitedstates/aframerwar/index.html

This photographic history created by the History Place displays photographs of African Americans from World War II with sections that include Breaking Barriers, The War in Europe, The Pacific War, Honors and Awards, and Women's Contribution.

**Real African American Heroes**

http://www.raahistory.com/

This site focuses on military leaders and positive role models. The site also provides access to full-text periodicals published by the Johnson Publishing Company.

**Tuskegee Airmen, Inc.**

http://www.tuskegeeairmen.org/

This organization's site was designed to give the history of and honor to the Tuskegee Airmen and provide a place for members to view events. The site lists graduates, airmen by squadrons, official documents, and combat statistics.

## POLITICS AND GOVERNMENT

**African Americans and American Politics**

http://exhibitions.nypl.org/african-americans-in
-politics/

Created by the New York Public Library's Schomburg Center for Research in Black Culture, this interactive site provides a survey of over two hundred years of the fight for African American participation in political America.

**Black Wall Street: African Americans in Government**

http://blackwallstreet.org/blk.resources.dir/go.html

This organization links to political news and directories of African American members of Congress, governors, lieutenant governors, and groups. Individual politician links direct users to official Web sites.

**InfoPlease: Notable African American Government Officials**

http://www.infoplease.com/spot/bhmpeople1.html

InfoPlease.com created a listing of biographies of notable African American government officials. Each biography includes other resources, examples of how to cite the Web page, and an image.

## RELIGION

### African American Religion

http://nationalhumanitiescenter.org/tserve/nineteen/
nkeyinfo/aareligion.htm

Provided by the National Humanities Center, this site takes an in-depth chronological view of the history of religion among African Americans. There are images of official documents, links to online resources, historian debates, and teacher resources.

### African American Religion: A Documentary History Project

http://www3.amherst.edu/~aardoc/menu.html

This documentary history project was founded in 1987 at Amherst College. It provides a comprehensive history of African American religion, "from the earliest African-European encounters along the west coast of Africa during the mid-fifteenth century to the present day." Bibliographies, documents, interpretive commentary, and research memoranda are or will be made available through this Web site; it is a work still in progress.

### Pew Forum: A Religious Portrait of African Americans

http://pewforum.org/A-Religious-Portrait-of-African
-Americans.aspx

This compilation of research analyzes African Americans and their connection to religion. This is an excellent resource for anyone in need of a study that uses statistics, charts, and tables of religious affiliations of African Americans by age, geography, education, and gender.

### ReligionLink: A Guide to African Americans and Religion

http://www.religionlink.com/tip_070108.php

A comprehensive guide to African Americans and religion, this site links to biographies, organizations, information on events, congregations, history, music, social issues, and Christian and non-Christian religions.

## SCIENTISTS

### The Faces of Science: African Americans in the Sciences

https://webfiles.uci.edu/mcbrown/display/faces.html

This Web site profiles African Americans who have contributed to the fields of science and engineering. This retrospective can serve as a pathfinder for present and future engineers and scientists by chronicling the history of science.

### NASA Quest: African American Astronauts

http://quest.nasa.gov/qchats/special/mlk00/
afam_astronauts.html

This section of the National Aeronautics and Space Administration (NASA) Quest site exhibits the former, current, and candidate African American astronauts and provides biographical information for each individual.

### Physicists of the African Diaspora

http://www.math.buffalo.edu/mad/physics/physics
-peeps.html

Provided by the State University of New York's University at Buffalo, this site lists profiles of African American physicists, astronomers, and astrophysicists.

## SPORTS

### Pro Football Hall of Fame: African Americans

http://www.profootballhof.com/history/general/african
-americans.aspx

This site lists pro football's African American pioneers, milestones, and firsts. The list is divided by time periods, such as pre-National Football Leauge years, 1920-1933, and 1946; firsts by African Americans in the modern era (post-World War II); and coaching firsts by African Americans. The site provides basic information.

## TEACHING RESOURCES

### Great Black Speakers

http://greatblackspeakers.com/

Founded in 2007, this bureau's site provides help for organizations, corporations, colleges, universities, and schools seeking African American speakers for events. Included are well-known entrepreneurs, actors, authors, journalists, and other public figures, as well as speakers who may need more exposure. Each speaker's biography is included with his or her profile.

### The Internet African American History Challenge

http://www.brightmoments.com/blackhistory/

Intended for teachers to use with their students, this Web site has three levels of quizzes that will test and sharpen knowledge of African American history.

### Scholastic: Top 10 African American Inventors

http://teacher.scholastic.com/activities/bhistory/inventors/

This site is an elementary school teacher's resource that provides biographical information on African American inventors such as Elijah McCoy, Lewis Latimer, and more.

### Smithsonian Education: Black History Teaching Resources

http://www.smithsonianeducation.org/educators/resource_library/african_american_resources.html

Provided by the Smithsonian Center for Education and Museum Studies, this site includes teaching resources, an African American history virtual tour, reading lists, and biographies. The Web site is the "gateway to the institution's educational resources and programs, publishing *Smithsonian in Your Classroom,* a journal for elementary and middle school educators, offering research opportunities and resources to the museum community, and conducting professional development programs for educators at all levels."

—*Kassundra Miller*

Great Lives from History

# Indexes

# CATEGORY INDEX

## LIST OF CATEGORIES

Abolitionism . . . . . . . . 1689
Art and Photography . . . . . 1689
Business . . . . . . . . . . . 1690
Civil Rights. . . . . . . . . 1690
Dance. . . . . . . . . . . . 1691
Diplomacy . . . . . . . . . 1691
Education. . . . . . . . . . 1691
Entertainment:
   Comedy . . . . . . . . . 1692
Entertainment:
   Minstrelsy. . . . . . . . 1692
Entertainment:
   Vaudeville. . . . . . . . 1692
Exploration and
   Pioneering. . . . . . . . 1692
Fashion. . . . . . . . . . . 1692
Film: Acting . . . . . . . . 1692
Film: Direction. . . . . . . 1693
Film: Music . . . . . . . . 1693
Film: Production . . . . . . 1693
Gay and Lesbian Issues . . . 1693
Government and
   Politics . . . . . . . . . 1693
Invention . . . . . . . . . . 1694

Journalism and
   Publishing. . . . . . . . 1694
Labor. . . . . . . . . . . . 1695
Law. . . . . . . . . . . . . 1695
Literature. . . . . . . . . . 1695
Medicine . . . . . . . . . . 1696
Military. . . . . . . . . . . 1696
Music: Bandleading . . . . 1696
Music: Blues . . . . . . . . 1696
Music: Boogie-woogie . . . . 1696
Music: Classical and
   Operatic . . . . . . . . . 1696
Music: Composition . . . . 1697
Music: Crossover. . . . . . 1697
Music: Folk and
   Country . . . . . . . . . 1697
Music: Funk . . . . . . . . 1697
Music: Gospel . . . . . . . 1697
Music: Hip-hop . . . . . . 1697
Music: Jazz. . . . . . . . . 1697
Music: Latin, Caribbean,
   and Reggae . . . . . . . 1698
Music: Pop. . . . . . . . . 1698
Music: Production . . . . . 1698

Music: Rhythm and
   Blues . . . . . . . . . . 1698
Music: Rock and Roll . . . . 1699
Music: Soul . . . . . . . . 1699
Music: Spirituals . . . . . . 1699
Music: Swing. . . . . . . . 1699
Philanthropy . . . . . . . . 1699
Poetry . . . . . . . . . . . 1699
Radio and Television. . . . . 1700
Religion and Theology. . . . 1700
Scholarship. . . . . . . . . 1700
Science and Technology . . . 1701
Social Issues . . . . . . . . 1701
Social Sciences. . . . . . . 1702
Sports: Baseball . . . . . . 1702
Sports: Basketball . . . . . 1702
Sports: Boxing . . . . . . . 1702
Sports: Football . . . . . . 1703
Sports: Golf and Tennis . . . 1703
Sports: Miscellaneous . . . . 1703
Sports: Olympics. . . . . . 1703
Sports: Track and Field . . . 1703
Theater . . . . . . . . . . . 1704
Women's Rights . . . . . . 1704

**ABOLITIONISM**
Allen, Richard, 36
Bell, James Madison, 140
Coker, Daniel, 388
Craft, William, 425
Crummell, Alexander, 435
Delany, Martin Robison, 481
Douglass, Frederick, 513
Forten, James, 606
Grimké, Charlotte L. Forten, 703
Hall, Prince, 716
Harper, Frances Ellen Watkins, 732
Jones, Absalom, 889
Menard, John Willis, 1048
Russwurm, John Brown, 1302
Scott, Dred, 1324
Singleton, Benjamin, 1366
Stewart, Maria, 1397

Truth, Sojourner, 1441
Tubman, Harriet, 1444
Walker, David, 1495

**ACTING.** *See* **FILM**

**ART AND PHOTOGRAPHY**
Alston, Charles, 40
Ball, James Presley, 84
Bannister, Edward Mitchell, 94
Barthé, Richmond, 107
Basquiat, Jean-Michel, 111
Bearden, Romare, 126
Campbell, E. Simms, 292
Casey, Bernie, 324
Chase-Riboud, Barbara, 339
Davis, Miles, 461
DeCarava, Roy, 476

Douglas, Aaron, 512
Hansen, Austin, 731
Johnson, Joshua, 874
Johnson, Sargent, 886
Johnson, William H., 888
Lawrence, Jacob, 961
Lee-Smith, Hughie, 971
Lewis, Edmonia, 980
Marshall, Kerry James, 1034
Parks, Gordon, Sr., 1155
Ringgold, Faith, 1258
Saar, Betye, 1306
Savage, Augusta, 1317
Tanner, Henry Ossawa, 1412
Van Der Zee, James, 1477
Williams, Billy Dee, 1565
Withers, Ernest, 1601

**BANDLEADING.** *See* **MUSIC**

**BASEBALL.** *See* **SPORTS**

**BASKETBALL.** *See* **SPORTS**

**BLUES.** *See* **MUSIC**

**BOOGIE-WOOGIE.** *See* **MUSIC**

**BOXING.** *See* **SPORTS**

**BUSINESS**
Abbott, Robert S., 5
Amos, Wally, 43
Banks, Tyra, 90
Baylor, Elgin, 121
Beard, Andrew Jackson, 125
Brimmer, Andrew Felton, 212
Carver, George Washington, 319
Chenault, Kenneth, 351
Collins, Marva, 403
Cooke, Sam, 415
Cuffe, Paul, 437
Dunn, Oscar James, 532
Evers-Williams, Myrlie, 568
Forten, James, 606
Fortune, Amos, 608
Garvey, Marcus, 635
Gaston, Arthur George, 637
Gordy, Berry, Jr., 672
Gourdine, Meredith C., 676
Graves, Earl G., Sr., 679
Handy, W. C., 727
Hobson, Mellody, 778
Jackson, Bo, 822
Jakes, T. D., 846
Jay-Z, 852
Jemison, Mae C., 858
Johnson, John H., 872
Johnson, Magic, 877
Johnson, Robert L., 884
Jordan, Michael, 909
Julian, Hubert Fauntleroy, 917
Micheaux, Oscar, 1055
Morgan, Garrett Augustus, 1075
Otis, Clarence, Jr., 1137
Pointe du Sable, Jean Baptiste, 1188
Puff Daddy, 1217
Rhone, Sylvia M., 1243

Rice, Condoleezza, 1245
Rice, Linda Johnson, 1249
Robinson, Sugar Ray, 1284
Shabazz, Ilyasah, 1332
Simmons, Kimora Lee, 1352
Simmons, Russell, 1354
Thompson, Larry D., 1428
Trotter, William Monroe, 1439
Walker, Madam C. J., 1500
West, Kanye, 1540
Winfrey, Oprah, 1597
Wonder, Stevie, 1605
Woods, Tiger, 1612

**CARIBBEAN MUSIC.** *See* **MUSIC**

**CIVIL RIGHTS**
Abernathy, Ralph David, 11
Anderson, Marian, 47
Baraka, Amiri, 96
Barry, Marion, 104
Bass, Charlotta Spears, 113
Bates, Daisy, 116
Bearden, Romare, 126
Bevel, James, 150
Bunche, Ralph, 262
Carmichael, Stokely, 305
Chaney, James, 330
Chavis, Benjamin, 341
Childress, Alice, 356
Cleage, Albert Buford, Jr., 369
Davis, Henrietta Vinton, 459
Dee, Ruby, 478
Douglass, Frederick, 513
Du Bois, W. E. B., 520
Dunn, Oscar James, 532
Edelman, Marian Wright, 540
Evers, Charles, 565
Evers, Medgar, 566
Evers-Williams, Myrlie, 568
Farmer, James L., Jr., 573
Forman, James, 602
Garvey, Marcus, 635
Gaston, Arthur George, 637
Gibson, Althea, 648
Hall, Prince, 716
Height, Dorothy, 752
Hooks, Benjamin, 789
Hope, John, 791
Houston, Charles Hamilton, 797

Hunter-Gault, Charlayne, 807
Innis, Roy, 817
Jackson, Jesse, 826
Jackson, Mahalia, 831
Jealous, Benjamin T., 853
Jordan, June, 907
Jordan, Vernon, 912
King, Coretta Scott, 939
King, Martin Luther, Jr., 941
Lawson, James, 964
Lewis, John Robert, 982
Lowery, Joseph, 1001
Marshall, Thurgood, 1037
Mays, Benjamin E., 1043
Meredith, James, 1049
Mfume, Kweisi, 1053
Mitchell, Clarence M., Jr., 1067
Morial, Dutch, 1077
Nash, Diane, 1102
Newton, Huey P., 1108
Nixon, E. D., 1116
Norton, Eleanor Holmes, 1119
Odetta, 1126
Parks, Rosa, 1157
Poitier, Sidney, 1190
Powell, Adam Clayton, Jr., 1196
Randolph, A. Philip, 1228
Robinson, Jackie, 1272
Robinson, Jo Ann Gibson, 1275
Sharpton, Al, 1337
Shuttlesworth, Fred, 1347
Simone, Nina, 1359
Trotter, William Monroe, 1439
Vivian, C. T., 1488
Walker, David, 1495
Walters, Alexander, 1508
Wells-Barnett, Ida B., 1533
White, Walter, 1552
Wilkins, Roy, 1560
Williams, Hosea, 1571
Williams, Robert Franklin, 1578
Withers, Ernest, 1601
Young, Whitney, 1637

**CLASSICAL AND OPERATIC.** *See* **MUSIC**

**COMEDY.** *See* **ENTERTAINMENT**

**COMPOSITION.** *See* **MUSIC**

COUNTRY MUSIC. *See* MUSIC

CROSSOVER MUSIC. *See* MUSIC

DANCE
Ailey, Alvin, 18
Allen, Debbie, 33
Bailey, Pearl, 71
Checker, Chubby, 347
Coles, Honi, 400
Dunham, Katherine, 530
Europe, James Reese, 559
Glover, Savion, 660
Hines, Gregory, 774
Jones, Bill T., 891
Juba, Master, 916
Kitt, Eartha, 944
Knowles, Beyoncé, 948
Mills, Florence, 1060
Mitchell, Arthur, 1064
Nicholas, Fayard and Harold, 1110
Nichols, Nichelle, 1114
Primus, Pearl, 1208
Rice, Jerry, 1247
Robinson, Bill, 1266
Robinson, Sugar Ray, 1284
Smith, Emmitt, 1379
Vereen, Ben, 1485

DIPLOMACY
Bunche, Ralph, 262
Douglass, Frederick, 513
Harris, Patricia Roberts, 737
Johnson, James Weldon, 868
Obama, Barack, 1121
Powell, Colin, 1199
Rice, Condoleezza, 1245
Shabazz, Betty, 1330
Wharton, Clifton Reginald, Jr., 1543
Young, Andrew, 1632

DIRECTION. *See* FILM

EDUCATION
Alexander, Elizabeth, 24
Alston, Charles, 40
Asante, Molefi Kete, 60
Baker, Ella, 75
Baker, Houston A., Jr., 77
Becton, Julius Wesley, Jr., 134

Bethune, Mary McLeod, 148
Bond, Horace Mann, 177
Bond, Julian, 179
Bradley, David, 196
Braun, Carol E. Moseley, 204
Brown, Charlotte Hawkins, 223
Brown, Claude, 225
Brown, Sterling A., 243
Brown, Tony, 246
Bunche, Ralph, 262
Burroughs, Nannie Helen, 273
Carter, Stephen L., 318
Carver, George Washington, 319
Cary, Lorene, 322
Cheek, James E., 349
Chisholm, Shirley, 359
Clark, Septima Poinsette, 365
Clarke, John Henrik, 367
Coachman, Alice, 384
Coker, Daniel, 388
Collins, Marva, 403
Collins, Patricia Hill, 405
Cosby, Bill, 422
Crummell, Alexander, 435
Dett, R. Nathaniel, 489
Dodson, Owen, 506
Douglas, Aaron, 512
Dove, Rita, 516
Drew, Charles R., 518
Du Bois, W. E. B., 520
Dunbar-Nelson, Alice, 527
Edelman, Marian Wright, 540
Elders, Joycelyn, 543
Emanuel, James A., 551
Evans, James Carmichael, 560
Farrakhan, Louis, 575
Fauset, Jessie Redmon, 582
Ferguson, Samuel, 584
Fontaine, William Thomas, 598
Forrest, Leon, 604
Franklin, John Hope, 617
Futrell, Mary Hatwood, 626
Gaines, Ernest J., 629
Gates, Henry Louis, Jr., 640
Giovanni, Nikki, 657
Gordon, Lewis, 668
Gordon-Reed, Annette, 670
Granville, Evelyn Boyd, 678
Gray, William H., III, 682
Grimké, Charlotte L. Forten, 703

Harris, Patricia Roberts, 737
Healy, Patrick F., 750
Hill, Anita, 764
Hilliard, Asa Grant, III, 768
Hooks, Bell, 788
Hope, John, 791
Jackson, Shirley Ann, 842
Jeffries, Leonard, 856
Johnson, Charles S., 862
Johnson, James Weldon, 868
Jordan, Barbara, 905
Just, Ernest Everett, 921
Karenga, Maulana, 923
Lawrence, Jacob, 961
Lawson, James, 964
Lee-Smith, Hughie, 971
Lorde, Audre, 997
McLean, Jackie, 1012
McWhorter, John, 1020
Madhubuti, Haki R., 1022
Marshall, Paule, 1035
Mays, Benjamin E., 1043
Meredith, James, 1049
O'Leary, Hazel R., 1130
Paige, Rod, 1146
Patterson, Frederick D., 1165
Poussaint, Alvin Francis, 1194
Raby, Albert, 1224
Reed, Ishmael, 1238
Revels, Hiram Rhoades, 1241
Rice, Condoleezza, 1245
Richards, Lloyd, 1251
Robinson, Jo Ann Gibson, 1275
Robinson, Spottswood W., III, 1282
Sanchez, Sonia, 1307
Savage, Augusta, 1317
Shabazz, Betty, 1330
Shepp, Archie, 1344
Simmons, Ruth, 1356
Slaughter, John Brooks, 1369
Smith, Anna Deveare, 1374
Smith, Barbara, 1376
Steele, Claude M., 1392
Steele, Shelby, 1395
Stewart, Maria, 1397
Terrell, Mary Church, 1416
Thomas, Vivien, 1427
Threadgill, Henry, 1430
Tolson, Melvin B., 1434
Walker, George, 1497

Walker, Margaret, 1503
Washington, Booker T., 1513
West, Cornel, 1535
Wharton, Clifton Reginald, Jr., 1543
Wideman, John Edgar, 1555
Williams, Daniel Hale, 1567
Williams, Hosea, 1571
Wilson, William Julius, 1593
Woodson, Carter G., 1615
Wright, Jane Cooke, 1619
Wright, Jeremiah, 1622
Young, Whitney, 1637

**ENTERTAINMENT: COMEDY**
Anderson, Eddie "Rochester," 45
Bailey, Pearl, 71
Cambridge, Godfrey, 286
Cedric the Entertainer, 325
Chappelle, Dave, 333
Checker, Chubby, 347
Cosby, Bill, 422
Crothers, Scatman, 428
Davis, Sammy, Jr., 466
Foxx, Jamie, 611
Foxx, Redd, 613
Goldberg, Whoopi, 662
Gregory, Dick, 688
Hall, Arsenio, 714
Lemon, Meadowlark, 972
Mabley, Moms, 1003
Mac, Bernie, 1005
Morris, Garrett, 1078
Murphy, Eddie, 1090
Pryor, Richard, 1214
Reid, Tim, 1240
Rock, Chris, 1286
Walker, Jimmie, 1498
Williams, Bert, 1563
Wilson, Flip, 1590

**ENTERTAINMENT: MINSTRELSY**
Aldridge, Ira Frederick, 22
Anderson, Eddie "Rochester," 45
Beavers, Louise, 129
Bland, James, 165
Fetchit, Stepin, 586
Handy, W. C., 727
Juba, Master, 916
Little Richard, 990
Mabley, Moms, 1003

McDaniel, Hattie, 1006
Morton, Jelly Roll, 1082
Rainey, Ma, 1226
Williams, Bert, 1563

**ENTERTAINMENT: VAUDEVILLE**
Anderson, Eddie "Rochester," 45
Bailey, Pearl, 71
Baker, Josephine, 78
Basie, Count, 109
Bethune, Blind Tom, 145
Blake, Eubie, 159
Bradford, Perry, 195
Davis, Sammy, Jr., 466
Fetchit, Stepin, 586
McDaniel, Hattie, 1006
Mills, Florence, 1060
Montgomery, Little Brother, 1071
Morton, Jelly Roll, 1082
Nicholas, Fayard and Harold, 1110
Robinson, Bill, 1266
Smith, Bessie, 1377
Waller, Fats, 1504
Williams, Bert, 1563
Williams, Mary Lou, 1574

**EXPLORATION AND PIONEERING**
Beckwourth, Jim, 132
Bush, George Washington, 277
Coker, Daniel, 388
Henson, Matthew Alexander, 761
Pointe du Sable, Jean Baptiste,
    1188

**FASHION**
Banks, Tyra, 90
Beckford, Tyson, 130
Carroll, Diahann, 312
Charles, Suzette, 338
Cleaver, Eldridge, 371
Griffith-Joyner, Florence, 699
Jay-Z, 852
Johnson, John H., 872
Knowles, Beyoncé, 948
L. L. Cool J., 952
Leslie, Lisa, 976
Parks, Gordon, Sr., 1155
Prince, 1210
Puff Daddy, 1217
Rice, Linda Johnson, 1249

Ross, Diana, 1291
Simmons, Kimora Lee, 1352
Tyson, Cicely, 1460
Williams, Serena, 1579
Williams, Venus, 1583

**FILM: ACTING**
Aaliyah, 1
Abdul-Jabbar, Kareem, 8
Allen, Debbie, 33
Anderson, Eddie "Rochester," 45
Angelou, Maya, 50
Bailey, Pearl, 71
Banks, Tyra, 90
Bassett, Angela, 115
Beavers, Louise, 129
Beckford, Tyson, 130
Belafonte, Harry, 136
Berry, Halle, 144
Blige, Mary J., 168
Brown, Jim, 237
Burton, LeVar, 275
Cambridge, Godfrey, 286
Cara, Irene, 296
Carey, Mariah, 301
Carroll, Diahann, 312
Carter, Nell, 316
Casey, Bernie, 324
Cedric the Entertainer, 325
Cheadle, Don, 343
Cosby, Bill, 422
Crothers, Scatman, 428
Dandridge, Dorothy, 442
Davis, Ossie, 464
Davis, Sammy, Jr., 466
Davis, Viola, 471
Dee, Ruby, 478
Dixon, Ivan, 499
Dutton, Charles S., 533
Epps, Omar, 552
Fetchit, Stepin, 586
50 Cent, 588
Fishburne, Laurence, 590
Foxx, Jamie, 611
Freeman, Morgan, 623
Glover, Danny, 658
Glover, Savion, 660
Goldberg, Whoopi, 662
Gooding, Cuba, Jr., 663
Gordon, Dexter, 665

Gossett, Louis, Jr., 674
Grier, Pam, 694
Guillaume, Robert, 706
Hall, Arsenio, 714
Hayes, Isaac, 746
Hines, Gregory, 774
Horne, Lena, 794
Houston, Whitney, 798
Hudson, Jennifer, 802
Ice Cube, 812
Jackson, Janet, 825
Jackson, Michael, 835
Jackson, Samuel L., 840
Johnson, Dwayne, 864
Jones, James Earl, 895
Keys, Alicia, 932
Kitt, Eartha, 944
Knowles, Beyoncé, 948
L. L. Cool J., 952
LaBelle, Patti, 953
Lee, Canada, 967
Lee, Spike, 969
Little, Cleavon, 989
Mac, Bernie, 1005
McDaniel, Hattie, 1006
Moore, Archie, 1073
Murphy, Eddie, 1090
Nichols, Nichelle, 1114
O'Neal, Shaquille, 1133
Perry, Tyler, 1173
Peters, Brock, 1175
Pickett, Bill, 1179
Poitier, Sidney, 1190
Prince, 1210
Pryor, Richard, 1214
Queen Latifah, 1221
Reid, Tim, 1240
Robeson, Paul, 1263
Robinson, Bill, 1266
Rock, Chris, 1286
Ross, Diana, 1291
Simpson, O. J., 1361
Smith, Will, 1385
Snipes, Wesley, 1386
Snoop Dogg, 1388
Strode, Woody, 1402
Taj Mahal, 1410
Townsend, Robert, 1438
Turner, Tina, 1455
Tyson, Cicely, 1460

Uggams, Leslie, 1468
Underwood, Blair, 1470
Usher, 1474
Vance, Courtney B., 1476
Van Peebles, Mario, 1480
Van Peebles, Melvin, 1482
Vereen, Ben, 1485
Washington, Denzel, 1515
Whitaker, Forest, 1548
Williams, Billy Dee, 1565
Williams, Vanessa, 1581
Winfield, Paul, 1595
Winfrey, Oprah, 1597
Woodard, Alfre, 1607
Wright, Jeffrey, 1620

**FILM: DIRECTION**
Allen, Debbie, 33
Angelou, Maya, 50
Burton, LeVar, 275
Casey, Bernie, 324
Dash, Julie, 445
Davis, Ossie, 464
Dixon, Ivan, 499
Dutton, Charles S., 533
Freeman, Morgan, 623
Ice Cube, 812
Lee, Spike, 969
Micheaux, Oscar, 1055
Murphy, Eddie, 1090
Parks, Gordon, Sr., 1155
Perry, Tyler, 1173
Poitier, Sidney, 1190
Pryor, Richard, 1214
Rashad, Phylicia, 1233
Reid, Tim, 1240
Rock, Chris, 1286
Singleton, John, 1367
Townsend, Robert, 1438
Underwood, Blair, 1470
Van Peebles, Mario, 1480
Van Peebles, Melvin, 1482
Washington, Denzel, 1515
Whitaker, Forest, 1548

**FILM: MUSIC**
Carter, Benny, 314
Ellington, Duke, 545
Hancock, Herbie, 725
Handy, W. C., 727

Hayes, Isaac, 746
Jones, Quincy, 899

**FILM: PRODUCTION**
Belafonte, Harry, 136
Cheadle, Don, 343
Dee, Ruby, 478
Ice Cube, 812
Micheaux, Oscar, 1055
Perry, Tyler, 1173
Peters, Brock, 1175
Reid, Tim, 1240
Rock, Chris, 1286
Smith, Will, 1385
Winfrey, Oprah, 1597

**FOLK MUSIC.** *See* **MUSIC**

**FOOTBALL.** *See* **SPORTS**

**FUNK.** *See* **MUSIC**

**GAY AND LESBIAN ISSUES**
Baldwin, James, 81
Barthé, Richmond, 107
Cliff, Michelle, 377
Davis, Angela, 448
Delany, Samuel R., 484
Dodson, Owen, 506
Grimké, Angelina Weld, 701
Lorde, Audre, 997
Parker, Pat, 1153
Rustin, Bayard, 1303
Smith, Barbara, 1376

**GOLF AND TENNIS.** *See* **SPORTS**

**GOSPEL MUSIC.** *See* **MUSIC**

**GOVERNMENT AND POLITICS**
Barry, Marion, 104
Becton, Julius Wesley, Jr., 134
Bethune, Mary McLeod, 148
Bond, Julian, 179
Bradley, Tom, 200
Braun, Carol E. Moseley, 204
Brooke, Edward W., 215
Brown, Dorothy Lavinia, 229
Brown, Ron, 241
Brown, Willie, 249

Bruce, Blanche Kelso, 251
Bunche, Ralph, 262
Burke, Yvonne Brathwaite, 267
Burris, Roland, 271
Cardozo, Francis Lewis, 298
Cheatham, Henry Plummer, 344
Chisholm, Shirley, 359
Clyburn, James E., 382
Conyers, John, Jr., 413
Davis, Benjamin J., 451
Dellums, Ron, 485
DePriest, Oscar, 488
Dinkins, David, 497
Douglass, Frederick, 513
Dunn, Oscar James, 532
Dymally, Mervyn, 535
Elders, Joycelyn, 543
Espy, Mike, 556
Evers, Charles, 565
Gray, William H., III, 682
Hamer, Fannie Lou, 717
Harris, Patricia Roberts, 737
Herman, Alexis M., 763
Holder, Eric, 779
Ifill, Gwen, 814
Innis, Roy, 817
Jackson, Jesse, 826
Jackson, Jesse, Jr., 829
Jackson, Maynard, 833
Jackson Lee, Sheila, 844
Jordan, Barbara, 905
Jordan, Vernon, 912
Keyes, Alan, 930
Lewis, John Robert, 982
Lowery, Joseph, 1001
Marshall, Thurgood, 1037
Menard, John Willis, 1048
Mfume, Kweisi, 1053
Morial, Dutch, 1077
Nagin, Ray, 1100
Norton, Eleanor Holmes, 1119
Obama, Barack, 1121
Obama, Michelle, 1124
O'Leary, Hazel R., 1130
Paige, Rod, 1146
Paterson, David A., 1159
Patrick, Deval, 1161
Pierce, Samuel R., Jr., 1183
Pinchback, P. B. S., 1184

Powell, Adam Clayton, Jr., 1196
Powell, Colin, 1199
Raby, Albert, 1224
Rangel, Charles, 1231
Revels, Hiram Rhoades, 1241
Rice, Condoleezza, 1245
Robinson, Spottswood W., III, 1282
Rustin, Bayard, 1303
Satcher, David, 1315
Sharpton, Al, 1337
Smalls, Robert, 1371
Steele, Michael, 1393
Terrell, Mary Church, 1416
Thomas, Clarence, 1418
Thompson, Larry D., 1428
Tucker, C. DeLores, 1447
Washington, Harold, 1518
Waters, Maxine, 1523
Watts, J. C., 1528
Weaver, Robert C., 1530
West, Togo, 1541
Wharton, Clifton Reginald, Jr., 1543
Wilder, L. Douglas, 1557
Wilkins, Roy, 1560
Williams, Hosea, 1571
Young, Andrew, 1632
Young, Coleman, 1635

**HIP-HOP.** *See* **MUSIC**

**INVENTION**
Alcorn, George Edward, 20
Banneker, Benjamin, 92
Beard, Andrew Jackson, 125
Blair, Henry, 158
Boykin, Otis, 193
Carver, George Washington, 319
Drew, Charles R., 518
Gourdine, Meredith C., 676
Julian, Percy Lavon, 919
Latimer, Lewis Howard, 959
Marchbanks, Vance Hunter, 1029
Matzeliger, Jan Ernst, 1041
Morgan, Garrett Augustus, 1075
Rillieux, Norbert, 1256
Walker, Madam C. J., 1500
Woods, Granville T., 1610

**JAZZ.** *See* **MUSIC**

**JOURNALISM AND PUBLISHING**
Abbott, Robert S., 5
Bass, Charlotta Spears, 113
Bates, Daisy, 116
Bradley, Ed, 198
Briggs, Cyril V., 210
Brown, Tony, 246
Bruce, John E., 254
Campbell, E. Simms, 292
Cary, Lorene, 322
Crouch, Stanley, 432
Douglass, Frederick, 513
Du Bois, W. E. B., 520
Dunbar-Nelson, Alice, 527
Fauset, Jessie Redmon, 582
Forrest, Leon, 604
Garnet, Henry Highland, 631
Gordon, Ed, 667
Graves, Earl G., Sr., 679
Gumbel, Bryant, 707
Haley, Alex, 711
Hobson, Mellody, 778
Hunter-Gault, Charlayne, 807
Ifill, Gwen, 814
Jealous, Benjamin T., 853
Johnson, Charles S., 862
Johnson, John H., 872
McWhorter, John, 1020
Madhubuti, Haki R., 1022
Meriwether, Louise, 1052
Page, Clarence E., 1145
Pitts, Leonard, 1187
Randolph, A. Philip, 1228
Reed, Ishmael, 1238
Rice, Linda Johnson, 1249
Robinson, Max, 1277
Roker, Al, 1287
Russwurm, John Brown, 1302
Schuyler, George S., 1321
Shaw, Bernard, 1340
Sowell, Thomas, 1390
Tolson, Melvin B., 1434
Trotter, William Monroe, 1439
Walrond, Eric, 1507
Wells-Barnett, Ida B., 1533
West, Dorothy, 1538
Williams, Juan, 1573

**LABOR**
Briggs, Cyril V., 210
Delany, Martin Robison, 481
Farmer, James L., Jr., 573
Mitchell, Clarence M., Jr., 1067
Murray, Pauli, 1095
Nixon, E. D., 1116
Randolph, A. Philip, 1228
Robeson, Paul, 1263
Rustin, Bayard, 1303

**LATIN MUSIC.** *See* **MUSIC**

**LAW**
Bolin, Jane Matilda, 175
Braun, Carol E. Moseley, 204
Brooke, Edward W., 215
Brown, Ron, 241
Burke, Yvonne Brathwaite, 267
Carter, Stephen L., 318
Clark, Kenneth, 363
Cochran, Johnnie, 386
Crenshaw, Kimberlé Williams, 426
Davis, Benjamin J., 451
DeFrantz, Anita, 479
Espy, Mike, 556
Flood, Curt, 596
Gordon-Reed, Annette, 670
Harris, Patricia Roberts, 737
Hill, Anita, 764
Holder, Eric, 779
Hooks, Benjamin, 789
Houston, Charles Hamilton, 797
Jackson Lee, Sheila, 844
Jordan, Barbara, 905
Jordan, Vernon, 912
Marshall, Thurgood, 1037
Morial, Dutch, 1077
Murray, Pauli, 1095
Norton, Eleanor Holmes, 1119
Obama, Michelle, 1124
O'Leary, Hazel R., 1130
Patrick, Deval, 1161
Pierce, Samuel R., Jr., 1183
Pinchback, P. B. S., 1184
Robinson, Randall, 1278
Robinson, Spottswood W., III, 1282
Steele, Michael, 1393
Thomas, Clarence, 1418

Thompson, Larry D., 1428
Washington, Harold, 1518
West, Togo, 1541
Wilkins, Roy, 1560
Williams, Willie L., 1584

**LESBIAN ISSUES.** *See* **GAY AND LESBIAN ISSUES**

**LITERATURE**
Alexander, Elizabeth, 24
Baldwin, James, 81
Bambara, Toni Cade, 86
Baraka, Amiri, 96
Barnes, Steven, 101
Barrax, Gerald William, 102
Bell, James Madison, 140
Bonner, Marita, 186
Bontemps, Arna, 188
Bradley, David, 196
Braithwaite, William Stanley, 202
Brooks, Gwendolyn, 217
Brown, Claude, 225
Brown, Elaine, 230
Brown, Sterling A., 243
Bullins, Ed, 260
Butler, Octavia E., 279
Campbell, Bebe Moore, 290
Carter, Stephen L., 318
Cary, Lorene, 322
Chase-Riboud, Barbara, 339
Chesnutt, Charles Waddell, 353
Childress, Alice, 356
Cliff, Michelle, 377
Clifton, Lucille, 378
Coleman, Wanda, 399
Cooper, J. California, 417
Cornish, Sam, 418
Cortez, Jayne, 420
Cullen, Countée, 439
Delany, Samuel R., 484
Dodson, Owen, 506
Douglass, Frederick, 513
Dove, Rita, 516
Du Bois, W. E. B., 520
Dumas, Henry, 523
Dunbar, Paul Laurence, 524
Dunbar-Nelson, Alice, 527
Ellison, Ralph, 548
Emanuel, James A., 551

Evans, Mari, 563
Fauset, Jessie Redmon, 582
Forrest, Leon, 604
Fuller, Charles, 625
Gaines, Ernest J., 629
Gayle, Addison, Jr., 645
Giovanni, Nikki, 657
Grimké, Angelina Weld, 701
Grimké, Charlotte L. Forten, 703
Haley, Alex, 711
Hamilton, Virginia, 720
Hansberry, Lorraine, 728
Harper, Frances Ellen Watkins, 732
Harper, Michael S., 734
Himes, Chester, 770
Hooks, Bell, 788
Hughes, Langston, 803
Hurston, Zora Neale, 808
Johnson, James Weldon, 868
Jones, Gayl, 893
Jordan, June, 907
Kelley, William Melvin, 926
Kennedy, Adrienne, 928
Kincaid, Jamaica, 934
Komunyakaa, Yusef, 949
Larsen, Nella, 957
Locke, Alain, 995
Lorde, Audre, 997
McKay, Claude, 1010
McMillan, Terry, 1014
Madhubuti, Haki R., 1022
Marshall, Paule, 1035
Meriwether, Louise, 1052
Morrison, Toni, 1080
Mosley, Walter, 1086
Murray, Albert, 1094
Myers, Walter Dean, 1097
Naylor, Gloria, 1105
Parker, Pat, 1153
Petry, Ann, 1177
Reed, Ishmael, 1238
Sanchez, Sonia, 1307
Schuyler, George S., 1321
Shange, Ntozake, 1335
Shepp, Archie, 1344
Smith, Barbara, 1376
Taylor, Mildred D., 1415
Tolson, Melvin B., 1434
Toomer, Jean, 1435
Walker, Alice, 1493

Walker, Margaret, 1503
Walrond, Eric, 1507
West, Dorothy, 1538
Wheatley, Phillis, 1545
Wideman, John Edgar, 1555
Williams, Robert Franklin, 1578
Wilson, August, 1587
Wright, Richard, 1625
Yerby, Frank, 1628
Young, Al, 1631

**MEDICINE**
Brown, Dorothy Lavinia, 229
Drew, Charles R., 518
Elders, Joycelyn, 543
Gayle, Helene Doris, 646
Jemison, Mae C., 858
Julian, Percy Lavon, 919
Marchbanks, Vance Hunter, 1029
Poussaint, Alvin Francis, 1194
Satcher, David, 1315
Thomas, Debi, 1421
Thomas, Vivien, 1427
Wattleton, Faye, 1526
Williams, Daniel Hale, 1567
Wright, Jane Cooke, 1619
Wright, Louis T., 1624

**MILITARY**
Allensworth, Allen, 38
Attucks, Crispus, 66
Becton, Julius Wesley, Jr., 134
Bolden, Charles F., Jr., 173
Bullard, Eugene Jacques, 259
Carney, William H., 309
Davis, Benjamin O., Sr., 452
Davis, Benjamin O., Jr., 455
Delany, Martin Robison, 481
Evans, James Carmichael, 560
Flipper, Henry Ossian, 595
Fox, John R., 609
Gregory, Frederick Drew, 690
Lawrence, Robert H., Jr., 963
Lawson, John, 966
Marchbanks, Vance Hunter, 1029
Miller, Dorie, 1058
Powell, Colin, 1199
Robinson, David, 1269
Smalls, Robert, 1371
West, Togo, 1541

Williams, Montel, 1576
Young, Coleman, 1635

**MINSTRELSY.** *See*
**ENTERTAINMENT**

**MUSIC.** *See* **FILM**

**MUSIC: BANDLEADING**
Armstrong, Louis, 57
Basie, Count, 109
Blakey, Art, 162
Braxton, Anthony, 206
Calloway, Cab, 283
Clinton, George, 380
Crothers, Scatman, 428
Davis, Miles, 461
Eckstine, Billy, 538
Ellington, Duke, 545
Europe, James Reese, 559
Fitzgerald, Ella, 592
Gillespie, Dizzy, 654
Hampton, Lionel, 723
Handy, W. C., 727
Jones, Quincy, 899
Joplin, Scott, 903
Morton, Jelly Roll, 1082
Oliver, King, 1132
Roach, Max, 1260
Rollins, Sonny, 1289
Shepp, Archie, 1344
Silver, Horace, 1349
Threadgill, Henry, 1430
Turner, Ike, 1451
Tyner, McCoy, 1458
Webb, Chick, 1531
Williams, Cootie, 1566

**MUSIC: BLUES**
Adderley, Cannonball, 15
Ammons, Gene, 41
Armstrong, Lillian Hardin, 55
Berry, Chuck, 141
Bland, Bobby Blue, 163
Bradford, Perry, 195
Broonzy, Big Bill, 220
Brown, Charles, 222
Carr, Leroy, 311
Crudup, Big Boy, 433
Diddley, Bo, 494

Dixon, Willie, 500
Dorsey, Thomas A., 510
Dumas, Henry, 523
Griffin, Johnny, 697
Handy, W. C., 727
Hooker, John Lee, 786
James, Etta, 847
King, B. B., 936
Little Walter, 992
Montgomery, Little Brother, 1071
Oliver, King, 1132
Professor Longhair, 1212
Rainey, Ma, 1226
Simone, Nina, 1359
Smith, Bessie, 1377
Taj Mahal, 1410
Turner, Big Joe, 1448
Turner, Ike, 1451
Waters, Muddy, 1525

**MUSIC: BOOGIE-WOOGIE**
Domino, Fats, 508
Hooker, John Lee, 786
Little Richard, 990
Montgomery, Little Brother, 1071
Smith, Huey "Piano," 1381
Sun Ra, 1407
Williams, Mary Lou, 1574

**MUSIC: CLASSICAL AND**
**OPERATIC**
Anderson, Marian, 47
Armstrong, Lillian Hardin, 55
Battle, Kathleen, 119
Bethune, Blind Tom, 145
Braxton, Anthony, 206
Burleigh, Harry T., 268
Guillaume, Robert, 706
Hancock, Herbie, 725
Hayes, Roland, 748
Jones, Sissieretta, 902
Kay, Ulysses, 925
McDonald, Audra, 1008
Marsalis, Wynton, 1032
Norman, Jessye, 1117
Price, Leontyne, 1202
Robeson, Paul, 1263
Simone, Nina, 1359
Still, William Grant, 1398
Walker, George, 1497

**MUSIC: COMPOSITION**
Armstrong, Lillian Hardin, 55
Bethune, Blind Tom, 145
Blake, Eubie, 159
Bland, James, 165
Bonds, Margaret Allison, 185
Bradford, Perry, 195
Braxton, Anthony, 206
Broonzy, Big Bill, 220
Brown, Ray, 239
Burleigh, Harry T., 268
Carter, Benny, 314
Charles, Ray, 336
Davis, Miles, 461
Dett, R. Nathaniel, 489
Dorsey, Thomas A., 510
Ellington, Duke, 545
Europe, James Reese, 559
Gillespie, Dizzy, 654
Hancock, Herbie, 725
Handy, W. C., 727
Hathaway, Donny, 739
Hayes, Isaac, 746
Hayes, Roland, 748
Johnson, James Weldon, 868
Jones, Quincy, 899
Joplin, Scott, 903
Kay, Ulysses, 925
Marsalis, Ellis, Jr., 1030
Marsalis, Wynton, 1032
Mingus, Charles, 1061
Monk, Thelonious, 1068
Morton, Jelly Roll, 1082
Nichols, Herbie, 1112
Oliver, King, 1132
Redding, Otis, 1235
Roach, Max, 1260
Rollins, Sonny, 1289
Russell, George, 1300
Shepp, Archie, 1344
Shorter, Wayne, 1345
Silver, Horace, 1349
Still, William Grant, 1398
Taj Mahal, 1410
Threadgill, Henry, 1430
Tyner, McCoy, 1458
Walker, George, 1497
Waller, Fats, 1504

**MUSIC: CROSSOVER**
Burke, Solomon, 265
Cooke, Sam, 415
Houston, Whitney, 798
Jackson, Michael, 835
McPhatter, Clyde, 1019
Richie, Lionel, 1252
Turner, Tina, 1455
Wilson, Jackie, 1592

**MUSIC: FOLK AND COUNTRY**
Belafonte, Harry, 136
Bland, James, 165
Broonzy, Big Bill, 220
Burke, Solomon, 265
Crudup, Big Boy, 433
Delany, Samuel R., 484
Dett, R. Nathaniel, 489
Neville, Aaron, 1106
Odetta, 1126
Pride, Charley, 1206
Rucker, Darius, 1294
Still, William Grant, 1398
Taj Mahal, 1410

**MUSIC: FUNK**
Brown, James, 234
Clinton, George, 380
Davis, Miles, 461
Gaye, Marvin, 643
Gray, Macy, 681
Hammer, M. C., 721
Hancock, Herbie, 725
Hayes, Isaac, 746
Prince, 1210

**MUSIC: GOSPEL**
Adams, Faye, 14
Adderley, Cannonball, 15
Brown, James, 234
Burke, Solomon, 265
Charles, Ray, 336
Chestnut, Cyrus, 355
Cooke, Sam, 415
Crouch, Andraé, 430
Dorsey, Thomas A., 510
Dumas, Henry, 523
Franklin, Aretha, 614
Green, Al, 684
Houston, Whitney, 798

Jackson, Mahalia, 831
Neville, Aaron, 1106
Redding, Otis, 1235

**MUSIC: HIP-HOP**
Aaliyah, 1
Babyface, 69
Blige, Mary J., 168
Brown, James, 234
Dr. Dre, 504
50 Cent, 588
Hammer, M. C., 721
Hill, Lauryn, 767
Ice Cube, 812
Jay-Z, 852
Jean, Wyclef, 855
Keys, Alicia, 932
L. L. Cool J., 952
O'Neal, Shaquille, 1133
Puff Daddy, 1217
Queen Latifah, 1221
Rihanna, 1255
Shakur, Tupac, 1333
Simmons, Joseph, 1350
Smith, Will, 1385
Snoop Dogg, 1388
Usher, 1474
West, Kanye, 1540

**MUSIC: JAZZ**
Adderley, Cannonball, 15
Ammons, Gene, 41
Armstrong, Lillian Hardin, 55
Armstrong, Louis, 57
Basie, Count, 109
Batiste, Alvin, 118
Blackwell, Edward, 156
Blake, Eubie, 159
Blakey, Art, 162
Bland, Bobby Blue, 163
Blanton, Jimmy, 167
Bonds, Margaret Allison, 185
Bradford, Perry, 195
Braxton, Anthony, 206
Brown, Clifford, 227
Brown, Ray, 239
Calloway, Cab, 283
Carney, Harry, 308
Carter, Benny, 314
Chestnut, Cyrus, 355

Cole, Nat King, 390
Cole, Natalie, 393
Coleman, Ornette, 396
Coltrane, Alice, 407
Coltrane, John, 409
Crothers, Scatman, 428
Crouch, Stanley, 432
Davis, Miles, 461
Davis, Sammy, Jr., 466
Dorsey, Thomas A., 510
Eckstine, Billy, 538
Ellington, Duke, 545
Fitzgerald, Ella, 592
Forrest, Leon, 604
Gillespie, Dizzy, 654
Gordon, Dexter, 665
Griffin, Johnny, 697
Hampton, Lionel, 723
Hancock, Herbie, 725
Hines, Earl, 772
Hinton, Milt, 776
Holiday, Billie, 781
Horne, Lena, 794
James, Etta, 847
Jones, Quincy, 899
Joplin, Scott, 903
Keys, Alicia, 932
McLean, Jackie, 1012
Marsalis, Ellis, Jr., 1030
Marsalis, Wynton, 1032
Mingus, Charles, 1061
Monk, Thelonious, 1068
Morton, Jelly Roll, 1082
Navarro, Fats, 1103
Neville, Aaron, 1106
Nichols, Herbie, 1112
Oliver, King, 1132
Parker, Charlie, 1151
Roach, Max, 1260
Rollins, Sonny, 1289
Russell, George, 1300
Sanders, Pharoah, 1314
Shepp, Archie, 1344
Shorter, Wayne, 1345
Silver, Horace, 1349
Simone, Nina, 1359
Stitt, Sonny, 1401
Threadgill, Henry, 1430
Turner, Big Joe, 1448
Tyner, McCoy, 1458

Vaughan, Sarah, 1483
Waller, Fats, 1504
Webb, Chick, 1531
Williams, Cootie, 1566

**MUSIC: LATIN, CARIBBEAN, AND REGGAE**
Belafonte, Harry, 136
Ellington, Duke, 545
Gillespie, Dizzy, 654
Hancock, Herbie, 725
Hill, Lauryn, 767
Jean, Wyclef, 855
McPhatter, Clyde, 1019
Professor Longhair, 1212
Queen Latifah, 1221
Rihanna, 1255
Russell, George, 1300
Silver, Horace, 1349
Taj Mahal, 1410

**MUSIC: POP**
Adams, Faye, 14
Babyface, 69
Bailey, Pearl, 71
Baker, Josephine, 78
Belafonte, Harry, 136
Cara, Irene, 296
Carey, Mariah, 301
Carter, Nell, 316
Checker, Chubby, 347
Cole, Nat King, 390
Cole, Natalie, 393
Cooke, Sam, 415
Davis, Sammy, Jr., 466
Diddley, Bo, 494
Europe, James Reese, 559
Green, Al, 684
Hammer, M. C., 721
Hancock, Herbie, 725
Horne, Lena, 794
Houston, Whitney, 798
Jackson, Janet, 825
Jackson, Michael, 835
Jones, Quincy, 899
Keys, Alicia, 932
King, B. B., 936
Kitt, Eartha, 944
LaBelle, Patti, 953
Price, Lloyd, 1204

Rihanna, 1255
Ross, Diana, 1291
Summer, Donna, 1405
Turner, Tina, 1455
Uggams, Leslie, 1468
Usher, 1474
Vaughan, Sarah, 1483
Vereen, Ben, 1485
Warwick, Dionne, 1510
Williams, Vanessa, 1581
Wonder, Stevie, 1605

**MUSIC: PRODUCTION**
Clinton, George, 380
Dixon, Willie, 500
Dr. Dre, 504
Gordy, Berry, Jr., 672
Hathaway, Donny, 739
Hill, Lauryn, 767
Jean, Wyclef, 855
Jones, Quincy, 899
Prince, 1210
Puff Daddy, 1217
Rhone, Sylvia M., 1243
Richie, Lionel, 1252
Robinson, Smokey, 1280
Simmons, Russell, 1354
Snoop Dogg, 1388
West, Kanye, 1540
Wonder, Stevie, 1605

**MUSIC: RHYTHM AND BLUES**
Aaliyah, 1
Adams, Faye, 14
Babyface, 69
Berry, Chuck, 141
Blackwell, Edward, 156
Bland, Bobby Blue, 163
Blige, Mary J., 168
Braxton, Toni, 208
Brown, Charles, 222
Brown, James, 234
Burke, Solomon, 265
Carey, Mariah, 301
Charles, Ray, 336
Cole, Natalie, 393
Coleman, Ornette, 396
Cooke, Sam, 415
Crudup, Big Boy, 433
Diddley, Bo, 494

Franklin, Aretha, 614
Gaye, Marvin, 643
Gray, Macy, 681
Green, Al, 684
Griffin, Johnny, 697
Hampton, Lionel, 723
Hancock, Herbie, 725
Hathaway, Donny, 739
Hayes, Isaac, 746
Hill, Lauryn, 767
Houston, Whitney, 798
Hudson, Jennifer, 802
India.Arie, 815
Jackson, Janet, 825
Jackson, Michael, 835
James, Etta, 847
Jean, Wyclef, 855
Jones, Quincy, 899
Keys, Alicia, 932
King, B. B., 936
Knight, Gladys, 946
Knowles, Beyoncé, 948
LaBelle, Patti, 953
Little Walter, 992
McPhatter, Clyde, 1019
Neville, Aaron, 1106
Price, Lloyd, 1204
Professor Longhair, 1212
Queen Latifah, 1221
Redding, Otis, 1235
Richie, Lionel, 1252
Rihanna, 1255
Robinson, Smokey, 1280
Summer, Donna, 1405
Taj Mahal, 1410
Turner, Ike, 1451
Turner, Tina, 1455
Usher, 1474
Williams, Vanessa, 1581
Wilson, Jackie, 1592
Wonder, Stevie, 1605

**MUSIC: ROCK AND ROLL**
Berry, Chuck, 141
Bland, Bobby Blue, 163
Crudup, Big Boy, 433
Diddley, Bo, 494
Gray, Macy, 681
Hendrix, Jimi, 758
Jackson, Janet, 825

James, Etta, 847
King, B. B., 936
Price, Lloyd, 1204
Prince, 1210
Professor Longhair, 1212
Rucker, Darius, 1294
Summer, Donna, 1405
Taj Mahal, 1410
Turner, Ike, 1451
Turner, Tina, 1455
Waters, Muddy, 1525

**MUSIC: SOUL**
Babyface, 69
Blige, Mary J., 168
Brown, James, 234
Burke, Solomon, 265
Carey, Mariah, 301
Charles, Ray, 336
Franklin, Aretha, 614
Gaye, Marvin, 643
Gray, Macy, 681
Green, Al, 684
Griffin, Johnny, 697
Hayes, Isaac, 746
Hill, Lauryn, 767
Houston, Whitney, 798
India.Arie, 815
James, Etta, 847
Jean, Wyclef, 855
Keys, Alicia, 932
Knight, Gladys, 946
Prince, 1210
Redding, Otis, 1235
Robinson, Smokey, 1280
Wilson, Jackie, 1592

**MUSIC: SPIRITUALS**
Battle, Kathleen, 119
Bowman, Sister Thea, 192
Dorsey, Thomas A., 510
Norman, Jessye, 1117
Odetta, 1126
Robeson, Paul, 1263

**MUSIC: SWING**
Basie, Count, 109
Blackwell, Edward, 156
Blanton, Jimmy, 167
Broonzy, Big Bill, 220

Calloway, Cab, 283
Carney, Harry, 308
Carter, Benny, 314
Ellington, Duke, 545
Fitzgerald, Ella, 592
Hampton, Lionel, 723
Hinton, Milt, 776
Oliver, King, 1132
Waller, Fats, 1504
Webb, Chick, 1531
Williams, Cootie, 1566

**OLYMPICS.** *See* **SPORTS**

**OPERA.** *See* **MUSIC**

**PHILANTHROPY**
Brown, Jim, 237
Cheatham, Henry Plummer, 344
Clemente, Roberto, 374
Cuffe, Paul, 437
Duncan, Tim, 528
Forten, James, 606
Gaston, Arthur George, 637
Graves, Earl G., Sr., 679
Holyfield, Evander, 784
Jealous, Benjamin T., 853
Latimer, Lewis Howard, 959
Rice, Linda Johnson, 1249
Robinson, David, 1269
Smith, Emmitt, 1379
Woods, Tiger, 1612

**PHOTOGRAPHY.** *See* **ART AND PHOTOGRAPHY**

**PIONEERING.** *See* **EXPLORATION AND PIONEERING**

**POETRY**
Alexander, Elizabeth, 24
Baldwin, James, 81
Baraka, Amiri, 96
Barrax, Gerald William, 102
Bell, James Madison, 140
Bontemps, Arna, 188
Braithwaite, William Stanley, 202
Brooks, Gwendolyn, 217
Brown, Sterling A., 243
Casey, Bernie, 324

Chase-Riboud, Barbara, 339
Clarke, John Henrik, 367
Cliff, Michelle, 377
Clifton, Lucille, 378
Coleman, Wanda, 399
Cornish, Sam, 418
Cortez, Jayne, 420
Cullen, Countée, 439
Dodson, Owen, 506
Dove, Rita, 516
Dunbar, Paul Laurence, 524
Dunbar-Nelson, Alice, 527
Emanuel, James A., 551
Evans, Mari, 563
Giovanni, Nikki, 657
Grimké, Angelina Weld, 701
Grimké, Charlotte L. Forten, 703
Harper, Frances Ellen Watkins, 732
Harper, Michael S., 734
Hughes, Langston, 803
Jones, Gayl, 893
Jordan, June, 907
Komunyakaa, Yusef, 949
Lorde, Audre, 997
McKay, Claude, 1010
Madhubuti, Haki R., 1022
Murray, Pauli, 1095
Parker, Pat, 1153
Reed, Ishmael, 1238
Sanchez, Sonia, 1307
Shange, Ntozake, 1335
Tolson, Melvin B., 1434
Walker, Alice, 1493
Walker, Margaret, 1503
Wheatley, Phillis, 1545
Young, Al, 1631

POLITICS. *See* GOVERNMENT AND
POLITICS

POP MUSIC. *See* MUSIC

PUBLISHING. *See* JOURNALISM
AND PUBLISHING

RADIO AND TELEVISION
Abernathy, Ralph David, 11
Barkley, Charles, 99
Barnes, Steven, 101
Bond, Julian, 179

Boykin, Otis, 193
Bradley, Ed, 198
Brown, Tony, 246
Campbell, Bebe Moore, 290
Frazier, Walt, 621
Gordon, Ed, 667
Gumbel, Bryant, 707
Hooks, Benjamin, 789
Ifill, Gwen, 814
Johnson, Magic, 877
Johnson, Robert L., 884
Mitchell, Brian Stokes, 1065
O'Neal, Shaquille, 1133
Owens, Terrell, 1143
Pitts, Leonard, 1187
Reed, Ishmael, 1238
Richards, Lloyd, 1251
Robinson, Max, 1277
Roker, Al, 1287
Sharpton, Al, 1337
Shaw, Bernard, 1340
Simpson, O. J., 1361
Smiley, Tavis, 1373
Smith, Anna Deveare, 1374
Smith, Emmitt, 1379
Strode, Woody, 1402
Vance, Courtney B., 1476
Williams, Juan, 1573
Williams, Montel, 1576

REGGAE MUSIC. *See* MUSIC

RELIGION AND THEOLOGY
Abernathy, Ralph David, 11
Ali, Noble Drew, 29
Allen, Richard, 36
Allensworth, Allen, 38
Bevel, James, 150
Brown, H. Rap, 232
Cleage, Albert Buford, Jr., 369
Coker, Daniel, 388
Cone, James H., 411
Crummell, Alexander, 435
Farrakhan, Louis, 575
Father Divine, 577
Ferguson, Samuel, 584
Gray, William H., III, 682
Gregory, Wilton D., 692
Hammer, M. C., 721
Healy, Patrick F., 750

Hooks, Benjamin, 789
Jackson, Jesse, 826
Jakes, T. D., 846
Jones, Absalom, 889
King, Martin Luther, Jr., 941
Lawson, James, 964
Lewis, John Robert, 982
Lincoln, C. Eric, 985
Lowery, Joseph, 1001
Malcolm X, 1024
Mays, Benjamin E., 1043
Muhammad, Elijah, 1088
Murray, Pauli, 1095
Revels, Hiram Rhoades, 1241
Shuttlesworth, Fred, 1347
Sullivan, Leon H., 1404
Turner, Henry McNeal, 1450
Vivian, C. T., 1488
Walters, Alexander, 1508
Wright, Jeremiah, 1622

RHYTHM AND BLUES. *See* MUSIC

ROCK AND ROLL. *See* MUSIC

SCHOLARSHIP
Abdul-Jabbar, Kareem, 8
Asante, Molefi Kete, 60
Baker, Houston A., Jr., 77
Bond, Horace Mann, 177
Bontemps, Arna, 188
Brown, Sterling A., 243
Clarke, John Henrik, 367
Collins, Patricia Hill, 405
Du Bois, W. E. B., 520
Franklin, John Hope, 617
Gates, Henry Louis, Jr., 640
Gayle, Addison, Jr., 645
Gordon, Lewis, 668
Gordon-Reed, Annette, 670
Jeffries, Leonard, 856
Karenga, Maulana, 923
Lincoln, C. Eric, 985
Locke, Alain, 995
McWhorter, John, 1020
Newton, Huey P., 1108
Primus, Pearl, 1208
Quarles, Benjamin, 1219
Schomburg, Arturo Alfonso, 1319
Sowell, Thomas, 1390

Steele, Shelby, 1395
West, Cornel, 1535
Wilson, William Julius, 1593
Woodson, Carter G., 1615

**SCIENCE AND TECHNOLOGY**
Alcorn, George Edward, 20
Banneker, Benjamin, 92
Beard, Andrew Jackson, 125
Blackwell, David Harold, 153
Blair, Henry, 158
Bluford, Guion, 171
Bolden, Charles F., Jr., 173
Boykin, Otis, 193
Carver, George Washington, 319
Coleman, Bessie, 394
Flipper, Henry Ossian, 595
Gourdine, Meredith C., 676
Granville, Evelyn Boyd, 678
Gregory, Frederick Drew, 690
Henson, Matthew Alexander, 761
Jackson, Shirley Ann, 842
Jemison, Mae C., 858
Johnson, Katherine G., 876
Julian, Hubert Fauntleroy, 917
Julian, Percy Lavon, 919
Just, Ernest Everett, 921
Latimer, Lewis Howard, 959
Lawrence, Robert H., Jr., 963
McNair, Ronald E., 1017
Marchbanks, Vance Hunter, 1029
Matzeliger, Jan Ernst, 1041
Morgan, Garrett Augustus, 1075
Rillieux, Norbert, 1256
Slaughter, John Brooks, 1369
Thomas, Vivien, 1427
Tyson, Neil deGrasse, 1464
Woods, Granville T., 1610
Wright, Jane Cooke, 1619

**SOCIAL ISSUES**
Abbott, Robert S., 5
Abernathy, Ralph David, 11
Allen, Richard, 36
Ashe, Arthur, 63
Attucks, Crispus, 66
Baker, Ella, 75
Baldwin, James, 81
Bambara, Toni Cade, 86
Baraka, Amiri, 96

Bates, Daisy, 116
Bell, James Madison, 140
Bethune, Mary McLeod, 148
Bevel, James, 150
Bond, Julian, 179
Briggs, Cyril V., 210
Brooks, Gwendolyn, 217
Brown, Elaine, 230
Brown, H. Rap, 232
Brown, Jim, 237
Brown, Tony, 246
Bruce, John E., 254
Burroughs, Nannie Helen, 273
Campanella, Roy, 288
Carmichael, Stokely, 305
Chaney, James, 330
Chavis, Benjamin, 341
Chesnutt, Charles Waddell, 353
Cinque, Joseph, 361
Clark, Septima Poinsette, 365
Cleaver, Eldridge, 371
Cliff, Michelle, 377
Coleman, Bessie, 394
Cortez, Jayne, 420
Crenshaw, Kimberlé Williams, 426
Crummell, Alexander, 435
Cuffe, Paul, 437
Davis, Angela, 448
Davis, Benjamin J., 451
Davis, Henrietta Vinton, 459
Delany, Martin Robison, 481
Du Bois, W. E. B., 520
Dunbar-Nelson, Alice, 527
Edelman, Marian Wright, 540
Evans, Mari, 563
Evers, Medgar, 566
Evers-Williams, Myrlie, 568
Farmer, James L., Jr., 573
Farrakhan, Louis, 575
Father Divine, 577
Fontaine, William Thomas, 598
Forman, James, 602
Forten, James, 606
Garnet, Henry Highland, 631
Garvey, Marcus, 635
Gates, Henry Louis, Jr., 640
Gayle, Helene Doris, 646
Giovanni, Nikki, 657
Gordon, Lewis, 668

Gregory, Wilton D., 692
Grimké, Charlotte L. Forten, 703
Hall, Prince, 716
Hamer, Fannie Lou, 717
Hansberry, Lorraine, 728
Harper, Frances Ellen Watkins, 732
Height, Dorothy, 752
Hemings, Sally, 754
Hill, Anita, 764
Hunter-Gault, Charlayne, 807
Innis, Roy, 817
Jackson, Jesse, 826
Jakes, T. D., 846
Jealous, Benjamin T., 853
Jeffries, Leonard, 856
Johnson, Rafer, 882
Jones, Bill T., 891
Karenga, Maulana, 923
Keyes, Alan, 930
King, Coretta Scott, 939
King, Martin Luther, Jr., 941
Lee, Canada, 967
Locke, Alain, 995
McWhorter, John, 1020
Malcolm X, 1024
Marshall, Paule, 1035
Meredith, James, 1049
Meriwether, Louise, 1052
Mfume, Kweisi, 1053
Mitchell, Clarence M., Jr., 1067
Morrison, Toni, 1080
Muhammad, Elijah, 1088
Newton, Huey P., 1108
O'Neil, Buck, 1136
Ringgold, Faith, 1258
Robinson, Max, 1277
Robinson, Randall, 1278
Rudolph, Wilma, 1295
Russwurm, John Brown, 1302
Rustin, Bayard, 1303
Saar, Betye, 1306
Sanchez, Sonia, 1307
Scott, Dred, 1324
Seale, Bobby, 1328
Shabazz, Betty, 1330
Shabazz, Ilyasah, 1332
Shuttlesworth, Fred, 1347
Singleton, Benjamin, 1366
Smiley, Tavis, 1373
Steele, Shelby, 1395

Stewart, Maria, 1397
Sullivan, Leon H., 1404
Terrell, Mary Church, 1416
Thomas, Clarence, 1418
Till, Emmett, 1432
Truth, Sojourner, 1441
Tubman, Harriet, 1444
Tucker, C. DeLores, 1447
Turner, Henry McNeal, 1450
Turner, Nat, 1453
Vesey, Denmark, 1487
Vivian, C. T., 1488
Walker, David, 1495
Walters, Alexander, 1508
Washington, Booker T., 1513
Waters, Maxine, 1523
Weaver, Robert C., 1530
West, Cornel, 1535
White, Walter, 1552
Wilkins, Roy, 1560
Wright, Louis T., 1624
Young, Andrew, 1632
Young, Coleman, 1635

**SOCIAL SCIENCES**
Asante, Molefi Kete, 60
Baker, Houston A., Jr., 77
Bond, Horace Mann, 177
Clark, Kenneth, 363
Clarke, John Henrik, 367
Collins, Patricia Hill, 405
Du Bois, W. E. B., 520
Dunham, Katherine, 530
Franklin, John Hope, 617
Gates, Henry Louis, Jr., 640
Hilliard, Asa Grant, III, 768
Hurston, Zora Neale, 808
Johnson, Charles S., 862
Lincoln, C. Eric, 985
Quarles, Benjamin, 1219
Sowell, Thomas, 1390
Steele, Claude M., 1392
Wharton, Clifton Reginald, Jr.,
    1543
Wilson, William Julius, 1593
Woodson, Carter G., 1615

**SOUL.** *See* **MUSIC**

**SPIRITUALS.** *See* **MUSIC**

**SPORTS: BASEBALL**
Aaron, Hank, 3
Baker, Dusty, 73
Banks, Ernie, 88
Bell, Cool Papa, 138
Blue, Vida, 170
Bonds, Barry, 182
Brock, Lou, 213
Campanella, Roy, 288
Carew, Rod, 300
Clemente, Roberto, 374
Doby, Larry, 502
Flood, Curt, 596
Gibson, Bob, 650
Gibson, Josh, 652
Griffey, Ken, Jr., 695
Gwynn, Tony, 708
Hammer, M. C., 721
Henderson, Rickey, 756
Jackson, Bo, 822
Jackson, Reggie, 838
Jeter, Derek, 860
Jordan, Michael, 909
Mays, Willie, 1045
O'Neil, Buck, 1136
Paige, Satchel, 1148
Pride, Charley, 1206
Robinson, Frank, 1270
Robinson, Jackie, 1272
Sanders, Deion, 1311
Thomas, Frank, 1423
Washington, Kenny, 1521
White, Bill, 1550
Wills, Maury, 1586

**SPORTS: BASKETBALL**
Abdul-Jabbar, Kareem, 8
Barkley, Charles, 99
Baylor, Elgin, 121
Billups, Chauncey, 152
Bryant, Kobe, 256
Chamberlain, Wilt, 327
Dawkins, Darryl, 474
Doby, Larry, 502
Duncan, Tim, 528
Erving, Julius, 554
Ewing, Patrick, 571
Frazier, Walt, 621
Garnett, Kevin, 633
Gibson, Bob, 650

Gossett, Louis, Jr., 674
Gwynn, Tony, 708
Hawkins, Connie, 740
Hayes, Elvin, 745
Howard, Dwight, 800
Iverson, Allen, 819
James, LeBron, 849
Johnson, Magic, 877
Johnson, Robert L., 884
Jones, Marion, 897
Jordan, Michael, 909
Joyner-Kersee, Jackie, 914
Lemon, Meadowlark, 972
Leslie, Lisa, 976
Lloyd, Earl, 994
Malone, Karl, 1027
Martin, Kenyon, 1039
Miller, Cheryl, 1057
Olajuwon, Hakeem, 1128
O'Neal, Shaquille, 1133
Owens, Chris, 1139
Paul, Chris, 1166
Pierce, Paul, 1181
Pippen, Scottie, 1186
Robertson, Oscar, 1261
Robinson, David, 1269
Russell, Bill, 1298
Thomas, Isiah, 1424
West, David, 1537
Wilkens, Lenny, 1558
Williams, Gus, 1569
Woodard, Lynette, 1609

**SPORTS: BOXING**
Ali, Muhammad, 26
Armstrong, Henry, 53
Bullins, Ed, 260
Charles, Ezzard, 334
Dixon, Willie, 500
Foreman, George, 600
Frazier, Joe, 620
Gordy, Berry, Jr., 672
Holyfield, Evander, 784
Johnson, Jack, 865
Lee, Canada, 967
Leonard, Sugar Ray, 974
Liston, Sonny, 987
Louis, Joe, 999
Miller, Dorie, 1058
Moore, Archie, 1073

Patterson, Floyd, 1163
Robinson, Sugar Ray, 1284
Tyson, Mike, 1462
Walcott, Jersey Joe, 1491
Wilson, Jackie, 1592

**SPORTS: FOOTBALL**
Allen, Damon, 31
Allen, Marcus, 34
Brown, Jim, 237
Brown, Tim, 245
Bryant, Antonio, 255
Campbell, Earl, 294
Casey, Bernie, 324
Davis, Ernie, 457
Dickerson, Eric, 493
Faulk, Marshall, 580
Greene, Joe, 686
Harris, Franco, 735
Hayes, Bob, 742
Jackson, Bo, 822
Johnson, Dwayne, 864
Johnson, Michael, 880
Lanier, Willie, 955
Lewis, Ray, 984
McNabb, Donovan, 1016
Owens, Terrell, 1143
Payton, Walter, 1168
Peete, Rodney, 1172
Pollard, Fritz, 1193
Reed, Ed, 1236
Rice, Jerry, 1247
Sanders, Barry, 1309
Sanders, Deion, 1311
Shell, Art, 1341
Simpson, O. J., 1361
Singletary, Mike, 1364
Smith, Emmitt, 1379
Strode, Woody, 1402
Taylor, Lawrence, 1413
Upshaw, Gene, 1472
Washington, Kenny, 1521
Watts, J. C., 1528
Wheatley, Tyrone, 1547
Woodson, Rod, 1617

**SPORTS: GOLF AND TENNIS**
Ashe, Arthur, 63
Elder, Lee, 542
Gibson, Althea, 648

Peete, Calvin, 1170
Williams, Serena, 1579
Williams, Venus, 1583
Woods, Tiger, 1612

**SPORTS: MISCELLANEOUS**
Davis, Shani, 469
Dawes, Dominique, 472
DeFrantz, Anita, 479
Gumbel, Bryant, 707
Johnson, Dwayne, 864
Murphy, Isaac Burns, 1093
Pickett, Bill, 1179
Robinson, Jackie, 1272
Scurry, Briana, 1326
Simms, Willie, 1357
Thomas, Debi, 1421
Winkfield, James, 1600

**SPORTS: OLYMPICS**
Ali, Muhammad, 26
Ashford, Evelyn, 65
Barkley, Charles, 99
Beamon, Bob, 123
Billups, Chauncey, 152
Boston, Ralph, 190
Bradley, Tom, 200
Calhoun, Lee, 282
Carlos, John, 303
Coachman, Alice, 384
Davenport, Willie, 446
Davis, Shani, 469
Dawes, Dominique, 472
DeFrantz, Anita, 479
Devers, Gail, 491
Evans, Lee, 562
Ewing, Patrick, 571
Foreman, George, 600
Garnett, Kevin, 633
Gourdine, Meredith C., 676
Griffith-Joyner, Florence, 699
Hayes, Bob, 742
Holyfield, Evander, 784
Howard, Dwight, 800
Johnson, Magic, 877
Johnson, Michael, 880
Johnson, Rafer, 882
Jones, Marion, 897
Jordan, Michael, 909
Joyner-Kersee, Jackie, 914

Leonard, Sugar Ray, 974
Leslie, Lisa, 976
Lewis, Carl, 978
Louis, Joe, 999
Malone, Karl, 1027
Moses, Edwin, 1084
Olajuwon, Hakeem, 1128
O'Neal, Shaquille, 1133
Owens, Jesse, 1140
Patterson, Floyd, 1163
Robertson, Oscar, 1261
Robinson, David, 1269
Rudolph, Wilma, 1295
Russell, Bill, 1298
Scurry, Briana, 1326
Smith, Tommie, 1382
Thomas, Debi, 1421
Tyus, Wyomia, 1466
Williams, Serena, 1579
Williams, Venus, 1583
Woodard, Lynette, 1609

**SPORTS: TRACK AND FIELD**
Ashford, Evelyn, 65
Beamon, Bob, 123
Boston, Ralph, 190
Calhoun, Lee, 282
Carlos, John, 303
Chamberlain, Wilt, 327
Coachman, Alice, 384
Davenport, Willie, 446
Devers, Gail, 491
Evans, Lee, 562
Gourdine, Meredith C., 676
Griffith-Joyner, Florence, 699
Hayes, Bob, 742
Jackson, Bo, 822
Johnson, Michael, 880
Johnson, Rafer, 882
Jones, Marion, 897
Joyner-Kersee, Jackie, 914
Lewis, Carl, 978
Moses, Edwin, 1084
Owens, Jesse, 1140
Rudolph, Wilma, 1295
Simpson, O. J., 1361
Smith, Tommie, 1382
Tyus, Wyomia, 1466
Wheatley, Tyrone, 1547

SWING. *See* MUSIC

TECHNOLOGY. *See* SCIENCE AND TECHNOLOGY

TELEVISION. *See* RADIO AND TELEVISION

TENNIS. *See* SPORTS

THEATER
Baraka, Amiri, 96
Bonner, Marita, 186
Braxton, Toni, 208
Childress, Alice, 356
Cooper, J. California, 417
Davis, Viola, 471
Dodson, Owen, 506
Fuller, Charles, 625
Grimké, Angelina Weld, 701
Hansberry, Lorraine, 728
Jones, Gayl, 893
Kennedy, Adrienne, 928

Mitchell, Brian Stokes, 1065
Richards, Lloyd, 1251
Sanchez, Sonia, 1307
Shange, Ntozake, 1335
Smith, Anna Deveare, 1374
Vance, Courtney B., 1476
Wilson, August, 1587
Wolfe, George C., 1603
Young, Al, 1631

THEOLOGY. *See* RELIGION AND THEOLOGY

TRACK AND FIELD. *See* SPORTS

VAUDEVILLE. *See* ENTERTAINMENT

WOMEN'S RIGHTS
Bambara, Toni Cade, 86
Bass, Charlotta Spears, 113
Bonner, Marita, 186
Burke, Yvonne Brathwaite, 267

Burroughs, Nannie Helen, 273
Clark, Septima Poinsette, 365
Coleman, Bessie, 394
Davis, Angela, 448
Harper, Frances Ellen Watkins, 732
Height, Dorothy, 752
Jordan, Barbara, 905
Jordan, June, 907
Lorde, Audre, 997
Marshall, Paule, 1035
Murray, Pauli, 1095
Parker, Pat, 1153
Robinson, Jo Ann Gibson, 1275
Smith, Barbara, 1376
Stewart, Maria, 1397
Terrell, Mary Church, 1416
Truth, Sojourner, 1441
Tubman, Harriet, 1444
Tucker, C. DeLores, 1447
Walker, Alice, 1493
Wattleton, Faye, 1526
Wells-Barnett, Ida B., 1533

# Personages Index

Aaliyah, 1-2

Aaron, Hank, 3-5, 73, 184, 1046, 1206; and M. C. Hammer, 721

Abbott, Cleveland, 384

Abbott, Robert S., 5-8, 390, 395

Abdul-Jabbar, Kareem, 8-11, 184, 741, 745, 878, 1262, 1383

Abernathy, Ralph David, 11-13, 263, 832; and James Bevel, 151; and Jesse Jackson, 827

Abrams, Muhal Richard, 206-207, 1430

Abzug, Bella, 569

Adams, Faye, 14-15

Adams, John, 67, 754

Adams, John Quincy, 362, 1162

Adderley, Cannonball, 15-17, 118, 462

Adderley Brothers, 336

Adler, Kurt, 120

Admiral, the. See Robinson, David

Adoff, Virginia Hamilton. See Hamilton, Virginia

African Roscius, The. See Aldridge, Ira Frederick

Agyeman, Jaramogi Abebe. See Cleage, Albert Buford, Jr.

Aiken, Loretta Mary. See Mabley, Moms

Ailey, Alvin, 18-20, 50

Air, 1431

Alabamians, 284

Albright, Madeleine, 1245

Alcindor, Lew. See Abdul-Jabbar, Kareem

Alcorn, George Edward, 20-21

Alcorn, James L., 1242

Alda, Alan, 465

Aldridge, Ira Frederick, 22-24

Alexander, Elizabeth, 24-25

Alexander, J. W., 416

Alexander, Margaret Walker. See Walker, Margaret

Ali, Laila, 28

Ali, Muhammad, 26-28, 373, 601, 1074, 1164, 1205, 1386; and

Joe Frazier, 620-621; and Sonny Liston, 988, 1492

Ali, Noble Drew, 29-30

Ali, Rashied, 410

Allen, Andrew Arthur "Tex," 1233

Allen, Betty, 185

Allen, Damon, 31-33

Allen, Debbie, 33-34, 1112, 1233

Allen, Henry, 1560

Allen, Marcus, 31, 34-36, 1169

Allen, Phog, 327

Allen, Ray, 634, 1182

Allen, Richard, 36-38, 389, 606, 889-890

Allensworth, Allen, 38-39

Alston, Charles, 40-41, 961, 1318

Althouse, Paul, 270

Altman, Robert, 137

Alton, Louise, 270

Amankwatia, Nana Baffour, II. See Hilliard, Asa Grant, III

Ambers, Lou, 54

Ames, Adelbart, 252

Amin, Idi, 818

Amin, Jamil Abdullah Al-. See Brown, H. Rap

Ammons, Albert, 41

Ammons, Gene, 41-43, 1401

Amos, John, 1499

Amos, Wally, 43-45

Anderson, Cornelius, 45

Anderson, Eddie "Rochester," 45-47

Anderson, Greg, 184

Anderson, Marian, 47-50, 270, 832, 1117, 1202; and Marian Wright Edelman, 540

Anderson, Theodore W., 154

Andrew, Joseph Maree. See Bonner, Marita

Angelou, Maya, 50-53, 286, 526, 1127; and Lorene Cary, 323; critique of, 399

Angry Blond Negro. See Briggs, Cyril V.

Answer, the. See Iverson, Allen

Anthony, Carmelo, 153

Anthony, Susan B., 515, 1445, 1447

Anthropologists; Katherine Dunham, 530-531; Zora Neale Hurston, 808-811; Pearl Primus, 1208-1209; William Julius Wilson, 1593-1594

Appiah, Kwame Anthony, 641

Arafat, Yasir, 828

Arie, India. See India.Arie

Aristide, Jean-Bertrand, 683, 1279

Arizmendi, Baby, 54

Arkestra, 1408-1409, 1430

Armstrong, Harry, 53

Armstrong, Henry, 53-55

Armstrong, Lillian Hardin, 55-57; and Louis Armstrong, 56, 58

Armstrong, Louis, 57-60, 195, 867; and Lillian Hardin Armstrong, 56; and Cab Calloway, 284; and Ella Fitzgerald, 593; and Lionel Hampton, 723; and Earl Hines, 773; and Milt Hinton, 777; and Billie Holiday, 781, 783; and Charles Mingus, 1062; and Ma Rainey, 1227; and Chick Webb, 1531

Armstrong, Neil, 876

Arriba. See Clemente, Roberto

Artist Formerly Known as Prince, the. See Prince

Arvey, Verna, 1400

Asante, Molefi Kete, 60-62

Asbury, Francis, 36

Ashe, Arthur, 63-64, 648-649

Ashford, Evelyn, 65-66, 700

Ashwood, Amy, 635

Assad, Hafez al-, 828

Astronauts; Guion Bluford, 171-173; Charles F. Bolden, Jr., 173-174; Frederick Drew Gregory, 690-692; Mae C. Jemison, 858-859; Robert H. Lawrence, Jr., 963-964; Ronald E. McNair, 1017-1019

Atkins, Chet, 1206
Atkins, Cholly, 400-402
Attucks, Crispus, 66-68, 1440
Atwater, Lee, 350
Auerbach, Red, 327, 1298
Ausbie, Herb "Geese," 1609
Avakian, George, 461
Aviators; Guion Bluford, 171-173; Charles F. Bolden, Jr., 173-174; Eugene Jacques Bullard, 259-260; Bessie Coleman, 394-396; Benjamin O. Davis, Jr., 455-457; Frederick Drew Gregory, 690-692; Hubert Fauntleroy Julian, 917-919; Robert H. Lawrence, Jr., 963-964
Ayers-Allen, Phylicia. See Rashad, Phylicia

Babyface, 69-70
Bacall, Lauren, 468
Bacharach, Burt, 1459, 1510-1511
Baer, Max, 1000, 1492
Bailey, Benny, 429
Bailey, Frederick Augustus Washington. See Douglass, Frederick
Bailey, Pearl, 71-73, 1003
Baker, Anita, 168
Baker, Dusty, 73-74
Baker, Ella, 75-76, 719
Baker, Etta, 1411
Baker, George, Jr. See Father Divine
Baker, Houston A., Jr., 77-78
Baker, Josephine, 78-81, 675, 1233
Balanchine, George, 1064
Baldwin, James, 81-84; and Maya Angelou, 51; and Eldridge Cleaver, 373; and Walter Dean Myers, 1098; and Emmett Till, 1433; and Richard Wright, 1627
Baldwin, Maria L., 223
Ball, James Presley, 84-85
Ball, Thomas, 980
Ballard, Florence, 1291
Bambaataa, Afrika, 1221
Bambara, Toni Cade, 86-88, 291
Bancroft, Hubert, 1320
Banks, Ernie, 88-90, 139, 1136

Banks, Tyra, 90-91
Banneker, Benjamin, 92-93
Bannister, Edward Mitchell, 94-95
Bar-Kays, 1235
Baraka, Amiri, 96-98, 397; and Sonia Sanchez, 1308; and August Wilson, 1588
Barbarin, Paul, 156
Bard of the Maumee. See Bell, James Madison
Barkley, Charles, 99-101, 152
Barnes, Steven, 101-102
Barnet, Charlie, 794, 1012
Barnett, Ross, 1050-1051
Barone, Joseph "Pep," 987
Barons of Rhythm, 109
Baroudi, Sam, 335
Barrax, Gerald William, 102-104
Barrow, Clyde, 622
Barrow, Joseph Louis. See Louis, Joe
Barry, Marion, 104-106, 150, 738, 1573
Barthé, Richmond, 107-108
Bartholomew, Dave, 508-509
Baryshnikov, Mikhail, 19, 1422
Baseball managers; Dusty Baker, 74; Cool Papa Bell, 139; Larry Doby, 503; Cito Gaston, 74; Buck O'Neil, 1136-1137; Frank Robinson, 1270-1272
Basie, Count, 109-111; and Gene Ammons, 42; and Milt Hinton, 777; and Billie Holiday, 782; and Albert Murray, 1095; and Big Joe Turner, 1448
Basketball coaches; Earl Lloyd, 994; Bill Russell, 1298-1299
Basquiat, Jean-Michel, 111-113, 1621
Bass, Charlotta Spears, 113-114
Bass, Joseph Blackburn, 113
Bass, Kingsley B., Jr. See Bullins, Ed
Bassett, Angela, 115-116, 591, 1015, 1457, 1477
Bates, Daisy, 116-118
Bates, Ellas Otha. See Diddley, Bo
Batiste, Alvin, 118-119
Batiste, Harold, 156

Batson, Florence, 269
Batt, John, 716
Battle, Kathleen, 119-121, 185, 356
Battle, Mike, 622
Baumfree, Isabella. See Truth, Sojourner
Baumgarten, David, 694
Bauzá, Mario, 655
Baylor, Elgin, 121-123
Beach Boys, 143
Beam, Abraham, 498
Beamon, Bob, 123-124, 191, 979, 1384
Beard, Andrew Jackson, 125-126
Bearden, Romare, 40, 126-128, 1588
Beasley, Myrlie Louise. See Evers-Williams, Myrlie
Beastie Boys, 1355
Beatles, 143, 373, 1475; and Chuck Berry, 142; and Fats Domino, 509; and Little Richard, 991
Beaty, Powhatan, 459
Beavers, Louise, 129-130, 1007
Beckford, Tyson, 130-132
Beckwith, Byron De La, 332, 568, 570
Beckwourth, Jim, 132-134
Becton, Julius Wesley. Jr., 134-135
Bee, Clair, 503
Bee Gees, 1475
Belafonte, Harry, 136-138, 314, 1078, 1126-1127; and Brock Peters, 1175
Bell, Alexander Graham, 960
Bell, Cool Papa, 138-140, 675
Bell, Demetrius, 1028
Bell, James Madison, 140-141
Bellotte, Pete, 1406
Bellson, Louis, 72
Bennett, Tony, 110
Bennett, William, 1447
Benny, Jack, 45
Bens, Franklin, 119
Benton, Thomas Hart, 254
Benton, Walter, 103
Berbick, Trevor, 1463
Bergman, Ingrid, 1155
Berlin, Irving, 593
Berman, Bess, 832

Bernadotte, Folke, 264

Bernstein, Leonard, 19, 727, 1033

Berry, Chu, 285, 315, 776

Berry, Chuck, 141-143, 496, 501, 848

Berry, Halle, 144-145, 841

Bertrand, Jimmy, 723

Bethune, Blind Tom, 145-147

Bethune, James, 145-146

Bethune, Mary McLeod, 148-150, 752-753, 1530

Bevel, Diane. See Nash, Diane

Bevel, James, 150-151, 1102, 1488

Beyoncé. See Knowles, Beyoncé

Biden, Joseph, 641, 765, 815, 1123

Big Cat, the. See Lloyd, Earl

Big Dipper, the. See Chamberlain, Wilt

Big E, the. See Hayes, Elvin

Big Hurt, the. See Thomas, Frank

Big O, the. See Robertson, Oscar

Big Ticket, the. See Garnett, Kevin

Biko, Steve, 1516

Billups, Chauncey, 152-153, 1181

Bird. See Parker, Charlie

Bird, Larry, 878-879

Bishop, Joey, 468

Bishop, William "Billy," 917

Black, Julian, 999

Black Babe Ruth, the. See Gibson, Josh

Black Eagle, the. See Julian, Hubert Fauntleroy

Black Herman, 1407

Black Mamba. See Bryant, Kobe

Black Mencken, the. See Schuyler, George S.

Black Patti, the. See Jones, Sissieretta

Black Patti Troubadours, 269, 902

Black Thomas Edison, the. See Woods, Granville T.

Black Ty Cobb, the. See Bell, Cool Papa

Black Venus. See Baker, Josephine

Blackbird of Harlem. See Mills, Florence

Blackburn, Jack "Chappie," 999, 1491

Blackwell, David Harold, 153-156

Blackwell, Edward, 156-157

Blackwell, Scrapper, 311

Blagojevich, Rod, 272

Blair, Henry, 158-159

Blair, William, 409

Blake, Eubie, 79, 159-161, 270

Blakey, Art, 162-163, 1260, 1346; and Jackie McLean, 1013

Blalock, Alfred, 1427

Bland, Bobby Blue, 163-164

Bland, James, 165-166

Blanton, Jimmy, 167-168

Blaze, Just, 852

Blazers, 222

Blige, Mary J., 168-169, 505, 852, 1217

Blind Tom. See Bethune, Blind Tom

Bloom, Allan, 930

Blount, Herman Poole. See Sun Ra

Blow, Kurtis, 1350, 1354

Blow, Sam. See Scott, Dred

Blue, Vida, 170-171

Blue Boy. See Bland, Bobby Blue

Blue Devils, 109, 167, 461

Blue Flames, 227

Bluebelles, 954

Bluford, Guion, 171-173, 1115

Boas, Franz, 809

Bobo, Willie, 725

Bocchicchio, Felix, 1491

Bocelli, Andrea, 169

Bogart, Humphrey, 468, 1492

Boghetti, Giuseppe, 48

Bojangles. See Robinson, Bill

Bolden, Buddy, 57

Bolden, Charles F., Jr., 173-174

Bolin, Jane Matilda, 175-177

Bonavena, Oscar, 27

Bond, Horace Mann, 177-179

Bond, Julian, 179-181, 603

Bonds, Barry, 182-184, 1047

Bonds, Bobby, 1047

Bonds, Margaret Allison, 185-186

Bonner, Marita, 186-187

Bontemps, Arna, 188-190, 441

Boone, Herman, 1517

Bork, Robert, 765

Bosh, Chris, 850

Boss of the Blues. See Turner, Big Joe

Boston, Ralph, 123, 190-192

Boswell Sisters, 592

Boulanger, Nadia, 900

Bowart, Walter, 1238

Bowdoin, James, 716

Bowers, Sam, 331-332

Bowman, Sister Thea, 192-193

Boyar, Burt, 468

Boyar, Jane, 468

Boyd, Evelyn. See Granville, Evelyn Boyd

Boyd, Julianne, 161

Boyer, Elisa, 416

Boykin, Otis, 193-194

Boyz II Men, 69, 302, 715

Boz's Juba. See Juba, Master

Brackett, Edward A., 980

Braddock, Jim, 1000

Bradford, Perry, 195-196

Bradley, Bill, 1536

Bradley, David, 196-197

Bradley, Ed, 198-199

Bradley, Mamie Till, 1432

Bradley, Tom, 200-202, 536, 1373

Brady, Mary Beattie, 1318

Braithwaite, William Stanley, 202-204

Braun, Carol E. Moseley, 204-206, 766, 907

Brawley, Benjamin, 203

Brawley, Tawana, 1338

Braxton, Anthony, 206-208

Braxton, Toni, 69, 131, 208-209

Brecht, Bertolt, 1336

Breckinridge, Frank, 107

Breedlove, Sarah. See Walker, Madam C. J.

Brenner, David, 1499

Brenston, Jackie, 1451

Bridger, Jim, 134

Briggs, Bunny, 775

Briggs, Cyril V., 210-212

Brimmer, Andrew Felton, 212-213

Britt, May, 468

Broadus, Charles "Doc," 600

Broadus, Cordozar Calvin, Jr. See Snoop Dogg

Brock, Lou, 213-215, 596, 757, 1136, 1586; and Cool Papa Bell, 139

Brock, Roslyn M., 180
Broglio, Ernie, 214
Bronze Venus. *See* Baker, Josephine
Brooke, Edward W., 215-217
Brooks, Gwendolyn, 217-220, 805; and Haki R. Madhubuti, 1022-1023; poet laureateship, 517; Pulitzer Prize, 516; and Emmett Till, 1433
Brooks, Mel, 333, 775, 989
Brooks, Robert Calvin. *See* Bland, Bobby Blue
Brooks, Samuel I. *See* Schuyler, George S.
Broonzy, Big Bill, 220-221, 1002
Brother Ray. *See* Charles, Ray
Brown, Betye Irene. *See* Saar, Betye
Brown, Bobby, 69, 799
Brown, Charles, 222-223
Brown, Charlotte Hawkins, 223-225
Brown, Chris, 1255
Brown, Claude, 225-227
Brown, Clifford, 227-229, 1103, 1260
Brown, Cynthia Stokes, 366
Brown, Dorothy Lavinia, 229-230
Brown, Drew "Bundini," 612
Brown, Elaine, 230-231
Brown, George W., 154
Brown, H. Rap, 232-234, 841
Brown, James, 234-236, 381, 726; and Al Sharpton, 1337; and Jackie Wilson, 1593
Brown, James Willie, Jr. *See* Komunyakaa, Yusef
Brown, Jim, 237-239, 387, 458, 969, 1311
Brown, John, 140, 980, 1366, 1445
Brown, John. *See* Russwurm, John Brown
Brown, Lavinia, 827
Brown, Lawrence, 1264
Brown, Nicole, 1363
Brown, Oliver, 1038
Brown, Oscar, Jr., 218
Brown, Paul, 238
Brown, Ray, 239-241, 593

Brown, Ron, 241-242, 763
Brown, Ruth, 14
Brown, Sterling A., 154, 243-245, 1227
Brown, Tim, 245-246, 1313
Brown, Tony, 246-248
Brown, Willie, 249-251
Brown Bomber. *See* Louis, Joe
Bruce, Blanche Kelso, 251-253
Bruce, John E., 254-255
Bruce, Richard, 1399
Bryant, Antonio, 255-256
Bryant, Carolyn, 1432
Bryant, Joe, 256, 258
Bryant, Kobe, 256-258, 850, 1134
Bryant, Roy, 1432
Bryant, Willie, 315
Buchanan, Charles, 284
Buchanan, James, 146
Bucketeers basketball team, 973
Buckeye Bullet, the. *See* Owens, Jesse
Bufano, Beniamino, 886
Buhaina, Abdullah ibn. *See* Blakey, Art.
Bukowski, Charles, 399
Bull-Dogger, the. *See* Pickett, Bill
Bullard, Eugene Jacques, 259-260
Bullet Bob. *See* Hayes, Bob
Bullins, Ed, 260-262
Bullock, Anna Mae. *See* Turner, Tina
Bumbry, Grace, 902
Bunche, Ralph, 262-265, 363
Burke, Solomon, 265-266
Burke, Valenza Pauline. *See* Marshall, Paule
Burke, Yvonne Brathwaite, 267-268, 764
Burleigh, Harry T., 268-271, 902
Burns, Isaac. *See* Murphy, Isaac Burns
Burns, Jesse Louis. *See* Jackson, Jesse
Burns, Ken, 433, 1033, 1136
Burns, Lugenia, 792
Burns, Tommy, 866
Burrell, Stanley Kirk. *See* Hammer, M. C.
Burris, Roland, 271-273

Burroughs, Nannie Helen, 273-275
Burton, LeVar, 275-277
Burton, Wayne, 1378
Bush, George H. W., 828, 1420
Bush, George W., 1123; and John Conyers, Jr., 414; and Eric Holder, 780; and Colin Powell, 1200; and Condoleezza Rice, 1246; and Larry D. Thompson, 1429; and Tina Turner, 1457; and Neil deGrasse Tyson, 1464; and Kanye West, 1540
Bush, George Washington, 277-279
Butler, Octavia E., 279-281
Butterbeans and Susie, 1003
Buttrick, Wallace, 792
Byrd, Bobby, 234
Byrd, Donald, 725
Byrd, Henry Roeland. *See* Professor Longhair

Cacchione, Pete, 452
Cade, Miltona Mirkin. *See* Bambara, Toni Cade
Cadillacs, 402
Calhoun, Arthur, 748
Calhoun, Lee, 282-283
Callender, Red, 1062
Calloway, Cab, 283-285, 401, 655, 776
Cambridge, Godfrey, 51, 286-288
Caminiti, Ken, 183
Campanella, Roy, 288-290
Campanis, Al, 1551
Campbell, Bebe Moore, 290-292
Campbell, E. Simms, 292-293
Campbell, Earl, 294-295, 493
Campbell, Ernestine, 991
Campbell, Milton, 882
Campbell, Robert, 482
Camus, Albert, 1097
Canegata, Leonard Lionel Cornelius. *See* Lee, Canada
Cannon, Nick, 303
Cantor, Eddie, 467
Cara, Irene, 296-297
Carbo, John Paul "Frankie," 987
Cardozo, Francis Lewis, 298-299
Carew, Rod, 300-301
Carey, Gordon, 574

Carey, Mariah, 301-303, 715

Carey, Mathew, 37

Carlos, John, 303-304, 562, 601, 1383-1384, 1466

Carmichael, Ralph, 431

Carmichael, Stokely, 305-307, 603, 719, 841, 983, 1230

Carnegie, Andrew, 1514

Carnera, Primo, 1000, 1492

Carney, Harry, 308-309

Carney, William H., 309-310

Carr, Leroy, 311-312

Carroll, Diahann, 312-314, 1191

Carson, Johnny, 714

Carter, Benny, 314-316, 777, 1068; and George Russell, 1300

Carter, Betty, 355

Carter, Jimmy, 827, 1130; and Yvonne Brathwaite Burke, 267; and Patricia Roberts Harris, 738; inauguration, 616; and Barbara Jordan, 906; Olympic boycott, 65, 1084, 1609; and John Brooks Slaughter, 1370; and Andrew Young, 1634

Carter, Nell, 316-317

Carter, Rubin, 1516

Carter, Stephen L., 318-319

Carter, Vince, 1181

Caruso, Enrico, 748, 1502

Carver, George Washington, 319-322; bust of, 108

Cary, Lorene, 322-323

Casey, Bernie, 324-325

Castle, Irene, 559

Castle, Vernon, 559

Caston, Leonard "Baby Doo," 501

Castro, Fidel, 306, 828, 1025

Catlett, Sid, 315

Cato, Gavin, 1339

Cedric the Entertainer, 325-327

Chamberlain, Wilt, 9, 258, 327-330, 1299; and Bill Russell, 1299

Chambers, Paul, 725

Chaney, Don, 745

Chaney, James, 330-332

Chapman, Traci, 445

Chappelle, Dave, 333-334, 1215

Charles, Ezzard, 334-335, 1001, 1492

Charles, Ray, 118, 265, 336-338, 612, 899; and Edward Blackwell, 156; and Sugar Ray Leonard, 974

Charles, Suzette, 338-339

Charleston, Oscar, 139

Chase-Riboud, Barbara, 339-341, 1259

Chavez, Hugo, 828

Chavis, Benjamin, 341-342

Cheadle, Don, 343-344, 1621

Cheatham, Doc, 396

Cheatham, Henry Plummer, 344-346

Checker, Chubby, 347-349

Cheek, James E., 349-350

Cheeks, Maurice, 555

Chenault, Kenneth, 351-353

Cheney, Dick, 1200

Cherry, Don, 157, 1289, 1314

Chesnutt, Charles Waddell, 353-355

Chess, Leonard, 142, 495, 992, 1525

Chess, Phil, 142

Chestnut, Cyrus, 355-356

Childress, Alice, 356-358

Childress, Alvin, 356

Chisholm, Shirley, 359-361, 486, 574, 1232

Chivington, John, 133

Chocolate Thunder. See Dawkins, Darryl

Christian, Charlie, 1152

Christopher, Mary. See West, Dorothy

Chudd, Lew, 508

Church, Frederick, 95

Church, Mary Eliza. See Terrell, Mary Church

Churchill, Winston, 1156

Cinque, Joseph, 361-363

Clapton, Eric, 70, 143, 937

Clark, Dick, 347

Clark, Jim, 1489

Clark, Kenneth, 363-365

Clark, Septima Poinsette, 365-367, 1571

Clarke, John Henrik, 367-369, 857

Clarke, Kenny, 1103, 1260

Classic Quartet, 1458

Clay, Cassius, Jr. See Ali, Muhammad

Clay, William L., Sr., 1278

Cleage, Albert Buford, Jr., 369-371

Cleaver, Eldridge, 231, 371-374, 603, 645, 1329

Clemens, Doug, 214

Clement, Jack, 1206

Clemente, Roberto, 374-376, 651

Cleveland, James, 616

Cliff, Michelle, 377-378

Clifton, Lucille, 378-379, 564

Clifton, Nat "Sweetwater," 994

Cline, Sir Rodney. See Carew, Rod

Clinton, Bill, 753, 828; and Maya Angelou, 52; and Carol E. Moseley Braun, 205; and Andrew Felton Brimmer, 212; and Shirley Chisholm, 360; and John Conyers, Jr., 414; and Joycelyn Elders, 544; and Mike Espy, 557; and James Farmer, 574; and William H. Gray III, 683; and Arsenio Hall, 715; and Alexis Herman, 763; and Eric Holder, 779-780; and Gwen Ifill, 814; inauguration, 336, 616; and Sheila Jackson Lee, 845; and Vernon Jordan, 913; and Walter Mosley, 1086; and Hazel R. O'Leary, 1131; and Rosa Parks, 1158; and Deval Patrick, 1162; and Togo West, 1542

Clinton, George, 380-381, 1389

Clinton, Hillary Rodham, 205, 845, 1122

Clouds of Joy, 1575

Clown Prince of Basketball. See Lemon, Meadowlark

Clyburn, James E., 382-384

Coachman, Alice, 384-385

Coburn, Tom, 1122

Cochran, Johnnie, 386-388, 1338, 1363

Coker, Abner, 875

Coker, Daniel, 388-390, 875

Colbert, Claudette, 129
Cole, Bob, 869
Cole, Nat King, 390-393, 415, 539
Cole, Natalie, 392-394
Coleman, Bessie, 260, 394-396
Coleman, Denardo, 398, 420-421
Coleman, Emmett. *See* Reed,
    Ishmael
Coleman, Katherine. *See* Johnson,
    Katherine G.
Coleman, Ornette, 156-157, 396-
    398, 410, 420; and Alvin
    Batiste, 118; and Edward
    Blackwell, 156; and Pharoah
    Sanders, 1314
Coleman, Wanda, 399-400
Coles, Honi, 400-402
Collegians, 15, 1110
Collins, Bootsy, 69
Collins, Marva, 403-405
Collins, Patricia Hill, 405-406
Colomby, Harry, 1070
Coltrane, Alice, 407-408, 410
Coltrane, John, 397, 409-411; and
    Cannonball Adderley, 17; and
    Alvin Batiste, 118; and Alice
    Coltrane, 407; and Miles Davis,
    461-462; and Michael S. Harper,
    734; and Pharoah Sanders,
    1314; and Archie Shepp, 1344;
    and Sonny Stitt, 1401; and
    McCoy Tyner, 1458
Combs, Sean "Puffy." *See* Puff
    Daddy
Comer, James P., 1195
Commodores, 1252-1254
Cone, James H., 411-413, 1451
Conley, Arthur, 265
Conroy, Jack, 189
Conyers, John, Jr., 413-415
Cooder, Ry, 1410
Cook, Alicia Augello. *See* Keys,
    Alicia
Cook, Mercer, 243
Cook, Will Marion, 185, 270
Cooke, Sam, 265, 415-417, 614,
    1019
Cooks, Patricia. *See* Parker, Pat
Coolidge, Calvin, 149, 460, 636
Cooper, Chuck, 994

Cooper, George W., 1266
Cooper, J. California, 417-418
Copland, Aaron, 1400
Copper, Anna Julian, 273
Coppola, Francis Ford, 836
Corea, Chick, 206, 1401, 1458
Cornish, James, 1568
Cornish, Sam, 418-419
Cornish, Samuel, 1302
Cortez, Diego, 111
Cortez, Jayne, 397, 420-422
Cosby, Bill, 422-424, 1234; and
    Herbie Hancock, 726; and
    Samuel L. Jackson, 840; and
    Bernie Mac, 1005; and Alvin
    Francis Poussaint, 1195; and
    Richard Pryor, 1214
Cosell, Howard, 785
Costa, Dino, 1040
Cotton Club Boys, 401
Cotton Pickers, 315
Counts, Dorothy, 83
Courlander, Harold, 712
Covey, James, 362
Cowlings, Al, 1362
Cox, Billy, 759
Craft, Ellen, 425-426
Craft, William, 425-426
Crawford, Joan, 1007
Cream, Arnold Raymond. *See*
    Walcott, Jersey Joe
Crenshaw, Kimberlé Williams,
    426-427
Creolettes, 847
Crichlow, Ernest, 1318
Critchlow, Cyril, 637
Cronkite, Walter, 1340
Crooks, Lesane Parish. *See* Shakur,
    Tupac
Crosby, Bing, 723, 777
Crothers, Scatman, 428-430
Crouch, Andraé, 430-431
Crouch, Stanley, 432-433, 1095
Crudup, Big Boy, 433-434
Crummell, Alexander, 435-437,
    482
Crump, E. H., 727
Cruz, Harold, 368
Cruz, Rolando, 272
Cuffe, Paul, 437-439

Cullen, Countée, 189, 203, 439-
    441, 1318; and Jessie Redmon
    Fauset, 583; and William Grant
    Still, 1399
Culp, Robert, 422
Curb, Mike, 201
Cuthbert, Julie, 491

Daley, Richard J., 272, 1224, 1519
Daley, Richard M., 1125, 1520
D'Amato, Cus, 988, 1163, 1462-
    1463
Dameron, Tadd, 461, 665, 1103
Dandridge, Dorothy, 137, 144, 442-
    444
Danforth, John C., 1419
Daniels, Lee, 169
Darin, Bobby, 777
Darrow, Clarence, 488
Dash, Julie, 445-446
Da Silva, Howard, 465
Davenport, Willie, 446-447
David, Hal, 1510
Davis, Al, 35, 1342
Davis, Alice Coachman. *See*
    Coachman, Alice
Davis, Angela, 324, 448-451, 514,
    1411
Davis, Arthur P., 243
Davis, Benjamin J., 451-452
Davis, Benjamin O., Sr., 452-456;
    and James A. Emanuel, 551
Davis, Benjamin O., Jr., 454-457
Davis, Bette, 1007
Davis, Carl, 1592
Davis, Clive, 933
Davis, Eddie "Lockjaw," 698,
    1401, 1567
Davis, Ernie, 457-459
Davis, Henrietta Vinton, 459-460
Davis, Jack, 282
Davis, Mary Lee, 382
Davis, Miles, 461-463; and
    Cannonball Adderley, 16-17;
    and Jimmy Blanton, 167; and
    John Coltrane, 409-410; and
    Herbie Hancock, 725; and John
    Lee Hooker, 787; and Jackie
    McLean, 1013; and Charlie
    Parker, 1152; and Max Roach,

1260; and Sonny Rollins, 1289; and Wayne Shorter, 1346; and Sonny Stitt, 1402; and Cicely Tyson, 1461

Davis, Ossie, 464-466, 478, 970

Davis, Roquel "Billy," 673, 1592

Davis, Sammy, Jr., 343, 466-469, 775

Davis, Shani, 469-470

Davis, Viola, 471-472

Dawes, Dominique, 472-474

Dawkins, Darryl, 474-475

Dawson, William, 173, 185, 1197

Dean, Dizzy, 1149

DeBarge, James, 825

Debs, Eugene V., 804

DeCarava, Roy, 476-477

Decatur, Stephen, 606

Dee, Ruby, 464-465, 478-479, 970

Deele, 69

Dees, Morris, 181

Def, Mos, 1621

DeFranco, Buddy, 162, 777

DeFrantz, Anita, 479-481

DeGaetano, Suzette. See Charles, Suzette

DeKnight, Freda, 1460

Delany, Martin Robison, 481-484

Delany, Samuel R., 102, 280, 484-485

De Lavallade, Carmen, 18

Dellums, Ron, 485-487

De Mille, Agnes, 401

Dempsey, Jack, 1000

DePasse, Suzanne, 1252

Deppe, Lois, 772

DePriest, Jessie, 488

DePriest, Oscar, 455, 488-489

Desdune, Clarence, 1071

Destiny's Child, 948

Dett, R. Nathaniel, 489-491, 1497

Deukmejian, George, 201

Devers, Gail, 491-493

Devine, Bing, 214, 650

Devine, Loretta, 1015

Diallo, Amadou, 1339

Diamond, Bill, 508

Dickens, Charles, 916

Dickerson, Carroll, 773

Dickerson, Eric, 493-494

Dickinson, Angie, 468

Diddley, Bo, 494-496, 824

Diddy. See Puff Daddy

Dietrich, Marlene, 1511

Diggs, Charles C., Jr., 1278

Dillinger, Daz, 1389-1390

Dinkins, David, 497-499, 818

Diop, Cheikh Anta, 62

Disciples, 431

Ditka, Mike, 1169

Dixie Duo, 160

Dixie Steppers, 78

Dixon, Ivan, 499-500

Dixon, Sharon Pratt, 105

Dixon, Willie, 434, 500-502, 993, 1071, 1525

Doby, Larry, 502-504, 1271

Dr. Dre, 504-506, 812, 1389; and George Clinton, 381; and Snoop Dogg, 1389

Doctor Funkenstein. See Clinton, George

Dr. J. See Erving, Julius

Dr. John, 266

Dodson, Owen, 441, 506-507

Dogg, Snoop, 387

Dolphy, Eric, 157, 207, 1062

Domino, Fats, 508-510

Dominoes. See Ward, Billy

Doob, Joseph, 154

Dorsey, Thomas A., 510-511, 831, 1227; and Ma Rainey, 1227

Douglas, Aaron, 127, 512-513

Douglas, Buster, 1463

Douglass, Frederick, 84, 513-515; and Charles Waddell Chesnutt, 354; and Henrietta Vinton Davis, 459; and Martin Robison Delany, 482; and Paul Laurence Dunbar, 525; and James Forten, 606; and Henry Highland Garnet, 632; and Lewis Howard Latimer, 959; and Edmonia Lewis, 981; and Benjamin Quarles, 1219; and Sojourner Truth, 1442

Dove, Billie, 781

Dove, Rita, 516-518

Drew, Charles R., 243, 518-519, 690

Drew, Timothy. See Ali, Noble Drew

Drexler, Clyde, 1128

Drifters, 1019, 1510

Drinkard Sisters, 1510

Driver, Wilsonia Benita. See Sanchez, Sonia

Du Bois, W. E. B., 520-522; and Julian Bond, 179; and William Stanley Braithwaite, 203; and Charles Waddell Chesnutt, 354; and Communist Party, 211; and Alexander Crummell, 436; daughter of, 440; documentary about, 87; "double consciousness" concept, 187, 870; and Aaron Douglas, 512; encyclopedia project, 641; and Marcus Garvey, 636; and Lorraine Hansberry, 729; and Harlem Renaissance, 805; and James Weldon Johnson, 870; and Claude McKay, 1011; and Paul Robeson, 1265; and Augusta Savage, 1317; "talented tenth", 7; and Eric Walrond, 1507; and Booker T. Washington, 1439, 1514

DuBose, Richard, 502

Dubuffet, Jean, 111

Dudley Regan, Caroline, 79

Due, Tananarive, 102

Duhamel, Marcel, 771

Dukakis, Michael, 828

Duke, David, 1051

Duke's Serenaders, 546

Dumars, Joe, 152

Dumas, Henry, 523-524

Dunbar, Paul Laurence, 204, 244, 524-526; and Alice Dunbar-Nelson, 527; and James Weldon Johnson, 869; and Arturo Alfonso Schomburg, 1320; and William Grant Still, 1399

Dunbar-Nelson, Alice, 525, 527-528

Duncan, Tim, 528-529

Dundee, Angelo, 27, 975

Dungy, Tony, 1343, 1618

Dunham, Katherine, 530-531, 944, 1064

Dunn, Oscar James, 532-533
Duran, Roberto, 975
Durante, Jimmy, 200
Durham, Eddie, 109
Durocher, Leo, 89
Dusky Demon, the. *See* Pickett, Bill
Dutton, Charles S., 533-535, 840
Duva, Lou, 785
Dyett, Walter, 390, 697
Dylan, Bob, 266, 1127, 1282, 1411, 1433
Dymally, Mervyn, 535-537

Eakins, Thomas, 1412
Earhart, Amelia, 395
Earth, Wind and Fire, 69
Eastman, Max, 1011
Easton, Sheena, 1211
Eastwood, Clint, 624, 1070, 1549
Eazy-E. *See* Wright, Eric "Eazy-E"
Eckstine, Billy, 538-540; and Gene Ammons, 41; and Art Blakey, 162; and Miles Davis, 461; and Fats Navarro, 1103; and Sonny Stitt, 1401; and Sarah Vaughan, 1483
Edelman, Marian Wright, 540-541
Edison, Thomas Alva, 321, 960, 1611
Edmonds, Kenneth "Babyface," 208
Edwards, Eli. *See* McKay, Claude
Edwards, Harry, 191
Edwards, James, 1595
Edwards, Vince, 822
Eisenhower, Dwight D., 761, 1156; and Louis Armstrong, 59; and Benjamin O. Davis, Sr., 454; and Little Rock Nine, 117; and Adam Clayton Powell, Jr., 1198
Elder, Lee, 542-543, 1171
Elders, Joycelyn, 543-545
Eldridge, Roy, 655
Electra, Carmen, 1211
Elizondo, Rene, Jr., 825
Elkus, Max, 334
Ellington, Duke, 545-548, 1448; and Alvin Ailey, 19; and Jimmy Blanton, 167; and Harry Carney,

308-309; and Benny Carter, 314; and Dexter Gordon, 665; and Lorraine Hansberry, 729; and Eartha Kitt, 945; and Florence Mills, 1060; and Thelonious Monk, 1069; and Max Roach, 1260; and Cootie Williams, 1566, 1575
Elliott, Bill, 1511
Elliott, Missy, 2, 1222
Elliott, Timbaland, 2
Ellis, Herb, 777
Ellison, Harlan, 280
Ellison, Ralph, 548-550, 605, 1094
Elmira Express. *See* Davis, Ernie
Emanuel, James A., 551-552
Eminem, 588-589, 721, 852; and Dr. Dre, 505
Empress of Soul. *See* Knight, Gladys
Empress of the Blues. *See* Smith, Bessie
Epperson, Lia, 854
Epps, Omar, 552-553
Ertegun, Ahmet, 265
Erving, Julius, 474, 554-556
Escalera, Irene. *See* Cara, Irene
Espy, Mike, 556-558
Esquerita, 990
Europe, James Reese, 559-560
Evans, Bill, 16
Evans, Gil, 461-462
Evans, James Carmichael, 560-561
Evans, Lee, 562-563
Evans, Mari, 563-564
Evans, Wanda. *See* Coleman, Wanda
Everett, Ronald McKinley. *See* Karenga, Maulana
Evers, Charles, 565-566
Evers, Medgar, 566-568; assassin of, 332, 570; brother of, 565-566; and Dick Gregory, 689; and James Meredith, 1050; murder of, 1360; and Archie Shepp, 1344; widow of, 568-570
Evers-Williams, Myrlie, 567, 568-570
Ewing, Patrick, 571-572, 1129

Fab Five Freddy, 1221
Fabian, 347
Fagan, Eleanora. *See* Holiday, Billie
Famous Flames, 234
Famous Hokum Boys, 220, 510
Fanon, Frantz, 306, 603, 669
Fard, Wallace D., 1088
Farmer, James L., Jr., 573-575, 818
Farrakhan, Louis, 342, 432, 575-576; and James Bevel, 151; and Tom Bradley, 201; and Malcolm X, 1026
Father Divine, 577-580; portrayal in drama, 507
Father MC, 168
Father of Black Liberation Theology. *See* Cone, James H.
Father of Chicago. *See* Pointe du Sable, Jean Baptiste
Father of Electrogasdynamics. *See* Gourdine, Meredith C.
Father of the Blues. *See* Handy, W. C.
Fats, Minnesota, 847
Faubus, Orval, 117
Faulk, Marshall, 580-581
Faulkner, William, 204, 630
Fauset, Jessie Redmon, 582-584, 805
Feeley, James Downer, 20
Feldman, Al, 592
Felious, Odetta. *See* Odetta
Fells, Augusta Christine. *See* Savage, Augusta
Fenty, Robyn Rihanna. *See* Rihanna
Ferguson, John, 1371
Ferguson, Samuel, 584-585
Ferrara, Abel, 1387
Fetchit, Stepin, 586-588
Fifth Dimension, 417
50 Cent, 588-590
Finley, Charles O., 170, 839
Firespitters, 421
First Lady of Jazz. *See* Fitzgerald, Ella
First Lady of Talk Shows. *See* Winfrey, Oprah
First Lady of the Struggle. *See* Bethune, Mary McLeod

Fishburne, Laurence, 324, 590-591, 1087, 1457

Fisher, George. *See* Peters, Brock

Fisk Jubilee Singers, 268, 270, 748

Fitzgerald, Ella, 592-594; and Louis Armstrong, 59; and Count Basie, 110; and Ray Brown, 240; and Sarah Vaughan, 1483; and Chick Webb, 1532

Flack, Roberta, 739-740, 767, 933

Flipper, Henry Ossian, 595-596

FloJo. *See* Griffith-Joyner, Florence

Flood, Curt, 215, 596-598

Flutie, Doug, 32

Fontaine, Joan, 137

Fontaine, William Thomas, 598-599

Football coaches; Fritz Pollard, 1193-1194; Art Shell, 1341-1343

Ford, Cheryl, 1028

Ford, Gerald, 1130, 1562

Ford, Henry, 321

Ford, Lawrence "Flying," 45

Ford-El, David, 30

Foreman, George, 27, 600-602, 621, 1074, 1205, 1492

Forman, James, 602-604

Forrest, Leon, 604-606

Forten, Charlotte Lottie. *See* Grimké, Charlotte L. Forten

Forten, James, 606-607

Fortune, Amos, 608-609

Fortune, T. Thomas, 254, 1509

Foster, Adelaide Towson, 1252

Fox, John R., 609-610

Foxx, Jamie, 337, 611-612

Foxx, Redd, 429, 613-614

Francois, Terry, 249

Frankie Lymon and the Teenagers, 380, 402

Franklin, Aretha, 69, 169, 614-617; and Donny Hathaway, 739; "Respect," 616, 1235

Franklin, Benjamin, 1546

Franklin, John Hope, 154, 617-619

Franklin, Kirk, 431

Frazier, E. Franklin, 154, 226; and Ralph Bunche, 262

Frazier, Joe, 27, 601, 620-621

Frazier, Walt, 621-622

Fredericks, Henry St. Clair, Jr. *See* Taj Mahal

Freed, Alan, 14

Freeman, Morgan, 404, 623-624, 840

Freeman, Ron, 562

Fresh Prince. *See* Smith, Will

Friedan, Betty, 569

Frost, Robert, 484

Fugard, Athol, 659

Fugees, 767-768, 855

Fuhrman, Mark, 387

Fuller, Charles, 625-626

Fuller, Gil, 656

Fuller, Hoyt, 645, 1023

Funk Mob, 381

Funkadelic, 381

Funnye, Doris, 817

Fuqua, Harvey, 643

Futrell, Mary Hatwood, 626-628

Gable, Clark, 1007

Gaines, Ernest J., 629-631

Gaines, LaDonna Adrian. *See* Summer, Donna

Gaither, Tom, 574

Gandhi, Mahatma, 150, 818, 940, 942, 964, 1230; and C. T. Vivian, 1488

Gans, Joe, 160

Garcia, Ceferino, 54

Garfield, James, 253, 1048

Garfinkel, Howard, 909

Garner, Erroll, 72

Garnet, Henry Highland, 631-633

Garnett, Kevin, 633-634, 1181-1182

Garrison, Jimmy, 397

Garrison, William Lloyd, 703, 1397, 1496; and Martin Robison Delany, 482; and Frederick Douglass, 514; and James Forten, 606; and Lewis Howard Latimer, 959; and Edmonia Lewis, 980; and William Monroe Trotter, 1439; and Sojourner Truth, 1442

Garrison, Zina, 649

Garvey, Marcus, 29, 635-637; and Cyril V. Briggs, 211; and John E. Bruce, 254; and John Henrik Clarke, 368; and Alexander Crummell, 436; and Henrietta Vinton Davis, 459; and Claude McKay, 1011; and Malcolm X, 1024; and "New Thought" philosophy, 578; and A. Philip Randolph, 1229; and Arturo Alfonso Schomburg, 1320; and George S. Schuyler, 1322; and James Van Der Zee, 1478; and Eric Walrond, 1507

Gaston, Arthur George, 637-639

Gaston, Cito, 74

Gates, Bill, 642

Gates, Bill and Melinda, 683

Gates, Darryl F., 1585

Gates, Henry Louis, Jr., 640-642; and Alex Haley, 713

Gatson, Daisy Lee. *See* Bates, Daisy

Gaulle, Charles de, 260

Gaye, Marvin, 402, 417, 643-644, 673, 848; and Usher, 1474

Gayle, Addison, Jr., 645-646

Gayle, Helene Doris, 646-647

Gayten, Paul, 508

Genius, the. *See* Charles, Ray

Gentleman of Boxing, the. *See* Patterson, Floyd

Georgia Minstrels, 165

Georgia Tom. *See* Dorsey, Thomas A.

Gershwin, George, 285, 401, 462

Getz, Stan, 1349, 1401

Giants of Jazz, 162, 1402

Gibbs, Terry, 407, 777

Gibson, Althea, 648-650

Gibson, Bob, 214, 596, 650-651

Gibson, Jo Ann. *See* Robinson, Jo Ann Gibson

Gibson, Josh, 139, 652-654, 1149-1150

Gibson, Josh, Jr., 653

Gibson, Kenneth, 97

Gibson, Tyrese, 1368

Gill, Johnny, 69

Gillespie, Dizzy, 654-656, 1301; and Art Blakey, 162; and Ray Brown, 240; and Cab Calloway, 285; and John Coltrane, 409; and Miles Davis, 461; and Ella Fitzgerald, 593; and Quincy Jones, 900; and Thelonious Monk, 1069; and Fats Navarro, 1103; and Charlie Parker, 1152; and Max Roach, 1260; and Sonny Stitt, 1401; and Sarah Vaughan, 1484; and Jackie Wilson, 1592

Gilmore, John, 1408

Giovanni, Nikki, 657-658

Girshick, Meyer Abraham, 154

Giuliani, Rudolph, 498

Givens, Robin, 1463

Gladys Knight and the Pips, 946

Glaser, Joe, 59

Glenn, John, 876

Glover, Danny, 658-660, 1471, 1608

Glover, Savion, 402, 660-661, 1459

Gluck, Alma, 270

Goldberg, Arthur, 597

Goldberg, Whoopi, 333, 662-663, 767, 1015; and Moms Mabley, 1004

Goldman, Ronald, 387, 1363

Goldwater, Barry, 216

Gomer, Nina, 521

Gooding, Cuba, Jr., 663-664

Goodman, Benny; and Harry Carney, 308; and Lionel Hampton, 723; and Milt Hinton, 777; and Chick Webb, 1532; and Cootie Williams, 1567, 1575

Goodman, Robert, 828

Gorbachev, Mikhail, 450

Gordon, Dexter, 41, 665-667, 725

Gordon, Ed, 667-668

Gordon, Lewis, 668-670

Gordon-Reed, Annette, 670-672

Gordy, Berry, Jr., 380, 672-674, 1291, 1592; and Marvin Gaye, 643; and Jackson Five, 835; and Smokey Robinson, 1281-1282; and Stevie Wonder, 1605

Gordy, Gwendolyn, 673

Gore, Altovise, 468

Gore, Lesley, 900

Gospel Starlighters, 234

Gospelaires, 1510

Gossett, Louis, Jr., 674-675

Gottlieb, Ed, 327-328

Gough, Eleanora. *See* Holiday, Billie

Gould, Joe, 1000

Gourdine, Meredith C., 676-677

Grahn, Judy, 1153

Grant, Carolyn, 1117

Grant, Ulysses S., 515

Granville, Evelyn Boyd, 678-679

Granz, Norman, 240, 593

Gravely, Samuel, 971

Graves, Earl G., Sr., 679-680

Graves, Howard, 1570

Gray, Frizell Gerald. *See* Mfume, Kweisi

Gray, Macy, 681-682

Gray, Perry O., 585

Gray, Wardell, 666

Gray, William H., III, 682-684

Greeley, Gus, 652

Green, Al, 684-686, 1457

Green, Paul, 1626

Greene, Claude D., 30

Greene, Joe, 686-687

Greene, Marion, 270

Greene, Thomas. *See* Bethune, Blind Tom

Greenfield, Elizabeth Taylor, 902

Greenlee, Gus, 1149

Greer, Sonny, 546

Gregory, Dick, 688-690, 1004

Gregory, Frederick Drew, 690-692

Gregory, Wilton D., 692-693

Gretzky, Wayne, 184

Grier, Pam, 287, 694-695

Grier, Rosey, 883

Griffey, Dick, 69

Griffey, Ken, Sr., 695

Griffey, Ken, Jr., 695-697

Griffin, Johnny, 697-698

Griffith-Joyner, Florence, 699-701, 897, 915

Grimké, Angelina Weld, 701-704

Grimké, Archibald, 701

Grimké, Charlotte L. Forten, 703-705

Grimké, Sarah, 704

Grit, Bruce. *See* Bruce, John E.

Grosz, George, 127

Guillaume, Robert, 465, 706-707

Guillory, Ben, 1471

Guitar Slim. *See* Jones, Eddie

Gumbel, Bryant, 707-708

Gumbel, Greg, 707

Gurdjieff, George, 1436

Guthrie, Woody, 1410

Guy, Buddy, 937

Gwynn, Tony, 708-710

Gypsy Sun and Rainbows, 759

Hacker, Marilyn, 484

Haden, Charlie, 157

Hagler, Marvin, 975

Hagood, Kenny "Pancho," 407

Haile Selassie, 731, 918, 1000

Hailey, Cedric "K-Ci," 169

Hakeem the Dream. *See* Olajuwon, Hakeem

Haley, Alex, 144, 276, 711-714, 1468; screen portrayal of, 895

Hall, Arsenio, 714-715, 1286

Hall, Juanita, 196

Hall, Prince, 716-717

Halstead, Oliver Willis, 490

Hamer, Fannie Lou, 717-720, 908

Hamilton, Anthony, 740

Hamilton, Virginia, 720-721

Hammer, M. C., 721-723

Hammerin' Hank. *See* Aaron, Hank.

Hammond, John, 781, 1448

Hampton, Lionel, 723-724; and Clifford Brown, 227; and Thomas A. Dorsey, 510; and Dexter Gordon, 665; and Johnny Griffin, 697; and Milt Hinton, 776; and Quincy Jones, 899; and Charles Mingus, 1062

Hancock, Herbie, 462, 725-726

Handlin, Oscar, 618

Handy, W. C., 392, 559, 727-728, 1227, 1399; and Thomas A. Dorsey, 510

Hankerson, Barry, 1

Hansberry, Lorraine, 368, 675, 728-730, 1234, 1251

Hansberry, William Leo, 368, 729

Hansen, Austin, 731-732

Hardin, Lillian Beatrice. *See* Armstrong, Lillian Hardin

Harding, Halley, 1522

Hardwick, Elizabeth, 893

Hardwick, Erwin, 542

Hardy, Nell Ruth. *See* Carter, Nell

Hare, Nathan, 226

Harlem Harlicans, 56

Harlem Stompers, 1531

Harper, Frances Ellen Watkins, 732-733

Harper, Michael S., 734-735, 893

Harrell, Andre, 168, 1217

Harris, Elinore. *See* Holiday, Billie

Harris, Franco, 735-737

Harris, Frank, 1011

Harris, Patricia Roberts, 737-738, 764

Harris, Phil, 429

Harris, Tracy, 1164

Harris, William Beasley, 737

Harrison, Benjamin, 253, 515, 1372

Hart, Cecilia, 896

Hart, Gary, 1246

Hart, Marvin, 866

Harvey, Steve, 325, 1355

Hastie, William H., 243

Hathaway, Donny, 739-740

Hatwood, Mary Alice Franklin. *See* Futrell, Mary Hatwood

Haughton, Aaliyah Dana. *See* Aaliyah

Havens, Richie, 675

Haverly, Jack, 165

Haverly's Genuine Colored Minstrels, 165

Hawkins, Adrienne Lita. *See* Kennedy, Adrienne

Hawkins, Charlotte Eugenia. *See* Brown, Charlotte Hawkins

Hawkins, Coleman, 1069, 1349; and Herbie Hancock, 725; and Milt Hinton, 777

Hawkins, Connie, 740-742

Hawkins, Jamesetta. *See* James, Etta

Hawkins, Yusef, 1339

Hayer, Thomas, 1026

Hayes, Bob, 742-744

Hayes, Elvin, 8, 745-746

Hayes, Isaac, 746-748

Hayes, Roland, 47, 748-750, 1498

Hayes, Rutherford B., 515, 520, 1509

Haynes, Euphemia Lofton, 678

Haynes, Marques, 973

Healy, Patrick F., 750-751

Hearst, William Randolph, 7

Heath, Jimmy, 409

Heavy D, 1217

Hefner, Hugh, 689

Heidelberg, Joe, 1597

Height, Dorothy, 752-753, 763

Helms, Jesse, 205, 1051

Helms, Jesse, Sr., 1578

Hemings, Sally, 670, 754-755; in fiction, 340; sister of, 1439

Hemus, Solly, 650

Henderson, Fletcher; and Lillian Hardin Armstrong, 56-58; and Benny Carter, 314; film depiction of, 468; and Ma Rainey, 1227; and Fats Waller, 1505; and Cootie Williams, 1566

Henderson, Horace, 314

Henderson, Michael, 463

Henderson, Rickey, 214, 756-758, 1586

Hendrix, Jimi, 381, 758-760, 937, 991, 1411

Henry, Aaron, 565, 719

Henry, Georgiana, 593

Henson, Jim, 137

Henson, Matthew Alexander, 761-762

Henthoff, Nat, 397

Herman, Alexis M., 763-764

Herman, Woody, 42

Herndon, Alice. *See* Childress, Alice

Herndon, Angelo, 451

Herzog, Arthur, Jr., 782

Hester, Lucille, 744

Hewlett, James, 22

Hickerson, John, 578

Hicks, William, 1156

Higgins, Billy, 725, 1289

Highway QC's, 415

Hill, Anita, 204, 427, 764-766, 1420

Hill, Herman, 1522

Hill, Lauryn, 767-768

Hill, Patricia. *See* Collins, Patricia Hill

Hilliard, Asa Grant, III, 768-770

Hilliard, Bob, 1510

Hilliard, David, 231

Himes, Chester, 464, 770-772

Hinds, Natalie. *See* Gray, Macy

Hines, Earl, 772-774; and Louis Armstrong, 58; and Art Blakey, 162; and Nat King Cole, 390; and Billy Eckstine, 538; and Dizzy Gillespie, 655; and Charlie Parker, 1152; and Sarah Vaughan, 1483

Hines, Gregory, 72, 161, 402, 774-775

Hines, Johnny, 53

Hinton, Milt, 285, 776-777

Hirt, Al, 1032

Historians; Arna Bontemps, 188-190; John Henrik Clarke, 367-369; John Hope Franklin, 617-619; Annette Gordon-Reed, 670-672; James Meredith, 1049-1051; Benjamin Quarles, 1219-1220; Arturo Alfonso Schomburg, 1319-1321; Carter G. Woodson, 1615-1617

Hite, Les, 723

Hitler, Adolf, 1000, 1141

Hobson, Mellody, 778-779

Hodges, Johnny, 167, 308-309, 546

Hoffman, Julius, 1329

Hogan, Wilbert, 156

Holder, Eric, 779-781

Holiday, Billie, 109, 666, 781-784, 1292; and Milt Hinton, 776; screen portrayal of, 1293

Holliday, Jennifer, 802

Holly, James Theodore, 584

Hollywood, DJ, 1354

Holmes, Eleanor Katherine. *See* Norton, Eleanor Holmes

Holmes, Hamilton "Hamp," 807

Holmes, Larry, 1171

Holmes, Odetta. *See* Odetta

Holte, Patricia Louise. *See* LaBelle, Patti

Holton, Kenneth, 781

Holty, Carl, 127

Holyfield, Evander, 601, 784-786, 1463

Hooker, John Lee, 495, 786-788

Hooker, John Lee, Jr., 787

Hooker, Zakiya, 787

Hooks, Bell, 788-789

Hooks, Benjamin, 789-791

Hootie and the Blowfish, 1294-1295

Hoover, Herbert, 149

Hoover, J. Edgar, 7, 372

Hoover, Lou Henry, 488

Hope, Elmo, 697

Hope, John, 791-793, 1043

Hope, Lugenia Burns, 792

Hopkins, Fred, 1431

Hopkinson, Nalo, 102

Hopper, Edward, 971

Horn, Mother, 81

Horne, Lena, 198, 794-796, 1469, 1506

Horton, Big Walter, 992

Horton, Myles, 150, 366

Hot Five, 55-56, 58-59, 773

Hot Seven, 58-59, 773

Hounsou, Djimon, 1353

House, Son, 1525

Houseman, John, 1621, 1626

Houston, Charles Hamilton, 797-798, 1037

Houston, Whitney, 69, 798-800, 1015, 1477, 1510, 1512

Hova. *See* Jay-Z

Howard, Dwight, 800-802, 850

Howard, Kathleen, 270

Howard, Theodore Roosevelt Mason, 567

Howells, William Dean, 525

Howlin' Wolf, 501

Hubbard, Freddie, 725

Hudson, Jennifer, 802-803

Huggins, Ericka, 1329

Huggins, Willis N., 368

Hughes, Langston, 563, 803-806, 949; and Arna Bontemps, 189; and Gwendolyn Brooks, 217; and Roy DeCarava, 477; and Ralph Ellison, 548; and James A. Emanuel, 551; and Jessie Redmon Fauset, 582; and Lorraine Hansberry, 729; library collection, 189; "The Negro Speaks of Rivers", 1208; and Odetta, 1127; and William Grant Still, 1399; and Margaret Walker, 1503

Hughley, D. L., 326

Hulmes, Helen, 109

Human Buzzsaw. *See* Armstrong, Henry

Human Torpedo. *See* Pollard, Fritz

Hunter, C. J., 898

Hunter-Gault, Charlayne, 323, 807-808

Hurston, Zora Neale, 564, 805, 808-811, 1538, 1603; and Moms Mabley, 1003

Hutcherson, Bobby, 1013

Hutton, Bobby, 372

Hyde, Roger Erik, 429

I Come for to Sing, 220

Ice Cube, 505, 812-813

Ickes, Harold, 49

Ifill, Gwen, 814-815

Imus, Don, 1339

India.Arie, 740, 815-816

Ink Spots, 415

Innis, Roy, 817-819

Iola. *See* Wells-Barnett, Ida B.

Iron Mike. *See* Tyson, Mike

Isaacs, Kendu, 169

Isley Brothers, 758

Iverson, Allen, 819-821, 1557

Jackson, Bo, 822-824, 1313

Jackson, Curtis James, III. *See* 50 Cent

Jackson, David, 134

Jackson, George, 324, 373, 448, 1411

Jackson, Henry, Jr. *See* Armstrong, Henry

Jackson, Howard, 886

Jackson, Janet, 825-826, 1112, 1334

Jackson, Jesse, 826-829; and Cannonball Adderley, 16; and Ron Brown, 242; and Roland Burris, 272; and Louis Farrakhan, 576; and Donny Hathaway, 740; and Roy Innis, 818; and Jesse Jackson, Jr., 830; and Alvin Francis Poussaint, 1195; and Al Sharpton, 1337; Washington, D.C., mayoral race, 105; and Maxine Waters, 1524

Jackson, Jesse, Jr., 827, 829-830

Jackson, Joseph, 825, 835

Jackson, Juanita, 753

Jackson, Katherine, 116, 825, 835

Jackson, Mahalia, 511, 614, 831-833, 1203, 1337

Jackson, Maynard, 833-834

Jackson, Melody. *See* Armstrong, Henry

Jackson, Michael, 387, 825, 835-837, 1112; and Quincy Jones, 836, 901; and Lionel Richie, 1253; tribute to, 52; and Jackie Wilson, 1593

Jackson, Milt, 240

Jackson, O'Shea. *See* Ice Cube

Jackson, Papa Charlie, 220

Jackson, Phil, 910, 1134

Jackson, Reggie, 838-840, 861; and M. C. Hammer, 721

Jackson, Samuel L., 840-842, 1368

Jackson, Shirley Ann, 842-843

Jackson Five, 825, 835-836, 901, 1253; and Babyface, 69

Jackson Lee, Sheila, 844-845

Jacobs, Mike, 1000

Jacquet, Illinois, 593, 724, 1113

Jagger, Mick, 266

Jakes, T. D., 846-847

Jam, Jimmy, 169, 825

Jam Master Jay. *See* Mizell, Jason

Jamerson, James, 673

James, Etta, 847-848, 1411; portrayal in film, 949

James, Jimmy. *See* Hendrix, Jimi

James, Larry, 562

James, LeBron, 849-851, 1135

Jamison, Judith, 19

Jarrell, Randall, 82

Jay-Z, 852-853, 1255-1256, 1355, 1540

Jazz Messengers; and Art Blakey, 162-163; and Clifford Brown, 227; and Johnny Griffin, 697; and Jackie McLean, 1013; and Wynton Marsalis, 1033; and Wayne Shorter, 1346; and Horace Silver, 1349; and McCoy Tyner, 1458

Jazzola Orchestra, 1531

Jazztet, 1458

Jealous, Benjamin T., 853-854

Jean, Wyclef, 767, 855-856

Jefferson, Blind Lemon, 787, 1588

Jefferson, Thomas, 670; and Benjamin Banneker, 92-93; descendants of, 754; and Sally Hemings, 340, 754-755, 1439; on Phillis Wheatley, 1546

Jeffries, Jim, 867

Jeffries, Leonard, 856-857

Jekyll, Walter, 1010

Jemison, Mae C., 858-859

Jenkins, Esau, 366

Jenkins, Louise. *See* Meriwether, Louise

Jeter, Derek, 860-862

Jimi Hendrix Experience, 759-760

Jimmy James and the Blue Flames, 759

Jockeys; Allen Allensworth, 38; Eugene Jacques Bullard, 259; Canada Lee, 967; Isaac Burns Murphy, 1093-1094; James Winkfield, 1600-1601

Jodeci, 169, 1217

Johansson, Ingemar, 1164

John, Elton, 169

John Paul II, 693, 937, 1158

Johnson, Andrew, 140-141, 483, 671

Johnson, Carol Diann. *See* Carroll, Diahann

Johnson, Caryn Elaine. *See* Goldberg, Whoopi

Johnson, Charles S., 792, 808, 862-864, 1507

Johnson, Columbus M., 1366

Johnson, Dennis, 1570

Johnson, Dwayne, 864-865

Johnson, Ernie, 100

Johnson, Fenton, 203

Johnson, Georgia Douglas, 808

Johnson, Jack, 865-868, 895, 1000, 1206

Johnson, James P., 195, 1068, 1504, 1566, 1575

Johnson, James Weldon, 868-871, 1318, 1553; and Gwendolyn Brooks, 217

Johnson, Jim, 867

Johnson, John H., 872-874

Johnson, Johnnie, 141

Johnson, Joshua, 874-875

Johnson, Judy, 139

Johnson, Katherine G., 876-877

Johnson, Lady Bird, 945

Johnson, Linda. *See* Rice, Linda Johnson

Johnson, Lyndon B., 943, 983; and Charles F. Bolden, Jr., 173; and H. Rap Brown, 232; and James L. Farmer, Jr., 574; funeral of, 1203; and Patricia Roberts Harris, 738; and Barbara Jordan, 906; and Moms Mabley, 1004; and Thurgood Marshall, 1038; and Adam Clayton Powell, Jr., 1198; and Leontyne Price, 1203; and Bayard Rustin, 1304; and Robert C. Weaver, 1530

Johnson, Magic, 10, 555, 877-880; HIV infection, 714

Johnson, Marguerite Annie. *See* Angelou, Maya

Johnson, Michael, 880-881

Johnson, Mordecai Wyatt, 262

Johnson, R. Walter, 63

Johnson, Rafer, 882-883

Johnson, Robert L., 884-886, 911

Johnson, Rosamond, 869

Johnson, Sargent, 886-887

Johnson, William H., 888-889

Johnson Gospel Singers, 831

Jolson, Al, 54, 1592

Jones, Absalom, 36, 606, 889-891

Jones, Bill T., 891-892

Jones, Booker T., 747

Jones, Eddie, 1381

Jones, Elvin, 162

Jones, Gayl, 893-894

Jones, James Earl, 895-896, 1476, 1517, 1589

Jones, Jane. *See* Wright, Jane Cooke

Jones, Jerry, 1380

Jones, Jo, 109

Jones, K. C., 1298

Jones, LeRoi. *See* Baraka, Amiri

Jones, Marion, 897-899

Jones, Minnie Lee. *See* Elders, Joycelyn

Jones, Quincy, 15, 240, 899-901; and Michael Jackson, 836, 901

Jones, Sam, 973

Jones, Sissieretta, 269, 902-903

Jones, Thad, 1401

Jones, Tom, 266

Jones Family Band, 78

Joplin, Janis, 1227

Joplin, Scott, 120, 903-905, 1021, 1431; film about, 287, 1565

Jordan, Barbara, 844, 905-907, 1633

Jordan, Eli, 1093

Jordan, Jenny Johnson, 883

Jordan, June, 907-909

Jordan, Louis, 195

Jordan, Mary, 270

Jordan, Michael, 100, 257, 849, 885, 909-912, 1028, 1128; and Scottie Pippen, 1186

Jordan, Taft, 1532

Jordan, Vernon, 241, 671, 912-913

Josephson, Barney, 782, 795

Jovi, Jon Bon, 417

Joyce, James, 550, 928, 1097

Joyland Revellers, 1071

Joyner, Al, Jr., 700, 914-915

Joyner, Marjorie, 1502

Joyner-Kersee, Jackie, 914-915

Juba, Master, 916-917

Judge, the. *See* Hinton, Milt

Judkins, Steveland Hardaway. *See* Wonder, Stevie

Jug. *See* Ammons, Gene

Juice, the. *See* Simpson, O. J.

Julian, Hubert Fauntleroy, 917-919

Julian, Percy Lavon, 919-920

Junior. *See* Griffey, Ken, Jr.

Just, Ernest Everett, 921-922

Kanter, Hal, 313

Karajan, Herbert von, 120

Karenga, Maulana, 62, 399, 923-925, 1023

Kay, Ulysses, 925-926

Keane, Johnny, 214, 596, 650

Keats, John, 440

Keepnews, Orrin, 1069

Kelley, William Melvin, 926-928

Kelly, Anna, 366

Kelly, R., 1

Kelly, Wynton, 462

Kennedy, Adam P., 929

Kennedy, Adrienne, 928-930

Kennedy, Jacqueline, 348, 1539; and Jackie Joyner-Kersee, 914

Kennedy, John F., 689; and Harry Belafonte, 138; civil rights bill, 1633; and Nat King Cole, 392; and Ernie Davis, 458; and Mervyn Dymally, 535; and James L. Farmer, Jr., 574; inauguration, 832; and Mahalia Jackson, 832; Malcolm X on, 1025; and Thurgood Marshall, 1038; and James Meredith, 1050; and segregation, 1561; and Robert C. Weaver, 1530

Kennedy, Robert F., 250, 738; assassination of, 883; and Benjamin Chavis, 341; and Medgar Evers, 565; and James L. Farmer, Jr., 574; and Earl G. Graves, Sr., 679; and Rafer Johnson, 883

Kennedy, Ted, 241

Kenny Clarke Septet, 16

Kenton, Stan, 656

Kersee, Bob, 491, 699, 914

Keyes, Alan, 930-931, 1122

Keys, Alicia, 932-933, 1474

Khan, Chaka, 69

Killen, Edgar Ray, 331-332

Killens, John O., 368; and Walter Dean Myers, 1098

Kimball, Florence Page, 1202

Kincaid, Jamaica, 934-936

King, B. B., 163, 434, 848, 936-938, 1411

King, Billy, 48

King, Coretta Scott, 13, 939-941, 1002, 1461; funeral of, 181; and Andrew Young, 1634

King, Don, 601, 975, 1205, 1338

King, Earl, 1381

King, Ed, 719

King, Martin Luther, Jr., 941-944, 1183; and Ralph David Abernathy, 12; and Maya Angelou, 51-52; assassination of, 235, 1572; and Harry Belafonte, 137; and James Bevel, 150; birthday holiday, 413-414, 940, 1519, 1606; and Carol Moseley Braun, 204; and Tony Brown, 247; and Benjamin Chavis, 341; and John Conyers, Jr., 413; and Ossie Davis, 465, 478; and Ruby Dee, 478; in drama, 357; film portrayals of, 1621; and James Forman, 603; and Aretha Franklin, 615, 619; and Arthur George Gaston, 639; and Dick Gregory, 689; "I Have a Dream" speech, 263, 690, 753, 832, 943, 1230, 1561; and Jesse Jackson, 827-828, 832; and Coretta Scott King, 939; and James Lawson, 964; and Joseph Lowery, 1002; and Malcolm X, 1025-1026; and Benjamin E. Mays, 1044; and Nichelle Nichols, 1115; and Odetta, 1126; paintings of, 1034; photographs of, 1155; poetry about, 523; and Albert Raby, 1224; and Jo Ann Gibson Robinson, 1276; and Bayard Rustin, 1304; screen portrayals of, 1596; and Al Sharpton, 1338; and Clarence Thomas,

1419; and C. T. Vivian, 1489; and Hosea Williams, 1572; and Ernest Withers, 1602; and Andrew Young, 1632-1633

King, Martin Luther, Sr., 841

King, Rodney, 201, 291, 1536, 1585

King of Dance. *See* Checker, Chubby

King of Pop. *See* Jackson, Michael

King of Ragtime. *See* Joplin, Scott

King of Rock and Soul. *See* Burke, Solomon

Kings of Rhythm, 1451-1452, 1455

Kirk, Andy, 1103

Kitt, Eartha, 944-946

Kittel, Frederick August. *See* Wilson, August

Knight, Gladys, 1, 402, 946-947; and Jackson Five, 835

Knight, Gwendolyn, 962

Knight, Marion "Suge," 505, 1389

Knight, Marva Delores. *See* Collins, Marva

Knowles, Beyoncé, 740, 853, 948-949

Koch, Ed, 498

Koenigswarter, Pannonica de, 1070

Kolax, King, 41

Komunyakaa, Yusef, 949-951

Korbel, Josef, 1245

Kristol, William, 1394

Krupa, Gene, 723, 1532

Krynicki, Nell. *See* Carter, Nell

Kuhn, Bowie, 597

Kunstler, William, 1329

Kunta Kinte, 275, 712-713

Kushner, Tony, 929

Kyles, Cedric Antonio. *See* Cedric the Entertainer

L. L. Cool J., 952-953, 1355

L. T. *See* Taylor, Lawrence

L.A. Four, 240

La Funque, Buckshot. *See* Adderley, Cannonball

Labelle, 954

LaBelle, Patti, 69, 953-955

LaChiusa, Michael John, 1009

Lady Day. *See* Holiday, Billie

LaFayette, Bernard, 1488
Lagerfeld, Karl, 1353
Laine, Frankie, 429
Lamothe, Ferdinand Joseph. *See* Morton, Jelly Roll
LaMotta, Jake, 1284
Land, Harold, 1260
Lane, Anna Houston. *See* Petry, Ann
Lane, Dick, 429
Lane, William Henry. *See* Juba, Master
Laney, Lucy Craft, 223, 792
Lanier, Willie, 955-957
Laroque, Nell. *See* Carter, Nell
LaRouche, Lyndon, 151
Larsen, Nella, 957-959
Lateef, Yusef, 16
Latimer, Lewis Howard, 959-960
Law, W. W., 1571
Lawford, Peter, 468
Lawrence, Jacob, 40, 127, 961-962, 1318; and George Washington Bush, 278
Lawrence, Martin, 1355
Lawrence, Robert H., Jr., 963-964
Lawson, James, 150, 964-966, 982, 1102, 1488
Lawson, John, 966-967
Leadbelly, 1127
Leadbitter, Mike, 1213
Lear, Norman, 706, 1499
Led Zeppelin, 501, 787
Ledbetter, Huddie. *See* Leadbelly
Lee, Albert, 143
Lee, Canada, 967-968
Lee, Don Luther. *See* Madhubuti, Haki R.
Lee, John C. H., 454
Lee, Johnny, 586
Lee, Minnie Joycelyn. *See* Elders, Joycelyn
Lee, Spike, 238, 969-970, 1332, 1387, 1438; and Ossie Davis, 465; and Samuel L. Jackson, 841
Lee, Ulysses, 243
Lee-Smith, Hughie, 971-972
Leland, Mickey, 844
Lemon, Meadowlark, 429, 972-974

Lennox, Annie, 686
Leonard, Sheldon, 422
Leonard, Sugar Ray, 974-976
Leslie, Lisa, 976-977
Levine, James, 119
Lewis, Carl, 978-980
Lewis, Edmonia, 980-981
Lewis, Jerry Lee, 496
Lewis, John, 461, 593
Lewis, John Robert, 150, 180, 982-984, 1433, 1488
Lewis, Lennox, 1463
Lewis, Norman, 127, 1318
Lewis, Ray, 984-985, 1365
Lewis, Smiley, 1381
Lewis, Terry, 169, 825
Lewis, Willie, 315
Lie, Trygve, 263-264
Lillie, Frank Rattray, 921
Limbaugh, Rush, 1016, 1394
Lincoln, Abbey, 500
Lincoln, Abraham, 869; and Martin Robison Delany, 483; and Frederick Douglass, 514; Emancipation Proclamation, 140, 1442; and Sojourner Truth, 1443; and Henry McNeal Turner, 1450
Lincoln, C. Eric, 985-986
Lindbergh, Charles, 917
Lindsay, Vachel, 805
Lion, Alfred, 1069
Liston, Sonny, 27, 601, 987-988, 1164; and Muhammad Ali, 1492
Little, Cleavon, 465, 989-990
Little, Malcolm. *See* Malcolm X
Little Giant. *See* Griffin, Johnny
Little Richard, 195, 496, 758, 848, 990-991, 1235, 1381; and Otis Redding, 1235
Little Rock. *See* Sanders, Pharoah
Little Vincent. *See* Burke, Solomon
Little Walter, 501, 992-993
Lloyd, Earl, 994-995
Lloyd, Harold, 1110
Locke, Alain, 995-996; and Charles Alston, 40; and Ralph Bunche, 262; and Aaron Douglas, 512; and Harlem Renaissance, 805; and Zora Neale Hurston, 808;

Rhodes Scholarship, 1555; and William Grant Still, 1399
Loeb, Jacques, 921
Logan, Harold, 1205
Lomax, Alan, 1083, 1525
Long, G. A., 789
Long Tall Friday, 1071
Longfellow, Henry Wadsworth, 524
Lorde, Audre, 997-999, 1376
Louis, Joe, 54, 72, 542, 649, 999-1001, 1194, 1273; and Jersey Joe Walcott, 1491-1492
Louis X. *See* Farrakhan, Louis
Lowery, Joseph, 1001-1002
Lucky Seven Trio, 400
Lugar, Richard, 1122
Lumumba, Patrice, 263, 929, 1025
Lundy, Benjamin, 1496
Lyle, Ron, 601

Ma, Yo Yo, 1033
Mabley, Moms, 72, 1003-1004
Mac, Bernie, 326, 1005, 1215
McCain, John, 815, 1123, 1200
McCall, Steve, 1431
McCarthy, Joseph, 795, 805
McCauley, Rose Louise. *See* Parks, Rosa
McCullough, Bernard Jeffrey. *See* Mac, Bernie
McDaniel, Ellas. *See* Diddley, Bo
McDaniel, Hattie, 663, 1006-1008
McDaniels, Darryl, 1350, 1354
McDonald, Freda Josephine. *See* Baker, Josephine
McDonald, James Solomon. *See* Burke, Solomon
McDuffie, Emmanuel, 655
McGhee, Brownie, 434
McGlown, Betty, 1291
McGwire, Mark, 183
McIntyre, Natalie Renee. *See* Gray, Macy
Mack, Craig, 1217
McKay, Claude, 1010-1012; and Arturo Alfonso Schomburg, 1320
McKinley, William, 253, 345-346
McKissick, Floyd, 574
MacLaine, Shirley, 468

McLean, Jackie, 1012-1013
Maclean, Malcolm, 1572
McLeod, Alice Lucille. *See* Coltrane, Alice
McLeod, Mary Jane. *See* Bethune, Mary McLeod
McMillan, Terry, 116, 1014-1015
MacMurray, Fred, 45
McNabb, Donovan, 1016-1017, 1143
McNair, Ronald E., 1017-1019
McNeil, Bill, 654
McPhatter, Clyde, 1019-1020, 1592
McShann, Jay, 141, 1152
McVeigh, Timothy, 199
McWhorter, John, 1020-1022
Madhubuti, Haki R., 1022-1024; and Sonia Sanchez, 1308
Madison, James, 438
Mahara's Minstrels, 727
Mailman, the. *See* Malone, Karl
Majors, Margaret Allison. *See* Bonds, Margaret Allison
Makaveli. *See* Shakur, Tupac
Make a Move, 1431
Makeba, Miriam, 136, 306
Malcolm X, 115, 1024-1027; and Maya Angelou, 51; daughter of, 1332-1333; and Ossie Davis, 465; death of, 52; and Ruby Dee, 478; and Louis Farrakhan, 575; in film, 1516; and Alex Haley, 711; and Martin Luther King, Jr., 1025-1026; and Elijah Muhammad, 1089; photographs of, 1155; screen portrayal of, 1516; and Betty Shabazz, 1025, 1330; and Wesley Snipes, 1387
Malone, Annie Turnbo, 1501-1502
Malone, Karl, 911, 1027-1028
Malone, Moses, 555
Man of Steal, the. *See* Henderson, Rickey
Mancini, Henry, 900
Mandela, Nelson, 624, 778, 940, 1065, 1192, 1250, 1279
Mandela, Winnie, 940
Manley, Effa, 503
Manning, Peyton, 184
Mao Zedong, 603

Marabel, Fate, 58, 1300
Marble, Alice, 648
Marbury, Stephon, 1181
Marchan, Bobby, 1382
Marchbanks, Vance Hunter, 1029-1030
Marciano, Rocky, 335, 1001, 1074, 1163, 1492
Marcuse, Herbert, 448
Marion, George, 1506
Marley, Bob, 1411
Marsalis, Branford, 1031-1032, 1402
Marsalis, Delfeayo, 1031
Marsalis, Ellis, Jr., 156, 1030-1032
Marsalis, Jason, 1031
Marsalis, Wynton, 59, 432, 1031-1033, 1095
Marshall, Kerry James, 1034-1035
Marshall, Paule, 1035-1036
Marshall, Ray, 763
Marshall, Thurgood, 619, 1037-1039, 1050, 1096, 1283; biographies of, 1573; and Stephen L. Carter, 318; screen portrayal of, 1192
Martin, Billy, 757, 839
Martin, Dean, 468
Martin, Denver Ed, 866
Martin, Joe, 26
Martin, Kenyon, 1039-1040
Martin, Roland, 7
Martinez, Chihuahua, 725
Marvelettes, 673, 1281
Marx, Karl, 448, 1535
Masekela, Hugh, 19
Mason, Charlotte Osgood, 805, 809
Master P, 1389
Mastin, Will, 466
Matadors, 1280-1281
Mathematicians; David Harold Blackwell, 153-156; Evelyn Boyd Granville, 678-679; Katherine G. Johnson, 876-877
Mathis, Buster, 620
Matzeliger, Jan Ernst, 1041-1042
Mavericks, Houston, 745
Maxim, Joey, 335, 1074, 1163, 1285, 1492
Mayfield, Curtis, 758

Maynard, Robert C., 1277
Mays, Benjamin E., 1043-1045
Mays, Willie, 4, 1045-1048, 1206; and Barry Bonds, 182; and O. J. Simpson, 1361
Mazama, Ama, 62
Meade, Eddie, 54
Meeropol, Abel, 782
Meier, Audrey, 431
Melba, Nellie, 270, 748
Melish, William, 448
Melony Hounds, 1006
Melrose, Lester, 434
Menard, John Willis, 1048-1049
Mencken, H. L., 1322
Meredith, James, 689, 1049-1051
Meriwether, Louise, 1052-1053
Metcalfe, Ralph, 1518, 1632
Method Man, 169
Meyers, Johnny, 832
Mfume, Kweisi, 181, 1053-1055
Micheaux, Oscar, 1055-1056, 1264, 1482
Michel, Prakazrel "Pras," 767
Mickey and Sylvia, 1456
Middleton, Benjamin Augustus. *See* Vereen, Ben
Middleton, Kenneth, 565
Mifflin, Warner, 37
Milam, J. W., 1432
Milburn, Ralph, 446
Miles, Buddy, 759
Milestone Jazzstars, 1290, 1458
Miley, Bubber, 546
Miller, Cheryl, 1057-1058
Miller, Dorie, 1058-1059
Miller, Edward Charles, 1044
Miller, George Washington, 1179
Miller, Maria W. *See* Stewart, Maria
Miller, Mitch, 1469
Miller, Theodore, 1266
Millinder, Lucky, 162
Mills, Florence, 1060-1061
Mingus, Charles, 397, 1013, 1061-1063; and Duke Ellington, 547; and Max Roach, 1260
Mint Condition, 208
Miracles, 402, 1291, 1606; and Smokey Robinson, 1280-1282

Missourians, 284
Mitchell, Arthur, 1064-1065
Mitchell, Brian Stokes, 471, 1065-1066
Mitchell, Clarence M., Jr., 1067-1068
Mitchell, Margaret, 1007
Mitchell, Mitch, 759
Mitchell, Parren, 1053
Mitchell, Willie, 685
Mizell, Jason, 588, 1350-1352, 1355
Modell, Art, 238
Modern Jazz Quartet, 240, 397
Mohammed, Khalid Shaikh, 780
Mohawk, Dee-Dee, 416
Moi, Daniel arap, 828
Molinas, Jack, 740
Moncur, Grachan, III, 1013, 1344
Monk, Thelonious, 206, 1068-1070, 1113; and Art Blakey, 162; and Johnny Griffin, 697
Monroe, Marilyn, 443, 468, 593
Montgomery, James, 1445
Montgomery, Little Brother, 1071-1072
Montgomery, Tim, 898
Mood, Alexander, 154
Moon, Warren, 32
Moonfixer. See Lloyd, Earl
Moonglows, 643
Moore, Alice Ruth. See Dunbar-Nelson, Alice
Moore, Archie, 335, 1073-1075, 1163
Moore, Eleanor, 265
Moore, Elizabeth Bebe. See Campbell, Bebe Moore
Moore, Johnny, 222, 1019
Moore, Maxine. See Waters, Maxine
Moore, Melba, 465
Moore, Oscar, 222
Moore, Tim, 1003
Moorer, Michael, 602
Moraga, Cherrie, 1376
Morehouse, Henry Lyman, 792
Morgan, Garrett Augustus, 1075-1076
Morgan, John Pierpont, 269

Morial, Dutch, 1077-1078
Morial, Marc, 1077, 1100
Moroder, Giorgio, 1406
Morris, Garrett, 1078-1080
Morris, Joe, 14, 697
Morris, Samuel, 578
Morris, Steveland. See Wonder, Stevie
Morrison, George, 1006
Morrison, Toni, 1080-1082; and Toni Cade Bambara, 87; and Claude Brown, 226; and Barbara Chase-Riboud, 340; and Leon Forrest, 605; and Gayl Jones, 893; and June Jordan, 908; and Emmett Till, 1433
Morrison, Van, 164, 266, 787, 1592
Morrow, George, 1260
Morton, Jelly Roll, 55, 1071, 1082-1084, 1213, 1575
Moscone, George, 250
Moses, Edwin, 1084-1085
Moses, Robert, 719
Mosley, Walter, 1086-1087
Moss, Carlton, 1399
Moss, Hajna O., 590
Moss, Paula, 1335
Moten, Benny, 109, 1133
Mother of Chemotherapy, the. See Wright, Jane Cooke
Moton, Robert, 321, 1165
Mott, Lucretia, 1447
Mottola, Tommy, 302
Mourning, Alonzo, 1040
Mouskouri, Nana, 136
Mr. Accuracy. See Peete, Calvin
Mr. B. See Eckstine, Billy
Mr. Big Shot. See Billups, Chauncey
Mr. Civil Rights. See Wilkins, Roy
Mr. Cub. See Banks, Ernie
Mr. Excitement. See Wilson, Jackie
Mr. Fourth Quarter. See Dickerson, Eric
Mr. Keene. See Aldridge, Ira Frederick
Mr. NAACP. See White, Walter
Mr. November. See Jeter, Derek
Mr. October. See Jackson, Reggie
Mr. Personality. See Price, Lloyd

Muhammad, Benjamin Chavis. See Chavis, Benjamin
Muhammad, Elijah, 27, 83, 575, 1024, 1088-1090
Muhammad, Kalot, 1089
Muhammad, Wallace D., 575, 1089
Mulligan, Gerry, 308, 461
Mulligan, Robert, 1175
Munson, Thurman, 839
Murphy, Eddie, 287, 663, 714, 1090-1092, 1215, 1438; and Chris Rock, 1286
Murphy, Isaac Burns, 1093-1094
Murray, Albert, 1094-1095
Murray, David, 1336
Murray, Pauli, 1095-1097
Muskie, Edmund S., 569
Mussolini, Benito, 1000
Muste, A. J., 573
Muti, Riccardo, 120
Myers, Walter Dean, 1097-1099
Myrdal, Gunnar, 5, 243, 262; and Kenneth Clark, 364

Nader, Ralph, 1536
Nagin, Ray, 1100-1101
Nance, Ray, 167
Nas, 740, 852-853
Nash, Diane, 61, 150-151, 982, 1102-1103, 1488
Nash, Keisha, 1549
Nate Dogg, 1388, 1390
Navarro, Fats, 227, 1103-1104
Naylor, Gloria, 1105-1106
Neal, Larry, 625; and Sonia Sanchez, 1308
Nelson, Prince Rogers. See Prince
Nemiroff, Lorraine Hansberry. See Hansberry, Lorraine
Nemiroff, Robert, 729
Neon Deion. See Sanders, Deion
Neumann, John von, 154
Neville, Aaron, 1106-1107
Neville Brothers, 1107
New York Contemporary Five, 1344
Newcombe, Don, 289
Newk. See Rollins, Sonny
Newman, Floyd, 746
Newton, Huey P., 372, 603, 1110, 1328

Nicholas, Fayard, 1110-1112
Nicholas, Harold, 442, 775, 1110-1112
Nicholas, Ulysses Domonick, 1110
Nicholas, Viola Harden, 1110
Nicholas Brothers. *See* Nicholas, Fayard, and Nicholas, Harold
Nichols, Herbie, 1112-1113
Nichols, James Thomas. *See* Bell, Cool Papa
Nichols, Nichelle, 275, 1114-1115
Niebuhr, Reinhold, 942
Nigerian Nightmare, the. *See* Olajuwon, Hakeem
Nighthawk, Robert, 501
Niven, Larry, 101
Nix, Robert, 683
Nixon, E. D., 12, 1116-1117
Nixon, Richard M., 1089, 1562; and Ralph Abernathy, 13; and James L. Farmer, 574; and Benjamin Hooks, 790; and Roy Innis, 817; and Barbara Jordan, 906; and Watergate, 906; and Stevie Wonder, 1606; and Whitney Young, 1638
Nkrumah, Kwame, 306, 368, 522, 929
Noone, Jimmie, 773
Norman, Jessye, 120, 185, 1117-1119
Norman, Peter, 304, 1384
Norton, Eleanor Holmes, 1119-1120
Notorious B.I.G., 116, 852, 1217, 1334, 1389; film about, 1218; murder of, 1217
Nottage, Cynthia DeLores. *See* Tucker, C. DeLores
Novak, Kim, 468
N.W.A., 505, 812-813; gangsta rap, 505

Obama, Barack, 737, 1121-1124; and Edward W. Brooke, 217; and Roland Burris, 272; and James E. Clyburn, 383; and Angela Davis, 450; and *Ebony* magazine, 873; and Henry Louis Gates, Jr., 641; and Eric Holder,

780; inauguration, 24-25, 616, 949, 1002, 1127, 1606; and Jesse Jackson, 829; and Jesse Jackson, Jr., 830; and Alan Keyes, 931; and Michelle Obama, 1124; and Deval Patrick, 1162; and Colin Powell, 1200; and Tavis Smiley, 1374; and Shelby Steele, 1396; vacated Senate seat, 272; and Stevie Wonder, 1606; and Jeremiah Wright, 1623
Obama, Michelle, 1121, 1124-1125
Occomy, Marita Odette Bonner. *See* Bonner, Marita
Ochocinco, Chad, 1144
Odets, Clifford, 468
Odetta, 1126-1127
Ogden, C. K., 1011
Ohno, Apolo Anton, 469
O'Jays, 402
Okino, Betty, 472
Olajuwon, Hakeem, 1128-1130
Old and New Dreams, 157
Old Mongoose, the. *See* Moore, Archie
O'Leary, Hazel R., 1130-1131
O'Leary, John F., 1130
Oliver, King, 1132-1133; and Lillian Hardin Armstrong, 55-57; and Louis Armstrong, 58; and Edward Blackwell, 156; and Thomas A. Dorsey, 510; and Ulysses Kay, 925; and Jelly Roll Morton, 1083
O'Malley, Peter, 1551
Onassis, Jacqueline Kennedy. *See* Kennedy, Jacqueline
O'Neal, Shaquille, 1136
Onedaruth. *See* Coltrane, John
O'Neil, Buck, 89, 1136-1137
O'Neill, Eugene, 1264
Ordettes, 954
Originator, the. *See* Diddley, Bo
Ory, Kid, 58, 1132
Osumare, Halifu, 1335
Otis, Clarence, Jr., 1137-1139
Otis, Johnny, 847
Owen, Chandler, 210, 1228
Owens, Chris, 1139-1140

Owens, Dana. *See* Queen Latifah
Owens, Jesse, 123, 190, 1140-1142; and Chris Owens, 1139
Owens, Terrell, 1143-1144

P-funk All-Stars, 381
Page, Clarence E., 1145-1146
Page, LaWanda, 613
Page, Walter, 109
Pahluk, Mahri. *See* Henson, Matthew Alexander
Paige, Rod, 1146-1148
Paige, Satchel, 139, 503, 1148-1151; and Josh Gibson, 653; and Buck O'Neil, 1136; screen portrayal of, 675
Palermo, Frank "Blinky," 987
Palin, Sarah, 815, 1123, 1200
Palmer, Alice Freeman, 223
Pankhurst, Sylvia, 1011
Papanek, Ernest, 225
Parham, Tiny, 776
Parker, Charlie, 409, 1151-1153; and Miles Davis, 461; depiction in *Bird*, 1153, 1549; and Dizzy Gillespie, 655-656; and Johnny Griffin, 697; and Jackie McLean, 1012; and Thelonious Monk, 1069; and Ishmael Reed, 1239; and Max Roach, 1260; and George Russell, 1301; and Archie Shepp, 1345; and Sonny Stitt, 1401; and Sarah Vaughan, 1484; and Cootie Williams, 1567
Parker, George W., 210
Parker, Pat, 1153-1154
Parks, Gordon, Sr., 1155-1156, 1479
Parks, Rosa, 12, 940, 943, 1116, 1127, 1157-1159; and John Conyers, Jr., 413
Parks, Suzan-Lori, 929, 1604, 1621
Parliaments, 380-381
Parrott, Russell, 606
Paterson, Basil, 1159
Paterson, David A., 1159-1161
Patrick, Deval, 1161-1162
Patterson, Floyd, 988, 1074, 1163-1165

Patterson, Frederick D., 260, 1165-1166
Patti, Adelina, 902
Paul, Chris, 1166-1168
Payne, Benny, 284
Payne, William, 39
Payton, Walter, 1168-1170, 1310
Peaches, 847
Peale, Charles Willson, 874
Peale, Rembrandt, 875
Pearson, Carlton, 846
Peary, Robert E., 761
Peebles, Melvin. See Van Peebles, Melvin
Peete, Calvin, 1170-1171
Peete, Rodney, 1172-1173
Pendergrass, Teddy, 539
Penniman, Richard Wayne. See Little Richard
Penny, Rob, 1588
Pequit, Alice, 438
Perkins, Kimora Lee. See Simmons, Kimora Lee
Perkins, Pinetop, 1451
Perry, Lincoln Theodore Monroe Andrew. See Fetchit, Stepin
Perry, Tyler, 675, 825, 1173-1174, 1461
Peters, Brock, 1175-1176
Peters, Charles Wesley, 259
Peters, Ronnie. See Adderley, Cannonball
Peterson, Oscar, 240, 593
Petry, Ann, 1177-1178
Pettiford, Oscar, 15, 899
Petty, Christine, 384
Phillips, Sam, 163
Phillips, Wendell, 1242, 1439
Phipps, Mamie, 363
Physicists; George Edward Alcorn, 20-21; Meredith C. Gourdine, 676-677; Evelyn Boyd Granville, 678-679; Shirley Ann Jackson, 842-843; Katherine G. Johnson, 876-877; Ronald E. McNair, 1017-1019; Neil deGrasse Tyson, 1464-1465
Pickett, Bill, 1179-1181
Picou, Tom, 7
Pieh, Sengbe. See Cinque, Joseph

Pierce, Paul, 634, 1181-1182
Pierce, Samuel R., Jr., 1183-1184
Pikl, Josef, 919
Pikl, Julian, 919
Pilgrim Travelers, 415
Pinchback, P. B. S., 1184-1185, 1435
Pinkett, Jada, 1386
Pinkney, Jerry, 783
Pinson, Vada, 596
Pippen, Scottie, 1186-1187
Pips. See Knight, Gladys
Piscator, Erwin, 136
Pitts, Leonard, 1187-1188
Platters, 593, 1280
Poet laureates; Amiri Baraka, 98; Gwendolyn Brooks, 218, 517; Sterling A. Brown, 244; Lucille Clifton, 379; Rita Dove, 516-517; Melvin B. Tolson, 1435; Al Young, 1631
Poinsette, Septima. See Clark, Septima Poinsette
Pointe du Sable, Jean Baptiste, 1188-1190
Poitier, Sidney, 464, 840, 900, 1190-1193, 1251, 1476; and Harry Belafonte, 136; and Alice Childress, 357; and Bill Cosby, 423; and Ivan Dixon, 499; in South Africa, 968; and Paul Winfield, 1595
Polk, Charles Peale, 874-875
Pollard, Fritz, 1193-1194, 1342, 1521
Pollard, Fritz, Jr., 1193
Poole, Elijah. See Muhammad, Elijah
Poplar, Ellen, 1626
Pops. See Armstrong, Louis
Porter, Countée LeRoy. See Cullen, Countée
Porter, David, 747
Posey, Cumberland, 652
Pournelle, Jerry, 101
Poussaint, Alvin Francis, 1194-1196
Powell, Adam Clayton, IV, 1232
Powell, Adam Clayton, Jr., 226, 691, 1196-1198, 1232, 1276;

newspaper column, 1178; and Leon H. Sullivan, 1404
Powell, Bud, 228, 1401; and Alice Coltrane, 407; and Dexter Gordon, 666; and Johnny Griffin, 697; and Jackie McLean, 1013; and Thelonious Monk, 1069
Powell, Chris, 227
Powell, Colin, 1199-1201, 1247; screen portrayal of, 1621
Powell, Mike, 124, 979
Powell, Richie, 228, 1260
Powers, Hiram, 980
Pozo, Chano, 656
Preminger, Otto, 443-444
Presley, Elvis, 69, 416, 1204; and Big Boy Crudup, 434; and Fats Domino, 509; and Jackie Wilson, 1593
Presley, Lisa Marie, 837
Preston, Billy, 430
Price, Cecil Ray, 331-332
Price, Florence, 185
Price, Leontyne, 185, 902, 1117, 1202-1204
Price, Lloyd, 1204-1205
Pride, Charley, 1206-1207, 1294
Pridgett, Gertrude Melissa Nix. See Rainey, Ma
Prime Time. See Sanders, Deion
Primettes, 1291
Primus, Pearl, 50, 1208-1209
Prince, 404, 1210-1212
Prince of Late Night. See Hall, Arsenio
Princess of Black Poetry. See Giovanni, Nikki
Prinze, Freddie, 429
Pritchett, Laurie, 942
Professor Longhair, 1212-1213
Prophet, Elizabeth, 1318
Prosser, Gabriel, 189
Prowse, Juliet, 468
Pryor, Richard, 287, 694, 1214-1216
Public Enemy, 812, 1355
Puff Daddy, 168, 721, 852, 1217-1218, 1234
Purvis, Robert, 703

Quarles, Benjamin, 1219-1220
Quarry, Jerry, 27
Queen Bess. *See* Coleman, Bessie
Queen Latifah, 1221-1223
Queen of Daytime TV. *See* Winfrey, Oprah
Queen of Disco. *See* Summer, Donna
Queen of Happiness. *See* Mills, Florence
Queen of Hip-Hop Soul. *See* Blige, Mary J.
Queen of Rock and Roll. *See* Turner, Tina
Queen of Soul. *See* Franklin, Aretha

Rabbit's Foot Minstrels, 1226
Raby, Albert, 1224-1226
Rackley, Alex, 1329
Radio disc jockeys; Ralph David Abernathy, 12; Jean-Michel Basquiat, 111; Ed Bradley, 198; Benjamin Chavis, 342; Charles Evers, 565; Redd Foxx, 613; Arsenio Hall, 714; Joe Heidelberg, 1597; B. B. King, 937; Kweisi Mfume, 1053; Studs Terkel, 832
Radio disc jockeys fictional, 1240
Raelettes, 336
Raft, George, 54
Rainey, Lawrence, 331-332
Rainey, Ma, 195, 1226-1228, 1589; and Thomas A. Dorsey, 510; and Bessie Smith, 1378
Rainey, William "Pa," 1226
Raitt, Bonnie, 222, 787, 1411
Randall, Eddie, 461
Randolph, A. Philip, 210, 753, 763, 790, 1116, 1228-1231; March on Washington, 1554; and Bayard Rustin, 1303; and George S. Schuyler, 1322; and Leon H. Sullivan, 1404
Rangel, Charles, 498, 1231-1233
Rashad, Phylicia, 33, 423, 1233-1235
"Rat Pack," 343, 468
Ray, Floyd, 1062
Ray, James Earl, 943

Raymond, Usher, 1486
Raymond, Usher Terry, IV. *See* Usher
Razaf, Andy, 1505
Reagan, Ronald, 627; and Eldridge Cleaver, 372; and John Conyers, Jr., 414; and Angela Davis, 448; and Eric Holder, 779; inauguration, 336; and Roy Innis, 818; and Jesse Jackson, 828; and Samuel R. Pierce, Jr., 1183; satire of, 1238; and Thomas Sowell, 1391
Real Deal, the. *See* Holyfield, Evander
Reb's Legion Club Forty-Fives, 723
Red Hot Peppers, 1083
Redding, Noel, 759
Redding, Otis, 417, 616, 991, 1072, 1235-1236; and Isaac Hayes, 747
Redman, Dewey, 157
Redman, John, 641-642
Reed, E. *See* Evans, Mari
Reed, Ed, 1236-1237
Reed, Ishmael, 1014, 1238-1240
Reed, Willis, 572, 622
Reeder, Eskew. *See* Esquerita
Reeder, Steven Quincy, Jr. *See* Esquerita
Reese, Della, 511
Reid, Antonio "L. A.," 69-70, 208
Reid, Rollins. *See* O'Leary, Hazel R.
Reid, Tim, 1240-1241
Reiss, Winold, 512
Reno, Janet, 779
Representatives, U.S.; Yvonne Brathwaite Burke, 267-268; Henry Plummer Cheatham, 344-346; Shirley Chisholm, 359-361; James E. Clyburn, 382-384; John Conyers, Jr., 413-415; Oscar DePriest, 488-489; Mervyn Dymally, 535-537; Mike Espy, 556-558; Sheila Jackson Lee, 844-845; Barbara Jordan, 905-907; John Robert Lewis, 982-984;

Revels, Hiram Rhoades, 1241-1243
Reverend Run. *See* Simmons, Joseph
Reynolds, Debbie, 16
Reynolds, Kate L., 1317
Rhone, Sylvia M., 1243-1244
Rhythm Pals, 401
Riboud, Marc, 339
Rice, Condoleezza, 1245-1247
Rice, Jerry, 1143, 1247-1249
Rice, Linda Johnson, 873, 1249-1250
Rich, Adrienne, 377
Rich, Buddy, 162
Rich, Marc, 780
Richards, Ann, 906
Richards, Lloyd, 115, 1251-1252, 1588
Richardson, Elaine Cynthia Potter. *See* Kincaid, Jamaica
Richie, Lionel, 836, 901, 1252-1254, 1292; and Cuba Gooding, Jr., 663
Richmond, Dannie, 1062
Rickey, Branch, 289, 1273
Ride, Sally, 1115
Riefenstahl, Leni, 1402
Righteous Brothers, 417
Rihanna, 853, 1255-1256
Riley, James Whitcomb, 524
Riley, Pat, 878, 1135
Rillieux, Norbert, 1256-1257
Ringgold, Faith, 1258-1259
Rinzler, Alan, 226
Rising Sons, 1410
Rivera, Diego, 40
Rivera, Geraldo, 818
Rivers, Joan, 714
Rizzo, Frank, 1584
Roach, Max, 162, 1260-1261; and Clifford Brown, 228; and Duke Ellington, 547; and Bill T. Jones, 892; and Charles Mingus, 1062; and George Russell, 1300
Roberson, Ida Mae, 440
Robert, Dehlco, 1071
Roberts, Patricia. *See* Harris, Patricia Roberts
Roberts, Ron, 491
Roberts, T. J., 75

Robertson, Oscar, 9, 1261-1263
Robertson, Robbie, 266
Robeson, Paul, 270, 1007, 1056,
    1191, 1194, 1251, 1263-1266;
    and Julian Bond, 179; and
    Benjamin J. Davis, 451; and
    Dizzy Gillespie, 656; and
    Lorraine Hansberry, 729; and
    Lena Horne, 796; and Canada
    Lee, 968; play about, 464; and
    Leontyne Price, 1202
Robey, Don, 163
Robinson, Bernice, 366, 382
Robinson, Bill, 195, 775, 1060,
    1110, 1266-1268, 1506
Robinson, Bojangles. *See*
    Robinson, Bill
Robinson, David, 529, 1269-1270
Robinson, Edward "Abie," 1522
Robinson, Frank, 596, 1270-1272
Robinson, Freddie Lee. *See*
    Shuttlesworth, Fred
Robinson, Harold B., 954
Robinson, Jackie, 1272-1275,
    1403, 1521; and Cool Papa Bell,
    139; and Roy Campanella, 289;
    and Larry Doby, 503; film
    portrayals of, 1471
Robinson, Jo Ann Gibson, 12,
    1275-1276
Robinson, John C., 918
Robinson, Mack, 1274
Robinson, Max, 1277-1278
Robinson, Michelle LaVaughn. *See*
    Obama, Michelle
Robinson, Noah Louis, 826
Robinson, Randall, 1277-1280
Robinson, Robert, 919
Robinson, Smokey, 402, 1019,
    1280-1282, 1291, 1606; and
    Usher, 1475
Robinson, Spottswood W., III,
    1282-1283; and Stephen L.
    Carter, 318
Robinson, Sugar Ray, 54, 335, 649,
    1284-1286
Roc. *See* Dutton, Charles S.
Rock, Chris, 287, 1135, 1215,
    1286-1287
Rock, the. *See* Johnson, Dwayne

Rockefeller, John D., 1514
Rockefeller, Nelson, 1183
Roddenberry, Gene, 1115
Rogers, Claudette, 1281
Rogers, Henry H., 1514
Rogers, J. A., 368
Rogers, Roy, 787
Rogers, Will, 587, 1007, 1179
Roker, Al, 1287-1289
Rolle, Esther, 1499
Rolling Stones, 142-143, 496, 501,
    787, 937, 1456, 1606; and Ike
    and Tina Turner, 1452
Rollini, Adrian, 308
Rollins, Sonny, 1260, 1289-1291
Ronstadt, Linda, 1107
Roosevelt, Eleanor, 49, 149, 465,
    753, 795, 968, 1530, 1553-1554;
    and Claude Brown, 226
Roosevelt, Franklin D., 49, 1229-
    1230, 1518, 1554; Black
    Cabinet, 148-149, 1530
Roosevelt, Theodore, 869, 1514;
    and Harry T. Burleigh, 270
Rose McClendon Players, 464
Rosenberg, Ethel and Julius, 478
Rosenwald, Julius, 107, 1317
Ross, Araminta. *See* Tubman,
    Harriet
Ross, Barney, 54
Ross, Betsy, 575
Ross, Diana, 402, 783, 1254, 1291-
    1293; and Berry Gordy, Jr., 673;
    and Jackson Five, 835; and
    Lionel Richie, 1253
Rostenkowski, Dan, 779
Round Mound of Rebound, the.
    *See* Barkley, Charles
Rowe, Debbie, 837
Roxborough, John "Roxy," 999
Roybal, Edward, 200
Rubin, Rick, 952, 1351, 1355
Rucker, Darius, 1294-1295
Rudd, Roswell, 1113, 1344
Rudolph, Wilma, 65, 1295-1297,
    1466
Rufus, James. *See* Forman, James
Rumsfeld, Donald, 1200
Run-D.M.C., 588, 1350-1352,
    1354-1355

Rush, Benjamin, 606, 889
Rush, Bobby, 1122
Rush, Otis, 501
Rushing, Jimmy, 110, 777
Russell, Bill, 9, 596, 745, 994,
    1298-1300; and Wilt
    Chamberlain, 328, 1299
Russell, George, 1300-1301
Russwurm, John Brown, 1302-
    1303
Rustin, Bayard, 1229, 1303-1305
Ruth, Babe, 3-4, 839
Ryan, Robert, 137

Saar, Betye, 1259, 1306-1307
Sadler, Dick, 601
Sagan, Carl, 1464
Sagittinanda, Turiya. *See* Coltrane,
    Alice
St. Hill, Shirley Anita. *See*
    Chisholm, Shirley
Sale, George, 792
Sampson, Edgar, 1532
Sampson, Ralph, 1128
Sanchez, Sonia, 1307-1309
Sanders, Barry, 1172, 1309-1311,
    1618
Sanders, Betty Dean. *See* Shabazz,
    Betty
Sanders, Deion, 1311-1313
Sanders, Pharoah, 408, 1314-1315
Sanford, John Elroy. *See* Foxx,
    Redd
Santana, Carlos, 408, 682, 787,
    1457
Saparo, Henry, 308
Saperstein, Abe, 328, 741, 973
Sarron, Petey, 54
Sartre, Jean-Paul, 669, 1626
Satcher, David, 1315-1317
Satchidananda, Swami, 408
Satchmo. *See* Armstrong, Louis
Saud, Sulaimon. *See* Tyner, McCoy
Saunders, Raymond, 127
Savage, Augusta, 961, 1317-1318
Savage, James, 154
Say Hey. *See* Mays, Willie
Sayers, Gale, 1565
Sayles, Thelma Lucille. *See*
    Clifton, Lucille

Scheffé, Henry, 154

Schippers, Thomas, 119

Schmeling, Max, 1000

Schoenberg, Arnold, 206

Schomburg, Arturo Alfonso, 368, 435, 1319-1321

Schroeder, Charles, 107

Schuller, Gunther, 397, 1063, 1301

Schurz, Carl, 532

Schuyler, George S., 1321-1323

Schwarzkopf, Norman, 1200

Science-fiction writers; and Steven Barnes, 101-102; and LeVar Burton, 276; and Octavia E. Butler, 279-281; and Samuel R. Delany, 484-485; and Walter Mosley, 1087; and George S. Schuyler, 1322-1323

Scott, Coretta. See King, Coretta Scott

Scott, Dred, 959, 1324-1325

Scott, Ed, 3

Scott, Hazel, 1469

Scott, Joe, 163

Scott, Tony, 1516

Scottsboro boys, 189, 1440

Scowcroft, Brent, 1246

Scruggs, Fay. See Adams, Faye

Scruggs, Mary Elfrieda. See Williams, Mary Lou

Sculptors; Richmond Barthé, 107-108; and Barbara Chase-Riboud, 339-341; Sargent Johnson, 886-887; Edmonia Lewis, 980-981; Betye Saar, 1306-1307; Augusta Savage, 1317-1318

Scurry, Briana, 1326-1327

Seabrooke-Powell, Georgette, 1318

Seagle, Oscar, 270

Seale, Bobby, 372, 1109, 1328-1330

Seattle Mariners, 695

Seeger, Pete, 220, 1126-1127

Seidenberg, Sid, 937

Selig, Bud, 1551

Selig's Mastodon Minstrels, 1563

Selznick, David O., 1007

Semi, Allen. See Larsen, Nella

Senators, U.S.; Carol E. Moseley Braun, 204-206; Edward W.

Brooke, 215-217; Blanche Kelso Bruce, 251-253; Roland Burris, 271-273; Barack Obama, 1121-1124; Hiram Rhoades Revels, 1241-1243

Sengstacke, John H., 7

Sepia Sinatra, the. See Eckstine, Billy

Severance, 774

Sex Pistols, 143

Seymour, William, 578

Shabazz, Betty, 115, 1329-1331; and Malcolm X, 1025

Shabazz, El-Hajj Malik el-. See Malcolm X

Shabazz, Ilyasah, 1332-1333

Shakira, 1606

Shakur, Tupac, 387, 552, 1222, 1333-1334, 1389

Shange, Ntozake, 623, 840, 929, 1335-1336

Shantz, Bobby, 214

Sharp, Granville, 1546

Sharper, Darren, 1237

Sharpton, Al, 818, 1337-1340, 1536

Shaw, Artie, 782

Shaw, Bernard, 1340-1341

Shaw, Irwin, 1000

Shaw, Robert Gould, 310, 704, 980

Shawn, William, 934

Shell, Art, 1193, 1341-1343

Shepard, Alan, 876

Shepp, Archie, 1344-1345

Shook, Karel, 1064

Shorter, Wayne, 462, 1345-1347

Showard, Derek, 726

Shuttlesworth, Fred, 1347-1348

Sifford, Charlie, 542

Silver, Horace, 162, 1349-1350

Simmons, Joseph, 1350-1352, 1354

Simmons, Kimora Lee, 1352-1353, 1355

Simmons, Michael, 277-278

Simmons, Russell, 1354-1355; Def Jam Recordings, 342; and L. L. Cool J., 952; portrayal in Kush Groove, 1470; and Joseph Simmons, 1350, 1353

Simmons, Ruth, 1356-1357

Simms, Willie, 1357-1359

Simone, Nina, 169, 933, 1359-1361

Simpson, India Arie. See India.Arie

Simpson, Nicole Brown, 387, 1363

Simpson, O. J., 387, 667, 1169, 1361-1364

Simpson, Ralph, 815

Sims, Sandman, 775

Sinatra, Frank, 110; and Sammy Davis, Jr., 467-468; and Ella Fitzgerald, 593; and Quincy Jones, 900; and Joe Louis, 1001

Singing Children, 415

Singletary, Mike, 1364-1365

Singleton, Benjamin, 1366-1367

Singleton, John, 115, 552, 663, 813, 1367-1369

Singleton, Zutty, 776

Sirhan, Sirhan, 883

Sisler, George, 1274

Sissle, Noble, 71, 79, 160, 270, 794

Slater, Andrew, 681

Slaughter, John Brooks, 1369-1370

Slocum, Paul. See Cuffe, Paul

Sly and the Family Stone, 381, 1456

Slyde, Jimmy, 775

Smalls, Robert, 1371-1372

Smiley, Tavis, 1373-1374

Smith, Ada "Bricktop," 1060

Smith, Anna Deveare, 1374-1375

Smith, Arthur Lee, Jr. See Asante, Molefi Kete

Smith, Barbara, 1376-1377

Smith, Bessie, 195, 727, 1377-1379; and Billie Holiday, 781; and Ma Rainey, 1227

Smith, Dean, 909

Smith, Emmitt, 1169, 1248, 1311, 1379-1380

Smith, George Allen. See Russell, George

Smith, Gerrit, 1445

Smith, Huey "Piano," 1381-1382

Smith, Hughie Lee. See Lee-Smith, Hughie

Smith, Jabbo, 776

Smith, James Todd. See L. L. Cool J.

Smith, Jedediah, 134

Smith, Kenny, 100

Smith, Lovie, 1343

Smith, Mamie, 195, 1227

Smith, Tommie, 304, 562, 601, 1382-1384, 1466

Smith, Walker, Jr. *See* Robinson, Sugar Ray

Smith, Will, 90, 1192, 1222, 1385-1386

Smith, Willie Mae Ford, 510

Smokin' Joe. *See* Frazier, Joe

Snipes, Wesley, 552, 1386-1388

Snoop Dogg, 715, 1388-1390; and Dr. Dre, 505

Snowden, Elmer, 546

Sobukwe, Robert, 1634

Sorvino, Al, 53

Sosa, Sammy, 183

Soul Stirrers, 416

Sowell, Thomas, 1390-1391; and Clarence Thomas, 1419

Soyinka, Wole, 465, 640

Space Trio, 1408

Sparkman, John, 1198

Spector, Phil, 1452, 1456

Spencer, Tim, 431

Speranzeva, Olga, 530

Sphinx of City Hall, the. *See* Bradley, Tom

Spielberg, Steven, 34, 464, 901, 1494

Spingarn, Arthur, 176

Spingarn, Joel, 1011

Spinks, Leon, 28

Spitzer, Eliot, 1160

Spurgeon, Charles Haddon, 862

Stackpole, Ralph, 886

Stanton, Elizabeth Cady, 515, 1447

Starr, Brenda K., 301

Starski, Lovebug, 1354

State Collegians, 167

Staubach, Roger, 743-744

Steele, Claude M., 1392-1393

Steele, Michael, 1393-1395

Steele, Shelby, 1395-1397

Stefani, Gwen, 505

Steichen, Edward, 477, 1000, 1479

Steinem, Gloria, 569

Sterling, Donald, 122

Stern, Bernhard, 996

Stevens, David, 713

Stevens, Moses, 542

Stevenson, Alexandra, 555

Stewart, Maria, 1397-1398

Still, William Grant, 727, 732, 925, 1398-1400, 1445

Stitt, Sonny, 1401-1402; and Gene Ammons, 41-42

Stockton, John, 1028

Stokes, Maurice, 324

Stokes, Moses, 1226

Stone, Sly, 726

Stoner, Fred, 27

Stoudamire, Damon, 1426

Stoute, Steven, 1217

Stowe, Harriet Beecher, 482; and Sojourner Truth, 1442

Strauss, Claude Levi, 1626

Strayhorn, Billy, 167, 547

Strode, Woody, 1402-1403, 1521-1522

Stubblefield, Ruth Jean. *See* Simmons, Ruth

Sturgis, Stokeley, 36

Styron, William, 1052

Sullivan, Ed, 416, 495, 1268

Sullivan, Leon H., 1404-1405

Summer, Donna, 1405-1407

Sumner, Charles, 1443

Sun Ra, 523, 1407-1409, 1430; and Pharoah Sanders, 1314

Supremes, 402, 954; and Diana Ross, 1291-1293

Suso, Foday Musa, 726

Sutton, Percy, 1232

Sweatman, Wilbur, 195

Sweetness. *See* Payton, Walter

Swinton, Harry, 1266

Sykes, Roosevelt, 1071

Taft, William H., 1514

Taj Mahal, 1410-1412; and John Lee Hooker, 787

Tajo, Italo, 119

Talk show hosts; Cannonball Adderley, 16; Tyra Banks, 91; Ossie Davis, 465; Whoopi Goldberg, 662; Ed Gordon, 667; Arsenio Hall, 714-715; Gwen Ifill, 815; Chad Ochocinco,

1144; Terrell Owens, 1144; Queen Latifah, 1222; Al Roker, 1287; Tavis Smiley, 1373; Montel Williams, 1576-1578; Oprah Winfrey, 1597-1600

Tampa Red, 1227; and Ma Rainey, 1227

Taney, Roger, 1325

Tanner, Henry Ossawa, 1318, 1412-1413

Tap dancers; Sammy Davis, Jr., 660; Savion Glover, 660-661; Gregory Hines, 660; Bill Robinson, 660, 1266-1268, 1284-1285

Tapia, Richard, 155

Tappan, Lewis, 362

Tarantino, Quentin, 694, 841

Tate, Erskine, 776

Tatum, Goose, 973

Taussig, Helen B., 1427

Tavernier, Bertrand, 666

Taylor, Cecil, 1344

Taylor, Clarence, 731

Taylor, Clarice, 1004

Taylor, Elizabeth, 836

Taylor, Farwell, 1062

Taylor, Jeanette, 195

Taylor, Koko, 501

Taylor, Lawrence, 1413-1415

Taylor, Mildred D., 1415-1416

Tchicai, John, 1344

Temple, Ed, 1466

Temple, Shirley, 1267-1268

Temptations, 402, 1281

Tennessee Jubilee Singers, 902

Terkel, Studs, 832

Terrell, Mary Church, 273, 1416-1418

Terrell, Tammi, 643

Terry, Clark, 461

Tex, Joe, 265

Thant, U, 264

Theodore, Grandwizard, 1354

Thomas, Clarence, 204, 427, 765, 1418-1421, 1428, 1573

Thomas, Debi, 1421-1423

Thomas, Frank, 1423-1424

Thomas, Isiah, 1424-1426

Thomas, Vivien, 1427-1428

Thomas, Walter "Foots," 396

Thompson, George, 1442

Thompson, Hale, 488

Thompson, John, 571, 819

Thompson, Larry D., 1428-1429

Thompson, Titanic, 542

Thoreau, Henry David, 927, 942

Thorogood, George, 143

Thorpe, Jim, 1313

Threadgill, Henry, 1430-1431

Three Black Aces, 45

Three Millers, 400

Thurmond, Strom, 205

Till, Emmett, 83, 179, 1432-1433, 1602; murder case, 199

Timberlake, Justin, 825

Tingle, William, 565

TLC, 69

Tolliver, James "Buster," 308

Tolson, Melvin B., 1434-1435

Tomlin, Mike, 1343

Tomlinson, LaDainian, 1169

Toney, Andrew, 555

Toomer, Jean, 243, 1435-1437; and Jessie Redmon Fauset, 583

Toure, Ahmed Sekou, 306

Toure, Kwame. See Carmichael, Stokely

Toussaint, Allen, 1106

Townes, Jeff, 1385

Townsend, Fannie Lou. See Hamer, Fannie Lou

Townsend, Robert, 1438-1439

Travolta, John, 137

Tristano, Lennie, 206, 1062

Trotter, William Monroe, 1439-1440

Trueheart, John, 1531

Truman, Harry S., 161, 560, 1229, 1265, 1554; and Mahalia Jackson, 832

Trusty, Henry. See Garnet, Henry Highland

Truth, Sojourner, 788, 1441-1443, 1447

Truth, the. See Pierce, Paul

Tubman, Harriet, 1444-1446, 1461

Tucker, Allyson, 1066

Tucker, C. DeLores, 1447-1448

Tucker, Jim, 994

Tucker, Sophie, 195

Tuell, Fay. See Adams, Faye

Tune, Tommy, 401

Tureaud, A. P., 1077

Turner, Big Joe, 1448-1449

Turner, Henry McNeal, 1450-1451

Turner, Ike, 163, 591, 1451-1453, 1455, 1457

Turner, Nat, 1241, 1453-1455

Turner, Tina, 1455-1458; and Ike Turner, 1452-1453

Tuskegee Airmen, 260, 1029, 1094, 1543; and Benjamin O. Davis, Jr., 455-457; and Coleman Young, 1636

Tutu, Desmond, 807, 1517

Twain, Mark, 146, 354

Twombly, Cy, 111

2Pac. See Shakur, Tupac

Tye, Colonel, 67

Tyler Rose, the. See Campbell, Earl

Tyner, McCoy, 407, 1458-1459

Tyson, Cicely, 404, 1078, 1460-1462, 1596

Tyson, Mike, 785, 1462-1464; and Evander Holyfield, 785

Tyson, Neil deGrasse, 1464-1465

Tyus, Wyomia, 1466-1467

Uggams, Leslie, 1468-1470

Underwood, Blair, 102, 1470-1471

United Nations Orchestra, 656

Unruh, Jesse, 250

Updike, John, 893

Upsetters, 990, 1235

Upshaw, Gene, 1342, 1472-1473

Usher, 1474-1475, 1606

Van Buren, Martin, 362

Vance, Courtney B., 115, 1476-1477

Van Der Zee, James, 1477-1479

Vandross, Luther, 302

Van Jones, Rochester. See Anderson, Eddie "Rochester"

Van Peebles, Mario, 115, 1286, 1387, 1480-1481

Van Peebles, Melvin, 286, 1480, 1482-1483

Van Vechten, Carl, 869

Van Wagenen, Isabella. See Truth, Sojourner

Varèse, Edgar, 1399

Vashon, John B., 481

Vaughan, Sarah, 539, 1483-1485

Vaughan, Stevie Ray, 937

Veeck, Bill, 503, 1149

Venuti, Joe, 777

Vereen, Ben, 1485-1486

Verrett, Shirley, 1009

Vesey, Denmark, 1487-1488, 1495

Vitale, John J., 987

Vitous, Miroslav, 1346

Vivian, C. T., 1488-1490

Vodery, Will, 1061

Wade, Dwyane, 850, 1135

Walcott, Derek, 1431

Walcott, Jersey Joe, 335, 1491-1493

Walcott, Louis Eugene. See Farrakhan, Louis

Walker, Alice, 445, 908, 1493-1495; and J. California Cooper, 417; and Zora Neale Hurston, 810

Walker, C. J., 713

Walker, David, 1397, 1495-1496

Walker, George, 270, 1497-1498, 1563-1564

Walker, Jimmie, 1498-1500

Walker, Kurt. See Blow, Kurtis

Walker, Madam C. J., 1500-1502

Walker, Margaret, 645, 712, 1503-1504

Walker, Nellie Marian. See Larsen, Nella

Walker, T-Bone, 786, 937

Walker, Will, 510

Wallace, Henry A., 729, 1265

Wallace, Ruby Ann. See Dee, Ruby

Wallace, Voletta, 116

Wallack, Henry, 22

Wallack, James, 22

Waller, Fats, 109, 239, 284, 546, 1504-1506

Walrond, Eric, 1507-1508

Walsh, Bill, 1248

Walters, Alexander, 345, 1508-1510

Walters, Barbara, 1201; and
  Edward W. Brooke, 216
Ward, Billy, 1019, 1592
Ward, Clara, 511, 614
Ward, Douglas Turner, 533
Warhol, Andy, 112
Warmoth, Henry Clay, 532
Warren, Butch, 725
Warren G, 1388, 1390
Warwick, Dionne, 1510-1512
Washington, Booker T., 638, 1513-
  1515; bust of, 108; and George
  Washington Carver, 320; and
  Charles Waddell Chesnutt, 354;
  criticisms of, 1439; and W. E. B.
  Du Bois, 521; and Marcus
  Garvey, 211, 635; and John
  Hope, 792; and Claude McKay,
  1010; and National Afro-
  American Council, 1509;
  philosophy of, 224, 521, 792;
  and Harriet Tubman, 1446; and
  Madam C. J. Walker, 1501; and
  Eric Walrond, 1507; and
  Alexander Walters, 1509
Washington, Craig, 844
Washington, Denzel, 343, 472,
  1086, 1191, 1438, 1476, 1515-
  1518
Washington, Desiree, 1463
Washington, Dinah, 613-614
Washington, George, 37, 67, 93
Washington, Harold, 605, 828,
  1146, 1225, 1518-1521
Washington, Kenny, 1521-1522;
  and Woody Strode, 1403
Washington, Pauletta Pearson, 1517
Washington, Walter, 104
Washingtonians, 308, 546
Waters, Ethel, 79, 313, 466, 1007,
  1468
Waters, Maxine, 1523-1524
Waters, Muddy, 142, 501, 992,
  1525-1526, 1621
Watkins, Frances Ellen. See Harper,
  Frances Ellen Watkins
Watkins, Gloria Jean. See Hooks,
  Bell
Watson, Perle Yvonne. See Burke,
  Yvonne Brathwaite

Wattleton, Faye, 1526-1528
Watts, J. C., 1528-1529
Wayans, Damon, 1005
Wayans, Keenan Ivory, 324
Wayans brothers, 1215
Waymon, Eunice Kathleen. See
  Simone, Nina
Weaver, Robert C., 1530-1531
Webb, Chick, 315, 592, 1531-1532;
  and Cootie Williams, 1566
Weber, Max, 521
Webster, Ben, 167, 285, 1012
Webster, Nicholas, 465
Weinberger, Caspar, 1200
Weinglass, Leonard, 1329
Welch, Raquel, 238
Welles, Orson, 945, 968, 1626
Wells, Dicky, 315
Wells, Junior, 993
Wells, Mary, 1281
Wells-Barnett, Ida B., 1533-1534
West, Cornel, 1535-1536
West, David, 1537-1538
West, Dorothy, 1538-1539
West, Kanye, 589, 612, 852-853,
  1256, 1540-1541
West, Mae, 129, 1007
West, Togo, 1541-1543
Westhead, Paul, 878
Wexler, Jerry, 265, 615
Wharton, Clifton Reginald, Jr.,
  1543-1544
Wheatley, Phillis, 1545-1547,
  1626
Wheatley, Tyrone, 1547-1548
Wheatrob, Tony, 812
Whispering Syncopators, 510
Whitaker, Forest, 1015, 1548-1550
White, Bill, 214, 1550-1552
White, Charles, 1034
White, Clarence Cameron, 270
White, George, 345
White, Slappy, 613
White, Walter, 1230, 1552-1554,
  1560
White, William, 606
Whitefield, George, 1545-1546
Whittaker, "Tampa Red," 510
Whittier, John Greenleaf, 524,
  704

Wideman, John Edgar, 1555-1557
Wiggins, Thomas. See Bethune,
  Blind Tom
Wilberforce Collegians, 1300
Wild Tchoupitoulas, 1106
Wildcats Jazz Band, 510, 1227
Wilder, L. Douglas, 1557-1558
Wilkens, Lenny, 1558-1559
Wilkins, Roy, 603, 1560-1562; and
  Jane Matilda Bolin, 176
Wilkinson, J. L., 1150
Wilks, Samuel, 154
Willard, Jess, 1000
Williams, Anthony, 105
Williams, Bert, 195, 270, 334,
  1061, 1563-1564
Williams, Billy Dee, 1565-1566
Williams, Cootie, 167, 1566-1567
Williams, Daniel Hale, 1567-1569
Williams, Dootsie, 613
Williams, Eddie, 222
Williams, Eugene, 862
Williams, Floyd "Horsecollar,"
  1112
Williams, Gus, 1569-1570
Williams, Hosea, 834, 983, 1571-
  1572
Williams, Joe, 110
Williams, Juan, 1573-1574
Williams, Martin, 397
Williams, Mary Lou, 1113, 1574-
  1576
Williams, Montel, 1576-1578
Williams, Paulette. See Shange,
  Ntozake
Williams, Ricky, 1016
Williams, Robert Franklin, 1578-
  1579
Williams, Robert Peter. See
  Guillaume, Robert
Williams, Sandy, 1532
Williams, Serena, 649, 1579-1581
Williams, Sidney, 1523
Williams, Spencer, 1505
Williams, Vanessa, 338, 1581-1582
Williams, Venus, 649, 1583-1584
Williams, Willie L., 1584-1585
Willis, Benjamin, 1224
Wills, Maury, 214, 1586-1587
Wilmington Ten, 341-342

Wilson, August, 115, 534, 840, 1234, 1517, 1587-1589; and Romare Bearden, 128; and Lloyd Richards, 1251
Wilson, Brian, 266
Wilson, Cootie, 1069
Wilson, Flip, 947, 1215, 1590-1591
Wilson, Harriet E., 641
Wilson, Jackie, 673, 1592-1593
Wilson, Josephine Beall, 253
Wilson, Lionel, 231
Wilson, Mary, 1291
Wilson, Nancy, 16, 714
Wilson, Teddy, 723
Wilson, William Julius, 1593-1594
Wilson, Woodrow, 1440, 1509
Wilt the Stilt. *See* Chamberlain, Wilt
Winehouse, Amy, 740
Winfield, Paul, 1595-1597
Winfrey, Florence. *See* Mills, Florence
Winfrey, Oprah, 785, 1173, 1597-1600; book club, 630, 1598; and Nikki Giovanni, 658; and South Africa, 816; and Tiger Woods, 1613
Winkfield, James, 1600-1601
Winter, Bud, 304, 562
Winter, Johnny, 1526
Withers, Ernest, 1601-1603
Witt, Katarina, 1422
Wizard, the. *See* Williams, Gus

Wofford, Chloe Anthony. *See* Morrison, Toni
Wolf, Simon, 1068
Wolfe, George C., 660, 1603-1604
Womack, Bobby, 416
Wonder, Stevie, 69-70, 547, 1605-1607
Wonder Children, 442
Woodard, Alfre, 1517, 1607-1608
Woodard, Lynette, 1609-1610
Woodbridge, Hudson. *See* Tampa Red
Wooden, John, 8
Woods, Earl, 542
Woods, Granville T., 1610-1612
Woods, Tiger, 542, 1612-1614
Woodson, Carter G., 1320, 1615-1617
Woodson, Rod, 1617-1619
Woodward, Nathan, 357
Work, John, III, 1525
Wrestlers; Dwayne Johnson, 864-865; Woody Strode, 1403; Neil deGrasse Tyson, 1464
Wright, Angela, 766
Wright, Archibald Lee. *See* Moore, Archie
Wright, Eric "Eazy-E," 505, 812
Wright, Isaac. *See* Coker, Daniel
Wright, Jane Cooke, 1619-1620, 1624
Wright, Jeffrey, 1620-1622
Wright, Jeremiah, 1622-1623
Wright, Jonathan J., 1372
Wright, Louis T., 1624-1625

Wright, Marian. *See* Edelman, Marian Wright
Wright, Orville, 524
Wright, Richard, 646, 1625-1627; and James Baldwin, 81; biographies of, 1503; and Ralph Ellison, 548; *Native Son*, 968; and Dorothy West, 1538
Wright, Wilbur, 524
Wu Tang Clan, 381
Wurf, Jerry, 574

Yang, C. K., 882
Yardbird. *See* Parker, Charlie
Yardbirds, 496, 787
Yearwood, Trisha, 1107
Yerby, Frank, 1628-1630
Yorty, Sam, 201
Young, Al, 1631-1632
Young, Andre Romelle. *See* Dr. Dre
Young, Andrew, 209, 719, 834, 1632-1635
Young, Coleman, 1635-1637
Young, Lester, 109, 782, 1012
Young, Whitney, 1044, 1637-1638
Young Jeezy, 853

Zane, Arnie, 891-892
Zawinul, Joe, 1346
Zea-Daly, Errol, 1415
Zooid, 1431
Zwerin, Charlotte, 1070

# SUBJECT INDEX

AACM. *See* Association for the Advancement of Creative Musicians

Aaliyah, 1-2

Aaron, Hank, 3-5, 73, 184, 1046, 1206; and M. C. Hammer, 721

Abbott, Cleveland, 384

Abbott, Robert S., 5-8, 390, 395

ABC-Paramount Records. *See* Paramount Records

Abdul-Jabbar, Kareem, 8-11, 184, 741, 745, 878, 1262, 1383

*Abeng* (Cliff), 377

Abernathy, Ralph David, 11-13, 263, 832; and James Bevel, 151; and Jesse Jackson, 827

Abolitionism, 84-85, 624, 632; and Joseph Cinque, 361-363. *See also List of Entries by Category*

*About Sarah* (television movie), 1241

*Above the Rim* (film), 1334

Abrams, Muhal Richard, 206-207, 1430

*Abuelita* (Basquiat), 111

Abyssinian Baptist Church, 81, 312, 731, 1196

Abzug, Bella, 569

Academy Awards; and Angela Bassett, 116, 1457; and Halle Berry, 145, 444; Best Actors, 344, 591, 612, 665, 1190, 1386, 1516-1517, 1549, 1595; Best Actresses, 116, 145, 313, 443-444, 1292-1293, 1461; Best Supporting Actors, 612, 623-624, 663, 674, 841, 1092, 1516; Best Supporting Actresses, 471, 662, 803, 1006-1007, 1222, 1598; and Irene Cara, 296; and Diahann Carroll, 313; ceremonies, 2, 662; and Don Cheadle, 344; and Dorothy Dandridge, 443-444; and Viola Davis, 471; directors, 1368; documentaries, 87, 180; and

Laurence Fishburne, 591, 1457; and Jamie Foxx, 337, 612; and Morgan Freeman, 623; and Charles Fuller, 625; and Whoopi Goldberg, 662; and Cuba Gooding, Jr., 663; and Dexter Gordon, 665; and Louis Gossett, Jr., 674; and Jennifer Hudson, 803; and Samuel L. Jackson, 841; and Hattie McDaniel, 1006-1007; and Eddie Murphy, 1092; and Sidney Poitier, 1190; and Queen Latifah, 1222; and Lionel Richie, 1253; and Diana Ross, 1292-1293; and John Singleton, 1368; and Will Smith, 1386; songs, 296, 1253, 1292, 1406, 1582, 1606; and Donna Summer, 1406; and Cicely Tyson, 1461; and Denzel Washington, 1516-1517; and Forest Whitaker, 1549; and Vanessa Williams, 1582; and Paul Winfield, 1595; and Oprah Winfrey, 1598; and Stevie Wonder, 1606

Ace Records, 1381

Acquired immunodeficiency syndrome, 935; and Arthur Ashe, 64; and Magic Johnson, 879; and Max Robinson, 1278; and Dionne Warwick, 1512; and Alfre Woodard, 1608

Ad-Lib Records, 1013

Adams, Faye, 14-15

Adams, John, 67, 754

Adams, John Quincy, 362, 1162

*Adarand Constructors, Inc. v. Peña*, 1420

Adderley, Cannonball, 15-17, 118, 462

Adderley Brothers, 336

*Address to Those Who Keep Slaves and Approve the Practice, An* (Allen), 37

Adler, Kurt, 120

Admiral, the. *See* Robinson, David

Adoff, Virginia Hamilton. *See* Hamilton, Virginia

*Advance* (newspaper), 1238

*Adventures of Huck Finn, The* (1993 film), 1476

*Adventures of Huckleberry Finn, The* (1960 film), 1074

Affirmative action, 818, 833, 1246, 1396, 1447, 1524; and Clarence Thomas, 1420

Afghanistan; Soviet invasion of, 65, 1246; U.S. invasion of, 965, 1123, 1201, 1247

AFL. *See* American Federation of Labor

*Africa and America* (Crummell), 436

*Africa Awakening* (Barthé), 108

*African, The* (Courlander), 712

African American Policy Forum, 427

African Blood Brotherhood, 210-211

African Grove theater, 22

African Growth and Opportunity Act of 2000, 1232

African Heritage Studies Association, 857, 924

African Methodist Episcopal Church, 141, 990, 1488; and Richard Allen, 36-38; and Daniel Coker, 388-390, 875; and James H. Cone, 411-412; and Hiram Rhoades Revels, 1241; and Henry Ossawa Tanner, 1412; theology of, 37; and Henry McNeal Turner, 1450-1451; and Denmark Vesey, 1487; and Alexander Walters, 1508-1510

African Methodist Episcopal Zion Church, 939; and Absalom Jones, 889-891

African Roscius, The. *See* Aldridge, Ira Frederick

*African Sleeping Sickness* (Coleman), 399
African Union, 62
"Africology," 62
Afro-American Association, 923, 1328
Afro-American League, 254
Afro-American Symphony (Still), 1399-1400
*Afrocentric Idea, The* (Asante), 62
*Afrocentric Manifesto, An* (Asante), 62
Afrocentricity, 60-61, 210, 769, 857, 1221
*Afrocentricity* (Asante), 61
Aftermath Entertainment, 505, 589
*Against the Ropes* (film), 553
Agency for International Development, U.S., 135, 769
*Agnes of God* (play), 313
Agyeman, Jaramogi Abebe. *See* Cleage, Albert Buford, Jr.
Ahmadiyya movement, 30, 1458
*Aida* (opera), 902, 1118, 1202-1203
AIDS. *See* Acquired immunodeficiency syndrome
Aiken, Loretta Mary. *See* Mabley, Moms
Ailey, Alvin, 18-20, 50
*Ain't I a Woman* (Hooks), 788-789
"Ain't I a Woman?" (Truth), 1442
*Ain't Misbehavin* (musical), 33, 316, 1505
"Ain't That Peculiar" (song), 1281
Air, 1431
Air Force Academy, U.S., 691
Akron Pros, 1193
*Al on America* (Sharpton), 1338
al-Qaeda, 1247
Alabama Christian Movement for Human Rights, 1347
Alabama State College, 11
Alabamians, 284
Aladdin Records, 222
Albright, Madeleine, 1245
Alcindor, Lew. *See* Abdul-Jabbar, Kareem
Alcorn, George Edward, 20-21
Alcorn, James L., 1242

Alcorn State University, 565, 567-568; and Hiram Rhoades Revels, 1241-1242
Alda, Alan, 465
Aldridge, Ira Frederick, 22-24
*Alex Haley's Queen* (television program), 713
Alexander, Elizabeth, 24-25
Alexander, J. W., 416
Alexander, Margaret Walker. *See* Walker, Margaret
Algeria, 231, 372, 448
*Ali* (film), 612
Ali, Laila, 28
Ali, Muhammad, 26-28, 373, 601, 1074, 1164, 1205, 1386; and Joe Frazier, 620-621; and Sonny Liston, 988, 1492
Ali, Noble Drew, 29-30
Ali, Rashied, 410
*Alice in Wonder* (Davis), 464
*All Eyez on Me* (Shakur), 1334
*All for You* (Jackson), 825
*All God's Chillun Got Wings* (O'Neill), 1264
All-Negro National Committee of Inquiry, 413
Allen, Andrew Arthur "Tex," 1233
Allen, Betty, 185
Allen, Damon, 31-33
Allen, Debbie, 33-34, 1112, 1233
Allen, Henry, 1560
Allen, Marcus, 31, 34-36, 1169
Allen, Phog, 327
Allen, Ray, 634, 1182
Allen, Richard, 36-38, 389, 606, 889-890
Allensworth, Allen, 38-39
Allensworth, California, 39
*Aloneness* (Brooks), 219
*Along This Way* (Johnson), 869-870
Alpha Kappa Alpha sorority, 1233
Alpha Phi Alpha fraternity, 215, 486, 566, 739, 1077
Alston, Charles, 40-41, 961, 1318
Althouse, Paul, 270
Altman, Robert, 137
Alton, Louise, 270
Alvin Ailey American Dance Theater, 18-19, 892, 1244

Amankwatia, Nana Baffour, II. *See* Hilliard, Asa Grant, III
Amateur Athletic Foundation, 480
Amateur Sports Act of 1978, 480
*Amazing Grace* (film), 1004
Ambers, Lou, 54
AME. *See* African Methodist Episcopal Church
*Amen Corner, The* (play), 82
American Academy of Arts and Sciences, 155, 892, 1247
American Anti-Slavery Society, 703, 1442
*American Bandstand* (television program), 234, 347
American Basketball Association, 329, 741, 745, 1262; and Julius Erving, 554-555
American Basketball League (men), 503, 741
American Basketball League (women), 915
American Civil Liberties Union, 1119
American Colonization Society, 436, 438, 482, 606, 637, 1302; and Daniel Coker, 389. *See also* Liberia
*American Dilemma, An* (Myrdal), 243, 263
American Express, 351-353
American Federation of Labor, 1229-1230
American Festival of Negro Art, 1238
American Football League, 1341, 1384
*American Gangster* (film), 479
*American Idol* (television program), 802, 1282
*American Mercury, The* (magazine), 1322
American Missionary Association, 223, 595, 863, 939, 986
American Moral Reform Society, 606
American Negro Academy, 435-436, 1320
American Negro Exposition, 1435

American Negro Theater, 357, 478, 1177, 1190

*American People* (Ringgold), 1259

American Professional Football Association, 1193

American Red Cross, 519, 1413

American Revolution, 437, 1258; African Americans in, 67; and Crispus Attucks, 66-68; and James Forten, 606; and Prince Hall, 716; and Jean Baptiste Pointe du Sable, 1188; and Phillis Wheatley, 1546

American Society of Composers, Authors, and Publishers, 165, 270, 948, 1095

American Tennis Association, 63, 648-649

American Women's Suffrage Association, 733

*America's Black Forum* (television program), 180

America's Independent Party, 931

*America's Next Top Model* (television program), 91, 1353

*AmeriKKKa's Most Wanted* (Ice Cube), 812-813

Ames, Adelbart, 252

Amin, Idi, 818

Amin, Jamil Abdullah Al-. *See* Brown, H. Rap

*Amistad* (film), 34, 340, 624

*Amistad* slave rebellion, 34, 340, 361-363, 1162

Ammons, Albert, 41

Ammons, Gene, 41-43, 1401

Amnesty International, 341, 854

Amos, John, 1499

Amos, Wally, 43-45

*Amos 'n' Andy* (television program), 357, 1003

Amsterdam News, The. *See New York Amsterdam News, The*

ANA. *See* American Negro Academy

*Anastasia* (film), 2

*And the Walls Came Tumbling Down* (Abernathy), 12-13

Anderson, Cornelius, 45

Anderson, Eddie "Rochester," 45-47

Anderson, Greg, 184

Anderson, Marian, 47-50, 270, 832, 1117, 1202; and Marian Wright Edelman, 540

Anderson, Theodore W., 154

Andrew, Joseph Maree. *See* Bonner, Marita

Andrew Young Foundation, 1634

Angelou, Maya, 50-53, 286, 526, 1127; and Lorene Cary, 323; critique of, 399

*Angels in America* (play), 1604, 1620-1621

Angola, 818, 1633-1634

Angry Blond Negro. *See* Briggs, Cyril V.

Anheuser-Busch, 1550

*Anna Lucasta* (film), 468

*Anna Lucasta* (play), 464

*Annie John* (Kincaid), 935

*Another Country* (Baldwin), 83

*Another Kind of Rain* (Barrax), 103

Answer, the. *See* Iverson, Allen

ANT. *See* American Negro Theater

Anthony, Carmelo, 153

Anthony, Susan B., 515, 1445, 1447

Anthropologists; Katherine Dunham, 530-531; Zora Neale Hurston, 808-811; Pearl Primus, 1208-1209; William Julius Wilson, 1593-1594

Anti-Defamation League, 1339

Any Body Can, 1074

*Any Given Sunday* (film), 238, 612, 953, 1414

Apartheid, South African, 219, 1383; and Arthur Ashe, 64; and Hugh Masekela, 19. *See also* South Africa

Apollo Records, 265, 832

Apollo Theater, 71; and James Brown, 234; and George Clinton, 380; and Ella Fitzgerald, 592; and Lauryn Hill, 767; and Hines Brothers, 774; and Jackson Five, 835; and Johnny Moore's Three Blazers, 222; and Moms Mabley, 1003; and Jackie McLean, 1012; and

Sonny Rollins, 1289; television show, 325, 767; and Leslie Uggams, 1468; and Sarah Vaughan, 1483; and Jimmie Walker, 1499; and Dionne Warwick, 1510; and Flip Wilson, 1590

*Appeal to the Colored Citizens of the World* (Walker), 1495-1496

Appiah, Kwame Anthony, 641

Arab-Israeli War, 603

Arafat, Yasir, 828

*Are Prisons Obsolete?* (Davis), 450

*Are You Experienced?* (Hendrix), 759-760

Arie, India. *See* India.Arie

Arista Records, 206, 208, 616, 798, 933, 1314, 1511

Aristide, Jean-Bertrand, 683, 1279

Aristocrat Records. *See* Chess Records

Arizmendi, Baby, 54

Arizona Cardinals, 1380

*Ark and the Ankh, The* (Dumas), 523

*Arkansas State Press, The* (newspaper), 116

Arkestra, 1408-1409, 1430

Armstrong, Harry, 53

Armstrong, Henry, 53-55

Armstrong, Lillian Hardin, 55-57; and Louis Armstrong, 56, 58

Armstrong, Louis, 57-60, 195, 867; and Lillian Hardin Armstrong, 56; and Cab Calloway, 284; and Ella Fitzgerald, 593; and Lionel Hampton, 723; and Earl Hines, 773; and Milt Hinton, 777; and Billie Holiday, 781, 783; and Charles Mingus, 1062; and Ma Rainey, 1227; and Chick Webb, 1531

Armstrong, Neil, 876

Arriba. *See* Clemente, Roberto

*Arsenio Hall Show, The* (television program), 714-715

Art Students League, 127, 972

Arthur Ashe Foundation, 64

Artist Formerly Known as Prince, the. *See* Prince

Artists for a New South Africa, 1471, 1608
Arvey, Verna, 1400
*As I Am* (Keys), 933
*As the World Turns* (television program), 767
ASALH. *See* Association for the Study of African American Life and History
Asante, Molefi Kete, 60-62
Asbury, Francis, 36
ASCAP. *See* American Society of Composers, Authors, and Publishers
*Ascension* (Sanders), 1314
Ashe, Arthur, 63-64, 648-649
Ashford, Evelyn, 65-66, 700
Ashwood, Amy, 635
*Aspects of Negro Life* (Douglas), 512
Assad, Hafez al-, 828
Associated Publishers, 1615
Associates in Negro Folk Education, 996
Association for Nubian Kemetic Heritage, 61
Association for Tennis Professionals, 64
Association for the Advancement of Creative Musicians, 206, 1430
Association for the Study of African American Life and History; and John Henrik Clarke, 369; and Benjamin Quarles, 1220; and Arturo Alfonso Schomburg, 1320; and Carter G. Woodson, 1615-1616
Association for the Study of Classical African Civilizations, 769
Association for the Study of Negro Life and History. *See* Association for the Study of African American Life and History
Association of Black Foundation Executives, 854
Association of Black Psychologists, 769, 1392

Association of Community Organizers for Reform Now, 499
Astronauts, 1115; Guion Bluford, 171-173; Charles F. Bolden, Jr., 173-174; Frederick Drew Gregory, 690-692; Mae C. Jemison, 858-859; Robert H. Lawrence, Jr., 963-964; Ronald E. McNair, 1017-1019. *See also* Aviators
*At the Bottom of the River* (Kincaid), 934
Atco Records, 739
Atkins, Chet, 1206
Atkins, Cholly, 400-402
Atlanta Baptist College. *See* Morehouse College
Atlanta Braves, 5, 73, 1312
"Atlanta Compromise" address (Washington), 1514
Atlanta Falcons, 494, 1312
Atlanta, Georgia; Black Action Strategies and Information Center, 1490; Black Image Theater Company, 840; board of education, 1553; city council, 983; Committee on Appeal for Human Rights, 179; Dexter Avenue Baptist Church, 12, 939, 941, 1275; Ebenezer Baptist Church, 940-942; Eighty-One Theater, 510, 1378; *Gone with the Wind* premiere, 1007; Hosea Feeds the Hungry and Homeless, 1572; House of Blues, 1173; Institute for the Black World, 940; mayors, 833, 1572, 1632, 1634; Olympic Games, 834, 1634; race riots, 1552; riot of 1906, 792. *See also* Morehouse College
*Atlanta Independent, The* (newspaper), 451
Atlanta University; and Ralph David Abernathy, 12; and Horace Mann Bond, 177; and William Stanley Braithwaite, 203; and W. E. B. Du Bois, 521-522; and John Hope, 791; and Whitney Young, 1638

Atlanta University Center, 793, 940
*Atlantic Monthly* magazine, 354
Atlantic Records, 336; and Toni Braxton, 209; and Solomon Burke, 265; and Cyrus Chestnut, 356; and Ornette Coleman, 397; and Aretha Franklin, 615; and Macy Gray, 681; and Clyde McPhatter, 1019; and Herbie Nichols, 1113; and Sylvia M. Rhone, 1243-1244; and Big Joe Turner, 1449
*Atlantis* space shuttle, 691
Attucks, Crispus, 66-68, 1440
Atwater, Lee, 350
Auerbach, Red, 327, 1298
Augusta Institute. *See* Morehouse College
Ausbie, Herb "Geese," 1609
*Autobiography of an Ex-Colored Man, The* (Johnson), 869-870
*Autobiography of Malcolm X, The* (Haley), 711
*Autobiography of Miss Jane Pittman, The* (Gaines), 630
*Autobiography of Miss Jane Pittman, The* (television movie), 630, 1461
*Autobiography of My Mother, The* (Kincaid), 935
Avakian, George, 461
Aviators; Guion Bluford, 171-173; Charles F. Bolden, Jr., 173-174; Eugene Jacques Bullard, 259-260; Bessie Coleman, 394-396; Benjamin O. Davis, Jr., 455-457; Frederick Drew Gregory, 690-692; Hubert Fauntleroy Julian, 917-919; Robert H. Lawrence, Jr., 963-964. *See also* Astronauts
*Axis* (Hendrix), 759
Ayers-Allen, Phylicia. *See* Rashad, Phylicia

*Baadasssss!* (film), 1481
Baby Phat, 1352-1353, 1355
Babyface, 69-70
Bacall, Lauren, 468
Bacharach, Burt, 1459, 1510-1511

"Back to Africa" movements; and Richard Allen, 37; and Blanche Kelso Bruce, 252; and John E. Bruce, 254; and James Forten, 606; and Marcus Garvey, 635-636; and John Brown Russwurm, 1303

*Bad* (Jackson), 836

*Bad Boy* (Myers), 1097

Bad Boy Records, 1217

*Bad Boys* (film), 1385

Baer, Max, 1000, 1492

*Bagdad Cafe* (television program), 989

*Bagpipe Lesson, The* (Tanner), 1412

Bahamas, 2, 689, 1523; Sidney Poitier, 1190-1193

Bailey, Benny, 429

Bailey, Frederick Augustus Washington. *See* Douglass, Frederick

Bailey, Pearl, 71-73, 1003

*Bailey's Café* (Naylor), 1105

Baker, Anita, 168

Baker, Dusty, 73-74

Baker, Ella, 75-76, 719

Baker, Etta, 1411

Baker, George, Jr. *See* Father Divine

Baker, Houston A., Jr., 77-78

Baker, Josephine, 78-81, 675, 1233

*Bal Nègre* (dance production), 945

Balanchine, George, 1064

BALCO. *See* Bay Area Laboratory Co-operative

Baldwin, James, 81-84; and Maya Angelou, 51; and Eldridge Cleaver, 373; and Walter Dean Myers, 1098; and Emmett Till, 1433; and Richard Wright, 1627

Baldwin, Maria L., 223

Ball, James Presley, 84-85

Ball, Thomas, 980

*Ballad of the Brown Girl, The* (Cullen), 440

Ballard, Florence, 1291

Ballet Negro, 530

*Baltimore Afro-American, The* (newspaper), 7, 127, 1067

Baltimore Black Sox, 1149

Baltimore Bullets. *See* Washington Bullets

Baltimore Orioles, 839, 1271-1272

Baltimore Ravens, 1313, 1365, 1618; and Ray Lewis, 984-985; and Ed Reed, 1236-1237

Bambaataa, Afrika, 1221

Bambara, Toni Cade, 86-88, 291

*Bamboozled* (film), 660, 969

*Banana Bottom* (McKay), 1011

Bancroft, Hubert, 1320

*Band of Angels* (film), 840

*Band of Gypsys* (Hendrix), 759

Bandung Conference, 1197

*Banjo* (McKay), 1011

*Banjo Lesson, The* (Tanner), 1412

Banks, Ernie, 88-90, 139, 1136

Banks, Tyra, 90-91

Banneker, Benjamin, 92-93

Bannister, Edward Mitchell, 94-95

Bar-Kays, 1235

Baraka, Amiri, 96-98, 397; and Sonia Sanchez, 1308; and August Wilson, 1588

Barbados, 1255

Barbarin, Paul, 156

*Barbershop* (film), 326, 813

Bard of the Maumee. *See* Bell, James Madison

Barkley, Charles, 99-101, 152

Barnes, Steven, 101-102

Barnet, Charlie, 794, 1012

Barnett, Ross, 1050-1051

Barone, Joseph "Pep," 987

Barons of Rhythm, 109

Baroudi, Sam, 335

Barrax, Gerald William, 102-104

Barrow, Clyde, 622

Barrow, Joseph Louis. *See* Louis, Joe

Barry, Marion, 104-106, 150, 738, 1573

Barthé, Richmond, 107-108

Bartholomew, Dave, 508-509

Baryshnikov, Mikhail, 19, 1422

Baseball managers; Dusty Baker, 74; Cool Papa Bell, 139; Larry Doby, 503; Cito Gaston, 74; Buck O'Neil, 1136-1137; Frank Robinson, 1270-1272

Basie, Count, 109-111; and Gene Ammons, 42; and Milt Hinton, 777; and Billie Holiday, 782; and Albert Murray, 1095; and Big Joe Turner, 1448

Basketball coaches; Earl Lloyd, 994; Bill Russell, 1298-1299

*Basquiat* (film), 1621

Basquiat, Jean-Michel, 111-113, 1621

Bass, Charlotta Spears, 113-114

Bass, Joseph Blackburn, 113

Bass, Kingsley B., Jr. *See* Bullins, Ed

Bassett, Angela, 115-116, 591, 1015, 1457, 1477

Bates, Daisy, 116-118

Bates, Ellas Otha. *See* Diddley, Bo

*Bates v. City of Little Rock*, 117

Batiste, Alvin, 118-119

Batiste, Harold, 156

*Batman* (television program), 945

Batson, Florence, 269

Batt, John, 716

Battle, Kathleen, 119-121, 185, 356

Battle, Mike, 622

Baumfree, Isabella. *See* Truth, Sojourner

Baumgarten, David, 694

Bauzá, Mario, 655

Bay Area Laboratory Co-operative, 184, 898

Baylor, Elgin, 121-123

Beach Boys, 143

Beam, Abraham, 498

Beamon, Bob, 123-124, 191, 979, 1384

Beard, Andrew Jackson, 125-126

Bearden, Romare, 40, 126-128, 1588

Beasley, Myrlie Louise. *See* Evers-Williams, Myrlie

Beastie Boys, 1355

Beat movement, 96-97

Beatles, 143, 373, 1475; and Chuck Berry, 142; and Fats Domino, 509; and Little Richard, 991

Beaty, Powhatan, 459

*Beauty and the Beast* (musical), 208

Beavers, Louise, 129-130, 1007
Bebop, 547; and Cannonball Adderley, 17; and Gene Ammons, 41-43; and Edward Blackwell, 156-157; and Art Blakey, 162; and Jimmy Blanton, 167; and John Coltrane, 409; and "cool jazz," 462; and Scatman Crothers, 429; and Miles Davis, 462; and Billy Eckstine, 538, 1103; and Dizzy Gillespie, 654-656; and Dexter Gordon, 666; and Johnny Griffin, 697-698; and Earl Hines, 773; and Quincy Jones, 899; and Charles Mingus, 1061-1063; and Thelonious Monk, 1069; and Fats Navarro, 1103-1104; and Charlie Parker, 409, 1151-1153; and Max Roach, 1260-1261; and Sonny Rollins, 1289; and Wayne Shorter, 1345; and Sonny Stitt, 1401-1402
Beckford, Tyson, 130-132
Beckwith, Byron De La, 332, 568, 570
Beckwourth, Jim, 132-134
Beckwourth Pass, 133
Becoming Dad (Pitts), 1187
Becton, Julius Wesley. Jr., 134-135
Bee, Clair, 503
Bee Gees, 1475
Before I Forget (Pitts), 1188
Bel Canto Foundation, 1575
Belafonte, Harry, 136-138, 314, 1078, 1126-1127; and Brock Peters, 1175
Bell, Alexander Graham, 960
Bell, Cool Papa, 138-140, 675
Bell, Demetrius, 1028
Bell, James Madison, 140-141
Bellotte, Pete, 1406
Bellson, Louis, 72
Beloved (Morrison), 1081
Beneath the Underdog (Mingus), 1063
Bennett, Tony, 110
Bennett, William, 1447
Benny, Jack, 45

Benny Goodman Story, The (film), 468
Bens, Franklin, 119
Benson (television program), 706-707
Benton, Thomas Hart, 254
Benton, Walter, 103
Berbick, Trevor, 1463
Bergman, Ingrid, 1155
Berlin, Irving, 593
Berman, Bess, 832
Bernadotte, Folke, 264
Bernie Mac Show, The (television program), 1005
Bernstein, Leonard, 19, 727, 1033
Berry, Chu, 285, 315, 776
Berry, Chuck, 141-143, 496, 501, 848
Berry, Halle, 144-145, 841
Bertrand, Jimmy, 723
BET. See Black Entertainment Television
Bethel Literary and Historical Association, 1417
Bethune, Blind Tom, 145-147
Bethune, James, 145-146
Bethune, Mary McLeod, 148-150, 752-753, 1530
Bethune-Cookman University, 149
Bethune-Dubois Institute, 1447-1448
Beulah (radio program), 1008
Beulah (television program), 129, 313, 429, 1008, 1468
Beulah Land Farms, 371
Bevel, Diane. See Nash, Diane
Bevel, James, 150-151, 1102, 1488
Beverly Hills Cop films, 1091-1092, 1286
Beyoncé. See Knowles, Beyoncé
Beyond Racism (Young), 1638
Biden, Joseph, 641, 765, 815, 1123
Big Cat, the. See Lloyd, Earl
Big Dipper, the. See Chamberlain, Wilt
Big E, the. See Hayes, Elvin
Big Hurt, the. See Thomas, Frank
Big O, the. See Robertson, Oscar
Big Sea, The (Hughes), 806
Big Ticket, the. See Garnett, Kevin

Biko, Steve, 1516
Bill and Melinda Gates Foundation, 683
Bill Cosby Show, The (television program), 423; and Quincy Jones, 900
Billups, Chauncey, 152-153, 1181
Bingo Long Traveling All Stars and Motor Kings, The (film), 1565
Bird. See Parker, Charlie
Bird (film), 1153, 1549
Bird, Larry, 878-879
Birdland, 227, 1152
Birmingham, Alabama; Sixteenth Street Baptist Church, 332
Birmingham Black Barons, 1046, 1149, 1206
Birmingham Children's March, 151, 1102
Birmingham Civil Rights Institute, 639, 1348
Birth of a Nation, The (film), 113, 702, 1440
Birth of the Cool (Davis), 461-462, 1260
Bishop, Joey, 468
Bishop, William "Billy," 917
Bitches Brew (Davis), 462, 725
Black, Julian, 999
Black Action Strategies and Information Center, 1490
Black Aesthetic, The (Gayle), 645
Black American Cinema Society, 500, 659, 1565
Black and Blue (musical), 402, 660
Black Arts movement; and Toni Cade Bambara, 88; and Mari Evans, 563; and Charles Fuller, 625; and Addison Gayle, Jr., 645-646; and Nikki Giovanni, 657; and Gayl Jones, 893; and William Melvin Kelley, 926, 928; and Haki R. Madhubuti, 1022-1023; and The Negro Digest, 927; and Sonia Sanchez, 1307-1308; and George S. Schuyler, 1323; and Survey Graphic, 996
Black Babe Ruth, the. See Gibson, Josh

"Black Beauty" (song), 1060
*Black Boy* (Wright), 1626
Black Cabinet, 149, 1530
Black Caucus of the American Library Association, 1087
*Black Christ and Other Poems, The* (Cullen), 440
Black Christian Nationalist Church, 369-371
Black Codes, 299
*Black Doctor, The* (play), 23
Black Eagle, the. *See* Julian, Hubert Fauntleroy
Black Eagle Associates, 918
Black Economic Union, 239
*Black Empire* (Schuyler), 1323
*Black Enterprise* magazine, 213, 639, 679-680, 778, 873
Black Entertainment Television, 885, 1357; and Cedric the Entertainer, 325; and Ed Gordon, 667-668; and Robert L. Johnson, 884-886; and Tavis Smiley, 1374
*Black Experience, The* (television program), 563
*Black Feeling, Black Talk* (Giovanni), 657
*Black Feminist Thought* (Collins), 405
Black Filmmakers Hall of Fame, 500, 588, 659, 1176, 1596
*Black Genius* (Mosley), 1087
*Black Girl* (film), 465
Black Herman, 1407
*Black History: Lost, Stolen, or Strayed* (television program), 587
Black History Month, 229-230, 1615-1616. *See also* Negro History Week
*Black Ice* (Cary), 322-323
"Black Internationale, The" (Schuyler), 1323
Black Inventors Hall of Fame, 677
*Black Judgment* (Giovanni), 657
Black Leadership Forum, 1002
Black liberation theology, 411-412, 1451. *See also* Cone, James H.
Black Mamba. *See* Bryant, Kobe

*Black Man, The* (newspaper), 1508
*Black Manhattan* (Johnson), 870
Black Mencken, the. *See* Schuyler, George S.
Black Messiah movement, 369, 370, 371
*Black Moses* (Hayes), 747
Black Muslims, 986. *See also* Nation of Islam
Black Nationalism, 97, 219, 261, 432; and Cyril V. Briggs, 210; and Stokely Carmichael, 306; and Albert Buford Cleage, Jr., 369-371; and Alexander Crummell, 435-437; and Henrietta Vinton Davis, 459-460; and Martin Robison Delany, 481-482; and Ralph Ellison, 550; and Marcus Garvey, 635-637, 1251; and hip-hop, 406; and Roy Innis, 817-818; and Malcolm X, 1024-1027; and Bayard Rustin, 1304; and George S. Schuyler, 1322; and Henry McNeal Turner, 1450; and Roy Wilkins, 1562
*Black No More* (Schuyler), 1322
Black Panther Party, 232, 1034, 1384; and Elaine Brown, 230-231; and H. Rap Brown, 233; and Ed Bullins, 261; and Stokely Carmichael, 306; and Eldridge Cleaver, 372-373; and Angela Davis, 448; and Lee Evans, 562; and James Forman, 603; and Huey P. Newton, 1108-1110; poetry about, 551; and Bobby Seale, 1328-1330; and Tupac Shakur, 1333-1334; and Cornel West, 1535
Black Patti, the. *See* Jones, Sissieretta
Black Patti Troubadours, 269, 902
Black Periodical Literature Project, 641
*Black Position, The* (magazine), 219
*Black Power* (Carmichael), 306
*Black Power and the American Myth* (Vivian), 1489

Black Power movement, 87, 841, 943; and Houston A. Baker, Jr., 77; and H. Rap Brown, 232-234; and Stokely Carmichael, 305-307; and Christian values, 412; and Eldridge Cleaver, 371-374; and George Clinton, 381; and James H. Cone, 411-412; and Angela Davis, 448-451; and Lee Evans, 562-563; and Addison Gayle, Jr., 645; and Samuel L. Jackson, 841; and Benjamin T. Jealous, 854; and Maulana Karenga, 923-925; and Malcolm X, 1027; and Huey P. Newton, 1108-1110; and A. Philip Randolph, 1230; and Ishmael Reed, 1238; and Betye Saar, 1307; and Bobby Seale, 1328-1330; and Archie Shepp, 1345; and August Wilson, 1588
*Black Reign* (Queen Latifah), 1222
*Black Religion* (Washington), 412
Black Second, 345
*Black Sports* (magazine), 707
Black Star Line, 459, 636-637
Black Strategy Center, 1489
Black Student Union, 659, 923
*Black Theology and Black Power* (Cone), 412
*Black Theology of Liberation, A* (Cone), 412
Black Thomas Edison, the. *See* Woods, Granville T.
*Black Thunder* (Bontemps), 189
Black Ty Cobb, the. *See* Bell, Cool Papa
*Black Unicorn, The* (Lorde), 998
*Black Unity* (Sanders), 1314
Black Venus. *See* Baker, Josephine
*Black Woman, The* (Bambara), 86
*Black Women Writers, 1950-1980* (Evans), 564
Blackbird of Harlem. *See* Mills, Florence
*Blackbirds* (musical), 1060, 1267
*Blackboard Jungle* (film), 1191-1192
Blackburn, Jack "Chappie," 999, 1491

Blackground Records, 1

*Blackman, The* (newspaper), 636

*Blacks, The* (play), 51, 286, 895, 1460

Blackwell, David Harold, 153-156

Blackwell, Edward, 156-157

Blackwell, Scrapper, 311

*Blade* films, 1387

Blagojevich, Rod, 272

Blair, Henry, 158-159

Blair, William, 409

*Blake* (Delany), 482

Blake, Eubie, 79, 159-161, 270

Blakey, Art, 162-163, 1260, 1346; and Jackie McLean, 1013. *See also* Jazz Messengers

Blalock, Alfred, 1427

Blalock-Taussig shunt procedure, 1427

*Blancs, Les* (play), 730

Bland, Bobby Blue, 163-164

Bland, James, 165-166

Blanton, Jimmy, 167-168

"Blaxploitation" films, 423, 465; and Jim Brown, 238; and Bernie Casey, 324; *Cotton Comes to Harlem*, 286; and Pam Grier, 694-695; spoofs of, 1286; and Melvin Van Peebles, 1482-1483

Blaze, Just, 852

Blazers, 222

*Blazing Saddles* (film), 110, 989

*Blessing the Boats* (Cliff), 379

Blige, Mary J., 168-169, 505, 852, 1217

*Blind Faith* (television movie), 1477

*Blind Man with a Pistol* (Himes), 771

Blind Tom. *See* Bethune, Blind Tom

Blood banking, 518-519

*Blood on the Fields* (Marsalis), 1033

*Bloodworth Orphans, The* (Forrest), 605

Bloom, Allan, 930

Blount, Herman Poole. *See* Sun Ra

Blow, Kurtis, 1350, 1354

Blow, Sam. *See* Scott, Dred

*Blow Up* (film), 725

Blue, Vida, 170-171

Blue Boy. *See* Bland, Bobby Blue

*Blue Chips* (film), 1135

Blue Devils, 109, 167, 461

Blue Flames, 227

Blue Note Records; and Dexter Gordon, 666; and Al Green, 686; and Johnny Griffin, 698; and Herbie Hancock, 725; and Jackie McLean, 1013; and Thelonious Monk, 1069; and Herbie Nichols, 1113; and Horace Silver, 1349; and McCoy Tyner, 1458

Blue Sky Records, 1526

Bluebelles, 954

Bluebird Records, 220, 434, 1071

*Blueprint, The* (Jay-Z), 1540

*Blues Book for Blue Black Magical Women, A* (Sanchez), 1308

*Blues Brothers, The* (film), 236, 285, 336, 616, 787

*Blues for Mr. Charlie* (play), 83

Blues Heaven Foundation, 501

*Blues Suite* (dance), 18

*Blues to the Bone* (James), 848

*Bluest Eye, The* (Morrison), 1080

Bluford, Guion, 171-173, 1115

*Blunted on Reality* (Fugees), 767, 855

Boas, Franz, 809

Bobo, Willie, 725

Bocchicchio, Felix, 1491

Bocelli, Andrea, 169

*Bodies of Water* (Cliff), 377

*Body and Soul* (1925 film), 1056, 1264

*Body and Soul* (1947 film), 968

*Bodyguard, The* (film), 799, 1107

Bogart, Humphrey, 468, 1492

Boghetti, Giuseppe, 48

Bojangles. *See* Robinson, Bill

*Bojangles* (television movie), 660, 775

Bolden, Buddy, 57

Bolden, Charles F., Jr., 173-174

Bolin, Jane Matilda, 175-177

*Bombing of Osage Avenue, The* (film), 87

Bonavena, Oscar, 27

Bond, Horace Mann, 177-179

Bond, Julian, 179-181, 603

Bonds, Barry, 182-184, 1047

Bonds, Bobby, 1047

Bonds, Margaret Allison, 185-186

Bonner, Marita, 186-187

Bontemps, Arna, 188-190, 441

"Boogie Chillen" (song), 786-787

Boomerang, 1091

*Boomerang* (film), 69, 208

Boone, Herman, 1517

*Bopha!* (film), 624, 715

Boricua Popular Army, 780

Bork, Robert, 765

*Boseman and Lena* (play), 478

Bosh, Chris, 850

Boss of the Blues. *See* Turner, Big Joe

Boston, Ralph, 123, 190-192

Boston Celtics, 850, 994; and Chauncey Billups, 152; and Wilt Chamberlain, 327; and Kevin Garnett, 634; and Shaquille O'Neal, 1135; and Paul Pierce, 1181-1182; and Bill Russell, 994, 1298-1299

*Boston Guardian, The* (newspaper), 1439

Boston Massacre, 66-68

Boswell Sisters, 592

Boulanger, Nadia, 900

Bowart, Walter, 1238

Bowdoin, James, 716

Bowers, Sam, 331-332

Bowman, Sister Thea, 192-193

Boxers. *See* List of Entries by Category under Sports: Boxing

*Boy at the Window* (Dodson), 507

*Boy X Man* (play), 261

Boyar, Burt, 468

Boyar, Jane, 468

*Boycott* (film), 1621

Boyd, Evelyn. *See* Granville, Evelyn Boyd

Boyd, Julianne, 161

Boyer, Elisa, 416

Boykin, Otis, 193-194

*Boyz N the Hood* (film), 115, 663-664, 813, 1368

Boyz II Men, 69, 302, 715
Boz's Juba. *See* Juba, Master
BPP. *See* Black Panther Party
Brackett, Edward A., 980
Braddock, Jim, 1000
Bradford, Perry, 195-196
Bradley, Bill, 1536
Bradley, David, 196-197
Bradley, Ed, 198-199
Bradley, Mamie Till, 1432
Bradley, Tom, 200-202, 536, 1373
"Bradley Effect," 201
Brady, Mary Beattie, 1318
Braithwaite, William Stanley, 202-204
Braun, Carol E. Moseley, 204-206, 766, 907
Brawley, Benjamin, 203
Brawley, Tawana, 1338
Braxton, Anthony, 206-208
Braxton, Toni, 69, 131, 208-209
Breast Cancer Research Foundation, 1254
Brecht, Bertolt, 1336
Breckinridge, Frank, 107
Breedlove, Sarah. *See* Walker, Madam C. J.
Brenner, David, 1499
Brenston, Jackie, 1451
*Brian's Song* (television movie), 1565
Bridger, Jim, 134
Briggs, Bunny, 775
Briggs, Cyril V., 210-212
*Brilliant Corners* (Monk), 1069
Brimmer, Andrew Felton, 212-213
*Bring in 'da Noise, Bring in 'da Funk* (musical), 660, 1604
Britt, May, 468
Broadus, Charles "Doc," 600
Broadus, Cordozar Calvin, Jr. *See* Snoop Dogg
Brock, Lou, 213-215, 596, 757, 1136, 1586; and Cool Papa Bell, 139
Brock, Roslyn M., 180
Broglio, Ernie, 214
Bronx Cavaliers, 300
Bronze Venus. *See* Baker, Josephine

*Bronzeville Boys and Girls* (Brooks), 219
Brooke, Edward W., 215-217
Brooklyn Dodgers, 288-289, 374; and Jackie Robinson, 1272-1275; and Maury Wills, 1586. *See also* Los Angeles Dodgers
Brooks, Gwendolyn, 217-220, 805; and Haki R. Madhubuti, 1022-1023; poet laureateship, 517; Pulitzer Prize, 516; and Emmett Till, 1433
Brooks, Mel, 333, 775, 989
Brooks, Robert Calvin. *See* Bland, Bobby Blue
Brooks, Samuel I. *See* Schuyler, George S.
Broonzy, Big Bill, 220-221, 1002
Brother Ray. *See* Charles, Ray
Brotherhood of Sleeping Car Porters, 485, 1116, 1229-1230
*Brothers* (film), 324, 1411
*Brothers and Sisters* (Campbell), 291
Brown, Betye Irene. *See* Saar, Betye
Brown, Bobby, 69, 799
Brown, Charles, 222-223
Brown, Charlotte Hawkins, 223-225
Brown, Chris, 1255
Brown, Claude, 225-227
Brown, Clifford, 227-229, 1103, 1260
Brown, Cynthia Stokes, 366
Brown, Dorothy Lavinia, 229-230
Brown, Drew "Bundini," 612
Brown, Elaine, 230-231
Brown, George W., 154
Brown, H. Rap, 232-234, 841
Brown, James, 234-236, 381, 726; and Al Sharpton, 1337; and Jackie Wilson, 1593
Brown, James Willie, Jr. *See* Komunyakaa, Yusef
Brown, Jim, 237-239, 387, 458, 969, 1311
Brown, John, 140, 980, 1366, 1445
Brown, John. *See* Russwurm, John Brown

Brown, Lavinia, 827
Brown, Lawrence, 1264
Brown, Nicole, 1363
Brown, Oliver, 1038
Brown, Oscar, Jr., 218
Brown, Paul, 238
Brown, Ray, 239-241, 593
Brown, Ron, 241-242, 763
Brown, Ruth, 14
Brown, Sterling A., 154, 243-245, 1227
Brown, Tim, 245-246, 1313
Brown, Tony, 246-248
Brown, Willie, 249-251
Brown Bomber. *See* Louis, Joe
*Brown Girl, Brownstones* (Marshall), 1036
*Brown v. Board of Education*, 82, 117, 364, 373, 382, 567, 1347, 1561; and John Hope Franklin, 619; and Charles Hamilton Houston, 797; and Zora Neale Hurston, 810; and Thurgood Marshall, 1037-1038; and Pauli Murray, 1096-1097; and Spottswood W. Robinson III, 1283
*Brownie's Book* (magazine), 582
*Brownsville Affair, The* (play), 625
Brownsville, Texas, incident, 6, 625
Bruce, Blanche Kelso, 251-253
Bruce, John E., 254-255
Bruce, Richard, 1399
Bryant, Antonio, 255-256
Bryant, Carolyn, 1432
Bryant, Joe, 256, 258
Bryant, Kobe, 256-258, 850, 1134
Bryant, Roy, 1432
Bryant, Willie, 315
BSL. *See* Black Star Line
*Bubblin' Brown Sugar* (musical), 401
Buchanan, Charles, 284
Buchanan, James, 146
*Buck and the Preacher* (film), 137, 1191
Bucketeers basketball team, 973
Buckeye Bullet, the. *See* Owens, Jesse

Buddah Records, 947, 1243

Buddhism, 788, 1346; and Romare Bearden, 127

Bufano, Beniamino, 886

Buffalo Bills, 1144, 1361-1363

Buffalo Soldiers, 454, 610, 659

Buhaina, Abdullah ibn. *See* Blakey, Art

Bukowski, Charles, 399

Bull-Dogger, the. *See* Pickett, Bill

Bullard, Eugene Jacques, 259-260

Bullet Bob. *See* Hayes, Bob

Bullins, Ed, 260-262

Bullock, Anna Mae. *See* Turner, Tina

Bumbry, Grace, 902

Bunche, Ralph, 262-265, 363

Burke, Solomon, 265-266

Burke, Valenza Pauline. *See* Marshall, Paule

Burke, Yvonne Brathwaite, 267-268, 764

Burleigh, Harry T., 268-271, 902

Burns, Isaac. *See* Murphy, Isaac Burns

Burns, Jesse Louis. *See* Jackson, Jesse

Burns, Ken, 433, 1033, 1136

Burns, Lugenia, 792

Burns, Tommy, 866

Burrell, Stanley Kirk. *See* Hammer, M. C.

Burris, Roland, 271-273

Burroughs, Nannie Helen, 273-275

Burton, LeVar, 275-277

Burton, Wayne, 1378

Bush, George H. W., 828, 1420

Bush, George W., 1123; and John Conyers, Jr., 414; and Eric Holder, 780; and Colin Powell, 1200; and Condoleezza Rice, 1246; and Larry D. Thompson, 1429; and Tina Turner, 1457; and Neil deGrasse Tyson, 1464; and Kanye West, 1540

Bush, George Washington, 277-279

*Bustin' Loose* (film), 1461

Butler, Octavia E., 279-281

Butterbeans and Susie, 1003

*Butterfly* (Carey), 302

Buttrick, Wallace, 792

Byrd, Bobby, 234

Byrd, Donald, 725

Byrd, Henry Roeland. *See* Professor Longhair

*Cabin in the Sky* (film), 795

Cable News Network, 7, 1340, 1573; and James Earl Jones, 896

Cacchione, Pete, 452

Cade, Miltona Mirkin. *See* Bambara, Toni Cade

*Cadillac Records* (film), 326, 949, 1621

Cadillacs, 402

Café Society, 795-796, 1208, 1448, 1575

Cakewalk, 270, 870, 1060, 1563; and Bert Williams, 1564

Calhoun, Arthur, 748

Calhoun, Lee, 282-283

California Angels, 301; and Bo Jackson, 824, 839; and Charley Pride, 1206

*California Eagle, The* (newspaper), 113

California gold rush, 133, 980

Callender, Red, 1062

Calloway, Cab, 283-285, 401, 655, 776

*Callus on My Soul* (Gregory), 690

Calypso music, 51, 1289; and Harry Belafonte, 136-137; and Louis Farrakhan, 575

Cambridge, Godfrey, 51, 286-288

Cameo-Parkway Records, 347

Caminiti, Ken, 183

Campanella, Roy, 288-290

Campanis, Al, 1551

Campbell, Bebe Moore, 290-292

Campbell, E. Simms, 292-293

Campbell, Earl, 294-295, 493

Campbell, Ernestine, 991

Campbell, Milton, 882

Campbell, Robert, 482

Camus, Albert, 1097

Canadian Football League, 31-33, 1403, 1528

Candid Records, 1344

*Cane* (Toomer), 1436-1437

Canegata, Leonard Lionel Cornelius. *See* Lee, Canada

Cannon, Nick, 303

Cantor, Eddie, 467

Capitol Records; and Nat King Cole, 391-393; and Miles Davis, 462; and Darius Rucker, 1294; and Tina Turner, 1457

*Captain EO* (film), 836

Cara, Irene, 296-297

*Carasmatic* (Cara), 296

Carbo, John Paul "Frankie," 987

Cardozo, Francis Lewis, 298-299

Carew, Rod, 300-301

Carey, Gordon, 574

Carey, Mariah, 301-303, 715

Carey, Mathew, 37

*Caribe Gold* (film), 1460

Carlos, John, 303-304, 562, 601, 1383-1384, 1466

*Carmen Jones* (film), 72, 137, 313, 443-444

*Carmen Jones* (musical), 1175

Carmichael, Ralph, 431

Carmichael, Stokely, 305-307, 603, 719, 841, 983, 1230

Carnegie, Andrew, 1514

Carnegie Hall, 308, 559; and Josephine Baker, 80; and Big Bill Broonzy, 220; and Honi Coles and Cholly Atkins, 401; and Billy Eckstine, 539; and Billie Holiday, 783; and Mahalia Jackson, 832; and Odetta, 1126; "Spirituals to Swing" concert, 1448

Carnera, Primo, 1000, 1492

Carney, Harry, 308-309

Carney, William H., 309-310

*Carnival of Rhythm* (film), 531

*Carolinian, The* (newspaper), 341

Carr, Leroy, 311-312

Carroll, Diahann, 312-314, 1191

"Carry Me Back to Old Virginny" (song), 166

Carson, Johnny, 714

Carter, Benny, 314-316, 777, 1068; and George Russell, 1300

Carter, Betty, 355

Carter, Jimmy, 827, 1130; and Yvonne Brathwaite Burke, 267; and John Conyers, Jr., 414; and Patricia Roberts Harris, 738; inauguration, 616; and Barbara Jordan, 906; Olympic boycott, 65, 1084, 1609; and John Brooks Slaughter, 1370; and Andrew Young, 1634

Carter, Nell, 316-317

Carter, Rubin, 1516

Carter, Stephen L., 318-319

Carter, Vince, 1181

Caruso, Enrico, 748, 1502

Carver, George Washington, 319-322; bust of, 108

Cary, Lorene, 322-323

*Casbah* (film), 945

Casey, Bernie, 324-325

*Cast the First Stone* (Himes), 771

Castle, Irene, 559

Castle, Vernon, 559

Caston, Leonard "Baby Doo," 501

Castro, Fidel, 306, 828, 1025

*Cat on a Hot Tin Roof* (play), 896, 1234

*Catherine Carmier* (Gaines), 630

Catholic Church. *See* Roman Catholic Church

Catlett, Sid, 315

Cato, Gavin, 1339

Cedric the Entertainer, 325-327

Centennial Exposition, 94-95, 981

Center for the Study of Urban Inequality, 1594

Centers for Disease Control and Prevention, 1316

Central Intelligence Agency, 1201, 1626

Chain gangs, 1304

*Challenge, The* (magazine), 1538

*Challenger* space shuttle, 172, 174, 691, 1018

Chamberlain, Wilt, 9, 258, 327-330, 1299; and Bill Russell, 1299

Chambers, Paul, 725

*Chambers v. Florida*, 1037

Chaney, Don, 745

Chaney, James, 330-332

*Chaneysville Incident, The* (Bradley), 197

*Change* (Ringgold), 1259

Chapman, Traci, 445

Chappelle, Dave, 333-334, 1215

*Chappelle's Show* (television program), 334

Charles, Ezzard, 334-335, 1001, 1492

Charles, Ray, 118, 265, 336-338, 612, 899; and Edward Blackwell, 156; and Sugar Ray Leonard, 974

Charles, Suzette, 338-339

Charleston, Oscar, 139

*Charleston Independent, The* (newspaper), 483

"Charleston Rag" (song), 160

Charlotte Bobcats; and Robert L. Johnson, 885; and Michael Jordan, 911

Charlotte Hornets, 885

Chase-Riboud, Barbara, 339-341, 1259

Chatham County Crusade for Voters, 1571

Chattanooga White Sox, 1148

Chavez, Hugo, 828

Chavis, Benjamin, 341-342

Che-Lumumba Club, 448

Cheadle, Don, 343-344, 1621

Cheatham, Doc, 396

Cheatham, Henry Plummer, 344-346

*Check and Double Check* (film), 546

Checker, Chubby, 347-349

Cheek, James E., 349-350

Cheeks, Maurice, 555

Cheikh Anta Diop International Conference, 61-62

Chenault, Kenneth, 351-353

Cheney, Dick, 1200

Cherry, Don, 157, 1289, 1314

Chesnutt, Charles Waddell, 353-355

Chess, Leonard, 142, 495, 992, 1525

Chess, Phil, 142

Chess Records; and Chuck Berry, 142; and Bo Diddley, 495; and Willie Dixon, 501; and Aretha Franklin, 614; and Little Walter, 993; and Muddy Waters, 1525

Chestnut, Cyrus, 355-356

Chicago; aldermen, 488-489; Black Arts Festival, 900; Democratic National Convention of 1968, 1329; founding of, 1188-1189; Grand Terrace, 773; Human Relations Commission, 1225; mayors, 272, 689, 1122, 1225, 1518-1521; Moorish Science Temple, 29; Palmer House, 185; riots, 858, 862; sit-ins, 204, 573; Sunset Club, 773; Trinity United Church of Christ, 1125, 1622; World's Fair, 524, 903

*Chicago* (film), 1222

Chicago Bears, 1343; and Walter Payton, 1168-1169; and Mike Singletary, 1364

Chicago Black Hawks, 1194

Chicago Bulls, 257, 329, 1028; and Michael Jordan, 909-912; and Scottie Pippen, 1186-1187

*Chicago Conservator, The* (newspaper), 1534

Chicago Cubs; and Dusty Baker, 74; and Ernie Banks, 88-89; and Lou Brock, 214; and Buck O'Neil, 89, 1136; and Sammy Sosa, 183

*Chicago Defender, The* (band), 776

*Chicago Defender, The* (newspaper), 217, 390, 395, 586, 602, 1432; and Robert S. Abbott, 5-8; band, 723; and Romare Bearden, 127; and Langston Hughes, 806

Chicago Open Housing Movement, 151, 965

Chicago White Sox; and Larry Doby, 503; and Bo Jackson, 823-824; and Michael Jordan, 911; and Frank Thomas, 1423-1424

*Chico and the Man* (television program), 429-430

Child Development Group of Mississippi, 718

*Child of Myself* (Parker), 1154

*Children of Ham, The* (Brown), 225-226

Children's Defense Fund, 540-541

Childress, Alice, 356-358

Childress, Alvin, 356

*Chinaberry* (Fauset), 583

Chisholm, Shirley, 359-361, 486, 574, 1232

Chivington, John, 133

*Chocolate City* (Clinton), 381

*Chocolate Dandies* (musical), 79

Chocolate Thunder. *See* Dawkins, Darryl

*Chosen Place, the Timeless People, The* (Marshall), 1036

Christian, Charlie, 1152

"Christlam," 373

*Christmas Is a Special Day* (Domino), 509

Christopher, Mary. *See* West, Dorothy

*Chronic, The* (Dr. Dre), 1389

Chudd, Lew, 508

Church, Frederick, 95

Church, Mary Eliza. *See* Terrell, Mary Church

Churchill, Winston, 1156

Cincinnati Bengals, 255, 1144, 1384

Cincinnati Reds, 695; and Dusty Baker, 74; and Curt Flood, 596; and Ken Griffey, Jr., 696; and Frank Robinson, 1271; and Deion Sanders, 1312

Cincinnati Royals, 1262

Cinque, Joseph, 361-363

Citizenship schools, 365-367, 1571-1572

*City of Angels* (television program), 1471

Civil Rights Act of 1957, 1067

Civil Rights Act of 1964, 574, 738, 1096, 1230, 1420, 1633; and Fred Shuttlesworth, 1347

Civil Rights movement; and Hank Aaron, 3; and Ralph David Abernathy, 11-13; and James

Bevel, 150-151; and Charles Evers, 565; and Lena Horne, 795; and Mahalia Jackson, 832; and James Meredith, 1051; and Rosa Parks, 1157; photographs of, 1602; and Frank Robinson, 1271

Civil War, 141; and James Presley Ball, 85; and Edward Mitchell Bannister, 94; Battle of Manassas, 146; Battle of Mobile Bay, 966; and Blind Tom Bethune, 146; and William H. Carney, 309-310; and George Washington Carver, 319; and Martin Robison Delany, 482; and Frederick Douglass, 514, 966; and Charlotte L. Forten Grimké, 704; and Lewis Howard Latimer, 959; and John Lawson, 966-967; and P. B. S. Pinchback, 1184; and Hiram Rhoades Revels, 1242; and Benjamin Singleton, 1366; and Robert Smalls, 1371-1372; studies of, 1219; and James Monroe Trotter, 1439; and Sojourner Truth, 1442; and Harriet Tubman, 1445; and Henry McNeal Turner, 1450

Civilian Conservation Corps; and Oscar DePriest, 488; and Gordon Parks, Sr., 1155; and Professor Longhair, 1212

*Claiming an Identity They Taught Me to Despise* (Cliff), 377

Clapton, Eric, 70, 143, 937

Clark, Dick, 347

Clark, Jim, 1489

Clark, Kenneth, 363-365

Clark, Septima Poinsette, 365-367, 1571

Clarke, John Henrik, 367-369, 857

Clarke, Kenny, 1103, 1260

Classic Quartet, 1458

*Claudine* (film), 313

Clay, Cassius, Jr. *See* Ali, Muhammad

Clay, William L., Sr., 1278

Cleage, Albert Buford, Jr., 369-371

Cleaver, Eldridge, 231, 371-374, 603, 645, 1329

Clef Club, 559

Clemens, Doug, 214

Clement, Jack, 1206

Clemente, Roberto, 374-376, 651

Cleveland, James, 616

Cleveland Association of Colored Men, 1076

Cleveland Browns, 237-238, 458; and Antonio Bryant, 255

*Cleveland Call, The* (newspaper), 1076

Cleveland Cavaliers, 849-850, 1475, 1559

Cleveland Cubs, 1149

Cleveland Indians; and Larry Doby, 503; and Satchel Paige, 1150; and Frank Robinson, 1271-1272

Cliff, Michelle, 377-378

Clifton, Lucille, 378-379, 564

Clifton, Nat "Sweetwater," 994

Cline, Sir Rodney. *See* Carew, Rod

Clinton, Bill, 753, 828; and Maya Angelou, 52; and Carol E. Moseley Braun, 205; and Andrew Felton Brimmer, 212; and Shirley Chisholm, 360; and John Conyers, Jr., 414; and Joycelyn Elders, 544; and Mike Espy, 557; and James Farmer, 574; and William H. Gray III, 683; and Arsenio Hall, 715; and Alexis Herman, 763; and Eric Holder, 779-780; and Gwen Ifill, 814; inauguration, 336, 616; and Sheila Jackson Lee, 845; and Vernon Jordan, 913; and Walter Mosley, 1086; and Hazel R. O'Leary, 1131; and Rosa Parks, 1158; and Deval Patrick, 1162; and Togo West, 1542

Clinton, George, 380-381, 1389

Clinton, Hillary Rodham, 205, 845, 1122

Clouds of Joy, 1575

Clown Prince of Basketball. *See* Lemon, Meadowlark

Clyburn, James E., 382-384

CNN. *See* Cable News Network

Coachman, Alice, 384-385

Coalition of American Public Employees, 574

Cobra Records, 501, 1072

Coburn, Tom, 1122

Cochran, Johnnie, 386-388, 1338, 1363

*Coffy* (film), 694

COINTELPRO. *See* Federal Bureau of Investigation, counterintelligence program

Coker, Abner, 875

Coker, Daniel, 388-390, 875

Colbert, Claudette, 129

Cold War, 963

Cole, Bob, 869

Cole, Nat King, 390-393, 415, 539

Cole, Natalie, 392-394

Coleman, Bessie, 260, 394-396

Coleman, Denardo, 398, 420-421

Coleman, Emmett. *See* Reed, Ishmael

Coleman, Katherine. *See* Johnson, Katherine G.

Coleman, Ornette, 156-157, 396-398, 410, 420; and Alvin Batiste, 118; and Edward Blackwell, 156; and Pharoah Sanders, 1314

Coleman, Wanda, 399-400

Coles, Honi, 400-402

*Colgate Comedy Hour, The* (television program), 467

*College Dropout, The* (West), 1540

Collegians, 15, 1110

Collins, Bootsy, 69

Collins, Marva, 403-405

Collins, Patricia Hill, 405-406

Colomby, Harry, 1070

*Color* (Cullen), 440

*Color Purple, The* (film), 431, 590, 659, 662, 901, 1494, 1598

*Color Purple, The* (musical), 1494

*Color Purple, The* (Walker), 1494

Colorado Rockies, 1551

*Colored American Magazine*, 202, 702

*Colored Museum, The* (play), 1603

Colored People's Constitutional Convention, 299, 1372

Colored Vaudeville Benevolent Association, 195

*Colored Woman in a White World, A* (Taylor), 1417

Colored Women's Democratic League, 127

Colored Women's League, 704

Coltrane, Alice, 407-408, 410

Coltrane, John, 397, 409-411; and Cannonball Adderley, 17; and Alvin Batiste, 118; and Alice Coltrane, 407; and Miles Davis, 461-462; and Michael S. Harper, 734; and Pharoah Sanders, 1314; and Archie Shepp, 1344; and Sonny Stitt, 1401; and McCoy Tyner, 1458

Columbia Records, 932; and Mariah Carey, 302; and Miles Davis, 461; and Destiny's Child, 948; and 50 Cent, 588-589; and Aretha Franklin, 615; and Marvin Gaye, 644; and Dexter Gordon, 666; and Herbie Hancock, 726; and W. C. Handy, 727; and Billie Holiday, 782; and Mahalia Jackson, 832; and Thelonious Monk, 1070; and Russell Simmons, 1355; and Bessie Smith, 1378; and Henry Threadgill, 1431; and Leslie Uggams, 1469

*Columbia* space shuttle, 173

Combahee River Collective, 1376

Combs, Sean "Puffy." *See* Puff Daddy

*Come Home Early, Child* (Dodson), 507

*Come On, People* (Cosby), 423

*Comedy* (Fauset), 583

Comer, James P., 1195

*Comic Relief* (television program), 333

*Comin' Uptown* (musical), 774

*Coming to America* (film), 663, 714-715, 896, 1091

Commission on Civil Rights, U.S., 1283

Commission on Immigration Reform, 906

Commission on Interracial Cooperation, 863; and John Hope, 792. *See also* Rosenwald Fund

Commission on Research in Black Education, 769

Committee on Political and Civil Rights, President's, 1096

Commodore Records, 782

Commodores, 1252-1254

*Commonwealth of Virginia v. George Crawford*, 797

*Commonwealth v. Jennison*, 716

Communism; and African Blood Brotherhood, 211; and Amiri Baraka, 96; and Cyril V. Briggs, 210-212; and Che-Lumumba Club, 448; and Angela Davis, 448-451; and Benjamin J. Davis, 451-452; and Ralph Ellison, 548; and Langston Hughes, 806; and Claude McKay, 1011; and A. Philip Randolph, 1229; and Paul Robeson, 1265; and Bayard Rustin, 1303; and Robert Franklin Williams, 1578; and Workers Party of America, 211; and Richard Wright, 1625-1627

Community Self-Determination Act of 1968, 818

Concerned Black Men, 779

*Conch* (online magazine), 1239

*Condition, Elevation, Emigration, and Destiny of the Colored People of the United States, Politically Considered, The* (Delany), 482

Cone, James H., 411-413, 1451

Confederate flag controversies, 205, 263, 1294

Confederate States of America, 146, 1371

Conference of Church Workers Among Colored People, 436

*Confession Stone, The* (Dodson), 507

*Confessions* (Usher), 1474

*Confessions of Nat Turner* (Turner), 1454
*Confessions of Nat Turner, The* (Styron), 1052
Congress of Racial Equality, 574, 1395; and James Baldwin, 83; and Stokely Carmichael, 305; and James Chaney, 330; and Benjamin Chavis, 341; and James L. Farmer, Jr., 573-575; and James Forman, 603; and Roy Innis, 817-819; and James Lawson, 964; and John Robert Lewis, 982; and Floyd Patterson, 1164; and Bayard Rustin, 1303; and Sonia Sanchez, 1308; and C. T. Vivian, 1489
Congressional Black Caucus, 205, 360, 1195, 1278, 1524; and Yvonne Brathwaite Burke, 267; and James E. Clyburn, 382-383; and John Conyers, Jr., 413; and Ron Dellums, 486; and Jesse Jackson, Jr., 829-830; and Kweisi Mfume, 1054; and Charles Rangel, 1232
Congressional Medal of Honor; William H. Carney, 310; John Fox, 610; John Lawson, 966
*Conjure Woman, The* (Chesnutt), 354
Conley, Arthur, 265
*Conquest* (Micheaux), 1055
Conroy, Jack, 189
*Constab Ballads* (McKay), 1010
*Content of Our Character, The* (Steele), 1395
Continental Basketball Association, 1139, 1426
*Control* (Jackson), 825
Conyers, John, Jr., 413-415
Cooder, Ry, 1410
Cook, Alicia Augello. *See* Keys, Alicia
Cook, Mercer, 243
Cook, Will Marion, 185, 270
Cook County Democratic Committee, 1518
Cooke, Sam, 265, 415-417, 614, 1019

Cookman Institute, 149, 1228
Cooks, Patricia. *See* Parker, Pat
"Cool jazz," 547, 1061, 1063; and Miles Davis, 462
Coolidge, Calvin, 149, 460, 636
Cooper, Chuck, 994
Cooper, George W., 1266
Cooper, J. California, 417-418
Coordinating Council of Community Organizations, 1224
*Copacetic* (Komunyakaa), 950
Copland, Aaron, 1400
Copper, Anna Julian, 273
*Copper Sun* (Cullen), 440
Coppola, Francis Ford, 836
CORE. *See* Congress of Racial Equality
Corea, Chick, 206, 1401, 1458
*Corner, The* (television program), 535
Cornish, James, 1568
Cornish, Sam, 418-419
Cornish, Samuel, 1302
*Correct Thing to Do, to Say, and to Wear, The* (Brown), 224
*Corregidora* (Jones), 893
Cortez, Diego, 111
Cortez, Jayne, 397, 420-422
Cosby, Bill, 422-424, 1234; and Herbie Hancock, 726; and Samuel L. Jackson, 840; and Bernie Mac, 1005; and Alvin Francis Poussaint, 1195; and Richard Pryor, 1214
*Cosby* (television program), 423
*Cosby Show, The* (television program), 423-424; and Angela Bassett, 115; and Samuel L. Jackson, 840; and Alicia Keys, 933; and Audra McDonald, 1009; and Alvin Francis Poussaint, 1195; and Phylicia Rashad, 1234; and Blair Underwood, 1470
Cosell, Howard, 785
Costa, Dino, 1040
Cotton Club, 546; and Josephine Baker, 79; and Cab Calloway, 284; and Duke Ellington, 1132; and Lena Horne, 794; and

Moms Mabley, 1003; and Nicholas Brothers, 1110; rivals of, 1505; and Bill Robinson, 1268
*Cotton Club, The* (film), 401, 775, 1403, 1480
Cotton Club Boys, 401
*Cotton Comes to Harlem* (film), 464, 613, 989
Cotton Pickers, 315
Cotton States and International Exposition, 1514
Council of Independent Black Institutions, 769
Council on Interracial Books for Children, 1098, 1415
*Countdown at Kusini* (film), 465
Counts, Dorothy, 83
Courlander, Harold, 712
Covey, James, 362
*Cowboys and Colored People* (Wilson), 1590
Cowlings, Al, 1362
Cox, Billy, 759
Craft, Ellen, 425-426
Craft, William, 425-426
*Crash* (film), 344
Crawford, Joan, 1007
"Crazy Blues" (song), 195
Cream, Arnold Raymond. *See* Walcott, Jersey Joe
Crenshaw, Kimberlé Williams, 426-427
*Creole Giselle* (ballet), 1065
Creolettes, 847
Crichlow, Ernest, 1318
*Crisis, The* (magazine), 7, 175, 188, 440, 512, 582, 957, 1320; and W. E. B. Du Bois, 521; and Roy Wilkins, 1561
Critchlow, Cyril, 637
Critical race theory, 426-427, 669
Critical Resistance, 450
Cronkite, Walter, 1340
Crooks, Lesane Parish. *See* Shakur, Tupac
Crosby, Bing, 723, 777
*Crossings* (Hancock), 726
Crothers, Scatman, 428-430
Crouch, Andraé, 430-431

Crouch, Stanley, 432-433, 1095
Crown Heights Riots, 498, 1339; in literature, 1375
Crudup, Big Boy, 433-434
Crummell, Alexander, 435-437, 482
Crump, E. H., 727
Crusade for Citizenship, 76
*Crusader, The* (magazine), 210-211
Cruz, Harold, 368
Cruz, Rolando, 272
*Cry Freedom* (film), 1516
*Cry, the Beloved Country* (1951 film), 968, 1191
*Cry, the Beloved Country* (1996 film), 896
*Cry, the Beloved Country* (musical), 1176
Cuffe, Paul, 437-439
Cullen, Countée, 189, 203, 439-441, 1318; and Jessie Redmon Fauset, 583; and William Grant Still, 1399
Culp, Robert, 422
Curb, Mike, 201
Cuthbert, Julie, 491
Cy Young Award; Vida Blue, 170-171; Bob Gibson, 651

*Daddy Was a Number Runner* (Meriwether), 1052
Daguerreotype, 84-85
*Dahomean: An Historical Novel, The* (Yerby), 1629
*Daily Worker, The* (newspaper), 211, 451, 1578, 1625
Daley, Richard J., 272, 1224, 1519
Daley, Richard M., 1125, 1520
Dallas Cowboys; and Antonio Bryant, 255; and Bob Hayes, 743-744; and Terrell Owens, 1143; and Deion Sanders, 1313; and Emmitt Smith, 1379-1380
D'Amato, Cus, 988, 1163, 1462-1463
Dameron, Tadd, 461, 665, 1103
*Damned of the Earth, The* (Fanon), 669
Dance Theatre of Harlem, 1064-1065

*Dancing with the Stars* (television program); Toni Braxton, 209; Irene Cara, 297; Macy Gray, 682; Evander Holyfield, 785; Jerry Rice, 1249; Emmitt Smith, 1380
Dandridge, Dorothy, 137, 144, 442-444
Danforth, John C., 1419
*Dangerous* (Jackson), 837
*Daniel in the Lions' Den* (Tanner), 1412
Daniels, Lee, 169
Darden Restaurants, 1137-1139
Darfur, 344, 659, 845
Darin, Bobby, 777
Darrow, Clarence, 488
Dash, Julie, 445-446
Da Silva, Howard, 465
Daughters of the American Revolution, 49
*Daughters of the Dust* (film), 445
*Dave Chappelle's Block Party* (film), 334
Davenport, Willie, 446-447
David, Hal, 1510
Davis, Al, 35, 1342
Davis, Alice Coachman. *See* Coachman, Alice
Davis, Angela, 324, 448-451, 514, 1411
Davis, Arthur P., 243
Davis, Benjamin J., 451-452
Davis, Benjamin O., Sr., 452-456; and James A. Emanuel, 551
Davis, Benjamin O., Jr., 454-457
Davis, Bette, 1007
Davis, Carl, 1592
Davis, Clive, 933
Davis, Eddie "Lockjaw," 698, 1401, 1567
Davis, Ernie, 457-459
Davis, Henrietta Vinton, 459-460
Davis, Jack, 282
Davis, Mary Lee, 382
Davis, Miles, 461-463; and Cannonball Adderley, 16-17; and Jimmy Blanton, 167; and John Coltrane, 409-410; and Herbie Hancock, 725; and John

Lee Hooker, 787; and Jackie McLean, 1013; and Charlie Parker, 1152; and Max Roach, 1260; and Sonny Rollins, 1289; and Wayne Shorter, 1346; and Sonny Stitt, 1402; and Cicely Tyson, 1461
Davis, Ossie, 464-466, 478, 970
Davis, Roquel "Billy," 673, 1592
Davis, Sammy, Jr., 343, 466-469, 775
Davis, Shani, 469-470
Davis, Viola, 471-472
Dawes, Dominique, 472-474
Dawkins, Darryl, 474-475
Dawson, William, 173, 185, 1197
*Day, The* (Babyface), 70
*Days of Our Lives* (television program), 399
Daytona Educational and Industrial Training School for Negro Girls, 149. *See also* Bethune-Cookman University
Dean, Dizzy, 1149
Death Row Records, 505, 1334, 1389
DeBarge, James, 825
Debs, Eugene V., 804
Debut Records, 1062
DeCarava, Roy, 476-477
Decathlon, 882-883
Decatur, Stephen, 606
Decca Records, 56-57, 467-468, 783, 831
*Decision, The* (television program), 850
*Declining Significance of Race, The* (play), 1594
Dee, Ruby, 464-465, 478-479, 970
Deele, 69
*Deep Cover* (film), 1389
"Deep River" (song), 270
Dees, Morris, 181
Def, Mos, 1621
*Def Comedy Jam* (television program), 325, 333, 1005; and Russell Simmons, 1355
Def Jam Recordings, 342, 853, 952-953, 1255; and Jay-Z, 852; and Russell Simmons, 1354-1355

*Def Poetry Jam* (television program), 1355

*Defiant Ones, The* (film), 499, 1191

DeFranco, Buddy, 162, 777

DeFrantz, Anita, 479-481

DeGaetano, Suzette. *See* Charles, Suzette

DeKnight, Freda, 1460

Delany, Martin Robison, 481-484

Delany, Samuel R., 102, 280, 484-485

De Lavallade, Carmen, 18

Dellums, Ron, 485-487

Delta Sigma Theta sorority, 569, 627, 737, 753, 763, 1330

De Mille, Agnes, 401

Democratic Party; 1964 National Convention, 76, 717-719, 738; 1968 National Convention, 180, 616, 719, 1329; 1972 National Convention, 267, 360, 1523; 1988 National Convention, 1634; 1992 National Convention, 763, 906; 2004 National Convention, 1122, 1125; 2008 National Convention, 803, 1122; and Julian Bond, 180; and Carol E. Moseley Braun, 205; and Ron Brown, 241-242, 249-251; and Yvonne Brathwaite Burke, 267; and Shirley Chisholm, 359-360; and James E. Clyburn, 382-383; and John Conyers, Jr., 413; and Ron Dellums, 486; and David Dinkins, 498; and Mervyn Dymally, 536; and Mike Espy, 556; and Myrlie Evers-Williams, 569; and Earl G. Graves, Sr., 679; and William H. Gray III, 683; and Patricia Roberts Harris, 738; and Alexis Herman, 763; and Roy Innis, 818; and Jesse Jackson, 828; and Jesse Jackson, Jr., 830; and Sheila Jackson Lee, 844; and Barbara Jordan, 905-906; and Kweisi Mfume, 1054; and E. D. Nixon, 1116; and Barack Obama, 1121-1124; and David Paterson, 1160; and Deval

Patrick, 1162; and Adam Clayton Powell, Jr., 1196-1198; and Charles Rangel, 1231-1233; and Condoleezza Rice, 1246; and Al Sharpton, 1337-1340; and C. DeLores Tucker, 1447; and Alexander Walters, 345, 1509; and Harold Washington, 1518-1521; and Maxine Waters, 1523; and Robert C. Weaver, 1530; and L. Douglas Wilder, 1557-1558

Dempsey, Jack, 1000

Denver Nuggets, 152-153, 820, 1040

DePasse, Suzanne, 1252

Deppe, Lois, 772

DePriest, Jessie, 488

DePriest, Oscar, 455, 488-489

Derby Records, 416

Desdune, Clarence, 1071

Destiny's Child, 948

Detroit; mayors, 1635-1637; riots, 371, 412

*Detroit Black Journal* (television program), 667

Detroit Lions, 1172, 1310

Detroit Pistons, 1186; and Chauncey Billups, 152-153; and Darryl Dawkins, 475; and Allen Iverson, 820; and Earl Lloyd, 994; and Isiah Thomas, 1425-1426

Detroit Tigers, 503

Dett, R. Nathaniel, 489-491, 1497

Deukmejian, George, 201

Devers, Gail, 491-493

*Devil in a Blue Dress* (film), 343

*Devil in a Blue Dress, The* (Mosley), 1086

*Devil's Music: The Life and Blues of Bessie Smith, The* (play), 1378

Devine, Bing, 214, 650

Devine, Loretta, 1015

Dexter Avenue Baptist Church, Atlanta, Georgia, 12, 939, 941, 1275

*Dhalgren* (Delany), 484

Diallo, Amadou, 1339

Diamond, Bill, 508

*Diary of a Mad Black Woman* (film), 1173, 1461

*Diary of a Mad Black Woman* (play), 1173

*Diary of Alicia Keys, The* (Keys), 933

*Diary of an African Nun* (film), 445

Dickens, Charles, 916

Dickerson, Carroll, 773

Dickerson, Eric, 493-494

Dickinson, Angie, 468

Diddley, Bo, 494-496, 824

Diddy. *See* Puff Daddy

*Die Hard with a Vengeance* (film), 841

*Die Nigger Die!* (Brown), 233

*Dien Cai Dau* (Komunyakaa), 950

Dietrich, Marlene, 1511

*Different Drummer, A* (Kelley), 927-928

*Different Kind of Christmas, A* (Haley), 713

*Diff'rent Strokes* (television program), 825, 1549

Diggs, Charles C., Jr., 1278

Digital Underground, 1333

Dillard University, 177, 1219, 1497, 1634

Dillinger, Daz, 1389-1390

Dinkins, David, 497-499, 818

Diop, Cheikh Anta, 62

*Dirty Dancing* (film), 401

*Dirty Dozen, The* (film), 238

*Dirty Mind* (Prince), 1211

Disc jockeys. *See* Radio disc jockeys

Disciples, 431

Disco music, 336, 381, 836, 945, 1233, 1351; and Donna Summer, 1405-1407

*Discovery* space shuttle, 172, 691

*Dissent* magazine, 226

*Distortion* (Simmons), 1352

Ditka, Mike, 1169

*Divine Comedy* (play), 507

*Divine Days* (Forrest), 605

Dixie Duo, 160

*Dixie Showboat* (television program), 429

Dixie Steppers, 78
*Dixie to Broadway* (musical), 1060
Dixon, Ivan, 499-500
Dixon, Sharon Pratt, 105
Dixon, Willie, 434, 500-502, 993, 1071, 1525
*Do the Right Thing* (film), 465, 969
*Do You!* (Russell), 1355
Doby, Larry, 502-504, 1271
*Doctor Dolittle* (film), 1092
*Dr. Dolittle 2* (film), 933
Dr. Dre, 504-506, 812, 1389; and George Clinton, 381; and Snoop Dogg, 1389
Doctor Funkenstein. *See* Clinton, George
Dr. J. *See* Erving, Julius
Dr. John, 266
*Doctrines and Disciplines of the African Methodist Episcopal Church* (Allen), 37
Dodson, Owen, 441, 506-507
*Does Your House Have Lions?* (Sanchez), 1308
Dogg, Snoop, 387
*Doggystyle* (Snoop Dogg), 505, 1389
Doggystyle Records, 1389
Doll League, 129
Dolphy, Eric, 157, 207, 1062
Domino, Fats, 508-510
Dominoes. *See* Ward, Billy
"Don't Be Cruel" (song), 69
*Don't Knock the Rock* (film), 990
*Don't Look Back* (Hooker), 787
"Don't You Just Know It" (song), 1381
Doob, Joseph, 154
Dooto Records, 613
*Dope Sick* (Myers), 1098
Dorsey, Thomas A., 510-511, 831, 1227; and Ma Rainey, 1227
Dos Antillas, Las, 1319
Double L Records, 1205
Douglas, Aaron, 127, 512-513
Douglas, Buster, 1463
Douglass, Frederick, 84, 513-515; and Charles Waddell Chesnutt, 354; and Henrietta Vinton Davis, 459; and Martin Robison

Delany, 482; and Paul Laurence Dunbar, 525; and James Forten, 606; and Henry Highland Garnet, 632; and Lewis Howard Latimer, 959; and Edmonia Lewis, 981; and Benjamin Quarles, 1219; and Sojourner Truth, 1442
Dove, Billie, 781
Dove, Rita, 516-518
*Dover Street to Dixie* (musical), 1060
*Down and Out in Beverly Hills* (film), 991
"Down Hearted Blues" (Smith), 1378
*DownBeat* magazine, 16; awards, 240, 309, 666, 1290; Hall of Fame, 17, 241
"Dream Team," 100, 572, 879, 910, 1269
*Dreamgirls* (film), 659, 802, 949, 1090, 1092
*Dreaming Emmett* (Morrison), 1081
*Dreams from My Father* (Obama), 1121
*Dred Scott v. Sandford*, 1324-1325
Drew, Charles R., 243, 518-519, 690
Drew, Timothy. *See* Ali, Noble Drew
Drexler, Clyde, 1128
Drifters, 1019, 1510
Drinkard Sisters, 1510
Driver, Wilsonia Benita. *See* Sanchez, Sonia
*Driving Miss Daisy* (film), 623
*Drop of Patience, A* (Kelley), 928
Du Bois, W. E. B., 520-522; and Julian Bond, 179; and William Stanley Braithwaite, 203; and Charles Waddell Chesnutt, 354; and Communist Party, 211; and Alexander Crummell, 436; daughter of, 440; documentary about, 87; "double consciousness" concept, 187, 870; and Aaron Douglas, 512; encyclopedia project, 641; and

Marcus Garvey, 636; and Lorraine Hansberry, 729; and Harlem Renaissance, 805; and James Weldon Johnson, 870; and Claude McKay, 1011; and Paul Robeson, 1265; and Augusta Savage, 1317; "talented tenth," 7; and Eric Walrond, 1507; and Booker T. Washington, 1439, 1514
DuBose, Richard, 502
Dubuffet, Jean, 111
Dudley Regan, Caroline, 79
Due, Tananarive, 102
Duhamel, Marcel, 771
Dukakis, Michael, 828
Duke, David, 1051
Duke Records, 163
Duke's Serenaders, 546
Dumars, Joe, 152
Dumas, Henry, 523-524
Dunbar, Paul Laurence, 204, 244, 524-526; and Alice Dunbar-Nelson, 527; and James Weldon Johnson, 869; and Arturo Alfonso Schomburg, 1320; and William Grant Still, 1399
Dunbar-Nelson, Alice, 525, 527-528
Duncan, Tim, 528-529
Dundee, Angelo, 27, 975
*Dunfords Travels Everywhere* (Kelley), 928
Dungy, Tony, 1343, 1618
Dunham, Katherine, 530-531, 944, 1064
Dunlap Colony, 1366
Dunn, Oscar James, 532-533
Duran, Roberto, 975
Durante, Jimmy, 200
Durham, Eddie, 109
Durocher, Leo, 89
Dusky Demon, the. *See* Pickett, Bill
*Dusky Sally* (play), 340
*Dust Tracks on a Road* (Hurston), 809
*Dutchman* (play), 97, 1595
Dutton, Charles S., 533-535, 840
Duva, Lou, 785

Dyett, Walter, 390, 697
Dylan, Bob, 266, 1127, 1282, 1411, 1433
Dymally, Mervyn, 535-537
*Dynasty* (television program), 313

Eakins, Thomas, 1412
Earhart, Amelia, 395
Earth, Wind and Fire, 69
*East Broadway Run Down* (Rollins), 1289
*East Side, West Side* (television program), 1461
*East Village Other, The* (newspaper), 1238
Eastman, Max, 1011
Eastman School of Music, 490, 925, 1497
Easton, Sheena, 1211
Eastwood, Clint, 624, 1070, 1549
Eazy-E. *See* Wright, Eric "Eazy-E"
*Ebony* magazine, 293, 312, 873, 1250
*Echo in My Soul* (Clark), 366
*Echo of Lions* (Chase-Riboud), 340
Eckstine, Billy, 538-540; and Gene Ammons, 41; and Art Blakey, 162; and Miles Davis, 461; and Fats Navarro, 1103; and Sonny Stitt, 1401; and Sarah Vaughan, 1483
Economic Opportunity Act of 1964, 718
Edelman, Marian Wright, 540-541
Edison, Thomas Alva, 321, 960, 1611
Edmonds, Kenneth "Babyface," 208
Edwards, Eli. *See* McKay, Claude
Edwards, Harry, 191
Edwards, James, 1595
Edwards, Vince, 822
EEOC. *See* Equal Employment Opportunity Commission
*Eight Men* (Wright), 1627
Eisenhower, Dwight D., 761, 1156; and Louis Armstrong, 59; and Benjamin O. Davis, Sr., 454; and Little Rock Nine, 117; and Adam Clayton Powell, Jr., 1198

El Saturn Records, 1408-1409
Elder, Lee, 542-543, 1171
Elders, Joycelyn, 543-545
Eldridge, Roy, 655
Electra, Carmen, 1211
*Electric Ladyland* (Hendrix), 759
Elektra Records, 1243-1244
*Element of Freedom, The* (Keys), 933
Elizondo, Rene, Jr., 825
Elkus, Max, 334
Ellington, Duke, 545-548, 1448; and Alvin Ailey, 19; and Jimmy Blanton, 167; and Harry Carney, 308-309; and Benny Carter, 314; and Dexter Gordon, 665; and Lorraine Hansberry, 729; and Eartha Kitt, 945; and Florence Mills, 1060; and Thelonious Monk, 1069; and Max Roach, 1260; and Cootie Williams, 1566, 1575
Elliott, Bill, 1511
Elliott, Missy, 2, 1222
Ellis, Herb, 777
Ellison, Harlan, 280
Ellison, Ralph, 548-550, 605, 1094
Elmira Express. *See* Davis, Ernie
Emancipation Proclamation, 140, 514, 705, 966, 1442; celebration of, 140, 981
*Emancipation Proclamation, The* (Franklin), 618
Emanuel, James A., 551-552
EmArcy Records, 16
Eminem, 588-589, 721, 852; and Dr. Dre, 505
*Emotions* (Carey), 302
*Emperor Jones, The* (film), 1194
*Emperor Jones, The* (O'Neill), 1264
*Emperor of Ocean Park, The* (Carter), 318
Empress of Soul. *See* Knight, Gladys
Empress of the Blues. *See* Smith, Bessie
*Empyrean Isles* (Hancock), 725
"End of the Road" (song), 69
*Endeavor* space shuttle, 859

"Endless Love" (song), 302, 1253, 1292
Enron, 1428-1429
Environmental Justice Braintrust, 383
Environmental racism, 342
Epic Records, 287, 836, 954; and Jackson Five, 836
Epperson, Lia, 854
Epps, Omar, 552-553
Equal Employment Opportunity Commission, 24, 765, 790, 1119, 1541; and Anita Hill, 765; and Clarence Thomas, 1420
Equal Rights Amendment, 360, 828, 906, 1447
Equal Rights Association, 515
*ER* (television program), 552
Eracism Foundation, 675
Ertegun, Ahmet, 265
Erving, Julius, 474, 554-556
Escalera, Irene. *See* Cara, Irene
Espy, Mike, 556-558
Esquerita, 990
*Esquire* magazine, 145, 293, 771
*Essence* magazine, 90, 1156; awards, 1015
Essence Music Festival, 169
Ethiopia, 918, 1000, 1323, 1331
*Eubie!* (musical), 161, 774
Europe, James Reese, 559-560
Evans, Bill, 16
Evans, Gil, 461-462
Evans, James Carmichael, 560-561
Evans, Lee, 562-563
Evans, Mari, 563-564
Evans, Wanda. *See* Coleman, Wanda
*Eva's Man* (Jones), 893
*Evening Shade* (television program), 465
Everett, Ronald McKinley. *See* Karenga, Maulana
Evers, Charles, 565-566
Evers, Medgar, 566-568; assassin of, 332, 570; brother of, 565-566; and Dick Gregory, 689; and James Meredith, 1050; murder of, 1360; and Archie Shepp, 1344; widow of, 568-570

Evers-Williams, Myrlie, 567, 568-570

"Every Little Step" (song), 69

*Everybody Hates Chris* (television program), 1287

"Everybody Plays the Fool" (song), 663, 1107

*Eve's Bayou* (film), 841

Ewing, Patrick, 571-572, 1129

Excelsior Records, 1062

Executive Order 9981, 454, 456, 1229

"Exodusters," 252, 1366

*Eyes on the Prize* (Williams), 1573

Fab Five Freddy, 1221

Fabian, 347

*Fabulosity* (Simmons), 1353

*Fabulous Miss Marie, The* (play), 261

Fagan, Eleanora. *See* Holiday, Billie

Fair Employment Practices Commission, 1229, 1231, 1554; and A. Philip Randolph, 1230

Fair Employment Practices Committee. *See* Fair Employment Practices Commission

Fair Housing Act of 1968, 216

*Fallen Angels* (Myers), 1098

*Fallen Aviator* (Barthé), 108

*Fame* (1980 film), 33, 296-297, 1386

*Fame* (2009 film), 34

*Fame* (television program), 34, 343, 825

*Family* (Cooper), 418

Famous Amos cookies, 43-45

Famous Flames, 234

Famous Hokum Boys, 220, 510

Fanon, Frantz, 306, 603, 669

Fantasy Records, 1126

Fard, Wallace D., 1088

Farm Security Administration, 1155

Farmer, James L., Jr., 573-575, 818

Farrakhan, Louis, 342, 432, 575-576; and James Bevel, 151; and Tom Bradley, 201; and Malcolm X, 1026

*Farrakhan Speaks* (radio program), 576

*Fast and Furious* (musical), 1003

*Fat Albert and the Cosby Kids* (television program), 423

*Fat Albert Rotunda* (Hancock), 726

"Fat Man, The" (song), 509

Father Divine, 577-580; portrayal in drama, 507

Father MC, 168

Father of Black Liberation Theology. *See* Cone, James H.

Father of Chicago. *See* Pointe du Sable, Jean Baptiste

Father of Electrogasdynamics. *See* Gourdine, Meredith C.

Father of the Blues. *See* Handy, W. C.

*Fatheralong: A Meditiation on Fathers and Sons, Race and Society* (Wideman), 1556

*Fatherhood* (Cosby), 423

Fats, Minnesota, 847

*Fats Waller's Rhythm Club* (radio program), 1505

Faubus, Orval, 117

Faulk, Marshall, 580-581

Faulkner, William, 204, 630

Fauset, Jessie Redmon, 582-584, 805

Fayetteville State University, 353

FBI. *See* Federal Bureau of Investigation

Federal Bureau of Investigation, 331, 918, 924, 1433, 1599; and Hank Aaron, 4; and Marion Barry, 105; and Charlotta Spears Bass, 114; and Black Panthers, 372; and H. Rap Brown, 233; and Willie Brown, 250; counterintelligence program, 231, 233, 372, 924; and Angela Davis, 449; and 50 Cent, 589; and Anita Hill, 765; and Samuel L. Jackson, 841; most wanted list, 449, 1579; and Elijah Muhammad, 1089; and Nation of Islam, 1026, 1089; and N.W.A., 505, 812; and James Earl Ray, 943; and Paul

Robeson, 1265; and Bayard Rustin, 1304; and Al Sharpton, 1338; suspected informants, 1329; and Robert Franklin Williams, 1579; and Ernest Withers, 1602; and Richard Wright, 1626

Federal Emergency Management Agency, 134-135

Federal Funding Accountability and Transparency Act of 2006, 1122

Federal Writers' Project, 243, 1503, 1625, 1628

Feeley, James Downer, 20

Feldman, Al, 592

Felious, Odetta. *See* Odetta

Fellowship of Reconciliation, 573, 964, 1303

Fells, Augusta Christine. *See* Savage, Augusta

FEMA. *See* Federal Emergency Management Agency

Female Anti-Slavery Society, 703

*Feminist Theory* (Hooks), 788

*Fences* (play), 472, 896, 1476, 1517, 1588-1589

Fenty, Robyn Rihanna. *See* Rihanna

*Feral Benga* (Barthé), 107

Ferguson, John, 1371

Ferguson, Samuel, 584-585

Ferrara, Abel, 1387

*Festivals and Funerals* (Cortez), 421

Fetchit, Stepin, 586-588

Fields of Flowers, 231

Fifth Dimension, 417

50 Cent, 588-590

Fifty-fourth Massachusetts Volunteer Infantry Regiment, 140, 310, 704-705, 1439

*Final Call, The* (newspaper), 576

Finley, Charles O., 170, 839

*Fire in the Flint, The* (White), 1553

*FIRE!!* magazine, 512

*Fire Next Time, The* (Baldwin), 83

*Fires in the Mirror* (play), 1375

*Firespitter* (Cortez), 421

Firespitters, 421

First African Baptist Church, 1397
First Lady of Jazz. *See* Fitzgerald, Ella
First Lady of Talk Shows. *See* Winfrey, Oprah
First Lady of the Struggle. *See* Bethune, Mary McLeod
Fishburne, Laurence, 324, 590-591, 1087, 1457
Fisher, George. *See* Peters, Brock
Fisk Jubilee Singers, 268, 270, 748
Fisk University; and Arna Bontemps, 189; Cravath Memorial Museum, 1320; and Aaron Douglas, 512; and W. E. B. Du Bois, 520; and John Hope Franklin, 617; and Evelyn Boyd Granville, 678-679; and Charles S. Johnson, 863; and James Weldon Johnson, 870; and Percy Lavon Julian, 919; and John Robert Lewis, 983; and Diane Nash, 1102; and Hazel R. O'Leary, 1130-1131; and Booker T. Washington, 1514; writers conference, 218
Fitzgerald, Ella, 592-594; and Louis Armstrong, 59; and Count Basie, 110; and Ray Brown, 240; and Sarah Vaughan, 1483; and Chick Webb, 1532
Five Spot Café, 397, 697, 1070
Flack, Roberta, 739-740, 767, 933
*Flashdance* (film), 296
*Flight* (White), 1553
*Flight to Canada* (Reed), 1238
Flipper, Henry Ossian, 595-596
FloJo. *See* Griffith-Joyner, Florence
Flood, Curt, 215, 596-598
Florida A&M University, 15, 336, 682, 1317
Flutie, Doug, 32
"Fly Me to the Moon" (song), 900
"Flying Home" (song), 724
Folies Bergères, 79
*Folks from Dixie* (Dunbar), 525
Fontaine, Joan, 137
Fontaine, William Thomas, 598-599

Football coaches; Fritz Pollard, 1193-1194; Art Shell, 1341-1343
*for colored girls who have considered suicide/ when the rainbow is enuf* (play), 1335-1336
*For Love of Imabelle* (Himes), 771
*For My People* (Walker), 1503
*For Us, the Living* (Evers-Williams), 569
Ford, Cheryl, 1028
Ford, Gerald, 1130, 1562
Ford, Henry, 321
Ford, Lawrence "Flying," 45
Ford-El, David, 30
Foreign Agents Registration Act of 1938, 522
Foreman, George, 27, 600-602, 621, 1074, 1205, 1492
*Forged Note, The* (Micheaux), 1055
Forman, James, 602-604
Forrest, Leon, 604-606
Fort Valley State College, 177
Forten, Charlotte Lottie. *See* Grimké, Charlotte L. Forten
Forten, James, 606-607
Fortune, Amos, 608-609
Fortune, T. Thomas, 254, 1509
40 Acres and a Mule, 970, 1332
*48 Hrs.* (film), 1091
Foster, Adelaide Towson, 1252
*Four Little Girls* (television program), 969
*Four Negro Poets* (Locke), 1011
*Four Shall Die* (film), 443
Fox, John R., 609-610
*Foxes of Harrow, The* (Yerby), 1629
Foxx, Jamie, 337, 611-612
Foxx, Redd, 429, 613-614
*Foxy Brown* (film), 694
*Fragments of the Ark* (Meriwether), 1052
France; and Josephine Baker, 79-80; and James Baldwin, 82-83; and Tyra Banks, 90; and Otis Boykin, 194; and Eugene Jacques Bullard, 259; and Bessie Coleman, 395; and

Countée Cullen, 440; and Chester Himes, 771-772; and Jack Johnson, 867; and Quincy Jones, 900; and Ernest Everett Just, 921; and Gordon Parks, Sr., 1156; and Norbert Rillieux, 1256-1257; and Henry Ossawa Tanner, 1412; and Eric Walrond, 1508; and Mary Lou Williams, 1575; and James Winkfield, 1600; and Richard Wright, 1626
Francois, Terry, 249
Frankie Lymon and the Teenagers, 380, 402
Franklin, Aretha, 69, 169, 614-617; and Donny Hathaway, 739; "Respect," 616, 1235
Franklin, Benjamin, 1546
Franklin, John Hope, 154, 617-619
Franklin, Kirk, 431
*Franklin v. Gwinett County Public Schools*, 766
*Frank's Place* (television program), 338, 1240
Frazier, E. Franklin, 154, 226; and Ralph Bunche, 262
Frazier, Joe, 27, 601, 620-621
Frazier, Walt, 621-622
Fredericks, Henry St. Clair, Jr. *See* Taj Mahal
*Free!* (Cary), 323
Free African Society, 36, 606, 889-890
*Free Enterprise* (Cliff), 377
*Free Jazz* (Coleman), 157, 397-398
Free jazz movement, 96; and John Coltrane, 410
*Free South* (newspaper), 1048
*Free Speech* (newspaper), 1533
Freed, Alan, 14
Freedmen's Bureau, 353, 483, 1443, 1450; and Oscar James Dunn, 532
Freedmen's Hospital, 518-519, 1029, 1568, 1624
Freedmen's Saving Bank, 253
*Freedom* (magazine), 729
Freedom Now Party, 370
*Freedom of Information* (dance), 892

Freedom Rides, 818; and James Bevel, 150; and Stokely Carmichael, 305; and James L. Farmer, Jr., 573-574; and James Lawson, 965; and John Robert Lewis, 982-983; and Diane Nash, 1102; play about, 623; poetry about, 218; and Bayard Rustin, 1304; and Fred Shuttlesworth, 1348; and C. T. Vivian, 1489; and Robert Franklin Williams, 1578

Freedom School campaign, 76, 331

Freedom Summer campaign, 76, 137, 330-331, 603, 718, 983

*Freedom's Journal* (newspaper), 1302, 1495

Freeman, Morgan, 404, 623-624, 840

Freeman, Ron, 562

Freemasonry, 1320, 1533; and Oscar James Dunn, 532; and Prince Hall, 716

French Foreign Legion, 259

Fresh Prince. *See* Smith, Will

*Fresh Prince of Bel-Air, The* (television program), 90, 343, 1066, 1222, 1385, 1582

Friedan, Betty, 569

*From Slavery to Freedom* (Franklin), 618

Frost, Robert, 484

Fugard, Athol, 659

Fugees, 767-768, 855

Fugitive Slave Act of 1850, 425, 482, 703

Fuhrman, Mark, 387

Fuller, Charles, 625-626

Fuller, Gil, 656

Fuller, Hoyt, 645, 1023

*Fullerton Street* (play), 1588

Funerary industry, 638, 831

Funk Mob, 381

Funkadelic, 381

Funnye, Doris, 817

*Funnyhouse of a Negro* (Kennedy), 929

Fuqua, Harvey, 643

Fur trade, 132, 277, 1188

Futrell, Mary Hatwood, 626-628

*Future of Africa, The* (Crummell), 436

*Future Shock* (Hancock), 726

Gable, Clark, 1007

Gaines, Ernest J., 629-631

Gaines, LaDonna Adrian. *See* Summer, Donna

Gaither, Tom, 574

Gambia, 712

Game theory, 154-155

Gandhi, Mahatma, 150, 818, 940, 942, 964, 1230; and C. T. Vivian, 1488

*Gang in Blue* (film), 1481

Gangsta rap, 130, 432, 852-853, 855, 885, 1334, 1447; and Dr. Dre, 504-506; and 50 Cent, 588-590; and M. C. Hammer, 722; and Ice Cube, 812-813; and Snoop Dogg, 1388-1390

Gans, Joe, 160

Garcia, Ceferino, 54

Garfield, James, 253, 1048

Garfinkel, Howard, 909

Garner, Erroll, 72

Garnet, Henry Highland, 631-633

Garnett, Kevin, 633-634, 1181-1182

Garrison, Jimmy, 397

Garrison, William Lloyd, 703, 1397, 1496; and Martin Robison Delany, 482; and Frederick Douglass, 514; and James Forten, 606; and Lewis Howard Latimer, 959; and Edmonia Lewis, 980; and William Monroe Trotter, 1439; and Sojourner Truth, 1442

Garrison, Zina, 649

Garvey, Marcus, 29, 635-637; and Cyril V. Briggs, 211; and John E. Bruce, 254; and John Henrik Clarke, 368; and Alexander Crummell, 436; and Henrietta Vinton Davis, 459; and Claude McKay, 1011; and Malcolm X, 1024; and "New Thought" philosophy, 578; and A. Philip Randolph, 1229; and Arturo

Alfonso Schomburg, 1320; and George S. Schuyler, 1322; and James Van Der Zee, 1478; and Eric Walrond, 1507

Gaston, Arthur George, 637-639

Gaston, Cito, 74

Gates, Bill, 642

Gates, Darryl F., 1585

Gates, Henry Louis, Jr., 640-642; and Alex Haley, 713

*Gathering of Old Men, A* (Gaines), 630

Gatson, Daisy Lee. *See* Bates, Daisy

Gaulle, Charles de, 260

Gaye, Marvin, 402, 417, 643-644, 673, 848; and Usher, 1474

Gayle, Addison, Jr., 645-646

Gayle, Helene Doris, 646-647

Gayten, Paul, 508

Geffen Records, 1389, 1406

*Gemini* (Giovanni), 657

Genius, the. *See* Charles, Ray

Gentleman of Boxing, the. *See* Patterson, Floyd

*Gentlemen Prefer Blondes* (musical), 401

George Washington Carver Foundation, 1165

Georgetown University, 750

Georgia Minstrels, 165

"Georgia on My Mind" (song), 336

Georgia Tom. *See* Dorsey, Thomas A.

Gershwin, George, 285, 401, 462

*Get On the Bus* (film), 534, 1005

*Get Rich or Die Tryin'* (50 Cent), 588-589

*Get Rich or Die Tryin'* (film), 471, 589

Getz, Stan, 1349, 1401

Ghana, 747; and Maya Angelou, 51; and John Henrik Clarke, 368; and W. E. B. Du Bois, 522; and Asa Grant Hilliard III, 769; and Adrienne Kennedy, 929

"Ghetto Qu'ran" (song), 589

*Ghost* (film), 662

*Ghost Talks, The* (film), 587

Giants of Jazz, 162, 1402

Gibbs, Terry, 407, 777

Gibson, Althea, 648-650

Gibson, Bob, 214, 596, 650-651

Gibson, Jo Ann. *See* Robinson, Jo Ann Gibson

Gibson, Josh, 139, 652-654, 1149-1150

Gibson, Josh, Jr., 653

Gibson, Kenneth, 97

Gibson, Tyrese, 1368

Gill, Johnny, 69

Gillespie, Dizzy, 654-656, 1301; and Art Blakey, 162; and Ray Brown, 240; and Cab Calloway, 285; and John Coltrane, 409; and Miles Davis, 461; and Ella Fitzgerald, 593; and Quincy Jones, 900; and Thelonious Monk, 1069; and Fats Navarro, 1103; and Charlie Parker, 1152; and Max Roach, 1260; and Sonny Stitt, 1401; and Sarah Vaughan, 1484; and Jackie Wilson, 1592

Gilmore, John, 1408

*Gimme a Break!* (television program), 316-317

*Gingertown* (McKay), 1011

Giovanni, Nikki, 657-658

*Giovanni's Room* (Baldwin), 82

*Girl Can't Help It, The* (film), 990

*Girl Like Me, A* (Rihanna), 1255

*Girl Without a Room* (film), 723

Girshick, Meyer Abraham, 154

Giuliani, Rudolph, 498

Givens, Robin, 1463

Gladys Knight and the Pips, 946

*Glance Away, A* (Wideman), 1555

Glaser, Joe, 59

Glenn, John, 876

*Glitter* (film), 302-303

*Glory* (film), 310, 624, 1516

Glover, Danny, 658-660, 1471, 1608

Glover, Savion, 402, 660-661, 1459

Gluck, Alma, 270

*Go Tell It on the Mountain* (Baldwin), 82

"God Bless the Child" (song), 782

*God Sends Sunday* (Bontemps), 189

*Godfather of Soul: An Autobiography, The* (Brown), 234

*Godfather of Soul, The* (Brown), 234

"Going Home" (song), 509

Goldberg, Arthur, 597

Goldberg, Whoopi, 333, 662-663, 767, 1015; and Moms Mabley, 1004

*Golden Boy* (Odets), 468

Golden State Warriors; and Ralph Sampson, 1129; and Gus Williams, 1569

Goldman, Ronald, 387, 1363

Goldwater, Barry, 216

Gomer, Nina, 521

*Gone Are the Days!* (film), 286, 465

*Gone Fishin'* (Mosley), 1086

*Gone with the Wind* (film), 45, 1007, 1521; and Martin Luther King, Jr., 941

*Good Fight, The* (Chisholm), 360

*Good Girl Gone Bad* (Rihanna), 1255

"Good Golly, Miss Molly" (song), 990

*Good Morning America* (television program), 708, 778, 1612

G.O.O.D. Music, 1541

*Good Times* (Clifton), 379

*Good Times* (television program), 33, 825, 1498-1499, 1591

Gooding, Cuba, Jr., 663-664

Goodman, Benny; and Harry Carney, 308; and Lionel Hampton, 723; and Milt Hinton, 777; and Chick Webb, 1532; and Cootie Williams, 1567, 1575

Goodman, Robert, 828

Gorbachev, Mikhail, 450

Gordon, Dexter, 41, 665-667, 725

Gordon, Ed, 667-668

Gordon, Lewis, 668-670

Gordon-Reed, Annette, 670-672

*Gordon's War* (film), 465

Gordy, Berry, Jr., 380, 672-674, 1291, 1592; and Marvin Gaye, 643; and Jackson Five, 835; and Smokey Robinson, 1281-1282; and Stevie Wonder, 1605

Gordy, Gwendolyn, 673

Gore, Altovise, 468

Gore, Lesley, 900

*Gorilla, My Love* (Bambara), 87

Gospel Starlighters, 234

Gospelaires, 1510

Gossett, Louis, Jr., 674-675

Gottlieb, Ed, 327-328

Gough, Eleanora. *See* Holiday, Billie

Gould, Joe, 1000

Gourdine, Meredith C., 676-677

Grahn, Judy, 1153

Grambling College, 1276

Grand Ole Opry, 1206-1207

Grant, Carolyn, 1117

Grant, Ulysses S., 515

Granville, Evelyn Boyd, 678-679

Granz, Norman, 240, 593

Gravely, Samuel, 971

Graves, Earl G., Sr., 679-680

Graves, Howard, 1570

Gray, Frizell Gerald. *See* Mfume, Kweisi

Gray, Macy, 681-682

Gray, Perry O., 585

Gray, Wardell, 666

Gray, William H., III, 682-684

*Greased Lightning* (film), 694

*Great Day in Harlem, A* (film), 777

Great Depression; art of, 971; and educational funding, 321, 464; effect on rural areas, 792, 1410, 1596; entertainment during, 161, 466; photographs of, 1155; and recording industry, 1083; and sports, 1000, 1149, 1491

*Great White Hope, The* (play), 895, 1078

Greeley, Gus, 652

Green, Al, 684-686, 1457

Green, Paul, 1626

*Green Is Blues* (Green), 685

Green Party, 231

*Green Pastures, The* (film), 45

*Green Power* (Gaston), 639

Greene, Claude D., 30

Greene, Joe, 686-687

Greene, Marion, 270

Greene, Thomas. *See* Bethune, Blind Tom

Greenfield, Elizabeth Taylor, 902

Greenlee, Gus, 1149

Greensboro, North Carolina, sit-ins, 179, 983

Greer, Sonny, 546

Gregory, Dick, 688-690, 1004

Gregory, Frederick Drew, 690-692

Gregory, Wilton D., 692-693

Gretzky, Wayne, 184

Grier, Pam, 287, 694-695

Grier, Rosey, 883

Griffey, Dick, 69

Griffey, Ken, Sr., 695

Griffey, Ken, Jr., 695-697

Griffin, Johnny, 697-698

Griffith-Joyner, Florence, 699-701, 897, 915

Grimké, Angelina Weld, 701-704

Grimké, Archibald, 701

Grimké, Charlotte L. Forten, 703-705

Grimké, Sarah, 704

Grit, Bruce. *See* Bruce, John E.

Grosz, George, 127

*Growing Up X* (Shabazz), 1332

*Grutter v. Bollinger*, 1420

*Guess Who's Coming to Dinner* (film), 1191

Guillaume, Robert, 465, 706-707

Guillory, Ben, 1471

Guinea, 306

Guitar Slim. *See* Jones, Eddie

Gulf War. *See* Persian Gulf War

Gullah, 5, 382, 445-446, 704

Gumbel, Bryant, 707-708

Gumbel, Greg, 707

G-Unit Records, 589

Gurdjieff, George, 1436

Guthrie, Woody, 1410

Guy, Buddy, 937

*Guys and Dolls* (musical), 33, 706

Gwynn, Tony, 708-710

Gymnasts, 472-474

Gypsy Sun and Rainbows, 759

Hacker, Marilyn, 484

Haden, Charlie, 157

Hagler, Marvin, 975

Hagood, Kenny "Pancho," 407

Haile Selassie, 731, 918, 1000

Hailey, Cedric "K-Ci," 169

Haines Institute, 148, 792

*Hair* (musical), 316, 1405, 1485

Haiti; and Richmond Barthé, 108; and Frederick Douglass, 515; and Katherine Dunham, 530-531; earthquake of 2010, 169, 383, 659, 801, 901, 1524; and William H. Gray III, 683; and Janet Jackson, 826; and Wyclef Jean, 855-856; and Jean Baptiste Pointe du Sable, 1188-1190; and resettlement movement, 37; revolution, 1487; and TransAfrica, 1279; and Denmark Vesey, 1487; voodoo, 809

Hakeem the Dream. *See* Olajuwon, Hakeem

Haley, Alex, 144, 276, 711-714, 1468; screen portrayal of, 895

*Half-Baked* (film), 333

Hall, Arsenio, 714-715, 1286

Hall, Juanita, 196

Hall, Prince, 716-717

Hall of Fame for Great Americans, 108

*Hallelujah, Baby!* (musical), 1078, 1469

Halstead, Oliver Willis, 490

Hamer, Fannie Lou, 717-720, 908

Hamilton, Anthony, 740

Hamilton, Virginia, 720-721

Hamitic League, 210

*Hamlet* (play), 989

Hammer. *See* Hammer, M. C.

Hammer, M. C., 721-723

Hammerin' Hank. *See* Aaron, Hank.

*Hammerman* (television program), 723

Hammond, John, 781, 1448

Hampton, Lionel, 723-724; and Clifford Brown, 227; and Thomas A. Dorsey, 510; and

Dexter Gordon, 665; and Johnny Griffin, 697; and Milt Hinton, 776; and Quincy Jones, 899; and Charles Mingus, 1062

Hampton Institute. *See* Hampton University

Hampton University, 5, 7, 364, 490, 1513

*Hancock* (film), 787, 1386

Hancock, Herbie, 462, 725-726

*Handbook of Black Studies* (Asante), 62

Handlin, Oscar, 618

Handy, W. C., 392, 559, 727-728, 1227, 1399; and Thomas A. Dorsey, 510

Hankerson, Barry, 1

Hansberry, Lorraine, 368, 675, 728-730, 1234, 1251

Hansberry, William Leo, 368, 729

Hansen, Austin, 731-732

*Harambee* (newspaper), 231

*Harder They Fall, The* (film), 1492

Hardin, Lillian Beatrice. *See* Armstrong, Lillian Hardin

Harding, Halley, 1522

Hardwick, Elizabeth, 893

Hardwick, Erwin, 542

Hardy, Nell Ruth. *See* Carter, Nell

Hare, Nathan, 226

Harlem; Abyssinian Baptist Church, 81, 312, 1196; art museums, 128; Art Workshop, 961, 1318; Black Arts Repertory Theater, 97-98; Commonwealth Council, 817; Community Art Center, 476, 961, 1318; Connie's Inn, 1505; in fiction, 771; Lincoln Theater, 18, 195; and *Manchild in the Promised Land*, 226; Minton's Playhouse, 167, 1068, 1260; Monroe's Uptown House, 168, 1112, 1260; Mural Project, 40, 961; photographs of, 476, 731-732, 1477-1479; riots, 907; Rockland Palace, 579; Rose McClendon Players, 464; Savoy Ballroom, 284, 308, 390, 592, 1531-1532; Uptown Arts Laboratory, 961;

Youth Council, 753. *See also* Apollo Theater; Cotton Club; New York City

*Harlem* (McKay), 1011

Harlem Artists' Guild, 512

*Harlem Book of the Dead, The* (Dodson), 507

Harlem Globetrotters; and Kareem Abdul-Jabbar, 9; animated television series, 429; and Ernie Banks, 88; and Cab Calloway, 284-285; and Wilt Chamberlain, 328; and Darryl Dawkins, 475; and Larry Doby, 502; and Althea Gibson, 649-650; and Connie Hawkins, 741; and Meadowlark Lemon, 972-974; and Lynette Woodard, 1609

Harlem Harlicans, 56

*Harlem Liberator, The* (newspaper), 211

*Harlem Nights* (film), 614, 715, 1091

*Harlem Quarterly*, 368

Harlem Renaissance; artists, 107-108, 512-513, 886-887, 961-962; and Richmond Barthé, 107; and Romare Bearden, 126; and Arna Bontemps, 188-189; and William Stanley Braithwaite, 204; and Cab Calloway, 284; and Cotton Club, 284; and Countée Cullen, 439-441; and Aaron Douglas, 512; and W. E. B. Du Bois, 521; and Alice Dunbar-Nelson, 527-528; and Duke Ellington, 546; and Jessie Redmon Fauset, 582-583; and Angelina Weld Grimké, 702; and Langston Hughes, 803-806; and Zora Neale Hurston, 808-811; and Charles S. Johnson, 862-863, 886; and James Weldon Johnson, 870-871; and Nella Larsen, 957-959; and Jacob Lawrence, 961-962; library collections, 189, 1319-1321; and Alain Locke, 995-996; and Claude McKay, 1010-1012; poets, 204, 217, 439-441,

506, 803-806; and Arturo Alfonso Schomburg, 1319-1321; and George S. Schuyler, 1322; and William Grant Still, 1398-1400; and Jean Toomer, 1435-1437; and Madam C. J. Walker, 1502; and Fats Waller, 1504; and Eric Walrond, 1507-1508; and Dorothy West, 1538-1539; and Walter White, 1553; and Carter G. Woodson, 1616. *See also Opportunity: Journal of Negro Life*

Harlem River Houses, 107

*Harlem Shadows* (McKay), 1011

Harlem Stompers, 1531

Harlem Writers Guild, 51-52, 368, 997, 1014, 1098

Harlem Youth Opportunities Unlimited, 364

Harper, Frances Ellen Watkins, 732-733

Harper, Michael S., 734-735, 893

Harpo Productions, 1598-1599

Harrell, Andre, 168, 1217

Harriet Tubman Award, 193

Harris, Elinore. *See* Holiday, Billie

Harris, Franco, 735-737

Harris, Frank, 1011

Harris, Patricia Roberts, 737-738, 764

Harris, Phil, 429

Harris, Tracy, 1164

Harris, William Beasley, 737

Harrison, Benjamin, 253, 515, 1372

Hart, Cecilia, 896

Hart, Gary, 1246

Hart, Marvin, 866

Hartford Artists' Collective, 1013

*Harvard Law Review*, 797, 1121

Harvey, Steve, 325, 1355

Hastie, William H., 243

*Hate That Hate Produced, The* (television program), 1025

Hathaway, Donny, 739-740

Hatwood, Mary Alice Franklin. *See* Futrell, Mary Hatwood

Haughton, Aaliyah Dana. *See* Aaliyah

Havens, Richie, 675

Haverly, Jack, 165

Haverly's Genuine Colored Minstrels, 165

Hawkins, Adrienne Lita. *See* Kennedy, Adrienne

Hawkins, Charlotte Eugenia. *See* Brown, Charlotte Hawkins

Hawkins, Coleman, 1069, 1349; and Herbie Hancock, 725; and Milt Hinton, 777

Hawkins, Connie, 740-742

Hawkins, Jamesetta. *See* James, Etta

Hawkins, Yusef, 1339

*Hawkins v. National Basketball Association*, 741

Hayer, Thomas, 1026

Hayes, Bob, 742-744

Hayes, Elvin, 8, 745-746

Hayes, Isaac, 746-748

Hayes, Roland, 47, 748-750, 1498

Hayes, Rutherford B., 515, 520, 1509

Haynes, Euphemia Lofton, 678

Haynes, Marques, 973

*He Is Arisen* (Bearden, 127

*Head Hunters* (Hancock), 726

Head Start program, 540, 662, 1494, 1523

Heal the World Foundation, 837

*Healer, The* (Hooker), 787

Health food, 689

Healy, Patrick F., 750-751

Hearst, William Randolph, 7

*Heart Is a Lonely Hunter, The* (film), 1460

*Heart of Happy Hollow, The* (Dunbar), 525

*Hearts of Dixie* (film), 587

Heath, Jimmy, 409

Heavy D, 1217

Hefner, Hugh, 689

Heidelberg, Joe, 1597

Height, Dorothy, 752-753, 763

Heisman Trophy; and Marcus Allen, 35; and Tim Brown, 245; and Earl Campbell, 294; and Ernie Davis, 458; and Bo

Jackson, 823; and Walter Payton, 1168; and Barry Sanders, 1310; and O. J. Simpson, 1361-1362
*Hello, Dolly!* (musical), 72, 285, 623, 1008
"Hello, Dolly!" (song), 59
Helms, Jesse, 205, 1051
Helms, Jesse, Sr., 1578
Hemings, Sally, 670, 754-755; in fiction, 340; sister of, 1439
Hemus, Solly, 650
Henderson, Fletcher; and Lillian Hardin Armstrong, 56-58; and Benny Carter, 314; film depiction of, 468; and Ma Rainey, 1227; and Fats Waller, 1505; and Cootie Williams, 1566
Henderson, Horace, 314
Henderson, Michael, 463
Henderson, Rickey, 214, 756-758, 1586
Hendrix, Jimi, 381, 758-760, 937, 991, 1411
Henry, Aaron, 565, 719
Henry, Georgiana, 593
Henson, Jim, 137
Henson, Matthew Alexander, 761-762
Henthoff, Nat, 397
Heptathlon, 914-915
Herman, Alexis M., 763-764
Herman, Woody, 42
Herndon, Alice. *See* Childress, Alice
Herndon, Angelo, 451
*Hero Ain't Nothin' but a Sandwich, A* (Childress), 357-358
*Hero Ain't Nothin' but a Sandwich, A* (film), 357
Herzog, Arthur, Jr., 782
Hester, Lucille, 744
Hewlett, James, 22
Hi Records, 685
Hickerson, John, 578
Hicks, William, 1156
Higgins, Billy, 725, 1289
*Higher Learning* (film), 90, 552, 813, 1368

Highlander Folk School, 150, 366, 1571
Highway QC's, 415
*Hill, The* (film), 464
Hill, Anita, 204, 427, 764-766, 1420
Hill, Herman, 1522
Hill, Lauryn, 767-768
Hill, Patricia. *See* Collins, Patricia Hill
*Hill Street Blues* (television program), 343, 663, 1549, 1607
Hilliard, Asa Grant, III, 768-770
Hilliard, Bob, 1510
Hilliard, David, 231
Himes, Chester, 464, 770-772
Hinds, Natalie. *See* Gray, Macy
Hinduism, 407-408, 964, 1314
Hines, Earl, 772-774; and Louis Armstrong, 58; and Art Blakey, 162; and Nat King Cole, 390; and Billy Eckstine, 538; and Dizzy Gillespie, 655; and Charlie Parker, 1152; and Sarah Vaughan, 1483
Hines, Gregory, 72, 161, 402, 774-775
Hines, Johnny, 53
Hinton, Milt, 285, 776-777
Hip Hop Summit Action Network, 342, 1355
Hirt, Al, 1032
Historians; Arna Bontemps, 188-190; John E. Bruce, 254-255; John Henrik Clarke, 367-369; John Hope Franklin, 617-619; Annette Gordon-Reed, 670-672; James Meredith, 1049-1051; Benjamin Quarles, 1219-1220; Arturo Alfonso Schomburg, 1319-1321; Carter G. Woodson, 1615-1617
*HIStory* (Jackson), 825, 837
Hite, Les, 723
Hitler, Adolf, 1000, 1141
Hitsville U.S.A., 673, 1281
Hobson, Mellody, 778-779
Hodges, Johnny, 167, 308-309, 546
Hoffman, Julius, 1329
Hogan, Wilbert, 156

*Hogan's Heroes* (television program), 500
Holder, Eric, 779-781
Holiday, Billie, 109, 666, 781-784, 1292; and Milt Hinton, 776; screen portrayal of, 1293
Holliday, Jennifer, 802
Holly, James Theodore, 584
Hollywood, DJ, 1354
Hollywood Bears, 1522
*Hollywood Shuffle* (film), 1438
Holmes, Eleanor Katherine. *See* Norton, Eleanor Holmes
Holmes, Hamilton "Hamp," 807
Holmes, Larry, 1171
Holmes, Odetta. *See* Odetta
Holte, Patricia Louise. *See* LaBelle, Patti
Holton, Kenneth, 781
Holty, Carl, 127
*Holy Koran of the Moorish Science Temple* (Ali), 29
Holyfield, Evander, 601, 784-786, 1463
*Home of the Brave* (1949 film), 1595
*Home of the Brave* (2006 film), 589, 841
*Home to Harlem* (McKay), 1011
*Homecoming, The* (play), 1588
*Homegirls and Handgrenades* (Sanchez), 1308
Homestead Grays, 139, 289, 652-653, 1149
*Homesteader, The* (film), 1055
*Homesteader, The* (Micheaux), 1055
"Honey Love" (song), 1019
Hooker, John Lee, 495, 786-788
Hooker, John Lee, Jr., 787
Hooker, Zakiya, 787
Hooks, Bell, 788-789
Hooks, Benjamin, 789-791
Hootie and the Blowfish, 1294-1295
Hoover, Herbert, 149
Hoover, J. Edgar, 7, 372
Hoover, Lou Henry, 488
Hope, Elmo, 697
Hope, John, 791-793, 1043

Hope, Lugenia Burns, 792
Hopkins, Fred, 1431
Hopkinson, Nalo, 102
Hopper, Edward, 971
Horn, Mother, 81
Horne, Lena, 198, 794-796, 1469, 1506
Horton, Big Walter, 992
Horton, Myles, 150, 366
Hosea Feeds the Hungry and Homeless, 1572
*Hot Buttered Soul* (Hayes), 747
*Hot Chocolates* (musical), 284, 1505
*Hot Feet* (musical), 1505
Hot Five, 55-56, 58-59, 773
Hot Seven, 58-59, 773
*Hotel Rwanda* (film), 344
*Hottentot Venus* (Chase-Riboud), 340
Hounsou, Djimon, 1353
*House* (television program), 553
House, Son, 1525
*House at Dies Drear, The* (Hamilton), 720
*House Behind the Cedars, The* (film), 1056
*House of Flowers* (musical), 18, 72, 313
House Select Committee on Assassinations, 267, 844
House Un-American Activities Committee, 795, 1265
Houseman, John, 1621, 1626
Houston, Charles Hamilton, 797-798, 1037
Houston, Whitney, 69, 798-800, 1015, 1477, 1510, 1512
Houston Rockets, 745; and Charles Barkley, 100; and Hakeem Olajuwon, 1128-1129; and Scottie Pippen, 1186
Hova. *See* Jay-Z
"How High the Moon" (song), 593
*How I Learned What I Learned* (play), 1589
*How Stella Got Her Groove Back* (film), 116
*How Stella Got Her Groove Back* (McMillan), 1015

Howard, Dwight, 800-802, 850
Howard, Kathleen, 270
Howard, Theodore Roosevelt Mason, 567
Howard University; and George Edward Alcorn, 20; and Houston A. Baker, Jr., 77; and Amiri Baraka, 96; and David Harold Blackwell, 154; and Sterling A. Brown, 243; and Ralph Bunche, 262; and Stokely Carmichael, 305; Charles Rangel International Affairs Program, 1233; and James E. Cheek, 349-350; Chenault commencement address, 352; and Lucille Clifton, 378; and Alexander Crummell, 436; and David Dinkins, 497; and Owen Dodson, 507; and Charles R. Drew, 518-519; and Katherine Dunham, 530; and John Hope Franklin, 618; and Patricia Roberts Harris, 737; and Charles Hamilton Houston, 797; and Percy Lavon Julian, 919; and Ernest Everett Just, 921; and Hughie Lee-Smith, 972; and Alain Locke, 995; and Benjamin E. Mays, 1044; and Pauli Murray, 1096; Phi Beta Sigma fraternity, 1470; and Spottswood W. Robinson III, 1283; and Thomas Sowell, 1391; and Booker T. Washington, 1514; and Carter G. Woodson, 1615
Howells, William Dean, 525
Howlin' Wolf, 501
HUAC. *See* House Un-American Activities Committee
Hubbard, Freddie, 725
Hudson, Jennifer, 802-803
Huggins, Ericka, 1329
Huggins, Willis N., 368
Hughes, Langston, 563, 803-806, 949; and Arna Bontemps, 189; and Gwendolyn Brooks, 217; and Roy DeCarava, 477; and Ralph Ellison, 548; and James A. Emanuel, 551; and Jessie

Redmon Fauset, 582; and Lorraine Hansberry, 729; library collection, 189; "The Negro Speaks of Rivers," 1208; and Odetta, 1127; and William Grant Still, 1399; and Margaret Walker, 1503
Hughley, D. L., 326
Hulmes, Helen, 109
Human Buzzsaw. *See* Armstrong, Henry
Human Torpedo. *See* Pollard, Fritz
Hunter, C. J., 898
Hunter-Gault, Charlayne, 323, 807-808
*Hurricane, The* (film), 1516
Hurricane Katrina, 383, 1167, 1537, 1572; and Fats Domino, 509; film about, 969; and Beyoncé Knowles, 949; and Ray Nagin, 1100-1101; and Aaron Neville, 1107; relief work, 383, 816, 1033, 1540
*Hurry Home* (Wideman), 1555
Hurston, Zora Neale, 564, 805, 808-811, 1538, 1603; and Moms Mabley, 1003
Hutcherson, Bobby, 1013
Hutton, Bobby, 372
Hyde, Roger Erik, 429

*I Am a Black Woman* (Evans), 563
*I Can Do Bad All by Myself* (film), 169
*I Can Do Bad All by Myself* (Perry), 1173
I Come for to Sing, 220
"I Have a Dream speech." *See* King, Martin Luther, Jr.
"I Heard It Through the Grapevine" (song), 643, 673
"I Just Called to Say I Love You" (song), 1606
*I Know I've Been Changed* (Perry), 1173
*I Know Why the Caged Bird Sings* (Angelou), 51-52, 1597; and Paul Laurence Dunbar, 526
"I Put a Spell on You" (song), 1360
*I Spy* (television program), 422

*I, Tina* (Turner), 1457
"I Want to Take You Higher" (song), 1456
Ice Cube, 505, 812-813
Ickes, Harold, 49
*If He Hollers Let Him Go* (Himes), 771
*If I Did It* (Simpson), 1363
Ifill, Gwen, 814-815
*Illustrated News, The* (newspaper), 370
*I'm Gonna Git You Sucka* (film), 324, 1286
"I'm Just Wild About Harry" (song), 160-161
*I'm Not Rappaport* (play), 465, 989
*I'm Your Baby Tonight* (Houston), 799
*Imitation of Life* (film), 129-130, 832, 1214
Imperial Records, 509, 1382
Impulse! Records, 1314, 1344, 1458
Imus, Don, 1339
*In Dahomey* (musical), 1564
In Friendship, 75
*In Living Color* (television program), 611, 1286
*In My Father's House* (Gaines), 630
*In Old Kentucky* (film), 587
*In Old Plantation Days* (Dunbar), 525
*In Our Lifetime?* (Gaye), 644
*In the Heat of the Night* (film), 900, 1191
*In the House* (television program), 953
*In the Mecca* (Brooks), 218
*In the New England Winter* (play), 261
*In the Night of the Heat* (Barnes), 102
*In the Spirit of Sojourner Truth* (play), 908
*In the Wine Time* (play), 261
*Incredibles, The* (film), 841
*Independence Day* (film), 1386
India.Arie, 740, 815-816
Indiana Pacers, 1426

Indianapolis Colts, 581, 1343
Indonesia, 1121, 1123
*Inglourious Basterds* (film), 841
Ink Spots, 415
*Innervisions* (Wonder), 1606
Innis, Roy, 817-819
*Inside Man* (film), 969
*Inside the NBA* (television program), 100
Institute for Black American Music, 900
Institute for the Black World, 940
International Cheikh Anta Diop Conference, 924
International Civil Rights Walk of Fame, 469, 1348
International Council of Women of Darker Races, 274
International Peace Mission, 577-580
Interscope, 589, 1217
*Into the Woods* (musical), 1582
*Introducing Dorothy Dandridge* (television movie), 144, 444
*Intuitive* (dance), 892
*Invictus* (film), 624
*Invisible Man* (Ellison), 549-550
Iola. *See* Wells-Barnett, Ida B.
Iraq, 1200-1201, 1246; and Bernard Shaw, 1341; U.S. invasion of, 693, 828, 845, 965, 1002, 1123, 1247, 1524, 1536
*Iron Ladies of Liberia* (film), 816
Iron Mike. *See* Tyson, Mike
Isaacs, Kendu, 169
Islam; and Kareem Abdul-Jabbar, 9; and al-Qaeda, 1247; and Muhammad Ali, 27, 29-30; and Amiri Baraka, 97; and Art Blakey, 162; and H. Rap Brown, 233; and Benjamin Chavis, 341-342; and "Christlam," 373; and Eldridge Cleaver, 372; and John Coltrane, 410; and Elijah Muhammad, 1088-1090; and Hakeem Olajuwon, 1129; and Sonia Sanchez, 1308; and Wesley Snipes, 1387; and McCoy Tyner, 1458; and Mike Tyson, 1463; and Denzel

Washington, 1516. *See also* Nation of Islam
*Island in the Sun* (film), 137
Island Records, 826
Isley Brothers, 758
Iverson, Allen, 819-821, 1557
Ivory Coast, 857

J Records, 933
*Jackie Brown* (film), 694, 841
Jackson, Bo, 822-824, 1313
Jackson, Curtis James, III. *See* 50 Cent
Jackson, David, 134
Jackson, George, 324, 373, 448, 1411
Jackson, Henry, Jr. *See* Armstrong, Henry
Jackson, Howard, 886
Jackson, Janet, 825-826, 1112, 1334
Jackson, Jesse, 826-829; and Cannonball Adderley, 16; and Ron Brown, 242; and Roland Burris, 272; and Louis Farrakhan, 576; and Donny Hathaway, 740; and Roy Innis, 818; and Jesse Jackson, Jr., 830; and Alvin Francis Poussaint, 1195; and Al Sharpton, 1337; Washington, D.C., mayoral race, 105; and Maxine Waters, 1524
Jackson, Jesse, Jr., 827, 829-830
Jackson, Joseph, 825, 835
Jackson, Juanita, 753
Jackson, Katherine, 116, 825, 835
Jackson, Mahalia, 511, 614, 831-833, 1203, 1337
Jackson, Maynard, 833-834
Jackson, Melody. *See* Armstrong, Henry
Jackson, Michael, 387, 825, 835-837, 1112; and Quincy Jones, 836, 901; and Lionel Richie, 1253; tribute to, 52; and Jackie Wilson, 1593
Jackson, Milt, 240
Jackson, O'Shea. *See* Ice Cube
Jackson, Papa Charlie, 220
Jackson, Phil, 910, 1134

Jackson, Reggie, 838-840, 861; and M. C. Hammer, 721

Jackson, Samuel L., 840-842, 1368

Jackson, Shirley Ann, 842-843

*Jackson Advocate, The* (newspaper), 854

Jackson Five, 825, 835-836, 901, 1253; and Babyface, 69

*Jackson Five, The* (television program), 835

Jackson Lee, Sheila, 844-845

Jackson State University, 1049, 1168, 1494, 1503

Jacobs, Mike, 1000

Jacquet, Illinois, 593, 724, 1113

Jagger, Mick, 266

Jakes, T. D., 846-847

Jam, Jimmy, 169, 825

Jam Master Jay. *See* Mizell, Jason

Jamaica, 108; and Harry Belafonte, 136-137; and Joseph Cinque, 363; and Michelle Cliff, 377-378; and Patrick Ewing, 571-572; and Henry Highland Garnet, 632; and Marcus Garvey, 635-637; and Lewis Gordon, 668-670; and Claude McKay, 1010-1012; and Terry McMillan, 1014; and John Willis Menard, 1049; and John Brown Russwurm, 1302-1303

Jamerson, James, 673

James, Etta, 847-848, 1411; portrayal in film, 949

James, Jimmy. *See* Hendrix, Jimi

James, Larry, 562

James, LeBron, 849-851, 1135

James E. Sullivan Award. *See* Sullivan Award winners

Jamison, Judith, 19

Jarrell, Randall, 82

JATP. *See* Jazz at the Philharmonic

Jay-Z, 852-853, 1255-1256, 1355, 1540

*Jazz* (Morrison), 1081

*Jazz* (television program), 433, 1033

Jazz at the Philharmonic, 240, 315, 593

*Jazz Immortal* (Brown), 228

Jazz Messengers; and Art Blakey, 162-163; and Clifford Brown, 227; and Johnny Griffin, 697; and Jackie McLean, 1013; and Wynton Marsalis, 1033; and Wayne Shorter, 1346; and Horace Silver, 1349; and McCoy Tyner, 1458. *See also* Blakey, Art

Jazz poetry, 421

Jazzola Orchestra, 1531

Jazztet, 1458

Jazztone Records, 1113

*Jazzvisions* (Hancock), 726

Jealous, Benjamin T., 853-854

Jean, Wyclef, 767, 855-856

*Jeb* (play), 478

Jefferson, Blind Lemon, 787, 1588

Jefferson, Thomas, 670; and Benjamin Banneker, 92-93; descendants of, 754; and Sally Hemings, 340, 754-755, 1439; on Phillis Wheatley, 1546

Jeffries, Jim, 867

Jeffries, Leonard, 856-857

Jekyll, Walter, 1010

*Jelly's Last Jam* (musical), 660, 775, 1065, 1083, 1234, 1485-1486, 1603

Jemison, Mae C., 858-859

Jenkins, Esau, 366

Jenkins, Louise. *See* Meriwether, Louise

"Jesus music" movement, 430

*Jet* (magazine), 873, 1250, 1432

Jeter, Derek, 860-862

Jimi Hendrix Experience, 759-760

Jimmy James and the Blue Flames, 759

*Jitney* (play), 1588

Jive Records, 1

*Jo Jo Dancer, Your Life Is Calling* (film), 1216

Jockeys; Allen Allensworth, 38; Eugene Jacques Bullard, 259; Canada Lee, 967; Isaac Burns Murphy, 1093-1094; James Winkfield, 1600-1601

Jodeci, 169, 1217

*Joe Turner's Come and Gone* (play), 115, 128, 534, 1588-1589

Johansson, Ingemar, 1164

John, Elton, 169

John Paul II, 693, 937, 1158

"Johnny B. Goode" (song), 141-142, 501

Johnson, Andrew, 140-141, 483, 671

Johnson, Carol Diann. *See* Carroll, Diahann

Johnson, Caryn Elaine. *See* Goldberg, Whoopi

Johnson, Charles S., 792, 808, 862-864, 1507

Johnson, Columbus M., 1366

Johnson, Dennis, 1570

Johnson, Dwayne, 864-865

Johnson, Ernie, 100

Johnson, Fenton, 203

Johnson, Georgia Douglas, 808

Johnson, Jack, 865-868, 895, 1000, 1206

Johnson, James P., 195, 1068, 1504, 1566, 1575

Johnson, James Weldon, 868-871, 1318, 1553; and Gwendolyn Brooks, 217

Johnson, Jim, 867

Johnson, John H., 872-874

Johnson, Johnnie, 141

Johnson, Joshua, 874-875

Johnson, Judy, 139

Johnson, Katherine G., 876-877

Johnson, Lady Bird, 945

Johnson, Linda. *See* Rice, Linda Johnson

Johnson, Lyndon B., 943, 983; and Charles F. Bolden, Jr., 173; and H. Rap Brown, 232; and James L. Farmer, Jr., 574; funeral of, 1203; and Patricia Roberts Harris, 738; and Barbara Jordan, 906; and Moms Mabley, 1004; and Thurgood Marshall, 1038; and Adam Clayton Powell, Jr., 1198; and Leontyne Price, 1203; and Bayard Rustin, 1304; and Robert C. Weaver, 1530

Johnson, Magic, 10, 555, 877-880; HIV infection, 714
Johnson, Marguerite Annie. *See* Angelou, Maya
Johnson, Michael, 880-881
Johnson, Mordecai Wyatt, 262
Johnson, R. Walter, 63
Johnson, Rafer, 882-883
Johnson, Robert L., 884-886, 911
Johnson, Rosamond, 869
Johnson, Sargent, 886-887
Johnson, William H., 888-889
Johnson Gospel Singers, 831
Johnson Publishing Company, 872-874, 1249-1250
Joint Chiefs of Staff, 1199-1200
Jolson, Al, 54, 1592
*Jonah's Gourd Vine* (Hurston), 809
Jones, Absalom, 36, 606, 889-891
Jones, Bill T., 891-892
Jones, Booker T., 747
Jones, Eddie, 1381
Jones, Elvin, 162
Jones, Gayl, 893-894
Jones, James Earl, 895-896, 1476, 1517, 1589
Jones, Jane. *See* Wright, Jane Cooke
Jones, Jerry, 1380
Jones, Jo, 109
Jones, K. C., 1298
Jones, LeRoi. *See* Baraka, Amiri
Jones, Marion, 897-899
Jones, Minnie Lee. *See* Elders, Joycelyn
Jones, Quincy, 15, 240, 899-901; and Michael Jackson, 836, 901
Jones, Sam, 973
Jones, Sissieretta, 269, 902-903
Jones, Thad, 1401
Jones, Tom, 266
Jones Family Band, 78
Jonestown, Guyana, massacre, 1154, 1340
Joplin, Janis, 1227
Joplin, Scott, 120, 903-905, 1021, 1431; film about, 287, 1565
Jordan, Barbara, 844, 905-907, 1633

Jordan, Eli, 1093
Jordan, Jenny Johnson, 883
Jordan, June, 907-909
Jordan, Louis, 195
Jordan, Mary, 270
Jordan, Michael, 100, 257, 849, 885, 909-912, 1028, 1128; and Scottie Pippen, 1186
Jordan, Taft, 1532
Jordan, Vernon, 241, 671, 912-913
*Josephine Baker Story, The* (television movie), 675
Josephson, Barney, 782, 795
*Journal of Black Poetry, The*, 432
*Journal of Negro History*, 1615
*Journey in Satchidananda* (Coltrane), 408
Journey of Reconciliation, 574
Jovi, Jon Bon, 417
Joyce, James, 550, 928, 1097
Joyland Revellers, 1071
Joyner, Al, Jr., 700, 914-915
Joyner, Marjorie, 1502
Joyner-Kersee, Jackie, 914-915
Juba, Master, 916-917
*Jubilee* (radio program), 794-795
*Jubilee* (Walker), 712, 1503
Judaism, 317, 467
Judge, the. *See* Hinton, Milt
*Judge Priest* (film), 1007
Judkins, Steveland Hardaway. *See* Wonder, Stevie
Jug. *See* Ammons, Gene
*Juice* (film), 552, 1334
Juice, the. *See* Simpson, O. J.
Juilliard School of Music, 926; and Miles Davis, 461; and Audra McDonald, 1009; and Wynton Marsalis, 1033; and Leontyne Price, 1202; and Nina Simone, 1360; and Leslie Uggams, 1469
*Julia* (television program), 313, 1596
Julian, Hubert Fauntleroy, 917-919
Julian, Percy Lavon, 919-920
Julius Rosenwald Fund. *See* Rosenwald Fund
*Jump for Joy* (musical), 1448
*Juneteenth* (Ellison), 549
*Jungle Fever* (film), 144, 841, 969

Junior. *See* Griffey, Ken, Jr.
Just, Ernest Everett, 921-922
*Just Around the Corner* (film), 1268

Kags Music Corporation, 416
*Kansas City* (film), 137
Kansas City Chiefs, 35, 955-956
Kansas City Monarchs, 1150; and Ernie Banks, 88; and Cool Papa Bell, 139; and Buck O'Neil, 1136; and Jackie Robinson, 1273
Kansas City Royals, 171, 823, 1136-1137
Kanter, Hal, 313
Kappa Alpha Psi fraternity, 1373
Karajan, Herbert von, 120
Karenga, Maulana, 62, 399, 923-925, 1023
*Karma* (Sanders), 1314
Kawaida, 62, 97, 923-924
Kay, Ulysses, 925-926
*Kazaam* (film), 1135
Keane, Johnny, 214, 596, 650
Keats, John, 440
"Keep A-Knockin'" (song), 195, 990
*Keep on Singin'* (Disciples), 431
*Keep Punching* (film), 54
*Keep Shufflin'* (musical), 1505
Keepnews, Orrin, 1069
Kelley, William Melvin, 926-928
Kelly, Anna, 366
Kelly, R., 1
Kelly, Wynton, 462
Kennedy, Adam P., 929
Kennedy, Adrienne, 928-930
Kennedy, Jacqueline, 348, 1539; and Jackie Joyner-Kersee, 914
Kennedy, John F., 689; and Harry Belafonte, 138; civil rights bill, 1633; and Nat King Cole, 392; and Ernie Davis, 458; and Mervyn Dymally, 535; and James L. Farmer, Jr., 574; inauguration, 832; and Mahalia Jackson, 832; Malcolm X on, 1025; and Thurgood Marshall, 1038; and James Meredith,

1050; and segregation, 1561; and Robert C. Weaver, 1530

Kennedy, Robert F., 250, 738; assassination of, 883; and Benjamin Chavis, 341; and Medgar Evers, 565; and James L. Farmer, Jr., 574; and Earl G. Graves, Sr., 679; and Rafer Johnson, 883

Kennedy, Ted, 241

Kenny Clarke Septet, 16

Kent Recording Company, 937, 1205

Kenton, Stan, 656

Kentucky Derby, 1093, 1357-1358, 1600

Kerner Commission, 247

Kersee, Bob, 491, 699, 914

Keyes, Alan, 930-931, 1122

Keys, Alicia, 932-933, 1474

Khan, Chaka, 69

Killen, Edgar Ray, 331-332

Killens, John O., 368; and Walter Dean Myers, 1098

Kimball, Florence Page, 1202

*Kimora* (television program), 1353

Kincaid, Jamaica, 934-936

*Kind of Blue* (Davis), 16, 410, 462-463, 1301

*Kindred* (Butler), 280

*King* (television movie), 1461, 1596

King, B. B., 163, 434, 848, 936-938, 1411

King, Billy, 48

King, Coretta Scott, 13, 939-941, 1002, 1461; funeral of, 181; and Andrew Young, 1634

King, Don, 601, 975, 1205, 1338

King, Earl, 1381

King, Ed, 719

King, Martin Luther, Jr., 941-944, 1183; and Ralph David Abernathy, 12; and Maya Angelou, 51-52; assassination of, 235, 1572; and Harry Belafonte, 137; and James Bevel, 150; birthday holiday, 413-414, 940, 1519, 1606; and Carol Moseley Braun, 204; and

Tony Brown, 247; and Benjamin Chavis, 341; and John Conyers, Jr., 413; and Ossie Davis, 465, 478; and Ruby Dee, 478; in drama, 357; film portrayals of, 1621; and James Forman, 603; and Aretha Franklin, 615, 619; and Arthur George Gaston, 639; and Dick Gregory, 689; "I Have a Dream" speech, 263, 690, 753, 832, 943, 1230, 1561; and Jesse Jackson, 827-828, 832; and Coretta Scott King, 939; and James Lawson, 964; and Joseph Lowery, 1002; and Malcolm X, 1025-1026; and Benjamin E. Mays, 1044; and Nichelle Nichols, 1115; and Odetta, 1126; paintings of, 1034; photographs of, 1155; poetry about, 523; and Albert Raby, 1224; and Jo Ann Gibson Robinson, 1276; and Bayard Rustin, 1304; screen portrayals of, 1596; and Al Sharpton, 1338; and Clarence Thomas, 1419; and C. T. Vivian, 1489; and Hosea Williams, 1572; and Ernest Withers, 1602; and Andrew Young, 1632-1633

King, Martin Luther, Sr., 841

King, Rodney, 201, 291, 1536, 1585

*King Hedley II* (play), 471

*King Lear* (play), 23, 478

King of Dance. *See* Checker, Chubby

*King of New York* (film), 590

King of Pop. *See* Jackson, Michael

King of Ragtime. *See* Joplin, Scott

King of Rock and Soul. *See* Burke, Solomon

King Records, 1019

Kings of Rhythm, 1451-1452, 1455

*Kings of Rock* (Run-D.M.C.), 1351

Kinte Foundation, 712

Kirk, Andy, 1103

"Kiss an Angel Good Morning" (song), 1207

*Kiss of the Spider Woman* (musical), 1582

Kitchen Table: Women of Color Press, 998, 1376

Kitt, Eartha, 944-946

Kittel, Frederick August. *See* Wilson, August

Knight, Gladys, 1, 402, 946-947; and Jackson Five, 835

Knight, Gwendolyn, 962

Knight, Marion "Suge," 505, 1389

Knight, Marva Delores. *See* Collins, Marva

Knowles, Beyoncé, 740, 853, 948-949

Koch, Ed, 498

Koch Records, 356

Koenigswarter, Pannonica de, 1070

Kolax, King, 41

Komunyakaa, Yusef, 949-951

*Kongi's Harvest* (film), 465

Korbel, Josef, 1245

Korean War; and Cannonball Adderley, 15; and Julius Wesley Becton, Jr., 134; and Bobby Blue Bland, 163; and James E. Cheek, 349; and John Conyers, Jr., 413; and W. E. B. Du Bois, 522; and Ernest J. Gaines, 630; and James Lawson, 964; and Vance Hunter Marchbanks, 1029; and Thurgood Marshall, 1037; and Willie Mays, 1046; and Dutch Morial, 1077; peace initiatives, 522; and Lloyd Price, 1205; and Charles Rangel, 1231; and Paul Robeson, 1265; and Thomas Sowell, 1390; and L. Douglas Wilder, 1557

Kristol, William, 1394

Krupa, Gene, 723, 1532

*Krush Groove* (film), 953, 1355, 1470

Krynicki, Nell. *See* Carter, Nell

Ku Klux Klan, 266, 455, 566, 1303; in *Birth of a Nation*, 702; civil rights worker murders, 330-332, 818; and William Thomas Fontaine, 598; and Malcolm X, 1024; and Medgar

Evers murder, 568; Mississippi girl murders, 332, 1245; National Anti-Klan Network, 1489; and Sidney Poitier, 1190; and Hiram Rhoades Revels, 1242; and Paul Robeson, 1265; and Fred Shuttlesworth, 1348; and Robert Franklin Williams, 1578; and James Winkfield, 1600; and Andrew Young, 1633
Kuhn, Bowie, 597
Kunstler, William, 1329
Kunta Kinte, 275, 712-713
Kushner, Tony, 929
Kwanzaa, 923-924, 1023
Kyles, Cedric Antonio. *See* Cedric the Entertainer

L. L. Cool J., 952-953, 1355
*L-Shaped Room, The* (film), 1175
*L Word, The* (television program), 465
L. T. *See* Taylor, Lawrence
L.A. Four, 240
La Funque, Buckshot. *See* Adderley, Cannonball
*L.A. Law* (television program), 343, 1470-1471
L.A. Rebellion, 445
Labelle, 954
LaBelle, Patti, 69, 953-955
LaChiusa, Michael John, 1009
*Lackawanna Blues* (film), 1604, 1621
*Ladies First* (Queen Latifah), 1222
*Ladies First: Revelations of a Strong Woman* (Queen Latifah), 1222
Lady Day. *See* Holiday, Billie
"Lady Madonna" (song), 509
*Lady Sings the Blues* (film), 673, 783, 1215, 1291, 1293
*Lady Sings the Blues* (Holiday), 783
LaFace Records, 69, 208-209
LaFayette, Bernard, 1488
Lagerfeld, Karl, 1353
*L'Ag'Ya* (ballet), 530
Laine, Frankie, 429

Lamothe, Ferdinand Joseph. *See* Morton, Jelly Roll
LaMotta, Jake, 1284
Land, Harold, 1260
*Land of Look Behind* (Cliff), 377
Lane, Anna Houston. *See* Petry, Ann
Lane, Dick, 429
Lane, William Henry. *See* Juba, Master
Laney, Lucy Craft, 223, 792
Langston Hughes Medal; Amiri Baraka, 97; Ishmael Reed, 1239
Lanier, Willie, 955-957
Laroque, Nell. *See* Carter, Nell
LaRouche, Lyndon, 151
Larsen, Nella, 957-959
Las Vegas; and Cholly Atkins, 402; and Louise Beavers, 129; and Toni Braxton, 209; and Nat King Cole, 391; and Dorothy Dandridge, 442; and Sammy Davis, Jr., 467-468; and Fats Domino, 509; and Redd Foxx, 613; and Richard Pryor, 1214; and Tupac Shakur, 1334; and O. J. Simpson, 1363
*Last Days of Louisiana Red, The* (Reed), 1238-1239
*Last King of Scotland, The* (film), 1548-1549
*Last Minstrel Show, The* (play), 774
Lateef, Yusef, 16
Latimer, Lewis Howard, 959-960
Laurinburg Institute, 654
Law, W. W., 1571
Lawford, Peter, 468
Lawrence, Jacob, 40, 127, 961-962, 1318; and George Washington Bush, 278
Lawrence, Martin, 1355
Lawrence, Robert H., Jr., 963-964
Lawson, James, 150, 964-966, 982, 1102, 1488
Lawson, John, 966-967
Leadbelly, 1127
Leadbitter, Mike, 1213
*Leaning Against the Sun* (Barrax), 103
Lear, Norman, 706, 1499

*Learning Tree, The* (Parks), 1156
Led Zeppelin, 501, 787
Ledbetter, Huddie. *See* Leadbelly
Lee, Albert, 143
Lee, Canada, 967-968
Lee, Don Luther. *See* Madhubuti, Haki R.
Lee, John C. H., 454
Lee, Johnny, 586
Lee, Minnie Joycelyn. *See* Elders, Joycelyn
Lee, Spike, 238, 969-970, 1332, 1387, 1438; and Ossie Davis, 465; and Samuel L. Jackson, 841
Lee, Ulysses, 243
Lee-Smith, Hughie, 971-972
Leland, Mickey, 844
Lemon, Meadowlark, 429, 972-974
Lennox, Annie, 686
Leonard, Sheldon, 422
Leonard, Sugar Ray, 974-976
*Les Miserables* (Hugo), 1435
Leslie, Lisa, 976-977
*Lesson Before Dying, A* (Gaines), 630
*Lethal Weapon* films, 659
*Let's Do It Again* (film), 423, 1191
*Let's Get It Started* (Hammer), 722
*Let's Roll* (James), 848
*Let's Stay Together* (Green), 685, 1457
*Letter from Birmingham City Jail* (King), 943
Levine, James, 119
Lewis, Carl, 978-980
Lewis, Edmonia, 980-981
Lewis, Jerry Lee, 496
Lewis, John, 461, 593
Lewis, John Robert, 150, 180, 982-984, 1433, 1488
Lewis, Lennox, 1463
Lewis, Norman, 127, 1318
Lewis, Ray, 984-985, 1365
Lewis, Smiley, 1381
Lewis, Terry, 169, 825
Lewis, Willie, 315
*Liberating Voices* (Jones), 894
*Liberation of Aunt Jemima, The* (Saar), 1306

*Liberator, The* (magazine), 1011

*Liberator, The* (newspaper), 482, 514, 703, 959, 1397, 1439; and James Forten, 606

Liberia, 149, 483, 637, 816, 1302; American immigrants, 389, 435-437, 482-483, 584-585, 1302-1303; arts center, 1208; and Mary McLeod Bethune, 149; and Benjamin O. Davis, Sr., 453-454; and Henrietta Vinton Davis, 460; and Ossie Davis, 464; and Henry Highland Garnet, 632; and Asa Grant Hilliard III, 769; libretto for, 1434; Peace Corps, 859; poet laureate, 1435; and John Brown Russwurm, 1302; and George S. Schuyler, 1322; slavery in, 863. *See also* American Colonization Society

Liberia College, 436

Lie, Trygve, 263-264

*Life and Times of Frederick Douglass, Written by Himself* (Douglass), 514

*Life* magazine, 293; and Dorothy Dandridge, 443; and Gordon Parks, Sr., 1155-1156

"Life on the Sea Islands" (Grimké), 704-705

*Lifeboat* (film), 968

*Lift Every Voice and Sing* (Savage), 1318

Light Records, 431

*Lilacs* (Walker), 1498

*Lilies of the Field* (film), 1190-1191

Lillie, Frank Rattray, 921

Limbaugh, Rush, 1016, 1394

Lincoln, Abbey, 500

Lincoln, Abraham, 869; and Martin Robison Delany, 483; and Frederick Douglass, 514; Emancipation Proclamation, 140, 1442; and Sojourner Truth, 1443; and Henry McNeal Turner, 1450

Lincoln, C. Eric, 985-986

Lincoln Institute, 177, 490, 1637

Lincoln Memorial, 48, 943, 1606; Anderson concert, 49

Lincoln Motion Picture Company, 1055

Lincoln University, 177, 598, 649, 704, 805, 1037, 1434

Lindbergh, Charles, 917

*Linden Hills* (Naylor), 1105

Lindsay, Vachel, 805

Linguistics, 1020-1022

Lion, Alfred, 1069

*Lion King, The* (film), 431, 706, 896

Liston, Sonny, 27, 601, 987-988, 1164; and Muhammad Ali, 1492

Literacy Volunteers of America, 44-45

Little, Cleavon, 465, 989-990

Little, Malcolm. *See* Malcolm X

*Little Colonel* (film), 1268

Little Giant. *See* Griffin, Johnny

Little Richard, 195, 496, 758, 848, 990-991, 1235, 1381; and Otis Redding, 1235

Little Rock. *See* Sanders, Pharoah

Little Rock Nine, 59, 116-118, 411

Little Vincent. *See* Burke, Solomon

Little Walter, 501, 992-993

*Littlest Rebel* (film), 1268

Live Aid benefit concert, 1351

"Living in America" (song), 234, 236

*Living Is Easy, The* (West), 1539

Lloyd, Earl, 994-995

Lloyd, Harold, 1110

Locke, Alain, 995-996; and Charles Alston, 40; and Ralph Bunche, 262; and Aaron Douglas, 512; and Harlem Renaissance, 805; and Zora Neale Hurston, 808; Rhodes Scholarship, 1555; and William Grant Still, 1399

Loeb, Jacques, 921

Logan, Harold, 1205

Lomax, Alan, 1083, 1525

*London Suite* (Waller), 1506

Long, G. A., 789

*Long Black Song* (Baker), 77

*Long Dream, The* (Wright), 1626

*Long Kiss Goodnight, The* (film), 841

Long Tall Friday, 1071

*Long Way from Home, A* (McKay), 1011

Longfellow, Henry Wadsworth, 524

Lorde, Audre, 997-999, 1376

Los Angeles; city council, 1373; Crips gang, 1388; Inner City Cultural Center, 186, 1595; mayors, 200-202; Police Department, 200-201, 386-387, 1585; riots of 1992, 201, 291, 1375; Sugar Hill neighborhood, 1007; Watts riot, 51, 267, 373, 432, 924, 943, 1034, 1137, 1306

Los Angeles Angels. *See* California Angels

Los Angeles Clippers, 122; and Elgin Baylor, 122

Los Angeles Dodgers, 73, 1522; and Maury Wills, 1586-1587. *See also* Brooklyn Dodgers

Los Angeles Lakers, 257, 850; and Kareem Abdul-Jabbar, 9; and Elgin Baylor, 122; and Kobe Bryant, 257-258; and Wilt Chamberlain, 329; and Magic Johnson, 877-880; and Karl Malone, 1028; and Shaquille O'Neal, 1134-1135

Los Angeles Raiders, 35, 246, 494, 823-824. *See also* Oakland Raiders

Los Angeles Rams, 324, 493, 1521-1522

*Los Angeles Sentinel* (newspaper), 1052

Los Angeles Sparks, 977

*Losing Isaiah* (film), 144, 841

*Losing the Race: Self-Sabotage in Black America* (McWhorter), 1021

*Lost Boundaries* (film), 968

*Lost Boys* (Marshall), 1034

*Lost Man, The* (film), 1596

*Lost Zoo, The* (Cullen), 440

*Loud* (Rihanna), 1256

Louis, Joe, 54, 72, 542, 649, 999-1001, 1194, 1273; and Jersey Joe Walcott, 1491-1492

Louis X. *See* Farrakhan, Louis

*Love and Basketball* (film), 553
*Love and Peace* (Silver), 1350
*Love Supreme, A* (Coltrane), 410, 1458
*Love Will Find a Way* (Sanders), 1314
*Lovers* (Babyface), 69
*Loving v. Virginia*, 1038
Lowery, Joseph, 1001-1002
"Lucille" (song), 990
Lucky Seven Trio, 400
*Lucy* (Kincaid), 935
Lugar, Richard, 1122
Lugar-Obama Nuclear Proliferation Act of 2007, 1122
Lumumba, Patrice, 263, 929, 1025
Lundy, Benjamin, 1496
Lyle, Ron, 601
*Lynchers, The* (Wideman), 1556
Lynching, 6, 210-211, 867, 1514, 1533; antilynching legislation, 527, 795, 1197; in Georgia, 1571; in literature, 630, 702, 870, 927, 1556; in Mississippi, 291, 565, 1432-1433, 1602; in music, 782; and National Association for the Advancement of Colored People, 870, 1553, 1561; in South Carolina, 654; in Tennessee, 617, 1533; in Texas, 249; and Emmett Till, 291, 1432-1433, 1602; and United Youth Committee Against Lynching, 753; and Ida B. Wells-Barnett, 1533-1534
Lyric Records, 270
*Lyrics of Lowly Life* (Dunbar), 525

*M. C. Higgins the Great* (Hamilton), 721
Ma, Yo Yo, 1033
*Ma Rainey's Black Bottom* (play), 115, 534, 1251, 1588-1589
Mabley, Moms, 72, 1003-1004
Mac, Bernie, 326, 1005, 1215
MacArthur Foundation ("genius") grants; Anthony Braxton, 207; Octavia E. Butler, 281; Stanley Crouch, 433; Henry Louis

Gates, Jr., 642; Virginia Hamilton, 720; Kerry James Marshall, 1034, 1036; Ishmael Reed, 1239; Anna Deavere Smith, 1375
*Macbeth* (play), 23, 459, 968, 989
McCain, John, 815, 1123, 1200
McCall, Steve, 1431
McCarthy, Joseph, 795, 805
McCauley, Rose Louise. *See* Parks, Rosa
McCullough, Bernard Jeffrey. *See* Mac, Bernie
McDaniel, Ellas. *See* Diddley, Bo
McDaniel, Hattie, 663, 1006-1008
McDaniels, Darryl, 1350, 1354
McDonald, Freda Josephine. *See* Baker, Josephine
McDonald, James Solomon. *See* Burke, Solomon
McDuffie, Emmanuel, 655
McGhee, Brownie, 434
McGlown, Betty, 1291
McGwire, Mark, 183
McIntyre, Natalie Renee. *See* Gray, Macy
Mack, Craig, 1217
McKay, Claude, 1010-1012; and Arturo Alfonso Schomburg, 1320
McKinley, William, 253, 345-346
McKissick, Floyd, 574
MacLaine, Shirley, 468
McLean, Jackie, 1012-1013
Maclean, Malcolm, 1572
McLeod, Alice Lucille. *See* Coltrane, Alice
McLeod, Mary Jane. *See* Bethune, Mary McLeod
McMillan, Terry, 116, 1014-1015
MacMurray, Fred, 45
McNabb, Donovan, 1016-1017, 1143
McNair, Ronald E., 1017-1019
McNeil, Bill, 654
McPhatter, Clyde, 1019-1020, 1592
McShann, Jay, 141, 1152
McVeigh, Timothy, 199
McWhorter, John, 1020-1022
*Made in Harlem* (musical), 195

*Madea Goes to Jail* (film), 472
*Madea's Family Reunion* (film), 1173
Madhubuti, Haki R., 1022-1024; and Sonia Sanchez, 1308
Madison, James, 438
Mafia, 284
Magic Johnson Enterprises, 879
Mahara's Minstrels, 727
*Mahogany* (film), 674, 1292
*Maiden Voyage* (Hancock), 725
Mailman, the. *See* Malone, Karl
*Major and Minors* (Dunbar), 525
*Major League* (film), 1387-1388
Major League Baseball; integration of, 502-503, 653, 1046, 1150, 1272-1275; reserve clause, 596-597. *See also individual teams and List of Entries by Category under Sports: Baseball*
*Major League II* (film), 552
Majors, Margaret Allison. *See* Bonds, Margaret Allison
Makaveli. *See* Shakur, Tupac
Make a Move, 1431
Makeba, Miriam, 136, 306
*Making of Black Revolutionaries, The* (Forman), 603
Malcolm X, 115, 1024-1027; and Maya Angelou, 51; daughter of, 1332-1333; and Ossie Davis, 465; death of, 52; and Ruby Dee, 478; and Louis Farrakhan, 575; in film, 1516; and Alex Haley, 711; and Martin Luther King, Jr., 1025-1026; and Elijah Muhammad, 1089; photographs of, 1155; screen portrayal of, 1516; and Betty Shabazz, 1025, 1330; and Wesley Snipes, 1387
*Malcolm X* (film), 115-116, 465, 969, 1332, 1516
*Malcolm X as Cultural Hero and Other Afrocentric Essays* (Asante), 61
Malone, Annie Turnbo, 1501-1502
Malone, Karl, 911, 1027-1028
Malone, Moses, 555
*Mama* (McMillan), 1014
*Mama Day* (Naylor), 1105

*Mama Flora's Family* (television program), 713

*Man Called White, A* (White), 1553

Man of Steal, the. *See* Henderson, Rickey

*Manchild in the Promised Land* (Brown), 225-226

Mancini, Henry, 900

*Mandela* (film), 659, 1607

Mandela, Nelson, 624, 778, 940, 1065, 1192, 1250, 1279

Mandela, Winnie, 940

Manley, Effa, 503

Mann Act of 1910, 142, 867

Manning, Peyton, 184

Mao Zedong, 603

"Maple Leaf Rag" (song), 903-904

Marabel, Fate, 58, 1300

Marble, Alice, 648

Marbury, Stephon, 1181

March Against Fear, 1050-1051

March on Washington for Jobs and Freedom (1963), 80; and James Baldwin, 83; and Daisy Bates, 117; and Harry Belafonte, 137; and James Bevel, 151; and Ralph Bunche, 263; and CORE, 818; and Ossie Davis, 465; and James L. Farmer, 574; and Dick Gregory, 690; and Dorothy Height, 753; and Lena Horne, 796; and Mahalia Jackson, 832; and Martin Luther King, Jr., 943; and John Robert Lewis, 983; Malcolm X on, 1025; and Diane Nash, 1103; and Odetta, 1126; and A. Philip Randolph, 1230; and Bayard Rustin, 1304; twentieth-anniversary march, 940; and Roy Wilkins, 1561

March on Washington Movement (1941), 1229

Marchan, Bobby, 1382

Marchbanks, Vance Hunter, 1029-1030

*Marching Blacks* (Powell), 1197

Marciano, Rocky, 335, 1001, 1074, 1163, 1492

Marcuse, Herbert, 448

Marion, George, 1506

*Mario's Green House* (television program), 1481

Mark Twain Prize for American Humor, 1215

*Mark Warnow's Hit Parade* (radio program), 315

Markov chains, 154

Marley, Bob, 1411

Marsalis, Branford, 1031-1032, 1402

Marsalis, Delfeayo, 1031

Marsalis, Ellis, Jr., 156, 1030-1032

Marsalis, Jason, 1031

Marsalis, Wynton, 59, 432, 1031-1033, 1095

Marshall, Kerry James, 1034-1035

Marshall, Paule, 1035-1036

Marshall, Ray, 763

Marshall, Thurgood, 619, 1037-1039, 1050, 1096, 1283; biographies of, 1573; and Stephen L. Carter, 318; screen portrayal of, 1192

Martin, Billy, 757, 839

Martin, Dean, 468

Martin, Denver Ed, 866

Martin, Joe, 26

Martin, Kenyon, 1039-1040

Martin, Roland, 7

Martin Luther King, Jr., Center for Nonviolent Social Change, 940

Martinez, Chihuahua, 725

Marvelettes, 673, 1281

Marx, Karl, 448, 1535

Mary Jane Entertainment, 169

Masekela, Hugh, 19

Mason, Charlotte Osgood, 805, 809

Massachusetts Anti-Slavery Society, 514

Massachusetts General Colored Association, 1495

*Massacre, The* (50 Cent), 589

*"Master Harold" . . . and the boys* (play), 659

Master P, 1389

Master Records, 546

Mastin, Will, 466

Matadors, 1280-1281

Mathematicians; David Harold Blackwell, 153-156; Evelyn

Boyd Granville, 678-679; Katherine G. Johnson, 876-877

Mathis, Buster, 620

*Matrix* films, 591, 1536

Matzeliger, Jan Ernst, 1041-1042

*Maude* (television program), 1499

Mavericks, Houston, 745

Maxim, Joey, 335, 1074, 1163, 1285, 1492

*Maybe You Never Cry Again* (Mac), 1005

"Maybellene" (song), 141

Mayfield, Curtis, 758

Maynard, Robert C., 1277

Mays, Benjamin E., 1043-1045

Mays, Willie, 4, 1045-1048, 1206; and Barry Bonds, 182; and O. J. Simpson, 1361

Mazama, Ama, 62

MCA Records, 674, 947

Meade, Eddie, 54

Mecca, 1026, 1129

*Meditations* (Sanders), 1314

Meeropol, Abel, 782

*Meet the Browns* (television program), 1174

Meier, Audrey, 431

Melba, Nellie, 270, 748

Melish, William, 448

Melony Hounds, 1006

Melotone Records, 1071

Melrose, Lester, 434

*Mementos* (Marshall), 1034

Memphis, Tennessee; Beale Street, 163, 746, 937; Full Gospel Tabernacle Church, 685; Lorraine Motel, 13, 827, 943; Middle Baptist Church, 790; sanitation worker strike, 13, 939, 943, 965, 1572

"Memphis Blues, The" (song), 727, 1227

Memphis Grizzlies, 1139

Memphis Red Sox, 139, 1136, 1206

*Men in Black* (film), 932, 1386

Menard, John Willis, 1048-1049

Mencken, H. L., 1322

Merchant Marines, 548

*Merchant of Venice, The* (play), 23

Mercury Records, 1020, 1212, 1354, 1484; and Quincy Jones, 900

*Mercy, Mercy, Mercy! Live at "The Club"* (Adderley), 16

Meredith, James, 689, 1049-1051

*Meridian* (Walker), 1494

Meriwether, Louise, 1052-1053

*Messenger, The* (newspaper), 210, 1228, 1322

Metcalfe, Ralph, 1518, 1632

*Meteor in the Madhouse* (Forrest), 605

Method Man, 169

*Metronome* magazine, 316; awards, 16, 240, 309, 467

Metropolitan Opera, 19, 49, 312, 954, 1118, 1202-1203; and Kathleen Battle, 120

Mexican War, 133

Meyers, Johnny, 832

MFDP. *See* Mississippi Freedom Democratic Party

Mfume, Kweisi, 181, 1053-1055

MGM Records, 1019

MIA. *See* Montgomery Improvement Association

Miami Dolphins, 1581

Miami Heat, 850, 1135

Micheaux, Oscar, 1055-1056, 1264, 1482

Michel, Prakazrel "Pras," 767

Mickey and Sylvia, 1456

Middleton, Benjamin Augustus. *See* Vereen, Ben

Middleton, Kenneth, 565

Mifflin, Warner, 37

*Migration of the Negro, The* (Lawrence), 962

Milam, J. W., 1432

Milburn, Ralph, 446

Miles, Buddy, 759

*Miles Ahead* (Davis), 462

Milestone Jazzstars, 1290, 1458

*Milestones* (Davis), 16, 410, 462

Miley, Bubber, 546

Military Academy, U.S., 595-596, 1029; and Benjamin O. Davis, Sr., 453; and Benjamin O. Davis, Jr., 455

Miller, Cheryl, 1057-1058

Miller, Dorie, 1058-1059

Miller, Edward Charles, 1044

Miller, George Washington, 1179

Miller, Maria W. *See* Stewart, Maria

Miller, Mitch, 1469

Miller, Theodore, 1266

Millinder, Lucky, 162

*Million Dollar Baby* (film), 624

Million Man March, 52, 151, 1488, 1623; and Benjamin Chavis, 341-342; and Louis Farrakhan, 576; and Maulana Karenga, 924

Million Woman March, 342

Mills, Florence, 1060-1061

Milwaukee Braves, 3

Milwaukee Brewers, 4, 301

Milwaukee Bucks, 9, 1262

*Mind of the Negro as Reflected in Letters Written During the Crisis, 1800-1860, The* (Woodson), 1616

Mingus, Charles, 397, 1013, 1061-1063; and Duke Ellington, 547; and Max Roach, 1260

Minneapolis Lakers, 122

Minnesota Timberwolves, 152, 634; and Kevin Garnett, 634

Minnesota Twins, 300-301

"Minnie the Moocher" (song), 284-285

Minstrelsy and vaudeville, 165. *See also in List of Entries by Category under Entertainment: Minstrelsy*

Mint Condition, 208

*Miracle in Harlem* (film), 587

Miracles, 402, 1291, 1606; and Smokey Robinson, 1280-1282

*Miseducation of Lauryn Hill, The* (Hill), 767

*Mis-education of the Negro, The* (Woodson), 1616

Miss America pageant, 338-339, 1102, 1581

*Miss Muriel and Other Short Stories* (Petry), 1178

Miss Teen America, 144

Miss Universe pageant, 694

Miss USA pageant, 144

Missionaries, 274, 362, 482; Mary McLeod Bethune, 148; Daniel Coker, 389; Alexander Crummell, 435-436; Samuel Ferguson, 584-585; Gloria Naylor, 1105

Mississippi Alliance for Progress, 718

*Mississippi Burning* (film), 332

Mississippi Freedom Democratic Party, 76, 717-719

Mississippi Freedom Project, 232

*Mississippi Masala* (film), 1516

Missouri Compromise of 1820, 1325

Missourians, 284

Mitchell, Arthur, 1064-1065

Mitchell, Brian Stokes, 471, 1065-1066

Mitchell, Clarence M., Jr., 1067-1068

Mitchell, Margaret, 1007

Mitchell, Mitch, 759

Mitchell, Parren, 1053

Mitchell, Willie, 685

Mizell, Jason, 588, 1350-1352, 1355

*Mo' Better Blues* (film), 841, 970, 1387, 1516

Modell, Art, 238

Modern Jazz Quartet, 240, 397

Modern Records, 163, 786, 848

*Moesha* (television program), 1005

Mohammed, Khalid Shaikh, 780

Mohawk, Dee-Dee, 416

Moi, Daniel arap, 828

Molinas, Jack, 740

"Mona Lisa" (song), 391, 393

Moncur, Grachan, III, 1013, 1344

"Money Honey" (song), 1019

Monk, Thelonious, 206, 1068-1070, 1113; and Art Blakey, 162; and Johnny Griffin, 697

Monroe, Marilyn, 443, 468, 593

*Monster* (Myers), 1098

*Monster's Ball* (film), 145, 444

*Montel Williams Show, The* (television program), 1577

Monterey Jazz Festival, 16, 397, 547, 759

Monterey Pop Festival, 1235

Montgomery, James, 1445

Montgomery, Little Brother, 1071-1072

Montgomery, Tim, 898

Montgomery bus boycott; and Ralph David Abernathy, 12; and Coretta Scott King, 939, 941, 943; and E. D. Nixon, 1116-1117; and Rosa Parks, 1157-1159; and Jo Ann Gibson Robinson, 1275-1276; and Bayard Rustin, 1304

Montgomery Improvement Association, 941, 943, 1116, 1275-1276, 1347

Montreal Jazz Festival, 157

Mood, Alexander, 154

Moon, Warren, 32

Moonfixer. See Lloyd, Earl

Moonglows, 643

Moore, Alice Ruth. See Dunbar-Nelson, Alice

Moore, Archie, 335, 1073-1075, 1163

Moore, Eleanor, 265

Moore, Elizabeth Bebe. See Campbell, Bebe Moore

Moore, Johnny, 222, 1019

Moore, Maxine. See Waters, Maxine

Moore, Melba, 465

Moore, Oscar, 222

Moore, Tim, 1003

Moorer, Michael, 602

*Moorish Guide* (newspaper), 29

Moorish Science Temple, 29-30

Moraga, Cherrie, 1376

Morehouse, Henry Lyman, 792

Morehouse College, 179, 792, 940; and John Hope, 793; and Samuel L. Jackson, 840-841; and Martin Luther King, Jr., 941; and Benjamin E. Mays, 1043-1045; and Edwin Moses, 1084; and David Satcher, 1315-1316

Morgan, Garrett Augustus, 1075-1076

Morgan, John Pierpont, 269

Morial, Dutch, 1077-1078

Morial, Marc, 1077, 1100

Moroder, Giorgio, 1406

Morris, Garrett, 1078-1080

Morris, Joe, 14, 697

Morris, Samuel, 578

Morris, Steveland. See Wonder, Stevie

Morris Brown College, 205, 800, 1450, 1571

Morrison, George, 1006

Morrison, Toni, 1080-1082; and Toni Cade Bambara, 87; and Claude Brown, 226; and Barbara Chase-Riboud, 340; and Leon Forrest, 605; and Gayl Jones, 893; and June Jordan, 908; and Emmett Till, 1433

Morrison, Van, 164, 266, 787, 1592

Morrow, George, 1260

Morton, Jelly Roll, 55, 1071, 1082-1084, 1213, 1575

Moscone, George, 250

Moses, Edwin, 1084-1085

*Moses, Man of the Mountain* (Hurston), 809

Moses, Robert, 719

Mosley, Walter, 1086-1087

Moss, Carlton, 1399

Moss, Hajna O., 590

Moss, Paula, 1335

Moten, Benny, 109, 1133

*Mother, The* (Barthé), 107

Mother of Chemotherapy, the. See Wright, Jane Cooke

Mothers Advocating Juvenile Justice, 231

*Mother's Quilt* (Ringgold), 1259

Moton, Robert, 321, 1165

Motown Records, 380, 402, 673, 815-816, 1291; and Cholly Atkins, 401; and Commodores, 1253; and Marvin Gaye, 643-644; and Berry Gordy, Jr., 672-674; and Jackson Five, 835-836; and Gladys Knight, 946; and Sylvia M. Rhone, 1243-1244;

and Lionel Richie, 1253; and Smokey Robinson, 1280-1282; Soul label, 946; and Supremes, 1291; and Stevie Wonder, 1605

*Motown 25* (television program), 836

Mott, Lucretia, 1447

Mottola, Tommy, 302

Mount Zion Methodist Church, 331

Mourning, Alonzo, 1040

Mouskouri, Nana, 136

MOVE bombing, 87, 683, 1556, 1584

"Move on Up a Little Higher (song), 832

Mozambique, 1633

Mr. Accuracy. See Peete, Calvin

Mr. B. See Eckstine, Billy

Mr. Big Shot. See Billups, Chauncey

Mr. Civil Rights. See Wilkins, Roy

Mr. Cub. See Banks, Ernie

Mr. Excitement. See Wilson, Jackie

Mr. Fourth Quarter. See Dickerson, Eric

Mr. Keene. See Aldridge, Ira Frederick

Mr. NAACP. See White, Walter

Mr. November. See Jeter, Derek

Mr. October. See Jackson, Reggie

Mr. Personality. See Price, Lloyd

*Mr. Potter* (Kincaid), 935

*Mr. Wonderful* (play), 468

*MTV Unplugged No. 2.0* (Hill), 768

Muhammad, Benjamin Chavis. See Chavis, Benjamin

Muhammad, Elijah, 27, 83, 575, 1024, 1088-1090

Muhammad, Kalot, 1089

Muhammad, Wallace D., 575, 1089

*Muhammad Speaks* (newspaper), 27, 605

*Mule Bone* (play), 809

*Mules and Men* (Hurston), 809

Mulligan, Gerry, 308, 461

Mulligan, Robert, 1175

Munson, Thurman, 839

Murphy, Eddie, 287, 663, 714, 1090-1092, 1215, 1438; and Chris Rock, 1286

Murphy, Isaac Burns, 1093-1094

Murray, Albert, 1094-1095

Murray, David, 1336

Murray, Pauli, 1095-1097

Museum of Modern Art; and Charles Alston, 40; and Romare Bearden, 127; and Barbara Chase-Riboud, 339; and Roy DeCarava, 477; and Martin Luther King, Jr., 1259; and Jacob Lawrence, 962

*Music Box* (Carey), 302

*Music of the Sun* (Rihanna), 1255

Muskie, Edmund S., 569

Muslim Mosque, Inc., 1026

Mussolini, Benito, 1000

Muste, A. J., 573

Muti, Riccardo, 120

*Mwandishi* (Hancock), 726

*My American Journey* (Powell), 1200

*My Bondage and My Freedom* (Douglass), 514

*My Brother* (Kincaid), 935

*My Children! My Africa!* (play), 1476

"My Favorite Things" (song), 410

*My Green Hills of Jamaica* (McKay), 1011

"My Guy" (song), 1281

*My Life with Martin Luther King, Jr.* (King), 939

*My Lives and How I Lost Them* (Cullen), 441

*My One and Only* (musical), 401

*My Way* (Usher), 1474

Myers, Walter Dean, 1097-1099

Myrdal, Gunnar, 5, 243, 262; and Kenneth Clark, 364

*Mystery, The* (newspaper), 482

Mystery and detective fiction writers; and Steven Barnes, 102; and Virginia Hamilton, 720; and Chester Himes, 770-772; and Walter Mosley, 1086-1087

NAACP. *See* National Association for the Advancement of Colored People

NACW. *See* National Association of Colored Women

Nader, Ralph, 1536

Nagin, Ray, 1100-1101

*Naked Gun* films, 1363

Nance, Ray, 167

*Narrative of the Life of Frederick Douglass, an American Slave* (Douglass), 514

Nas, 740, 852-853

NASA. *See* National Aeronautics and Space Administration

Nash, Diane, 61, 150-151, 982, 1102-1103, 1488

Nash, Keisha, 1549

Nashville, Tennessee; sit-ins, 61, 150, 1102, 1488

Nashville Christian Institute, 60

*Nat King Cole Show* (television program), 392

Nate Dogg, 1388, 1390

Nation of Islam, 27, 30, 1308; and Benjamin Chavis, 341-342; and Louis Farrakhan, 575-576; and Malcolm X, 1024-1027; and Malcolm X assassination, 1332; and Betty Shabazz, 1330-1331. *See also* Islam

National Academy of Sciences, 155, 920, 1594

National Action Network, 1339

National Aeronautics and Space Administration, 1018; and George Edward Alcorn, 20; and Guion Bluford, 171-173; and Charles F. Bolden, Jr., 174; and Evelyn Boyd Granville, 678; and Frederick Drew Gregory, 691; and Mae C. Jemison, 859; and Katherine G. Johnson, 876-877; and Robert H. Lawrence, Jr., 963; and Ronald E. McNair, 1017-1019; and Vance Hunter Marchbanks, 1029; and Nichelle Nichols, 1115; and Neil deGrasse Tyson, 1464

National Afro-American Council, 254, 345, 1509

National Alliance Against Racism and Political Repression, 450

National Anti-Klan Network, 1489

National Association for the Advancement of Colored People, 129, 306, 702; and Ella Baker, 75, 80; and Daisy Bates, 117; and Jane Matilda Bolin, 176; and Julian Bond, 179-180; and Cyril V. Briggs, 211; and Willie Brown, 249; and James Chaney, 330; and Benjamin Chavis, 341-342; and Charles Waddell Chesnutt, 354; and Shirley Chisholm, 359; and Septima Poinsette Clark, 365-366; and James E. Clyburn, 382; and W. E. B. Du Bois, 521-522; and Charles Evers, 565, 567; and Medgar Evers, 566-568; and Myrlie Evers-Williams, 568-570; and James L. Farmer, Jr., 574; and Jessie Redmon Fauset, 582; and Stepin Fetchit, 587; and James Forman, 603; and Patricia Roberts Harris, 737; and Benjamin Hooks, 789-791; and John Hope, 792; and Charles Hamilton Houston, 797; and Benjamin T. Jealous, 853-854; and James Weldon Johnson, 870; and Vernon Jordan, 913; and Martin Luther King, Jr., 941; and Sonny Liston, 988; and Claude McKay, 1011; and Thurgood Marshall, 1037-1038; and Kweisi Mfume, 1053-1054; and Clarence M. Mitchell, Jr., 1067-1068; Montgomery bus boycott, 12; and Garrett Augustus Morgan, 1076; and Dutch Morial, 1077; and E. D. Nixon, 1116; and Rosa Parks, 1157; and Floyd Patterson, 1164; and Frank Robinson, 1271, 1274; and Spottswood W. Robinson III, 1283; and Fred Shuttlesworth, 1347; sit-in campaign, 1096, 1571; and Mary Church Terrell, 1417; and Till murder case, 1433; and C. DeLores Tucker, 1447; and Alexander Walters, 1509; and

Booker T. Washington, 1514; and Robert C. Weaver, 1530; and Walter White, 1552-1554; and Roy Wilkins, 1560-1562; and Hosea Williams, 1571, 1578; and Louis T. Wright, 1624; and Whitney Young, 1638. *See also* Spingarn Medal

National Association for the Advancement of Colored People Legal Defense and Education Fund, 642, 779, 854, 912, 1050, 1077, 1162, 1283

National Association of Black Journalists, 199, 668, 807, 873, 908, 1188, 1277; and Bernard Shaw, 1341

National Association of Black Media Producers, 247

National Association of Black Social Workers, 769

National Association of Colored Women, 149, 274, 733, 794, 1417, 1534; and Madam C. J. Walker, 1502

National Association of Negro Musicians, 48, 185

National Association of Social Workers, 1638

National Association of Wage Earners, 274

National Baptist Convention, 273-274, 510, 831-832

National Basketball Association; integration of, 994. *See also individual teams and List of Entries by Category under Sports: Basketball*

National Basketball Association Players Association, 1426

National Black Feminist Organization, 1376

National Black Sisters' Conference, 193

National Conservatory of Music, 269, 902

National Convention of Gospel Choirs and Choruses, 511

National Council for Black Studies, 62, 769, 924

National Council of Negro Women, 148-149, 752-753, 796, 1330

National Education Association, 626-627

National Emigration Convention, 482

National Equal Rights League, 1440

National Equality March, 181

National Football League, 1193. *See also individual teams and List of Entries by Category under Sports: Football*

National Football League Players Association, 1472-1473

National Freedmen's Relief Association, 1443

National Inventors Hall of Fame, 126, 321, 1257

National League of Republican Colored Women, 274

National Low Income Housing Coalition, 217

National Medal of Arts; Romare Bearden, 128; Harry Belafonte, 138; Gwendolyn Brooks, 218; Ray Charles, 336; Roy DeCarava, 477; Fats Domino, 509; Lionel Hampton, 724; Wynton Marsalis, 1033; Arthur Mitchell, 1065; Odetta, 1127; Gordon Parks, Sr., 1156; Leontyne Price, 1203; Lloyd Richards, 1252; Smokey Robinson, 1282

National Medical Association, 1569

National Negro Business League, 1514

National Negro Congress, 753, 1229

National Newspapers Publishers Association, 854

National Organization for Women, 205, 360, 367, 1095-1096

National Political Congress of Black Women, 360, 1447

National Rifle Association, 818

National Science Foundation, 1369

National Training School for Women and Girls, 274

National Urban League, 274, 1044, 1067; and Ron Brown, 241; and Charles S. Johnson, 862; and Robert L. Johnson, 884; and Vernon Jordan, 913; and Eric Walrond, 1507; and Whitney Young, 1637-1638

National Women's Political Caucus, 205, 569, 719

National Youth Administration, 149, 1208, 1273

Native American reservations, 10, 1055, 1415

*Native Son* (play), 968

*Native Son* (Wright), 82, 1625, 1627

Naval Academy, U.S., 173-174, 681, 1269, 1576

Navarro, Fats, 227, 1103-1104

Naylor, Gloria, 1105-1106

NCNW. *See* National Council of Negro Women

Neal, Larry, 625; and Sonia Sanchez, 1308

Negro Actors' Guild, 1268

Negro American Labor Council, 1230

*Negro Art* (Locke), 996

"Negro Art-Hokum, The" (Schuyler), 1322

*Negro Caravan, The* (Brown), 244

Negro Dance Group, 530

*Negro Digest, The* (magazine), 523, 873, 927

Negro Ensemble Company, 625, 840, 1516

Negro History Week, 451-452, 1616. *See also* Black History Month

*Negro in American Culture, The* (Locke), 996

*Negro in American Fiction, The* (Brown), 244

*Negro in Chicago, The* (Johnson), 862

Negro League Baseball Museum, 1136

Negro Leagues, 289; Hank Aaron, 3-4; Ernie Banks, 88; Cool Papa Bell, 138-140; Roy Campanella, 288; Larry Doby, 502-504; documentary about, 675; in film, 1565; Josh Gibson, 652-654; Willie Mays, 1046; Buck O'Neil, 1136-1137; Satchel Paige, 1148-1151; photographs of, 1602; Charley Pride, 1206; Jackie Robinson, 1273; Kenneth S. Washington, 1521. *See also individual teams and players*

Negro National Labor Union, 483

*Negro Poetry and Drama* (Brown), 244

Negro Society for Historical Research, 1320

*Negro Soldier, The* (film), 454

"Negro Speaks of Rivers, The" (Hughes), 804, 1208

Negro Women, Inc., 1178

*Negro World, The* (newspaper), 636, 1507

*Negroes with Guns* (Williams), 1579

Nelson, Prince Rogers. *See* Prince

Nemiroff, Lorraine Hansberry. *See* Hansberry, Lorraine

Nemiroff, Robert, 729

Neon Deion. *See* Sanders, Deion

*Neon Vernacular* (Komunyakaa), 950

*Neon Vernacular: New and Selected Poems* (Komunyakaa), 950

Neumann, John von, 154

Neverland Ranch, 836

Neville, Aaron, 1106-1107

Neville Brothers, 1107

New Black Cinema movement, 969

*New Challenge, The* (magazine), 1538

New England Anti-Slavery Society, 1397, 1496

*New Faces* (musical), 945

*New Jack City* (film), 1480

"New jack swing," 70

New Jersey Nets; and Darryl Dawkins, 474; and Julius Erving, 555; and Jay-Z, 852; and Kenyon Martin, 1039-1040

*New Kind of Family, A* (television program), 825

*New Masses* (journal), 548

*New Negro, The* (Locke), 809, 996, 1320

New Negro movement, 210, 886, 996, 1228; and Eric Walrond, 1507

*New Negro Poets, U.S.A.* (Hughes), 997

New Orleans; Dryades Street boycott, 1077; Hurricane Katrina, 383, 1100-1101; mayors, 1077-1078, 1100-1101; Storyville, 57-58, 1082, 1132; World Cotton Centennial, 253

*New Orleans* (film), 783

New Orleans Hornets, 1167, 1537

New Orleans Jazz, 122

*New Orleans Tribune, The* (newspaper), 532-533

New Thought movement, 577-578

*New World A-Coming* (play), 507

*New York Age, The* (newspaper), 870, 1533

*New York Amsterdam News, The* (newspaper), 210, 451, 731, 926, 1177

*New York Beat* (film), 111

New York Brown Bombers, 1194

New York City; African Burial Ground, 340; African Free School, 631; African Grove theater, 22; Association of Community Organizers for Reform Now, 499; Bamboo Inn, 308; Birdland, 227, 1152; Black Bottom Club, 1531; Colored Orphan Asylum, 592; Cosmopolitan Club, 141; Crown Heights Riots, 498, 1339, 1375; Hell's Kitchen, 1284; Human Rights Commission, 1119; mayors, 497-499, 1339; Temple Emanu-El, 270; Temple Number Seven, 575; Tin Palace, 432; World's Fair, 623, 1003, 1318. *See also* Harlem

New York Contemporary Five, 1344

New York Foundation, 421, 1106

New York Giants (baseball), 1550; and Willie Mays, 1045-1048; and Maury Wills, 1586

New York Giants (football); and Lawrence Taylor, 1413-1415; and Tyrone Wheatley, 1548

*New York Independent News, The*, 1194

New York Knicks, 1426, 1559; and Nat "Sweetwater" Clifton, 994; and Patrick Ewing, 571-572; and Walt Frazier, 621-622; and Louis Gossett, Jr., 674

New York Mets; and Willie Mays, 1047; and Charley Pride, 1206

New York Nets, 554; and Julius Erving, 555

New York Public Library; murals, 512; Schomburg Collection, 1320

New York Renaissance Big Five, 10

*New York Times, The*, 1183

*New York Times v. Sullivan*, 1183

New York Yankees, 1551; and Rickey Henderson, 757; and Reggie Jackson, 839; and Derek Jeter, 860-862; and Deion Sanders, 1312

*New Yorker, The*, 83, 293, 516, 807, 934

Newark Eagles, 289, 503, 838, 1150

Newcombe, Don, 289

Newk. *See* Rollins, Sonny

Newman, Floyd, 746

Newport Folk Festival, 937, 1126-1127

Newport Jazz Festival, 401; and Art Blakey, 162; and Ray Brown, 240; and Miles Davis, 461; and Duke Ellington, 547; and McCoy Tyner, 1458; and Muddy Waters, 1526; and Mary Lou Williams, 1575

Newton, Huey P., 372, 603, 1110, 1328

*Nguzo Saba*, 924

Niagara Movement, 791-792, 1417, 1440, 1514; and W. E. B. Du Bois, 520-522

Nicaragua, 869; and Roberto Clemente, 376

Nicholas, Fayard, 1110-1112

Nicholas, Harold, 442, 775, 1110-1112

Nicholas, Ulysses Domonick, 1110

Nicholas, Viola Harden, 1110

Nicholas Brothers. *See* Nicholas, Fayard, and Nicholas, Harold

Nichols, Herbie, 1112-1113

Nichols, James Thomas. *See* Bell, Cool Papa

Nichols, Nichelle, 275, 1114-1115

Niebuhr, Reinhold, 942

Nigeria, 465, 962, 1208; and James Meredith, 1050; and Hakeem Olajuwon, 1128-1129

Nigerian Nightmare, the. *See* Olajuwon, Hakeem

*Night Gallery* (television program), 464

*Night in Havana, A* (film), 656

Nighthawk, Robert, 501

*1996* (Naylor), 1106

*1999* (Prince), 1211

Niven, Larry, 101

Nix, Robert, 683

Nixon, E. D., 12, 1116-1117

Nixon, Richard M., 1089, 1562; and Ralph Abernathy, 13; and James L. Farmer, 574; and Benjamin Hooks, 790; and Roy Innis, 817; and Barbara Jordan, 906; and Watergate, 906; and Stevie Wonder, 1606; and Whitney Young, 1638

Nkrumah, Kwame, 306, 368, 522, 929

No Child Left Behind Act of 2002, 1147

No Limit Records, 1389

*No Telephone to Heaven* (Cliff), 377

*No Way Out* (film), 478, 1190

Nobel Peace Prize; Ralph Bunche, 264; Martin Luther King, Jr., 939, 943; Barack Obama, 1123, 1536

Nobel Prize in Literature; Toni Morrison, 1081; Wole Soyinka, 465, 640

Nonviolent Action Group, 232

Noone, Jimmie, 773

Norman, Jessye, 120, 185, 1117-1119

Norman, Peter, 304, 1384

North Carolina Agricultural and Technical College, 179, 827, 1017

*North Star, The* (newspaper), 482, 513-514

Norton, Eleanor Holmes, 1119-1120

*Notes of a Native Son* (Baldwin), 82

*Notes on the State of Virginia* (Jefferson), 92

*Nothing but a Man* (film), 499-500

Notorious B.I.G., 116, 852, 1217, 1334, 1389; film about, 1218; murder of, 1217

Nottage, Cynthia DeLores. *See* Tucker, C. DeLores

Novak, Kim, 468

NOW. *See* National Organization for Women

*Now Is the Time to Open Your Heart* (Walker), 1495

*Now Is Your Time!* (Myers), 1098

Nuclear Regulatory Commission, U.S., 843

*Nutty Professor, The* (film), 333, 1092

*Nutty Professor II: The Klumps* (film), 825

N.W.A., 505, 812-813; gangsta rap, 505

*O* magazine, 445

*Oak and Ivy* (Dunbar), 524

Oakland Athletics; and Vida Blue, 170-171; and M. C. Hammer, 721; and Rickey Henderson, 757; and Reggie Jackson, 838-839; and Frank Thomas, 1424

Oakland Police Department, 1109

Oakland Raiders, 736; and Jerry Rice, 1249; and Art Shell, 1341-1343; and Gene Upshaw, 1472; and Tyrone Wheatley, 1548; and Rod Woodson, 1618. *See also* Los Angeles Raiders

Oaktown Records, 722

Obama, Barack, 737, 1121-1124; and Edward W. Brooke, 217; and Roland Burris, 272; and James E. Clyburn, 383; and Angela Davis, 450; and *Ebony* magazine, 873; and Henry Louis Gates, Jr., 641; and Eric Holder, 780; inauguration, 24-25, 616, 949, 1002, 1127, 1606; and Jesse Jackson, 829; and Jesse Jackson, Jr., 830; and Alan Keyes, 931; and Michelle Obama, 1124; and Deval Patrick, 1162; and Colin Powell, 1200; and Tavis Smiley, 1374; and Shelby Steele, 1396; vacated Senate seat, 272; and Stevie Wonder, 1606; and Jeremiah Wright, 1623

Obama, Michelle, 1121, 1124-1125

Occomy, Marita Odette Bonner. *See* Bonner, Marita

*Ocean's Eleven* (film), 468

Ochocinco, Chad, 1144

*Odds Against Tomorrow* (film), 137

Odets, Clifford, 468

Odetta, 1126-1127

*Of Love and Dust* (Gaines), 630

*Of New Horizons* (Kay), 925

*Off the Wall* (Jackson), 836, 901

Office of Economic Opportunity, 382

*Officer and a Gentleman, An* (film), 675

Ogden, C. K., 1011

"Oh Lady Be Good" (song), 593

Ohno, Apolo Anton, 469

O'Jays, 402

Okeh Records; and Perry Bradford, 195; and Big Bill Broonzy, 220; and Earl Hines, 773; and Billie Holiday, 783; and Little Brother Montgomery, 1071; and Bessie

Smith, 1378; and Fats Waller, 1505

Okino, Betty, 472

*Oklahoma!* (musical), 401

Olajuwon, Hakeem, 1128-1130

Old and New Dreams, 157

Old Mongoose, the. *See* Moore, Archie

Ole Miss. *See* University of Mississippi

O'Leary, Hazel R., 1130-1131

O'Leary, John F., 1130

Oliver, King, 1132-1133; and Lillian Hardin Armstrong, 55-57; and Louis Armstrong, 58; and Edward Blackwell, 156; and Thomas A. Dorsey, 510; and Ulysses Kay, 925; and Jelly Roll Morton, 1083

Olivia Records, 1154

Olympic Project for Human Rights, 9, 191, 304, 1383

Olympics boycotts, 480; 1968, 9, 191, 304, 1383; 1980, 65, 979, 1084, 1609

*Om* (Sanders), 1314

O'Malley, Peter, 1551

*Omni-Americans, The* (Murray), 1094

"On Being Young—A Woman—and Colored" (Bonner), 186

*On How Life Is* (Gray), 681

*On These I Stand* (Cullen), 441

*On Whitman Avenue* (play), 968

Onassis, Jacqueline Kennedy. *See* Kennedy, Jacqueline

*100 Rifles* (film), 238

"One O'Clock Jump" (song), 109

*One Way to Heaven* (Cullen), 440

O'Neal, Shaquille, 1136

Onedaruth. *See* Coltrane, John

O'Neil, Buck, 89, 1136-1137

O'Neill, Eugene, 1264

Operation Breadbasket, 16, 827, 900, 1337

Operation Crossroads, 856-857

Operation PUSH, 272, 827-828, 900, 1195

"Opossum Up a Gum Tree" (song), 23

*Opportunity: Journal of Negro Life*, 188, 808, 1320; and Sterling A. Brown, 243; and Countée Cullen, 440; and Aaron Douglas, 512; and Charles S. Johnson, 862; and Alain Locke, 995; and Eric Walrond, 1507; writing contests, 440, 809, 1538

*Optimistic Do-Nut Hour, The* (radio program), 1007

Ora Nell Records, 992

Ordettes, 954

Organization of Afro-American Unity, 1026

Organization of Women Writers of Africa, 421

Original Amateur Hour. *See Ted Mack's Original Amateur Hour*

*Original Kings of Comedy, The* (film), 326, 1005

*Original Kings of Comedy, The* (Lorde), 1005

Originator, the. *See* Diddley, Bo

Orlando Magic, 555, 850; and Dwight Howard, 800-802; and Shaquille O'Neal, 1134

Ory, Kid, 58, 1132

Osumare, Halifu, 1335

*Othello* (film), 591

*Othello* (play), 23, 896, 1264, 1621

Otis, Clarence, Jr., 1137-1139

Otis, Johnny, 847

*Our Nig* (Wilson), 641

*Our World* (magazine), 1035

*Outsider, The* (Wright), 926, 1626

*Outta Season* (Turners), 1456

Owen, Chandler, 210, 1228

Owens, Chris, 1139-1140

Owens, Dana. *See* Queen Latifah

Owens, Jesse, 123, 190, 1140-1142; and Chris Owens, 1139

Owens, Terrell, 1143-1144

P-funk All-Stars, 381

Pacemakers, 194

Page, Clarence E., 1145-1146

Page, LaWanda, 613

Page, Walter, 109

Pahluk, Mahri. *See* Henson, Matthew Alexander

Paige, Rod, 1146-1148

Paige, Satchel, 139, 503, 1148-1151; and Josh Gibson, 653; and Buck O'Neil, 1136; screen portrayal of, 675

*Palace Council* (Carter), 318

Palermo, Frank "Blinky," 987

Palestine Liberation Organization, 828, 1634

Palin, Sarah, 815, 1123, 1200

Palmer, Alice Freeman, 223

*Palmerstown, USA* (television program), 713

Pan-African Congresses, 522

Pan African Orthodox Christian Church, 370-371

Pan-American Games, 190, 214, 491, 785, 978

Panama, 300

Pankhurst, Sylvia, 1011

*Panther* (film), 115, 1481

Papanek, Ernest, 225

*Parable of the Talents* (Butler), 280

Paramount Records; and Thomas A. Dorsey, 510; and Quincy Jones, 900; and Little Brother Montgomery, 1071; and Lloyd Price, 1205; and Ma Rainey, 1227

Parham, Tiny, 776

*Paris Blues* (film), 313

Parker, Charlie, 409, 1151-1153; and Miles Davis, 461; depiction in *Bird*, 1153, 1549; and Dizzy Gillespie, 655-656; and Johnny Griffin, 697; and Jackie McLean, 1012; and Thelonious Monk, 1069; and Ishmael Reed, 1239; and Max Roach, 1260; and George Russell, 1301; and Archie Shepp, 1345; and Sonny Stitt, 1401; and Sarah Vaughan, 1484; and Cootie Williams, 1567

Parker, George W., 210

Parker, Pat, 1153-1154

Parks, Gordon, Sr., 1155-1156, 1479

Parks, Rosa, 12, 940, 943, 1116, 1127, 1157-1159; and John Conyers, Jr., 413

Parks, Suzan-Lori, 929, 1604, 1621

Parkway Records, 992

Parliaments, 380-381

Parrott, Russell, 606

*Passing* (Larsen), 958

Paterson, Basil, 1159

Paterson, David A., 1159-1161

Pathé Records, 270, 559

Patrick, Deval, 1161-1162

*Patternmaster* (Butler), 280

Patterson, Floyd, 988, 1074, 1163-1165

Patterson, Frederick D., 260, 1165-1166

Patti, Adelina, 902

Paul, Chris, 1166-1168

*Pawnbroker, The* (film), 900, 1176

Payne, Benny, 284

Payne, William, 39

*Payne v. Tennessee*, 1039

Payton, Walter, 1168-1170, 1310

Peace and Freedom Party, 372

Peace Corps; and Harry Belafonte, 138; and Asa Grant Hilliard III, 769; and Mae C. Jemison, 859; and Albert Raby, 1225; and Mildred D. Taylor, 1415

Peaches, 847

Peale, Charles Willson, 874

Peale, Rembrandt, 875

Peanut products, 321

*Pearl Bailey Show, The* (television program), 72

Pearson, Carlton, 846

Peary, Robert E., 761

Peebles, Melvin. *See* Van Peebles, Melvin

Peete, Calvin, 1170-1171

Peete, Rodney, 1172-1173

Pendergrass, Teddy, 539

*Pennies from Heaven* (film), 723, 1399

Penniman, Richard Wayne. *See* Little Richard

Pennsylvania Abolition Society, 606

Penny, Rob, 1588

People United to Save Humanity. *See* Operation PUSH

People's Association for Human Rights, 1579

*People's Voice, The* (newspaper), 1178

Pequit, Alice, 438

Perkins, Kimora Lee. *See* Simmons, Kimora Lee

Perkins, Pinetop, 1451

Perry, Lincoln Theodore Monroe Andrew. *See* Fetchit, Stepin

Perry, Tyler, 675, 825, 1173-1174, 1461

Persian Gulf War, 360, 1341; and Colin Powell, 1200

Peters, Brock, 1175-1176

Peters, Charles Wesley, 259

Peters, Ronnie. *See* Adderley, Cannonball

Peterson, Oscar, 240, 593

Petry, Ann, 1177-1178

Pettiford, Oscar, 15, 899

Petty, Christine, 384

Phat Farm, 1352-1353, 1355

Phelps-Stokes Fund, 863, 1166

Phi Beta Sigma fraternity, 1470

Phi Delta Kappa, 678

"Phi Slamma Jamma," 1128-1129

Philadelphia; African Episcopal Church, 890; Afro-American Arts Theatre, 625; Art Sanctuary Community Lecture and Performance Series, 323; Beulah Baptist Church, 954; Centennial Exposition, 94-95, 981; Richard Allen Homes, 422; MOVE bombing, 87, 683, 1556, 1584; New Years Day Mummers parade, 166; Police Department, 1584; Progress Plaza, 1404; Red Rooster Club, 1458; riots, 1404; Solomon's Temple, 265; Standard Theater, 1110; Zion Baptist Church, 1404

Philadelphia Abolitionist Society, 36

Philadelphia Eagles, 1016, 1143, 1172

*Philadelphia Fire* (Wideman), 1556

*Philadelphia Negro, The* (Du Bois), 521

Philadelphia Phillies; and Roy Campanella, 289; and Curt Flood, 597

Philadelphia 76ers; and Charles Barkley, 99; and Wilt Chamberlain, 329; and Darryl Dawkins, 474; and Julius Erving, 555; and Allen Iverson, 819

Philadelphia Warriors; and Wilt Chamberlain, 327-329

Philanthropic Society, 93, 481

Phillips, Sam, 163

Phillips, Wendell, 1242, 1439

Philosophy; black self-determination, 210, 234; black self-improvement, 672; Christian liberation, 1535; conceptual pragmatism, 598; existentialism, 668-670, 1626; Kawaida, 62, 923; Marxism, 97, 522; New Thought, 578; nonviolence, 150-151, 939-940, 942, 964, 1074; racial uplift, 224; socialism, 306-307, 603; teachers, 436, 448, 598-599, 995

Phipps, Mamie, 363

Phoenix Suns, 741; and Charles Barkley, 100; and Shaquille O'Neal, 1135

*Phylon* (journal), 522

Physicists; George Edward Alcorn, 20-21; Meredith C. Gourdine, 676-677; Evelyn Boyd Granville, 678-679; Shirley Ann Jackson, 842-843; Katherine G. Johnson, 876-877; Ronald E. McNair, 1017-1019; Neil deGrasse Tyson, 1464-1465

Pi Lambda Phi fraternity, 561, 856

*Piano Lesson, The* (play), 128, 840

Pickett, Bill, 1179-1181

Picou, Tom, 7

Pieh, Sengbe. *See* Cinque, Joseph

Pierce, Paul, 634, 1181-1182

Pierce, Samuel R., Jr., 1183-1184

Pikl, Josef, 919

Pikl, Julian, 919

Pilgrim Travelers, 415

Pilots. *See* Aviators

Pinchback, P. B. S., 1184-1185, 1435

Pinkett, Jada, 1386

Pinkney, Jerry, 783

Pinson, Vada, 596

Pippen, Scottie, 1186-1187

Pips. *See* Knight, Gladys

Piscator, Erwin, 136

*Pissstained Stairs and the Monkey Man's Wares* (Cortez), 421

*Pithecanthropus Erectus* (Mingus), 1062

Pitts, Leonard, 1187-1188

*Pittsburgh Courier* (newspaper), 7, 731, 1165, 1322

Pittsburgh Crawfords, 139, 652, 1149

Pittsburgh Pirates, 182, 184, 374-375, 1587

Pittsburgh Steelers, 686-687, 735-737, 1343, 1548, 1617-1618

*Plan B* (Himes), 771

Planned Parenthood, 1526-1528

Plantation Club, 79

*Plantation Revue* (musical), 1060

*Planter*, SS, 1371

Plasma storage, 518-519

Platters, 593, 1280

Playboy Club, 689

*Playboy* magazine, 293, 694; and Alex Haley, 711

*Playing in the Dark* (Morrison), 1081

*Playlist* (Babyface), 70

*Please Hammer, Don't Hurt 'Em* (Hammer), 722

*Plessy v. Ferguson*, 1358, 1561

*Plum Bun* (Fauset), 583

*Plum Bun: A Novel Without a Moral* (Fauset), 583

*Poems of Love and Life* (Latimer), 960

*Poems on Various Subjects, Religious and Moral* (Wheatley), 1546

Poet laureates; Amiri Baraka, 98; Gwendolyn Brooks, 218, 517; Sterling A. Brown, 244; Lucille Clifton, 379; Rita Dove, 516-

517; Melvin B. Tolson, 1435; Al Young, 1631

*Poetic Justice* (film), 825, 1334, 1368

Poinsette, Septima. *See* Clark, Septima Poinsette

Pointe du Sable, Jean Baptiste, 1188-1190

Poitier, Sidney, 464, 840, 900, 1190-1193, 1251, 1476; and Harry Belafonte, 136; and Alice Childress, 357; and Bill Cosby, 423; and Ivan Dixon, 499; in South Africa, 968; and Paul Winfield, 1595

Polar exploration, 761-762

*Political Status of the Negro in the Age of FDR, The* (Bunche), 263

Polk, Charles Peale, 874-875

Pollard, Fritz, 1193-1194, 1342, 1521

Pollard, Fritz, Jr., 1193

*Polly* (television program), 34

Poole, Elijah. *See* Muhammad, Elijah

Poor People's Campaign, 13, 51, 540, 939

Poplar, Ellen, 1626

Pops. *See* Armstrong, Louis

*Porgy and Bess* (film), 72, 443-444, 468, 499, 1175

*Porgy and Bess* (opera), 1078; and Maya Angelou, 51; and Cab Calloway, 285; and Miles Davis, 462; and Nichelle Nichols, 1114; and Brock Peters, 1175; and Leontyne Price, 1202; and Nina Simone, 1360; and Dorothy West, 1538

*Pork Chop Hill* (film), 1403

Port Royal Experiment, 704

Porter, Countée LeRoy. *See* Cullen, Countée

Porter, David, 747

Portland Baseline Essays, 769

Portland Trail Blazers, 1186, 1559

Posey, Cumberland, 652

*Possessing the Secret of Joy* (Walker), 1494

Postage stamps, U.S.; Mary McLeod Bethune, 150; and Ralph Bunche, 264; George Washington Carver, 321; Roberto Clemente, 376; Bessie Coleman, 396; *Cosby Show, The*, 423; Charles R. Drew, 519; Ella Fitzgerald, 594; Patricia Roberts Harris, 738; Matthew Alexander Henson, 761; Billie Holiday, 783; Ernest Everett Just, 922; Jan Ernst Matzeliger, 1042; Bill Pickett, 1181; Otis Redding, 1236

Pournelle, Jerry, 101

Poussaint, Alvin Francis, 1194-1196

Powell, Adam Clayton, IV, 1232

Powell, Adam Clayton, Jr., 226, 691, 1196-1198, 1232, 1276; newspaper column, 1178; and Leon H. Sullivan, 1404

Powell, Bud, 228, 1401; and Alice Coltrane, 407; and Dexter Gordon, 666; and Johnny Griffin, 697; and Jackie McLean, 1013; and Thelonious Monk, 1069

Powell, Chris, 227

Powell, Colin, 1199-1201, 1247; screen portrayal of, 1621

Powell, Mike, 124, 979

Powell, Richie, 228, 1260

*Powerful Long Ladder* (Dodson), 507

Powers, Hiram, 980

Pozo, Chano, 656

Prairie View State College, 134-135, 1165

*Praisesong for the Widow* (Marshall), 1036

*Preacher's Wife, The* (film), 775, 799, 1254, 1476, 1516

*Precious* (film), 169, 301, 303, 1174

Preminger, Otto, 443-444

Presidential Medal of Freedom; Hank Aaron, 3, 5; Pearl Bailey, 72; Eubie Blake, 161; Edward W. Brooke, 217; James E.

Cheek, 350; Roberto Clemente, 376; Bill Cosby, 424; Marian Wright Edelman, 541; Ella Fitzgerald, 594; Aretha Franklin, 616, 619; Dorothy Height, 753; Benjamin Hooks, 791; John H. Johnson, 873; Barbara Jordan, 906; Joseph Lowery, 1002; Clarence M. Mitchell, Jr., 1067; Buck O'Neil, 1137; Frederick D. Patterson, 1166; Sidney Poitier, 1192; Colin Powell, 1201; Leontyne Price, 1203; Frank Robinson, 1271

President's Council on Physical Fitness and Sports, 191, 473, 700

Presley, Elvis, 69, 416, 1204; and Big Boy Crudup, 434; and Fats Domino, 509; and Jackie Wilson, 1593

Presley, Lisa Marie, 837

Prestige Records, 43, 461, 1013, 1069

Preston, Billy, 430

*Presumed Innocent* (film), 1621

Price, Cecil Ray, 331-332

Price, Florence, 185

Price, Leontyne, 185, 902, 1117, 1202-1204

Price, Lloyd, 1204-1205

*Price of a Child* (Cary), 323

*Pride* (Cary), 323

Pride, Charley, 1206-1207, 1294

Pride, Inc., 104

Pridgett, Gertrude Melissa Nix. *See* Rainey, Ma

Prime Time. *See* Sanders, Deion

Primettes, 1291

*Primitive, The* (Himes), 771

Primus, Pearl, 50, 1208-1209

Prince, 404, 1210-1212

Prince of Late Night. *See* Hall, Arsenio

Princess of Black Poetry. *See* Giovanni, Nikki

Prinze, Freddie, 429

Priority Records, 1389

Prison abolitionism, 450

*Prisoner, The* (Hancock), 726

Pritchett, Laurie, 942

*Private Dancer* (Turner), 1457

Pro Football Hall of Fame, 744

Professor Longhair, 1212-1213

Progressive Party, 729, 1265

Prophet, Elizabeth, 1318

Prosser, Gabriel, 189

"Proud Mary" (song), 1452, 1456-1457

Prowse, Juliet, 468

Pryor, Richard, 287, 694, 1214-1216

Public Allies, 1125

Public Enemy, 812, 1355

Puff Daddy, 168, 721, 852, 1217-1218, 1234

Pulitzer Prizes; Gwendolyn Brooks, 217-218; John Coltrane, 411; Stanley Crouch, 433; Rita Dove, 516; Duke Ellington, 548; Charles Fuller, 625; Annette Gordon-Reed, 671; Alex Haley, 712; Yusef Komunyakaa, 950; Wynton Marsalis, 1032-1033; Thelonious Monk, 1070; Toni Morrison, 1080-1081; Clarence E. Page, 1145-1146; Leonard Pitts, 1187; Alice Walker, 1493-1494, 1497-1498; August Wilson, 1587, 1589

Pullman sleeping car porters, 6, 45, 371, 1229; Matthew Alexander Henson, 762; Benjamin E. Mays, 1043; Oscar Micheaux, 1055; E. D. Nixon, 1116

*Pulp Fiction* (film), 841-842

*Purlie* (musical), 33, 465, 989

*Purlie Victorious* (Davis), 286, 464-465

*Purple Flower, The* (play), 187

*Purple Rain* (film), 1211

Purvis, Robert, 703

PUSH. *See* Operation PUSH

"Put a Little Love in Your Heart" (song), 686

*Put and Take* (musical), 195

Quarles, Benjamin, 1219-1220

Quarry, Jerry, 27

*Queen* (television movie), 144

Queen Bess. *See* Coleman, Bessie

Queen Latifah, 1221-1223

Queen of Daytime TV. *See* Winfrey, Oprah

Queen of Disco. *See* Summer, Donna

Queen of Happiness. *See* Mills, Florence

Queen of Hip-Hop Soul. *See* Blige, Mary J.

Queen of Rock and Roll. *See* Turner, Tina

Queen of Soul. *See* Franklin, Aretha

*Queen of the Damned* (film), 2

*Quicksand* (Larsen), 957

*Quiet Storm, A* (Robinson), 1281

Rabbit's Foot Minstrels, 1226

Raby, Albert, 1224-1226

*Race Matters* (West), 1536

*Rachel* (play), 701-702

Rackley, Alex, 1329

*Radio* (film), 664

*Radio* (L. L. Cool J.), 952

Radio disc jockeys; Ralph David Abernathy, 12; Jean-Michel Basquiat, 111; Ed Bradley, 198; Benjamin Chavis, 342; Charles Evers, 565; Redd Foxx, 613; Arsenio Hall, 714; Joe Heidelberg, 1597; B. B. King, 937; Kweisi Mfume, 1053; Studs Terkel, 832

Radio disc jockeys fictional, 1240

*Radio Free Dixie* (radio program), 1579

*Radio Golf* (play), 1588-1589

Raelettes, 336

Raft, George, 54

*Rage in Harlem, A* (film), 775

*Rage in Harlem, A* (Himes), 771

*Ragtime* (musical), 1009, 1066

Ragtime music, 58-59; and Eubie Blake, 159, 161; and Duke Ellington, 545; and Earl Hines, 773; and Scott Joplin, 903-905; and Little Brother Montgomery, 1071; and Jelly Roll Morton,

1082-1083; and King Oliver, 1132

Rainbow Coalition, 828

Rainey, Lawrence, 331-332

Rainey, Ma, 195, 1226-1228, 1589; and Thomas A. Dorsey, 510; and Bessie Smith, 1378. *See also Ma Rainey's Black Bottom*

Rainey, William "Pa," 1226

*Raisin* (musical), 33

*Raisin in the Sun, A* (film), 478, 729, 1191

*Raisin in the Sun, A* (play), 317, 464, 499, 675, 728-729, 1009, 1217, 1234, 1251

*Raising of Lazarus* (Tanner), 1413

Raitt, Bonnie, 222, 787, 1411

*Ramparts* magazine, 372

Randall, Eddie, 461

Randolph, A. Philip, 210, 753, 763, 790, 1116, 1228-1231; March on Washington, 1554; and Bayard Rustin, 1303; and George S. Schuyler, 1322; and Leon H. Sullivan, 1404

Rangel, Charles, 498, 1231-1233

Rashad, Phylicia, 33, 423, 1233-1235

"Rat Pack," 343, 468

*Rated R* (Rihanna), 1255

*Raw* (film), 1438

*Ray* (film), 337, 612

Ray, Floyd, 1062

Ray, James Earl, 943

Raymond, Usher Terry, IV. *See* Usher

*Raymond v. Raymond* (Usher), 1475

Razaf, Andy, 1505

RCA Records; and Harry Belafonte, 136; and Jimmy Blanton, 167; and Sam Cooke, 416; and Lena Horne, 795; and Little Richard, 990; and Charley Pride, 1206; and Diana Ross, 1292

RCA Victor. *See* RCA Records

*Reading Rainbow* (television program), 276, 662

*Ready from Within: Septima Clark and the Civil Rights Movement* (Clark), 366

Reagan, Ronald, 627; and Eldridge Cleaver, 372; and John Conyers, Jr., 414; and Angela Davis, 448; and Eric Holder, 779; inauguration, 336; and Roy Innis, 818; and Jesse Jackson, 828; and Samuel R. Pierce, Jr., 1183; satire of, 1238; and Thomas Sowell, 1391

Real Deal, the. *See* Holyfield, Evander

*Real McCoy, The* (Tyner), 1458

*Real Sports with Bryant Gumbel* (television program), 708

*Rebecca of Sunnybrook Farm* (film), 1268

*Rebellion in Rhyme* (Clarke), 368

*Rebop* (television program), 276

Reb's Legion Club Forty-Fives, 723

*Reckless Eyeballing* (Reed), 1238

Reconstruction, 1509

*Recycle* (play), 1588

Red Hot Peppers, 1083

Redding, Noel, 759

Redding, Otis, 417, 616, 991, 1072, 1235-1236; and Isaac Hayes, 747

Redman, Dewey, 157

Redman, John, 641-642

Reed, E. *See* Evans, Mari

Reed, Ed, 1236-1237

Reed, Ishmael, 1014, 1238-1240

Reed, Willis, 572, 622

Reeder, Eskew. *See* Esquerita

Reeder, Steven Quincy, Jr. *See* Esquerita

Reese, Della, 511

*Reflections of an Affirmative Action Baby* (Carter), 318

Reggae music, 381, 402, 767, 1221

Reid, Antonio "L. A.," 69-70, 208

Reid, Rollins. *See* O'Leary, Hazel R.

Reid, Tim, 1240-1241

Reiss, Winold, 512

*Remember the Titans* (film), 1517

Reno, Janet, 779

Reparation movement, 603, 923, 1279

Representatives, U.S.; Yvonne Brathwaite Burke, 267-268; Henry Plummer Cheatham, 344-346; Shirley Chisholm, 359-361; James E. Clyburn, 382-384; John Conyers, Jr., 413-415; Ron Dellums, 485-487; Oscar DePriest, 488-489; Mervyn Dymally, 535-537; Mike Espy, 556-558; William H. Gray III, 682-684; Jesse Jackson, Jr., 829-830; Sheila Jackson Lee, 844-845; Barbara Jordan, 905-907; John Robert Lewis, 982-984; John Willis Menard, 1048-1049; Kweisi Mfume, 1053-1055; Eleanor Holmes Norton, 1119-1120; Adam Clayton Powell, Jr., 1196-1198; Charles Rangel, 1231-1233; Robert Smalls, 1371-1372; Maxine Waters, 1523-1524; J. C. Watts, 1528-1529; Andrew Young, 1632-1635

Reprise Records, 613

Republic of New Afrika, 1579

Republican Party; and James Madison Bell, 141; and Edward W. Brooke, 216; and Blanche Kelso Bruce, 252-253; and John E. Bruce, 254; and Henry Plummer Cheatham, 345; and Eldridge Cleaver, 373; and Frederick Douglass, 515; 1892 National Convention, 345; and Charles Evers, 565; and Lionel Hampton, 724; and Roy Innis, 817; and James Weldon Johnson, 869; and Alan Keyes, 930; and John Willis Menard, 1048; and James Meredith, 1051; and Samuel R. Pierce, Jr., 1183; and P. B. S. Pinchback, 1184-1185; and Colin Powell, 1200; and Condoleezza Rice, 1246; and Robert Smalls, 1372; and Thomas Sowell, 1391; and

Michael Steele, 1393-1395; and Clarence Thomas, 1419; and Alexander Walters, 1509; and J. C. Watts, 1528-1529
"Respect" (song), 616, 1235
*Revelations* (dance), 19
Revels, Hiram Rhoades, 1241-1243
Reverend Run. *See* Simmons, Joseph
Revilot Records, 380
*Revolutionary Petunias, and Other Poems* (Walker), 1494
*Revolutionary Suicide* (Newton), 1108-1109
Revolutionary War. *See* American Revolution
*Revue nègre, La* (musical), 79
Reynolds, Debbie, 16
Reynolds, Kate L., 1317
*Rhetoric of Black Revolution* (Asante), 61
*Rhetoric of Revolution* (Asante and Rich), 61
Rhodes scholars; Benjamin T. Jealous, 854; Alain Locke, 995, 1555; John Edgar Wideman, 1555
Rhodesia, 1383, 1633-1634. *See also* Zimbabwe
Rhone, Sylvia M., 1243-1244
Rhythm Pals, 401
Riboud, Marc, 339
Rice, Condoleezza, 1245-1247
Rice, Jerry, 1143, 1247-1249
Rice, Linda Johnson, 873, 1249-1250
Rich, Adrienne, 377
Rich, Buddy, 162
Rich, Marc, 780
Richards, Ann, 906
Richards, Lloyd, 115, 1251-1252, 1588
Richardson, Elaine Cynthia Potter. *See* Kincaid, Jamaica
Richie, Lionel, 836, 901, 1252-1254, 1292; and Cuba Gooding, Jr., 663
Richmond, Dannie, 1062
Rickey, Branch, 289, 1273
Ride, Sally, 1115

*Ride 'em Cowboy* (film), 593
Riefenstahl, Leni, 1402
*Right Stuff, The* (Williams), 1582
Righteous Brothers, 417
Rihanna, 853, 1255-1256
Riley, James Whitcomb, 524
Riley, Pat, 878, 1135
Rillieux, Norbert, 1256-1257
Ringgold, Faith, 1258-1259
Rinzler, Alan, 226
*Riot* (Brooks), 219
Rising Sons, 1410
"River Deep, Mountain High" (song), 1452, 1456-1457
Rivera, Diego, 40
Rivera, Geraldo, 818
Rivers, Joan, 714
Riverside Records, 16, 56, 698, 1069
Rizzo, Frank, 1584
*RL's Dream* (Mosley), 1087
Roach, Max, 162, 1260-1261; and Clifford Brown, 228; and Duke Ellington, 547; and Bill T. Jones, 892; and Charles Mingus, 1062; and George Russell, 1300
Roberson, Ida Mae, 440
Robert, Dehlco, 1071
Roberts, Patricia. *See* Harris, Patricia Roberts
Roberts, Ron, 491
Roberts, T. J., 75
Robertson, Oscar, 9, 1261-1263
Robertson, Robbie, 266
*Robertson v. National Basketball Association*, 1262
Robeson, Paul, 270, 1007, 1056, 1191, 1194, 1251, 1263-1266; and Julian Bond, 179; and Benjamin J. Davis, 451; and Dizzy Gillespie, 656; and Lorraine Hansberry, 729; and Lena Horne, 796; and Canada Lee, 968; play about, 464; and Leontyne Price, 1202
Robey, Don, 163
Robey Theater Company, 1471
*Robin and the Seven Hoods* (film), 468
*Robin Hood* (film), 333

Robinson, Bernice, 366, 382
Robinson, Bill, 195, 775, 1060, 1110, 1266-1268, 1506
Robinson, Bojangles. *See* Robinson, Bill
Robinson, David, 529, 1269-1270
Robinson, Edward "Abie," 1522
Robinson, Frank, 596, 1270-1272
Robinson, Freddie Lee. *See* Shuttlesworth, Fred
Robinson, Harold B., 954
Robinson, Jackie, 1272-1275, 1403, 1521; and Cool Papa Bell, 139; and Roy Campanella, 289; and Larry Doby, 503; film portrayals of, 1471
Robinson, Jo Ann Gibson, 12, 1275-1276
Robinson, John C., 918
Robinson, Mack, 1274
Robinson, Max, 1277-1278
Robinson, Michelle LaVaughn. *See* Obama, Michelle
Robinson, Noah Louis, 826
Robinson, Randall, 1277-1280
Robinson, Robert, 919
Robinson, Smokey, 402, 1019, 1280-1282, 1291, 1606; and Usher, 1475
Robinson, Spottswood W., III, 1282-1283; and Stephen L. Carter, 318
Robinson, Sugar Ray, 54, 335, 649, 1284-1286
Roc. *See* Dutton, Charles S.
*Roc* (television program), 534, 611
Roc-a-Fella Records, 852-853
Rock, Chris, 287, 1135, 1215, 1286-1287
Rock, the. *See* Johnson, Dwayne
Rockefeller, John D., 1514
Rockefeller, Nelson, 1183
"Rocket 88" (song), 1451
"Rockin' Pneumonia and the Boogie Woogie Flu" (song), 1381
Roddenberry, Gene, 1115
Rodeo, 1179-1181
*Roe v. Wade*, 1527

Rogers, Claudette, 1281

Rogers, Henry H., 1514

Rogers, J. A., 368

Rogers, Roy, 787

Rogers, Will, 587, 1007, 1179

Roker, Al, 1287-1289

*Roll of Thunder, Hear My Cry* (Taylor), 1416

Rolle, Esther, 1499

Rolling Stones, 142-143, 496, 501, 787, 937, 1456, 1606; and Ike and Tina Turner, 1452

Rollini, Adrian, 308

Rollins, Sonny, 1260, 1289-1291

Roman Catholic Church; and Kareem Abdul-Jabbar, 8-9; and Richmond Barthé, 107; and Sister Thea Bowman, 192-193; and LeVar Burton, 275; and Wilton D. Gregory, 692-693; and Patrick F. Healy, 750-751; in Liberia, 585; and Claude McKay, 1011; sexual abuse crisis, 693; and Mary Lou Williams, 1575

Ronstadt, Linda, 1107

"Rooney Rule," 1343

Roosevelt, Eleanor, 49, 149, 465, 753, 795, 968, 1530, 1553-1554; and Claude Brown, 226

Roosevelt, Franklin D., 49, 1229-1230, 1518, 1554; Black Cabinet, 148-149, 1530

Roosevelt, Theodore, 869, 1514; and Harry T. Burleigh, 270

Roost Records, 136

*Root, The* (online magazine), 642

*Roots* (Haley), 276, 711-712

*Roots* (television program); and Maya Angelou, 52; and LeVar Burton, 276; and Lou Gossett, Jr., 675; and Quincy Jones, 901; and Cicely Tyson, 1461; and Leslie Uggams, 1468-1469; and Ben Vereen, 1485

*Roots: The Gift* (television movie), 713

*Roots: The Next Generations* (television program), 296, 713, 1066, 1251, 1596

*Roots: The Saga of an American Family* (Haley); historicity of, 713

*Rope and Faggot* (White), 1553

*Rosa Parks Story, The* (television movie), 116, 445

Rose McClendon Players, 464

Rosenberg, Ethel and Julius, 478

Rosenberg Foundation, 854

Rosenwald, Julius, 107, 1317

Rosenwald Fund, 177, 189, 530, 678, 863, 962. *See also* Commission on Interracial Cooperation

*Rosewood* (film), 343, 1368

Ross, Araminta. *See* Tubman, Harriet

Ross, Barney, 54

Ross, Betsy, 575

Ross, Diana, 402, 783, 1254, 1291-1293; and Berry Gordy, Jr., 673; and Jackson Five, 835; and Lionel Richie, 1253

Rostenkowski, Dan, 779

*Rotary Action* (dance), 891

*'Round Midnight* (film), 666

Round Mound of Rebound, the. *See* Barkley, Charles

Rowe, Debbie, 837

Roxborough, John "Roxy," 999

Royal Society of London, 321

Roybal, Edward, 200

Rubin, Rick, 952, 1351, 1355

*Ruby's Bucket of Blood* (television movie), 116

Rucker, Darius, 1294-1295

Rudd, Roswell, 1113, 1344

Rudolph, Wilma, 65, 1295-1297, 1466

Rufus, James. *See* Forman, James

*Rufus Jones for President* (film), 466

*Rules of Engagement* (film), 1471

"Rumble in the Jungle," 601, 1074, 1205

Rumsfeld, Donald, 1200

Run-D.M.C., 588, 1350-1352, 1354-1355

*Running a Thousand Miles to Freedom* (Craft), 425

*Run's House* (television program), 1350, 1352

Rush, Benjamin, 606, 889

Rush, Bobby, 1122

Rush, Otis, 501

Rush Artistic Management Company, 1354

Rushing, Jimmy, 110, 777

Russell, Bill, 9, 596, 745, 994, 1298-1300; and Wilt Chamberlain, 328, 1299

Russell, George, 1300-1301

Russwurm, John Brown, 1302-1303

Rustin, Bayard, 1229, 1303-1305

Ruth, Babe, 3-4, 839

Rwanda genocide, 344

Ryan, Robert, 137

*Rythm Mastr* (Marshall), 1034

Saar, Betye, 1259, 1306-1307

Sadler, Dick, 601

Sagan, Carl, 1464

Sagittinanda, Turiya. *See* Coltrane, Alice

*St. Elsewhere* (television program), 1517

St. Hill, Shirley Anita. *See* Chisholm, Shirley

*St. Louis Blues* (film), 392, 727, 832, 1378

St. Louis Browns, 139, 1150

St. Louis Cardinals; and Lou Brock, 213-215; and Curt Flood, 596-597; and Bob Gibson, 650-651; and Bill White, 1550

St. Louis Hawks, 1558

St. Louis Rams, 581

St. Louis Stars, 138

*St. Louis Woman* (musical), 72, 441

St. Vincent-St. Mary High School, 849-850

Sale, George, 792

*Sally Hemings* (Chase-Ribaud), 340

*Salt Eaters, The* (Bambara), 87

Sampson, Edgar, 1532

Sampson, Ralph, 1128

San Antonio Spurs, 529, 850; and Tim Duncan, 528-529; and

David Robinson, 1269

San Diego Padres, 708-710

San Diego Rockets, 745

San Francisco 49ers; and Antonio Bryant, 255; and Bernie Casey, 324; and Terrell Owens, 1143; and Jerry Rice, 1248-1249; and Deion Sanders, 1312; and O. J. Simpson, 1363; and Mike Singletary, 1365; and Rod Woodson, 1618

San Francisco Giants; and Dusty Baker, 74; and Vida Blue, 171; and Barry Bonds, 182-184; and Willie Mays, 1045-1048; and Frank Robinson, 1272; and Deion Sanders, 1313

San Jose State College, 191, 304, 562, 1382

Sanchez, Sonia, 1307-1309

Sanders, Barry, 1172, 1309-1311, 1618

Sanders, Betty Dean. See Shabazz, Betty

Sanders, Deion, 1311-1313

Sanders, Pharoah, 408, 1314-1315

Sanford, John Elroy. See Foxx, Redd

Sanford and Son (television program), 613, 706, 1215, 1499

"Santa Baby" (song), 944-945

Santana, Carlos, 408, 682, 787, 1457

Saparo, Henry, 308

Saperstein, Abe, 328, 741, 973

SAR Records, 416

Sarron, Petey, 54

Sartre, Jean-Paul, 669, 1626

Satcher, David, 1315-1317

Satchidananda, Swami, 408

Satchmo. See Armstrong, Louis

Saturday Night Live (television program); and Julian Bond, 180; and Ray Charles, 336; and Garrett Morris, 1079-1080; and Eddie Murphy, 1090-1091; and Chris Rock, 1286; and Snoop Dogg, 1389; and Robert Townsend, 1438

Saud, Sulaimon. See Tyner, McCoy

Saunders, Raymond, 127

Savage, Augusta, 961, 1317-1318

Savage, James, 154

Savage Holiday (Wright), 1626

"Save the Last Dance for Me" (song), 1019

Savoy Records, 1113, 1344

Say Hey. See Mays, Willie

Say It Loud (television program), 682

"Say It Loud—I'm Black and I'm Proud" (song), 234-235

Sayers, Gale, 1565

Sayles, Thelma Lucille. See Clifton, Lucille

SBK Records, 1282

Scat singing, 782; Louis Armstrong, 59; Cab Calloway, 284-285; Scatman Crothers, 429; Ella Fitzgerald, 593; Dizzy Gillespie, 656

Scepter Records, 1510-1511

Scheffé, Henry, 154

Schippers, Thomas, 119

Schmeling, Max, 1000

Schoenberg, Arnold, 206

Schomburg, Arturo Alfonso, 368, 435, 1319-1321

Schomburg Center for Research in Black Culture, 254, 1320, 1566; Hansen's Harlem exhibition, 731

School Daze (film), 465, 590, 841, 970

Schroeder, Charles, 107

Schuller, Gunther, 397, 1063, 1301

Schurz, Carl, 532

Schuyler, George S., 1321-1323

Schwarzkopf, Norman, 1200

Science-fiction writers; and Steven Barnes, 101-102; and LeVar Burton, 276; and Octavia E. Butler, 279-281; and Samuel R. Delany, 484-485; and Walter Mosley, 1087; and George S. Schuyler, 1322-1323

SCLC. See Southern Christian Leadership Conference

SCOPE. See Summer Community Organization and Political Education

Score, The (Fugees), 767

Scorpion King, The (film), 865

Scott, Coretta. See King, Coretta Scott

Scott, Dred, 959, 1324-1325

Scott, Ed, 3

Scott, Hazel, 1469

Scott, Joe, 163

Scott, Tony, 1516

Scott v. Sandford, 1324-1325

Scottsboro boys, 189, 1440

Scowcroft, Brent, 1246

Scruggs, Fay. See Adams, Faye

Scruggs, Mary Elfrieda. See Williams, Mary Lou

Sculptors; Richmond Barthé, 107-108; and Barbara Chase-Riboud, 339-341; Sargent Johnson, 886-887; Edmonia Lewis, 980-981; Betye Saar, 1306-1307; Augusta Savage, 1317-1318

Scurry, Briana, 1326-1327

Sea Birds Are Still Alive, The (Bambara), 87

Seabrooke-Powell, Georgette, 1318

Seagle, Oscar, 270

Seale, Bobby, 372, 1109, 1328-1330

Search for Education, Elevation, and Knowledge, 86, 498, 1498

Seattle Mariners, 695, 1587

Seattle Seahawks, 1249

Seattle SuperSonics, 1299, 1558; and Gus Williams, 1569-1570

Second Coming, The (film), 1470

Secret Life of Bees, The (film), 933

Seeger, Pete, 220, 1126-1127

SEEK. See Search for Education, Elevation, and Knowledge

Seidenberg, Sid, 937

Selective Patronage Movement, 1404

Selig, Bud, 1551

Selig's Mastodon Minstrels, 1563

Selma-to-Montgomery march; and James Baldwin, 83; and James Bevel, 151; and Ralph Bunche,

263; and Billy Eckstine, 539; and John Hope Franklin,, 619; and Martin Luther King, Jr., 943; and John Robert Lewis, 983; and Joseph Lowery, 1002; and Diane Nash, 1102; and Odetta, 1127; and Charles Rangel, 1232; and Fred Shuttlesworth, 1348; and C. DeLores Tucker, 1447; and C. T. Vivian, 1489; and Andrew Young, 1633-1634

Selznick, David O., 1007

Semi, Allen. *See* Larsen, Nella

Seminole Wars, 133

Senate, U.S.; and Blanche Kelso Bruce, 253

Senators, U.S.; Carol E. Moseley Braun, 204-206; Edward W. Brooke, 215-217; Blanche Kelso Bruce, 251-253; Roland Burris, 271-273; Barack Obama, 1121-1124; Hiram Rhoades Revels, 1241-1243

Senegal, 531

Sengstacke, John H., 7

*Sepia* magazine, 312

Sepia Sinatra, the. *See* Eckstine, Billy

September 11, 2001, terrorist attacks, 1201; and Amiri Baraka, 98; and Kenneth Chenault, 352; and Sheila Jackson Lee, 845; and Leonard Pitts, 1187; and Colin Powell, 1200; and Condoleezza Rice, 1246; and Larry D. Thompson, 1429; and Jeremiah Wright, 1623

*Seraph on the Suwanee* (Hurston), 810

*Sergeant Rutledge* (film), 1403

*Sergeants Three* (film), 468

*Sesame Street* (television program), 656, 660, 896

*Seven Guitars* (play), 471

*Seventeen* magazine, 291, 339, 798, 997

Seventh-day Adventists, 188

*Seventy-two Hour Hold* (Campbell), 291

Severance, 774

Sex Pistols, 143

*Sextant* (Hancock), 726

Seymour, William, 578

Shabazz, Betty, 115, 1329-1331; and Malcolm X, 1025

Shabazz, El-Hajj Malik el-. *See* Malcolm X

Shabazz, Ilyasah, 1332-1333

*Shadow Dancing* (Meriwether), 1052

*Shadow of the Plantation* (Johnson), 863

*Shaft* (1971 film), 747, 1156

*Shaft* (2000 film), 841, 933, 1414, 1621

*Shake Sugaree* (Taj Mahal), 1411

Shakira, 1606

Shakur, Tupac, 387, 552, 1222, 1333-1334, 1389

Shange, Ntozake, 623, 840, 929, 1335-1336

Shantz, Bobby, 214

*Shape of Jazz to Come, The* (Coleman), 397-398

*Shaq Vs.* (television program), 1135

Sharp, Granville, 1546

Sharper, Darren, 1237

Sharpton, Al, 818, 1337-1340, 1536

Shaw, Artie, 782

Shaw, Bernard, 1340-1341

Shaw, Irwin, 1000

Shaw, Robert Gould, 310, 704, 980

Shaw University, 75, 179, 349-350, 964, 1219

Shawn, William, 934

Shays' Rebellion, 716

*She Hate Me* (film), 465, 969

Shell, Art, 1193, 1341-1343

Shepard, Alan, 876

Shepp, Archie, 1344-1345

*She's Gotta Have It* (film), 969

Shoe-lasting machine, 1041, 1042

Shook, Karel, 1064

*Shooter* (Myers), 1098

Shorter, Wayne, 462, 1345-1347

*Show Boat* (film), 587, 1007

*Show Boat* (musical), 1078, 1264

Showard, Derek, 726

*Showing My Color* (Page), 1146

*Shrek* films, 1092

Shrine of the Black Madonna, 370

*Shuffle Along* (musical), 79, 159-161, 390, 1060

Shuttlesworth, Fred, 1347-1348

Sierra Leone; and Joseph Cinque, 361; and Daniel Coker, 388-389; colonization movement, 438; and Paul Cuffe, 437-439; Peace Corps, 859

Sifford, Charlie, 542

*Sign in Sidney Brustein's Window, The* (play), 729

*Signifying Monkey, The* (Gates), 641-642

Silver, Horace, 162, 1349-1350

*Silver Streak* (film), 1215

Silveto Records, 1350

Simmons, Joseph, 1350-1352, 1354

Simmons, Kimora Lee, 1352-1353, 1355

Simmons, Michael, 277-278

Simmons, Russell, 1354-1355; Def Jam Recordings, 342; and L. L. Cool J., 952; portrayal in *Krush Groove*, 1470; and Joseph Simmons, 1350, 1353

Simmons, Ruth, 1356-1357

Simms, Willie, 1357-1359

*Simon and Simon* (television program), 1240

Simone, Nina, 169, 933, 1359-1361

*Simple Speaks His Mind* (Hughes), 806

Simpson, India Arie. *See* India.Arie

Simpson, Nicole Brown, 387, 1363

Simpson, O. J., 387, 667, 1169, 1361-1364

Simpson, Ralph, 815

Sims, Sandman, 775

Sinatra, Frank, 110; and Sammy Davis, Jr., 467-468; and Ella Fitzgerald, 593; and Quincy Jones, 900; and Joe Louis, 1001

*Sinfonietta* (Kay), 925

*Sing Along with Mitch* (television program), 1469

Singing Children, 415

*Singing in the Comeback Choir* (Campbell), 291
Singletary, Mike, 1364-1365
Singleton, Benjamin, 1366-1367
Singleton, John, 115, 552, 663, 813, 1367-1369
Singleton, Zutty, 776
*Sinister Wisdom* magazine, 377
Sirhan, Sirhan, 883
Sisler, George, 1274
Sissle, Noble, 71, 79, 160, 270, 794
"Sissy Blues" (song), 1227
*Sister Outsider: Essays and Speeches* (Lorde), 998
Sit-ins, 383, 567; Chicago, 204, 573; Greensboro, North Carolina, 179, 983; Nashville, Tennessee, 61, 150, 964, 982, 1102, 1488; Washington, D.C., 1096; and Robert Franklin Williams, 1578
"(Sittin' on) The Dock of the Bay" (song), 1235
*Six Degrees of Separation* (play), 1476
Sixteenth Street Baptist Church bombing, 448, 690, 969, 1245
*60 Minutes* (television program), 193, 404, 668; and Ed Bradley, 198-199
*Ski Party* (film), 235
"Skylark" (song), 538
Slater, Andrew, 681
Slaughter, John Brooks, 1369-1370
Slave rebellions, 607, 1049, 1241, 1496; and Joseph Cinque, 361-363; and Nat Turner, 1453-1455; and Denmark Vesey, 1487-1488
Slaves and former slaves; Richard Allen, 36-38; Allen Allensworth, 38-39; Crispus Attucks, 66-68; Andrew Jackson Beard, 125-126; Blind Tom Bethune, 145-147; Blanche Kelso Bruce, 251-253; John E. Bruce, 254-255; George Washington Carver, 319-322; Henry Plummer Cheatham, 344-346; Joseph Cinque, 361-363;

Daniel Coker, 388-390; William and Ellen Craft, 425-426; Martin Robison Delany, 481-484; Frederick Douglass, 513-515; Henry Ossian Flipper, 595-596; Amos Fortune, 608-609; Henry Highland Garnet, 631-633; Prince Hall, 716-717; Sally Hemings, 754-755; Absalom Jones, 889-891; Dred Scott, 1324-1325; Benjamin Singleton, 1366-1367; Robert Smalls, 1371-1372; Sojourner Truth, 1441-1443; Harriet Tubman, 1444-1446; Nat Turner, 1453-1455; Denmark Vesey, 1487-1488; Alexander Walters, 1508-1510; Booker T. Washington, 1513-1515; Ida B. Wells-Barnett, 1533-1534
*Slave's Revenge, A* (play), 22
*Slaves Today* (Schuyler), 1322
Slocum, Paul. *See* Cuffe, Paul
Sly and the Family Stone, 381, 1456
Slyde, Jimmy, 775
*Small Place, A* (Kincaid), 935
Smalls, Robert, 1371-1372
Smiley, Tavis, 1373-1374
Smith, Ada "Bricktop," 1060
Smith, Anna Deveare, 1374-1375
Smith, Arthur Lee, Jr. *See* Asante, Molefi Kete
Smith, Barbara, 1376-1377
Smith, Bessie, 195, 727, 1377-1379; and Billie Holiday, 781; and Ma Rainey, 1227
Smith, Dean, 909
Smith, Emmitt, 1169, 1248, 1311, 1379-1380
Smith, George Allen. *See* Russell, George
Smith, Gerrit, 1445
Smith, Huey "Piano," 1381-1382
Smith, Hughie Lee. *See* Lee-Smith, Hughie
Smith, Jabbo, 776
Smith, James Todd. *See* L. L. Cool J.
Smith, Jedediah, 134

Smith, Kenny, 100
Smith, Lovie, 1343
Smith, Mamie, 195, 1227
Smith, Tommie, 304, 562, 601, 1382-1384, 1466
Smith, Walker, Jr. *See* Robinson, Sugar Ray
Smith, Will, 90, 1192, 1222, 1385-1386
Smith, Willie Mae Ford, 510
Smith Act of 1940, 452
Smithsonian Institution, 28, 1220, 1566
Smokin' Joe. *See* Frazier, Joe
SNCC. *See* Student Nonviolent Coordinating Committee
Snipes, Wesley, 552, 1386-1388
Snoop Dogg, 715, 1388-1390; and Dr. Dre, 505
Snowden, Elmer, 546
*Soap* (television program), 706-707
Sobukwe, Robert, 1634
Socialist Party, 1228-1230
Society of Midland Authors, 605
Soda Pop Records, 70
*Soldier's Play, A* (play), 625, 840
*Soldier's Story, A* (film), 625, 955, 1438, 1516
*Soledad Brother* (Jackson), 448
Soledad Prison, 372, 448
*Solid Gold* (television program), 714, 1512
*Sometimes My Mommy Gets Angry* (Campbell), 291
*Sonata Mulattica* (Dove), 516-517
*Song of Solomon* (Morrison), 1081
*Song of the Trees* (Taylor), 1415
*Songs in A Minor* (Keys), 933
*Songs in the Key of Life* (Wonder), 1606
*Songs of Jamaica* (McKay), 1010
*Songs of the Big City* (McPhatter), 1020
Sony Records, 836
*Sophisticated Gents, The* (television movie), 1596
*Sophisticated Ladies* (musical), 775
Sorvino, Al, 53
Sosa, Sammy, 183
*Soul* (magazine), 1187

*Soul Food* (film), 70, 1582
*Soul of the Game* (television movie), 1471
*Soul on Fire* (Cleaver), 373
*Soul on Ice* (Cleaver), 372-373
Soul Stirrers, 416
*Soul Train* (television program), 69, 714-715, 836, 955
Soulbird Records, 816
*Soulfully* (Disciples), 431
*Souls of Black Folk: Essays and Sketches, The* (Du Bois), 521
*Sounder* (film), 1461, 1596; and Taj Mahal, 1410; Paul Winfield, 1596
South Africa, 486; apartheid, 683, 791, 1002, 1279, 1383, 1404-1405, 1523; *Cry, the Beloved Country*, 968; and William H. Gray III, 683; and Charlayne Hunter-Gault, 807; and Jesse Jackson, 828; and Coretta Scott King, 940; and Oprah Winfrey, 816; and Andrew Young, 1634. *See also* Apartheid, South African
*South Park* (television program), 747
*South Street* (Bradley), 196
Southern Christian Leadership Conference; and Ralph David Abernathy, 12-13; and Maya Angelou, 51; and Ella Baker, 76; and James Bevel, 150-151; and Julian Bond, 179; and Benjamin Chavis, 341; Citizenship Education Project, 366; and Septima Poinsette Clark, 366; creation of, 942; and Fannie Lou Hamer, 718; and Benjamin Hooks, 790; and Jesse Jackson, 827-828; and Coretta Scott King, 939, 941-944; and Joseph Lowery, 1002; and Diane Nash, 1102; organization of, 12; and Albert Raby, 1224; and Fred Shuttlesworth, 1348; and C. T. Vivian, 1489; and Hosea Williams, 1571-1572; and Andrew Young, 1633

Southern County Progress, Inc., 718
*Southern Cross, The*, 950
Southern Poverty Law Center, 181, 570
*Southern Road* (Brown), 243-244
Soviet Union, 1229; breakup of, 487; and Angela Davis, 450; and Langston Hughes, 805-806; and Claude McKay, 1011; and Adam Clayton Powell, Jr., 1197; and Condoleezza Rice, 1246; and Paul Robeson, 1264-1265; and Dorothy West, 1538
Sowell, Thomas, 1390-1391; and Clarence Thomas, 1419
Soyinka, Wole, 465, 640
Space shuttle program, 172, 691, 876; *Atlantis*, 691; *Challenger*, 172, 174, 691, 1018; *Columbia*, 173; *Discovery*, 172, 691; *Endeavor*, 859
Space Trio, 1408
Spanish Civil War, 1264
Sparkman, John, 1198
Sparta Agricultural and Industrial Institute, 1436
*Spartacus* (film), 1403
*Speaking Truth to Power* (Hill), 765
Specialty Records, 1204, 1381
Spector, Phil, 1452, 1456
Speed skaters, 469-470
Spelman College, 180, 424, 507, 540, 793, 1493, 1498; and Ruth Simmons, 1356
Spencer, Tim, 431
Speranzeva, Olga, 530
Sphinx of City Hall, the. *See* Bradley, Tom
Spielberg, Steven, 34, 464, 901, 1494
Spingarn, Arthur, 176
Spingarn, Joel, 1011
Spingarn Medal; Alvin Ailey, 19; William Stanley Braithwaite, 203; Harry T. Burleigh, 270; Sammy Davis, Jr., 467; Earl G. Graves, Sr., 680; Benjamin Hooks, 791; John Hope, 793;

Vernon Jordan, 913; Percy Lavon Julian, 920; Ernest Everett Just, 922; Jacob Lawrence, 962; John Robert Lewis, 983; Clarence M. Mitchell, Jr., 1067; Gordon Parks, Sr., 1156; Arturo Alfonso Schomburg, 1320; Carter G. Woodson, 1616; Louis T. Wright, 1624, 1626
Spinks, Leon, 28
Spitzer, Eliot, 1160
*Spook Show, The* (Goldberg), 662
*Sport of the Gods, The* (Dunbar), 525-526
*Sports Night* (television program), 706
*Spring in New Hampshire, and Other Poems* (McKay), 1011
Spurgeon, Charles Haddon, 862
Stackpole, Ralph, 886
"Stagger Lee" (song), 1205
Stamps. *See* Postage stamps, U.S.
Stanton, Elizabeth Cady, 515, 1447
*Star Search* (television program), 1, 714, 1474
Star Talent Records, 1213
*Star Trek* (television program), 275, 1114; and Martin Luther King, Jr., 1115; novels, 102
*Star Trek: Deep Space Nine* (television program), 1176
*Star Trek: The Next Generation* (television program), 276, 662, 859
*Star Wars* films; and Samuel L. Jackson, 841; and James Earl Jones, 896; and Billy Dee Williams, 1565
Starr, Brenda K., 301
Starski, Lovebug, 1354
State Collegians, 167
Staubach, Roger, 743-744
Stax Records, 746, 748, 1235
*Steel* (film), 1135
Steele, Claude M., 1392-1393
Steele, Michael, 1393-1395
Steele, Shelby, 1395-1397
Steeplechase Records, 666
Stefani, Gwen, 505

Steichen, Edward, 477, 1000, 1479
Steinem, Gloria, 569
Sterling, Donald, 122
Stern, Bernhard, 996
*Stevedore* (play), 968
Stevens, David, 713
Stevens, Moses, 542
Stevenson, Alexandra, 555
Stewart, Maria, 1397-1398
Still, William Grant, 727, 732, 925, 1398-1400, 1445
*Stir Crazy* (film), 1191, 1215
Stitt, Sonny, 1401-1402; and Gene Ammons, 41-42
Stockton, John, 1028
Stokes, Maurice, 324
Stokes, Moses, 1226
*Stompin' at the Savoy* (television movie), 34
*Stomping the Blues* (Murray), 1095
Stone, Sly, 726
Stoner, Fred, 27
*Stormy Weather* (film), 531, 795, 1111, 1267, 1399, 1506
*Stormy Weather* (musical), 1469
Stoudamire, Damon, 1426
Stoute, Steven, 1217
Stowe, Harriet Beecher, 482; and Sojourner Truth, 1442
*Straight Outta Compton* (N.W.A.), 505, 812
"Strange Fruit" (song), 781-783, 1208
Strauss, Claude Levi, 1626
Strayhorn, Billy, 167, 547
*Street, The* (Petry), 1178
*Strength of Gideon, and Other Stories, The* (Dunbar), 525
*Strictly for Dixie* (radio program), 795
*Strictly 4 My N.I.G.G.A.Z.* (Shakur), 1334
*Stride Toward Freedom* (King), 942
Strode, Woody, 1402-1403, 1521-1522
Stubblefield, Ruth Jean. *See* Simmons, Ruth
Student National Medical Association, 647

Student Nonviolent Coordinating Committee, 331, 965, 1489; and Molefi Kete Asante, 61; and Ella Baker, 76; and Marion Barry, 104; and James Bevel, 150; and Julian Bond, 179; and H. Rap Brown, 232-233; and Stokely Carmichael, 305-306; and James Forman, 602-604; and Fannie Lou Hamer, 718; and Martin Luther King, Jr., 942; and John Robert Lewis, 982-983; and Diane Nash, 1102
Studio 306, 127
Sturgis, Stokeley, 36
Styron, William, 1052
Suez Canal Crisis, 263
Sugar-refining industry, 1256-1257
*Sula* (Morrison), 1080
Sullivan, Ed, 416, 495, 1268
Sullivan, Leon H., 1404-1405
Sullivan Award winners; Florence Griffith-Joyner, 700; Rafer Johnson, 882; Edwin Moses, 1085; Wilma Rudolph, 1296
Sullivan Principles, 1404
Summer, Donna, 1405-1407
Summer Community Organization and Political Education, 1571-1572
Sumner, Charles, 1443
Sun Ra, 523, 1407-1409, 1430; and Pharoah Sanders, 1314
Sun Records, 163, 434
*Sun Valley Serenade* (film), 442
*Sunset Boulevard* (play), 313
*Superman III* (film), 1215
*Suppression of the African Slave Trade to the United States of America, 1638-1870, The* (Du Bois), 520
Supreme Court, U.S., justices, 1037-1039, 1418-1421
Supremes, 402, 954; and Diana Ross, 1291-1293
Surgeon General, U.S., 543-545
*Survivor* (Destiny's Child), 948
Suso, Foday Musa, 726

Sutton, Percy, 1232
Swahili, 62, 924; names, 371, 469, 726, 1023
Sweatman, Wilbur, 195
*Sweet Flypaper of Life, The* (DeCarva and Hughes), 477
*Sweet Summer: Growing Up with and Without My Dad* (Campbell), 291
*Sweet Sweetback's Baadasssss Song* (film), 1480-1482
Sweetness. *See* Payton, Walter
*Swing It* (musical), 161
Swing Time Records, 336
Swinton, Harry, 1266
Sykes, Roosevelt, 1071

Taft, William H., 1514
Taj Mahal, 1410-1412; and John Lee Hooker, 787
Tajo, Italo, 119
*Take a Giant Step* (play), 286, 674, 1565
*Take Me Back* (Disciples), 431
*Takin' Off* (Hancock), 725
*Taking of Miss Janie, The* (Bullins), 261
Talk show hosts; Cannonball Adderley, 16; Tyra Banks, 91; Ossie Davis, 465; Whoopi Goldberg, 662; Ed Gordon, 667; Arsenio Hall, 714-715; Gwen Ifill, 815; Chad Ochocinco, 1144; Terrell Owens, 1144; Queen Latifah, 1222; Al Roker, 1287; Tavis Smiley, 1373; Montel Williams, 1576-1578; Oprah Winfrey, 1597-1600
*Talking Back* (Hooks), 788
*Talking Book* (Wonder), 1606
*Tamango* (film), 443
*T.A.M.I. Show, The* (television program), 235
Tamla Records, 1281. *See also* Motown Records
Tampa Bay Buccaneers, 246, 255-256, 823, 1548
Tampa Red, 1227; and Ma Rainey, 1227
Taney, Roger, 1325

Tanner, Henry Ossawa, 1318, 1412-1413

*Tap* (film), 660, 775

*Tap Dance Kid, The* (musical), 660

Tap dancers; Honi Coles and Cholly Atkins, 400-402; Sammy Davis, Jr., 660; Savion Glover, 660-661; Gregory Hines, 660, 774-775; Master Juba, 916-917; Fayard and Harold Nicholas, 1110-1112; Bill Robinson, 660, 1266-1268, 1284-1285

Tapia, Richard, 155

Tappan, Lewis, 362

*Tar Baby* (Morrison), 1081

*Tar Beach* (Ringgold), 1259

Tarantino, Quentin, 694, 841

Task Force for Small Business, 677

*Taste of Power, A* (Brown), 231

Tate, Erskine, 776

Tatum, Goose, 973

*Tauhid* (Sanders), 1314

Taussig, Helen B., 1427

Tavernier, Bertrand, 666

Taylor, Cecil, 1344

Taylor, Clarence, 731

Taylor, Clarice, 1004

Taylor, Elizabeth, 836

Taylor, Farwell, 1062

Taylor, Jeanette, 195

Taylor, Koko, 501

Taylor, Lawrence, 1413-1415

Taylor, Mildred D., 1415-1416

Tchicai, John, 1344

*Tears for Water* (Keys), 933

*Ted Mack's Original Amateur Hour* (television program); and Louis Farrakhan, 575; and Gladys Knight, 946

TelArc Records, 356

"Tell It Like It Is" (song), 1106

*Tell My Horse* (Hurston), 809

*Temperatures Rising* (television program), 989

Temple, Ed, 1466

Temple, Shirley, 1267-1268

Temple Number Seven, 575

*Temple of My Familiar, The* (Walker), 1494

Temptations, 402, 1281

*Tender Lover* (Babyface), 70

Tennessee Jubilee Singers, 902

*Tenspeed and Brown Shoe* (television program), 1486

Terkel, Studs, 832

Terrell, Mary Church, 273, 1416-1418

Terrell, Tammi, 643

Terry, Clark, 461

Tex, Joe, 265

*Tha Doggfather* (Snoop Dogg), 1389

*Thank God It's Friday* (film), 1406

*Thankful Poor, The* (Tanner), 1412

Thant, U, 264

*That Nigger's Crazy* (Pryor), 1214

"That's All Right" (song), 434

"That's What Friends Are For" (song), 947, 1511-1512

Theater Owners Booking Association, 195, 510, 1071, 1378

*Their Eyes Were Watching God* (Hurston), 809-810

*Their Eyes Were Watching God* (television movie), 564, 1598

*Thelonious Monk: Straight, No Chaser* (film), 1070

*Them Dirty Blues* (Adderley), 17

*Thembi* (Sanders), 1314

Theodore, Grandwizard, 1354

"There Goes My Baby" (song), 1019

*There Is a Tree More Ancient than Eden* (Forrest), 605

*There Is a Tree More Ancient than Eden* (play), 605

*There Is Confusion* (Fauset), 583

*Things That I Do in the Dark* (Jordan), 908

"Think" (song), 616

*Third Fourth of July, The* (Cullen), 441

*Third Life of Grange Copeland, The* (Walker), 1494

Third World Cinema Corporation, 464

Third World Press, 1022-1023

*This Is Another Day* (Disciples), 431

*This Is It* (film), 837

Thomas, Clarence, 204, 427, 765, 1418-1421, 1428, 1573

Thomas, Debi, 1421-1423

Thomas, Frank, 1423-1424

Thomas, Isiah, 1424-1426

Thomas, Vivien, 1427-1428

Thomas, Walter "Foots," 396

*Thomas and Beulah* (Dove), 516-517

Thompson, George, 1442

Thompson, Hale, 488

Thompson, John, 571, 819

Thompson, Larry D., 1428-1429

Thompson, Titanic, 542

Thoreau, Henry David, 927, 942

Thorogood, George, 143

Thorpe, Jim, 1313

Threadgill, Henry, 1430-1431

Three Black Aces, 45

*3 Girls 3* (television program), 33

Three Millers, 400

"Thrill Is Gone, The" (song), 937

"Thrilla in Manila," 621

*Thriller* (Jackson), 836, 901

Thurmond, Strom, 205

*. . . tick . . . tick . . . tick . . .* (film), 324

Tide Collective, 1153

Till, Emmett, 83, 179, 1432-1433, 1602; murder case, 199

Timberlake, Justin, 825

*Timbuktu!* (musical), 945

*Tin Angel, The* (Odetta), 1126

Tingle, William, 565

"Tisket, a Tasket, A" (song), 592-593, 1532

TLC, 69

*To Be Equal* (Young), 1638

*To Be Young, Gifted, and Black* (play), 730

*To Die for the People* (Newton), 1109

*To Hell with Dying* (Walker), 1494

*To Kill a Mockingbird* (film), 1175

*To Sir, with Love* (film), 1191-1192

*Today Show* (television program), 180, 613, 668, 707-708, 1287-1288

Tolliver, James "Buster," 308

Tolliver's Circus, 1226-1227
Tolson, Melvin B., 1434-1435
Tomlin, Mike, 1343
Tomlinson, LaDainian, 1169
*Tommy* (film), 1456
Tommy Boy Records, 1221-1222
Toney, Andrew, 555
*Tonight Show, The* (television program), 161, 416, 774, 1064; and Bill Cosby, 422; and Arsenio Hall, 715; and Flip Wilson, 1590
*Tony Brown's Journal* (television program), 247, 248
Toomer, Jean, 243, 1435-1437; and Jessie Redmon Fauset, 583
*Topdog/Underdog* (play), 1604, 1621
*Torchlight for America, A* (Farrakhan), 576
Toronto Raptors, 1129, 1426, 1559
*Touched by an Angel* (television program), 52, 317, 393, 1158, 1596
Toure, Ahmed Sekou, 306
Toure, Kwame. *See* Carmichael, Stokely
Toussaint, Allen, 1106
*Toussaint L'Ouverture* (Lawrence), 961
"Toward a Black Feminist Criticism" (Smith), 1376
Townes, Jeff, 1385
Townsend, Fannie Lou. *See* Hamer, Fannie Lou
Townsend, Robert, 1438-1439
*Trading Places* (film), 1091
*Train Whistle Guitar* (Murray), 1094
*Trance of Seven Colors, The* (Sanders), 1314
TransAfrica Forum, 659, 1277-1280
*Transracial Communication* (Asante), 61
Travolta, John, 137
*Treemonisha* (Joplin), 120
Triangle Shirtwaist Factory fire, 1075
*Tribeca* (television program), 591

Trinidad, 530, 917, 1208
Tristano, Lennie, 206, 1062
*Tropic Death* (Walrond), 1507
Trotter, William Monroe, 1439-1440
*Trouble Man* (film), 1596
*Troubled Island* (Still), 1400
*True Colors* (television program), 989
Trueheart, John, 1531
Truman, Harry S., 161, 560, 1229, 1265, 1554; and Mahalia Jackson, 832
Trusty, Henry. *See* Garnet, Henry Highland
Truth, Sojourner, 788, 1441-1443, 1447
Truth, the. *See* Pierce, Paul
Tubman, Harriet, 1444-1446, 1461
Tucker, Allyson, 1066
Tucker, C. DeLores, 1447-1448
Tucker, Jim, 994
Tucker, Sophie, 195
Tuell, Fay. *See* Adams, Faye
Tulsa, Oklahoma, riots, 211
Tune, Tommy, 401
Tureaud, A. P., 1077
Turn 2 Foundation, 861
Turner, Big Joe, 1448-1449
Turner, Henry McNeal, 1450-1451
Turner, Ike, 163, 591, 1451-1453, 1455, 1457
Turner, Nat, 1241, 1453-1455
Turner, Tina, 1455-1458; and Ike Turner, 1452-1453
Turntable Records, 1205
Tuskegee Airmen, 260, 1029, 1094, 1543; and Benjamin O. Davis, Jr., 455-457; and Coleman Young, 1636
Tuskegee Institute. *See* Tuskegee University
Tuskegee Institute Singers, 270
Tuskegee University, 225, 253, 270, 435, 464, 863; and George Washington Carver, 320-321; and Alice Coachman, 385; and Benjamin O. Davis, Jr., 455-456; and Rita Dove, 517; and W. E. B. Du Bois, 521; and

Ralph Ellison, 548; and Barbara Jordan, 905; and Claude McKay, 1010; and Frederick D. Patterson, 1165-1166; and Lionel Richie, 1252-1253; satire of, 957; and Betty Shabazz, 1330; and Booker T. Washington, 1513-1515
"Tutti Frutti" (song), 990
Tutu, Desmond, 807, 1517
Twain, Mark, 146, 354
*Twelve Million Black Voices* (Wright), 1626
*25th Hour* (film), 969
*Twilight* (play), 1375
Twist (dance), 347-348
*Two Trains Running* (play), 840
*Two Wings to Veil My Face* (Forrest), 605
Twombly, Cy, 111
2Pac. *See* Shakur, Tupac
*2Pacalypse Now* (Shakur), 1334
Tye, Colonel, 67
*Tyler Perry's House of Payne* (television program), 1174
Tyler Rose, the. *See* Campbell, Earl
Tyner, McCoy, 407, 1458-1459
Tyson, Cicely, 404, 1078, 1460-1462, 1596
Tyson, Mike, 785, 1462-1464; and Evander Holyfield, 785
Tyson, Neil deGrasse, 1464-1465
Tyus, Wyomia, 1466-1467

UFO Schio, 1609
Uggams, Leslie, 1468-1470
*Ugly Betty* (television program), 1582
*Unbought and Unbossed* (Chisholm), 359-360
UNCF. *See* United Negro College Fund
*Uncle Tom's Cabin* (film), 129
*Uncle Tom's Cabin* (Stowe), 82, 482, 1238
*Uncle Tom's Children* (Wright), 1625
*Under the Oaks* (Bannister), 94-95
Underground Railroad, 309, 797, 1412; Bedford, Pennsylvania,

196; Chatham, Ontario, 140; fiction about, 713, 720; Philadelphia, 703; and Harriet Tubman, 1444-1446; West Chester, Pennsylvania, 1303; Windsor, Ontario, 1366

Underwood, Blair, 102, 1470-1471

"Unexpectedly" (song), 195

"Unforgettable" (song), 391, 393

*Unforgettable . . . with Love* (Cole), 393

UNICEF. *See* United Nations Children's Fund

United Auto Workers, 413

United Church of Christ, 341, 1125, 1622

United Farm Workers, 13

United Golf Association, 542

United Nations; and Pearl Bailey, 72; and Mary McLeod Bethune, 149; and David Harold Blackwell, 155; and Ralph Bunche, 263-264; and Benjamin O. Davis, Jr., 456; and Helene Doris Gayle, 647; and Danny Glover, 659; and Colin Powell, 1201; and Russell Simmons, 1355; and Dionne Warwick, 1512; and Walter White, 1554; and Andrew Young, 1634

United Nations Children's Fund, 138, 591, 647, 816, 1461

United Nations Messenger of Peace, 1033, 1606

United Nations Orchestra, 656

United Negro College Fund, 149, 360, 1606; creation of, 1165; and William H. Gray III, 683-684; and Vernon Jordan, 913; and Frederick D. Patterson, 1165-1166; and Linda Johnson Rice, 1250

United Service Organizations, 161, 429, 490, 547, 614, 771, 795; and Pearl Bailey, 72; and Lena Horne, 795; and Kenny Washington, 1522

United States Lawn Tennis Association, 63, 648-649

United Youth Committee Against Lynching, 753

Universal Negro Improvement Association, 211, 1229; and Cyril V. Briggs, 211; and Henrietta Vinton Davis, 459-460; and Marcus Garvey, 635-637; and Malcolm X, 1024; photographs of, 1478; and Arturo Alfonso Schomburg, 1320; writing contest, 1507

Universal Records, 1243-1244, 1281

University of Mississippi, 1602; and James Meredith, 1049-1051

*Unpredictable* (Foxx), 612

Unruh, Jesse, 250

*Up from Slavery* (Washington), 635, 1514

Updike, John, 893

Upsetters, 990, 1235

Upshaw, Gene, 1342, 1472-1473

Uptown Records, 168, 1217

*Uptown Saturday Night* (film), 137, 423

Urban League. *See* National Urban League

Us organization, 924

Usher, 1474-1475, 1486, 1606

USO. *See* United Service Organizations

Utah Jazz, 475, 1027-1028

*Vampire in Brooklyn* (film), 1092

Van Buren, Martin, 362

Vance, Courtney B., 115, 1476-1477

Van Der Zee, James, 1477-1479

Vandross, Luther, 302

Van Jones, Rochester. *See* Anderson, Eddie "Rochester"

Van Peebles, Mario, 115, 1286, 1387, 1480-1481

Van Peebles, Melvin, 286, 1480, 1482-1483

Van Vechten, Carl, 869

Van Wagenen, Isabella. *See* Truth, Sojourner

Varèse, Edgar, 1399

Variety Records, 546

Vashon, John B., 481

Vaudeville and mistrelsy, 165

Vaughan, Sarah, 539, 1483-1485

Vaughan, Stevie Ray, 937

Veeck, Bill, 503, 1149

Vee-Jay Records, 787

*Venus Hottentot, The* (Alexander), 25

Venuti, Joe, 777

Vereen, Ben, 1485-1486

Verrett, Shirley, 1009

Verve Records, 593, 783

Vesey, Denmark, 1487-1488, 1495

"Vicksburg Blues" (song), 1071-1072

*Victory* (Jacksons), 836

*Victory Over Myself* (Patterson), 1164

Vietnam War, 1579; and Muhammad Ali, 27; antiwar movement, 180, 232, 377, 486, 943, 1126, 1230, 1633; and Julius Wesley Becton, Jr., 135; and Guion Bluford, 172; and Charles F. Bolden, Jr., 174; and Julian Bond, 180; and Ed Bradley, 198-199; and Stokely Carmichael, 306-307; and John Conyers, Jr., 414; and Ron Dellums, 486; and Frederick Drew Gregory, 691; and Martin Luther King, Jr., 943, 1633; and Eartha Kitt, 945; and Yusef Komunyakaa, 950; and Clarence E. Page, 1145; and Colin Powell, 1199; and A. Philip Randolph, 1230; and Henry Threadgill, 1431; and Andrew Young, 1633

*Vietnam War Story* (television movie), 1387

*View, The* (television program), 662

*Village, The* (Fuller), 625

*Village Life* (Hancock), 726

Virgin Records, 303, 825

Virginia Squires, 554

VISTA. *See* Volunteers in Service to America

Vitale, John J., 987

Vitous, Miroslav, 1346

Vivian, C. T., 1488-1490
Vocalion Records, 220, 308, 311, 1072, 1448
Vodery, Will, 1061
*Vogelfängerin, Die* (Jones), 894
*Vogue* magazine, 798, 803, 977, 1156, 1353
Volunteers in Service to America, 382
Voting Rights Act of 1965, 151; and Ralph David Abernathy, 13; and John Conyers, Jr., 414; and Martin Luther King, Jr., 943; and Joseph Lowery, 1002; and Fred Shuttlesworth, 1347; and Harold Washington, 1520

Wade, Dwyane, 850, 1135
Wagner-Van Nuys Anti-Lynching bill, 1553
*Waiting to Exhale* (film), 69, 115, 208, 775, 1549
*Waiting to Exhale* (McMillan), 1014-1015
Walcott, Derek, 1431
Walcott, Jersey Joe, 335, 1491-1493
Walcott, Louis Eugene. *See* Farrakhan, Louis
Walk to Freedom, 247
Walker, Alice, 445, 908, 1493-1495; and J. California Cooper, 417; and Zora Neale Hurston, 810
Walker, David, 1397, 1495-1496
Walker, George, 270, 1497-1498, 1563-1564
Walker, Jimmie, 1498-1500
Walker, Kurt. *See* Blow, Kurtis
Walker, Madam C. J., 713, 1500-1502
Walker, Margaret, 645, 712, 1503-1504
Walker, Nellie Marian. *See* Larsen, Nella
Walker, T-Bone, 786, 937
Walker, Will, 510
Wallace, Henry A., 729, 1265
Wallace, Ruby Ann. *See* Dee, Ruby

Wallace, Voletta, 116
Wallack, Henry, 22
Wallack, James, 22
Waller, Fats, 109, 239, 284, 546, 1504-1506
Walrond, Eric, 1507-1508
Walsh, Bill, 1248
Walter and Connie Payton Foundation, 1169
Walters, Alexander, 345, 1508-1510
Walters, Barbara, 1201; and Edward W. Brooke, 216
*Waltz of the Stork* (play), 1480
War of 1812, 277, 438, 606
War on Poverty, 383, 600, 1198, 1637-1638
Ward, Billy, 1019, 1592
Ward, Clara, 511, 614
Ward, Douglas Turner, 533
Warhol, Andy, 112
Warmoth, Henry Clay, 532
Warner Bros. Records, 1210-1211, 1511; and Prince, 1211
Warren, Butch, 725
Warren G, 1388, 1390
Warwick, Dionne, 1510-1512
Washington, Booker T., 638, 1513-1515; bust of, 108; and George Washington Carver, 320; and Charles Waddell Chesnutt, 354; criticisms of, 1439; and W. E. B. Du Bois, 521; and Marcus Garvey, 211, 635; and John Hope, 792; and Claude McKay, 1010; and National Afro-American Council, 1509; philosophy of, 224, 521, 792; and Harriet Tubman, 1446; and Madam C. J. Walker, 1501; and Eric Walrond, 1507; and Alexander Walters, 1509
Washington, Craig, 844
Washington, D.C.; board of education, 1417; Freedmen's Hospital, 518-519, 1029, 1568, 1624; Lincoln Memorial, 48-49, 943, 1606; mayors, 104-106, 738; segregated schools, 1242; sit-ins, 1096; surveying of, 93

Washington, Denzel, 343, 472, 1086, 1191, 1438, 1476, 1515-1518
Washington, Desiree, 1463
Washington, Dinah, 613-614
Washington, George, 37, 67, 93
Washington, Harold, 605, 828, 1146, 1225, 1518-1521
Washington, Kenny, 1521-1522; and Woody Strode, 1403
Washington, Pauletta Pearson, 1517
Washington, Walter, 104
Washington Bullets, 745
Washington Elite Giants, 289
Washington Redskins; and Donovan McNabb, 1016-1017; and Deion Sanders, 1313
Washington Research Project, 540
Washington Senators, 597
Washington Wizards, 885; and Michael Jordan, 911
Washingtonians, 308, 546
Watergate scandal, 906
*Watermelon Man* (film), 286-287, 1482
Waters, Ethel, 79, 313, 466, 1007, 1468
Waters, Maxine, 1523-1524
Waters, Muddy, 142, 501, 992, 1525-1526, 1621
Watkins, Frances Ellen. *See* Harper, Frances Ellen Watkins
Watkins, Gloria Jean. *See* Hooks, Bell
Watson, Perle Yvonne. *See* Burke, Yvonne Brathwaite
Wattleton, Faye, 1526-1528
Watts, J. C., 1528-1529
Watts riot, 51, 267, 373, 432, 924, 943, 1034, 1137, 1306
Wayans, Damon, 1005
Wayans, Keenan Ivory, 324
Wayans brothers, 1215
Waymon, Eunice Kathleen. *See* Simone, Nina
*We a BaddDDD People* (Sanchez), 1308
"We Are the World" (song), 336, 826, 836, 901, 1511; and Lionel Richie, 1253

"We Shall Overcome" (song), 832, 1126

*Weary Blues, The* (Hughes), 805

Weather Report, 462, 1345-1346

Weather Underground, 399

Weaver, Robert C., 1530-1531

Webb, Chick, 315, 592, 1531-1532; and Cootie Williams, 1566

Weber, Max, 521

Webster, Ben, 167, 285, 1012

Webster, Nicholas, 465

Weinberger, Caspar, 1200

Weinglass, Leonard, 1329

Welch, Raquel, 238

Welles, Orson, 945, 968, 1626

Wells, Dicky, 315

Wells, Junior, 993

Wells, Mary, 1281

Wells-Barnett, Ida B., 1533-1534

West, Cornel, 1535-1536

West, David, 1537-1538

West, Dorothy, 1538-1539

West, Kanye, 589, 612, 852-853, 1256, 1540-1541

West, Mae, 129, 1007

West, Togo, 1541-1543

West African Students Union, 636

West Point. *See* Military Academy, U.S.

*West Side Story* (musical), 33

Westhead, Paul, 878

Wexler, Jerry, 265, 615

Wharton, Clifton Reginald, Jr., 1543-1544

"What a Wonderful World" (song), 59

*What's Going On?* (Gaye), 644

*What's Love Got to Do with It* (film), 115-116, 590-591, 1457

"What's Love Got to Do With It" (song), 1457

Wheatley, Phillis, 1545-1547, 1626

Wheatley, Tyrone, 1547-1548

Wheatrob, Tony, 812

*When the Levees Broke* (film), 969

*Where Does the Day Go?* (Myers), 1098

Whispering Syncopators, 510

Whitaker, Forest, 1015, 1548-1550

White, Bill, 214, 1550-1552

White, Charles, 1034

White, Clarence Cameron, 270

White, George, 345

White, Slappy, 613

White, Walter, 1230, 1552-1554, 1560

White, William, 606

White Citizens Councils, 391, 567

*White Man, Listen!* (Wright), 1626

*White Man's Burden* (film), 137

*White Men Can't Jump* (film), 1387

Whitefield, George, 1545-1546

Whittaker, "Tampa Red," 510

Whittier, John Greenleaf, 524, 704

"Who's Lovin' You" (song), 767

*Why Blacks Kill Blacks* (Poussaint), 1195

*Why Did I Get Married?* (film), 825, 1174

*Why Did I Get Married Too?* (film), 826

*Why Do Fools Fall in Love* (Ross), 1292

Wideman, John Edgar, 1555-1557

Wiggins, Thomas. *See* Bethune, Blind Tom

Wilberforce College; and Benjamin O. Davis, Sr., 453; and Martin Robison Delany, 482; and W. E. B. Du Bois, 521; and Frances Ellen Watkins Harper, 732; and Leontyne Price, 1202; and George Russell, 1300; and William Grant Still, 1399; and Mary Church Terrell, 1417; and William Julius Wilson, 1593

Wilberforce Collegians, 314, 1300

*Wild Seed* (Butler), 280

Wild Tchoupitoulas, 1106

Wild Tree Press, 418

*Wildcats* (film), 953, 1387

Wildcats Jazz Band, 510, 1227

Wilder, L. Douglas, 1557-1558

Wilkens, Lenny, 1558-1559

Wilkins, Roy, 603, 1560-1562; and Jane Matilda Bolin, 176

Wilkinson, J. L., 1150

Wilks, Samuel, 154

Willard, Jess, 1000

Williams, Anthony, 105

Williams, Bert, 195, 270, 334, 1061, 1563-1564

Williams, Billy Dee, 1565-1566

Williams, Cootie, 167, 1566-1567

Williams, Daniel Hale, 1567-1569

Williams, Dootsie, 613

Williams, Eddie, 222

Williams, Eugene, 862

Williams, Floyd "Horsecollar," 1112

Williams, Gus, 1569-1570

Williams, Hosea, 834, 983, 1571-1572

Williams, Joe, 110

Williams, Juan, 1573-1574

Williams, Martin, 397

Williams, Mary Lou, 1113, 1574-1576

Williams, Montel, 1576-1578

Williams, Paulette. *See* Shange, Ntozake

Williams, Ricky, 1016

Williams, Robert Franklin, 1578-1579

Williams, Robert Peter. *See* Guillaume, Robert

Williams, Sandy, 1532

Williams, Serena, 649, 1579-1581

Williams, Sidney, 1523

Williams, Spencer, 1505

Williams, Vanessa, 338, 1581-1582

Williams, Venus, 649, 1583-1584

Williams, Willie L., 1584-1585

Willis, Benjamin, 1224

Wills, Maury, 214, 1586-1587

*Wilmington Advocate, The* (newspaper), 527

Wilmington Ten, 341-342

Wilson, August, 115, 534, 840, 1234, 1517, 1587-1589; and Romare Bearden, 128; and Lloyd Richards, 1251

Wilson, Brian, 266

Wilson, Cootie, 1069

Wilson, Flip, 947, 1215, 1590-1591

Wilson, Harriet E., 641

Wilson, Jackie, 673, 1592-1593

Wilson, Josephine Beall, 253

Wilson, Lionel, 231

Wilson, Mary, 1291

Wilson, Nancy, 16, 714

Wilson, Teddy, 723

Wilson, William Julius, 1593-1594

Wilson, Woodrow, 1440, 1509

Wilt the Stilt. *See* Chamberlain, Wilt

Winehouse, Amy, 740

Winfield, Paul, 1595-1597

Winfrey, Florence. *See* Mills, Florence

Winfrey, Oprah, 785, 1173, 1597-1600; book club, 630, 1598; and Nikki Giovanni, 658; and South Africa, 816; and Tiger Woods, 1613

Winkfield, James, 1600-1601

Winter, Bud, 304, 562

Winter, Johnny, 1526

Winter Olympics, 469-470, 1085, 1421-1422

*Wire, The* (television program), 535

Withers, Ernest, 1601-1603

*Within Our Gates* (film), 1056

*Without a Song* (Rollins), 1290

Witt, Katarina, 1422

*Wiz, The* (film), 796, 836, 1292

Wizard, the. *See* Williams, Gus

*WKRP in Cincinnati* (television program), 1240

WNBA. *See* Women's National Basketball Association

Wofford, Chloe Anthony. *See* Morrison, Toni

Wolf, Simon, 1068

Wolfe, George C., 660, 1603-1604

Womack, Bobby, 416

*Woman Called Moses, A* (film), 1461

*Womanslaughter* (Parker), 1154

*Women of Brewster's Place, The* (Naylor), 1105-1106

*Women of Brewster's Place, The* (television program), 1598

Women's Christian Temperance Union, 733

Women's International League for Peace and Freedom, 939, 1308

Women's National Basketball Association, 898, 915, 977, 1028, 1057, 1609

Women's Political Council, 12

Women's Professional Soccer, 1327

Women's Rights Convention, 515

Women's United Soccer Association, 1327

Wonder, Stevie, 69-70, 547, 1605-1607

Wonder Children, 442

*Wonders of the African World* (television program), 641-642

Woodard, Alfre, 1517, 1607-1608

Woodard, Lynette, 1609-1610

Woodbridge, Hudson. *See* Tampa Red

Wooden, John, 8

Woods, Earl, 542

Woods, Granville T., 1610-1612

Woods, Tiger, 542, 1612-1614

Woods Electric Company, 1611

Woodson, Carter G., 1320, 1615-1617

Woodson, Rod, 1617-1619

Woodstock Festival, 759

Woodward, Nathan, 357

Word Up Records, 1385

Work, John, III, 1525

Workers Party of America, 211

*Workin' on the Chain Gang* (Mosley), 1087

Works Progress Administration, 161, 512, 731, 1600; Federal Art Project, 887, 1318; Federal Writers' Project, 1539; Harlem Mural Project, 40, 961; Music Copying Project, 925

World Cotton Centennial, 253

World Series; and Reggie Jackson, 839

*World View of Race* (Bunche), 262

World War I; aviators, 395; and black newspapers, 210; and Big Bill Broonzy, 220; and Eugene Jacques Bullard, 259; and Bessie Coleman, 395; and James Reese Europe, 559; and Arthur George Gaston, 638; and Charles Hamilton Houston, 797; and Charles S. Johnson, 862,

867; and Chandler Owen, 1228; and A. Philip Randolph, 1228; and Henry Ossawa Tanner, 1413; and Louis T. Wright, 1624

World War II; and Charles Alston, 40; and Josephine Baker, 78-79; and Julius Wesley Becton, Jr., 134; and Mary McLeod Bethune, 149; and black newspapers, 210; and Eubie Blake, 161; and Edward W. Brooke, 215; and Dorothy Lavinia Brown, 229; and Eugene Jacques Bullard, 259; and Ralph Bunche, 263; and Benjamin O. Davis, Sr., 452-455; and Benjamin O. Davis, Jr., 456-457; and Ossie Davis, 464; and Sammy Davis, Jr., 467; and David Dinkins, 497; and James A. Emanuel, 551; and James Carmichael Evans, 560; and Charles Evers, 565; *Fallen Aviator* sculpture, 108; and James L. Farmer, Jr., 574; films about, 238, 464; and John R. Fox, 609-610; and Alex Haley, 711; and Benjamin Hooks, 790; and Lena Horne, 795; Japanese American internment, 217; and Hubert Fauntleroy Julian, 918; and Ernest Everett Just, 922; and B. B. King, 936; and Canada Lee, 968; and Hughie Lee-Smith, 971; and C. Eric Lincoln, 986; and Hattie McDaniel, 1007; and Vance Hunter Marchbanks, 1029; and Dorie Miller, 1058-1059; and Albert Murray, 1094; and Negro Leagues, 1150; and Herbie Nichols, 1112; and Adam Clayton Powell, Jr., 1196; and Professor Longhair, 1212; and Lloyd Richards, 1251; and Paul Robeson, 1264; and Bayard Rustin, 1304; and Sun Ra, 1408; and Hosea Williams, 1571; and Ernest Withers, 1601; and Frank

Yerby, 1628; and Whitney Young, 1637. *See also* Tuskegee Airmen

WorldCom, 1428-1429

WPA. *See* Works Progress Administration

Wrestlers; Dwayne Johnson, 864-865; Woody Strode, 1403

*Wretched of the Earth* (Fanon), 306

Wright, Angela, 766

Wright, Archibald Lee. *See* Moore, Archie

Wright, Eric "Eazy-E," 505, 812

Wright, Isaac. *See* Coker, Daniel

Wright, Jane Cooke, 1619-1620, 1624

Wright, Jeffrey, 1620-1622

Wright, Jeremiah, 1622-1623

Wright, Jonathan J., 1372

Wright, Louis T., 1624-1625

Wright, Marian. *See* Edelman, Marian Wright

Wright, Orville, 524

Wright, Richard, 646, 1625-1627; and James Baldwin, 81; biographies of, 1503; and Ralph

Ellison, 548; *Native Son*, 968; and Dorothy West, 1538

Wright, Wilbur, 524

Wu Tang Clan, 381

Wurf, Jerry, 574

Yang, C. K., 882

Yardbird. *See* Parker, Charlie

Yardbirds, 496, 787

Yearwood, Trisha, 1107

Yéle Haiti Foundation, 856

Yerby, Frank, 1628-1630

*Yes, I Can* (Davis), 468

"Yet Do I Marvel" (Cullen), 440

*Yo! MTV Raps* (television program), 1221

Yorty, Sam, 201

Yoruba, 62, 482, 641, 924

"You Send Me" (song), 416

Young, Al, 1631-1632

Young, Andre Romelle. *See* Dr. Dre

Young, Andrew, 209, 719, 834, 1632-1635

Young, Coleman, 1635-1637

*Young, Gifted, and Black* (Franklin), 616

Young, Lester, 109, 782, 1012

Young, Whitney, 1044, 1637-1638

*Young and the Restless, The* (television program), 1176, 1254

Young Communist League, 368, 1333

Young Jeezy, 853

*Your Blues Ain't Like Mine* (Campbell), 291

*Your Hit Parade* (radio program), 592

Zane, Arnie, 891-892

Zawinul, Joe, 1346

Zea-Daly, Errol, 1415

*Zeely* (Hamilton), 720

*Ziegfeld Follies* (musical), 79, 1111, 1564

Zimbabwe, 940, 1607, 1634. *See also* Rhodesia.

Zooid, 1431

*Zooman and the Sign* (play), 625

Zwerin, Charlotte, 1070